BRITISH WRITERS

BRITISH WRITERS

Edited under the auspices of the British Council

IAN SCOTT-KILVERT

General Editor

VOLUME III

DANIEL DEFOE

TO

THE GOTHIC NOVEL

CHARLES SCRIBNER'S SONS / NEW YORK

Library of Congress Cataloging in Publication Data

Main entry under title:

British writers.

Includes bibliographies and index.
CONTENTS: v. 1. William Langland to the English
Bible.—v. 2. Thomas Middleton to George Farquhar.
—v. 3. Daniel Defoe to the Gothic Novel.
1. English literature—History and criticism.
2. English literature—Bio-bibliography.   3. Authors,
English—Biography.   I. Scott-Kilvert, Ian.   II. Great
Britain. British Council.
PR85.B688   820′.9   78-23483
ISBN 0-684-15798-5 (v. 1)
ISBN 0-684-16407-8 (v. 2)
ISBN 0-684-16408-6 (v. 3)

Editorial Staff

List of Subjects in Volume III

Introduction

British Writers is designed as a work of reference to complement *American Writers*, the six-volume set of literary biographies of authors past and present, which was first published in 1974. In the same way as its American counterpart, which first appeared in the form of individual pamphlets published by the University of Minnesota Press, the British collection originates from a series of separate articles entitled *Writers and Their Work*. This series was initiated by the British Council in 1950 as a part of its worldwide program to support the teaching of English language and literature, an activity carried on both in the English-speaking world and in many countries in which English is not the mother tongue.

The articles are intended to appeal to a wide readership, including students in secondary and advanced education, teachers, librarians, scholars, editors, and critics, as well as the general public. Their purpose is to provide an introduction to the work of writers who have made a significant contribution to English literature, to stimulate the reader's enjoyment of the text, and to give students the means to pursue the subject further. The series begins in the fourteenth century and extends to the present day, and is printed in chronological order according to the date of the subject's birth. The articles are far from conforming to a fixed pattern, but speaking generally each begins with a short biographical section, the main body of the text being devoted to a survey of the subject's principal writings and an assessment of the work as a whole. Each article is equipped with a selected bibliography that records the subject's writings in chronological order, in the form both of collected editions and of separate works, including modern and paperback editions. The bibliography concludes with a list of biographical and critical publications, including both books and articles, to guide the reader who is interested in further research. In the case of authors such as Chaucer or Shakespeare, whose writings have inspired extensive criticism and commentary, the critical section is further subdivided and provides a useful record of the new fields of research that have developed over the past hundred years.

British Writers is not conceived as an encyclopedia of literature, nor is it a series of articles planned so comprehensively as to include every writer of historical importance. Its character is rather that of a critical anthology possessing both the virtues and the limitations of such a grouping. It offers neither the schematized form of the encyclopedia nor the completeness of design of the literary history. On the other hand it is limited neither by the impersonality of the one nor the uniformity of the other. Since each contributor speaks with only one voice out of many, he is principally concerned with explaining his subject as fully as possible rather than with establishing an order of merit or making "placing" comparisons (since each contributor might well "place" differently). The prime task is one of presentation and exposition rather than of assigning critical praise or censure. The contributors to the first volume consist of distinguished literary scholars and critics—later volumes include contributions by poets, novelists, historians, and biographers. Each writes as an enthusiast for his subject, and each sets out to explain what are the qualities that make an author worth reading.

At the beginning of the eighteenth century, which this volume surveys, Augustan culture was already firmly rooted, though drawing little nourishment from crown or court. This was a period—as with the Augustan era in Rome—of reconciliation and reconstruction, a healing of the wounds inflicted by civil wars and religious feuds. The Glorious Revolution of 1688 had been effected with a minimum of bloodshed—and with it a notable shift in power from the nobleman to the entrepreneur or merchant. The governing class was still drawn from the landowners, but henceforth their interests (and their genealogy) would become more closely allied with those of the rising commercial classes, the latter having discovered that "an estate is a pond, but a trade is a spring." The result, for a half-century or more, was a remarkable political equilibrium, which tempted visitors such as Voltaire or Jean Jacques Rousseau to see England as a utopia by comparison with the absolute monarchies of the Continent: Voltaire's *Lettres philosophiques* was strictly banned in France.

In religious matters we find a broader tolerance, accompanied by a widespread aversion to the doctrines of single-minded fanatics or "enthusiasts." A century of religious upheaval was seen to have resulted in a general impasse in which every sectarian remained convinced that his dogma alone represented the true word. The need, then, was for a faith acceptable to reasonable individuals, and in the early years of the period, at least, the findings of science supported belief in an ordered universe directed by divinely framed laws. Science was no longer regarded as forbidden knowledge, but as the enlightened study of the works of God. What need of the old guidance by revelation if nature, when examined by the astronomers and physicists, provided evidence of the divine purpose on every hand? As Alexander Pope put it in his epitaph on Sir Isaac Newton:

> Nature and Nature's laws lay hid in night:
> God said, Let Newton be, and all was light.

In the social and cultural sphere, the forces of change expressed themselves in the rapid rise of a leisured middle class (including its wives and daughters) with an urgent need to educate itself and develop its taste: in the centralization of intellectual and artistic enterprise within the capital; the foundation of newspapers and periodicals; the replacement of the court, the aristocratic patron, or the coterie by a homogeneous bourgeois public, and hence the emergence of the professional writer, who draws his livelihood from a wide readership. The classics of the age—*Robinson Crusoe, Gulliver's Travels, Tom Jones, Rasselas, Tristram Shandy,* and Gray's "Elegy"—were immediately hailed by just such a public, "the common reader" of Samuel Johnson's phrase. At first it was the periodical essayists who supplied the demand for education and guidance at a time when the Renaissance manuals of civilized behavior were replaced by the discreet advice of the

Tatler or *Spectator* on manners, morals, literature, and taste: later this educative function spread to the novelists.

Daniel Defoe, the subject of the opening essay, was the first, though a somewhat rough-textured specimen, of the new man of letters—one associated with the city rather than the fashionable town. Dissenter, trader, pamphleteer, one-man newspaper, secret agent, expert on the underworld, and finally novelist, he did not write his first novel, *Robinson Crusoe,* until he was nearly sixty, and even thereafter judged it best to present his fiction under the "true story" guise of history or autobiography. Few critics would disagree concerning Defoe's extraordinary gift of making his fictions plausible and convincing; but many have questioned whether he was a writer capable of moral and artistic discrimination or merely a reporter with a prodigious capacity for assembling relevant details. James Sutherland's essay strongly argues the case that Defoe's stories take possession of our minds to a degree that proves him to be both a moralist and an artist.

Jonathan Swift and Alexander Pope are the giants of Augustan prose and verse satire. The life and work of each illustrate some of the contradictions contained within the Augustan scheme of values, and suggest how delicately balanced were the apparent stability and optimistic assurance of the times. Both writers, as these essays point out, had their roots deep in the seventeenth century: they were perhaps on this account the more skeptical of the Augustan vision of a benevolent and harmonious universe and the more painfully aware of the human imperfections immediately to hand. Swift is described in Norman Jeffares' essay as a man who moved between moods—at some moments prone to annihilating anger, at others to the desire for "mirth and society." Ian Jack considers that Pope's finest achievements, apart from the early *Rape of the Lock,* are to be found in late works such as the *Imitations of Horace* and the fourth book of *The Dunciad.* These poems contain some of his most brilliant character sketches and demonstrate his consummate mastery in fusing thought and image. But they were written at a time when the very epithet "Augustan" had taken on a derogatory meaning for the poet, and when the abuses of the era of Robert Walpole had inspired his final offensive against "The dull, the proud, the wicked and the mad."

The generation that followed Defoe approached fiction from a different starting point. While Defoe excelled at making the singular and arduous adventures of his heroes and heroines plausible, Samuel Richardson and Henry Fielding were more interested in exploring the everyday situations and dilemmas of ordinary people and giving them significance. R. F. Brissenden discusses Richardson's choice of the letter-writing convention with special reference to *Clarissa Harlowe*, which he sees as the only work of fiction of tragic dimensions produced in the eighteenth century. Fielding, who also claimed to have inaugurated a new kind of fiction, preferred an altogether broader social canvas. In describing Fielding's conception of the prose comic epic, John Butt remarks that the guiding principle for the whole sequence of adventures, both in *Joseph Andrews* and in *Tom Jones*, is the display of the ridiculous or, in other words, the exposure of the difference between being and seeming. Butt also makes it clear how much the author's fiction benefited from his training and experience as a journalist and as a man of the theater. The early novels of Tobias Smollett transport us to scenes of violence and brutality that are remarkable even in that unsqueamish age. Laurence Brander can fairly claim that these works excel in their sympathetic and comic characterization of seafaring men, but a majority of readers may prefer his enthusiasm for *Humphrey Clinker* as a panoramic record of the England of George III seen at a mellower stage of Smollett's career. Laurence Sterne, although chronologically a member of this quartet of classic eighteenth-century novelists, belongs to quite a different fictional tradition. D. W. Jefferson examines the nature of his humor and its links with prescientific writers on the grotesque, such as François Rabelais and Robert Burton: he commends the delicacy of Sterne's narrative technique and, above all, his power to convey the total absorption of his characters in their private worlds.

The career of Dr. Johnson, which spanned the four middle decades of the century, forms the centerpiece of this volume. Sir Sydney Roberts' essay deals with Johnson's character and personal qualities as well as with his writings. He assesses Johnson's best-known literary achievements—the poems, *Rasselas*, the *Dictionary*, the edition of Shakespeare, and *The Lives of the English Poets* —but he also singles out the less familiar essays and sketches contributed to the *Rambler* and the *Idler* as essential reading for an understanding of Johnson's position in the world of letters of his time.

The remarkable discoveries made during the last half-century in the archives at Malahide and Fetter-cairn have revolutionized our knowledge of James Boswell, who is now revealed as a master of autobiography as well as of biography. Philip Collins' study first explores Boswell's personality and examines his journals on their own considerable merits, and then discusses the use made of them in composing the greatest of English biographies. He remarks that Boswell did much to create a number of the encounters with Johnson that he recorded, and when making comparisons with later biographies, he notes that Boswell's is a picture, not an interpretation, and makes its effect through a host of minute particulars rather than by generalizations.

In 1756 Joseph Warton, a schoolmate of William Collins, published the essay *On the Genius of Pope*, which is mainly laudatory but contains the words: "The Sublime and the Pathetic are the two chief nerves of all genuine poesy. What is there transcendently sublime or pathetic in Pope?" Both the statement and the question were to reverberate far into the future. At that moment, they marked a decided shift away from the canons of Augustan taste and toward the concepts of "sensibility" and "the sublime," which were already having their effect upon the writers of the mid-century: the essay appeared a year before Edmund Burke's *Enquiry into the Origin . . . of the Sublime and Beautiful*. Poets in particular were then searching for new models of style of a more original or primitive kind. They turned toward ancient epic and lyric—especially to Greek, Hebrew, Scandinavian, and Celtic poetry, literatures untouched by the civilization of Rome; while within the native tradition there was a renewal of interest in the poetry of Edmund Spenser and John Milton. Hence the experiments of Gray and Collins at writing odes in Pindaric meters, and the attempt to combine in such poems as Gray's *Progress of Poesy* or Collins' *Ode on the Popular Superstitions of the Highlands* a stylized eighteenth-century diction with a heightened emotional tone: hence too, in the succeeding decade, the immense popularity of the "discovered" poems of Ossian and of Thomas Percy's *Reliques of Ancient English Poetry*. Gray's "Elegy" achieves a consummate blending of the old and the new prescriptions; it is recognizably Augustan in diction and tone—hence its appeal to Johnson—while its presentation of the solitary and melancholy poet discloses its affinity with the new currents of feeling.

William Cowper by no means shared Gray's taste for university life and, still less, that of Collins for the metropolis. He stands apart from his contemporaries as a poet who is much less concerned with the literary past than with direct observation of his rural and domestic surroundings—"fireside enjoyments, home-born happiness." Norman Nicholson, himself a poet of the countryside, discusses the paradoxes of Cowper's career and the surprisingly wide range of his writing, which encompassed not only the intimate and affectionate observations of nature and the rollicking gaiety of his ballad of John Gilpin, but also the torment of his last composition, *The Castaway*, a poem agonizingly expressive of the religious terrors that periodically threatened his reason. George Crabbe, a generation younger than Cowper, also drew his inspiration from the pattern of rural life and remained uninfluenced by the contemporary literary fashions of the capital. He earned early fame with his narrative poem *The Village*, deliberately composed in contrast to Oliver Goldsmith's sentimental *The Deserted Village*: "By such examples taught, I paint the Cot/As Truth will paint it, and as Bards will not."

Crabbe was predominantly a narrative poet, and R. L. Brett's study concludes that it is the lesser known collections of *Tales*, written thirty years or more after *The Village*, which best illustrate his skill in tracing the development of individual characters and contain the finest examples of his narrative art.

During the last quarter of the eighteenth century, political and economic factors acted with increasing speed to disturb the balance upon which the Augustan social and cultural order had rested. A season of thaw and flux had arrived, and a spirit of change was abroad—at first enthusiastically greeted by those who felt confident of the supremacy of reason and the perfectibility of man. The success of the American Revolution, the convening of the Estates-General at Versailles, and the fall of the Bastille could be seen as decisive harbingers of reform and as checks to the power of the Hanoverian, Bourbon, and other autocratic regimes. On the economic plane, the action of English landlords in enclosing the common land—on which villagers had pastured their livestock since medieval times—had coincided with the invention of mechanical methods of textile production. These developments impoverished great numbers of the rural population, whose livelihood had depended upon small-scale agriculture supplemented by cottage industry, and forced them to seek employment in the cities.

In this period the poets were the first imaginative writers to explore experiences and states of mind that lay beyond the pale of polite urban society.

This was not only on the grounds of "a man's a man for a' that," in Robert Burns's phrase, or "a man who does not wear fine clothes can feel deeply," in William Wordsworth's, but also because of the conviction that the profoundest emotions could best be communicated by means of simple and direct language. David Daiches' essay on Burns notes how Scotland's national poet has become a cult figure for his compatriots, though in a manner quite different from that in which Shakespeare is seen by the English. Burns is cherished for having found for his countrymen their natural voice and for having given poetic expression to the vitality of the popular speech and the richness of the popular culture: in consequence his sentimental passages have been overpraised and his image as an unlettered peasant overemphasized. The true strength of his writing, it is argued, lies in his genius for song, both in original composition and in the adaptation of traditional folk lyrics, in the exuberant wit and eloquence of his satire, and in the wonderful fertility of epithet and metaphor displayed in his language. William Blake's poetry sprang from a view of the world even more conspicuously at odds with that of the Augustans. J. B. Beer's essay examines the nature of Blake's imagination. It remarks on his faculty of "eidetic vision," the ability to apprehend physical images more vivid than those of the natural world, and his conviction of the importance of the poetic and prophetic character of man rather than the philosophic and experimental one—hence his rebellion against the view of reality taken by contemporary rationalist thinkers, which seemed to him to reduce the world to quantitative measurement and to perceptions limited by the five physical senses. In analyzing some of the most celebrated lyrics, such as "London," the essay notes one of the most characteristic qualities of Blake's poetry: a vision of the world that, although far from naive, is as if one were looking at it for the first time.

In the field of historical and political writing, this volume includes two authors who have achieved classic status: Edward Gibbon and Edmund Burke. It is Gibbon's exact control of his material that makes him unique among English narrative historians in Dame Veronica Wedgwood's judgment: the deliberate lowering of the tone of the final page of his *History* provides a striking illustration. Her essay offers an appreciation of *The Decline and Fall* on two planes: as a monument of historical scholarship and as a literary and stylistic masterpiece. The American War of Independence and the French Rev-

INTRODUCTION

olution were the two major historical landmarks of Burke's lifetime, and his response to these events forms the essence of his political beliefs. T. E. Utley regards Burke's conciliatory speech on American taxation, delivered in 1775, as the greatest of his career. He considers that Burke's powers of expression both as a conversationalist and as an orator won him an influence that far exceeded that of any public office he attained. As for posterity, he points out that Burke's writings, though constantly studied, have never become the possession of any political party, and he remains the greatest of English political philosophers of moderation.

Arnold Hare's study of Richard Brinsley Sheridan reviews the dramatist's acknowledged masterpieces and places his comedy in relation to the theatrical history and conventions of the period. Many critics have treated Sheridan's political and theatrical activities as completely separate segments of his life. This study notes the reasons for Sheridan's adoption of a political career, examines his brilliant gifts as a public speaker in relation to passages in *The Critic* and in his last play, *Pizarro*, and finds a connection between his oratorical style and the changes in taste that were overtaking the theater by the end of the eighteenth century.

Finally, Brendan Hennessy's survey of the Gothic novel discusses the appeal of the supernatural, the mysterious, and the horrific as an international aesthetic phenomenon that expressed itself in music and in the visual arts as well as in literature. Hennessy points out that the elements that compose the "Gothic taste" were active not only in the transitional period between the eighteenth and nineteenth centuries, but have also manifested themselves at intervals up to the present day.

The series was founded by Laurence Brander, then director of publications, at the British Council. The first editor was T. O. Beachcroft, himself a distinguished writer of short stories. His successors have been the late Bonamy Dobrée, formerly Professor of English Literature at the University of Leeds; Geoffrey Bullough, Professor Emeritus of English Literature, King's College, London, and author of *The Narrative and Dramatic Sources of Shakespeare*; and since 1970 the present writer. To these founders and predecessors *British Writers* is deeply indebted for the design of the series, the planning of its scope, and the distinction of their editorship, and I personally for many years of friendship and advice, and invaluable experience, generously shared.

—Ian Scott-Kilvert

Chronological Table

CHRONOLOGICAL TABLE

Philadelphia founded

Death of Sir Thomas Browne

1683 The Ashmolean Museum, the world's first public museum, opens at Oxford

Death of Izaak Walton

1685–1688 Reign of James II

1685 Rebellion and execution of James Scott, duke of Monmouth

John Gay born

1686 The first book of Newton's *Principia—De motu corporum*, containing his theory of gravitation—presented to the Royal Society

1687 James II issues the Declaration of Indulgence

Dryden's *The Hind and the Panther*

Death of Edmund Waller

1688 James II reissues the Declaration of Indulgence, renewing freedom of worship and suspending the provisions of the Test Act

Acquittal of the seven bishops imprisoned for protesting against the Declaration

William of Orange lands at Torbay, Devon

James II takes refuge in France

Death of John Bunyan

Alexander Pope born

1689 Parliament formulates the Declaration of Rights

William and Mary accept the Declaration and the crown

The Grand Alliance concluded between the Holy Roman Empire, England, Holland, and Spain

War declared against France

King William's War, 1689–1697 (the first of the French and Indian Wars)

Samuel Richardson born

1689–1702 Reign of William III

1690 James II lands in Ireland with French support, but is defeated at the battle of the Boyne

John Locke's *Essay Concerning Human Understanding*

1692 Salem witchcraft trials

Death of Sir George Etherege

1694 George Fox's *Journal*

Voltaire (François Marie Arouet) born

Death of Mary II

1695 Congreve's *Love for Love*

Death of Henry Vaughan

1697 War with France ended by the Treaty of Ryswick

Vanbrugh's *The Relapse*

1698 Jeremy Collier's *A Short View of the Immorality and Profaneness of the English Stage*

1699 Fénelon's *Les Aventures de Télémaque*

1700 Congreve's *The Way of the World*

Defoe's *The True-Born Englishman*

Death of John Dryden

1701 War of the Spanish Succession, 1701–1714 (Queen Anne's War in America, 1702–1713)

Death of Sir Charles Sedley

1702 Clarendon's *History of the Rebellion* (1702–1704)

Defoe's *The Shortest Way with the Dissenters*

1702–1714 Reign of Queen Anne

1703 Defoe is arrested, fined, and pilloried for writing *The Shortest Way*

Death of Samuel Pepys

1704 John Churchill, duke of Marlborough, and Prince Eugene of Savoy defeat the French at Blenheim

Capture of Gibraltar

Swift's *A Tale of a Tub* and *The Battle of the Books*

The *Review* founded (1704–1713)

1706 Farquhar's *The Recruiting Officer*

Deaths of John Evelyn and Charles Sackville, earl of Dorset

1707 Farquhar's *The Beaux' Stratagem*

Act of Union joining England and Scotland

Death of George Farquhar

Henry Fielding born

1709 The *Tatler* founded (1709–1711)

Nicholas Rowe's edition of Shakespeare

Samuel Johnson born

Marlborough defeats the French at Malplaquet

Charles XII of Sweden defeated at Poltava

1710 South Sea Company founded

First copyright act

1711 Swift's *The Conduct of the Allies*

The *Spectator* founded (1711–1712; 1714)

Marlborough dismissed

CHRONOLOGICAL TABLE

David Hume born

1712 Pope's *The Rape of the Lock* (cantos I–II)

Jean Jacques Rousseau born

1713 War with France ended by the Treaty of Utrecht

The *Guardian* founded

Swift becomes dean of St. Patrick's, Dublin

Addison's *Cato*

Laurence Sterne born

1714 Pope's expanded version of *The Rape of the Lock* (cantos I–V)

1714–1727 Reign of George I

1715 The Jacobite rebellion in Scotland

Pope's translation of Homer's *Iliad* (1715–1720)

Death of Louis XIV

1716 Death of William Wycherley

Thomas Gray born

1717 Pope's *Eloisa to Abelard*

David Garrick born

Horace Walpole born

1718 Quadruple Alliance (Britain, France, the Netherlands, the German Empire) in war against Spain

1719 Defoe's *Robinson Crusoe*

Death of Joseph Addison

1720 Inoculation against smallpox introduced in Boston

War against Spain

The South Sea Bubble

Defoe's *Captain Singleton* and *Memoirs of a Cavalier*

1721 Tobias Smollett born

William Collins born

1722 Defoe's *Moll Flanders, Journal of the Plague Year*, and *Colonel Jack*

1724 Defoe's *Roxana*

Swift's *The Drapier's Letters*

1725 Pope's translation of Homer's *Odyssey* (1725–1726)

1726 Swift's *Gulliver's Travels*

Voltaire in England (1726–1729)

Death of Sir John Vanbrugh

1727–1760 Reign of George II

1728 Gay's *The Beggar's Opera*

Pope's *The Dunciad* (books I–II)

Oliver Goldsmith born

1729 Swift's *A Modest Proposal*

Edmund Burke born

Deaths of William Congreve and Sir Richard Steele

1731 Navigation improved by introduction of the quadrant

Pope's *Moral Essays* (1731–1735)

Death of Daniel Defoe

William Cowper born

1732 Death of John Gay

1733 Pope's *Essay on Man* (1733–1734)

Lewis Theobald's edition of Shakespeare

1734 Voltaire's *Lettres philosophiques*

1737 Edward Gibbon born

1738 Johnson's *London*

1740 War of the Austrian Succession, 1740–1748 (King George's War in America, 1744–1748)

George Anson begins his circumnavigation of the world (1740–1744)

Frederick the Great becomes king of Prussia (1740–1786)

Richardson's *Pamela* (1740–1741)

James Boswell born

1742 Fielding's *Joseph Andrews*

Edward Young's *Night Thoughts* (1742–1745)

Pope's *The New Dunciad* (book IV)

1744 Johnson's *Life of Mr. Richard Savage*

Death of Alexander Pope

1745 Second Jacobite rebellion, led by Charles Edward, the Young Pretender

Death of Jonathan Swift

1746 The Young Pretender defeated at Culloden

Collins' *Odes on Several Descriptive and Allegorical Subjects*

1747 Richardson's *Clarissa Harlowe* (1747–1748)

Franklin's experiments with electricity announced

Voltaire's *Essai sur les moeurs*

1748 War of the Austrian Succession ended by the Peace of Aix-la-Chapelle

Smollett's *Adventures of Roderick Random*

David Hume's *Enquiry Concerning Human Understanding*

Montesquieu's *L'Esprit des lois*

1749 Fielding's *Tom Jones*

Johnson's *The Vanity of Human Wishes*

CHRONOLOGICAL TABLE

Bolingbroke's *Idea of a Patriot King*
1750 The *Rambler* founded (1750–1752)
1751 Gray's *Elegy Written in a Country Churchyard*
Fielding's *Amelia*
Smollett's *Adventures of Peregrine Pickle*
Denis Diderot and Jean le Rond d'Alembert begin to publish the *Encyclopédie* (1751–1765)
Richard Brinsley Sheridan born
1752 Thomas Chatterton born
1753 Richardson's *History of Sir Charles Grandison* (1753–1754)
Smollett's *The Adventures of Ferdinand Count Fathom*
1754 Hume's *History of England* (1754–1762)
Death of Henry Fielding
George Crabbe born
1755 Lisbon destroyed by earthquake
Fielding's *Journal of a Voyage to Lisbon* published posthumously
Johnson's *Dictionary of the English Language*
1756 The Seven Years' War against France, 1756–1763 (the French and Indian War in America, 1755–1760)
William Pitt the elder becomes prime minister
Johnson's proposal for an edition of Shakespeare
1757 Robert Clive wins the battle of Plassey, in India
Gray's "The Progress of Poesy" and "The Bard"
Burke's *Philosophical Enquiry into the Origin of Our Ideas of the Sublime and Beautiful*
Hume's *Natural History of Religion*
William Blake born
1758 The *Idler* founded (1758–1760)
1759 Capture of Quebec by General James Wolfe
Johnson's *History of Rasselas, Prince of Abyssinia*
Voltaire's *Candide*
The British Museum opens
Sterne's *The Life and Opinions of Tristram Shandy* (1759–1767)
Death of William Collins

Mary Wollstonecraft born
Robert Burns born
1760 James Macpherson's *Fragments of Ancient Poetry Collected in the Highlands of Scotland*
William Beckford born
1760–1820 **Reign of George III**
1761 Jean Jacques Rousseau's *Julie, ou la nouvelle Héloïse*
Death of Samuel Richardson
1762 Rousseau's *Du Contrat social* and *Émile*
Catherine the Great becomes czarina of Russia (1762–1796)
1763 The Seven Years' War ended by the Peace of Paris
Smart's *A Song to David*
1764 James Hargreaves invents the spinning jenny
1765 Parliament passes the Stamp Act to tax the American colonies
Johnson's edition of Shakespeare
Walpole's *The Castle of Otranto*
Thomas Percy's *Reliques of Ancient English Poetry*
Blackstone's *Commentaries on the Laws of England* (1765–1769)
1766 The Stamp Act repealed
Swift's *Journal to Stella* first published in a collection of his letters
Goldsmith's *The Vicar of Wakefield*
Smollett's *Travels through France and Italy*
Lessing's *Laokoon*
Rousseau in England (1766–1767)
1768 Sterne's *A Sentimental Journey through France and Italy*
The Royal Academy founded by George III
First edition of the *Encyclopaedia Britannica*
Death of Laurence Sterne
1769 David Garrick organizes the Shakespeare Jubilee at Stratford-upon-Avon
Sir Joshua Reynolds' *Discourses* (1769–1790)
Richard Arkwright invents the spinning water frame
1770 Boston Massacre
Burke's *Thoughts on the Cause of the Present Discontents*

Goldsmith's *The Deserted Village*
Death of Thomas Chatterton

1771 Deaths of Thomas Gray and Tobias Smollett

1773 Boston Tea Party
Goldsmith's *She Stoops to Conquer*
Johann Wolfgang von Goethe's *Götz von Berlichingen*

1774 The first Continental Congress meets in Philadelphia
Goethe's *Sorrows of Young Werther*
Death of Oliver Goldsmith

1775 American War of Independence begins with the battles of Lexington and Concord
Johnson's *Journey to the Western Islands of Scotland*
Sheridan's *The Rivals* and *The Duenna*
Beaumarchais's *Le Barbier de Séville*
James Watt and Matthew Boulton begin building steam engines in England

1776 American Declaration of Independence
Gibbons' *Decline and Fall of the Roman Empire* (1776–1788)
Adam Smith's *Inquiry into the Nature and Causes of the Wealth of Nations*
Thomas Paine's *Common Sense*
Death of David Hume

1777 Maurice Morgann's *Essay on the Dramatic Character of Sir John Falstaff*
Sheridan's *The School for Scandal* first performed (published 1780)

1778 The American colonies allied with France
Britain and France at war
Captain James Cook discovers Hawaii
Deaths of Jean Jacques Rousseau and Voltaire

1779 Johnson's *Prefaces to the Works of the English Poets* (1779–1781); reissued in 1781 as *The Lives of the Most Eminent English Poets*
Sheridan's *The Critic*
Samuel Crompton invents the spinning mule
Death of David Garrick

1780 The Gordon riots in London

1781 Charles Cornwallis surrenders at Yorktown

Immanuel Kant's *Critique of Pure Reason*
Friedrich von Schiller's *Die Räuber*

1782 Cowper's "The Journey of John Gilpin" published in the *Public Advertiser*
Pierre de Laclos's *Les Liaisons dangereuses*
Rousseau's *Confessions* published posthumously

1783 American War of Independence ended by the Definitive Treaty of Peace, signed at Paris
Blake's *Poetical Sketches*
Crabbe's *The Village*
William Pitt the younger becomes prime minister

1784 Beaumarchais's *Le Mariage de Figaro* first performed (published 1785)
Death of Samuel Johnson

1785 Warren Hastings returns to England from India
Boswell's *The Journal of a Tour of the Hebrides, with Samuel Johnson, LL.D.*
Cowper's *The Task*
Edmund Cartwright invents the power loom

1786 William Beckford's *Vathek* published in English (originally written in French in 1782)
Burns's *Poems Chiefly in the Scottish Dialect*
Wolfgang Amadeus Mozart's *The Marriage of Figaro*
Death of Frederick the Great

1787 The Committee for Abolition of the Slave Trade founded in England
The Constitutional Convention meets at Philadelphia; the Constitution is signed
Mozart's *Don Giovanni*
Schiller's *Don Carlos*

1788 The trial of Hastings begins on charges of corruption of the government in India
The Estates-General of France summoned
U. S. Constitution is ratified
George Washington elected president of the United States

CHRONOLOGICAL TABLE

Giovanni Casanova's *Histoire de ma fuite* (first manuscript of his memoirs)

1789 The Estates-General meets at Versailles

The National Assembly (Assemblée Nationale) convened

The fall of the Bastille marks the beginning of the French Revolution

First U.S. Congress meets in New York

Blake's *Songs of Innocence*

Jeremy Bentham's *Introduction to the Principles of Morals and Legislation*

Gilbert White's *Natural History of Selborne*

1790 Congress sets permanent capital city site on Potomac River

First U.S. Census

Burke's *Reflections on the Revolution in France*

Blake's *The Marriage of Heaven and Hell*

Edmund Malone's edition of Shakespeare

Death of Benjamin Franklin

1791 French royal family's flight from Paris and capture at Varennes; imprisonment in the Tuileries

Bill of Rights is ratified

Thomas Paine's *The Rights of Man* (1791–1792)

Boswell's *The Life of Johnson*

Burns's *Tam o' Shanter*

1792 The Prussians invade France and are repulsed at Valmy

September massacres

The National Convention declares royalty abolished in France

Washington reelected without opposition

New York Stock Exchange opens

Wollstonecraft's *Vindication of the Rights of Women*

1793 Trial and execution of Louis XVI and Marie Antoinette

France declares war against England

The Committee of Public Safety (Comité de Salut Public) established

Eli Whitney devises the cotton gin

William Godwin's *An Enquiry Concerning Political Justice*

1794 Execution of Georges Danton and Maximilien de Robespierre

Paine's *The Age of Reason* (1794–1796)

Blake's *Songs of Experience*

Ann Radcliffe's *The Mysteries of Udolpho*

Death of Edward Gibbon

1795 The government of the Directory established (1795–1799)

Hastings acquitted

Death of James Boswell

1796 Napoleon Bonaparte takes command in Italy

Matthew Lewis' *The Monk*

John Adams elected president

Death of Robert Burns

1797 The peace of Campo Formio: extinction of the Venetian Republic

X. Y. Z. Affair

Deaths of Edmund Burke, Mary Wollstonecraft, and Horace Walpole

1798 Napoleon invades Egypt

Horatio Nelson wins the battle of the Nile

Wordsworth and Coleridge's *Lyrical Ballads*

Thomas Malthus' *Essay on the Principle of Population*

1799 Napoleon becomes first consul

Sheridan's *Pizarro*

1800 Thomas Jefferson and Aaron Burr defeat John Adams in the presidential election

Library of Congress established

Death of William Cowper

1804 Napoleon crowned emperor of the French

Jefferson reelected

1807 Aaron Burr tried for treason; is acquitted

1808 James Madison is elected president

1812 War of 1812 (1812–1814)

Napoleon invades Russia; retreats from Moscow in winter

Madison reelected

1814 Napoleon abdicates and is exiled to Elba; Bourbon restoration with Louis XVIII

1815 Napoleon returns to France (the Hundred Days); is defeated at Waterloo and exiled to St. Helena

CHRONOLOGICAL TABLE

1816 James Monroe elected president
Death of Richard Brinsley Sheridan
1820 Monroe reelected
1821 Death of Napoleon
1825 John Quincy Adams elected president
by the House of Representatives

1827 Death of William Blake
1828 Andrew Jackson elected president
1831 Nat Turner slave revolt crushed in
Virginia
1832 Jackson reelected
Death of George Crabbe

List of Contributors

JOHN BEER. Reader in English Literature, University of Cambridge. Publications include *Blake's Humanism; Blake's Visionary Universe; Coleridge's Poetic Intelligence; Wordsworth and the Human Heart; Wordsworth in Time;* and editions of Coleridge's *Poems; Coleridge's Variety*, the bicentenary volume; and (with G. K. Das) *E. M. Forster: A Human View*, the Forster Centenary Studies. **William Blake.**

LAURENCE BRANDER. Lecturer in English, University of Lucknow (1927–1939); BBC Representative, New Delhi (1942–1945); Director, Publications Department, the British Council (1948–1962). Publications include *George Orwell; Somerset Maugham; E. M. Forster: A Critical Study;* and *Aldous Huxley: A Critical Study*. **Tobias Smollett.**

RAYMOND LAURENCE BRETT. G. F. Grant Professor of English, University of Hull. Publications include *The Third Earl of Shaftesbury; Reason and Imagination; An Introduction to English Studies; Fancy and Imagination;* and editions of *Poems of Faith and Doubt: The Victorian Age; S. T. Coleridge;* and *Andrew Marvell: Tercentenary Essays*. **George Crabbe.**

ROBERT FRANCIS BRISSENDEN. Reader in English, Australian National University, Canberra; Visiting Fellow, William Andrews Clark Memorial Library, University of California at Los Angeles (1970–1971); Chairman, Literature Board of the Australian Council (1978–   ). Publications include *Virtue in Darkness: Studies in the Novel of Sentiment from Richardson to Sade;* and critical monographs and articles on Australian and American writing. **Samuel Richardson.**

JOHN BUTT. Professor of English Literature, University of Edinburgh (1959–1965). Publications include *The Augustan Age* and *The Mid-Eighteenth Century*, vol. VIII of the *Oxford History of English Literature*. Editor of the *Twickenham Edition of the Poems of Alexander Pope*. **Henry Fielding.**

PHILIP ARTHUR WILLIAM COLLINS. Professor of English Literature, University of Leicester; Visiting Professor, University of California at Berkeley and Columbia University. Publications include *James Boswell; Dickens and Crime; Dickens and Education;* and *Reading Aloud: A Victorian Métier*. Editor of *Dickens: The Critical Heritage*. **James Boswell.**

DAVID DAICHES. Professor of English Literature, Cornell University (1946–1951); Lecturer in English, University of Cambridge (1951–1961); Professor of English and Dean of the School of English and American Studies, University of Sussex (1961–1977). Publications include *Robert Burns; Robert Burns and His World; A Critical History of English Literature; The Novel and the Modern World; The Paradox of Scottish Culture; Critical Approaches to Literature; Sir Walter Scott and His World; R. L. Stevenson;* and (with A. K. Thorlby) *Literature and Western Civilization*. **Robert Burns.**

OSWALD DOUGHTY. Formerly Professor of English Literature, University of Capetown. Publications include *D. G. Rossetti: A Victorian Romantic;* and editions of *The Poems of D. G. Rossetti* and (with J. R. Wahl) *The Letters of D. G. Rossetti*. **William Collins.**

ARNOLD HARE. Reader in Theater History, University of Bristol. Publications include *The Georgian Theatre in Wessex; Theatre Royal Bath—The Orchard Street Calendar 1750–1805; George Frederick Cooke—the Actor and the Man;* and "English Comedy" in *Comic Drama—the European Heritage*. Contributor to *Enciclopedia dello Spettacolo*. **Richard Brinsley Sheridan.**

BRENDAN HENNESSY. Publications include *A Dictionary of the Theatre* and articles and interviews on contemporary fiction and drama for the *Times* (London), *Daily Telegraph,* and *Transatlantic Review.* **The Gothic Novel.**

ARTHUR RALEIGH HUMPHREYS. Professor of English Literature, University of Leicester (1947–1976); Visiting Fellow, Folger Shakespeare Library, Washington, D. C. (1959–1960; 1961–1962; 1964), Huntington Library, San Marino, California (1978–1979); Visiting Professor, Bogazici University, Istanbul (1979–1980). Publications include *The Augustan World*; "Henry Fielding," "Tobias Smollett," "Samuel Johnson," "The Literary Scene," and "Architecture and Landscape" in the *Pelican Guide to English Literature: From Dryden to Johnson; and editions of Henry IV, Pts 1 and 2; Henry V; Henry VIII; and Robinson Crusoe.* **Sir Richard Steele and Joseph Addison.**

IAN ROBERT JAMES JACK. Reader in English Poetry, University of Cambridge (1973–1976); Professor of English, University of Cambridge (1976–   ). Publications include *Augustan Satire; English Literature 1815–1832,* vol. X of the *Oxford History of English Literature; Keats and the Mirror of Art; Browning's Major Poetry;* and editions of Laurence Sterne's *A Sentimental Journey* and *The Poetical Works of Robert Browning,* Oxford English Texts series. General Editor of the Clarendon edition of the Brontë novels. **Alexander Pope.**

ALEXANDER NORMAN JEFFARES, FRSL, FAHA. Professor of English Language and Literature, University of Adelaide (1951–1956); Professor of English Literature, University of Leeds (1957–1974); Professor of English Literature, University of Stirling (1974–   ). Editor of *A Review of English Literature* (1960–1967); *A Review of International English Literature* (1970–1972); Vice Chairman, Scottish Arts Council; Life President, International Association for the Study of Anglo-Irish Literature. Publications include *W. B. Yeats, Man and Poet; A Commentary on the Collected Poems of W. B. Yeats;* (with A. S. Knowland) *A Commentary on the Collected Plays of W. B. Yeats;* and editions of *Fair Liberty Was All His Cry,* a tercentenary tribute to Jonathan Swift; *Jonathan Swift,* Modern Judgments series; *In Excited Reverie,* a centenary tribute to W. B. Yeats; *W. B. Yeats: The Critical Heritage;* and

A Goldsmith Selection: She Stoops to Conquer. **Oliver Goldsmith; Jonathan Swift.**

DOUGLAS WILLIAM JEFFERSON. Professor of English Literature, University of Leeds (1970–1977). Publications include *Henry James,* Writers and Critics series; *Henry James and the Modern Reader;* "Laurence Sterne" in the *Pelican Guide to English Literature: From Dryden to Johnson;* and *Jane Austen's Emma.* **Laurence Sterne.**

ROBERT WYNDHAM KETTON-CREMER, FRSL. Reid Lecture, University of Cambridge (1957); Warton Lecture, British Academy (1959); Lamont Memorial Lecture, Yale University (1960). Publications include *Horace Walpole; Norfolk Portraits;* and *Thomas Gray.* **Thomas Gray.**

NORMAN CORNTHWAITE NICHOLSON. Publications include *Five Rivers; A Local Habitation; Selected Poems; The Old Man of the Mountains* (drama); *Portrait of the Lakes* (topography); and editions of *A Choice of Cowper's Verse* and *An Anthology of Modern Religious Verse.* **William Cowper.**

SIR SYDNEY CASTLE ROBERTS. Master of Pembroke College, University of Cambridge (1949–1958); Vice Chancellor, University of Cambridge (1949–1951); Secretary to the Syndics of the Cambridge University Press (1922–1948). Publications include *The Story of Dr. Johnson; A History of the Cambridge University Press; Samuel Johnson, Moralist;* and *Dr. Johnson and Others.* **Samuel Johnson.**

JAMES SUTHERLAND. Professor of English Literature, University of London, Birkbeck College (1936–1944), Queen Mary College (1944–1951), University College (1951–1967); Visiting Professor, Harvard University, Indiana University, University of Pittsburgh, New York University, and University of California at Los Angeles; Walter Scott Lectures, Edinburgh University (1952); Clark Lectures, University of Cambridge (1956); Alexander Lectures, Toronto University (1956). Editor of *Review of English Studies* (1940–1947). Publications include *Defoe* (biography); *Defoe: A Critical Study; A Preface to Eighteenth Century Poetry; English Satire; English Literature of the Late Seventeenth Century,* vol. VII of the *Oxford History of English Literature;* editions of Alexander Pope's *The Dun-*

ciad; The Oxford Book of English Talk; and *The Oxford Book of Literary Anecdotes.* **Daniel Defoe.**

THOMAS EDWIN UTLEY, CBE. Leader-writer *Sunday Times* (London) (1945–1947), *Times* (London) (1948–1954), *Daily Telegraph* (1964–   ). Publications include *Essays in Conservatism; The Conservatives and the Critics; Edmund Burke; Enoch Powell;* and *What Laws May Cure.* **Edmund Burke.**

DAME CICELY VERONICA WEDGWOOD, DBE, OM. Honorary Fellow, Lady Margaret College, University of Oxford, University College, London, and London School of Economics; Member, Institute for Advanced Study, Princeton University. Publications include *The Thirty Years' War; Seventeenth Century English Literature; Poetry and Politics;* and *The Trial of Charles I.* **Edward Gibbon.**

OLIVER WARNER, FRSL. Deputy Director, Publications Department, the British Council (1948–1963). Publications include *A Portrait of Lord Nelson; Trafalgar; Great Seamen;* and *Great Sea Battles.* **John Gay.**

DANIEL DEFOE

(ca. 1660-1731)

James Sutherland

"A few days ago died Daniel Defoe, Snr, a person well known for his numerous writings." These words, from the *Universal Spectator* of 1 May 1731, express very fairly the contemporary estimate of Defoe. Nothing here about the author of *Robinson Crusoe* and half a dozen other works of fiction that are still read today; only a comprehensive reference to his numerous writings, and the whole obituary disposed of in a single sentence. The notion that he would be remembered, more than two centuries after his death, as a famous English author would have seemed extravagant to most of his contemporaries. Joseph Addison, yes; and Alexander Pope, without a doubt—they were cultured men and correct writers who had addressed themselves to the polite society of London, and who had subscribed to, and in a large degree created, the literary standards of the age in which they lived. But though Defoe was as well known as either of them, and his works as widely read, his literary idiom was much less refined, and his public altogether less select. Pope did not hesitate to give him a place in the *Dunciad* along with the other Grub Street scribblers, and it is unlikely that many of his readers lifted an eyebrow at finding Defoe in such company.

The contemporary reader is apt to feel that whatever a classic may be, it cannot be a book that has entertained him with almost no effort on his part; and in the earliest references to the author of *Robinson Crusoe* and *Moll Flanders* there is always that half-mocking or patronizing tone with which the twentieth-century reader is apt to refer to any bestselling author. "There is not an old woman that can go to the price of it," he was told shortly after the publication of *Robinson Crusoe*, "but buys thy *Life*

[Quotations from *A Journal of the Plague Year* and *Colonel Jack* are from G. H. Maynardier, ed., *The Works*. Those from *Robinson Crusoe* and *Moll Flanders* are from the respective Everyman's Library editions.]

and Adventures, and leaves it as a legacy with the *Pilgrim's Progress*, the *Practice of Piety*, and *God's Revenge against Murther* to her posterity."

Yet we happen to know that Pope's real opinion of Defoe was much more favorable than the allusion in the *Dunciad* would lead us to expect. On one occasion, when the conversation turned to Defoe, Pope showed that he was fully alive to his remarkable gifts as a writer. "The first part of *Robinson Crusoe* is very good," he remarked. "Defoe wrote a vast many things; and none bad, though none excellent except this. There is something good in all he has written." Pope's brief estimate is wonderfully just. He had the candor to admit that Defoe's writings had given him pleasure, and the fairness to allow that this pleasure was due to the merit of Defoe, and not to some good-natured condescension on the part of his reader. It is clear, too, that he was much more familiar with Defoe's writings than the reader of the present day is likely to be. There are indeed "a vast many things" (John Robert Moore in his bibliography credits him with over five hundred separate titles), and so far as this iceberg still floats in the twentieth century, it is the fictitious narratives, written in his later life that still appear above the surface. The other seven-eighths are, for the ordinary reader, hopelessly submerged.

It is no use complaining about the modern neglect of Defoe's miscellaneous writings; we must accept Samuel Johnson's dictum that "about things on which the public thinks long it commonly attains to think right." Yet it is a pity that more of Defoe's work is not still read, for there is "something good in all he has written." One might go further and claim that, whereas in his prose fiction Defoe is not much more than a fascinating primitive, in his controversial and journalistic writings he is one of the great English masters. Most of these writings are too deeply imbedded in their contemporary setting to be immediately intelligible to the modern reader, and yet there is a quality in Defoe's style that keeps them obstinately alive. It is mainly a matter of spiritual energy, a natural alertness and liveliness that kept him at a high pitch of intensity as he put his thoughts on paper. He spent his whole writing life of nearly half a century advocating causes, persuading men to change their minds, to abandon some established prejudice, to consult their own best interest; and on every occasion he wrote with utter conviction. He not only meant what he said but believed that it was tremendously important it should be said, and that it was his business in life to say it. God had given him the insight—on such matters as trade, religious strife, and so on—that had been denied to other men, and he must publish the truth as he knew it.

All this has a familiar sound: it is the voice of the Puritan. Defoe in fact came of good Puritan stock. His earliest surviving compositions are contained in a manuscript volume, now in the Huntington Library, and they consist of a number of pious poems (undoubtedly his own work) and a series of abstracts of sermons he had heard. His father intended him for the ministry, but in his early twenties he became a partner in a haberdashery, and before long he was trading in wine, tobacco, and other commodities. Yet Defoe's Puritan ancestry and Nonconformist upbringing left a permanent impression on his mind and character. Much of his writing in the *Review* and elsewhere is like nothing so much as an unusually lively sermon. He never lost the earnestness and the stubborn conviction of having an "inner light" that are at once the source of the Puritan's strength and of his limitation. But when a man cares about things as much as Defoe did, he is unlikely to be dull. He can easily be wrong; he may be narrowminded; he may be needlessly repetitive; he may be too exclamatory and overwilling to preach. But he is never likely to bore his readers, and at his best he will have the same absolute dominion over them as the Mariner had over the Wedding Guest.

I

WHAT Defoe wrote was intimately connected with the sort of life he led, with the friends and enemies he made, and with the interests natural to a merchant and a Dissenter. About 1680, he began his adventurous career as a London merchant. In a few years he was trading in a large way, and the natural culmination of his career at this stage would have been to become Sir Daniel Defoe, lord mayor of London. But serious losses at sea and a tendency to launch indiscreetly beyond his financial depth combined to ruin the rising young merchant. In 1692 his affairs became hopelessly entangled, and he found himself bankrupt to the extent of £17,000. He recovered quickly from this misfortune, as he was to recover from many another, started a brick and tile factory near Tilbury, and in a few years had paid most of his creditors in full. And then the second blow fell. This time the trouble was due not to speculation or overtrading but to the fact that in 1703 he was arrested for writing an indiscreet political pamphlet, *The Shortest Way with the Dissenters*. When he was released from prison, his brick and tile business was ruined, and for the second time he was declared a bankrupt.

His entry into the world of politics was perhaps inevitable. Defoe was never content to remain for long in the realm of impersonal thought; he had a dangerous way of applying his mind to parties and persons. One of his earliest and liveliest pamphlets, *The Poor Man's Plea* (1698), illustrates well his fondness for walking on controversial ground. Under William and Mary, various laws had been passed to encourage a reformation in manners; but, though these laws were in the statute book, they could have little effect so long as many of the magistrates led dissolute lives themselves. What could be done about blasphemy, for example, when a magistrate "shall punish a Man for Drunkenness, with a *God damn him, set him in the Stocks*"? Worse still was the tendency of justices to discriminate between the rich and the poor:

These are all Cobweb Laws, in which the small Flies are catch'd, and great Ones break thro'. My Lord Mayor has whipt about the poor Beggars, and a few scandalous Whores have been sent to the House of Correction; some Alehouse-keepers and Vintners have been fin'd for drawing Drink on the Sabbath-Day; but all this falls upon us, of the Mob, the poor *Plebeii*, as if all the Vice lay among us, for we do not find the Rich Drunkard carry'd before my Lord Mayor, nor a Swearing Lewd Merchant. *The Man with a Gold Ring and Gay Cloaths* may Swear before the Justice, or at the Justice, may reel home through the open streets, and no Man take any notice of it; but if a poor Man get drunk, or swears an Oath, he must to the Stocks without Remedy.

This is the authentic voice of Defoe, the voice

that was to entertain and exasperate his contemporaries for the next thirty years. "England's watchdog" was the name given to William Cobbett in the early nineteenth century, and the phrase would equally well have fitted Defoe a hundred years earlier. He never pulled his verbal punches; and the words he used were so lively, so direct and colloquial, so immediately and devastatingly intelligible, that they seem to belong to the spoken rather than to the written word and to come straight "home to men's business and bosoms."

From this point onward, Defoe was drawn gradually deeper into the world of political controversy. In the last years of the seventeenth century, King William was patiently trying to arouse the country to an awareness of what the ambitions of the French king, Louis XIV, meant for English liberties, and Defoe published a series of effective pamphlets in favor of William's policy of containment. William appears to have been Defoe's one real hero, and when in 1700 the king's Dutch favorites, who came to England with him in 1688, were attacked by John Tutchin in a grumbling poem, *The Foreigners*, Defoe replied with his own far more popular—and, indeed, more famous—poem, *The True-Born Englishman*. And then the wheel of fortune turned again. The unexpected death of the king checked Defoe's rising fortunes, and the outlook for himself and his fellow Dissenters changed overnight for the worse.

During the reign of William and Mary, the Dissenters had been left more or less unmolested; but with the accession of Queen Anne, the High Tories came into their own, or believed they had, and proceeded to act on that assumption. A bill designed to penalize the Dissenters much more severely quickly passed through the House of Commons, but it met with considerable opposition from the House of Lords. Excitement in both houses and in the country at large was now running high, and some violent and intolerant sermons by High Church divines (notably one preached at Oxford by Dr. Henry Sacheverell) served to increase the public commotion. In December 1702, when the controversy was at its height, an anonymous pamphlet called *The Shortest Way with the Dissenters* put the case against the dissenting body in terms even more outrageous than any that Sacheverell had dared to use. "I do not prescribe fire and faggot," wrote the anonymous author, but in fact he stopped only a little short of those drastic remedies:

'Tis vain to trifle in this matter. The light, foolish handling of them by Mulcts, Fines etc., 'tis their Glory and their Advantage. If the Gallows instead of the Counter, and the Gallies instead of the Fines, were the Reward of going to a Conventicle, to preach or hear, there wou'd not be so many Sufferers. The Spirit of Martyrdom is over; they that will go to Church to be chosen Sheriffs and Mayors would go to forty Churches rather than be Hang'd.

This must have been music to the ears of the High Tories; but even the most stupid of them could not have remained deluded for long. On 3 January a warrant was issued for the arrest of the author of *The Shortest Way*. The government had found out who he was and duly named him. He was Daniel Defoe—"a middle-sized man, about forty years old, of a brown complexion, and dark-brown coloured hair, but wears a wig; a hooked nose, a sharp chin, grey eyes, and a large mole near his mouth."

The perpetrator of a successful hoax is rarely popular with those in authority, and Defoe was now to suffer severely for what was perhaps the cleverest thing he ever wrote. To expose the utter extravagance of the High Tory attitude to the Dissenters, he had slightly exaggerated the language used by the Tory diehards, and produced a completely successful reductio ad absurdum. Faced with the unexpected consequences of his ingenious intervention, Defoe went into hiding; but on 20 May 1703 he was discovered in the house of a French weaver and taken off to prison. He was to receive no mercy. On 9 July he was sentenced to stand three times in the pillory, to pay a considerable fine, to remain in prison during the queen's pleasure, and to find securities for his good behavior for the next seven years. It seems clear that this harsh sentence was a cumulative one, earned not merely for writing *The Shortest Way* but for his other political and literary misdemeanors over the past few years.

This unwelcome experience completely altered the course of Defoe's life. It drove him finally into political journalism, and it led him into that strange underground sort of life he was to lead for the next twenty years. On the man himself, his experience as a prisoner in Newgate almost certainly made a deep and lasting impression; and it seems likely that his keen interest in the lives and minds of rogues and criminals dates from this period. It is worth noticing too that in *The Shortest Way* Defoe had already perfected a technique that was to serve him again and again when he took to writing his fictitious narratives late in life: the technique of putting himself in someone else's shoes and proceeding to write consistently from that person's point of view. There is no fundamental difference between mimicking the outlook and idiom of an intolerant Tory and adopting the intellectual and moral attitudes and the literary style of a Robinson Crusoe or a Moll Flanders. That, at any rate, was Defoe's habitual method of writing prose fiction; it is a developed form of "make-believe."

Early in November 1703, Defoe was a free man again. He owed his release to Robert Harley, who was soon to become one of the two secretaries of state. Harley must have had his eye on Defoe for some time; for, during the course of the summer, he had written to one of his fellow ministers to say that Defoe's pen might be very useful to the new government. What followed is hard to state in a few words without giving a false impression. In the next few years Defoe's enemies frequently accused him of being a mere tool of Harley's, a mercenary scribbler who wrote for hire whatever Harley wanted at the moment. He certainly worked faithfully for Harley, but not quite in that fashion. He always claimed to be "a constant follower of moderate principles, a vigorous opposer of hot measures of *all* parties." In working for Harley, he was in little danger of betraying those principles; he was in fact working with Harley.

The first unmistakable indication that Defoe was at large again was the appearance, on 19 February 1704, of the first number of his famous periodical, the *Review*. He kept it going until 11 June 1713, for the greater part of the time as a triweekly paper (Monday, Thursday, Saturday). From this pulpit he could address his fellow Englishmen on all the topics nearest to his heart, but especially on trade. For over ten years he wrote almost every word of the *Review* himself, wherever he might be at the time and whatever else he might be doing. Yet he also found time to write numerous pamphlets on current affairs, and several substantial books, including *The Consolidator* (1705), a political allegory, *Jure Divino* (1706), an ambitious political poem in twelve books, and his *History of the Union* (1709), a folio running to over seven hundred pages.

Even all this writing was no more than the product of such leisure as he could snatch from other and more constant employments. Quite early in their odd relationship, Harley employed Defoe as a sort of secret service agent. Defoe was dispatched on various tours through the country districts to report on how the counties and boroughs felt toward the government. Later, in 1706, Harley sent him to Edinburgh on the eve of the negotiations for the Union, and Defoe supplied him with long and interesting reports on the Scots, whom he found to be a "hardened, refractory, and terrible people." When Harley fell from power early in 1708, Defoe continued to act in much the same capacity for the earl of Godolphin; and when Godolphin was replaced by Harley in 1710, the old relationship between the two men was at once resumed and remained unbroken until Queen Anne dismissed Harley from office a few days before her death on 1 August 1714.

With the death of the queen, the political scene was once more completely transformed. The Whigs swept into power and were never to be out of office again in Defoe's lifetime. Defoe, who had identified himself more and more closely in recent years with the moderate Toryism of Harley (now a prisoner in the Tower), found himself almost as lonely as his own Robinson Crusoe. In the spring of 1715 he published an autobiographical narrative, *An Appeal to Honour and Justice*, intended as a vindication of his political conduct. His health, it would seem, was failing; for he wrote pathetically of being now "very near to the great Ocean of Eternity," and his publisher added a note stating that the author had been "seiz'd with a violent fit of apoplexy" and was now in "a weak and languishing condition." There might never, then, have been a *Robinson Crusoe* at all, and Defoe's life might have closed in gloom and defeat. On the contrary, he was about to enter on his most remarkable decade as an author.

But first of all he succeeded in making peace with the Whig leaders, and they found a job for him that only he could do. Although the Tories were out of office, and the Jacobites in a hopeless minority, their various newspapers were still an active source of annoyance, and even of some danger, to the new government. With the approval of the Whig secretary of state, Defoe posed as a Tory, under the displeasure of the government, and got a job as a translator of foreign news on the most virulent of all the Tory papers, *Mist's Weekly Journal*. As this experienced journalist became more and more necessary to Mist, he appears to have gotten the running of the paper into his hands, and to have used his position to tone down its asperities, or, as he put it himself, to "disable" and "enervate" it, "so as to do no mischief, or give any offence to the government." This remarkable piece of double-crossing appears to have worked successfully for several years. It was a new kind of secret service, with the same leading actor, but with a different cast. The best that can be said in defense of Defoe's conduct is that he was still faithful to his principle of moderation. "I have been faithful," he might have claimed, "after my fashion."

He was now writing more busily than ever. With the appearance of *Robinsoe Crusoe*, on 25 April 1719, he entered on six remarkable years of fiction writing, ending rather than culminating in 1725 with *A New Voyage Round the World*. His annus mirabilis was undoubtedly 1722, which saw the publication of *Moll Flanders*, *A Journal of the Plague Year*, and *Colonel Jack*. But a glance at the bibliography will show that those works of fiction were only part of his total output. In his last few years he turned from fiction to write such books as his *Tour Thro' the Whole Island of Great Britain*, *The Complete English Tradesman*, *The Political History of the Devil*, as well as various works on the supernatural and on moral and social questions. When he died in the spring of 1731 he was at work on another long book, *The Compleat English Gentleman*. His mind was as fresh and vigorous as ever, but at last it had worn out its tenement of clay.

II

WHEN Defoe turned, in the last decade of his life, from fact to fiction, the change was not so abrupt as it might appear. For one thing, his fiction is remarkably like fact. That he invented most of the facts seems almost irrelevant; it is still the factual that interests him. Often, too, he found his information in some book he had been reading and applied it, or adapted it, to his own purposes. The process may be seen at its simplest in his *Journal of the Plague Year*. In this absorbing day-to-day account of the Great Plague of 1665 ("written by a citizen who continued all the while in London"), Defoe is drawing freely on such printed sources as the weekly bills of mortality, contemporary accounts of the plague, accounts of earlier London plagues, and no doubt on what he had heard in later life from old people who had actually lived through that dreadful summer in London. Out of the material at his disposal he wrote an eyewitness account so convincing that it is hard to believe the *Journal* is not authentic, and that the writer had not shared in the awful experiences he describes. There is an even chance that Defoe was in London during the plague, but, as he would have been only a small boy, not yet five years old, his memories of it could not have been very extensive. Given his facts, he is a master at making truth seem even truer. No one surpasses Defoe at turning reading to the uses of fiction, appropriating it to some particular context, making it come alive and appear to be a matter of personal recollection. "I remember," he will tell us, "and while I am writing this story I think I hear the very sound of it . . . ," and so on, to an account of a distracted mother shrieking out as she discovers the fatal plague tokens on her daughter's thighs. More subtly, he will occasionally admit to some uncertainty about his facts or figures. ("It is so long ago that I am not certain, but I think the mother never recovered, but died in two or three weeks after.") On such occasions we are expected to admire the honesty and reliability of the narrator: since he is not absolutely sure he refuses to make it up, and so when he does commit himself to a definite statement, we may be sure it is accurate. But Defoe's favorite method of authenticating his narrative is to overwhelm us with details so trivial, and so apparently irrelevant, that we feel the only possible reason for being given them at all must be that they are true. We are told by the citizen–author of the *Journal* how nervous people were about touching anything that might have come in contact with an infected person, and he gives us an example of the way in which one Londoner dealt with this problem:

When I came to the Post-House, as I went to put in my Letter, I saw a Man stand in one Corner of the Yard, and talking to another at a Window, and a third had open'd a Door belonging to the Office. In the middle of the Yard lay a small Leather Purse, with two Keys hanging at it, and money in it, but no Body would meddle with it. I ask'd how long it had lain there; the Man at the Window said it had lain almost an Hour, but that they had not meddled with it because they did not know but the Person who dropt it might come back to look for it. I had no such need of Money, nor was the Sum so big, that I had any Inclination to meddle with it, or to get the Money at the hazard it might be attended with; so I seem'd to go away, when the Man who had open'd the door said he would take it up, but so, that if the right Owner came for it he should be sure to have it. So he went in and fetched a pail of Water, and set it down hard by the Purse; then went again and fetch'd some Gun-powder, and cast a good deal of Powder upon the Purse, and then made a Train from that which he had thrown loose upon the Purse; the Train reached about two Yards; after this he goes in a third time, and fetches out a pair of Tongs red-hot, and which he had prepar'd, I suppose, on purpose; and first setting Fire to the Train of Powder, that sing'd the Purse, and also smoak'd the Air sufficiently. But he was not content with that, but he then takes up the Purse with the Tongs, holding it so long till the Tongs burnt thro' the Purse, and then he shook the Money out into the Pail of Water, so he carried it in. The Money, as I remember, was about thirteen Shillings, and some smooth Groats and Brass Farthings. (p. 117)

Like so much in Defoe, this is a description of something happening, and he makes an immediate bid for our attention and our credulity by his careful setting of the event: the man standing in one corner of the yard talking to the man who is looking out of the window, and the man who has just opened a door in the post office. In the middle of the yard, cleverly framed in empty space, the purse —small, made of leather, and with two keys attached to it. Not quite so memorable, perhaps, as the print of a naked foot on the shore that Crusoe came upon one day, but with something of the same isolation and unexpectedness. From the conversation that follows we get the impression that, in normal circumstances, any one of the four men would have pocketed the purse if no one else had been passing at the time, but, as several people are now involved, a good deal of fuss is made about seeing to it that "if the right Owner came for it he should be sure to have it." Defoe is now ready to describe the process of disinfection, and he does so with his usual attention to detail ("the Train reached about two Yards"), and an air of naive conjecture (the red-hot tongs had been "prepar'd, I suppose, on purpose"). And if anyone is still unconvinced, he must surely yield to the shattering authenticity of "as I remember, . . . about thirteen Shillings, and some smooth Groats and Brass Farthings." So firmly has Defoe held our attention that it never occurs to us to wonder how the man in the post office happened to have gunpowder handy, or how the narrator knew that the sum of money in the purse was not "so big" before he had seen the purse opened.

This circumstantial method is to be found in all of Defoe's fictitious narratives; it is the way he thinks a story should be told. As a means of giving fiction

the appearance of truth, it is certainly not economical; but it works, and the cumulative effect is overwhelming. When Colonel Jack treats the handsome young widow to supper at a Rochester inn, he gives her

what the House afforded, which was a couple of Partridges, and a very good Dish of stew'd Oysters; they brought us up afterward a Neat's Tongue and a Ham that was almost quite cut down, but we eat none of it, for the other was fully enough for us both, and the Maid made her Supper of the Oysters we had left, which were enough. (vol. II, p. 103)

When Moll Flanders and Colonel Jack enumerate the pieces of cloth or silverware that they have lifted from some shop, or when Roxana and Moll take stock of their worldly possessions, we have the same satisfied dwelling upon solid objects; the luxuries and necessities with which civilized man has surrounded himself, the things that can be bought and sold. In his imaginative writing Defoe is still very much the merchant, aware of quality and price, deeply interested in all the material evidence of civilization. His characters live in a world of pots and pans and tankards and spoons, of druggets and silks, watches and periwigs. With some writers, the solid weight of this environment would be enough to crush all the life out of the characters; but moving about in this dense undergrowth of material facts are bright-eyed, lively men and women to whom Defoe has somehow imparted his own restless energy and his own indomitable will to live. Our interest never stops short with what Moll stole; we become interested in how the theft was carried out, how Moll felt while she was about her business, and ultimately in Moll herself. And all the time Defoe is asking for more than our interest: he wants our belief. He is at his old game of make-believe, and the illusion is often complete. The author fades from our consciousness, and we are aware only of a shipwrecked sailor, or a rogue, or a whore, endlessly communicative, tirelessly repetitive, and completely self-absorbed. All this is as Defoe would have it be. *The Life and Strange Surprizing Adventures of Robinson Crusoe, of York, Mariner* was "written by himself"; *The Memoirs of a Cavalier*, "written threescore years ago by an English gentleman"; *The Fortunes and Misfortunes of the Famous Moll Flanders*, "written from her own memorandums," and so on. The pretense of actuality no doubt made these and other of Defoe's books sell more readily; but it may also have consoled him for having abandoned the truth of history and politics for the more profound but less obvious truth of imaginative literature.

On any count, much of the material in his fictitious narratives, like that in *A Journal of the Plague Year*, is true enough. *Robinson Crusoe* was based on the adventures of Alexander Selkirk, a Scottish sailor who had lived alone on the island of Juan Fernandez for over four years until he was rescued by Captain Woodes Rogers in 1709. Whether Defoe had actually talked with Selkirk or not, he could have read the account published in 1712 by Woodes Rogers, or that in Steele's periodical, the *Englishman*, in the following year. Given the situation of the solitary mariner on a desert island, Defoe could bring to bear on it much of the factual information he had obtained from his reading of travel books. In this way he made use of Richard Hakluyt's *Voyages*, William Dampier's *New Voyage Round the World*, Robert Knox's *An Historical Relation of the Island of Ceylon*, and similar works. When his library was sold after his death, the advertisement drew attention to "several hundred Curious, Scarce Tracts on . . . Husbandry, Trade, Voyages, Natural History, Mines, Minerals, etc." Much of the purely factual material out of which Defoe wove his narratives no doubt lay to hand in his library at Stoke Newington.

For *Moll Flanders* and *Colonel Jack*, he probably relied much less on his reading than on firsthand information. In 1720 he had begun writing for John Applebee's *Weekly Journal*, and through Applebee, who specialized in publishing the last dying speeches of criminals, he probably had ready access to Newgate and interviewed many of the prisoners awaiting sentence or already condemned. Like any other London citizen, too, he could (and no doubt did) attend the sessions of oyer and terminer, where he could listen to the idiomatic talk of highwaymen and pickpockets and become familiar with their ready invention at moments of crisis, their evasiveness, and the highly factual turn they gave their stories from the dock. If, for instance, he could have been present in September 1734, when Sarah Goffin and Thomas Edesbury were indicted for stealing a silver cup and a candlestick from a burning house (a similar incident occurs in *Moll Flanders*), he would have heard Edesbury's characteristically circumstantial account of his doings:

And so she came to ask me where Tom Gilpin was.—"You bitch," says I, "you have most reason to know where he is, for you were with him last."—And then she and I went through Temple Bar into Fleet-street, and turn'd down Chancery-lane, and so came to Fetter-lane, and then to Shoe-lane, and down Harp-Alley to Fleet-ditch, and up Fleet-lane to the Old-Bailey, and cross Newgate-street to Giltspur-street, and through Pye-Corner into Smithfield, and so to Long-lane, and cross Aldersgate-street to Barbican, and then down Red-Cross-street and up White-Cross-street to Jemmit's brandy-shop; and there we drank together, and she left the things and then we parted.

We might be listening to Colonel Jack; and indeed Edesbury's narrative is oddly like several similar accounts in the story of that young vagabond:

Pulling me by the Sleeve, "Run, Jack," says he, "for our Lives"; and away he Scours, and I after him, never resting or scarce looking about me, till we got quite up into Fenchurch-street, thro' Lime-street, into Leadenhall-street, down St. Mary-Axe to London-Wall, then thro' Bishopsgate, and down Old Bedlam into Moorfields.

Whatever means he may have used, Defoe had arrived at a thorough knowledge of the underworld of London. He knew, for example, how the professional thief tends to specialize in certain lines of theft, and not just grab whatever lies to hand. "The Comrade she helped me to," says Moll, "dealt in three sorts of Craft; viz. Shop-lifting, stealing of Shop-Books and Pocket-Books, and taking off Gold Watches from the Ladies' Sides; and this last she did so dexterously that no Woman ever arriv'd to the Perfection of that Art so as to do it like her." Moll's innocent admiration here reminds one of the rustic in the village pub remembering a departed friend: "Ah, poor old George! he shoved a beautiful ha'penny." As usual, Defoe managed to make Moll's words sound authentic. He had clearly thought a good deal about the mind of the criminal: his tendency to live from day to day, his fondness for some kind of celebration as soon as he gets any money, the gradual hardening of conscience as crime becomes habitual, and the persistence nonetheless of certain queer personal standards of what is fair and what is not.

It is clear that Defoe's idea of a fictitious narrative was that it should present either unusual people or abnormal situations (pirates, soldiers of fortune, rogues, a shipwrecked sailor, a plague-stricken city). But when he pleases he is quite capable of giving us a glimpse of a normal middle-class family that anticipates later novelists such as Samuel Richardson or Fanny Burney. Moll Flanders, abandoned by gypsies, was adopted by a family in Colchester, and has grown to be a handsome young woman. She becomes the mistress of the elder brother in the household, while the younger brother, ignorant of this liaison, wants to marry her. When the elder brother wishes to break off his intrigue with Moll, she becomes ill, and therefore the object of increased attention. The daughters of the family resent the fuss that is being made about her; and Moll tells us what she overheard one day downstairs:

Alas, says the old Lady, that poor Girl! I am afraid she will never be well. Well! says the elder Brother, how should Mrs. Betty be well? they say she is in Love. I believe nothing of it, says the old Gentlewoman. I don't know, says the elder Sister, what to say to it; they have made such a rout about her being so Handsome, and so Charming, and I know not what, and that in her hearing too, that has turn'd the Creature's Head, I believe, and who knows what possessions may follow such Doings? For my part I don't know what to make of it.

Why Sister, you must acknowledge she is very Handsome, says the elder Brother. Ay, and a great deal Handsomer than you, Sister, says Robin, and that's your mortification. Well, well, that is not the Question, says his Sister; the Girl is well enough, and she knows it well enough; she need not be told of it to make her Vain.

We are not a talking of her being Vain, says the elder Brother, but of her being in Love; it may be she is in Love with herself: it seems my Sisters think so.

I would she was in Love with me, says Robin; I'd quickly put her out of her Pain. What d'ye mean by that, Son? says the old Lady: how can you talk so? . . . Fye, Brother, says the second Sister, how can you talk so? Would you take a Creature that has not a Groat in the World? Prethee child, says Robin, Beauty's a Portion, and good humour with it is a double Portion; I wish thou hadst half her Stock of both for thy Portion. So there was her Mouth stop'd. (pp. 37–38)

Such a passage is as good as any in Richardson; and indeed Defoe is not always given enough credit for his close observation of contemporary manners and his lively interest in human behavior. In the early pages of *Colonel Jack*, he draws a memorable picture of a London waif, with some unusual glimpses into the mind of a young boy. Once or twice (for example, in the episode in which little Jack hides his money in a hollow tree, and it drops to the bottom out of his reach) it is easy to suppose that Defoe is drawing upon memories of his own childhood. At all events, the reality of such incidents is sometimes startling.

Of all his characters, the one who seems to be furthest from any experience that Defoe could have had, or from what would seem likely to interest him, is Roxana. Yet she, too, is firmly based on reality. Defoe has given us what must be one of the earliest studies in prose fiction of a gold digger. Roxana is the type of woman who attracts one man after another, but who (unlike Moll Flanders) has no warmth of feeling for any of them; she is selfish but not ungenerous, cold and hardhearted but perfectly agreeable. So far she is entirely consistent, but she is certainly more credible as the wife of the brewer or as the mistress of the jeweler, who is next in succession, than in the socially superior whoredom of her later years. When Roxana becomes the mistress of a prince, Defoe is out of his depth, and can do little more than recount her travels in France and Italy and enumerate the presents she receives from her royal lover.

But in one important point *Roxana* shows an advance on any of Defoe's earlier stories: it has a more highly developed plot. The form of all his works of fiction is that of an autobiographical narrative told by the hero or heroine. Time passes, sometimes slowly, sometimes in disconcerting jerks. "It concerns the Story in hand very little," Moll has a way of saying, "to enter into the farther particulars of the Family, or of myself, for the five Years that I liv'd with this Husband,—only to observe that I had two Children by him, and that at the end of the five Years he Died." When we come upon such a passage, we know that Defoe feels he has exhausted the possibilities of one episode and is now getting ready for a change of scene and some new characters. New characters, indeed, continually make their appearance, and the old ones, having served their fictional purpose by crossing the path of the hero or heroine, either die or just fade out. It is true that Moll meets again with her Lancashire husband, and the story is all the better for it; but Defoe's normal method of securing our attention is to develop an unusual and dramatic situation (*Robinson Crusoe, A Journal of the Plague Year*) or open up a succession of lively adventures (*Captain Singleton, Moll Flanders, Colonel Jack*), rather than construct a plot sufficiently integrated to arouse the anticipation of the reader, and generate the tension that develops when the lives of different characters cross and recross. In *Roxana*, at last, we do get something of that sort. The brewer husband turns up again in Paris and gives Roxana some cause for anxiety. But more important is the honest Dutch jeweler whom she eventually marries, after a lapse of a few years; and most telling of all is the awkward reappearance of one of her daughters, just after Roxana has married her Dutchman and become a countess. The tension aroused by this persistent girl is considerable, and we follow with increasing anxiety Roxana's attempts to keep out of her way, and the efforts of the faithful, and now murderous, Amy to get rid of her. For once we can feel that Defoe is seeing life as something more than an isolated series of events, and that, however little he may have put it to work in his fiction, he has a sense of the past.

The incident of Roxana and her neglected daughter had its appeal to the Puritan in Defoe. Here was an example of one's sins coming home to roost. Defoe's moral sincerity in these tales of thieves and adventurers has often been called into question; and critics have suggested that his primary aim in writing them was to achieve the highest possible level of sensation and, in consequence, a maximum sale for his books. The moral observations that fall from time to time from the lips of Moll or Roxana or Colonel Jack were only, it is suggested, put in to give those stories an appearance of decency: the real thing is the thieving and whoring, the risks and the escapes and the spectacle of vice triumphant, of wickedness getting away with it. But this is to take too simple a view of Defoe's mixed motives. It must be conceded that his title pages offer no evidence of the author's moral intentions. *The Fortunes and Misfortunes of the Famous Moll Flanders, etc., who was born in Newgate, and during a Life of continu'd Variety, for Threescore Years, besides her Childhood, was Twelve Year a Whore, five times a Wife (whereof once to her own Brother), Twelve Year a Thief, Eight Year a Transported Felon in Virginia, at last grew Rich, liv'd Honest, and died a Penitent*—such a title page was surely drawn up with only one idea in mind: to catch the eye of the idle apprentice as he loitered past the bookstall. It can be granted, too, that Defoe's moral interpolations are often perfunctory, and sometimes a little forced. But when Moll, no longer a young woman, is picked up by a gentleman in his cups, spends the night with him ("as for the bed, etc. I was not much concerned about that part"), and then robs him of his gold watch, purse, and periwig (the records of the sessions of oyer and terminer are full of just such cases in the 1720's and 1730's), her reflections are perfectly in character, and Defoe's moral intention is above suspicion. "There is nothing so absurd," Moll remarks,

so surfeiting, so ridiculous, as a Man heated by Wine in his Head, and a wicked Gust in his Inclination together; he is in the possession of two Devils at once, and can no more govern himself by his Reason than a Mill can grind without Water. . . . As for me, my Business was his Money, and what I could make of him; and after that, if I could have found out any way to have done it, I would have sent him safe home to his House and to his Family, for 'twas ten to one but he had an honest virtuous Wife, and innocent Children, that were anxious for his Safety, and would have been glad to have gotten him Home, and taken care of him, till he was restor'd to himself: and then with what Shame and Regret would he look back upon himself! how would he reproach himself with associating himself with a Whore! . . . Would such Gentlemen but consider the contemptible Thoughts which the very Women they are concern'd with, in such Cases as these, have of them, it wou'd be a Surfeit to them. . . .

(pp. 194–195)

There are none of the allurements of vice here: Moll is talking plain, harsh good sense; and Defoe means every word of it. His autobiographical form forced him to put such observations into the mouth of his chief character, where they do not always carry conviction (though here they do). If he had been writing in his own person, and therefore making those comments on his own account, his moral sincerity might have been accepted more readily. His own attitude to his erring heroes and heroines is never a simple one, for he is at once moralist and artist. "These are deplorable people," the moralist tells him—and Defoe agrees. "But how interesting they are!" the artist whispers in his ear, "how clever at doing what they can do! what a powerful instinct for survival they have! how adaptable, how tough, how resilient!"—and again, fortunately for the liveliness and humanity of his stories, Defoe has to agree. But the best reason for believing that he is never indifferent to the moral obliquity of his characters is the extent to which their stories fasten on our minds. If Defoe himself had not been so sharply aware of right and wrong, if he had not felt all the time he was writing *Moll Flanders* and *Roxana* that these women were breaking the moral law, that they were "wild outcasts of society," whose way of life was chaotic and unprofitable—if, in fact, he had not himself been shocked by such goings-on—he would never have succeeded in holding our attention as he does. He was not, perhaps, a very religious man; he gives the impression of having thought in terms of right and wrong rather than of good and evil. But he certainly had a strong preference for good conduct, a regular and well-ordered life, and "the single talent well employed"; and if he spent so much of his time describing the very antithesis of these things, it was because he contemplated them with a kind of reluctant fascination.

III

It is in *Robinson Crusoe* that Defoe's limited and practical ideals find positive expression. In most of his stories the hero is an isolated character pitting his wits against society, getting the better of his fellows by fraud or theft, or by taking advantage of their carelessness or their moral weakness. Here, however, in his first and most famous story, the hero is matching his wits and his resolution with the forces of nature; and the energy that in a Moll Flanders is purely destructive, or at best acquisitive, is here applied to constructive ends, and to producing order and a primitive culture out of the wasteful and unprofitable profusion of nature. In the process Crusoe is building up some sort of good life and developing all that is best in his character. Crusoe's success is due to the sturdy qualities in his character, to his own unaided efforts, to his courage and patience, to his practical skill and his intelligent persistence. He has his defeats, as he has his triumphs, but he allows neither to deflect him from his sober progress toward security and prosperity. He has most of the qualities of the "complete English tradesman," without having anyone to trade with.

In the hard oyster shell of Crusoe's character some sort of religious feeling is gradually secreted as a result of the constant fretting of circumstance on his consciousness. In recent years several critics have suggested that we ought to take Crusoe's religious utterances more seriously than it has been customary to take them; and it has been claimed that his account of the various stages in his religious development—from original sin to spiritual hardening and then, at last, through physical and mental suffering to a gradual repentance and ultimate conversion—follows closely the traditional pattern of seventeenth-century spiritual autobiographies. Crusoe's concern with omens and portents and his conviction that more than once he has owed his survival to the direct intervention of Providence were also traditional features of this literary genre. It is significant, too, how often Crusoe's descriptions of his actual physical vicissitudes recall the kind of imagery so often found in the autobiographies of converted sinners. Taking all such facts into account, we may agree that it is in Crusoe's progress from the careless self-indulgence of the natural man (when he conversed with sinners like himself, "wicked and profane to the last degree") to a life of reason and introspection and, ultimately, of faith in God, that we may find the structural unity of *Robinson Crusoe.*

But because Crusoe is what Defoe has made him, his conversion leaves the main lines of his character essentially unaffected. He remains as practical and self-reliant as before, believing that God helps those who help themselves. Like everything else about him on the island, his religion is homemade and not of the finest quality; it amounts perhaps to little more than "Count your blessings," but it is sound, it works, and it will stand up to daily use. It is noticeable that even when Crusoe has become convinced that there is a special Providence watching over him, Defoe never allows him—isolated though he is—to become a tragic figure. He meets the blows of fate, not with some heroic gesture or poetical declamation, but with little bursts of practical activity; he strikes no attitudes, he hardly ever dramatizes his difficulties. When, on one of his early visits to the wreck, he finds some gold and silver and pieces of eight, Defoe allows him a conventionally high-flown exclamation about the worthlessness of money. But almost at once Crusoe is made to check this extravagance:

I smil'd to my self at the Sight of this Money. "O drug!" said I aloud, "what art thou good for? Thou art not worth to me—no, not the taking off of the Ground; one of those Knives is worth all this Heap: I have no Manner of use for thee; e'en remain where thou art, and go to the Bottom, as a Creature whose Life is not worth saving." However, upon Second Thoughts, I took it away. . . . (pp. 43–44)

Had Crusoe tossed the money into the sea, we should have felt at once that Defoe had introduced a false note, for it was clearly a guiding principle with Crusoe that "you never know when a thing may come in handy." It is on such practical lines that Crusoe is built, and he proceeds by trial and error, continually learning from his mistakes and profiting from past experience. In its profoundest aspect this famous story is a triumph of character.

But the bracing moral tone of *Robinson Crusoe*, however important an element it may be in the total impact made by Defoe's narrative, hardly accounts for its continuing popularity for more than two hundred years. Defoe, in fact, has gratified some of the most permanent desires of the human heart and has helped his readers to recapture many of the forgotten pleasures of childhood—the pleasure of "playing house," of making things, of keeping animals, of watching things grow, of finding things and keeping them because one found them first, of sailing in rafts and boats, and so on. Crusoe, forced by circumstances to begin anew and do everything for himself, also compels us in our turn to look, as if for the first time, at all sorts of everyday objects "of which, for the common view, custom had bedimmed all the lustre, had dried up the sparkle and the dewdrops."

Robinson Crusoe owes much of its appeal, too, to the imaginative value of its situation: the desert island, and the shipwrecked mariner, utterly alone. (The reader's interest begins to flag when other men appear on the island.) Dr. Johnson went so far as to observe of *Gulliver's Travels* that "when once you have thought of big men and little men, it is very easy to do all the rest"; and on similar grounds some might seek to attribute the success of *Robinson Crusoe* to its subject. But Defoe deserves great credit for the way in which he treated it. This was just the sort of thing he could do best—think himself into a situation and live in imagination the life of another person. He has a remarkable intuition for the difficulties and frustrations that a man in Crusoe's position would have to cope with: the things too heavy to lift or the want of proper tools. When he tries to break off a piece from the great roll of lead he has discovered in the ship's hold, he has to abandon the attempt, for "as it lay about a Foot and a half in the Water, I could not make any Blow to drive the Hatchet."

Perhaps the most remarkable instance of Defoe's imaginative understanding of his hero occurs in the description of how Crusoe undertakes to build a canoe, or piragua. Fired by this new idea, he sets to work immediately with his wretched tools and toils incessantly. First he fells a huge cedar tree ("I ques-

tion much whether Solomon ever had such a one for the Building of the Temple at Jerusalem"), then he spends several months hewing off the branches and hacking out the inside, "till I had brought it to be a very handsome Periagua, and big enough to have carry'd six and twenty Men." When at last it is finished, after so many months of wearisome work, he is naturally delighted with it. It is only now that Crusoe realizes what he should have thought of at the very beginning: the piragua lies about a hundred yards from the shore, and the ground slopes uphill to the creek. Even then he will not believe that all his labor has been thrown away; he thinks of cutting a canal for it, and even starts the digging. But when he begins to make some calculations about length and depth, he finds that "by the Number of Hands I had, being none but my own, it must have been ten or twelve Years before I should have gone through with it." Anyone who thinks this incident fantastic surely forgets that even sensible people occasionally saw off the branch on which the ladder is resting. Defoe's psychology here is entirely sound: he knew how a fixed idea is capable of blinding a person to all secondary considerations. Crusoe's idea is to get off the island, and, with this sudden realization of how that might be accomplished, he goes to work on his large seagoing canoe without another thought. It is all so odd, and yet so natural, that once again we have the feeling it must have actually happened.

There is one final reason why *Robinson Crusoe* strikes with greater force than any of Defoe's other stories. If it can hardly be said to have a plot, it has at least the sort of action that carries the reader forward until he reaches a conclusion. A man was cast upon a desert island: somehow he must have been rescued, because it is his own narrative that we are reading. How did it all happen? and how did he manage to keep alive until his rescuers reached the island? In *Robinson Crusoe*, Defoe has hit upon a situation that only asks to be worked out; the episodes will arise naturally from the situation, and the situation is such that it can lead naturally to a complete change in the hero's outlook, and ultimately to a solution of all his troubles. There is all the difference in the world between this sort of story, which generates its own power, and the loose, picaresque narratives that Defoe went on to write afterward, where the interest can only be maintained by throwing a fresh log on the fire as the flames die down.

Although Defoe tried to claim in his *Serious Reflections During the Life and Surprizing Adventures of Robinson Crusoe* that the book was an allegory of his own life, Robinson Crusoe is not Daniel Defoe. And yet, more than any other of his books, it is a kind of daydream in which the author and his hero dissolve into one another. If Defoe had ever found himself alone on a desert island, he would undoubtedly have set about making the best of his circumstances. It is true that he could never have been happy without pen, ink, and plenty of paper; but perhaps he would have found all that he wanted in the captain's cabin. What we can be certain of is that he would never have given in. When the Spaniard was complimenting Crusoe on the way in which he had struggled with his misfortunes, he told him that he had noticed how "Englishmen had a greater presence of mind in their distress than any people that ever he met with." Defoe, an Englishman by birth, a tradesman by choice, and a writer almost by force of circumstances, had shown this presence of mind often enough in his troubled career, and a courage that matched his capacity for getting into trouble. He had the courage of the active man and the patient fortitude of the tradesman—the English tradesman sweeping up the broken glass from his shopfront the morning after an air raid. But this tradesman was a man of genius and a dreamer, whose dreams were of fair women and gallant, gay highwaymen, of pirates, of little children who were pickpockets, of the silent, plague-stricken streets of his beloved London, of shipwrecks, and desert islands, and the lost traveler under the hill.

SELECTED BIBLIOGRAPHY

I. BIBLIOGRAPHY. J. R. Moore, *A Checklist of the Writings of Daniel Defoe* (Bloomington, Ind., 1960; 2nd ed., Hamden, Conn., 1971); *Daniel Defoe, 1660–1731. Commemoration in Stoke Newington of the Tercentenary of His Birth: An Exhibition of Books, Pamphlets, Views and Portraits . . . Presented by the Public Libraries Committee, 7th to 28th May 1960* (London, 1960), published by the Stoke Newington Borough Council, includes a useful section of works on Defoe and his writings. Detailed bibliographical information can also be found in the appropriate volumes of the *Cambridge Bibliography of English Literature* and the *Oxford History of English Literature*.

II. COLLECTED AND SELECTED WORKS. *A Collection of the Writings of the Author of the True Born English-Man* (London, 1703), the pirated ed.; *A True Collection of the Writings of the Author of the True Born English-man* (London, 1703); *A Second Volume of the Writings of the Author of the True-Born Englishman* (London, 1705); Sir W. Scott, ed., *The Novels*, 12 vols. (Edinburgh, 1810); *The Novels and Miscellaneous Works*, 20 vols. (London, 1840–1841), with a biographical memoir by John Ballantyne; *The Works*, 3 vols. (London, 1840–1843), with a memoir of Defoe's life and writings by W. C. Hazlitt; *The Novels and Miscellaneous Works*, 6 vols. (London, 1854–1856); J. Keltie, ed., *The Works . . . with Chalmers' Life of the Author* (Edinburgh, 1869); H. Morley, ed., *The Earlier Life and the Chief Earlier Works* (London, 1889); G. A. Aitken, ed., *Romances and Narratives*, 16 vols. (London, 1895); G. H. Maynadier, ed., *The Works*, 16 vols. (New York, 1903–1904); *Novels and Selected Writings*, 14 vols. (Oxford, 1927–1928), the Shakespeare Head ed.; R. Manvell, ed., *Selections from the Prose of Daniel Defoe* (London, 1953); G. H. Healey, ed., *Letters* (Oxford, 1955); J. T. Boulton, ed., *Daniel Defoe* (London–New York, 1965); M. F. Shugrue, ed., *Selected Poetry and Prose of Daniel Defoe* (New York, 1968); J. R. Sutherland, ed., *Robinson Crusoe and Other Writings* (Boston, 1968); L. A. Curtis, ed., *The Versatile Defoe: An Anthology of Uncollected Writings by Daniel Defoe* (London, 1979).

III. SEPARATE WORKS. *The Meditations of Daniel Defoe* [London, 1681], early verse, first printed in G. H. Healey, ed. (Cummington, Mass., 1946); *A New Discovery of an Old Intreague* (London, 1691), verse; *An Essay upon Projects* (London, 1697), commentary, twelve essays on miscellaneous topics, mainly economic; *An Enquiry into the Occasional Conformity of Dissenters in Cases of Preferment* (London, 1697), pamphlet; *The Poor Man's Plea* (London, 1698), pamphlet; *An Argument Shewing that a Standing Army, with Consent of Parliament, Is Not Inconsistent with a Free Government* (London, 1698), pamphlet.

The Two Great Questions Consider'd. I. What the French King Will Do, with Respect to the Spanish Monarchy. II. What Measures the English Ought to Take (London, 1700), pamphlet; *The Pacificator: A Poem* (London, 1700), verse; *The Six Distinguishing Characters of a Parliament-Man* (London, 1700), pamphlet; *The True-Born English-man: A Satyr* (London, 1700), verse; *The Free-Holders Plea against Stock-Jobbing Elections of Parliament-Men* (London, 1701), pamphlet; *The Villainy of Stock-Jobbers Detected* (London, 1701), pamphlet; *Legion's Memorial to the House of Commons* (London, 1701), broadsheet; *The History of the Kentish Petition* (London, 1701), pamphlet; *The Mock-Mourners: A Satyr, by Way of Elegy on King William* (London, 1702), verse; *Reformation of Manners: A Satyr* (London, 1702), verse; *The Shortest Way with the Dissenters: or, Pro-*

posals for the Establishment of the Church (London, 1702), pamphlet; More Reformation: A Satyr upon Himself, by the Author of the True Born English-Man (London, 1703), verse; A Hymn to the Pillory (London, 1703), verse; The Shortest Way to Peace and Union (London, 1703), pamphlet; More Short-Ways with the Dissenters (London, 1704), pamphlet; The Storm: or, A Collection of the Most Remarkable Casualties and Disasters Which Happen'd in the Late Dreadful Tempest, Both by Sea and Land (London, 1704), narrative; Giving Alms No Charity, and Employing the Poor a Grievance to the Nation (London, 1704), pamphlet; A Review of the Affairs of France: and of All Europe, as Influenc'd by That Nation (London, 1704–1713), politics and trade, issued in parts, a complete facs. in 22 vols. by A. W. Secord, ed. (New York, 1938), see also W. L. Payne, comp., Index to Defoe's Review (New York, 1948) and W. L. Payne, comp. and ed., The Best of Defoe's Review (New York, 1951); The Consolidator: or, Memoirs of Sundry Transactions from the World in the Moon (London, 1704), satire.

The Experiment: or, The Shortest Way with the Dissenters Exemplified (London, 1705), pamphlet; The Dyet of Poland: A Satyr (London, 1705), verse; A True Relation of the Apparition of One Mrs. Veal, the Next Day after Her Death, to One Mrs. Bargrave at Canterbury, the 8th of September, 1705 (London, 1706), pamphlet; Jure Divino: A Satyr, in Twelve Books (London, 1706), verse; Caledonia: A Poem in Honour of Scotland, and the Scots Nation (Edinburgh, 1706; another ed., London, 1707), verse; The History of the Union of Great Britain (Edinburgh, 1709), history; The Present State of the Parties in Great Britain: Particularly an Enquiry into the State of the Dissenters in England (London, 1712), politics; Reasons against the Succession of the House of Hanover (London, 1713), pamphlet, this and the two pamphlets immediately below were ironical in title and in much of their content; And What if the Pretender Should Come? Or, Some Considerations of the Advantages and Real Consequences of the Pretender's Possessing the Crown of Great Britain (London, 1713), pamphlet; An Answer to a Question That No Body Thinks of, viz., but What if the Queen Should Die? (London, 1713), pamphlet; The Secret History of the White Staff, Being an Account of Affairs under the Conduct of Some Late Ministers (London, 1714–1715), politics, published in three parts and later issued as one pamphlet.

An Appeal to Honour and Justice, Tho' It Be of His Worst Enemies . . . : Being a True Account of His Conduct in Publick Affairs (London, 1715), autobiography; The Family Instructor (London, 1715; 2nd vol., 1718), moral and religious dialogues; The History of the Wars of His Present Majesty Charles XII King of Sweden (London, 1715), history; Minutes of the Negotiations of Monsr. Mesnager, at the Court of England (London, 1717), politics; The Life and Strange Surprizing Adventures of Robinson Crusoe, of York, Mariner (London, 1719), novel, also in A. Ross, ed. (Harmondsworth, 1965), and J. D. Crowley, ed. (London, 1972); The Farther Adventures of Robinson Crusoe (London, 1719), novel; The Anatomy of Exchange-Alley: or, A System of Stock-Jobbing (London, 1719), commentary on stock-jobbing; The King of Pirates: Being an Account of the Famous Enterprises of Captain Avery, the Mock King of Madagascar (London, 1719), narrative; Memoirs of a Cavalier: or, A Military Journal of the Wars in Germany, and the Wars in England (London, 1720), fictitious narrative, also in J. T. Boulton, ed. (London, 1973); The Life, Adventures, and Pyracies of the Famous Captain Singleton (London, 1720), novel, also in J. R. Sutherland, ed. (London, 1963), and S. K. Kumar, ed. (London, 1969); Serious Reflections During the Life and Surprizing Adventures of Robinson Crusoe: With His Vision of the Angelick World. Written by Himself (London, 1720), commentary.

The Fortunes and Misfortunes of the Famous Moll Flanders (London, 1721), novel, also in J. R. Sutherland, ed. (New York, 1959), B. Dobrée and H. Davis, eds. (London, 1961), J. P. Hunter, ed. (New York, 1970), and G. Starr, ed. (London, 1971); Due Preparations for the Plague (London, 1722), commentary; Religious Courtship: Being Historical Discourses, on the Necessity of Marrying Religious Husbands and Wives Only (London, 1722), moral and religious dialogues; A Journal of the Plague Year (London, 1722), fictitious narrative, also in A. Burgess and C. Bristow, eds. (Harmondsworth, 1966); The History and Remarkable Life of the Truly Honourable Col. Jacque, Commonly Call'd Col. Jack (London, 1722), novel, also in S. H. Monk, ed. (London, 1965); The Fortunate Mistress: or, A History of the Life and Vast Variety of Fortunes of Mademoiselle de Beleau, Afterwards Call'd the Countess de Wintselsheim, in Germany, Being the Person Known by the Name of the Lady Roxana, in the Time of King Charles II (London, 1724), novel; The Great Law of Subordination Consider'd: or, The Insolence and Unsufferable Behaviour of Servants in England Duly Enquir'd Into (London, 1724), commentary; A General History of the Robberies and Murders of the Most Notorious Pyrates (London, 1724), also a second vol. entitled The History of the Pyrates (London, 1728); A Tour Thro' the Whole Island of Great Britain, Divided into Circuits or Journies, 3 vols. (London, 1724–1727), travel, also in G. D. H. Cole, ed., 2 vols. (London, 1927), revised by D. C. Browning, ed. (London, 1963), P. Rogers, ed. (Harmondsworth, 1966); A Narrative of All the Robberies, Escapes, &c. of John Sheppard (London, 1724), narrative.

A New Voyage Round the World, by a Course Never Sailed Before (London, 1725), narrative of an imaginary voyage; Every-Body's Business, Is No-Body's Business; or, Private Abuses, Publick Grievances; Exemplified in the *Pride, Insolence and Exorbitant Wages of Our Women-Servants, Footmen Etc.* (London, 1725), commentary; *The Complete English Tradesman*, 2 vols. (London, 1726–1727), economics, a guide for young tradesmen; *The Political History of the Devil, As Well Ancient As Modern* (London, 1726), religion and the occult; *A General History of Discoveries and Improvements, in Useful Arts* (London, 1727), economics, published in four parts; *The Protestant Monastery: or, A Complaint against the Brutality of the Present Age* (London, 1727), commentary; *A System of Magick; or, A History of the Black Art* (London, 1727), the occult; *Conjugal Lewdness: or, Matrimonial Whoredom* (London, 1727), commentary; *An Essay on the History and Reality of Apparitions* (London, 1727), the occult; *A New Family Instructor* (London, 1727); *Augusta Triumphans: or, The Way to Make London the Most Flourishing City in the Universe* (London, 1728), education and moral reform; *A Plan of the English Commerce* (London, 1728), economics; *The Military Memoirs of Capt. George Carleton* (London, 1728), narrative, Defoe's authorship has been questioned; *Madagascar: or, Robert Drury's Journal* (London, 1729), travel; K. D. Bülbring, ed., *The Compleat English Gentleman* (London, 1895), educational treatise.

IV. SELECTED EDITIONS OF SEPARATE WORKS. *Robinson Crusoe*, in J. R. Sutherland, ed. (Boston, 1968), J. D. Crowley, ed. (London, 1972), and M. Shinagel, ed. (New York, 1975); *Memoirs of a Cavalier*, in J. T. Boulton, ed. (London, 1972); *Captain Singleton*, in S. K. Kumar, ed. (London, 1969); *Moll Flanders*, in J. R. Sutherland, ed. (Boston, 1959), G. A. Starr, ed. (London, 1971), and E. Kelly, ed. (New York, 1972); *A Journal of the Plague Year*, in L. A. Landa, ed. (London, 1969); *Colonel Jack*, in S. H. Monk, ed. (London, 1965); *Roxana*, in J. Jack, ed. (London, 1964); *A General History of the Pyrates*, in M. Schonhorn, ed. (London, 1972).

V. BIOGRAPHICAL AND CRITICAL STUDIES. G. Chalmers, *Life of Daniel Defoe* (London, 1785), first separate ed., with author's name (London, 1790); W. Wilson, *Memoirs of the Life and Times of Daniel Defoe*, 3 vols. (London, 1830); W. Lee, *Daniel Defoe: His Life and Recently Discovered Writings*, 3 vols. (London, 1869), valuable for inclusion of material from periodicals in vols. II and III; W. Minto, *Daniel Defoe* (London, 1879), in the English Men of Letters series; T. Wright, *The Life of Daniel Defoe* (London, 1894; enl. ed., 1931); W. P. Trent, *Daniel Defoe: How to Know Him* (Indianapolis, 1916); P. Dottin, *Daniel Defoe et ses romans*, 3 vols. (Paris, 1924); A. W. Secord, *Studies in the Narrative Method of Defoe* (Urbana, Ill., 1924); J. Sutherland, *Defoe* (London, 1937; 3rd ed., 1971); J. R. Moore, *Defoe in the Pillory, and Other Studies* (Bloomington, Ind., 1939); F. L. Watson, *Daniel Defoe* (London, 1952); I. Watt, *The Rise of the Novel: Studies in Defoe, Richardson and Fielding* (London, 1957); J. R. Moore, *Daniel Defoe: Citizen of the Modern World* (Chicago, 1958).

A. W. Secord, *Robert Drury's Journal and Other Studies* (Urbana, Ill., 1961); M. E. Novak, *Economics and the Fiction of Daniel Defoe* (Berkeley–Los Angeles, 1962); M. E. Novak, *Defoe and the Nature of Man* (London, 1963); G. A. Starr, *Defoe and Spiritual Autobiography* (Princeton, 1965); J. P. Hunter, *The Reluctant Pilgrim: Defoe's Emblematic Method and Quest for Form* (Baltimore, 1966); M. Shinagel, *Daniel Defoe and Middle-Class Gentility* (Cambridge, Mass., 1968); R. M. Baine, *Daniel Defoe and the Supernatural* (Athens, Ga., 1968); J. J. Richetti, *Popular Fiction Before Richardson: Narrative Patterns 1700–1739* (Oxford, 1969); F. H. Ellis, ed., *Twentieth-Century Interpretations of Robinson Crusoe* (Englewood Cliffs, N. J., 1969); R. C. Elliot, ed., *Twentieth-Century Interpretations of Moll Flanders* (Englewood Cliffs, N. J., 1970); G. A. Starr, *Defoe and Casuistry* (Princeton, N. J., 1971); J. R. Sutherland, *Daniel Defoe: A Critical Study* (Cambridge, Mass., 1971); E. A. James, *Daniel Defoe's Many Voices: A Rhetorical Study of Prose Style and Literary Method* (Amsterdam, 1972); P. Rogers, ed., *Defoe: The Critical Heritage* (London, 1972); J. J. Richetti, *Defoe's Narratives: Situations and Structures* (Oxford, 1975); E. Zimmerman, *Defoe and the Novel* (Berkeley, Calif., 1975); M. Byrd, ed., *Daniel Defoe: A Collection of Critical Essays* (Englewood Cliffs, N. J., 1976); P. Earle, *The World of Defoe* (London, 1976).

JONATHAN SWIFT
(1667-1745)

A. Norman Jeffares

A. Norman Jeffares

LIFE

JONATHAN SWIFT was born in Dublin on 30 November 1667. His father was the fifth son of Thomas Swift, vicar of Goodrich and rector of Bridstow, in Herefordshire, and an ardent royalist who had been ejected from his two livings and imprisoned by the Cromwellians. After Thomas' death, the Swifts, attracted by the possibilities of making themselves lucrative careers, removed to Ireland. But Swift's father died in the March or April before his son's birth, and the widow had merely twenty pounds a year on which to live. Swift described his parents' marriage as "on both sides very indiscreet, for his wife brought her husband little or no fortune, and his death happening so suddenly before he could make a sufficient establishment for his family." He remarked that he felt the consequences of that marriage, not only through the whole course of his education but during the greatest part of his life. He did not have a home in the ordinary sense of the word; and when he was about a year old his wet nurse took him from Dublin to Whitehaven (of which she was a native), where he stayed for nearly three years. Swift thought he had been in effect kidnapped by the nurse because she "was extremely fond of the infant," and his mother sent orders he was not to hazard another sea voyage back to Dublin until he "could be better able to bear it."

When Swift returned to Ireland he did not stay long with his mother. She returned to her home in Leicestershire with his sister, and Swift was then brought up by his uncles in Ireland. He was sent, probably at the age of six, to Kilkenny College, an excellent school established by the Ormonde family. He entered Trinity College, Dublin, on 24 April 1682. His tutor was St. George Ashe, who later became provost and subsequently held several

[All quotations are from H. Davis, ed., *The Prose Works* (Oxford, 1939-1964) and H. Williams, ed., *The Poems* (Oxford, 1937).]

bishoprics. Swift's own account of his undergraduate days gives a gloomy picture:

. . . by the ill treatment of his nearest relations, he was so discouraged and sunk in his spirits, that he too much neglected some parts of his academic studyes, for which he had no great relish by nature, and turned himself to reading history and poetry. So that when the time came for taking his degree of batchelor, although he had lived with great regularity and due observance of the statutes, he was stopped of his degree for dullness and insufficiency, and at last admitted in a manner little to his credit, which is called in that college *speciali gratia*.

Swift had found being a poor relation humiliating. When he was young he had wanted to be famous. His unhappiness is recorded in a memory of one youthful moment of frustration, itself an example of other events and emotions:

I remember when I was a little boy, I felt a great fish at the end of my line which I drew up almost on the ground, but it dropt in, and the disappointment vexeth me to this very day, and I believe it was the type of all my future disappointments.

In fact he had the best possible education in Ireland; and he had not done so badly at Trinity College as he made out in his old age. He found the curriculum dull; the most likely career to which it led—the Anglican Church of Ireland—did not necessarily offer the prospect of rapid advancement: and he was short of money. He spent nearly seven years at Trinity and was about to take his master's degree when public events intervened.

The tensions of impending revolution no doubt explain some of Swift's unsettled state as a student. Admonished for neglect of duties and for "frequenting the town" in March 1687, he started tumults at Trinity and, with five others, insulted the junior dean in November of that year, for which their degrees were suspended, and they had to beg the junior dean's pardon publicly on bended knees. James II's appointment of Richard Talbot, earl of

Tyrconnel, as lord lieutenant led to a withdrawal of the college's annual grant when the authorities refused to appoint a Roman Catholic to a fellowship on the king's orders. Most of the fellows and students, Swift among them, joined the general exodus of Protestants for England and Scotland.

After staying some time with his mother in Leicester, Swift became private secretary to Sir William Temple in 1689. Temple had family connections with Ireland. His grandfather had been provost of Trinity College, Dublin; his father, Sir John Temple, was educated there, became master of the rolls in Ireland, but eventually lived in London; Temple himself was elected to the Irish convention of 1660 and became a member of the Dublin Parliament in 1661. He pursued a diplomatic career, and was the architect of the Triple Alliance between England, Sweden, and the United Provinces; he next served as ambassador to Holland, where he became a close friend of William of Orange. Finally, in dislike of public life, he retreated to the country in 1681. Temple's effect on Swift was profound, for his experience of court life and diplomacy and the elegant mode of life he created at Moor Park, his country home in Surrey, enlarged the young man's horizons and, no doubt, his ambitions. After Swift had experienced his first attack of what we now know as Ménière's disease (its etiology was not fully recognized until 1861; its symptoms are giddiness, vomiting, deafness, and noises in the head), he returned briefly to Ireland. He thought his giddiness had been caused by eating too many apples (his later deafness he put down to the effects of a severe cold), and the doctors thought the effects of the English climate might have caused his illness. But he was soon back. Life at Moor Park, in a dependent position, was not enough for him. Not unnaturally, he wanted to make his own way in the world and Temple was "less forward" than Swift hoped in aiding him to obtain a position in the church. But he had "a scruple of entering the church meerly for support" so, once he had managed to get Temple to offer him a minor clerkship in the office of the master of the rolls in Ireland, he felt he could enter the church from choice rather than necessity. He refused the clerkship and left Moor Park in May 1694. Sir William Temple was "extremely angry" and still would not promise the young man anything firmly.

Swift returned to Ireland, not realizing that he would have difficulty in becoming ordained. There was a need to explain why he had not entered the church at once after taking his degree. What had he been doing in England? He had to humble himself, to write to Temple for a testimonial testifying to his good life and behavior, and giving the reasons for his leaving Temple's household. (Temple's sister, Lady Giffard, endorsed the ensuing dignified appeal to Temple as Swift's "penitential" letter.) Temple wrote in support of his former secretary; and Swift was ordained as deacon in October 1694, and as priest in January 1695. Two weeks later he became prebend of Kilroot. He found the experience of living in a rural parish in Northern Ireland with but a few parishioners, and surrounded by Presbyterians, disheartening, and he gave up the living at Temple's persuasion and returned to Moor Park in 1696.

In 1699, Temple died without having obtained a living for Swift in England, as he had promised he would, and so Swift again traveled to Ireland, this time as chaplain to the earl of Berkeley (who had become one of the three Lords Justice). The following year he was appointed vicar of Laracor, in County Meath, and became a prebend of Dunlavin in St. Patrick's Cathedral in Dublin. Again he was in a parish very thinly peopled with Church of Ireland Protestants, but this time he was surrounded by Catholics. He liked the place, and set about gardening, planting and improving his grounds.

When he was at Kilroot he had courted Jane Waring of Belfast, whom he knew as Varina. It was a curious courtship. He wrote her eloquent letters; but she did not fancy living in Kilroot on Swift's income. He managed to extricate himself by asking her to commit herself immediately when he was going back to Moor Park in 1696, though he was obviously fairly confident she would not do so. He had realistic views about marriage. He had earlier been involved in heavy flirtations in Leicester, but regarded himself as naturally temperate; and there were always "a thousand household thoughts" to drive matrimony out of his mind whenever it chanced to enter it. In 1699 he wrote a series of seventeen resolutions entitled "When I come to be old," the first, fifth, and fifteenth of which are part of what John Forster calls in his biography "the mystery" of Swift's life; they are: "Not to marry a young woman"; "Not to be fond of children, or let them come near me hardly"; "Not to hearken to flatteries, nor conceive I can be beloved by a young woman; *et eos qui haereditatem captant, odisse ac vitare.*[1] When Swift was once more in Laracor, in 1700, Varina wrote to inquire why he had not visited her in Belfast, and, in effect, he dismissed her in a devastating letter full of challenging questions: as to whether she had good enough health, the ability to manage a household on perhaps less than £300 a year, and an adequate inclination to his person and humors for marriage with him. There was another reason for ending their relationship. He had first met Esther Johnson, whom he later called Stella, at Moor Park, when she was a child of thirteen (some critics have agreed that Sir William Temple may have been her father); he now persuaded her to move to Ireland in 1701 with her friend and companion, Rebecca Dingley. He had taught Stella at Moor Park; she was intelligent, truthful, and courageous: she fitted into his idea of friendship. He never saw her alone, though the two ladies lived at Laracor and in his Dublin residences when he was not there. It was an unusual relationship. Swift wrote on 20 April 1704 to William Tisdall, a clergyman and friend of his who wished to marry Stella, that if his own fortunes and humor "served me to think of that state, I should certainly among all persons on earth, make your choice; because I never saw that person whose conversation I entirely valued but hers; this was the utmost I ever gave way to." When he wrote to her, he addressed his letters to both ladies, and his close and tender friendship with Stella lasted, with perhaps one break, until her death in 1728.

Swift was in London with Berkeley in 1701, and he then wrote his first political pamphlet, *A Discourse of the Contests and Dissensions between the Nobles and the Commons in Athens and Rome.* He praised the Whig leaders, Baron Somers and the earl of Halifax (disguised under Roman names), and the following year Swift let himself be known in London as the author. He made several visits to England between 1701 and 1704. In 1704 came the anonymous publication of *A Tale of a Tub* and *The Battle of the Books* (even in the fifth edition the anonymity was kept up), though the identity of the author was known to Swift's peers. Swift intended *A Tale of a Tub* as a satire on what he thought the gross contemporary corruptions in religion and learning: in it he satirized the worldliness of Rome and the immoderacy of the Presbyterians and Nonconformists. He was himself a churchman of the center, though he called himself a "high churchman." Although he thought the Church of England far from perfect, it was the best church he knew; its doctrine and discipline were moderate and cautious. It offered the middle way between Rome and Puritanism. He valued the Anglican church as the voice of reason, and reason seemed very necessary in an age when the Stuarts and the Puritans had recently tried to seize power: both royalist and Puritan causes were regarded as leading to absolutism and tyranny. But Swift knew that man's management of Christianity was all too human; and he was not above exercising his wit on religious absurdity, while remaining a good churchman.

During the period from 1707 to 1709, Swift was in London endeavoring to persuade the Whig government to grant a concession—remission of the firstfruits[2] and tithes—to the Church of Ireland. His efforts were unsuccessful, and he was also disappointed in his attempts to gain preferment. It was hinted to him that the remission of the firstfruits might be granted if the Test Act were to be repealed in Ireland. The Whigs' policy was to repeal the sacramental Test; and by removing it in Ireland they might have a useful example to support removal of the measure in England also. It was an act that excluded non-Anglicans from political power. Through its operation the Dissenters and Catholics could not, for instance, accept commissions in the army and the militia. Swift, however, was deeply concerned about the position of the Anglican church. He believed there was a danger of upsetting what had been achieved; he disliked the potential for corruption that might be generated by change; equilibrium was a condition for the continuance of the Anglican church and balanced government. But in Ireland the number of Protestant churchmen in the Pale[3] was small, the Establishment was insecure, and Swift felt the Dissenters of Scottish descent in the north had an innate industry and bravery as well as "a most formidable notion of episcop[ac]y," which they thought, "as most surely they did," three degrees worse than popery. It is clear from *A*

---

[1]Translation: "and to hate and avoid those who practice legacy-hunting."

[2]The first year's income or profits, formerly paid by each new holder of a benefice, or any office of profit, to some superior.

[3]That part of Ireland over which English jurisdiction was established.

Letter from a Member of the House of Commons in Ireland to a Member of the House of Commons in England Concerning the Sacramental Test (which Swift dated as being written from Dublin in December 1708) that his distrust of the Presbyterians was far greater than any worry about the Catholics, who had, after all, been defeated:

'Tis agreed among naturalists that a lion is a larger, a stronger, and more dangerous enemy than a cat; yet if a man were to have his choice, either a lion at his foot, bound fast with three or four chains, his teeth drawn out, and his claws pared to the quick, or an angry cat in full liberty at his throat; he would take no long time to determine.

It was probably in the summer of 1708 that Swift's friendship with Joseph Addison ripened into close intimacy: it was then that he complained of increased governmental work preventing Addison from meeting him as often as he would wish: their respect and liking for each other was mutual. Addison had inscribed a copy of his *Travels in Italy* (1705) to "the most Agreeable Companion, the Truest friend and the Greatest Genius of his Age"; and Swift regarded Addison as the man who had "worth enough to give reputation to our age." A remark is attributed to Swift that when he and Addison spent an evening together they "neither of them ever wished for a third person": they were, however, often in the company of wits (largely Whigs), and Swift also formed a friendship with Addison's friend and schoolfellow Richard Steele. He aided Steele in the creation of the *Tatler* and wrote pieces for it. Ambrose Philips and Matthew Prior were other friends of this period, and he had met many other literary figures in the coffeehouse society of the time, in which his schoolfellow William Congreve, a member of the Whigs' Kit Kat Club, also moved freely. Yet another friend was Charles Ford, a smart young intellectual and Irish landowner.

In the summer of 1709 Swift returned to Ireland in a depressed state. The symptoms of Ménière's disease, the giddiness, nausea, deafness, and noises in his head, continued throughout his life, and there are many entries in his memoranda book that show his occasional utter despair, two poignant examples being the entries for April 1709—"Small giddy fitt and swimming in the head MD [his name for Stella] and God help me"—and July 1710—"Terrible fitt.

God knows what may be the event. Better towards the end." Despite these attacks, he enjoyed his time at Laracor, planting trees, improving his garden, mending his canal. He had much social life. Addison was secretary to the lord lieutenant, and Swift saw a good deal of him in Dublin, introducing him to Stella—they liked each other—and there were many other friends with whom to dine and play cards.

When, somewhat reluctantly ("I never went to England with so little desire in my life"), he returned to London in 1710, things began to change. Though the letters to Stella and Miss Dingley continued with all their openness, their constant account of his doings and ideas, they did not convey the complication of a new friendship he began or, perhaps, drifted into with Esther Vanhomrigh. His relationship (he was forty-two, she twenty) with Esther—he called her Hessy or Vanessa—was based on a teasing, didactic, almost fatherly concern for her intellectual and moral development: and she (whose father was dead) found it irresistible. He dined frequently at the Vanhomrighs' in the autumn and winter of 1710; in the spring, Mrs. Vanhomrigh set aside a room for him. Stella was surprised at his frequenting them; he replied in a letter, jocosely but perhaps also defensively, "You say they are of no consequence: why, they keep as good female company as I do male; I see all the drabs of quality at this end of town with them. . . ." On the one hand, he taught Vanessa to despise orthodox views of conventional behavior; on the other, he valued discretion; he was probably quite sure of his own propriety, he had no intention of marrying, but he did enjoy his intimate friendship with this attractive girl. It is possible that she declared her love for him in 1712; it was probably in the autumn of 1713 that he wrote the poem *Cadenus and Vanessa*, which gives us an idea of his evasive tactics when Vanessa indicated her preference for passion rather than a Platonic friendship:

> But friendship in its greatest height
> A constant, rational delight
> On virtue's basis fix'd to last,
> When love's allurements long are past;
> Which gently warms but cannot burn;
> He gladly offers in return:
> His want of passion will redeem,
> With gratitude, respect, esteem:
> With that devotion we bestow
> When goddesses appear below.   (780–789)

Conversations with Vanessa, those meetings "over a pott of coffee or an orange and sugar in the sluttery,[4] which I have so often found to be the most agreeable chamber in the world," provided a relief from the world of politics, where Swift was rapidly becoming so successful. The new Tory ministry realized the value of his combination of cold reason and explosive logic and agreed to remission of the firstfruits (though Swift did not get the credit for this). He became a close friend of Robert Harley and Henry St. John and was put in charge of the Tory journal *Examiner*. This was the beginning of his period of political power.

After the Tory administration came into office, Swift had used his influence on behalf of Whig writers, as he told Stella in a letter:

And do you know I have taken more pains to recommend the Whig wits to the favour and mercy of the ministers than any other people. Steele I have kept in his place; Congreve I have got to be used kindly, and secured. Rowe I have recommended and got a promise of a place. Philips I could certainly have provided for, if he had not run party mad and made me withdraw my recommendation; and I got Addison so right at first, that he might have been employed, and have partly secured him the place he has; yet I am worse used by that faction than any man.   (18 December 1812)

He tried to reconcile Steele and Harley, but Steele did not keep the appointment. Later in 1713 he quarreled fiercely with Swift. Relations with Addison were not easy because of party differences, and John Arbuthnot, the queen's physician, became Swift's closest companion and friend. He shared Swift's love of hoaxes, of paradox, of irony. Swift had met him at Windsor. His friendship with the ministers had led him to court, where he had a wide range of acquaintances. He dined with the great, indeed he was included in the Society, a dining club set up by St. John for men of "wit and interest," whose members called each other "brother." Another grouping, the Scriblerus Club, was made up of leading writers, Swift, John Arbuthnot, Alexander Pope, John Gay, and Thomas Parnell, who allowed Harley and St. John to attend their meetings. A love of satiric literature and erudite jesting was shared by these authors, and their meetings obviously gave Swift very great pleasure. It was an ex-

[4]A workroom.

citing period in his life, and portions of "The Author upon Himself" convey this:

Swift had the sin of wit, no venial crime;
Nay 'twas affirm'd he sometimes dealt in rhyme.
Humour and mirth had place in all he writ;
He reconcil'd divinity and wit:
He moved and bow'd, and talk'd with too much grace;
Nor show'd the parson in his gait or face;
Despis'd luxurious wines and costly meat;
Yet still was at the tables of the great;
Frequented lords; saw those that saw the queen,
At Child's or Truby's never once had been.   (9–18)

Though he did not bother to frequent the favorite taverns of the clergy, Child's and Truby's, he worked hard for his view of how the interests of church and state should be preserved. His skill as a political propagandist greatly aided the acceptance of Tory policies and, notably, his attacks on the duke of Marlborough, which helped to bring about the conclusion of the war against France. *The Conduct of the Allies*, which went through many editions, supplied the arguments for the debate in the House of Commons: as he told Stella, "The Resolutions printed t'other day in the Votes are almost quotations from it; and would never have passed, if that book had not been written." But his pen had harmed his own career as well as Marlborough's, for *A Tale of a Tub* had been described to Queen Anne as profane. The "royal prude," as Swift called her, was reluctant that he should occupy high office in the church. He had used this phrase in a lampoon upon the duchess of Somerset, the mistress of the robes, who henceforth became his implacable enemy. This was partly because Swift had published the third part of Sir William Temple's *Memoirs* against the wishes of the family; these reflected upon the character of Lord Essex, husband of the duchess' favorite aunt. So he was not given the fat English deanery or slim bishopric he desired, but instead was made dean of St. Patrick's Cathedral, Dublin, in April 1713. Swift regarded this post as a kind of exile, deeply regretting the distance from his friends in London. He was back in London in September, vainly trying to patch up affairs between the two estranged Tory leaders, then withdrew to the country in May 1714 to stay with a friend in Berkshire, hoping to be made historiographer royal. He offered to accompany Harley, now earl of Oxford, to Herefordshire, for Viscount Bolingbroke (St. John) had won and Oxford had been dismissed by the queen.

Then the queen died, and the Whigs were back in power with the Hanoverian king enthroned.

Returning to Ireland in August, Swift occupied himself with administration. "You are to understand," he wrote to Pope,

that I live in the corner of a vast unfurnished house. My family consists of a steward, a groom, a helper in the stable, a footman, and an old maid, who are all at board wages, and when I do not dine abroad, or make an entertainment, which last is very rare, I eat a mutton-pie, and drink half a pint of wine. My amusements are defending my small dominions against the Archbishop, and endeavouring to reduce my rebellious choir.

He worked on *Gulliver's Travels* and, after about three years, had found congenial company in two young clergymen who were wits and scholars, Thomas Sheridan and Patrick Delany. It was not as brilliant a society as he had left in London, he wrote to Pope in 1722:

The best and greatest part of my life, until these eight years, I spent in England, there I made my friendships, and there I left my desires. I am condemned for ever to another country; what is in prudence to be done?

A crisis arose in his relationship with Vanessa, who had crossed to Ireland in 1714, despite the stern warning he had given her in England, "If you are in Ireland while I am there, I shall see you very seldom. It is not a place for any freedom, but where everything is known in a week, and magnified a hundred degrees." She seemed to have accepted earlier his conditions for friendship; but despite his warnings she was importunate; and he reminded her again that he would see her seldom. There was some final break, perhaps because she realized that the friendship with Stella came first with him. In June he vanished to the south of Ireland for several months. Vanessa had died, on 31 May 1723, making no mention of him in her will. He was in the depths of depression when he wrote to Pope in September:

I read the most trifling books I can find, and whenever I write, it is upon the most trifling subjects; but riding, waking, and sleeping take up eighteen of the twenty-four hours. I procrastinate more than I did twenty years ago, and have several things to finish which I put off to twenty years hence.

Irish politics roused him from his inertia, the Drapier[5] was born, and *Gulliver's Travels* finished. He wrote a famous letter to Pope about them on 29 September 1725, which contained his rationale as man and writer:

I have ever hated all nations, professions and communities, and all my love is towards individuals: for instance, I hate the tribe of lawyers, but I love Counsellor Such-a-one, and Judge Such-a-one. . . . But principally I hate and detest that animal called man, although I heartily love John, Peter, Thomas, and so forth.

He arrived in London in 1726, took up his old friendships after twelve years, and argued Ireland's case unsuccessfully with Sir Robert Walpole.

He was deeply disturbed at the news of Stella's illness and wrote some letters, to his vicar, John Worrall, to James Stopford, and to Richard Brinsley Sheridan, that show how affected he was. "We have been perfect friends these thirty-five years," he wrote, explaining how he had realized how ill she was and how much her death would mean to him. "I am of the opinion that there is not a greater folly than to contract too great and intimate a friendship, which must always leave the survivor miserable." He tried to rationalize the situation, but Stella "excelled in every good quality," and he confessed that "violent friendship is much more lasting, and as much engaging, as violent love." She recovered, but the ordeal of her death was deferred only for a year. In that year he offered her a last birthday poem:

From not the greatest of divines
Accept for once some serious lines.

In this he allowed his affection to have its head. He was again in London—his last visit to England—in 1727 and was himself ill when the news of Stella's being again in a precarious state reached him in September. Ill as he was, he rushed off to Holyhead as soon as he could, only to find himself, with wind and tide unfavorable for a week, raging at the delay. Stella died in January, and he immediately wrote an account of her life, finding it impossible to attend the burial service, the lights of which he saw through the deanery window as he recorded Stella's

---

[5]Swift adopted the persona of an imagined Dublin shopkeeper, M. B. Drapier, for his famous Drapier *Letters*.

qualities. This brief biography is haunting in its simplicity and sorrow.

Swift's last years were filled with more activity on behalf of Ireland. To this period belongs *A Modest Proposal* (1729) and *Verses on the Death of Dr. Swift* (1731), virtually a posthumous survey of his own life. He was also involved in *A Complete Collection of Genteel and Ingenious Conversations* and the *Directions to Servants* (posthumously published, 1745). He was often ill now, irascible at times, and yet his fierce anger flared out as effectively as ever in "The Legion Club," his scathing attack on the Dublin Parliament. His popularity, he wrote to Pope, was "wholly confined to the common people who are more constant than those we miscall our betters." When he walked the streets, he was received with acclaim, his seventieth birthday celebrated with illuminations, bonfires, and salutes of guns. And yet his attitude to the "ordinary" people of Ireland was ambivalent, indeed paradoxical; while condemning their governors, he despised them for their inability to help themselves. As his friend Arbuthnot recorded, he was a sincere, honest man who spoke truth when others were afraid to speak it. He himself wrote of his hate

> Whose lash just Heaven had long decreed
> Shall on a day make sin and folly bleed.

At the age of fifty, Swift had said to Edward Young, when gazing at an elm tree withered and decayed in its upper branches, "I shall be like that tree: I shall die at the top." His memory went; a letter, written in 1740 to his cousin Mrs. Whiteway, described his miserable state: extremely deaf and full of pain. He was "so stupid and confounded" he could not express the mortification he was under in body and mind. He was sure his days would be few. He lived another five years, legally declared of unsound mind in May 1742, not capable of taking care of his person or fortune. He died on 19 October 1745, and was buried in St. Patrick's Cathedral, with the Latin epitaph he wrote for himself placed over his grave. Yeats's version of it gives us the essence of the man:

> Swift has sailed into his rest;
> Savage indignation there
> Cannot lacerate his breast.
> Imitate him if you dare,
> World-besotted traveller; he
> Served human liberty.

THE PROSE SATIRES

SWIFT finished "the greatest part" of *A Tale of a Tub* in 1696 and published it anonymously in 1704. It was wrapped around in the mystery with which Swift loved to tease his readers; he seems to have assumed a false identity—a persona. In the fourth document, fitted in between "The Dedication to Lord Somers" and "The Epistle Dedicatory . . . to Prince Posterity," and entitled "The Bookseller to the Reader," it is stated that no satisfaction can be given as to the author, the bookseller being credibly informed that the publication is "without his knowledge" and whether the author had finished it or intended to fill up the defective places "is like to remain a secret." This challenging the curiosity of readers about the identity of the supposed author was matched by the mass of learned allusions in which the book abounds. The supposed annotator says, "I believe one of the Author's Designs was to set curious Men a-hunting thro Indexes and enquiring for Books out of the Common Road." He issued a warning to those "whom the *Learned* among Posterity will appoint for Commentators upon this elaborate Treatise" and, as Professor Nichol Smith, himself one of Swift's most notable modern editors, remarked, "the modern editor must always be conscious of the shade of Swift finding amused pleasure in the false surmises that send him searching on the wrong track, and when the hunt is successful, as often by luck as by skill, in the explanations that sometimes come perilously near to pedantry."

Swift's reading was extremely wide and in his own words "indefatigable"; he kept commonplace books, he abstracted from authors, he epitomized, but ultimately he was his own man, skeptical yet creative, insisting proudly that he had not borrowed hints from any other writers in the world. His originality is borne out by his own style, highly individual even in the midst of its mocking parodies. In *A Tale of a Tub* Swift involved himself in satirizing abuses in religion with digressions that mocked abuses in learning, literature, and language. He wrote in the manner of earlier seventeenth-century prose writers, echoing their complexity and the magnificent manner of their rhetoric. The following passage on man's fancy is characteristic: it is metaphysical in its imaginative energy, its paradoxical exaggeration, and contradictory in that it condemns the very fancy or free imagination that gives it exuberant life:

AND, whereas the mind of Man, when he gives the Spur and Bridle to his Thoughts, doth never stop, but naturally sallies out into both extremes of High and Low, of Good and Evil; his first flight of fancy, commonly transports Him to Idea's of what is most Perfect, finished, and exalted; till having soared out of his own Reach and Sight, not well perceiving how near the Frontiers of Height and Depth, border upon each other; With the same Course and Wing, he falls down plum into the lowest Bottom of Things; like one who travels the *East* into the *West*; or like a strait line drawn by its own length into a Circle. Whether a Tincture of Malice in our Natures, makes us fond of furnishing every bright Idea with its Reverse; Or, whether Reason reflecting upon the Sum of Things, can, like the Sun, serve only to enlighten one half of the Globe, leaving the other half, by Necessity, under the Shade and Darkness; Or, whether Fancy, flying up to the imagination of what is Highest and Best, becomes over-shot, and spent, and weary, and suddenly falls like a dead Bird of Paradise, to the Ground. (sec. VIII, p. 99)

He could draw upon earlier writers. For instance, this passage from *Antony and Cleopatra* (IV. xiv):

> Sometimes we see a cloud that's dragonish;
> A vapour sometime like a bear or a lion,
> A tower'd citadel, a pendant rock,
> A forked mountain, or blue promontory
> With trees upon't, that nod unto the world
> And mock our eyes with air . . .

was pressed into his service:

If I should venture in a windy Day, to affirm to *Your Highness*, that there is a large Cloud near the *Horizon* in the Form of a *Bear*, another in the *Zenith* with the Head of an *Ass*, a third to the Westward with Claws like a *Dragon*; and *Your Highness* should in a few Minutes think fit to examine the Truth, 'tis certain, they would all be changed in Figure and Position, new ones would arise, and all we could agree upon would be, that Clouds there were, but that I was grossly mistaken in the *Zoography* and *Topography* of them.

Swift was a firm believer in common sense; he wrote as a wit and a literary man. He naturally deflated what he thought dangerous and stupid. Thus he moved to a simpler style when he recounted the actual tale. This is the allegorical story—it begins "Once upon a time"—of the man "who had Three Sons by one Wife, and all at a Birth, neither could the Mid-Wife tell certainly which was the Eldest." The father leaves his triplet sons each a coat, instructing them not to alter them in any way. These coats represent the Christian faith; the sons Peter, Martin, and Jack, the three churches: Peter, the Roman Catholic; Martin, the Lutheran, which becomes the Anglican after the Reformation; and Jack, the Calvinist. Peter departs from the terms of the will after ingenious interpretations of it, so that silver fringes, embroidery, and shoulder knots are added. He hides the will and goes mad. The others, ejected from his house, get copies of the will and realize how they have departed from its conditions. Martin takes away as much as he can of the added decoration without damaging the original cloth; but Jack damages his coat by tearing off the extra material, being more bent on removing Peter's influence than keeping to the will. Peter's belief in the infallibility of the pope and Jack's in his own interpretation of the Bible lead to corruption in religion; but Martin, who represents the Anglicanism in which Swift believed, is rational in his attitude to religion—the compromise achieved was between Christianity and the world, and based upon the actual historical situation. The dangers to the Anglican position from Catholicism and Dissent were added to by the effects of the Deists, notably John Locke, the author of the *Essay Concerning Human Understanding*, and the Skeptics, notably Thomas Hobbes, author of *Leviathan*. Swift attacked both viewpoints in *A Tale of a Tub*, particularly in the Digression on Madness. Ironically he praises man's capacity for self-delusion:

. . . when a Man's Fancy gets *Astride* on his Reason, when Imagination is at Cuffs with the Senses and Common Understanding, as well as Common Sense, is Kickt out of Doors; the first Proselyte he makes, is Himself, and when that is once compass'd, the Difficulty is not so great in bringing over others; A Strong Delusion always operating from *without*, as vigorously as from *within*. For, Cant and Vision are to the Ear and Eye, the same as Tickling is to the Touch. Those Entertainments and Pleasures we most value in life, are such a *Dupe* and play the Wag with the Senses. (sec. IX, p. 108)

Swift had developed his own style: he depended in part upon lulling his reader into false security and then exposing the falsity of his reasoning, his happiness that *"is a perpetual Possession of being well Deceived."* There is a passage that praises the pursuit of truth despite the pain this may cause:

And therefore, in order to save the Charges of all such expensive Anatomy for the time to come; I do here think fit to inform the Reader that in such Conclusions as these, Reason is certainly in the Right; and that in most Corporeal Beings which have fallen under my cognizance, the *Outside* hath been infinitely preferable to the *In*: Whereof I have been farther convinced from some late Experiments. Last week I saw a Woman *flay'd* and you will hardly believe how much it altered her Person for the worse. (sec. IX, p. 109)

Despite the anonymity of its authorship, *A Tale of a Tub*, reprinted twice in 1704 and again in 1705, made Swift's reputation, but it marred his career in the church, for, although we can now see its essential morality, it offended many by what Francis Atterbury called its "profane strokes." Swift defended it in the Apology that prefaced the fifth edition of 1710; but he had not perhaps fully realized how few people could—and still can—accept a relationship between satire and genuine religion such as that which he put forward with what Nigel Dennis has described as "so much coarseness and vehemence." He had to create an audience for his particular invention, the persona, the "author"; his apparent irreverence, his variety of viewpoint, and his shatteringly satiric comments on stupidity have meant that the audience has sometimes shared Queen Anne's unamused disapproval. And Swift knew it. He wrote in "The Life and Character of Dean Swift" in 1731:

> 'Tis own'd he was a *Man of Wit-*,
> Yet many a *foolish thing* he writ-;
> And, sure he must be deeply learn'd-!
> That's more than ever I discern'd-;
> I know his nearest friends complain
> He was too *airy* for a *Dean*.   (74–79)

Along with *A Tale of a Tub* was published *The Battle of the Books*, which reflects some of Swift's unease at the corruptions he thought had invaded English life and letters after the Civil War: he was particularly concerned about the corruption of the language. He had also a certain skepticism about the value of the new sciences. His defense of Sir William Temple's essay *Of Ancient and Modern Learning* (1690) involved him in an argument in which Temple had cited *Aesop's Fables* and the *Epistles of Phalaris* to prove the superiority of the ancients in prose. William Wotton defended the modern age in his *Reflections upon Ancient and Modern Learning* (1694), and Richard Bentley argued in the second edition of that book that neither the *Fables* nor the

Epistles were as old as Temple thought. Robert Boyle supported Temple, and Swift joined in the fray—but was strongly aware of what *was* important: he used the mock heroic form to allow sufficient distance from the actual controversy. Into his account of the battle in St. James's Library (Bentley had been keeper there) he introduced a digression—the fable of the spider and the bee, which was based upon a proverb frequently used in the seventeenth century: "where the bee sucks honey, the spider sucks poison." Temple had used the image of the bee in his essay "Of Poetry" (1690), and Swift, after dismissing the spider as a symbol of modernity, produced an echo of Temple's poem in praise of the bee, ending with an elegant phrase that was itself echoed a century and a half later by Matthew Arnold in *Culture and Anarchy*:

> . . . As for *Us*, the *Ancients*, We are content with the *Bee*, to pretend to Nothing of our own beyond our *Wings* and our *Voice*: this is to say, our *Flights* and our *Language*; For the rest, whatever we have got, has been infinite Labor, and search, and ranging thro' every corner of Nature: The Difference is, that instead of *Dirt* and *Poison*, we have rather chose to fill our Hives with *Honey* and *Wax*, thus furnishing Mankind with the two Noblest of Things, which are *Sweetness* and *Light*.   (p. 151)

The spider represents the overweening, self-sufficient pride of an age concerned with artifice, rejecting the wisdom of the past, relying on intellect to create new ways of thought. Swift looked back to "the peaceable part" of the reign of Charles I as the highest period of politeness in England, and when he measured by that standard the world of his own time, he found it sadly lacking:

> Whether is the nobler Being of the two, That which by a lazy Contemplation of Four Inches round; by an overweening Pride which feeding and engendering on itself, turns all into Excrement and Venom; producing nothing at last, but Fly-bone and a Cobweb: Or That, which, by an universal Range, with long Search, much Study, true Judgement, and Distinction of Things, brings home Honey and Wax.   (p. 151)

Swift wrote most of *Gulliver's Travels* between 1721 and 1725, not, as used to be thought, between 1714 and 1720 (a theory that led to the idea that Swift wrote the book on his return to Ireland in disappointment, and that the fourth book was the culmination of his misanthropy. The fourth book, in fact, was written before the third). Some parts may possibly derive from earlier drafts associated with a project of the Scriblerus Club to produce the *Memoirs of Martin Scriblerus* (1741), the satiric remembrances of an invented traveler.

The first edition, printed in London by Benjamin Motte, appeared in 1726; two editions followed in 1727, though Swift was dissatisfied with the text and himself later corrected the version published in 1735 by the Dublin printer George Faulkner (the third in a four-volume edition of Swift's *Works*). Swift's friend Gay wrote to him describing it as "the conversation of the whole town" since its publication, with all agreed "in liking it extremely." And he alluded to the fiction that Swift had nothing to do with it:

'Tis generally said that you are the author, but I am told, the Bookseller declares he knows not from what hand it came. From the highest to the lowest it is universally read, from the Cabinet-council to the Nursery.

Swift himself enjoyed the situation. In a letter to Mrs. Howard he remarked that he could not understand a letter of hers "till a bookseller sent me the Travells of one Captain Gulliver, who proved a very good Explainer, although at the same time, I thought it hard to be forced to read a Book of seven hundred Pages in order to understand a Letter of fifty lines."

Gulliver's Travels begins with two prefatory items, "A Letter from Captain Gulliver to His Cousin Sympson" and "The Publisher to the Reader." These are designed to give authenticity to the accounts of Gulliver's four voyages that follow. Swift was writing in well-established genres, the traveler's tale, and parodies of it. He drew upon a very entertaining parody of fabulous voyages (such as those we find in the *Odyssey* and elsewhere in classical literature)—probably the first of its kind—written by Lucian in the second century A.D. The hero of Lucian's *True History* had many adventures, including being blown up to the moon and living for two years inside a whale. Sir Thomas More's introduction to *Utopia* (1516), the fourth and fifth books of François Rabelais (*ca.* 1552; *ca.* 1564), and Cyrano de Bergerac's *L'Autre monde on les états et empires de la lune* (1657) were other works of this nature, while Daniel Defoe's *Robinson Crusoe* (1719), written two years before *Gulliver's Travels* was begun, put the traveler's tale into the form of a realistic novel. Travelers' tales of

his own time were also parodied by Swift—notably William Dampier's *A New Voyage Round the World* (1697) and *A Voyage to New Holland* (1703–1709).

The *Travels* appeal to the reader on many levels. There is the simple attraction of the story. It is funny; it is filled with ingenious inventions; and it is exciting. Swift used a literary genre in order to criticize his contemporaries, and he also produced profound comments on human life in general. The story shows us humanity from four different points of view. In the first book Gulliver, among the Lilliputians, sees mankind as ridiculously small. In the second book, he is himself minute in comparison with the Brobdingnagians. For instance, when Gulliver is brought home by the farmer and shown to his wife, she screams and runs back "as women in England do at the sight of a Toad or a Spider." He is terrified of falling off their thirty-foot-high table, and is disgusted by the sight of a nurse with a monstrous breast feeding a Brobdingnagian baby. In the third book, the absurdity of human activities is seen from a commonsensical attitude, the whole book being a species of science fiction in its attitude to time, its mockery of philosophical belief in progress, its dislike of government by experts, its ridicule of experimental science. The fourth book describes rational animals, the Houyhnhnms; they regard mankind as irrational, as bestial as the Yahoos. Swift, as he wrote to Pope in 1725, had "got Materials Towards a Treatis proving the falsity of that Definition *animal rationale*; and to show it should be only *rationis capax*. Upon this great foundation of Misanthropy (though not in Timon's manner) the whole building of my Travells is erected" (*Correspondence*, book III). Since he considered man capable of reason but not a rational creature (like the Houyhnhnms), Swift did not hate mankind, as has sometimes been alleged, indeed as he wrote to Pope "it is *vous autres* who hate them because you would have them reasonable Animals, and are angry for being disappointed" (*Correspondence*, book III).

We need to remember, as we read the *Travels*, that Gulliver is not Swift; he is an invented character, and not always an admirable one. He himself is an object as much as an instrument of satire. This is true also of the characters in the first voyage, though there are different views on how the allegory is to be worked out in terms of English politics in the early eighteenth century. For example, Sir Charles Firth and A. E. Case have offered different identifications of the ministers at the Lilliputian court; and scholars have theorized at length on the likely identities of Bolgolam and Reldresal, and on whether Flimnap, the court treasurer, who is the most expert at a rope dance, is Sir Robert Walpole or perhaps Lord Godolphin. It is easier for the general reader to realize that the High heels, the majority party, are the Tories, and the Low heels, favored by the emperor, the Whigs. The religious parties, the Big Endians and the Little Endians (who break their eggs at the large or the small end respectively), represent the Catholics and the Protestants, and while Lilliput is obviously England, Blefuscu resembles France.

The Lilliputians are cruel, and gradually their treacherous nature is revealed, as we can see them (and, of course, human vice and stupidity) from a detached distance. But the tables are turned in Brobdingnag, where our human weaknesses become obvious in relation to the giants and the crude insensitivity of some of them. There are exceptions to this: for Glumdalclitch is consistently kind to Gulliver, and the king expresses his horror at European modes of life and the corruptions of Gulliver's society. Though the king is also kind, taking Gulliver into his hands and stroking him gently, his comment on the historical account Gulliver has given him of the politics of Europe in the last century is one of revulsion, "protesting it was only an Heap of Conspiracies, Rebellions, Murders, Massacres, Revolutions, Banishments; the very worst Effects that Avarice, Rage, Madness, Hatred, Envy, Lust, Malice, and Ambition could produce." The king continues:

"As for yourself . . . who have spent the greatest part of your Life in travelling; I am well disposed to hope you may hitherto have escaped many vices of your country. But, by what I have gathered from your own Relation, and the Answers I have with much Pains wringed and extorted from you; I cannot but conclude the Bulk of your Natives, to be the most pernicious Race of little odious Vermin that Nature ever suffered to crawl upon the Surface of the Earth."
(ch. VI)

Gulliver finds the physical presence of the Brobdingnagians repulsive, but his attempt to ingratiate himself with the king, by giving him an account of gunpowder and offering to build cannon for him, is received with intellectual horror:

He was amazed how so impotent and groveling an Insect as I (these were his Expressions) could entertain such inhuman Ideas, and in so familiar a Manner as to appear wholly unmoved at all the Scenes of Blood and Desolation, which I had painted as the Common Effect of those destructive Machines, whereof he said, some evil Genius, Enemy to Mankind, must have been the first Contriver.
(ch. VII)

And he commanded Gulliver, as he valued for his life, never to mention this secret anymore.

Swift enjoyed himself in parodying the scientists and projectors of the Royal Society in his account of the grand Academy of Lagado in the third book; he mocked the experiments on animals (blood transfusion had been unsuccessfully performed on a dog, and Swift recounts an experiment of deflating and inflating a dog's intestines by the insertion of a bellows in its anus—"the Dog died on the Spot, and we left the Doctor endeavouring to recover him by the same operation") as well as current theories of language. The flying island anticipated science fiction. And for sheer horror little can match the depressing account of the Struldbrugs, immortal, yet regarded as dead in law after eighty, forgetful. "They were not only opinionative, peevish, covetous, morose, vain, talkative, but uncapable of Friendship and dead to all natural affection. . . . Beside the usual Deformities in extreme old Age, they acquired an additional Ghastliness in Proportion to their Number of Years, which is not to be described. . . ."

It is the fourth book of the *Travels* that has caused most critical ink to be spilled. Here Swift splits human qualities between the Houyhnhnms and the Yahoos, the former rational, benevolent, and the latter brutish, selfish. The argument is not complete, for we see an occasional comic view of the horses, though Gulliver treats them with respect and reverence, accepting their view of him as a Yahoo, yet trying to meet their approval and his own self-approval by imitating "their gait and gesture which is now grown into a *Habit*, and my Friends often tell me in a blunt Way, that I *trot like a Horse*; which, however, I take for a great compliment: Neither shall I disown, that in speaking I am apt to fall into the Voice and manner of the *Houyhnhnms*, and hear my self ridiculed on that Account without the least Mortification."

Gulliver is banished from the Houyhnhnms' island by the horses and when he returns—saved by a benevolent and truly Christian Portuguese captain, Don Pedro, who persuaded him that his duty is to return to his family—we are given Swift's complex, ironic attitude to his relatively simple creation.

As soon as I entered the House, my Wife took me in her Arms, and kissed me; at which, having not been used to the Touch of that odious Animal for so many Years, I fell in a Swoon for almost an Hour. At the Time I am writing, it is five Years since my last Return to *England*: During the first Year I could not endure my Wife or Children in my Presence, the very Smell of them was intolerable; much less could I suffer them to eat in the same Room. To this Hour they dare not presume to touch my Bread, or drink out of the same Cup; neither was I ever able to let one of them take me by the Hand. The first money I laid out was to buy two young Stone-Horses, which I keep in a good Stable, and next to them the Groom is my greatest Favourite; for I feel my Spirits revived by the Smell he contracts in the Stable. My horses understand me tolerably well; I converse with them at least four Hours every day. (ch. IX)

In the last chapter we realize that Gulliver is himself suffering from what he attacks in others—pride. He is oversimplistic; and his misanthropy and misogyny are absurd. Swift's own view of humanity is larger, ultimately, than the rational, satiric view of man Gulliver put forward in his *Travels*.

TORY PROPAGANDA IN ENGLAND AND HISTORICAL WRITINGS

SWIFT was well received in London by the new, largely Tory, cabinet led by Harley and St. John in 1710. His apprehensions about the future position of the Anglican church after the Whigs' Toleration Act of 1689 had been expressed in *The Sentiments of a Church-of-England Man* (1704), *An Argument to Prove that the Abolishing of Christianity in England, May, as Things Stand, be Attended with some Inconveniences* (1708), and *A Project for the Advancement of Religion and the Reformation of Manners* (1709). His ability to write matched what Harley told Swift was the great difficulty of the new ministry, "the want of some good pen, to keep up the spirit raised in the people, to assert the principles, and justify the proceedings of the new ministers." And so from November 1710 onward Swift wrote for the *Examiner* those pungent and persuasive articles that had such an effect on a small, though highly influential, readership. The gentry, the clergy, and business and professional men were generally tired of the war against France and the taxes raised for it; they were suspicious of the Whigs' attitude to the Anglican church; they feared for the position of the crown. There was a rift between landed and financial interests. It was obvious to Swift, and he made it equally clear to his readers:

Let any man observe the equipages in this town; he shall find the greater number who make a figure, to be a species of man quite different from any that were ever known before the Revolution, consisting either of Generals or Colonels, or of such whose whole fortunes lie in funds and stocks: so that power, which according to the old maxim, was used to follow land, is now gone over to money.

The only answer to a situation where, as Swift put it, "through the contrivance and cunning of stock-jobbers, there has been brought in such a complication of knavery and cozenage, such a mystery of iniquity, and such an unintelligible jargon of terms to involve it in, as were never known in any other age or country of the world; was the conclusion of a peace." And Swift's *Examiner* of 23 November 1710 attacked the duke of Marlborough, "the great Commander," and also his wealth. In December he turned to Marlborough's request for lifetime employment in the post of captain-general. This, he argued, was criminal.

The *Examiner* was most influential, but it had served its purpose by July 1711. The delicate secret negotiations for peace went on; jealousies had developed between Harley and St. John; Marlborough had to be deceived into thinking the war could be prosecuted. Swift returned to England during the height of Grub Street pamphleteering, when the secret negotiations had reached their climax, and then his pamphlet *The Conduct of the Allies and of the Late Ministry in Beginning and Carrying on the Present War* was published on 27 November 1711. This devastating attack on Marlborough put forward a conspiratorial view, that the war had been a deception practiced by Marlborough and the Whigs:

We have been fighting to raise the wealth and grandeur of a particular family; to enrich usurers and stockjobbers; and to cultivate the pernicious design of a faction by destroying the Landed Interest. The nation begins to think these blessings are not worth fighting for any longer, and therefore desires a peace.

The pamphlet had an immediate effect, and further editions carried its message to more and more readers; it culminated in Marlborough's dismissal on the last day of the year, and this led the way to the Peace of Utrecht. Swift recorded the captain-general's fall in "The Widow and Her Cat"; he respected the achievements of Marlborough, despite his own detestation of war. The whole story is one of the power of the printed word, and, as Winston Churchill pointed out in his life of Marlborough, those "were not days when public men could afford to disdain the Press."

The Tory ministry, despite Swift's efforts to patch up some peace between Oxford and Boling-broke, appeared to be doomed. Swift thought "A Ship's Crew quarelling in a Storm, or while their Enemies are within gun shott" was but a "faint Idea of this fatal Infatuation." So he wrote *Some Free Thoughts upon the Present State of Affairs* (1714), which supported St. John's policies. Swift's last statements of the Tory point of view were *The History of the Four Last Years of Queen Anne* and his *Memoirs Relating to that Change which happened in Queen Anne's Ministry in the year 1710;* but the death of the queen, who had thwarted his ambition of preferment in England, brought in George I and the Whigs. To his historical writings Swift brought a firm belief, reinforced by Temple's experience and views, that history depended upon individuals, and a firm conviction that divine intervention could, no matter how hopeless the position of church and state, alter the history of England. He possessed a superb historical perspective, his knowledge of the past illuminated, he believed, his attitude to the present, and his desire to get the record straight by preserving facts was part of his historiographical method.

IRISH ANTICOLONIAL WRITINGS

SWIFT returned to Ireland to become dean of St. Patrick's Cathedral in 1713; twenty years later he referred to the greatest unhappiness of his life: "I mean, my banishment to this miserable country." Not only did he miss his literary friends in Lon-

don—Pope, Prior, Arbuthnot, and Gay; not only did he regret not being virtually at the center of political power; but he disliked being, in effect, a colonial, in "wretched Dublin, in miserable Ireland." He had earlier recorded his feelings in *The Story of the Injured Lady*, written in 1707 but not published till after his death. In this he had deplored the effect of English legislation on Ireland, particularly on the Irish wool trade. The "injured lady" (Ireland) alleges she has been undone by the gentleman (England), "half by Force and half by Consent after Solemn Vows and Protestations of Marriage": she has been jilted in favor of an inferior rival (Scotland). The Act of Union of 1707 between England and Scotland was something many of the governing Anglo-Irish would then have wished repeated in a union between England and Ireland. Swift's answer to Ireland's plight was that since the gentleman had got possession of her person, obliged her to place her estate under the management of his servants, and reduced her and her tenants to poverty, she should act legally, have the same steward (i.e., the king), and regulate her household "by such methods as you shall both agree to." This stemmed from the ideas of William Molyneux, a philosopher and member of the Irish Parliament, whose *The Case of Ireland Being Bound by Acts of Parliament in England, Stated* (1698) had put the view that Ireland had its own Parliament and owed allegiance to the king, but not to the Parliament at Westminster. Swift also argued that Ireland should assert her rights to export her goods where she wished, and he attacked the appointment of Englishmen to office in Ireland.

During Swift's first years in the deanery, he had no wish to play any part in Irish politics, but in 1720 his *Proposals for the Universal Use of Irish Manufacture . . .* put the case for using Irish goods and avoiding importation from England, which had restricted Irish trade. He had much sympathy with the plight of the Dublin weavers, though he thought that Ireland had the right remedies at hand, if she would use them. His polemical style had lost none of its force:

the fable, in *Ovid*, of *Arachne* and *Pallas*, is to this Purpose. The Goddess had heard of one *Arachne*, a young Virgin, very famous for *Spinning* and *Weaving:* They both met upon a Tryal of Skill; and *Pallas* finding herself almost equalled in her own Art, stung with Rage and Envy, knockt her *Rival* down, turned her into a *Spyder*, enjoining her to *spin* and *weave* for ever, *out of her own Bowels*, and *in a very narrow Compass.* I confess, that from a Boy, I always pitied poor *Arachne*, and could never heartily love the Goddess, on account of so *cruel and unjust a Sentence*; which, however, is *fully executed* upon *Us* by *England*, with further Additions of *Rigor* and *Severity.* For the greatest part of our *Bowels* and *Vitals* is extracted, without allowing us the Liberty of *spinning* and *weaving* them.

The government prosecuted the printer, but though this prosecution was dropped, the pamphlet did not have much direct success. Swift entered the fray again, when there seemed some chance of rallying and encouraging opposition to a patent granted to an English ironmaster, William Wood, in July 1722, to allow him to coin copper money for Ireland. The Irish Privy Council, the Lords Justice, the commissioners of revenue, and the two Irish houses of Parliament had declared against the patent; and Swift made devastating attacks on the project, in the adopted persona of a Dublin shopkeeper, M. B. Drapier, in a series of letters, the first of which was entitled *A Letter to the Shop-Keepers, Tradesmen, Farmers, and Common-People of Ireland* (1724), while the fourth was addressed to "the Whole People of Ireland." By this phrase Swift probably meant the Irish Protestant "garrison"; in his own words, the "true English people of Ireland"; those whom he was to describe in his letter of June 1737 to Pope as "the English gentry of this kingdom," as opposed to the "savage old Irish." While arguing that the people of Ireland are and ought to be as free as their brethren in England ("Am I a *Free-Man* in *England*, and do I become a *Slave* in Six Hours by crossing Channel?"), attacking the theory that Ireland was *"a depending kingdom,"* and destroying any credibility that might have attached to Wood's coinage, he was creating an active public opinion, and in September 1725 it was announced that Wood's patent had been withdrawn. Swift had become a popular Irish hero, an Irish patriot.

Irish affairs, however, despite the defeat of Wood's coinage, did not greatly change, as the pessimistic attitude that permeates *A Short View of the State of Ireland* (1727–1728) indicated. There followed a series of bad harvests—"three years dearth of corn, and every place strowed with beggars . . . the kingdom is absolutely undone," as Swift described the situation to Pope in a letter of 11 August 1729—and his sense of horror is recorded in what is perhaps the most stirring satire, *A Modest Proposal for Preventing the Children of Ireland from Being Burdensome, and for Making Them Beneficial* (1729). In this he argues his case as if he were an economist, putting forward his politico-economic project coolly and reasonably, with statements of the situation and some persuasive statistics. His appeal to the reader on moral grounds makes his suggestion for a solution of the Irish problem the more devastating when he reveals in a matter-of-fact manner:

I have been assured by a very knowing *American* of my Acquaintance in *London*; that a young healthy Child, well nursed, is, at a Year old, a most delicious, nourishing and wholesome Food: whether *Stewed, Roasted, Baked,* or *Boiled*; and, I make no doubt, that it will equally serve in a *fricasie,* or *Ragoust.*

The scheme is carefully calculated:

I do therefore humbly offer it to *publick Consideration* that of the Hundred and Twenty Thousand Children already computed, Twenty thousand may be reserved for Breed. . . . That the remaining Hundred thousand may, at a Year old, be offered in Sale to the *Persons of Quality* and *Fortune*, through the Kingdom; always advising the Mothers to let them suck plentifully in the last Month, so as to render them plump and fat for a good Table.

The *Modest Proposal* records Swift's disgust with the poverty of Ireland, but he thought that Irish apathy and selfishness and greed created it as much as English policy. His *saeva indignatio*, his fierce indignation, emerges through his scathingly ironic use of metaphor:

I grant this food will be somewhat dear, and therefore very *proper for Landlords*; who, as they have already devoured most of the parents, seem to have the best title to the children.

THE PROSE STYLE AND SWIFT'S SATIRE

In *Gulliver's Travels* Swift wrote of the style of the Brobdingnagians, which he described as "clear, masculine and smooth but not florid; for they avoid nothing more than multiplying unnecessary words, or using various expressions." This description could be applied to his own writing after *A Tale of a*

Tub, when he allowed his sense of comedy, irreverence, and particularly parody its head. He became deeply disturbed about the degeneration of the English language in his own day; he thought the peaceable part of King Charles I's reign was the time when English was at its best. This was very different from the attitude of those who had altered the language for the purposes of scientific communication, those who had produced the close, naked speech praised by Thomas Sprat in his *History of the Royal Society*. Swift thought that

During the Usurpation, Such an Infusion of Enthusiastick Jargon prevailed in every Writing, as was not shaken off in many Years after. To this succeeded that Licentiousness which entered with the *Restoration*; and from infecting our Religion and Morals, fell to corrupt our Language: Which last was not like to be much improved by those who, at that Time, made up the Court of King Charles the Second; either such who had followed him in his Banishment, or who had been altogether conversant in the Dialect of those *Fanatick Times.*

Swift tended to associate language with history, with politics, with religion. He wrote on English in *Tatler* No. 280 (1710) and his *Proposal for Correcting, Improving and Ascertaining the English Tongue* (1712), his *Letter to a Young Gentleman . . .* (1720), and his *Complete Collection of Genteel and Ingenious Conversation . . .* (1738) show his concern with language. For his political purposes and for his pamphlets, he needed a middle style, which would, in effect, avoid the extremes of decadent courtier or disloyal dissenter, of licentiousness and fanaticism. He thought that an academy, founded on the example of the Académie Française, might act prescriptively, to define correct English and fix it—a thing we now think virtually impossible to achieve. But for him language was not only associated with history, politics, and religion: it was part and parcel of morality as he saw it. So clarity was to be sought above all: "propriety and correctness of speech." What this meant in his case was the right word in the right place. He distrusted rhetoric that appealed to passion: his own plain style was nonetheless rhetorical, designed to provoke, to vex, to rouse. He translated arguments into literal terms; he pursued them to their limits. He was aware of his audience; he offered it concrete examples that could be understood. He is said to have summoned his servants, had his proofs read aloud to them, and then to have altered his writing until the servants fully understood it. He aimed, then, not only at the educated classes but at ordinary intelligent people; he therefore had to use an English that was, above all, normal—that is to say uneccentric, commonplace, simple, and generally acceptable; a prose that could evoke decent, tolerant responses and could, paradoxically, provide a vehicle for what is perhaps Swift's main contribution to English literature, his departure from the normal, the peculiarly powerful irony that carried his satire so effectively.

Satire in Swift's hands was a great cleansing force: it shifted the rubbish, it cut clear channels through the corruption of his own day—the hypocrisy and cant, the sheer stupidity and dullness of many of his contemporaries—and it remains with us, for the things he attacked are with us still. He was profoundly aware of the absurdities of human life; he found injustice and irrationality revolting; and he dwelt with disgust upon the ugly, unhygienic aspects of eighteenth-century life. And yet he had two main approaches: he described one as lashing vice, the other as ridiculing. The latter was natural for "a man of mirth," as many of his friends saw him, exuberant in his invention and sense of comic absurdity.

He could rail directly at the men whom he distrusted or disliked: this kind of satire runs the risk of seeming abusive or crude, and his other methods better stand the test of time. His indirect methods of irony led him into impersonating his enemies, or to achieving his effects indirectly with a deadpan style, or else to either diminishing or inflating an enemy's argument. And there was his habit of shifting his style from the reasonable and urbane to the disturbingly violent. He could also surprise his readers by omitting normal or expected human qualities, notably, for instance, in *A Modest Proposal*, which avoids any humanitarian sense of pity. This is part of one of his techniques—of being allusive, or forcing the reader to face for himself the problems presented by the printed word. In short, his methods possess immense variety, informed by that intensity of feeling he brought to bear on the temporary and the lasting issues of his age. The imperishable qualities of his satire are in part achieved by the quality of his imagination that imbues his inventions with the qualities of fact and of reality, and, therefore, even now, with that of convincing contemporaneity.

JONATHAN SWIFT

THE POETRY

SWIFT'S poetry has an engaging directness: he wrote occasional poems to amuse himself and others, to pay tribute and to denigrate, to capture details of the life about him, and to justify himself. He regarded his verses as written "upon trifles," though they were never composed "without a moral view." Trifles they may have seemed to him, but the total impact of his poetry gives us insight into the way his mind worked, shows us his skill with words (the fun he got out of punning and out of rhyming, not always very precisely) as well as his sense of realism. In the "Ode to Mr. Congreve" he offered advice:

> Beat not the dirty paths where vulgar feet have trod
> But give the vigorous fancy room.

And he took his own advice to heart. His fancy played with a wide range of subjects, and he could parody well-trodden, heroic, or pastoral paths with acute irony, as well as adapting classical models—notably, poems of Horace—to his own uses.

What beats through all his verse, even the early odes, is the accent of direct speech. The formal structure of the Pindaric ode that he used in his early poems was not suitable in his kind of poetry; yet in the "Ode to Sir William Temple" he contrived to convey his genuine respect and, at the close of that poem, to express his own feelings. Nature, he says, has tied him to the Muse's galleys:

> In vain I strive to cross this spacious main,
> In vain I try and pull the oar
> And when I almost reach the shore
> Strait the Muse turns the helm, and I launch out again;
>   And yet to feed my pride,
> Whene'er I mourn, stops my complaining breath
> With promise of a mad reversion after death.

He offers Temple the tribute of a humbler Muse:

> Nature the hidden spark did at my birth infuse
> And kindled first with Indolence and Ease,
> And since too oft debauch'd by praise,
> 'Tis now grown an incurable Disease:
> In vain to quench this foolish fire I try
> In Wisdom and Philosophy;
> In vain all wholesome Herbs I sow,
> Where nought but weeds will grow.
> Whate'er I plant (like Corn on barren Earth)

> By an equivocal Birth
> Seeds and runs up to Poetry.   (192–198; 202–212)

This should be contrasted with a poem of 1733, "On Poetry: A Rhapsody," which exhibits an old man's frenzy:

> Not Beggar's Brat, on Bulk begot;
> Not Bastard of a Pedlar *Scot*;
> Not Boy brought up to cleaning shoes,
> The Spawn of Bridewell, or the Stews;
> Not Infants dropt, the spurious Pledges
> Of Gipsies littering under Hedges,
> Are so disqualified by Fate
> To rise in *Church* or Law, or State,
> As he, whom Phebus in his Ire
> Hath blasted with poetick Fire.   (33–42)

These early odes show his desire to get below surface appearances: they contain his fierce awareness of human mortality. For him poetry was a means of clarifying, even of condensing, experience, of arriving at truth. But it had to seem casual—paradoxically, both concise and conversational, direct and clear. Thus in two poems, "A Description of the Morning" and "A Description of a City Shower" (both published in the *Tatler* in 1710, Nos. 9 and 238 respectively), he gives an impression of movement and noise, assembling details into a general and convincing pattern of city life, ironically mocking, in the process, aspects of heroic and pastoral poetry. The rhythm and the rhymes give an urgency to the lines on the shower:

> Now from all Parts the swelling Kennels flow,
> And bear their Trophies with them go:
> Filth of all Hues and Odours seem to tell
> What Streets they sailed from, by the Sight and Smell.
> They, as each Torrent drives, with rapid Force
> From *Smithfield*, or *St. Pulchre's* shape their Course,
> And in huge Confluent join at *Snow-Hill Ridge*,
> Fall from the *Conduit* prone to *Holborn-Bridge*.
> Sweepings from Butchers Stalls, Dung, Guts, and Blood,
> Drown'd Puppies, stinking Sprats, all drench'd in Mud,
> Dead Cats and Turnip-Tops come tumbling down the
>   Flood.   (53–63)

Here Swift is insisting upon the crude reality of ordinary objects. Human attitudes to life are captured equally well in the speech he created in colloquial monologues—as, for example, the famous "Humble Petition of Frances Harris" (1710) with all its breathless account of the loss of her money:

Now you must know because my Trunk has a very
    bad lock
Therefore all the Money, I have, which, *God*
    knows, is a very small stock,
I keep in a Pocket ty'd about my Middle, next
    my smock.
So when I went to put up my Purse, as *God* would
    have it, my smock was unript,
And, instead of putting it into my Pocket, down it
    slipt . . .   (5–9)

And the poem moves to her real problem, the possible loss of the chaplain as a husband. No less effective is a later poem in this genre, "Mary the Cook-Maid's Letter to Mr. Sheridan" (1718), which captures the rattling speech of a forthright Irish servant.

Swift adopted octosyllabic couplets, and in so doing found the right form for expressing himself. The directness and control of his lines are noteworthy. He wrote some political poems during his stay in London: these lampoons were clever, notably the attack on Marlborough in "A Fable of the Widow and Her Cat" (1712) or "The Virtues of Sid Hamett the Magician's Rod" (1710) on Lord Godolphin. He continued his attack on Marlborough, even after his death, in "A Satyrical Elegy on the Death of a Late Famous General":

Let pride be taught by this rebuke
How very mean a thing's a Duke
From all his ill-got Honours flung
Turn'd to that dirt from whence he sprung. (29–34)

These poems chimed with his political prose, and later, when he was involved in combating Wood's halfpence with *The Drapier's Letters*, his poems (of 1724–1725) again displayed a satiric liveliness of invention, a vitality of interpretation, which emerged in the bursting vigor of "Mad Mullinix and Timothy" (1728) and "A Character, Panegyric, and Description of the Legion Club" (written in 1736), a comment on the Irish Parliament, matched only by the bitter view expressed in "Ireland" (1727).

Before Swift settled in Dublin, as dean of St. Patrick's, he wrote *Cadenus and Vanessa*, his longest poem, in 889 lines, an account of his relationship (Cadenus is an anagram of *decanus*, Latin for dean) with Esther Vanhomrigh. This poem contrasts Vanessa's perfections and the imperfections of contemporary women that correspond to the failings of society, by means of setting this moral fable in a mythological setting where the two sexes dispute before Venus. The poem tells of Cadenus' surprise at Vanessa's falling in love with him:

Vanessa, not in Years a Score
Dreams of a Gown of forty-four;
Imaginary Charms can find,
In Eyes with Reading almost blind;
Cadenus now no more appears
Declin'd in Health, advanc'd in Years.
She fancies Musick in his Tongue
Nor further looks but thinks him Young. (525–532)

He is flattered, but his dignity and age forbid him to engage in love:

But friendship in its greatest Height,
A constant, rational Delight,
On Virtue's Basis fix'd to last,
When Love's allurements long are past;
Which gently warms but cannot burn;
He gladly offers in return.   (780–785)

Vanessa sees the situation of pupil and tutor is reversed:

But what success Vanessa met,
Is to the world a Secret yet:
Whether the Nymph to please her Swain,
Talks in a high Romantick Strain;
Or whether he at last descends
To like with less Seraphick Ends;
Or, to compound the Business, whether
They temper Love and Books together;
Must never to Mankind be told,
Nor shall the conscious Muse unfold.   (818–827)

The poem pays its compliments to Vanessa, but the interest for us is its autobiographical account of the problems of one of Swift's close relationships. Swift's friendship with Stella gave rise to revealing poems, some written for her birthdays, in which he pays tribute to her character, her intelligence, and her care for him. In these he pays her compliments ("On Stella's Birth-day, Written A.D. 1718–[19]"), praises her kindness ("To Stella, Visiting Me in My Sickness"), stresses their friendship:

Thou *Stella* wert no longer young
When first for thee my Harp I strung;
Without one Word of Cupid's Darts,
Of killing Eyes, or bleeding Hearts:
With Friendship and Esteem possesst,
I ne'er admitted Love a guest. . . .
    ("To Stella, Who Collected and
        Transcribed His Poems," 9–14)

Other poems stress the lasting quality of her intellect ("Stella's Birthday, Written A.D. 1720–21"), tease her ("Stella's Distress on the 3rd Fatal Day of October 1723," rewritten as "Stella at Wood-Park") when she finds her Dublin lodgings small after staying at Wood Park, praise her for missing him on her birthday—a self-pitying poem ("To Stella . . . Written on the Day of Her Birth, but not on the Subject, When I Was Sick in Bed") on his being fifty-six, she forty-three ("Stella's Birth Day, 1725"), on her being too thin ("A Receipt to Restore Stella's Youth, Written in the Year 1724–5"), and, perhaps the most moving of all, as Stella was dying in 1727 ("Stella's Birthday, March 13, 1727"):

> This Day whate'er the fates decree,
> Shall still be kept with Joy by me:
> This Day then, let us not be told,
> That you are sick and I grown old,
> Nor think on our approaching ills,
> And talk of Spectacles and Pills;
> To morrow will be time enough
> To hear such mortifying stuff.
> Yet since from Reason may be brought
> A better and more pleasing thought,
> Which can in spite of all Decays
> Support a few remaining Days:
> From not the gravest of Divines,
> Accept for once some serious lines
> Although we now can form no more
> Fond schemes of Life, as here to fore;
> Yet you, while Time is running fast,
> Can look with Joy on what is past. . . .

Perhaps the deepest sign of his care for Stella is to be found in "Holyhead, September 25, 1717," the moody, angry poem he wrote when, deeply anxious about her "On whom my fears and hopes depend," he was held up by contrary winds:

> Lo here I sit at holy head
> With muddy ale and mouldy bread
> All Christian vittals stink of fish
> I'm where my enemies would wish. . . .

Swift's last poems return to his basic interest in the difference between truth and illusion. "The Problem," a poem of 1699, deals with the animal side of love, and such poems as 'The Lady's Dressing Room" (1732) stress his loathing of untidiness and lack of hygiene. "A Beautiful Young Nymph Going to Bed" (1734) develops the attack on appearance and reality by showing how Erinna dismantles her

artificial aids at night while "Strephon and Chloe" (1734), describing Strephon's shock at discovering that his bride is all too human, stresses the need for maintaining decency.

Swift did not accept a persona in poetry as in prose. Thus his attitude toward himself appears unequivocally in several poems. "The Author upon Himself" (1714) was a straightforward, if ironic, account of his life in London, and his retiring from political life, "The Life and Character of Dr. Swift" (1731) exhibited a frank desire to weigh up his achievement, albeit laughingly, but the "Verses on the Death of Dr. Swift" (1739) had its sadness as it considered how quickly he will be forgotten. While playing cards the ladies

> Receive the news in doleful dumps,
> The Dean is dead, (and what is *Trumps*?)
> Then Lord have mercy on his Soul
> (Ladies I'll venture for the *Vole*)
> Six Deans they say must bear the Pall
> (I wish I knew what *King* to call). . . .

He defended his satire and his moral view, remarked how he had exposed the fool and lashed the knave:

> Yet malice never was his Aim
> He lash'd the Vice but spar'd the Name.

And finally, ironically, he linked himself yet again with the land he hated:

> He gave the little Wealth he had,
> To build a House for Fools and Mad:
> And show'd by one satyric Touch,
> No nation wanted it so much.
> (227–231; 459–460; 479–483)

THE CORRESPONDENCE

SWIFT's letters have an immediacy about them; they too reflect his desire to write unaffectedly and intimately, and they are written in a graphic, lively style. He provided his recipients with what he might have offered them in conversation. Thus he seems to talk out loud to Stella and her friend Rebecca Dingley in the *Journal to Stella*. He returns from his days among the great and relaxes in telling the ladies in Dublin about the events of his day in London, as well as relaying the gossip of the town.

From them we can piece together his care over money, coupled with his generosity, his fiery independence, his desire to be treated like a lord. He could tell Stella how he called on Secretary St. John and told him "never to appear cold to me, for I would not be treated like a school boy." St. John "took all right; said I had reason" and would have had Swift dine with him "to make up matters; but I would not. I don't know, but I would not." Stella knew him well. He had taught her to despise the shows of the world; so to her he could recount his sorrows—the death of Lady Ashburnham, for instance. He could scold her and tease her, and demand from her news of his garden in Ireland, of his fruit trees and willows and the trout stream.

Swift emerges from these letters in all his complexity, coarse and sensitive, proud yet ready to serve; humanly despairing and yet ready to endure. To Stella he could be imperious and instructive, gay and scathing, tender and scathing, tender and tolerant. We hear of his health, his troubles with servants, his forebodings about the government.

In letters to others we learn of his domestic situation, as dean in Dublin, for instance; he is often depressed by the effects of Ménière's disease, yet energetically taking vast exercise. There is one charming vignette:

I often ride out in fair weather, with one of my servants laden with a Joynt of meat and a bottle of wine, and Town bread, who attends me to some rural parson 5 or 6 miles round this Town.

There were many letters to Archbishop King, filled with the latest political views, yet discreet, for he knew well the man to whom he was writing. There were the letters to his younger friend Charles Ford, and the jesting, punning letters to Sheridan. Swift wrote many letters: and through them, as through his poems, there runs a nimbleness and drive, whether he is dispensing a moral view or enjoying some piece of raillery. The taut language of his letters reinforces his desire for simplicity; they are always concise. They range from statesmanship to literary satire; to his friends he showed his jocosity, his natural inventiveness, and, at times, his moods of deep depression.

He fought for health. There is a touching letter to Charles Ford advising him to take exercise and be temperate for his health's sake. In this Swift argues that life is not of much value but health is

everything. For his part, he wrote, he labored for daily health "as often and almost as many hours as a workman does for daily bread, and like a common labourer can but just earn enough to keep life and soul together." It was to Ford he wrote that he had finished *Gulliver's Travels* and was transcribing them. As always there is the query of how far to accept his literal meaning, for he commented on them: "they are admirable Things, and will wonderfully mend the World." And in a letter to Pope he wrote a sentence that does more to explain him than the writings of most commentators:

All my endeavours from a boy, to distinguish myself, were only for want of a great title and fortune, that I might be used like a Lord by those who have an opinion of my parts—whether right or wrong, it is no great matter, and so the reputation of wit or great learning does the office of a blue ribbon, or of a coach and six horses.

THE ULTIMATE ACHIEVEMENT

LORD BATHURST, writing in 1730 of Swift's achievement in his time, summed up his success in words that are still useful:

You have overturned and supported Ministers. You have set Kingdoms in a flame by your pen. Pray, what is there in that but having the knack of hitting the passions of mankind?

A fair comment and query; but it does not solve the problem of the elusive man behind the masks. Swift remains elusive, apt to rouse the passions of his readers into admiration or dislike. The evils of existence, as Bonamy Dobrée well put it, are combated with laughter by men such as Swift, who balance their critical, satiric spirits and their savage indignation with an exuberant, fantastic humor. And when there was no need for indignation at the irrationality and injustice of men, when reasonableness prevailed and life ran in smooth social currents, the humor was urbane, teasing where tacit, protective affection existed; creating mirth out of irony when fierce passions were temporarily lulled. Swift moved between moods, as Vanessa knew to her cost: she recorded how he could shake her with prodigious awe so that she trembled with fear, but at other times her soul was revived by the charming compassion that shone through Swift's soul. His saeva indignatio was matched by what Ford called his capacity "for mirth and society"; and Arbuthnot once wrote that it was not Swift's wit and good conversation that he valued him for, but for being a sincere, honest man and speaking truth when others were afraid to do so.

SELECTED BIBLIOGRAPHY

Detailed bibliographical information will also be found in the appropriate volume of the *Cambridge Bibliography of English Literature* and the *Oxford History of English Literature*.

I. BIBLIOGRAPHY. H. Teerink, *A Bibliography of the Writings in Prose and Verse* (The Hague, 1937), revised by A. H. Scouten, ed. (Philadelphia, 1963), a comprehensive work that supersedes W. S. Jackson's bibliography in T. Scott, ed., *Prose Works*, vol. XII (London, 1908) and contains extensive lists of doubtful and supposititious writings as well as of critical and biographical studies; L. L. Hubbard, *Contributions towards a Bibliography of "Gulliver's Travels"* (London, 1922); H. Williams, *The Motte Editions of "Gulliver's Travels"* (London, 1925), see also Sir H. Williams' authoritative bibliography of the early eds. in his ed. of *Gulliver's Travels* (First Edition Club, 1926); D. M. Berwick, *The Reputation of Swift, 1781–1882* (Philadelphia, 1941); L. A. Landa and J. E. Tobin, comps., *Jonathan Swift: A List of Critical Studies, 1895–1945* (New York, 1945), a valuable guide to numerous articles in learned journals, with an account by D. H. Davis of Swift MSS in American libraries; *The Rothschild Library*, 2 vols. (London, 1954), contains full descriptions of the important collection of printed books, pamphlets, and MSS by Swift formed by Lord Rothschild, with references to bibliographical studies of separate works published since Teerink; M. Voigt, *Swift and the Twentieth Century* (Detroit, 1964); J. J. Stathis, comp., *A Bibliography of Swift Studies 1945–1965* (Nashville, 1967); A. Norman Jeffares, ed., *Fair Liberty Was All His Cry* (London, 1967), includes C. Lamont's "A Checklist of Critical and Biographical Writings on Jonathan Swift, 1945–65."

II. COLLECTED WORKS. *Miscellanies in Prose and Verse* (London, 1711), the earliest collection of Swift's writings, apart from a sixteen-page pamphlet (1710), a number of unauthorized and pirated Swiftian "Miscellanies" of varied content were published during the following quarter of a century; *Miscellanies in Prose and Verse*, 3 vols. (London, 1727), these vols. of the "Swift-Pope Miscellanies" were extended by a 4th vol. (1732) and 5th vol. (1735), in 6-vol. ed. (1736), in 13 vols. (1751); *The Drapier's Miscellany* (Dublin, 1733), miscellaneous pieces in verse and prose relating to the Irish economy; *Works*, 4 vols. (Dublin, 1735), published by Faulkner with Swift's tacit approval, extended to 6 vols. (1738), 8 vols. (1746), 11 vols. (1763), and 20 vols. (1769); *Poetical Works* (Dublin, 1736), a separate reprint of Faulkner's 2nd ed. of *Works*, vol. II (above), a number of separate eds. of Swift's poetical works were published during the eighteenth century and his poems were included in the well-known series edited by Bell et al.; J. Hawkesworth, ed., *Works* (London, 1755–1775), a rival of Faulkner's ed., published simultaneously in 6 quarto vols. and 12 octavo vols., subsequently extended by 8 quarto vols. and 13 octavo vols., also published later in 27 eighteenmo vols.; T. Sheridan, ed., *Works*, 17 vols. (London, 1784), based on Hawkesworth's text.

Works, 19 vols. (London, 1801, 24 duodecimo vols., 1803), Sheridan's ed. corrected and revised by J. Nichols; Sir W. Scott, ed., *Works*, 19 vols. (Edinburgh, 1814; 2nd ed., 1824; repr., 1883), vol. I contains Scott's long biographical essay; T. Scott, ed., *Prose Works*, 12 vols. (London, 1897–1908), vol. XII is W. S. Jackson's bibliography; H. Davis, ed., *The Drapier's Letters to the People of Ireland against Receiving Wood's Halfpence* (Oxford, 1935), the definitive ed.; H. Davis, ed., *Prose Works*, 15 vols. (Oxford, 1939–1964), the definitive Shakespeare Head ed., with valuable intros. and bibliographical and textual notes; H. Williams, ed., *Poems*, 3 vols. (Oxford, 1937; 2nd ed., rev., 1958), the definitive ed.; J. Horrell, ed., *Collected Poems*, 2 vols. (London, 1958), in the Muses' Library.

III. SELECTED WORKS. Among the many selections from Swift's writings, ranging from school texts to deluxe limited eds. and including vols. in such series as Everyman's Library and Collins' Classics, the following are noteworthy: W. A. Eddy, ed., *Satires and Personal Writings* (London, 1932); J. Hayward, ed., *Gulliver's Travels and Selected Prose and Verse* (London, 1934), the Nonesuch Press ed.; J. Hayward, ed., *Selected Prose Works* (London, 1949), the Cresset Library ed.

IV. LETTERS. *Letters to and from Dr. J. Swift, 1714–1738* (Dublin, 1741), also published as Faulkner's ed. of *Works*, vol. VII; J. Hawkesworth, ed., *Letters* (London, 1766); J. Hawkesworth and D. Swift, eds., *Letters*, 6 vols. (London, 1768–1769), published as part of Hawkesworth's ed. of *Works*; G. B. Hill, ed., *Unpublished Letters* (London, 1899); A. M. Freeman, ed., *Vanessa and Her Correspondence with Swift* (London, 1921), the first publication of the "love letters" of Swift and Esther Vanhomrigh; D. Nichol Smith, *Letters to Charles Ford* (Oxford, 1935), edited for the first time from the originals, now for the most part in *The Rothschild Library*; H. Williams, ed., *The Journal to Stella*, 2 vols. (Oxford, 1948), the definitive ed., the letters to Esther Johnson were first printed, more or less inaccurately, in Hawkesworth's *Works*, vol. X, letters 1 and 41–65, and in vol. XII, letters 2–40; later eds. are G. A. Aitken, ed. (London, 1901), F. Ryland, ed. (London, 1905), which is vol. II of T. Scott's ed. of *Works*, and J. K. Moorhead, ed. (London, 1924), in Everyman's Library; H. Williams, ed., *The Correspondence of Jonathan Swift*, 5 vols. (Oxford, 1963–1965).

V. SEPARATE WORKS. This section does not include single pieces printed as broadsides or as folio halfsheets; contributions to periodicals (e.g., *The Tatler* and *The Examiner*) and to books by other writers, for which see H. Davis, ed., *Prose Works* and H. Williams, ed., *Poems*; or any of the numerous doubtful or supposititious works that at various times have been ascribed to Swift. For titles of the latter see Teerink's *Bibliography* (above) and the excellent short-title list by H. Williams in the *Cambridge Bibliography of English Literature*.

A Discourse of the Contests and Dissensions between the Nobles and the Commons in Athens and Rome (London, 1701), politics; *A Tale of a Tub* [and *The Battle of the Books*] (London, 1704), polemical satire, annotated ed. with plates (1710); *The Battle of the Books* was Swift's contribution to the famous quarrel of the ancients and the moderns, the definitive ed. of both works is A. Guthkelch and D. Nichol Smith, eds. (Oxford, 1920); *Predictions for the Year 1708* (London, 1708), parody, the first of several jesting satires against almanac-makers (and one, Partridge, in particular) written under the pseudonym of Isaac Bickerstaff during 1708–1709; *A Project for the Advancement of Religion and the Reformation of Manners* (London, 1709), moral instruction; *A Letter . . . Concerning the Sacramental Test* (London, 1709), church politics; *Baucis and Philemon* (London, 1709), verse, Swift's first separately printed poem, reprinted with other poems and with the prose parody *A Meditation upon a Broom-Stick* (London, 1710).

The Examiner (London, 1710–1711), political journalism, 32 weekly issues, beginning with No. 14, 26 Oct. 1710, written by Swift; *A Short Character of . . . [the Earl of Wharton]* (London, 1711), invective; *Some Remarks upon a Pamphlet* (London, 1711), politics; *A New Journey to Paris* (London, 1711), politics; *A Learned Comment upon Dr. Hare's Excellent Sermon* (London, 1711), church politics; *The Conduct of the Allies* (London, 1712), politics, the definitive ed. was edited, with intro. and notes, by C. B. Wheeler (Oxford, 1916); *Some Advice Humbly Offer'd to the Members of the October Club* (London, 1712), politics; *Some Remarks on the Barrier Treaty* (London, 1712), politics; *A Proposal for Correcting . . . the English Tongue* (London, 1712), criticism; *Some Reasons to Prove that No Person Is Obliged by His Principles as a Whig, etc.* (London, 1712), politics; *A Letter of Thanks . . . to the . . . Bishop of S. Asaph* (London, 1712), church politics; *Mr. C[olli]n's Discourse of Free-Thinking* (London, 1713), polemics; *Part of the Seventh Epistle of the First Book of Horace Imitated* (London,

1713), verse; *The Importance of the Guardian Considered* (London, 1713), politics; *The First Ode of the Second Book of Horace Paraphras'd* (London, 1713), verse; *The Publick Spirit of the Whigs* (London, 1714), politics; *An Argument to Prove that the Abolishing of Christianity in England, etc.* (London, 1717), first published in *Miscellanies* (London, 1711).

A Proposal for the Universal Use of Irish Manufacture (London, 1720), political economy, *A Defence of English Commodities* (London, 1720), an answer to this pamphlet, was probably written by Swift; *A Letter . . . to a Gentleman Designing for Holy Orders* (London, 1720), criticism; *The Swearer's Bank* (London, 1720), satire; *The Bubble* (London, 1721), verse; *A Letter of Advice to a Young Poet* (Dublin, 1721), criticism, long ascribed to Swift but probably not by him; *Some Arguments against Enlarging the Power of the Bishops* (London, 1723), church politics; *A Letter to the Shop-Keepers* (London, 1724), political economy, the first of the celebrated Drapier's letters; *A Letter to Mr. Harding the Printer* (London, 1724), political economy, the second of Drapier's letters; *Some Observations upon a Paper* (London, 1724), political economy, the third of Drapier's letters; *A Letter to the Whole People of Ireland* (London, 1724), political economy, the fourth of Drapier's letters; *A Letter to . . . Viscount Molesworth* (London, 1724), political economy, the fifth and last of Drapier's letters, which were published together in *Fraud Detected: or, The Hibernian Patriot* (Dublin, 1725); the definitive ed. of *Drapier's Letters* was H. Davis, ed. (Oxford, 1935); *The Birth of Manly Virtue* (London, 1725), verse; *Cadenus and Vanessa: A Poem* (London, 1726), verse; [*Gulliver's*] *Travels into Several Remote Nations of the World*, 2 vols. (London, 1726), satirical fantasy, Faulkner's text (*Works*, vol. III), which was revised with Swift's cooperation, was first reprinted in modern times in the Nonesuch ed. of *Swift*, and later in the Cresset Library *Swift*, in the Shakespeare Head *Swift*, vol. XI, and in Collins' Classics; the definitive ed. of the text of the first ed. (1726) was elaborately edited by H. Williams for the First Edition Club (1926); *A Short View of the State of Ireland* (Dublin, 1727–1728), political economy; *An Answer to a Paper Called "A Memorial of the Poor Inhabitants"* (Dublin, 1728), political economy; *The Intelligencer* (Dublin, 1728), political journalism, 20 weekly numbers by Swift and Sheridan, published as a single vol. (1729), No. 19 printed separately as *A Letter . . . to a Country Gentleman in the North of Ireland* (1736); *A Modest Proposal* (Dublin, 1729), sociological satire; *The Journal of a Dublin Lady* (Dublin, 1729), verse, reprinted in London as *The Journal of a Modern Lady*; *A Panegyric on . . . Dean Swift* (Dublin, 1729–1730), verse.

An Epistle to . . . Lord Carteret (Dublin, 1730), politics; *An Epistle upon an Epistle* (Dublin, 1730), verse; *A Libel on D[octor] D[elany]* (London, 1730), verse; *A Vindica-*

tion of . . . *Lord Carteret* (London, 1730), politics; *Traulus*, 2 parts (Dublin, 1730), verse; *Horace, Book I: Ode XIV* (Dublin, 1730), verse; *A Soldier and a Scholar* (London, 1732; repr., Dublin, 1732), verse, reprinted as *The Grand Question Debated; Considerations upon Two Bills* (London, 1732), church politics; *An Examination of Certain Abuses* (Dublin, 1732), sociological satire, the title of the London ed. begins *City Cries, Instrumental and Vocal . . .* ; *The Lady's Dressing Room* (London, 1732), verse; *The Advantages Proposed by Repealing the Sacramental Test* (Dublin, 1732), church politics; *An Elegy on Dicky and Dolly* (Dublin, 1732), verse; *The Life and Genuine Character of Doctor Swift. Written by Himself* (London, 1733), verse; *On Poetry: A Rapsody* (London, 1733), verse; *The Presbyterians' Plea of Merit* (Dublin, 1733), church politics; *Some Reasons against the Bill for Settling the Tyth of Hemp by a Modus* (Dublin, 1734), political economy; *An Epistle to a Lady . . . also a Poem . . . Called the Universal Passion* (London, 1734), verse; *A Beautiful Young Nymph Going to Bed* (London, 1734), verse, also contains "Strephon and Chloe" and "Cassinus and Peter"; *A Proposal for Giving Badges to the Beggars . . . of Dublin* (Dublin, 1737), sociology; *An Imitation of the Sixth Satire of the Second Book of Horace* (London, 1738), verse, written in 1714 and completed by Pope; *The Beasts' Confession to the Priest* (Dublin, 1738), verse; *A Complete Collection of Genteel and Ingenious Conversation* (London, 1738), social satire, published under the pseudonym of Simon Wagstaff; *Verses on the Death of Dr. Swift. Written by Himself* (London, 1739), verse, incorporates part of *The Life and Genuine Character . . .* (above), the text of the 4 folio eds. of 1739, published by Bathurst in London, is inferior to the text of the 6 octavo eds. published in Dublin by Faulkner in the same year.

Some Free Thoughts upon the Present State of Affairs (Dublin, 1741), politics; *Three Sermons* (London, 1744), theology, a fourth sermon was added to the 2nd ed. of the same year; *Directions to Servants* (Dublin, 1745), social satire; *Brotherly Love: A Sermon* (Dublin, 1754), theology; *The History of the Four Last Years of the Queen* (London, 1758), history; *Polite Conversation* (London, 1963), with intro., notes, and extensive commentary by E. Partridge; S. Le Brocquy, ed., *Stella's Birth-Days: Poems* (Dublin, 1967).

VI. Biography and Criticism. *Memoirs [of Laetitia Pilkington]*, 3 vols. (London, 1748–1754), lively but somewhat fanciful firsthand reminiscences; John Earl of Orrery, *Remarks on the Life and Writings of Jonathan Swift* (London, 1752), see also P. Delany's more important *Observations on Lord Orrery's Remarks* (London, 1754); J. Hawkesworth, *Life of Dr. Swift* (Dublin, 1755), first printed in Hawkesworth's ed. of *Works*, vol. I; *An Essay upon the Life, Writings and Character of Dr. Jonathan Swift* (London, 1735), by Swift's cousin Deane Swift; W. H. Dilworth, *Life* (London, 1758); S. Johnson,

Life, in his *Lives of the Poets*, vol. III (London, 1781); T. Sheridan, *Life* (London, 1784); J. Barrett, *Essay on the Earlier Part of the Life of Swift* (London, 1808); Sir W. Scott, *Memoirs of Jonathan Swift*, 2 vols. (Paris, 1826), first printed in Scott's ed. of *Works*, vol. I; Sir W. Wilde, *The Closing Years of Dean Swift's Life* (London, 1849); W. M. Thackeray, *The English Humourists of the 18th Century* (London, 1851), contains a famous essay on Swift; L. Prévost-Paradol, *Jonathan Swift: sa vie et ses oeuvres* (Paris, 1856); J. Forster, *Life* (London, 1875), only vol. I was published, the Forster Collection in the library of the Victoria and Albert Museum contains important manuscript and printed material by and relating to Swift; L. Stephen, *Swift* (London, 1882), in the English Men of Letters series; H. Craik, *Life* (London, 1882; 2 vols., 1894); J. C. Collins, *Jonathan Swift: A Bibliographical and Critical Study* (London, 1893); G. P. Moriarty, *Dean Swift and His Writings* (London, 1893); R. A. King, *Swift in Ireland* (London, 1895).

The Orrery Papers, 2 vols. (London, 1903); C. Whibley, *Swift* (London, 1917), the Leslie Stephen lecture; C. H. Firth, "The Political Significance of *Gulliver's Travels*" in *Proceedings of the British Academy* (1919–1920); W. A. Eddy, *Gulliver's Travels: A Critical Study* (Princeton, 1923); S. Goulding, *Swift en France* (Paris, 1924); E. Pons, *Swift: Les années de jeunesse et "Le Conte du Tonneau"* (Strasbourg, 1925), the first installment of a massive but incomplete critical biography; F. E. Ball, *Swift's Verse* (London, 1928); A. Huxley, *Do What You Will* (London, 1929), contains an essay on Swift; C. Van Doren, *Swift* (London, 1931); H. Williams, *Dean Swift's Library* (London, 1932), contains a facsimile of the catalog of Swift's library; S. Gywnn, *The Life and Friendships of Dean Swift* (London, 1933), a popular biography; W. D. Taylor, *Jonathan Swift: A Critical Essay* (London, 1933); W. B. Yeats, *The Words upon the Window Pane: A Play in One Act* (Dublin, 1934), a play about a seance in which the spirit of Swift appears, the intro. has many comments on Swift, whom Yeats read with deep interest in the 1920's and 1930's; S. Leslie, *The Script of Jonathan Swift and Other Essays* (Philadelphia, 1935); C. Looten, *La Pensée Religieuse de Swift et ses antinomies* (Lille, 1935); R. Quintana, *The Mind and Art of Jonathan Swift* (London, 1936; rev., 1953), an important critical study; M. B. Gold, *Swift's Marriage to Stella* (Cambridge, Mass., 1937), a careful analysis of all the available evidence relating to this vexed problem; B. Newman, *Jonathan Swift* (London, 1937); B. Dobrée, ed., *From Anne to Victoria* (London, 1937), valuable essay on Swift by J. Hayward; R. W. Jackson, *Jonathan Swift, Dean and Pastor* (London, 1939).

H. Davis, *Stella* (New York, 1942); R. W. Jackson, *Swift and His Circle* (Dublin, 1945); L. A. Landa and J. E. Tobin, *Jonathan Swift: A List of Critical Studies Published from 1895 to 1945* (New York, 1945); A. E. Case,

Four Essays on "Gulliver's Travels" (Princeton, 1945), defends the 1726 text against Faulkner's revised text of 1735; E. Hardy, The Conjured Spirit: Swift: A Study in the Relationship of Swift, Stella and Vanessa (London, 1949); H. Davis, The Satire of Jonathan Swift (New York, 1947); G. Orwell, Shooting an Elephant (London, 1950), includes the essay "Politics vs. Literature" on Gulliver; M. K. Starkman, Swift's Satire on Learning in "A Tale of a Tub" (Princeton, 1952); M. Johnson, The Sin of Wit: Jonathan Swift as a Poet (Syracuse, 1950); B. Fitzgerald, The Anglo-Irish: Three Representative Types: Cork, Ormonde, Swift, 1602–1745 (London, 1952), F. R. Leavis, The Common Pursuit (London, 1952), contains an important study entitled "Swift's Irony"; H. Williams, The Text of "Gulliver's Travels" (London, 1953), the Sanders lectures, a defense of Faulkner's text of 1735; J. M. Bullitt, Jonathan Swift and the Anatomy of Satire: A Study of Satirical Technique (Cambridge, Mass., 1953); M. Price, Swift's Rhetorical Art: A Study in Structure and Meaning (New Haven, 1953); J. M. Murry, Jonathan Swift: A Critical Biography (London, 1954); W. M. Ewald, Jr., The Masks of Jonathan Swift (London, 1954), a study of the personae adopted by Swift; L. A. Landa, Swift and the Church of Ireland (London, 1954), an important piece of research; R. Quintana, Swift: An Introduction (Oxford, 1955; ppb. ed., 1962), a masterly condensation; P. Greenacre, Swift and Carroll (New York, 1955), a psychological study according to Freudian principles; M. M. Foot, The Pen and the Sword (London, 1957); I. Ehrenpreis, The Personality of Jonathan Swift (London, 1958); D. Johnston, In Search of Swift (Dublin, 1959); K. Williams, Jonathan Swift and the Age of Compromise (London, 1959).

R. Paulson, Theme and Structure in Swift's "Tale of a Tub" (New Haven, 1960); D. F. R. Wilson, Dean Swift (Dublin, 1960); C. A. Beaumont, Swift's Classical Rhetoric (Athens, Ga., 1961); B. A. Goldgar, The Curse of Party: Swift's Relations with Addison and Steele (Lincoln, Nebr., 1961); P. Harth, Swift and Anglican Rationalism: The Religious Background of "A Tale of a Tub" (Chicago, 1961); O. W. Ferguson, Jonathan Swift and Ireland (Urbana, Ill., 1962); J. Fletcher, Samuel Beckett et Jonathan Swift: vers une étude comparée (Toulouse, 1962); S. Le Brocquy, Cadenus: A Reassessment . . . of the Relationship between Swift, Stella and Vanessa (Dublin, 1962); J. L. Snethlage, Jonathan Swift: De Englese Voltaire (The Hague, 1962); N. S. Subramanyam, Jonathan Swift (Allahabad, 1962); I. Ehrenpreis, Swift: The Man, His Works and the Age (London, 1962–   ), vol. I: Mr. Swift and His Contemporaries, vol. II: Dr. Swift; J. A. Mazzeo, ed., Reason and Imagination (London, 1962), contains an essay by R. S. Crane on book 4 of Gulliver's Travels; J. Traugott, ed., Discussions of Jonathan Swift (Boston, 1962); W. A. Eddy, "Gulliver's Travels": A Critical Study (New York, 1963); E. W. Rosenheim, Swift and the Satirist's Art (London, 1963); H. Davis, Jonathan Swift (New York, 1964), contains essays on Swift's satire and other studies; H. Davis, Jonathan Swift: Essays on His Satire and Other Studies (London, 1964); N. Dennis, Jonathan Swift: A Short Character (New York, 1964; London, 1965); P. Frédérix, Swift, le véritable Gulliver (Paris, 1964); E. Tuveson, Swift: A Collection of Critical Essays (Englewood Cliffs, N.J., 1964); M. Voight, Swift and the Twentieth Century (Detroit, 1964).

C. A. Beaumont, Swift's Use of the Bible: A Documentation and Study in Allusion (Athens, Ga., 1965); D. Donoghue, ed., Swift Revisited (Cork, 1965); M. E. Novak, The Uses of Irony: Papers on Defoe and Swift (Los Angeles, 1966), includes H. Davis' "Swift's Use of Irony"; J. G. Gilbert, Jonathan Swift: Romantic and Cynic Moralist (London, 1966); R. J. MacHugh and P. W. Edwards, eds., Jonathan Swift, 1667–1967: A Dublin Tercentenary Tribute (Dublin, 1967); P. Wolff-Windegg, Swift (Stuttgart, 1967); L. T. Milic, A Quantitative Approach to the Style of Jonathan Swift (The Hague, 1967); R. I. Cook, Jonathan Swift as a Tory Pamphleteer (London, 1967); G. Y. Goldberg, Jonathan Swift and Contemporary Cork (Cork, 1967); A. N. Jeffares, ed., Fair Liberty Was All His Cry: A Tercentenary Tribute to Jonathan Swift (London, 1967); A. N. Jeffares, ed., Swift: Modern Judgements (London, 1968); B. Vickers, comp. and ed., The World of Jonathan Swift: Essays for the Tercentenary (Oxford, 1968); K. Williams, Jonathan Swift (London, 1968), the Profiles in Literature series; S. Le Brocquy, Swift's Most Valuable Friend (Dublin, 1968); D. Donoghue, Jonathan Swift: A Critical Introduction (Cambridge, 1969); W. A. Speck, Swift (London, 1969), the Literature in Perspective series; K. Williams, ed., Swift: The Critical Heritage (London, 1970); D. Donoghue, ed., Jonathan Swift: A Critical Anthology (Harmondsworth, 1971); C. J. Rawson, ed., Swift (London, 1971); D. Ward, Jonathan Swift: An Introductory Essay (London, 1973); C. J. Rawson, ed., Gulliver and the Gentle Reader: Studies in Swift and Our Time (London, 1973); R. Gravil, ed., Swift: "Gulliver's Travels": A Casebook (London, 1974); A. L. Rowse, Jonathan Swift: Major Prophet (London, 1975), a lively biography, particularly good about Swift's relationships with Stella and Vanessa; C. T. Probyn, ed., Jonathan Swift: The Contemporary Background (Manchester, 1978) and The Art of Jonathan Swift (London, 1978).

SIR RICHARD STEELE
(1672-1729)

JOSEPH ADDISON
(1672-1719)

A. R. Humphreys

THE PERIODICAL ESSAYIST

It is a salutary principle, in judging a work of art, not to confuse its historical with its aesthetic importance. Anyone writing on the eighteenth-century periodical essay, even at its best in the *Tatler* and the *Spectator*, needs to remind himself of this principle; here is a case where the historical importance is very great but where the modern reader, if led to expect more than a charming humor and vivacity, is likely to feel cheated. Induced to expect too much, he will dismiss what he finds as too little.

Yet in doing so he will miss much in a delightful minor mode that is worth having, as well as a historical phenomenon that can give much food for reflection. Let us take this latter point first. In Britain's cultural life, few alliances have been more fruitful than that between the writers and the readers of these essays, few relationships more thoughtfully and responsibly adjusted. To study the best Augustan[1] periodicals leaves one, if not responding to a profound literary achievement, at least admiring the skill with which enlightenment was spread on a broad front of morals and letters. This was achieved by authors who gave their public what it wanted (they had to), but gave it something consistently better than it could have imagined. Entertainment went hand in hand with improvement; if human nature demanded amusement, it had its better self to be considered too. There is here a code of behavior, as well as a skill of achieve-

ment, which in our own times, and with our own standards of practice, should cause us an earnest and critical self-searching.

For what was happening was the direct and highly effective application to social life, and to a popular audience, of the best efforts literary men could bring to bear. By the late seventeenth century many forces were striving for a peaceful society, for a widely disseminated intelligent culture, and for a prose that would communicate clearly and pleasantly. Yet these forces strove against great odds, and one of the impressive things about the period is the ardor with which writers fought for better things. When violent politicians were "throwing Whig and Tory at one another" (the phrase is from the antifanatic statesman George Savile, marquess of Halifax), unity and sanity were needed; when the focus of culture was wavering between court and city, and a large but ill-defined reading public was coming into view, a common basis of intelligence was needed; and when prose was seeking to free itself from uncertain tone, technique, and aim, an assured acceptable style was needed. To see how the periodical essayists attended to these needs it is necessary to glance briefly at some historical circumstances.

First are the political and religious circumstances. From 1685 to 1715 there were thirty years of danger. In 1688, James II, swiftly deposed and exiled by a revolution, was replaced by his daughter Mary II and her foreign husband William III. James's son was further excluded from the throne by the importation of a second foreign ruler, George I of Hanover, in 1714; and in 1715 an abortive invasion was attempted in his favor. Party rancor was fierce. Of the political temper about 1690 Halifax writes:

---

[1]This term refers to the most accomplished period of a literature, like that in Rome under the Emperor Augustus; it normally indicates the period 1680–1750 in English literature.

There is a flying Squadron on both sides, that are afraid the World should agree, that raise angry Apparitions to keep Men from being reconciled, like Wasps that fly up and down, buzz and sting to keep Men unquiet.

Party journalism, seen at its strongest in Jonathan Swift's *Examiner* papers (1710–1711), was bitter in the early eighteenth century, and Daniel Defoe in his *Review* of 2 August 1712 draws a picture of extreme dissension:

What Distractions in what we expect! What Disorder in what we feel! What Confusion of Counsels! What Division of Parties! What Animosities in these Disputes! And in General what Clashings of Interest are to be found just now, among all the People of this Age! How are the Blessings of Charity, good Neighbourhood, Natural Affections, Civility, good Manners, and in short every Temper necessary to maintain Peace and Prosperity among a Society of People sunk and gone among us!

An equal danger showed itself in religious as in political affairs (the two were often connected), a danger that had exploded in the Civil War (1642–1649) and that still showed itself in violent sermons by High Church extremists and recriminations by the Dissenters against whom they were directed. Here again, men of goodwill felt the need for reconciliation. "No other thing is the better for being *Sower*; and it would be hard that religion should be so, which is the best of things," Halifax observed. His belief was shared by enlightened churchmen—the Latitudinarians (men of the Broad Church movement, who were inspired by the spiritual ideals of the Cambridge Platonists)—who propounded charity and toleration under their renowned leader John Tillotson, archbishop of Canterbury, and whose mildness Gilbert Burnet's *History of My Own Times* (first volume, 1723; second volume, 1734) contrasted with the "narrower thoughts and fiercer temper" of their opponents. In these circumstances Sir Richard Steele and Joseph Addison worked for latitude; the *Tatler* and the *Spectator*, as Samuel Johnson put it, "were published at a time when two parties, loud, restless and violent . . . were agitating the nation: to minds heated with political contest they supplied cooler and more inoffensive reflections."

Men of sense were not content with hauling the nation back from the brink of disaster; they had a large campaign of improvement to promote. There were triumphs of the new science to proclaim; there was a civilized literary style to practice; there was a busy and advancing civic life to record; there was a whole morality of social conduct to explore in relation to the growing demand for harmony. It was this complex of tasks that the periodical essayists undertook.

EVOLUTION OF THE ESSAY

THE evolution of the essay form first needs a comment. Montaigne's *Essais* (1580) had established the word "essay," and a taste for the form; his method, though resulting sometimes in a long composition, is characteristically easygoing, almost haphazard. In the essay "Of Democritus and Heraclitus" he remarks:

The judgement is a tool adapted for all subjects, and meddles with everything. Therefore, for these trials I make of it, I grasp at any kind of opportunity. . . . I take the first subject that chance offers; they are all equally good to me. And I never purpose to treat them exhaustively.

This is, in fact, the typical method of the essay writer. The first English practitioner was Francis Bacon, whose first ten *Essays* appeared in 1597—"grains of salt which will rather give an appetite than offend with satiety," he called them. Pithy, aphoristic, and stiff at first, Bacon developed in later essays such as "Atheism," "Superstition," and "Truth" a majestic and continuous eloquence. Yet one is not quite at ease with him; eloquent he may be, but with a magisterial eloquence. Nearer to Montaigne's familiar reflectiveness, and the easy manner of the Augustans, are the *Essayes* (in two series, 1600 and 1601) of Sir William Cornwallis. They reach no great heights; they are a personal and honest self-examination, a friendly and unassuming communication. But it is interesting to note this early naturalization in English of the friendly, private manner we credit rather to Abraham Cowley sixty years later, and the readable social advice we credit rather to the Augustans. The essay "Of Discourse" contains, though in a more picturesque idiom, advice an Augustan might well have given:

A Gentleman should talk like a Gentleman, which is, like a wise man. His knowledge ought to be general: it becomes him not to talk of one thing too much or to be weighed down with any particular profession. . . . One knowledge is but one part of a house, a bay-window or a gable-end. Who builds his house so maimed, much less himself? No, be complete.

Cornwallis seems to foreshadow some aspects of Sir Thomas Browne, like the whimsical revelations of *Religio Medici*, the improving precepts of *Christian Morals*; this familiar, Montaigne-like commentary became a favorite mode in the seventeenth century and has ever since remained so. One of its most pleasant exponents was Cowley in his *Discourses by Way of Essays* (1668). Like Horace (whom he often echoes, and translates) he praises the middle way of life, and the following Horatian passage exemplifies the lightness of his tone and touch:

I know very many men will despise, and some pity me, for this humour as a poor-spirited fellow; but I'm content and, like Horace, thank God for being so. . . . I confess, I love littleness almost in all things. A little convenient Estate, a little cheerful House, a little Company, and a very little Feast, and if ever I were to fall in love again (which is a great Passion, and therefore I hope I have done with it) it would be, I think, with Prettiness, rather than with Majestical Beauty!

("Of Greatness")

Friendly anecdotes, agreeable displays of his reading, rallying comment on social life, and unfailing charm—these ingredients make his essays a landmark in appealing discourse. They are too light to carry ideas far; instead, they while away the time in good sense and cultured companionship.

Cowley's distinction includes a clear and natural style. The periodical essay could not have arisen without such a style, and its evolution is one of the most notable achievements in English literature after 1660 (though not entirely unknown before). Its first monument is John Dryden's *Essay of Dramatick Poesy* (1668), which is good conversation and fair-minded argument. In the preface to the *Fables* (1700), his last prose work, Dryden refers to "the practice of honest Montaigne," and his own personal commentary, frank manner, well-stored mind, and roaming spirited intelligence recall his predecessor. By the time he wrote the preface, with its famous praise of Chaucer, prose was prepared for all the purposes of social comment, discussion, and entertainment. By that time other writers had

practiced it well, like Tillotson in his sermons, and Halifax in his cogent *Advice to a Daughter* and *Character of a Trimmer*, and Swift's employer, the once-esteemed diplomat Sir William Temple, whom Johnson (overgenerously) called "the first writer who gave cadence to English prose." "Temple," remarks Oliver Goldsmith in the *Bee* (24 November 1759), "wrote always like a man of sense and a gentleman; and his style is the model by which the best prose writers in the reign of Queen Anne formed theirs." "Very harmonious and sweet, full of Spirit and *Raciness of Wit*" was the view of John Hughes in his *Of Style* (1698). Temple's most admired work consists of four essays in the second part of *Miscellanea* (1690)—"Upon Ancient and Modern Learning," "Upon the Gardens of Epicurus," "Upon Heroick Virtue," and "Upon Poetry"—and for the scholar these are still interesting specimens of what the enlightened man of the period thought. Temple uses the essay as a methodical demonstration of serious subjects; he goes through his book learning and treats his topics academically, "like popular lectures," Sir Edmund Gosse devastatingly comments, "by a very ignorant man who presumes upon his genteel appearance and elegant delivery." His matter is now unimportant, but his manner at best has wit and charm, with a good-tempered easy thoughtfulness that was to mean much to Steele and Addison. He can be favorably represented by his best-known passage, the end of the essay "Of Poetry":

I know very well that many who pretend to be Wise, by the Form of being Grave, are apt to despise both Poetry and Music, as Toys and Trifles too light for the Use or Entertainment of serious Men. But whoever find themselves wholly insensible to their Charms, would I think do well to keep their own Counsel, for fear of Reproaching their own Temper, and bringing the Goodness of their Natures, if not their Understandings, into Question. . . . When all is done, Human Life is at the greatest and best but like a froward Child, that must be play'd with, and Humor'd a little, to keep it quiet, till it falls asleep, and then the Care is over.

Gosse, rightly severe on Temple's contents, is rightly impressed by his style. "If we must not say that Addison was taught by Temple," he observes, "at least it was Temple who taught the public to be ready for Addison." That was no small contribution to public taste.

The credit for establishing the social essay in the periodical, the particular vehicle Steele and Addison were to use, is largely Defoe's. Other men had worked toward it. Sir Roger L'Estrange's *Observator* papers (1681–1687) had question-and-answer dialogues that somewhat dramatized problems of the day, though in a violent party spirit. Edward (Ned) Ward's monthly *London Spy* (November 1698–April 1700), supposedly written by a country scholar who has "found an itching inclination in myself to visit London," describes what he finds there in a lively grotesque way, like the Elizabethan satirists on the one hand (Robert Greene, Thomas Nashe, or Ben Jonson), and the picaresque novelist such as Tobias Smollett on the other. It is vivid, and highly entertaining, but not "polite" letters; one thinks rather of William Hogarth's brilliant caricatures. The same may be said of Tom Brown's agreeable *Amusements Serious and Comical* (1700). The most promising performer before Defoe was his brother-in-law, the bookseller John Dunton, who has been rather too decisively called the father of English journalism. Dunton started the *Athenian Mercury* on 17 March 1690, originally called the *Athenian Gazette*; its title echoed St. Paul's remark that the Athenians "spent their time in nothing else, but either to tell or to hear some new thing." Besides news, the paper contained answers to correspondents, and in them Dunton provided numerous brief essays on social, ethical, and intellectual topics. On these (especially on such as are apt to arouse prejudice, like religion, superstition, and the status of women) he is thoroughly enlightened, a vigorous propagandist for the increasingly vocal conscience of the middle classes.

Defoe drew up his remarkable *Review* (February 1704–June 1713) on similar lines. In the first number he explained that the news ("real History, and just observation") would be followed by "a little Diversion," and this diversion, originally called "*Mercure Scandale*: or advice from the Scandalous Club" (later merely "Advice from the Scandal Club") was to be "*A Weekly History* of Nonsense, Impertinence, Vice and Debauchery." Starting as satire on rival newswriters it soon turned into commentary on social folly, seeking its main targets in drunkenness, inhuman magistrates, the folly of dueling, civil violence (with the outrages of the hooligan "Mohocks"), and the evils of seduction, adultery, and prostitution. As a Whig Dissenter, Defoe was against High Church extremists, but his paper's political tone was quite moderate (much more so than Swift's *Examiner*), and he did his best to spread common sense in political as in social conduct. In a practical, citizenly way, and with the religious earnestness of the Nonconformist, for nine years he urged moderation, humanity, and good behavior on his readers, and sometimes encouraged them to good literature, as when he paid tribute to Addison's *Spectator* papers on "the famous Mr. Milton" (29 March 1712). The title of the club is more titillating than its activities; the "Scandalous Club" is not in itself scandalous, nor does Defoe spread "scandalous" stories. The club is a court of reference, a company of sensible men, who adjudicate on incidents reported to them. These incidents Defoe describes with unfailing realism even when, as sometimes happens, they are allegorical, like the splendidly told story of the "young Lady brought before the Society this Week, in a very strange Condition," wasting away, unfashionably dressed, friendless, expelled from home, excluded from society, shunned in her walks, left "the last of her House, and afraid she should be the last in the Nation." "Her Name," we learn, "was *Modesty*" (8 August 1704). Defoe writes unaffectedly, directly, convincingly; the "Club" device allowed his subjects to be dramatized and was an important lead for future clubs like that of the *Spectator*; and his vivacious but responsible treatment of social morals proved, as his modern editor observes, "an important civilising force among simple readers."[2] He showed what the periodical could do.

THE TATLER

It is with the *Tatler* that the periodical and its essays really emerge into distinction. Steele was one of the remarkable writers of genius with whom Ireland provided England (others, in the eighteenth century, were George Farquhar, Swift, George Berkeley, Goldsmith, Edmund Burke, Laurence Sterne, and Richard Brinsley Sheridan; William Congreve, though born in Yorkshire, had his education at Kilkenny and Dublin). Educated at Oxford, a cap-

[2]Arthur Wellesley Secord, ed., the Facsimile Text Society edition, 22 vols. (New York, 1938). The most convenient form in which to study the *Review* is in W. L. Payne, ed., *The Best of Defoe's Review* (New York, 1951)—a most useful selection.

tain in the Life Guards, writer of comedies, and a political journalist, Steele was a man of warm, impulsive, generous temper, given to heavy drinking and plagued by debts, but, with all his improvidence, an endearing person. His paper ran from April 1709 to January 1711 (271 issues) and, like Defoe's *Review*, was published, the first number explains, on Tuesday, Thursday, and Saturday "for the convenience of the post"—that is, the mail coaches leaving London on those days for the country. The title, the supposed author Isaac Bickerstaff announces, has been taken to honor "the Fair Sex," for the *Tatler* was to appeal not only to the predominantly masculine tastes for politics and economics served by previous papers, but to women as well, and was to comment in a familiar, friendly way on matters of general social interest. Each contribution was to come from the most appropriate source, from the coffeehouse or chocolate house identified with that particular interest: accounts of "Gallantry, Pleasure, and Entertainment" from the fashionable White's Chocolate-House; literary matters from Will's, which Dryden had established as the center of letters; learning from the Grecian, haunt of the clergy; foreign and home news from St. James's, the center of political Whiggery. Above the text appeared the famous motto from Juvenal—*Quicquid agunt Homines nostri Farrago Libelli*—translated in the collected edition as

> Whate'er men do, or say, or think, or dream,
> Our motley paper seizes for its theme.

The *Tatler*'s range is not quite as wide as its motto suggests. It keeps to the normal range of social comedy, pathos, and moral improvement; as Samuel Johnson observes in the *Life of Addison*, its authors are the first "masters of common life," determined to "survey the track of daily conversation and free it from thorns and prickles, which tease the passer though they do not wound him." But within that familiar range it gradually creates a wonderfully complete picture, and the charm with which it does so differentiates it from its predecessors. "The exceptional feature of *The Tatler*," Peter Smithers comments in his biography of Addison, "was its air of gentlemanly unconcern, its appeal to the world of fashion, and hence, subtly, to that of unfashion." By the multiplicity of its social portraits (continued in later journals) it created a lively comic population of great vivacity and interest.

Addison detected the person of Steele behind the pseudonym of Bickerstaff, and began to contribute with No. 18. He had been a friend of Steele's since school and Oxford days, and had become well known for political and literary work. Both men tried their hands at comedies for the stage, but they show themselves far better comic dramatists in the essay form, in the animated social scenes and the entertaining persons who populate their pages. Neither tried the novel (which, indeed, was not truly created until Defoe produced *Robinson Crusoe* in 1719), but the spirit and manner of domestic-social fiction—as Henry Fielding was to provide it in *Joseph Andrews*, Goldsmith in *The Vicar of Wakefield*, and Jane Austen in all of her novels—begins to rise from the crisscross of relationships and events in the affairs of the Bickerstaffs (Isaac and his half-sister Jenny), whose comic genealogy by Heneage Twisden appears in the *Tatler* No. 11, and who, among their Staff ancestors, from their native county of Staffordshire, count Falstaff as a forebear.

The aims of the *Tatler*—entertainment and improvement—were strikingly furthered by its authors' ability to place their ideas in concrete situations, to discuss ethical, political, or commercial subjects in realistic or allegorical stories, and in living characterization. Sir Leslie Stephen, in *English Literature and Society in the Eighteenth Century*, points out that the philosophical trend of the time was making intellectual discourse abstract. The periodical essayists reversed this trend; they embedded it in real life. And they did so with a natural ease. Earlier "character" writers such as Sir Thomas Overbury and John Earl had presented vivid social types as set pieces, extracted from the context of normal life. Steele and Addison worked differently. Their portrait gallery is in action, and their moral commentary arises from a living scene. Open the *Tatler* or the *Spectator* where one will, one meets not stiff set descriptions but vivacious dramatic scenes, amusing on the whole, but sometimes (for both Steele and Addison were men of feeling) pathetic and touching. The following, brief as it is, may serve to show the social comedy in action; it is the sketch of the "Pretty Fellow" in the *Tatler* No. 21, and it follows the portrait of Sophronius, "a gentleman of sweet disposition," whose natural, unaffected bearing "that animal we call a pretty fellow" tries unsuccessfully to imitate:

Jack Dimple is his [Sophronius'] perfect mimic, whereby he is, of course, the most unlike him of all men living. Sophronius just now passed into the inner room directly forward: Jack comes as fast after as he can for the right and left looking-glass, in which he had but just approved himself by a nod at each, and marched on. He will meditate within for half an hour, until he thinks he is not careless enough in his air, and come back to the mirror to recollect his forgetfulness.

This has the right economy, the right bantering note, the right familiar style. The manner is skillful; no one could take offense at the humor, but everyone must ask himself whether he looks thus to an amused observer who nevertheless does not plume himself on his superiority, but who represents the pleasant good sense that everyone should approve. The "Pretty Fellow" is Addison's creation, and the fuller sketch of him in No. 24 helped to make the paper very popular; the same number, in addition to the lively comedies of the "Pretty Fellow," "Very Pretty Fellow," and "Happy Fellow," contains the famous account of the Toasts of the Town, with an anecdote of their origin in Bath, and the rival claims of the vivacious Mistress Gatty and the grave Mistress Frontlet. Addison is not always to modern tastes, least of all in his sermonizing (nor was he, in this respect, to all his contemporaries; "a parson in a tye-wig," the sardonic Bernard Mandeville called him). But for his social comedy, and for Steele's, there must be high praise; there is a spiritedness of fun, a lightness of touch, and an affectionateness of humor that compare well with the same qualities in Goldsmith, William Cowper, or Charles Lamb.

The *Tatler* began with short-winded essays and very miscellaneous contents, including current news. But the last "Continental Intelligence" occurs in No. 83, and as the paper won its hold it concentrated on the social and moral essay, reduced the contents to two themes, or even one, with correspondingly greater fullness, and introduced a generous sprinkling of literary discussion, usually by Addison. Much of this concerns classical reading, but there are comments on plays of Shakespeare and passages of Milton, and treatments of subjects like "the sublime" (No. 43), the expression of grief in tragedy (No. 47), true and false wit (No. 62), the treatment of love (No. 90), the moral power of poetry (No. 98), and poetical commonplaces (Nos. 106, 143, and 163, the particularly amusing paper on Ned Softly).

Though this criticism came mostly from Addison, there is no need here to distinguish methodically between his work and that of Steele, who wrote the majority of the *Tatler* essays. What is more important is the achievement of the paper as a whole. And its liveliest modern impact is made not by its literary criticism but by its social comedy. The material is dramatized excellently, like the entertaining account of Tom Wildair and his father (No. 60), or the philandering Tom Varnish (No. 136), or the visit made to Bickerstaff by some country grandees (No. 86), or the satire on dappers, mettled fellows, coffeehouse statesmen, and others (No. 96), or the political upholsterer (No. 155), or Ned Softly (No. 163). A portrait like the following, in No. 96, is as lively as anything a dramatist could stage:

About two days ago I was walking in the Park and accidentally met a rural Squire . . . with a carriage and behaviour made entirely out of his own head. He was of a bulk and stature larger than ordinary, had a red coat, flung open to show a gay calamanco waistcoat. His periwig fell in a very considerable bush upon each shoulder. His arms naturally swang at an unreasonable distance from his sides; which, with the advantage of a cane that he brandished in a great variety of irregular motions, made it unsafe for any one to walk within several yards of him. In this manner he took up the whole Mall, his spectators moving on each side of it, whilst he cocked up his hat, and marched directly for Westminster.

When Mr. Bickerstaff wishes to reprehend swearing he will do so not in a formal exhortation but in a discussion at his club with a friend, providing a lively anthology of illustrative curses and a richly comic tableau of irate coach passengers in a traffic jam (No. 137). When he discourages sour tempers between husbands and wives he presents the tart comedy of trivial dissension in a dramatic conversation piece (No. 150). And to provide a social context he draws the members of his Trumpet Club (No. 132), Bickerstaff with four garrulous veterans—"the talkative humour of old men"—though the full development of the club idea had to await the *Spectator*.

Characteristically, the Trumpet Club paper ends with a moral reflection on age and wisdom—characteristically, because the *Tatler* does more than hold a mirror up to nature. Steele's first publication, *The Christian Hero* (1701), sought to discover "why the Pagan struts, and the Christian sneaks." Dedicated to his commanding officer, Lord Cutts, as one not sullied by "the fashionable Vice of Exploding [pooh-poohing] Religion," it pleaded not for unthinking credulity but for real religious

SIR RICHARD STEELE AND JOSEPH ADDISON

responsibility. Christianity, not pagan stoicism, is the creed for the man of courage; the life of Christian conscience is better than any amount of classical virtue; and "a certain neglected book which is call'd . . . THE SCRIPTURE" is the best guide to conduct. Steele is one of the earliest and most attractive propagandists for social sympathy, and his generous sense of human nature makes him argue for it warmly, persuasively, though still clearheadedly. He wants a harmonious social life, on religious principles:

God presses us by a Natural Society to a close Union with each other, which is methinks a sort of enlargement of our very selves, when we run into the Ideas, Sensations, and Concerns of our Brethren.

Dedicating to Arthur Maynwaring the first volume of the collected *Tatler*, he explains that he has made it his aim "to pull off the disguises of cunning, vanity, and affectation." When in No. 271 he winds up his task as Bickerstaff he asserts that "the general purpose of the whole has been to recommend truth, innocence, honour, and virtue, as the chief ornaments of life." In No. 3 Bickerstaff says he is "of the 'Society for the Reformation of Manners'"; he is an enemy of viciousness and boorishness—"for, merely as a well-bred man, I cannot bear these enormities." What impressed the reading public was the stress that "as a well-bred man" he laid on decency. Dunton and Defoe had done so, as plebeian journalists; Jeremy Collier, who forcefully arraigned the indecencies of Restoration comedy in his *Immorality and Profaneness of the English Stage* (1698), did so as a High Church parson and was widely supported by the godly. But little had been heard from well-bred men, though, contemporaneously with Steele, one of the best bred, the third earl of Shaftesbury (1671–1713), was writing some extremely elegant persuasives to virtue, collected as his *Characteristicks* in 1711. Moral improvement coming from a popular periodical, urged with politeness, humor, and intelligence, was a new thing—how new, and how influential, John Gay reveals in *The Present State of Wit* (1711):

It would have been a jest, some time since, for a man to have asserted that anything witty could be said in praise of a married state, or that Devotion and Virtue were any way necessary to the character of a Fine Gentleman. . . . His [Bickerstaff's] writings have set all our Wits and Men of Letters on a new way of Thinking. . . . Every one of

them writes and thinks much more justly than they did some time since.

The reformed wits, it will be noticed, now think "more justly" than before, more in accordance with true humanity. The *Tatler* and the *Spectator* hold vice, cynicism, ungenerosity, and infidelity to be distortions of man's real self; in *Tatler* No. 111 Addison objects to La Rochefoucauld as one concerned "to depreciate human nature." Fashion and sophistication have gone wrong, as they habitually do. Dr. Johnson's tribute to Addison applies equally to the joint "Bickerstaff" personality Addison shared with Steele:

He not only made the proper use of wit himself, but taught it to others; and from this time it has been generally subservient to the cause of reason and of truth. He has dissipated the prejudice that had long connected gaiety with vice, and easiness of manner with laxity of principles. He has restored virtue to its dignity, and taught innocence not to be ashamed.

What did the *Tatler* do in this regard? It never for long overlooked its moral duty of enlightening as well as its commercial necessity of interesting. In No. 96 Addison mentions "a false opinion, that what I write is designed rather to amuse and entertain, than convince or instruct." Amusingly, but instructively also, he then distinguishes "living" from "dead" men (those with from those without useful lives). "In short," he concludes, "whoever resides in the world without having useful business in it, and passes away an age without ever thinking on the errand for which he was sent hither, is to me a dead man." Common failings and vulgarities are laughed at—practical joking, swearing and vulgar colloquialism, coquetry and pose, the frivolity of society ladies, affected dress, fashionable extravagances of deportment, boorishness, selfishness, swashbuckling, pedantry or dandyism, commercial meanness or narrow-mindedness, and a hundred other impediments to the good society. At the same time evils, as well as follies, are discredited—the recklessness of gambling, the inhumanity of seduction and of dueling, the brutality of hooliganism, the hideousness of cruelty to animals as well as to men. On such subjects the *Tatler*, though not invariably grave in manner (after all, it had to allure its readers), speaks quite forthrightly. Steele had shown courage in courting his fellow officers' mockery by writing *The Christian Hero*; Addison was more discreet, even demure; but neither of them was prepared to let decency and humanity go by default. So in No. 134, having gained the readers' attention with an amusing petition from an incarcerated cock, Steele goes on to show up cockfighting, bear-baiting, and similar popular sports for the ugly things they are. "The virtues of tenderness, compassion, and humanity," he concludes,

are those by which men are distinguished from brutes, as much as by reason itself; and it would be the greatest reproach to any nation, to distinguish itself from all others by any defect in these particular virtues. . . . When any of these ends [safety, convenience, or nourishment] are not served in the destruction of a living creature, I cannot but pronounce it a great piece of cruelty, if not a kind of murder.

While on the one hand vices are condemned, on the other hand goodness is exalted. In No. 74 Steele prints a letter from a correspondent protesting against destructive or venomous forms of satire and praising "your designed attempt of 'raising merit from obscurity, celebrating virtue in distress and attacking vice in another method, by setting innocence in a proper light.'" Satire abounds in these papers but (as will have been seen) it is satire to tease rather than to infuriate its victims. It may not have turned the vicious from their courses, but it doubtless prevented waverers from following them. And the satire is coupled with encouragements to goodness. Studies of "the noble character of Verus the magistrate" (No. 14), Sophronius the true gentleman (No. 21), Paulo the generous merchant (No. 25), Aspasia the ideal woman (Nos. 42, 49), the value of good breeding (No. 30)—these and many other studies of virtue, often drawn from real life and only thinly disguised, are dispersed through the essays. The institutions of the good society are to be defended against fashionable denigration. "The Wits of this Island, for some fifty years past, instead of correcting the vices of the age, have done all they could to inflame them," Steele protests (No. 159). Marriage, marital harmony, obedience to conscience rather than worldliness, charity, and religious earnestness have been the butts of ridicule. To Steele in particular, devotedly warmhearted toward his wife (his endearments in his letters are delightful), married love was one of the saving values of life. Again and again the *Tatler* speaks out in its favor, as it does also in favor of honor toward women in general. Probably the best-known phrase anywhere in Steele's work is that which concludes

the following praise of Lady Elizabeth Hastings, under the guise of Aspasia (*Tatler* No. 49):

In this accomplished lady, love is the constant effect, because it is never the design; yet, though her mien carries much more invitation than command, to behold her is an immediate check to loose behaviour; and to love her is a liberal education.

The "Scene of Domestic Felicity" (No. 95), the "Happiness . . . secured in the Married State" (No. 104), the "Characters of an Affectionate Couple" (No. 150)—these and similar papers have a charm of sentiment one hardly expects before Goldsmith. Steele is particularly good at these family companionships. If his best-known single phrase comes in the Aspasia extract above, his best-known single passage is in No. 181, on his childhood memories of his father's death. This has a truth and tenderness of feeling that anticipate Lamb.

THE REGULATION OF VIRTUE

BENEATH the social humor, beneath the generous feeling, there is something deeper. The *Tatler*, like its immediate successors the *Spectator* and the *Guardian*, and Dr. Johnson's *Rambler* and *Idler* later, does not hesitate to recommend religious faith. Among Aspasia's virtues it is related that "without the least affectation she consults retirement, the contemplation of her own being, and that supreme Power which bestowed it. . . . She goes on in a steady course of uninterrupted piety and virtue" (No. 42—the passage is Congreve's). Good conscience alone "can make us pass our days in our own favour and approbation" (No. 48). No. 111, "On the Prevalence of Irreligious Principles," is a midnight meditation on current "looseness of principles" fostered supposedly by would-be scientists and modish "freethinkers." In No. 108 Addison seeks in the arts of life ("the very design of dress, good-breeding, outward ornaments and ceremony . . . as indeed every art and science") the means "to lift up human nature, and set it off to advantage." He concludes:

But there is nothing which favours and falls in with this natural greatness and dignity of human nature so much as religion, which does not only promise the entire refinement of the mind, but the glorifying of the body, and the immortality of both.

Few tasks are more taxing than to retain a large public for moral exhortations. The *Guardian* (No. 87, 20 June 1713) confessed that "the grave Discourses which I sometimes give the Town do not win so much Attention as lighter Matters." Here the *Tatler*'s strategy was very skillful, and the judgment in linking gravity and frivolity was admirable. As Gay's tribute shows, it was immediately effective. This was largely, one surmises, because of the utter blandness of its assumption, or purported assumption, that of course men of sense were men of virtue; that virtue, though it needed cultivation, was natural to the gentleman. The tone of this assumption may sometimes seem too nonchalant; for instance, No. 5 recommends Swift's *Project for the Advancement of Religion* as "written with the spirit of one who has seen the world enough to undervalue it with good-breeding." "Good-breeding," one may feel, has not much to do with religion's undervaluing of the world. Yet Steele and Addison might well reply in the words "Bickerstaff" uses to explain his light tone in attacking dueling, that "you have chiefly to do with that part of mankind which must be led into reflection by degrees, and you must treat this custom with humour and raillery to get an audience" (No. 26). On these same grounds Johnson defends Addison against the charge of superficiality—"his instructions were such as the character of his readers made proper." Many otherwise unremarkable essays have an amiable presentation of such qualities as modesty, kindliness, and reverence, to encourage the conclusion that "life without the rules of morality is a wayward, uneasy being . . . but under the regulation of virtue, a reasonable and uniform habit of enjoyment" (No. 49). The recommendation of virtue as "enjoyment" is part of the temper of the times. Religion inspired "the soul's calm sunshine and the heartfelt joy" (Pope); a benevolent God attached happiness to the practice of goodness. "Religion is a cheerful thing," Halifax had remarked, "so far from being always at *Cuffs* with *Good Humour*, that it is inseparably united to it." Conventionally, the code of pleasure was that of the rake; Steele and Addison wished to equate it with virtue, and virtue with religion. Man was to be, as Shaftesbury recommended, in "the sweetest disposition" when he thought of spiritual things; religion was to be treated not with the fiery or the gloomy ardors of the seventeenth century but with an air of sweetness and light. Social and religious virtues were to coincide; good sense, good nature, good conscience, even "that inferior art of life and behaviour called good-breeding," were things of Christian even more than of pagan morals. In the next century Cardinal John Henry Newman was to insist on a difference of category— "Liberal Education makes not the Christian . . . but the gentleman." But the *Tatler* insists rather on the equivalence among the three terms. The true gentleman, liberally educated, is to be the true Christian; equally, the true Christian, liberally educated, is to be the true gentleman. And as Steele concluded his enterprise he expressed happily the outlook and manner of the periodical he had created (No. 271):

I must confess it has been a most exquisite pleasure to me to frame characters of domestic life, and put those parts of it which are at least observed into an agreeable view; to inquire into the seeds of vanity and affection, to lay before the readers the emptiness of ambition: in a word, to trace human life through all its mazes and recesses, and show much shorter methods than men ordinarily practise, to be happy, agreeable, and great.

THE SPECTATOR

HARDLY had the *Tatler* expired (January 1711) than the *Spectator* came to birth (March 1711), published six times weekly until December 1712 (555 numbers) and revived in 1714 thrice weekly for a further eighty. It is more famous than its forerunner, and its principal author, Addison, makes a greater, though not more attractive, literary figure than Steele. Son of a clerical father who became dean of Lichfield, educated with Steele at Charterhouse and at Oxford, he became a good classical scholar, a good Latin poet, and a fellow of Magdalen College. While Steele was serving in the Guards, Addison was preparing himself for a diplomatic career by traveling in Europe (1699–1704), and thereafter he held some prominent political offices, being undersecretary of state (1705), member of Parliament (1708–1719), chief secretary to the lord lieutenant of Ireland (1708–1710), and a secretary of state (1718). His verse gained him fame when he celebrated Marlborough's victory at Blenheim in *The Campaign* (1705); his high-minded classical tragedy, *Cato*, had a dazzling reception (1713). But were it not for his essays, Addison's literary reputation would be insignificant; into them, diluted and sweetened for popular consumption, went his classical and modern reading, his study of philosophy and natural science, reflections culled from French critics, and indeed anything that might make learning "polite."

Despite his career, Addison preferred to be a man of letters rather than a man of affairs. The *Tatler* and the *Spectator* show few signs of journalism's normal interest in news, and indeed on the whole they avoided it. The *Spectator*, being a sequel, lacks a touch of the *Tatler*'s exhilarating freshness, but from the beginning it had an advantage in being sure of its aim. Instead of the sheaf of short essays with which the *Tatler* had begun, it consists generally of a single one, which allows some length of presentation. The social portraits, good-humored raillery, and moral improvement that the *Tatler* had evolved were the *Spectator*'s aims too; it took its stand on a firm idea of what human nature needed. As Addison observed in No. 10:

I shall leave it to my Reader's consideration, whether it is not much better to be let into the knowledge of one's self than to hear what passes in Muscovy or Poland; and to amuse ourselves with such writings as tend to the wearing out of ignorance, passion and prejudice, than such as naturally conduce to inflame hatreds, and make enmities irreconcileable.

Whereas the *Tatler* had included some foreign news, the *Spectator* concerns itself throughout with the social scene and with moral and intellectual themes. "The knowledge of one's self" is that of the best self; it does not include partisanship, and "Mr. Spectator," though leaning occasionally to the Whigs (for example, in No. 3 "The Vision of Public Credit") dissociates himself from political strife. "A man makes an odious and despicable figure, that is violent in a party," he remarks (No. 58); "there cannot be a greater judgment befall a country than such a dreadful spirit of division as rends a government into two distinct people [nations]" (No. 125). Nor does "the knowledge of one's self" include self-centeredness of interest or specialization—among which is included rakishness, the specialization of pleasure. "Bar him [the rake] the play-house, a catalogue of the reigning beauties, and an account of a few fashionable distempers that have befallen him, and you strike him dumb" (No. 105). Mr. Spectator would echo Cornwallis—"Be complete." The standards Dryden had laid down in prefacing the *Miscellaneous Essays* (1692) of Charles de St. Évremond are now not only achieved in essay style but are to be the measures of man in society— "Fineness of Expression and a Delicateness of Thought, the Easiness of a Gentleman, the Exact-

ness of a Scholar, and the Good Sense of a Man of Business."

But lest this all sound too general and abstract, the same point is to be made here as was made about the *Tatler*, that the material is vividly realized in the social scene. The very first account of Mr. Spectator reads like the opening of an autobiographical novel (No. 1):

I was born to a small Hereditary Estate,[3] which I find, by the Writings of the Family, was bounded by the same Hedges and Ditches in *William* the Conqueror's Time that it is at present, and has been delivered down from Father to Son whole and entire, without the Loss or Acquisition of a single Field or Meadow, during the Space of six hundred Years. There goes a Story in the Family, that when my Mother was gone with Child of me about three Months, she dreamt that she was brought to Bed of a Judge: Whether this might proceed from a Law-Suit which was then depending in the Family, or my Father's being a Justice of the Peace, I cannot determine; for I am not so vain as to think it presaged any Dignity that I should arrive at in my future Life, though that was the Interpretation which the Neighbourhood put upon it. The Gravity of my Behaviour at my very first Appearance in the World, and all the Time that I sucked, seemed to favour my Mother's Dream: For, as she has often told me, I threw away my Rattle before I was two Months old, and would not make use of my Coral 'till they had taken away the Bells from it.

Thereafter, Mr. Spectator tells his readers, he has been a studious and silent schoolboy and college scholar, an observant traveler, and a quiet onlooker at social resorts, "rather as a Spectator on mankind than as one of the Species"; from points of discreet advantage he comments on the lives of others. Yet, onlooker though he may be, he immediately surrounds himself with company, the famous Spectator Club drawn first by Steele in No. 2 and by its varied interests improving greatly on the *Review*'s Scandal Club and the *Tatler*'s Trumpet Club. At its head is Sir Roger de Coverley, the jovial, eccentric, kindly, elderly, Tory country squire. Then there is Sir Andrew Freeport, "a merchant of great eminence," embodying city interests, Whig commerce, and progressiveness; then an Inner Temple lawyer; then Captain Sentry, "a gentleman of great courage, good understanding, but invincible modesty";

[3]This account is fictional. It is true that Addison was born in the remote West Country village of Milston, in Wiltshire, where his father, Lancelot Addison, was rector; but the "estate," a church living, was not and could not be hereditary. In fact his father came from Westmorland in the north of England.

then Will Honeycomb, a sociable man-about-town; and finally "a clergyman, a very philosophic man, of general learning, great sanctity of life, and the most exact good-breeding." The club is not, in fact, much used as a device, though Sir Roger is developed through a series of papers that is the *Spectator*'s most enduring attraction;[4] but it symbolizes the range and sympathy of outlook that the paper displayed, appreciative equally of professional worth, social manners, and religious seriousness, and of the old-fashioned country Tory and the enterprising city merchant (both types apt to be butts of satire). Addison speaks of the club as "very luckily composed of such persons as are engaged in different ways of life," so that different members of the public may be assured "that there is always somebody present who will take care of their respective interests" (No. 34). The club reminded readers, in an age of sectarian passion, that they should live together as a family, reproving real vice but looking on harmless differences of outlook and interest as a rich variegation of the nation's essential unity.

The *Spectator*, even more than the *Tatler*, is famous for the variety and vividness of its social panorama. The scope of London's life, and something of the country's, is mirrored—coffeehouse life with its debates, news sheets, clubs of common interests (even the common interests of oddities), and indeed its whole routine (Sir Roger sits down to "a clean pipe, a paper of tobacco, a dish of coffee, and the supplement" [of Defoe's *Review*]). We observe street scenes; commercial houses (No. 69 creates a splendid pattern of Royal Exchange activity and the romance behind the process of trade); moneyed and trading interests (Nos. 21 and 108 recommend business); theaters with accounts of performers and performances (and fun at the extravagances of the reigning Italian opera); current gossip; street cries; churches great and small; the ships and traffic of the Thames; fashions and fashionable affectations; and, beyond the town, the country with its sports, superstitions, and the comedy of its old-fashioned social life. The figure of Sir Roger flits through these scenes with his amiable eccentricities, tiffing good-humoredly with Sir Andrew at the club, distrusting any but elderly coachmen, engaging none but war-

wounded ferrymen when he goes on the Thames, discoursing in old-fashioned commonplaces upon the great men buried in Westminster Abbey, choosing to stay at uncomfortable Tory inns rather than comfortable Whig ones, and so on.

The series in which Mr. Spectator visits Sir Roger in the country (Nos. 106–132) provides an attractive picture of country manners. The Coverley household is served by veteran retainers who have grown old in Sir Roger's service, and indeed by veteran dogs and horses too; his old valet de chambre is like a brother, his butler is gray-haired, his coachman has "the looks of a privy counsellor." They love him, as he does them and indeed all his tenants, after whose welfare he solicitously inquires when he meets them at church. His chaplain is a venerable and kindly man, a good shepherd to his flock, an equally good backgammon opponent for Sir Roger, a seeker of charity for his parishioners but never for himself. Sir Roger is seen in his occupations and amusements, guiding his estate, conversing with fellow country gentlemen like Will Wimble, the expert in matters of game, or the acquaintances whose touchiness over precedence he must not offend. He is presented in his portrait gallery with his ancestors, in his hall with the trophies of the chase, on the judgment bench as a justice of the peace, having his palm read and pocket picked by gypsies, furnishing the church with texts and hassocks and prayer books as well as keeping the congregation in order, and being "a little puzzled" as to whether an old crone is a witch or not. We walk through his fields, attend his church services, are romantically impressed by a ruined abbey on his grounds, with aged elms and a rookery, and feel "a certain transport which raises us above ordinary life" in his country scenes. One of the brightest papers, No. 116, is by neither Addison nor Steele but Addison's cousin Eustace Budgell; it is a truly delightful account of Sir Roger's pack of hounds and a hunting scene, a vivid, lively, colorful, and traditionally English episode.

In No. 16 Addison had set his target high—"It is not my intention to sink the dignity of this my paper with reflections upon red heels or topknots, but rather to enter into the passions of mankind and to correct those depraved sentiments that give birth to all those little extravagancies which appear in their dress and behaviour." But this, though true, is too restrictive. In the first place, a large part of the paper's charm lies in its red heels, topknots, and so on—in the vivid externals of life; and in the second,

---

[4]The main series runs from No. 106 to No. 132, but Sir Roger makes scattered appearances up to No. 517 when Addison, foreseeing the end of the paper, caused his death to be reported to save him from maltreatment by other pens.

it goes higher than "little extravagancies." A famous statement of aims in No. 10 speaks of bringing philosophy out "to dwell in clubs and assemblies, at tea-tables and in coffee-houses." "Philosophy" is a comprehensive term for many kinds of knowledge and wisdom, and on many matters the *Spectator* conveys to its readers the best thought of its time. If its treatment is somewhat glib, Johnson's defense is still a just one, that "that general knowledge which now [1779] circulates in common talk was in his time rarely to be found . . . and in the female world any acquaintance with books was distinguished only to be censured." Delicate tactics of presentation were called for; as the *Tatler* had assumed it to be self-evident that self-respect and virtue go together, so the *Spectator* purports to assume that self-respect naturally goes with intelligence and a taste for "polite writing" (No. 58). By this simple flattery Addison and his collaborators were able to introduce a large circle of readers to such subjects as the criticism of tragedy (Nos. 39, 40, 42, 44), true and false wit (Nos. 23, 38, 59–63), recommendations of ballad simplicity (Nos. 70, 74), the morality or immorality of comedy (Nos. 65, 270, 446), "the Pleasures of the Imagination" (Nos. 411–421, a very significant and long-influential set on the subjects that inspire the mind), and a repeated treatment of Milton (over twenty papers between Nos. 267 and 463).

Not least impressive of the *Spectator*'s campaigns was that by which it popularized science, "the new philosophy," as a reinforcement of religious faith. No. 120 sees in the natural adaptation of animals a demonstration of God's beneficence; No. 387 rejoices in the beauties the microscope reveals in the minutest creatures; No. 393 asserts that natural philosophy "raises such rational admiration in the soul as is little inferior to devotion." In No. 465 Addison quotes Psalm 19—"The heavens declare the glory of God; and the firmament sheweth his handiwork"—and ends with his fine hymn on the stars in their courses, "The spacious firmament on high." No. 565 again quotes the Psalms (Psalm 8—"When I consider thy heavens, the work of thy fingers: the moon and the stars, which thou hast ordained"), and then dwells on the vastness of stellar space as astronomy was revealing it, concluding with confidence in God's omnipresence and omniscience.[5] The presiding geniuses of the new thought are saluted: Copernicus, René Descartes, Francis

Bacon, John Locke, Christiaan Huygens, Robert Boyle, and particularly Isaac Newton, still alive and boundlessly revered. In the *Guardian* No. 175, Steele adds William Derham, author of *Physico-Theology* (1713), who "does, as with a wand, show us the wonders and spectacles of all nature, and the particular capacities with which all living creatures are endowed for their several ways of life." Most important of all, science fed faith and imagination too. The finest of many statements of its power, in these papers, is Addison's praise in the *Spectator* No. 420 of "the authors of the new philosophy" for demonstrating, through the whole range from infinitesimally small to infinitely vast, the wonders of God in creation, by which we are "confounded with the immensity and magnificence of nature." On such themes the *Spectator* achieves a high eloquence.

A few years earlier it would have seemed inconceivable that such extended intellectual themes should appear in a popular journal, and if the language is somewhat bland the conviction of purpose behind it is impressive. It is equally so in the many papers that encourage social harmony and good sense, that "endeavour to enliven morality with wit, and to temper wit with morality" (No. 10), or satirize national prejudices (No. 50), or attack political violence (No. 125), or recommend good nature (Nos. 169, 177), or meditate on the transience of life (No. 26, on the tombs in Westminster Abbey; No. 159, the "Vision of Mirza," on life and death). The tone may be light, but it induces a serious idea, as when amusing anecdotes of credulous superstitions lead to recommendations of confidence in a merciful God (Nos. 7, 12), or light comedy on political passions in women turns into a plea for true womanly distinction at home (Nos. 57, 81). In particular, Addison, the "parson in a tyewig," campaigned for charitable religion against narrow fanatics or mocking skeptics.[6] In No. 445 he spoke with sturdy confidence of his aims and methods:

If I have any other merit in me, it is that I have new-pointed all the batteries of ridicule. They have been generally planted against persons who have appeared serious rather than absurd; or at best, have aimed rather at what is unfashionable than what is vicious. For my

---

[5]To similar effect are Nos. 571, 580, 590, and 628.

[6]For example, in Nos. 93, 106, 111, 112, 147, 185, 186, 201, 257, 356, 378, 381, 441, 459, 461, 465, 519, 531, 538, 543, 571, and 600; the list is far from exhaustive.

own part, I have endeavoured to make nothing ridiculous that is not in some measure criminal. I have set up the immoral man as the object of derision. In short, if I have not formed a new weapon against vice and irreligion, I have at least shown how that weapon may be put to a right use.

LATER PERIODICALS

STEELE's and Addison's subsequent periodicals can only be touched on. Between the suspension of the *Spectator* in December 1712 and its resumption in June 1714, Steele launched the *Guardian*, which ran daily from March to October 1713 (175 issues). Addison came in with No. 67 (having been preoccupied with his tragedy *Cato*) and thereafter wrote more than fifty papers. The most distinguished of the other contributors were Pope and Berkeley. The *Guardian* is not particularly distinguishable from the *Tatler* or the *Spectator*: the formula had been found satisfactory and the recipe continued as before. "The Guardian" himself is an elderly gentleman, "Nestor Ironside," friend of the country family of the Lizards and guardian to an excellent young landowner, Sir Harry Lizard, whose kindly but efficient estate owning is the model for other country gentlemen (No. 6). This family circle, under the excellent Lady Aspasia (No. 2), with her lively daughters (No. 5) and variously gifted sons (No. 13), gives Steele the chance he likes for domestic sentiment, coming appropriately from the kindly, elderly Nestor. One other portrait is notable, that of the wealthy merchant Mr. Charwell (No. 9), retiring to a country estate and increasing the countryside's prosperity with a practical wisdom that would have pleased Defoe. The range of the *Guardian* is the normal one: there are outright attacks on seduction (Nos. 17, 45, 123), dueling (Nos. 20, 129), and cruelty (No. 61, by Pope), and particularly an earnest but witty campaign by Berkeley (seconded by Steele) for a benign religious faith and against freethinkers. The tone of this latter campaign is light, for tactical reasons—"I must not be rough to gentlemen and ladies, but speak of sin as a gentleman," says Steele demurely (No. 17); even so, it considerably reduced the paper's popularity. Good miscellaneous essays are those on the miseries of the poor, and charity (Nos. 79, 166), charity schools (No. 105), rival periodical essayists (No. 98), natural phenomena as evidence of God's goodness (Nos. 103, 169, 175), and natural taste in gardens (No. 173, by Pope). Some papers discuss literature and poetic style (Nos. 4, 12, 15, 16, 25), and Thomas Tickell contributed five on the pastoral (Nos. 22, 23, 28, 30, 32). His praise of Ambrose Philips roused Pope to send anonymously to Steele the very humorous No. 40, an ironic puff for Philips' pastorals at the expense of Pope's own. Not penetrating the irony, Steele sought Pope's permission before publishing and was gravely encouraged to proceed. This paper, with Pope's famous "Receipt to make an Epic Poem" (No. 78), is the *Guardian*'s most entertaining exercise in comedy.

Steele launched several papers of less significance—the *Reader* (1714), *Town Talk* (1715), *Chitchat* (1716), the *Tea-Table* (1716), and, as his last venture, the *Theatre* (1720). Addison was to assist in one other, the *Lover* (February–May 1714), though of forty numbers he furnished only two. The main theme of this is one dear to Steele, "the softer affections of the mind" (No. 1), and the main contents relate to affairs of the heart, a novel and attractively managed bias of interest. Addison contributed No. 10, on women and their craze for the newly fashionable chinaware ("playthings for women of all ages"), and No. 39, on the love-crossed Will Wormgood, and on Theophrastus' *Characters* as translated by Budgell.

Steele's further relationship with Addison was less happy. Suddenly terminating the *Guardian*, he started the *Englishman* without Addison's aid (two series with a total of ninety-five numbers; October 1713–February 1714; July–November 1715). This calls itself "a sequel of the GUARDIAN" and claims to have taken over Nestor Ironside's assets. The first series keeps up some *Guardian* traits with appearances of the Lizard family and the usual comic, pathetic, or moralizing papers on social and religious topics, though the most interesting single number relates the adventures of Alexander Selkirk, the shipwrecked sailor (No. 26), and perhaps prompted Defoe to write *Robinson Crusoe*. But intermittently through the first series, and unremittingly through the second, runs "a particular regard to the Protestant interest in the world" (No. 53), a strong Whig campaign against the Tory *Examiner*, the pope, Louis XIV, and the exiled Stuart line. "This Paper," Steele admits in winding up the first series, "has exposed me to much Hatred and Invective," but politics had gripped him, and it was a political quarrel that estranged the former friends.

Addison himself was meanwhile proving to be a party publicist of skill; his *Whig Examiner* (September–October 1712; five numbers) counterblasts the Tory *Examiner*, which, it says, should rather be called the *Executioner*. In it Addison shows, as Johnson remarks, "all the force of gay malevolence and humorous satire." Much more important was his *Free-Holder* (December 1715–June 1716; fifty-five numbers). This stoutly supports the new Hanoverian king, George I, praising him as guardian of civil liberties and constitutional government, and it attacks the "Popish Pretender" and despotic power. "Every Englishman," it asserts, "will be a good subject to King George, in proportion as he is a good Englishman, and a lover of the constitution of his country" (No. 18). The paper's great merit is that it is written with much dignity and spirit, and a rollicking good humor. In circumstances of pressing political crisis, when other men were angry and bitter, Addison shows his best qualities; he is extremely amusing, but reasonable and constructive too. In No. 8 he addresses not only irritated politicians but society women at their tea tables, and does so with little of the irritating patronage that is elsewhere disagreeable in him:

It happens very luckily for the interest of the Whigs, that their enemies acknowledge the finest women of Great Britain to be of their party. The Tories are forced to borrow their toasts from their very antagonists, and can scarce find beauties enough of their own side, to supply a single round. . . . One may, indeed, sometimes discover among the malignants of the sex a face that seems to have been naturally designed for a Whig lady: but then it is so often flushed with rage, or soured with disappointments, that one cannot but be troubled to see it thrown away upon the owner. Would the pretty malecontent be persuaded to love her king and country, it would diffuse a cheerfulness through all her features and give her quite another air.

Among the best-known *Free-Holders*, and rich examples of partisan comedy, are the three papers on the Tory foxhunter (Nos. 22, 44, 47), the ludicrous, blundering reactionary countryman with all the comic ignorance of rustic bigotry, whom the Whigs liked to equate with the Tory squirearchy.

Addison, then, as well as Steele, could show his powers in politics. Unfortunately, in the last year of his life (1719), Steele and he quarreled over a point of constitutional procedure, in the *Plebeian* and the *Old Whig* respectively. No journals could have been much shorter-lived: the *Plebeian* ran for four

issues, the *Old Whig* for two. But the damage was done; the old friends were estranged, and before a reconciliation could take place, Addison died. Steele, harassed by debts, left London for Wales, and there, isolated, died in 1729.

CONCLUSION

IF any literary form is the particular creation and the particular mirror of the Augustan age in England it is the periodical essay. It was immensely popular; the *Cambridge Bibliography of English Literature* lists ninety periodicals founded between the *Tatler* in 1709 and 1720. Nathan Drake's *Essays Illustrative of The Tatler* (1805) enumerates 221 papers in the *Tatler* tradition current during the eighteenth century, though of course many were almost stillborn. "It may well be called the age of Counsellors, when every Blockhead who could write his own name attempted to inform and amuse the public," said Lewis Theobald. Circulations are hard to calculate; modern scholars put Defoe's *Review* somewhere between 3,000 (which Addison claims in No. 10) and 9,000 at its height. Each of the many copies displayed in coffeehouses would be read by many readers, so the effect of the papers would far outstrip their relatively small circulation.

The modern response to them is naturally cooler than the contemporary, for reasons that must almost always apply to ephemeral writing. And while Steele's personality still appeals warmly, Addison's has lost much favor since the idolizing Victorian days when Thomas Macaulay confessed for him "a sentiment as much like affection as any sentiment can be which is inspired by one who has been sleeping a hundred and twenty years in Westminster Abbey." "Always a somewhat superior person," say A. E. Dyson and John Butt;[7] "undoubtedly something of a prig," comments Bonamy Dobrée. T. S. Eliot feels "something very like antipathy" for him; C. S. Lewis thinks he would be "the most hated of our writers" if he were not so little read. There is something in this; the historical estimate is bound to put him higher than the literary one. "Neither Steele nor Addison is really a great writer," is Oliver Elton's verdict.[8] Yet even the literary estimate, though discovering in the

[7]In *Augustans and Romantics* (London, 1940), p. 57.
[8]In *The Augustan Ages* (London, 1899), p. 295.

essays little that is for all time, must admit the responsibility of aim, the comprehensiveness of grasp, and often the richness of comedy, that these papers show. The didacticism, with the genteel tone and the patronizing "fair-sexing it," may indeed irritate, but any modern journal that in three years produced a cultural revolution comparable with that the *Tatler* or the *Spectator* achieved would be a remarkably welcome phenomenon. The modern writer is not likely to follow Johnson's famous advice and "give his days and nights to the volumes of Addison"; it is nevertheless true that Addison developed prose with great skill, a skill excellently analyzed in Jan Lannering's *Studies in the Prose Style of Joseph Addison* (1951). His easy continuity and coherence were what prose was looking for, after the more spasmodic, even if more spirited, manner of even his greatest contemporaries like Dryden and Swift. From a study of his work and Steele's we may gain, first, an intimate, varied, and vivid picture of Augustan society, and, second, a renewed faith that men and women of intelligence, by striving for the good society, can bring it nearer, and indeed must do so.

SELECTED BIBLIOGRAPHY

I. BIBLIOGRAPHY. Detailed bibliographical information can also be found in the appropriate volume of the *Cambridge Bibliography of English Literature* and the *Oxford History of English Literature*. R. S. Crane and F. B. Kaye, *A Census of British Newspapers and Periodicals, 1620–1800* (Chapel Hill, N. C., 1927); K. K. Weed and R. P. Bond, *Studies in British Newspapers and Periodicals from Their Beginning to 1800: A Bibliography* (Chapel Hill, N. C., 1946).

II. COLLECTIONS AND ANTHOLOGIES. A. Chalmers, *The British Essayists; with Prefaces, Historical and Biographical*, 45 vols. (London, 1802–1803); R. Lynam, ed., *The British Essayists*, 30 vols. (London, 1827); G. Carver, ed., *Periodical Essays of the Eighteenth Century* (New York, 1930); M. G. Segar, ed., *Essays from Eighteenth Century Periodicals* (London, 1947).

III. GENERAL STUDIES. N. Drake, *Essays Biographical, Critical, and Historical, Illustrative of the Tatler, etc.*, 3 vols. (London, 1805); W. C. Hazlitt, *The English Comic Writers* (London, 1819); J. Spence, *Literary Anecdotes*, S. W. Singer, ed. (London, 1820); W. M. Thackeray, *The English Humourists of the Eighteenth Century* (London, 1853); L. Stephen, *English Literature and Society in the Eighteenth Century* (London, 1904); H. Walker, *The English Essay and Essayists* (London, 1915); G. S. Marr, *The Periodical Essayists of the Eighteenth Century* (London, 1923); W. Graham, *English Literary Periodicals* (New York, 1930), contains a useful bibliography; A. Beljame, *Men of Letters and the English Public, 1660–1744*, E. O. Lorimer, trans., B. Dobrée, ed. (London, 1948), originally published in French (Paris, 1881); R. P. Bond, *Contemporaries of the Tatler and Spectator* (Los Angeles, 1954), the Augustan Reprint Society; W. B. Ewald, *The Newsmen of Queen Anne* (London, 1956); D. H. Bond and W. R. McLeod, eds., *Newsletters to Newspapers: Eighteenth-Century Journalism* (Morgantown, W. Va., 1977), includes important essays on Addison and Steele.

IV. ESSAYISTS. *Before Defoe*: F. Bacon, *Essayes* (London, 1597; enl. eds., 1612, 1625); W. Cornwallis, *Essays* (London, 1600, 1601), in D. C. Allen, ed. (Baltimore, 1946); J. Florio, trans., *The Essayes, or Morall, Politike, and Militairie Discourses of Lo: Michaell de Montaigne* (London, 1603); T. Sprat, ed., *The Works of Mr. Abraham Cowley* (London, 1668), in A. R. Waller, ed., 2 vols. (Cambridge, 1905–1906); W. Temple, *Miscellanea*, 3 parts (London, 1680, 1690, 1701), the second is the most relevant to the periodical essay; R. L'Estrange, *The Observator, in Question and Answer* (London, 1681–1687); J. Dunton, *The Athenian Gazette; or, Casuistical Mercury, Resolving All the Most Nice and Curious Questions Proposed by the Ingenious* (London, 1690–1697), retitled *The Athenian Mercury* with the second number though each vol. bore the whole original title, anthologized as *The Athenian Oracle*, 3 vols. (London, 1704); E. (Ned) Ward, *The London Spy* (London, 1698–1700), in A. L. Hayward, ed. (London, 1927), with some expurgation; T. Brown, *Amusements Serious and Comical* (London, 1700), in A. L. Hayward, ed. (London, 1927), with other works; W. P. Ker, ed., *The Essays of John Dryden*, 2 vols. (Oxford, 1900); J. E. Spingarn, ed., *Essays on Ancient and Modern Learning and on Poetry by Sir William Temple* (Oxford, 1909); W. A. Raleigh, ed., *The Complete Works of George Savile, First Marquess of Halifax* (Oxford, 1912); G. Kitchen, *Sir Roger L'Estrange: A Contribution to the History of the Press in the Seventeenth Century* (London, 1913); F. J. C. Hearnshaw, ed., *Social and Political Ideas of Some English Thinkers of the Augustan Age* (London, 1928); C. Marburg, *Sir William Temple: Seventeenth-Century "Libertin"* (Chicago, 1929); H. E. Woodbridge, *Temple: The Man and His Work* (New York, 1940); H. W. Troyer, *Ned Ward of Grub Street* (Cambridge, Mass., 1946).

Defoe: D. Defoe, *A Weekly Review of the Affairs of France* (London, 1704–1713), continued successively as *A Review of the Affairs of France* and *A Review of the State of the English Nation*, in A. W. Secord, ed., 22 vols. (New York, 1938), complete facs. repr. for Facsimile Text Society, *Index* by W. L. Payne (New York, 1948); W. L. Payne, ed., *The Best of Defoe's "Review": An Anthology* (New York, 1951), contains a useful intro.; J. Sutherland,

Defoe (London, 1937), see also Sutherland's essay in this vol.; F. Watson, *Defoe* (London, 1952); J. T. Boulton, ed., *Selected Writings of Daniel Defoe* (London, 1965; repr. Cambridge, 1975); J. Sutherland, *Daniel Defoe: A Critical Study* (Cambridge, Mass., 1971).

Steele: R. Steele, *The Christian Hero: An Argument Proving that No Principles but Those of Religion Are Sufficient to Make a Great Man* (London, 1701), in R. Blanchard, ed. (Oxford, 1932), with a good intro.; "Isaac Bickerstaff" [R. Steele, J. Addison, et al.], *Tatler* (12 Apr. 1709–2 Jan. 1711), 271 nos. of which Steele wrote about 188 alone and shared about 36 with Addison, often repr. either with other periodicals (see "Collections and Anthologies" above) or separately as in G. A. Aitkin, ed., 4 vols. (London, 1898–1899), selections in Everyman's Library; "Mr. Spectator" [J. Addison, R. Steele, et al.], *Spectator* (1 Mar. 1711–6 Dec. 1712; 18 June–29 Sept. 1741), 635 nos. of which Steele wrote about 236 nos., often repr. either with other periodicals (see "Collections and Anthologies" above) or separately as in Bohn's Standard Library (London, 1854–1856), G. G. Smith, ed., 8 vols. (London, 1897–1899), and in Everyman's Library—D. F. Bond, ed., 5 vols. (Oxford, 1965), with intro. and notes, the definitive ed.; *Guardian* (12 Mar.–1 Oct. 1713), 175 nos. of which Steele wrote 82, repr. with other periodicals (see "Collections and Anthologies" above); *The Englishman: Being the Sequel to the Guardian* (6 Oct. 1713–15 Feb. 1714), 57 nos. of which Steele wrote 41, in R. Blanchard, ed. (Oxford, 1955), contains a good intro.; *The Englishman: Volume II* (11 July–21 Nov. 1715), all 38 nos. by Steele, included in R. Blanchard's ed. above; "Marmaduke Myrtle, Gent." [R. Steele], *Lover* (25 Mar.–27 May 1714), 40 nos. including 2 by Addison; *Reader* (22 Apr.–10 May 1714), 9 nos. including 2 by Addison; *Town-Talk* (17 Dec. 1715–13 Feb. 1716), 9 nos.; R. Blanchard, ed., *Periodical Journalism, 1714–1716* (Oxford, 1959), reprints *Lover, Reader*, and *Town-Talk*; *Plebeian* (14 Mar.–6 Apr. 1719), 4 nos.; *Theatre* (2 Jan.–5 Apr. 1720), 28 nos., in J. Loftis, ed. (Oxford, 1962); J. Gay, *The Present State of Wit* (London, 1711), in D. F. Bond, ed. (Ann Arbor, Mich., 1947), the Augustan Reprint Society, repr. in E. Arber, ed., *An English Garner*, vol. VI (Birmingham, 1883); N. Drake, *Essays . . . Illustrative of the Tatler*, 3 vols. (London, 1805); A. Dobson, *Selections* (London, 1885), contains an intro.; A. Dobson, *Richard Steele* (London, 1886); G. A. Aitkin, *Richard Steele*, 2 vols. (London, 1889), the standard biography.

L. E. Steele, *Selected Essays* (London, 1902); W. Connely, *Sir Richard Steele* (London, 1934); C. Winton, *Captain Steele* (London, 1964); D. F. Bond, ed., *Critical Essays from "The Spectator"* (London, 1970); C. Winton, *Sir Richard Steele, M. P.: The Later Career* (Baltimore, 1970); R. P. Bond, *"The Tatler": The Making of a Literary Journal* (Cambridge, Mass., 1971); D. McDonald, ed., *Joseph Addison and Richard Steele: Selected Essays from "The Tatler," "The Spectator," and "The Guardian"* (Indianapolis, 1971); D. Kay, *Short Fiction in "The Spectator"* (University, Ala., 1975).

Addison: *Tatler*, see under "Steele" above, Addison wrote about 46 nos. alone and about 36 with Steele; *Whig Examiner* (14 Sept.–12 Oct. 1710), 5 nos.; *Spectator*, see under "Steele" above, Addison wrote about 298 nos.; *Guardian*, see under "Steele" above, Addison wrote about 51 nos.; *Lover*, see under "Steele" above, Addison wrote 2 nos.; *Reader*, see under "Steele" above, Addison wrote 2 nos.; *Free-Holder* (23 Dec. 1715–29 June 1716), 55 nos., in J. Lenehy, ed. (Oxford, 1979), with intro. and notes, the definitive ed.; *Old Whig* (19 Mar.–2 Apr. 1719), 2 nos.; T. Tickell, ed., *Works*, 4 vols. (London, 1721), in R. Hurd, ed., 6 vols. (London, 1811), repr. in the Bohn Standard Library, 6 vols. (1854–1856); S. Johnson, *Lives of the English Poets* (London, 1779–1781); T. B. Macaulay, *Critical and Historical Essays* (London, 1843); J. R. Green, ed., *Essays* (London, 1880); W. J. Courthope, *Addison* (London, 1884), in the English Men of Letters series; W. Lewin, ed., *The Lover, with Other Papers of Steele and Addison* (London, 1887); A. Symons, ed., *Sir Roger de Coverley, and Other Essays from "The Spectator"* (London, 1905); A. Dobson, *Selected Essays* (London, 1906); J. G. Fraser, ed., *Essays*, 2 vols. (London, 1915); B. Dobrée, *Essays in Biography, 1680–1726* (Oxford, 1925); W. Graham, ed., *Letters* (Oxford, 1941); *Essays on the Eighteenth Century Presented to David Nichol Smith* (Oxford, 1945), contains an essay by C. S. Lewis on Addison; J. Lannering, *Studies in the Prose Style of Joseph Addison* (Uppsala, 1951); P. Smithers, *The Life of Joseph Addison* (Oxford, 1954; repr. 1968), the standard life; E. A. Bloom and L. D. Bloom, *Joseph Addison's Sociable Animal: In the Marketplace, on the Hustings, in the Pulpit* (Providence, 1971); J. Loftis, ed., *Essays in Criticism and Literary Theory* (Northbrook, Ill., 1975).

Swift: T. Scott, ed., *The Prose Works of Jonathan Swift*, vol. IX (London, 1902), contains Swift's contributions to the *Tatler*, the *Examiner*, the *Spectator*, and the *Intelligencer*; H. Davis, ed., *Political Tracts, 1711–1713* (Oxford, 1951), contains some *Examiner* papers, this and three following collections are separate vols. in the Shakespeare Head ed. of *The Prose Works of Jonathan Swift*; H. Davis and I. Ehrenpreis, *Political Tracts, 1713–1719* (Oxford, 1953), contains Swift's onslaught on Steele, "The Importance of the *Guardian* Considered"; J. M. Murry, *Jonathan Swift* (London, 1955; rev. ed., 1965; repr. 1979); H. Davis, *The Examiner and Other Pieces Written in 1710–1711* (Oxford, 1957), contains an excellent intro.; H. Davis, *Bickerstaff Papers* (Oxford, 1957), contains some *Tatler* papers; I. Ehrenpreis, *Swift: The Man, His Works, the Age*: vol. I, *Mr. Swift and His Contemporaries* (London, 1962); vol. II, *Dr. Swift* (London, 1967), the standard biography, third vol. in progress.

JOHN GAY

(1685-1732)

Oliver Warner

INTRODUCTION

JOHN GAY lives mainly through the continued attraction of his most successful work, *The Beggar's Opera*, though it is not his only claim to remembrance. He was a friend of Sir Richard Steele, Alexander Pope, and Jonathan Swift; he wrote the libretto for Handel's *Acis and Galatea*; and one of his earlier biographers was Samuel Johnson. Reprints of his poems, complete or in selection, have proliferated from his own day to the present. His monument by John Michael Rysbrack in Westminster Abbey carries an epitaph by Pope as well as the flippant couplet composed by Gay himself: "Life is a jest, and all things show it:/I thought so once, and now I know it." "I have always observed," wrote Washington Irving,

that the visitors to the Abbey remain longest about the simple memorials in the Poets' Corner. A kinder and fonder feeling takes the place of that cold curiosity or vague admiration with which they gaze on the splendid monuments of the great and the heroic. They linger about there as about the tombs of friends and companions.

(Sketch Book)

Irving, a kindly American visitor, wrote early in the nineteenth century, but there has been a significant change in Gay's case. His memorial has now been elevated, or relegated, to the triforium, to make room for weightier, or later, admissions. He himself would not have cared much, for, today as always, the mood in which he is read is likely to derive from affection, not duty. If we enjoy him, it is for himself, and not with any idea of shining example.

An amusing illustration of this occurs in one of the more celebrated scenes in James Boswell's *Life of Samuel Johnson*. The year was 1775 and Johnson, with Boswell, Sir Joshua Reynolds, and others, was looking over the books of a certain Mr. Cambridge.

It was the evening when Boswell remarked to Reynolds that, in argument, Johnson had "no formal preparation, no flourishing with his sword; he is through your body in an instant." The talk turned to Gay, Johnson asserting that no man was ever made a rogue by being present at *The Beggar's Opera*. Then, said Boswell, reconsidering the matter, and "collecting himself, as it were, to give a heavy stroke," he added: "There is in it such a *labefaction* of all principles, as may be injurious to morality." While he "pronounced this response," said Boswell, "we sat in a comical sort of restraint, covering a laugh, which we were afraid might burst out."

Had Gay been present, it is unlikely that he would have been so self-controlled. He would have given full play to his mirth; and, seeing this, Johnson might even have laughed at his own ponderosity.

LIFE

GAY was born at Barnstaple, Devon, during the reign of Charles II, of a respectable family long settled there. He was baptized on 16 September 1685. By the age of ten he was an orphan, but an uncle seems to have taken good care of him, and he was so well taught at the local grammar school that he kept a love for the classics all his life. The translations he made from Ovid's *Metamorphoses* are creditable, and a copy of Horace, with annotations in his beautiful script, survives.

London was the obvious place for a young man with a taste for learning and with literary ambitions, but the employment his uncle found for him as apprentice to a silk dealer was uncongenial. Gay's reaction was positive: he sought the acquaintance of authors, began to write, and at the age of twenty-three published anonymously his first poem, which was in praise of wine. By the year 1712 he had found his first patron. He became secretary or domestic steward to the duchess of Monmouth, widow of the ill-starred rebel who had been beheaded in the year that Gay was born. The duchess, who later married the earl of Cornwallis, had many more years to live, but Gay did not stay with her long. In 1714 Swift helped to get him employment in the household of Lord Clarendon, with whom he went to Hanover, where the elector was about to succeed to the throne of Britain as King George I. In the same year Gay published *The Shepherd's Week*, mocking the older pastoral style, and two years later *Trivia: or, The Art of Walking the Streets of London*.

In an unpretentious way, the author had now made something of a name for himself, and his reputation steadily grew. He could generally rely on some form of salaried service in a noble household, or even government employment, and his character and amiability were such that to the end of his life he was never without an attentive patron.

In 1717 Gay was at Aix with the earl of Bath; a little later he was "rambling from place to place" on the Continent, and making so many useful friends that when, in 1720, his *Poems* appeared in two quarto volumes, with a frontispiece by the architect William Kent, Lord Burlington and Lord Chandos subscribed for fifty copies each, and Lords Bathurst and Warwick for ten. The profits, which were at least £1,000, were invested in the South Sea Company, and when that speculation burst in the famous Bubble, Gay, who had been urged to sell out but unwisely held on, was said to have lost £20,000. It was therefore somewhat ironical that his next employment, which lasted almost until the end of his life, should have been in the official post of lottery commissioner, at a salary of £120 a year.

Gay, who never married, depended for society almost entirely on his aristocratic benefactors. Lord Burlington was his frequent host, but his closest friends were the duke and duchess of Queensberry, and he grew attached to their Wiltshire home, Amesbury Abbey. He was also given lodgings in Whitehall, where he entertained such guests as Swift.

Some years before his visit to Gay, Swift had written to Pope, giving it as his view that "the Pastoral ridicule is not exhausted," and that "a porter, footman or chairman's pastoral might do well, or what think you of a Newgate pastoral among the whores and thieves there?" The matter was put to the test, for by 1727 *The Beggar's Opera* was completed, and although it was refused at Drury Lane, John Rich, who was the manager at Lincolns Inn Fields—and was of the same mind as the duke of Queensberry that it would be either a huge success or an utter flop—took a chance on it and found his courage triumphantly justified. The first performance was on Valentine's Day 1728, and by the end of the year the printed version had run through two editions.

The current joke was that the play made Gay rich and Rich gay: in fact, Gay netted almost £694 from four "author's nights," but Rich made thousands, and continued to reap profits, for *The Beggar's Opera*, after a run of over sixty performances, which was sensational for the time, was soon transported to Dublin and elsewhere, playing to entranced audiences.

Gay was quick with the sequel, *Polly* (1729), but it was forbidden the stage by the lord chamberlain, from whom there was then no appeal. This caused Queensberry to withdraw from court, and might have been a blow for the author had he not done well from the sale of the text, for to ban *Polly* from the stage was to help it in the bookshops. Over 10,000 copies were printed within a few months, and Gay received £1,200 as his profits. It was almost his last sustained work. His health was giving increasing concern to his friends, and after writing some additional fables for a series begun in 1728 and a classical opera, *Achilles*, and seeing *Acis and Galatea*, which he had written many years earlier, produced at the Haymarket, he died suddenly in London in 1732, leaving what was then the not inconsiderable sum of £6,000.

The Queensberrys had proved Samaritans. Not only had they taken Gay's part over *Polly*, but they had carefully husbanded his resources, allowing no further Bubble speculations. Had he lived longer it is likely that he would have continued to prosper, for he was only forty-seven and at the height of his fame and success; his work was so much to the taste of the day that it continued to be reprinted. Gay aimed to please, and his wish was granted.

EARLY POEMS

GAY's first serious attempt to win recognition as a poet of more than occasional flights was made in

1714, when he published *The Shepherd's Week*. This work was in the tradition of which Pope had written:

A pastoral is an imitation of the action of a shepherd, or one considered under that character. The form of this imitation is dramatic, or narrative, or mixed of both; the fable is simple, the manners not too polite nor too rustic: the thoughts are plain, yet admit a little quickness and passion, but that short and flowing: the expression humble, yet as pure as the language will afford; neat, but not florid; easy, and yet lively. In short, the fable, manners, thoughts, and expressions, are full of the greatest simplicity in nature.

(*A Discourse on Pastoral Poetry*, 1704)

The exemplar in the pastoral mode was Theocritus of Syracuse, who wrote in the third century B.C. His *Idylls* were imitated later by Vergil and by poets of every country to which the tradition descended. By the reign of Elizabeth I the taste was beginning to spread to England. Shakespeare's *As You Like It* and John Fletcher's *The Faithful Shepherdess* were within a sphere that was developed by Milton in *Comus*, and enjoyed a considerable vogue in the later seventeenth and early eighteenth centuries, particularly in the hands of Pope.

The six pastorals contained in *The Shepherd's Week*—one for each weekday—were partly designed to make fun of Ambrose Philips, a Shropshire versifier now forgotten, whose work, though feeble enough, excited the jealousy and enmity of Pope and of Richard Blackmore, a writer buried still deeper in oblivion.

In a mannered proem or foreword, Gay explained:

That principally, courteous reader, whereof I would have thee to be advised, (seeing I depart from the vulgar usage) is touching the language of my shepherds; which is, soothly to say, such as is neither spoken by the country maiden nor the courtly dame; nay, not only such as in the present times is not uttered, but was never uttered in times past; and, if I judge aright, will never be uttered in times future. . . . Granted also it is, that in this my language, I seem unto my self, as a *London* mason, who calculateth his work for a term of years, when he buildeth with old materials upon a ground-rent that is not his own, which soon turneth to rubbish and ruins. . . .

This argues no very high claim for the work, which would indeed have been foreign to Gay's·

nature; yet his rustics do in fact have a rough correspondence with reality; his shepherdesses actually milk cows and clean out pigsties. The straight descriptions, though inviting mirth and even ridicule, bear the impress of direct knowledge of country pursuits, and an individual poetic quality. The opening of "Tuesday, or The Ditty" is a fair enough example:

Young *Colin Clout*, a lad of peerless meed,
Full well could dance, and deftly tune the reed;
In ev'ry wood his carrols sweet were known,
At ev'ry wake his nimble feats were shown.
When in the ring the rustick routs he threw,
The damsels pleasures with his conquests grew;
Or when aslant the cudgel threats his head,
His danger smites the breast of ev'ry maid,
But chief of *Marian. Marian* lov'd the swain,
The Parson's maid, and neatest of the plain.
Marian, that soft could stroke the udder'd cow,
Or lessen with her sieve the barley mow;
Marbled with sage the hard'ning cheese she press'd,
And yellow butter *Marian's* skill confess'd;
But *Marian* now devoid of country cares,
Nor yellow butter nor sage cheese prepares.
For yearning love the witless maid employs,
And *Love*, say swains, *all busie heed destroys.*
Colin makes mock at all her piteous smart,
A lass, who *Cic'ly* hight, had won his heart,
Cic'ly the western lass who tends the kee,[1]
The rival of the Parson's maid was she.
In dreary shade now *Marian* lyes along,
And mixt with sighs thus wails in plaining song.
    Ah woful day! ah woful noon and morn!
When first by thee my younglings white were shorn,
Then first, I ween, I cast a lover's eye,
My sheep were silly, but more silly I.
Beneath the shears they felt no lasting smart,
They lost but fleeces while I lost a heart.   (1–30)

The burlesque attitude to rustic life is explained in the titles: "Monday, or The Squabble"; "Tuesday, or The Ditty"; "Wednesday, or The Dumps"; "Thursday, or The Spell"; "Friday, or The Dirge"; "Saturday, or The Flights." "An Alphabetical Catalogue of Names, Plants, Flowers, Fruits, Birds, Beasts, Insects and Other Material Things Mentioned in These Pastorals" suggests just how seriously the matter is to be taken.

As a Londoner by necessity, if not by birth, or perhaps by inclination, Gay has much to say in

---

[1]Cows.

JOHN GAY

Trivia: or, The Art of Walking the Streets of London (1716), which is exactly what it states, a practical, lighthearted guide to the negotiation of the capital in early Georgian days. There is none of Johnson's power and splendor in his poem on the same subject[2] of twenty years or so later:

> Here malice, rapine, accident, conspire,
> And now a rabble rages, now a fire;
> Their ambush here relentless ruffians lay,
> And here the fell attorney prowls for prey:
> Here falling houses thunder on your head,
> And here a female atheist talks you dead.   (13–18)

Instead:

> Through winter streets to steer your course aright,
> How to walk clean by day, and safe by night,
> How jostling crouds, with prudence to decline,
> When to assert the wall, and when resign.   (I. 1–4)

Marginal notes are briefly descriptive: Of Shoes; Of Coats; Of Canes; Of the Weather; Implements proper for female Walkers; What Trades prejudicial to Walkers; To whom to give the Wall; To whom to refuse the Wall; Of whom to enquire the Way; Of narrow Streets; The Pleasure of walking through an Alley; Inconveniences that attend those who are unacquainted with the Town; Remarks on the Crys of the Town; Of avoiding Paint; How to know a Whore; Of Watchmen; Of Rakes. And if a present-day pedestrian, patiently awaiting his signal to cross the street, or, taking his life in his hands, essaying an independent dash, should be tempted to think nostalgically of the easier times of his ancestors, Gay for one had an eye wide open to the different perils of his more leisurely age:

Of Crossing the Street
> If wheels bar up the road, where streets are crost,
> With gentle words the coachman's ear accost:
> He ne'er the threat, or harsh command obeys,
> But with contempt the spatter'd shoe surveys.
> Now man with utmost fortitude thy soul,
> To cross the way where carts and coaches roll;
> Yet do not in thy hardy skill confide,
> Nor rashly risque the kennel's spacious stride;
> Stay till afar the distant wheel you hear,
> Like dying thunder in the breaking air;
> Thy foot will slide upon the miry stone,
> And passing coaches crush thy tortur'd bone,

> Or wheels enclose the road; on either hand
> Pent round with perils, in the midst you stand,
> And call for aid in vain; the coachman swears,
> And car-men drive, unmindful of thy prayers.
> Where wilt thou turn? ah! whither wilt thou fly?
> On ev'ry side the pressing spokes are nigh.
> So sailors, while *Charybdis'* gulph they shun,
> Amaz'd on *Scylla's* craggy dangers run.

One of the liveliest descriptions concerns a fire, and at a time when the Great Fire of London was a mere half-century in the past and therefore well within living memory, it is interesting to note the equipment of the fire fighter and the acceptance of the practice of demolition by gunpowder to prevent a conflagration from spreading.

> But hark! distress with screaming voice draws nigh'r,
> And wakes the slumb'ring street with cries of fire.
> At first a glowing red enwraps the skies,
> And born by winds the scatt'ring sparks arise;
> From beam to beam the fierce contagion spreads;
> The spiry flames now lift aloft their heads,
> Through the burst sash a blazing deluge pours,
> And splitting tiles descend in rattling show'rs.
> Now with thick crouds th'enlighten'd pavement swarms,
> The fire-man sweats beneath his crooked arms,
> A leathern casque his vent'rous head defends,
> Boldly he climbs where thickest smoak ascends;
> Mov'd by the mother's streaming eyes and pray'rs,
> The helpless infant through the flame he bears . . .
> See forceful engines spout their levell'd streams,
> To quench the blaze that runs along the beams;
> The grappling hook plucks rafters from the walls,
> And heaps on heaps the smoaky ruine falls . . .
> Hark! the drum thunders! far, ye crouds, retire:
> Behold! the ready match is tipt with fire,
> The nitrous store is laid, the smutty train
> With running blaze awakes the barrell'd grain;
> Flames sudden wrap the walls; with sullen sound
> The shatter'd pile sinks on the smoaky ground.

Gay sums up his scope and purpose in *Trivia* in a few modest lines, and it is tolerably certain that students of urban life and customs of the past will continue to find pleasure in his observation:

> Consider, reader, what fatigues I've known,
> The toils, the perils of the wintry town;
> What riots seen, what bustling crouds I bor'd,
> How oft' I cross'd where carts and coaches roar'd;
> Yet shall I bless my labours, if mankind
> Their future safety from my dangers find.
> (III. 165–184; 353–386; 393–398)

[2]"London."

57

JOHN GAY

OCCASIONAL VERSE AND FABLES

GAY's occasional verse is often pleasing, and in song he is generally at his best, as in the ballad "Sweet William's Farewell to Black-ey'd Susan" (1720), with its spirited opening, the vitality of which is sustained through eight stanzas:

> All in the *Downs* the fleet was moor'd,
>   The streamers waving in the wind,
> When black-ey'd *Susan* came aboard.
>   Oh! where shall I my true love find!
> Tell me, ye jovial sailors, tell me true
> If my sweet *William* sails among the crew.
>
> *William*, who high upon the yard,
>   Rock'd with the billows to and fro,
> Soon as her well-known voice he heard,
>   He sigh'd and cast his eyes below:
> The cord slides swiftly through his glowing hands,
> And, (quick as lightning,) on the deck he stands.
>
> So the sweet lark, high pois'd in air,
>   Shuts close his pinions to his breast,
> (If, chance, his mate's shrill call he hear)
>   And drops at once into her nest.
> The noblest Captain in the *British* fleet,
> Might envy *William's* lip those kisses sweet.
>
> O, *Susan*, *Susan*, lovely dear,
>   My vows shall ever true remain;
> Let me kiss off that falling tear,
>   We only part to meet again.
> Change, as ye list, ye winds; my heart shall be
> The faithful compass that still points to thee.

More often chosen for anthologies is "To a Lady on Her Passion for Old China," with its conclusion, so approved by lyric poets:

> Love, *Laura*, love, while youth is warm,
> For each new winter breaks a charm;
> And woman's not like *China* sold,
> But cheaper grows in growing old;
> Then quickly chuse the prudent part,
> Or else you break a faithful heart.   (67–72)

One occasional poem, "The Birth of the Squire" (1720), has so much more sting than most works of its kind that perhaps Gay had a particular case in mind: certainly, whatever his feelings as to the nobility, his patrons, he never seems to have had much tenderness for the lesser gentry who then controlled so much of England, as one of his plays, *The What D'Ye Call It*, which will claim attention in its place, bears witness.

Rural characters conspire, at his birth, to bring the future squire pleasure:

> Ye sylvan Muses, loftier strains recite,
> Not all in shades, and humble cotts delight.
> Hark! the bells ring; along the distant grounds
> The driving gales convey the swelling sounds;
> Th' attentive swain, forgetful of his work,
> With gaping wonder, leans upon his fork.
> What sudden news alarms the waking morn?
> To the glad Squire a hopeful heir is born.
> Mourn, mourn, ye stags; and all ye beasts of chase,
> This hour destruction brings on all your race:
> See the pleas'd tenants duteous off'rings bear,
> Turkeys and geese and grocer's sweetest ware;
> With the new health the pond'rous tankard flows,
> And old *October* reddens ev'ry nose.

His hero's career does not belie the promise. Nimrod is his saint, and when the time comes for education:

> How shall his spirit brook the rigid rules,
> And the long tyranny of grammar schools?
> Let younger brothers o'er dull authors plod,
> Lash'd into *Latin* by the tingling rod;
> No, let him never feel that smart disgrace:
> Why should he wiser prove than all his race?

Amours follow:

> The milk-maid (thoughtless of her future shame)
> With smacking lip shall raise his guilty flame.

Later there is Parliament, where he "snores debates away," and the magistrates' bench, where he becomes the terror of the poaching breed. All the while, he drinks, and in a final vision Gay delivers his creation back to his Maker:

> Methinks I see him in his hall appear,
> Where the long table floats in clammy beer,
> 'Midst mugs and glasses shatter'd o'er the floor,
> Dead-drunk his servile crew supinely snore;
> Triumphant, o'er the prostrate brutes he stands,
> The mighty bun:per trembles in his hands;
> Boldly he drinks, and like his glorious Sires,
> In copious gulps of potent ale expires.
>
> (1–14; 43–48; 51–52; 101–108)

JOHN GAY

Gay's *Fables* obey the conventions of a genre that has been popular since man first began to savor the pleasures of formal literature, and possibly long before that time. Strictly speaking, the fable is a short story in either prose or verse whose characters are generally, though not necessarily, animals, insects, fish, or birds, and that points a moral, sometimes ironically.

The earliest extant collection of fables is in Sanskrit, the ancient and sacred language of India, and in Western literature the best-known examples derive from Aesop, who is believed to have lived in the sixth century B.C. and whose work was preserved and developed by later writers, including Phaedrus, a Thracian in the service of the emperor Augustus, and by Saint Maximus. The mode was used by Marie de France in the twelfth century, and was brought to perfection by Jean de La Fontaine (1621–1695).

In English literature the fable form had been exploited by many earlier writers, including Geoffrey Chaucer, John Lydgate, and Robert Henryson, and it experienced a revival in the seventeenth and eighteenth centuries, a notable practitioner being Matthew Prior (1664–1721), whose work preceded that of Gay.

Gay's examples, some fifty of which were published in 1727 and a further sixteen, posthumously, in 1738, are on the whole similar to the bulk of his verse, pleasing, yet without the passion with which, at his best, he can infuse his lines; and the morals are often as arguable as in more classical examples. One of the shortest, "The Wild Boar and the Ram," which contains an original idea, is representative of the rest:

> Against an elm a sheep was ty'd,
> The butcher's knife in blood was dy'd;
> The patient flock, in silent fright,
> From far beheld the horrid sight;
> A savage Boar, who near them stood,
> Thus mock'd to scorn the fleecy brood.
>   All cowards should be serv'd like you.
> See, see, your murd'rer is in view;
> With purple hands and reeking knife
> He strips the skin yet warm with life:
> Your quarter'd sires, your bleeding dams,
> The dying bleat of harmless lambs
> Call for revenge, O stupid race!
> The heart that wants revenge is base.
>   I grant, an ancient Ram replys,
> We bear no terror in our eyes,
> Yet think us not of soul so tame,

> Which no repeated wrongs inflame;
> Insensible of ev'ry ill,
> Because we want thy tusks to kill.
> Know, Those who violence pursue
> Give to themselves the vengeance due,
> For in these massacres they find
> The two chief plagues that waste mankind.
> Our skin supplies the wrangling bar,
> It wakes their slumb'ring sons to war,
> And well revenge may rest contented,
> Since drums and parchment were invented. (1–28)

An advertisement prefaced to the extended edition of 1738 states:

These FABLES were finished by Mr. GAY, and intended for the Press, a short time before his Death; when they were left, with his other Papers, to the care of his noble Friend and Patron, the DUKE OF QUEENSBERRY: His Grace has accordingly permitted them to the Press, and they are here printed from the Originals in the Author's own Handwriting. We hope they will please equally with his former Fables, though mostly on Subjects of a graver and more political Turn: they will certainly shew Him to have been (what he esteemed the best Character) a Man of a truly honest Heart, and a sincere Lover of his Country.

The later fables are in general longer but not noticeably graver than the original series. "The Pack Horse and the Carrier," a fair example, is dedicated to a young nobleman and it enjoins him not to rely on any virtue in his ancestors. Noblesse oblige: it is necessary to remint the phrase in every generation:

> Superior worth your rank requires,
> For that mankind reveres your sires:
> If you degen'rate from your race,
> Their merits heighten your disgrace. (43–46)

The moral is pointed by the complaint of a packhorse, through his own demerits reduced to that status, who is snorting in his stall at the viler breeding of his companions. How can he tolerate their propinquity?

> Vain-glorious fool, (the Carrier cry'd,)
> Respect was never paid to pride.
> Know 'twas thy giddy, wilful heart
> Reduc'd thee to this slavish part.
> Did not thy headstrong youth disdain
> To learn the conduct of the rein? . . .
> Ask all the carriers on the road,

They'll say thy keeping's ill-bestowed.
Then vaunt no more thy noble race,
That neither mends thy strength or pace.
What profits me thy boast of blood?
An ass hath more intrinsick good.
By outward show let's not be cheated:
An ass should like an ass be treated.

(81–86; 93–100)

PLAYS

GAY had made various earlier attempts at writing for the stage before he turned his attention to a "Newgate pastoral." They met with small success, though they gave him experience of what was appropriate for the theater. *The Mohocks*, a "Tragi-Comical Farce" on the subject of the wellborn bullies who, calling themselves by the name of a fierce Indian tribe, roved the town by night and terrorized the watch, attacking quiet citizens and insulting women, was printed in 1712 but never produced. It contains one song in Act I, scene i, prophetic of those that were to appear in later works:

> Come fill up the Glass,
> Round, round, let it pass,
> 'Till our Reason be lost in our Wine:
> Leave Conscience's Rules
> To Women and Fools,
> This only can make us divine.

Chorus.   Then a *Mohock*, a *Mohock* I'll be,
> No Laws shall restrain
> Our libertine Reign,
We'll riot, drink on, and be free.

> We will scower the Town,
> Knock the Constable down,
Put the Watch and the Beadle to flight:
> We'll force all we meet
> To kneel down at our Feet,
And own this great Prince of the Night.

Chorus.   Then a *Mohock*, a *Mohock*, etc.

> The Grand Seignior shall own
> His Seraglio outdone,
For all Womankind is our booty;
> No Condition we spare
> Be they Brown, Black or Fair
We make them fall down, and do Duty.

Chorus.   Then a *Mohock*, a *Mohock*, etc. . . .

Not much can be said for the pastiche *The Wife of Bath*, which was actually staged in 1713, for the surviving fragments are such doggerel as to make Chaucer twirl in his grave—and the next venture was little better. This was a tragi-comi-pastoral farce, called *The What D'Ye Call It*. It made a brief appearance in 1715, and it was followed, two years later, by a comedy, *Three Hours After Marriage*, which was produced at the Theatre Royal, Gay acknowledging help from Pope and from their mutual friend Dr. John Arbuthnot.

Only the prologue, epilogue, and fragments of *Three Hours After Marriage* are printed in the standard edition of Gay's work, and they are unremarkable. *The What D'Ye Call It*, though fully preserved, gives no indication of the qualities that would blossom in *The Beggar's Opera*. There is pace and vivacity, but it is clear that the author was attempting too much, and the text reads more like a charade than a piece worthy of professional actors.

Using the framework of a play within a play, Gay makes fun of rustic characters, and above all country justices, not in the spirit of Shakespeare in *Henry IV*, but in that of a more degenerate age. A squire has got a girl into trouble, and his intention is to cause an innocent man, enamored of someone else, to make an honest woman of her or go to the wars. The victim refuses, and is duly drafted as a soldier, in which capacity he is soon due to go before a firing squad for running away. Ghosts of those they have punished or otherwise injured haunt the justices, and it is soon made plain that the methods of the press-gang were as obnoxious in the Hanoverian army as in the navy. After a number of extravagant twists of fortune, the condemned is reprieved, lovers are joined together in more or less holy matrimony, and all ends in a dance.

Most of the play is written in decasyllabic rhymed verse, the rest in prose; and there is one ballad, "'Twas when the seas were roaring," that shows Gay's felicity in composing lines to be sung, but there is little to prepare the reader for the triumph to come.

Finally, there is Gay's only tragedy, *The Captives*. He read this aloud to the princess of Wales: it was published in 1724, and it was acted at Drury Lane. It would be natural to expect that this blank verse play, in which the prosody is slipshod, and in which there is not a single memorable passage, would prove insufferable to modern taste, yet, however flat the lines, the plot carries them along.

Phraortes, king of Media, has beaten the Persians in battle and has taken prisoner Sophernes, a prince whom he treats with great consideration. Hydarnes and other Persians plot against Phraortes' life, but Sophernes takes no part in this. His sorrows are concentrated on his captive state, and on the loss of Cylene, his wife, who has supposedly been carried off to slavery or been slain in battle.

Phraortes' queen, Astarbe, secretly detests her husband, though she wields most of the royal power. Her affections center upon Sophernes, to whom she offers freedom if he will fly with her. The wretched man refuses, and Astarbe's revenge is to have him condemned for plotting against the king. At this point, Cylene returns in disguise to the Median capital, and tells a tale of such piteous wrongs done to her through Sophernes that the king agrees that she should be his executioner. When the time comes for her to visit Sophernes in his dungeon, she reveals her true identity and begs her husband to fly: she will pay the forfeit. Sophernes, though he reluctantly obeys, secretly returns to the palace in time to save the king's life from the real conspirator. The queen's misfeasances are exposed, and she stabs herself. Sophernes and Cylene are happily reunited.

The final lines, which should be moving, give a fair indication of the quality of the whole:

Sophernes. What I did was due.
  I've only paid a debt of gratitude;
  What would your bounty more?—you've giv'n me all.
  For in these arms I ev'ry wish possess.
Phraortes. Life is a voyage, and we with pain and labour
  Must weather many a storm to reach the port.
Sophernes. Since 'tis not giv'n to mortals to discern
  Their real good and ill; let men learn patience:
  Let us the toils of adverse fate sustain,
  For through that rugged road our hopes we gain.

(V. ix. 23–30)

It is sad that so respectable a plot should be so feebly clothed, line after line reading like a botched translation of one of the Greek masters; and it is with some amusement that the reader discovers a passage in the fulsome and well-turned letter to the princess of Wales who had to endure the author's declamation: "If it had the good fortune to gain Your ROYAL HIGHNESS's approbation," wrote Gay,

I have been often reflecting to what to impute it, and I think, it must have been the Catastrophe of the fable, the rewarding virtue, and the relieving the distressed: For that could not fail to give you some pleasure in fiction, which, it is plain, gives you the greatest in reality; or else Your ROYAL HIGHNESS would not (as you always have done) make it your daily practice.

THE BEGGAR'S OPERA

IN the four years that separate the last of Gay's earlier theatrical attempts and the composition of his masterpiece, he made an immense advance in technical skill. *The Beggar's Opera* is assured throughout: there is no faltering, no redundancy. Even the prose rises consistently above anything Gay had been able to sustain in his earlier work. From the Beggar's opening line: "If Poverty be a title to Poetry, I am sure no-body can dispute mine," to Macheath's final song: "Thus I stand like a Turk, with his doxies around," there is no doubt that the author has full control of his material, and that the audience, if the players and singers do their part, will be held captive.

The reasons are manifold. To begin with—surprise; and the start that Gay afforded his own age must be imagined to be far greater than anything we are now likely to experience, when the theater has been the subject of experiment, some of it outrageous, for generations. Setting and characters were truly novel. This was a piece where rogues were rogues, and if they came to grief it was because they were betrayed for money by their accomplices, not because they were overtaken by justice. An analogy with current politics was perceived, and was intended. As the Beggar says: "Through the whole piece you may observe such a similitude of manners in high and low life, that it is difficult to determine whether (in the fashionable vices) the fine gentlemen imitate the gentlemen of the road, or the gentlemen of the road the fine gentlemen."

What in fact helped to spark *The Beggar's Opera* was the career of Jonathan Wild, the course of which had opened people's minds to the ramifications of crime in London. Wild's life was brief but sensational. He had originally worked as a bucklemaker but found thieving so profitable that he not only turned himself into the leader and brains of a large corporation of thieves and pickpockets, but actually opened offices in various parts of London for the recovery and restoration of property stolen by his dependents.

Such ingenuity was worthy of a better cause. Wild, having enjoyed considerable success, since he found the authorities very bribable, was at last charged and convicted. He was hanged at Tyburn in 1725. Daniel Defoe, ever quick to seize upon a character or an event that would enable him to turn a penny or so by means of the printing press, published an account of Wild's "Life and Actions" shortly after his execution. Gay revived the excitement while it was still fairly fresh, and some years later, in 1743, Henry Fielding made Wild the peg for a study of "greatness" (as distinct from "goodness") in a satirical romance.

As with the less, so with the greater. *The Beggar's Opera* was written and produced during the long regime of Sir Robert Walpole as prime minister to the early Hanoverians; Walpole, who openly bought the votes of members of Parliament, rewarded his supporters with sinecures, and had no use for enthusiasm. The opera is, in fact, the capital city in miniature, leaving out those decent, unobtrusive folk who in every age have somehow contrived to keep moral standards from disappearing altogether.

With the sole exception of Polly Peachum, the characters, men and women alike, go further than being merely amoral. The men send their fellows to the gallows at a nod, almost with zest, and they are just as liable to be betrayed themselves. Peachum, Polly's father and a central figure in the play, calculates matters of life and death without a trace of sentiment or compunction, the scales balanced on his ledger; and an edge is given to his remarks by the knowledge that the Newgate of Gay's time was much as in the play, and that men, women, and even children could be and were hanged, or at best sent to work in the slave plantations of the West Indies, for what would now be termed petty theft. If the characters work against society, they also work against one another: they hang together only until they hang separately.

In contrast to this realistic spice is the absurdly romantic constancy of Polly in her love for the highwayman Macheath, and the engagingly innocent airs to which Gay sets his songs, most of them traditional. The public had grown tired of the fashionable Italian opera, sung by artists often of unprepossessing appearance in a language that the majority did not understand. Refreshingly, Gay's English was as clear as a stream, and although he employed a German, Dr. Johann Christoph Pepusch, to write bases, the tunes were familiar and beloved.

Finally, and here again the opera was happily different from the mode then in fashion, Gay knew when to leave off. The moment must be before, not after, listeners have had enough. Like Oliver Twist, they must ask for more.

William Congreve, an old and brilliant hand at the stage who had long given up writing plays, predicted, Pope said, that *The Beggar's Opera* would "either take greatly, or be damned confoundedly," which was exactly the view taken by Rich and Queensberry. Even before the end of the first act, Pope and other friends of Gay had heard the duke of Argyle, sitting in the next box, exclaim: "It will do—it must do—I see it in the eyes of them." The duke was a sound judge, and he was not deceived.

The Beggar and the Player having ended their preliminaries, the fourth scene opens upon Peachum, sitting at a table before his accounts. He sings:

> Through all the employments of life
>   Each neighbour abuses his brother;
> Whore and Rogue they call Husband and Wife:
>   All professions be-rogue one another:
> The Priest calls the Lawyer a Cheat,
>   The Lawyer be-knaves the Divine;
> And the Statesman, because he's so great,
>   Thinks his trade as honest as mine.

The tone is set, and when Filch enters, the audience is fully prepared for the review of the pickpocketing gang—Crook-finger'd Jack; Wat Dreary, alias Brown Will; Harry Paddington; Slippery Sam; Mat of the Mint; Tom Tipple; Robin of Bagshot, alias Gordon, alias Bluff Bob, alias Carbuncle, alias Bob Booty—whose fingers swell the store of Peachum's stolen goods.

Booty, who has been put down on Peachum's blacklist, inspires a defense from the woman who is Mrs. Peachum by courtesy, not by virtue of marriage, and she adds a note of sentiment that—though it will not be sustained in her own case—finds an echo in a younger bosom:

Mrs. Peachum. You know, my dear, I never meddle in matters of Death; I always leave those affairs to you. Women indeed are bitter bad judges in these cases, for they are so partial to the brave that they think every man handsome who is going to the Camp or the Gallows.

Presently, Macheath comes under consideration. He is of altogether different mettle from the rest, and Polly's mother is aware that her daughter's affections are already engaged. But Peachum will have none of it. As he says: "My daughter to me should be like a court-lady to a minister of state, a key to the whole gang."

Polly's first song, delivered when her father approaches her to learn how far matters have gone, "Virgins are like the fair flower in its lustre," is as fine as anything Gay composed for the part. It is quickly answered by her mother, who has found out the truth from Filch: the girl is actually married. "Can you support the expence of a husband, hussy, in gaming, drinking and whoring," she asks:

have you money enough to carry on the daily quarrels of man and wife about who shall squander most? There are not many husbands and wives, who can bear the charges of plaguing one another in a handsome way. If you must be married, could you introduce no-body into our family, but a highwayman! Why, thou foolish jade, thou wilt be as ill us'd, and as much neglected, as if thou hadst married a Lord! (I. viii)

Song succeeds song in reproach and animation:

O *Polly*, you might have toy'd and kist.
By keeping Men off, you keep them on.

Polly: But he so teaz'd me,
    And he so pleas'd me,
What I did, you must have done.

"Well, *Polly*," says Mrs. Peachum, "as far as one woman can forgive another, I forgive thee.—your father is too fond of you, hussy." "Then," says Polly, "all my sorrows are at an end." "A mighty likely speech in troth," replies her mother, "for a wench who is just married!"

Indeed, Mrs. Peachum is right, for in family conclave Peachum enunciates what he holds to be the proper advantage of marriage—that it may lead to widowhood:

The comfortable estate of widowhood, is the only hope that keeps up a wife's spirits. Where is the woman who would scruple to be a wife, if she had it in her power to be a widow whenever she pleas'd? If you have any views of this sort, *Polly*, I shall think the match not so very unreasonable. (I. x)

Even Mrs. Peachum is forced to agree that "to have Macheath peach'd is the only thing could ever make me forgive her"—a lively qualification of her earlier gesture to her daughter.

It was at this stage that Polly, with her song:

O ponder well! be not severe;
    So save a wretched wife!
For on the rope that hangs my dear
    Depends poor *Polly's* life.

first brought the house down. The original singer was Lavinia Fenton, an actress of such beauty and talent that she won the love of the duke of Bolton, who in due time made her his duchess.

The first act ends with the entrance of Macheath, who swears eternal constancy to Polly, their duet being one of the prettiest in the opera:

Macheath: Were I laid on *Greenland's* coast,
And in my arms embrac'd my lass;
Warm amidst eternal frost,
Too soon the half year's night would pass.

Polly: Were I sold on *Indian* soil,
Soon as the burning Day was clos'd,
I could mock the sultry toil,
When on my charmer's breast repos'd.

Macheath: And I would love you all the day,
Polly: Every night would kiss and play,
Macheath: If with me you'd fondly stray
Polly: Over the Hills and far away.

The critic was perceptive who thought "Over the Hills and far away" to be one of the most evocative lines in poetry, but the next scene is indoors, and heavy with the fumes of wine and the smoke from tobacco: it is a tavern near Newgate where members of Peachum's gang are drinking. The ruffians include some not already noted in Peachum's ledger—for instance, there is Jemmy Twitcher, whose name was to be bestowed, with opprobrium, on the fourth earl of Sandwich, an unpopular first lord of the admiralty later in the century; and there are Nimming Ned and Ben Budge. "Fill ev'ry glass," they sing, "for wine inspires us, / And fires us / With courage, love and joy." They await Macheath, preparatory to an adventure on the Western Road, but when the highwayman enters it is to report a difference with Peachum, and to give orders that the others must act on their own. No sooner is he by himself than he sings "If the heart of a man is deprest with cares"—and then calls for women.

There enter Mrs. Coaxer, Dolly Trull, Mrs. Vixen, Betty Doxy, Jenny Diver, Mrs. Slammerkin, Suky Tawdry, and Molly Brazen, the Ladies of the Town, and in an instant the music of a cotillion, and the song "Youth's the season made for joys," show that Macheath's troubles are not very taxing and that, free as ever with his money, his pleasures will be much the same as before.

Alas, Jenny Diver for one is in Peachum's pay, and she betrays her red-coated customer. Peachum himself enters with constables, and Macheath is taken off to prison. He sings:

> At the Tree I shall suffer with pleasure,
> At the Tree I shall suffer with pleasure,
>   Let me go where I will,
>   In all kinds of ill,
> I shall find no such Furies as these are. (II. v)

The audience echo him, but Newgate under Lockit and his turnkeys is as venal as the rest of London, and the victim is soon bargaining for a lighter set of fetters. Lucy Lockit is another matter. Macheath has got her into trouble and now, it seems, he is in her power. She demands marriage. She will save him—provided there is no truth in the rumor of his affair with Polly.

Peachum and Lockit are meanwhile in conference, and their discussion is such as to make the song appropriate:

> When you censure the age,
> Be cautious and sage,
> Lest the Courtiers offended should be:
>   If you mention vice or bribe,
>   'Tis so pat to all the tribe;
> Each cries—That was levell'd at me. (II. x)

The pair soon quarrel, until Peachum, with his "Brother, brother, we are both in the wrong—we shall both be losers in the dispute—for you know we have it in our power to hang each other . . . " calls a halt, and they make it up.

Macheath is quickly at work with plans for squaring Lockit, saying to Lucy: "If I could raise a small sum—Would not twenty guineas, think you, move him?—Of all the arguments in the way of business, the perquisite is the most prevail-ing—Your father's perquisites for the escape of prisoners must amount to a considerable sum in the year. Money well tim'd, and properly apply'd, will do anything."

Matters become complicated when Polly appears. She and Lucy inevitably squabble, and Macheath sings his famous lament:

> How happy could I be with either,
>   Were t'other dear charmer away!
> But while you thus teaze me together,
>   To neither a word will I say. (II. xiii)

The scene ends with Lucy relenting and Macheath once more free. But not for long, for the third and last act unfolds the hero's second betrayal, this time on the information of Diana Trapes. Lucy later tries, without success, to poison Polly with a glass of cordial, while Macheath suffers reincarceration from which there is this time no escape. Not only so, but all his women and their offspring come to see his fate.

When the curtain falls, the following dialogue ensues:

Player: But honest friend, I hope you don't intend that *Macheath* shall be really executed.

Beggar: Most certainly, Sir.—To make the piece perfect, I was for doing strict poetical Justice.—*Macheath* is to be hang'd; and for the other personages in the Drama, the Audience must have suppos'd they were all either hang'd or transported.

Player: Why, then, friend, this is a down-right deep Tragedy. The catastrophe is manifestly wrong, for an Opera must end happily.

Beggar: Your objection, Sir, is very just; and is easily remov'd. For you must allow, that in this kind of Drama, 'tis no matter how absurdly things are brought about—So—you rabble there—run and cry a Reprieve—let the prisoner be brought back to his wives in triumph. (III. xvi)

Even this is not quite good enough, for what about poor Polly? Macheath on his brief return—before transportation, for he cannot be wholly excused punishment—says: "Ladies, I hope you will give me leave to present a Partner to each of you"—sweeping his hand toward the Rabble. "And (if I may without offence) for this time, I take *Polly* for mine.—And for life, you Slut,—for we were really marry'd.—As for the rest.—But at present keep your own secret."

The way is open for a sequel.

JOHN GAY

POLLY *AND* ACHILLES

GAY has generally been referred to as an indolent man, but the last years of his life show a burst of creative activity and achievement. *The Beggar's Opera*, however delectably it reads and stages, is an affair involving thought and craftsmanship, and there is invention and character-drawing calling for sustained energy.

Gay meant to exploit every bit of the fame he had won from his hit. Ballad-opera in his manner had caught on, and it would last, for it was particularly suited to the English taste—a fact that Gilbert and Sullivan were to rediscover in the next century. As for Polly, she had stolen more hearts than that of the duke of Bolton. She must have an opera of her own, and so it was.

By 1729 the text was at the printer, but before that, bureaucracy intervened. No doubt far too many shafts in *The Beggar's Opera* had struck home. Gay wrote in his preface:

'Twas on SATURDAY morning DECEMBER 7TH, 1728, that I waited upon the Lord Chamberlain; I desir'd to have the honour of reading the Opera to his Grace, but he order'd me to leave it with him, which I did upon expectation of having it return'd on the Monday following, but I had it not 'till THURSDAY DECEMBER 12TH, when I receiv'd it from his Grace with this answer; that it was not allow'd to be acted, but commanded to be supprest. This was told me in general without any reasons assign'd, or any charge against me of my having given any particular offence.

It was rumored that the new king, George II, though not much inclined to what he described as "Boetry and Bainting," had given the lord chamberlain direct orders on the subject of Mr. Gay: but even he could not interdict the printing of a piece that, in Gay's words, "was to lash in general the reigning and fashionable vices, and to recommend and set virtue in as amiable a light as I could; to justify and vindicate my own character, I thought my-self obliged to print the Opera without delay in the manner I have done."

The Poet and Player who appear at the opening speak a few lines of plain truth:

Poet: A SEQUEL to a Play is like more last words. 'Tis a kind of absurdity; and really, Sir, you have prevail'd upon me to pursue this subject against my judgment.

1st Player: Be the success as it will, you are sure of what you have contracted for; and upon the inducement of gain no body can blame you for undertaking it.

The principal characters are Polly, Ducat, a West Indian planter, and a much disguised Macheath. Polly has followed her husband in his exile, but Macheath, with his usual agility, has run away from the plantation to which he has been condemned, and is thought dead, though he is in fact disguised as Morano, chief of the local pirates. Mrs. Trapes, another character from the earlier success, who now exercises the calling of procuress, tries to sell Polly to the amorous Ducat, and Polly is saved from dishonor by an attack by the pirates on the settlement. Disguised as a man, she joins the loyal Caribs, helps to beat off the attack, takes Morano prisoner, but learns his identity too late to save him from execution. In the end she marries an Indian prince, a conclusion about as unsatisfactory as could be imagined. It is scarcely surprising that those who have attempted to revive *Polly* have sometimes taken liberties with the original; it almost asks for it, though it is by no means without merit on its own account, and more than one of the songs are in Gay's best style. If the milieu had been such as to give the author reasonable scope, instead of being mere "theater," it could have become worthy of its predecessor, though sequels are too often, as the poet describes them, "a kind of absurdity."

In point of fact, Gay was trying the establishment rather hard. For instance, Act I is no further advanced than the fourth scene when Mrs. Trapes, of all people, is made to sing as follows:

In pimps and politicians
  The genius is the same;
Both raise their own conditions
  On others' guilt and shame:
With a tongue well-tipt with lyes
Each the want of parts supplies,
And with a heart that's all disguise
  Keeps his schemes unknown.
Seducing as the devil,
  They play the tempter's part,
And have, when most they're civil,
  Most mischief in their heart.
Each a secret commerce drives,
First corrupts and then connives,
And by his neighbour's vices thrives,
  For they are all his own.

There is, moreover, shrewd truth in the verses:

When kings by their huffing
Have blown up a squabble,

All the charge and cuffing
Light upon the rabble.
Thus when Man and Wife
By their mutual snubbing,
Kindle civil strife,
Servants get the drubbing.

Gay's worldly sense is well shown in Jenny Diver's song:

When gold is in hand,
It gives us command;
It makes us lov'd and respected.
'Tis now, as of yore,
Wit and sense, when poor,
Are scorn'd, o'erlook'd and neglected.
Tho' peevish and old
If women have gold,
They have youth, good-humour and beauty:
Among all mankind
Without it we find
Nor love, nor favour nor duty. (II. x)

Again, not many politicians would read with much pleasure Polly's own contribution in Act II:

The sportsmen keep hawks, and their quarry they gain;
Thus the woodcock, the partridge, the pheasant is slain.
What care and expence for their hounds are employ'd!
Thus the fox, and the hare, and the stag are destroy'd.
The spaniel they cherish, whose flattering way
Can as well as their masters cringe, fawn and betray.
Thus stanch politicians, look all the world round,
Love the men who can serve as hawk, spaniel or hound. (II. xii)

Considering how little such interpolations have to do with the ostensible plot of the opera, it is easy enough to understand the lord chamberlain's decision not to allow it on the stage, while its success in printed form is not surprising. If the ban was unjust, it was all too natural, since one of the victims of the play was confirming the satirist's diagnosis by his own behavior.

If attempts have been made to make something of *Polly* on the stage, such neglect has befallen *Achilles*, the opera published shortly after Gay's death, that although it was performed at the Theatre Royal, Covent Garden, it is unlikely for it to be revived. The theme is Achilles in petticoats. His mother, Thetis, clothes him thus, in order to save him from the perils of the siege of Troy. His adventures are ludicrous—sought after by Lycomedes, whom he spurns, and loved by Deidamia, of

whom he takes advantage, Achilles, it is almost needless to say, in the end goes off to the wars, having, in his own phrase, heard his mother's advice and followed his own.

The scenes, though sometimes fair enough, are not the equal even of the best of *Polly*. The songs, in which Gay was usually so assured, are as a whole lackluster, for he was clearly tired. There is one that deserves such small preservation as may be afforded by a current tribute:

Think of Dress in ev'ry Light;
'Tis Woman's chiefest Duty;
Neglecting that, our selves we slight
And undervalue Beauty.
That allures the Lover's Eye,
And graces ev'ry Action;
Besides, when not a Creature's by,
'Tis inward Satisfaction. (III. vii)

CONCLUSION

THE standard edition of *The Poetical Works of John Gay*, by Geoffrey Faber, was published in 1926, when the version of *The Beggar's Opera* staged by Nigel Playfair at the Lyric Theatre, Hammersmith (so long-lasting a success as to have become a London institution), was still fresh in memory. It is fitting that Faber should be quoted in judgment on an author to whose text he applied such scrupulous attention. "Like all men of his age," he wrote, "Gay likes to feel his feet on the firm earth; and if at times the irresistible breath of song lifts him off it, he is not carried far. No counterfeit Olympus for him; the lower slopes of a friendly Parnassus, where his playful ironic fancy breathes a congenial air—these are his spiritual home."

Gay tried verse, and did well enough; he tried moralizing, and found favor; then, gathering his strength, he combined his gifts in a flawless ballad-opera, and every generation has thanked him for it.

SELECTED BIBLIOGRAPHY

I. COLLECTED AND SELECTED WORKS. *Poems on Several Occasions*, 2 vols. (London, 1720; rev. ed., 1731), revision supervised by Gay; *Plays* (London, 1760); *The Works*, 4 vols. (Dublin, 1770); *Plays* (London, 1772);

Poems and Fables, 2 vols. (Aberdeen, 1772); The Works, 4 vols. (London, 1772); The Poetical Works, 3 vols. (London, 1777); The Poetical, Dramatic, and Miscellaneous Works, 6 vols. (London, 1795), includes a reprint of S. Johnson's account of Gay first published in his Lives of the English Poets (London, 1779); The Poetical Works, 2 vols. (Boston, 1854); J. Underhill, ed., The Poetical Works, 2 vols. (London, 1893), in the Muses Library; The Plays, 2 vols. (London, 1923), in the Abbey Classics series; Poems (London, 1923), with an intro. by F. Bickley, in the Abbey Classics series; G. C. Faber, ed., The Poetical Works (Oxford, 1926), the standard text, including plays and fragments, with a bibliography; A. Ross, ed., Selected Poems (London, 1950); C. F. Burgess, ed., Letters (Oxford, 1966); V. A. Dearing and C. E. Beckwith, eds., Poetry and Prose (London, 1975), in the Oxford English Texts series.

II. SEPARATE WORKS. Wine: A Poem (London, 1708), published anonymously; The Present State Of Wit, in a Letter to a Friend in the Country (London, 1711); The Mohocks: A Tragi-Comical Farce (London, 1712); Rural Sports: A Poem (London, 1713); The Wife of Bath: A Comedy (London, 1713); The Fan: A Poem (London, 1713); The Shepherd's Week: In Six Pastorals (London, 1714), verse; The What D'Ye Call It: A Tragi-Comi-Pastoral Farce (London, 1715); Trivia: or, The Art of Walking the Streets of London (London, 1716), verse; Three Hours After Marriage: A Comedy (London, 1717); An Epistle to Her Grace Henrietta, Duchess of Marlborough (London, 1722), verse; The Captives: A Tragedy (London, 1724); To a Lady on Her Passion for Old China (London, 1725), verse; Fables, 2 vols. (London, 1727-1738), additional fables published in 6th ed. (1738), repr. of 1727 ed., Scolar Press ed. (London, 1969); The Beggar's Opera (London, 1727), ballad-opera, an ed. containing the music first appeared in 1728, also in E. V. Roberts, ed., Regents Restoration Drama series (Lincoln, Nebr.-London, 1969); Polly (London, 1729), ballad-opera; Acis and Galatea: An English Pastoral Opera (London, 1732), published anonymously; Achilles: An Opera (London, 1733); The Distress'd Wife: A Comedy (London, 1743).

III. SOME BIOGRAPHICAL AND CRITICAL STUDIES. W. C. Hazlitt, Lectures on the English Poets (London, 1818), includes an account of Gay; W. M. Thackeray, English Humourists of the Eighteenth Century (London, 1853); L. Melville, Life and Letters of John Gay, 1685-1732 (London, 1921); F. Kidson, The Beggar's Opera, Its Predecessors and Successors (London, 1922); W. H. Irving, John Gay's London, Illustrated from the Poetry of the Time (Cambridge, Mass., 1928); O. Sherwin, Mr. Gay: Being a Picture of the Life and Times of the Author of "The Beggar's Opera" (New York, 1929); F. W. Bateson, English Comic Drama, 1700-1750 (London, 1929); W. Empson, Some Versions of Pastoral (London, 1936); P. F. Gaye, John Gay: His Place in the Eighteenth Century (London, 1938); W. H. Irving, John Gay: Favorite of the Wits (Durham, N. C., 1940); A. P. Herbert, Mr. Gay's London: With Extracts from the Proceedings of the Sessions of the Peace . . . in the Years 1732 and 1733 (London, 1948); J. L. Clifford and L. A. Landa, eds., Pope and His Contemporaries: Essays Presented to George Sherburn (London, 1949), includes a study of Gay by J. R. Sutherland; S. M. Armens, John Gay: Social Critic (New York, 1954); A. Forsgren, John Gay: Poet "of a Lower Order": Comments on His Rural Poems and Other Early Writings (Stockholm, 1964); P. M. Spacks, John Gay (New York, 1965).

ALEXANDER POPE
(1688-1744)

Ian Jack

WHEN William Hazlitt began his fourth lecture on the English poets by saying that John Dryden and Alexander Pope were the great masters of the artificial style of poetry in English, as Geoffrey Chaucer, Edmund Spenser, William Shakespeare, and John Milton were of the natural, he lent his authority to a false distinction that survived in literary histories until the other day. The legend has grown up—and few territories of human thought are as fertile in legends as literary criticism—that between the Restoration and the late eighteenth century English poetry was diverted from its main channel. Matthew Arnold went so far as to rule that Dryden and Pope, "though they may write in verse, though they may in a certain sense be masters of the art of versification . . . are not classics of our poetry, they are classics of our prose." As late as 1933, A. E. Housman asserted that "there was a whole age of English in which the place of poetry was usurped by something very different which possessed the proper and specific name of wit." In making this statement he was not only taking his cue from Arnold; he was also (whether consciously or not) harking back to Hazlitt's unsatisfactory distinction between poetry that is "natural" and poetry that is "artificial."

The change that has come over English poetry in the last fifty years has brought with it a revolution in critical perspective. In reaction against what they feel to have been the excessive respect of the later nineteenth century for the work of the romantics, modern poets have turned to the age of John Donne for their inspiration. As a result, such features of decadent romantic theory as the exaggerated insistence on "inspiration" and on the difference between the genius and the ordinary man, the distrust of imitation in poetry, the preference of emotion to thought, of spontaneity to controlled form—all these have begun to be cleared away into the lumber-room of discarded ideas. This explains the fact that

the new enthusiasm for the poetry of the metaphysicals has brought in its wake a new and vital interest in the poetry of the Augustans.

Attempts have even been made to trace a close affinity between the poetry of Pope and that of Donne. In an influential essay on William Collins, Middleton Murry claimed that Pope was not only a master of wit "in the Augustan sense, the verbal epigram of an extraordinarily alert mind," but also of "Wit in the best Metaphysical sense—namely, the striking expression of deep psychological perceptions." And in the chapter on "The Line of Wit" in F. R. Leavis' *Revaluation*, Pope occupies an honorable place beside Ben Jonson, Donne, and Andrew Marvell. Yet a moment's reflection will show that Murry's definitions of "wit" are inadequate, and that such resemblances as exist between Pope and Donne are greatly outweighed by the differences. I suggest that it may be more profitable to reverse the position of Hazlitt and to consider Pope as belonging to the same great tradition of English poetry as Spenser and Milton: what may be termed, in the widest sense, the Renaissance tradition. The true contrast, as it seems to me, is not between Pope and the poets who preceded him, but between Pope and his successors of the romantic age. That English poetry will never return to the romantic tradition it is perhaps too early to be certain; but at the moment all the omens are against it, and the modern reader can approach the poetry of Pope unhindered by the preconceptions that misled the readers of the nineteenth century.

In nothing is the contrast between Pope and the greatest of the romantic poets more evident than in their attitudes to earlier poetry. William Wordsworth despised most of the poetry written in the century before his own, and came to regard it as his mission to lead English poets back to the forceful simplicity of an earlier age. If Pope had written an essay on poetry as a preface to a volume of his own work, it would have been very different in tone from the celebrated preface to the second edition of *Lyrical Ballads*. As the *Essay on Criticism*, his letters, and the records of his conversation make abundantly clear, Pope considered the development of poetry in the age before his own as a matter for rejoicing. He shared the view of his contemporaries that Dryden had evolved a poetic idiom superior to that of any earlier poet, and proclaimed that he had learned the art of versification wholly from him. This does not mean that he was ignorant of the poetry written before the Restoration, or contemptuous of it (as Nicolas Boileau-Despréaux was of most of the poetry written before his own time). On the contrary, it would hardly be an exaggeration to say that Pope had read everything of value in earlier English poetry, so far as it was available in his day. Spenser was one of his earliest favorites; with Milton he was intimately conversant; Shakespeare he came to know with the familiarity of an editor. He was something of a collector of old books, numbered among his friends several of the scholars who were beginning to chart the course of English literary development, and himself made notes toward what would have been the first history of English poetry.[1] But it did not occur to him to turn back from the road along which Dryden had traveled with such acclamation; he rather felt that it was his task to use Dryden's discoveries as a basis for further exploration.

As we read Pope's early poems, in which we are watching one of the readiest learners English poetry has ever known serving his apprenticeship, we are fortunate in being able to turn (for a background) to the *Anecdotes* collected by his friend Joseph Spence. This has proved a disappointing book to those who have looked in it for something comparable to the indiscretions of Samuel Pepys or the rounded humanity of James Boswell's portrait of Samuel Johnson; yet to the student of poetics it is an invaluable document, for it gives us, in Pope's own words, an account of his early education, his reading, and his opinions. It is largely due to Spence that Pope is the first English poet of whose methods of composition we have reliable information.

If it were not for Spence, the fact that Pope's first considerable publication was his *Pastorals* might suggest that his career as a writer opened almost too

discreetly. But the *Anecdotes* make it clear that Pope was as ambitious as any poet could be in his boyish experiments. When he was about twelve, he told Spence, he "wrote a kind of play, which I got to be acted by my schoolfellows. It was a number of speeches from the *Iliad*; tacked together with verses of my own" (*Anecdotes*, ed. Singer, p. 276). Soon afterward he began an epic poem that was yet more ambitious, including as it did "an under-water scene in the first book." In this poem, of which some 4,000 lines were written, Pope "endeavoured to collect all the beauties of the great epic writers into one piece: there was Milton's style in one part, and Cowley's in another; here the style of Spenser imitated, and there of Statius; here Homer and Vergil, and there Ovid and Claudian." Imitation was of the essence of these early attempts, and when Pope wrote his *Pastorals* imitation remained his lodestar. These four poems mark his arrival at years of poetic discretion. It had become clear to him by now, one may suppose, that his boyish rage for rhyming was to lead to his lifetime's vocation; it was time for him to lay aside the grandiose imaginings of boyhood and settle down to study his art in earnest. Precisely when the *Pastorals* were written, we do not know: they were published in Jacob Tonson's *Miscellany* in 1709, but they were written at least in part three years earlier, when Pope was seventeen or eighteen. Early work as they are, these poems in watercolor reveal a poet who has already made himself master of one sort of versification, and whose descriptive powers—as in this passage from "Autumn"—are astonishingly mature:

> Here where the *Mountains* less'ning as they rise,
> Lose the low Vales, and steal into the Skies;
> While lab'ring Oxen, spent with Toil and Heat,
> In their loose Traces from the Field retreat;
> While curling Smokes from Village-Tops are seen,
> And the fleet Shades glide o'er the dusky Green.
> (59–64)

Pope's descriptive power is one of the striking features of his early poems, and it is interesting to notice that he was not only a good judge of painting but was actually a painter himself. In his middle twenties—a fact emphasized by the late Norman Ault—he spent some eighteen months studying in the studio of his friend Charles Jervas, who was a fashionable portrait painter. The letters he wrote at this time contain some amusing references to his own apprenticeship to the art. "They tell us," he

---

[1] Printed in Ruffhead's *Life of Alexander Pope* (London, 1769), pp. 424–425.

wrote to one friend, "when St. Luke painted, an Angel came & finish'd the work; and it will be thought here after, that when I painted, the devil put the last hand to my pieces, they are so begrimed and smutted. 'Tis however some mercy that I see my faults. . . ."

While it is interesting to speculate about Pope's attainments as a painter, what is permanently significant is the value to his poetry of this apprenticeship to paint. "I begin to discover Beauties that were till now imperceptible to me," he wrote in another letter. "Every Corner of an Eye, or Turn of a Nose or Ear . . . have charms to distract me." In *Windsor Forest* it is his interest in landscape painting that is most evident:

> There, interspers'd in Lawns and op'ning Glades,
> Thin trees arise that shun each others Shades.
> Here in full Light the russet Plains extend;
> There wrapt in Clouds the blueish Hills ascend;
> Ev'n the wild Heath displays her Purple Dies,
> And 'midst the Desart fruitful Fields arise.
>
> (21–26)

The same interest in colors and effects of light and shade is one of the features of *The Temple of Fame*:

> Of bright, transparent Beryl were the Walls,
> The Friezes Gold, and Gold the Capitals:
> As Heaven with Stars, the Roof with Jewels glows,
> And ever-living Lamps depend in Rows.
>
> (141–144)

Throughout Pope's work one finds passages that betray the painter's eye, and his references to the technique of painting are numerous and exact.

When the first collection of his poems appeared, in 1717, Pope's love of luxury and color could not have been overlooked, nor his growing mastery of the heroic couplet. A number of the poems included, however, went far beyond exhibiting his mastery of technique. The epistle "Eloisa to Abelard," to which both Joseph Warton and Johnson assigned a very high place among Pope's poems, is interesting because it deals with a subject with which he was not often to deal, passionate sexual love: the whole poem has a hectic quality that is dramatically appropriate. Even finer is the "Elegy to the Memory of an Unfortunate Lady"; whoever the lady may have been, if she existed at all, this is one of the greatest elegiac poems in the language. As she has

died at her own hand, the lady may not be buried in consecrated ground; but what of this? asks the poet:

> What tho' no sacred earth allow thee room,
> Nor hallow'd dirge be mutter'd o'er thy tomb?
> Yet shall thy grave with rising flow'rs be drest,
> And the green turf lie lightly on thy breast:
> There shall the morn her earliest tears bestow,
> There the first roses of the year shall blow;
> While Angels with their silver wings o'ershade
> The ground, now sacred by thy reliques made.
>
> (61–68)

Pope never wrote more tenderly than in this poem, or with a surer control of tone.

Yet the gem of the 1717 edition remains to be mentioned, *The Rape of the Lock*, of which the original version had been published in 1712, and the much expanded version (which we read now) two years later. This is the poem that Hazlitt described as "the most exquisite specimen of *fillagree* work ever invented" and that even Housman thought possibly the most perfect long poem in the language. The description on the title page, "An Heroi-Comical Poem," has misled some readers into imagining that the comic assault is leveled against heroic poetry; but in fact a mock heroic poem is no more a satire on heroic poetry than mock turtle soup is a satire on real turtle soup. The suggestion for the poem came from a quarrel that had arisen between two wealthy Catholic families in consequence of a stolen curl. When Pope was asked to write something that would restore everyone to good humor, it occurred to him to emphasize the triviality of the whole affair by describing it in the full pomp and splendor of epic verse. No poet has ever succeeded so well in "using a vast force to lift a feather" (as Pope himself described it in the postscript to his translation of the *Odyssey*). The style of the closing lines of canto II, for example,

> With beating Hearts the dire Event they wait,
> Anxious, and trembling for the Birth of Fate,

would be splendidly appropriate at a crucial moment in an epic poem; when we realize that "the Birth of Fate" is to be no more than the snipping off of a lock of hair, the result is high comedy. And yet something of the mastery of the poem is due to the fact that it is not simply and wholly ironical. When Pope wrote the line,

> *Belinda* smil'd, and all the World was gay,
>
> (II. 52)

he was not being as directly ironical as Dryden had been when he described the "goodly Fabrick" of Thomas Shadwell. The effect of comparing a fat poetaster to Hannibal and Augustus is bluntly sarcastic: that of comparing a beautiful girl to the sun is (in this instance) satirical, yet the comparison has its own imaginative truth. In *The Rape of the Lock* Pope plays with the traditional imagery of lovesick poets, and while his treatment hints at the absurdity of their conventions it is clear that he is enjoying the license this gives his imagination. He demonstrates the superficiality of Belinda's world of fashion and scandal, of petty vanities and trivial, mean absurdities; but he does not deny its transitory beauty—the beauty of which the sylphs, the inspired addition to the later version, are in some sort the symbol. Satire is absent from some of the descriptive passages of the poem, for, as Pope pointed out, "since inanimate and irrational beings are not objects of censure . . . these may be elevated as much as you please, and no ridicule follows." This is true of the description of the coffee-equipage in canto III, which is reminiscent rather of Vergil's use of epic style in the *Georgics* to describe the lives of bees than of the directly satiric method of *MacFlecknoe*:

> For lo! the Board with Cups and Spoons is crown'd,
> The Berries crackle, and the Mill turns round.
> On Shining Altars of *Japan* they raise
> The silver Lamp . . .
>
> (105–108)

Any satirical intention that there may be here is unimportant: the reader enjoys the game by which the things of everyday become transformed into objects of an unfamiliar beauty.

It would be a great mistake to ignore the moral of the poem, which is explicitly stated in Clarissa's speech in the last canto, and which holds the component parts in a close-knit unity; yet seldom has a moral been enforced with more delicacy and tact. Lytton Strachey wrote of Pope as if he were above all things the poet of hatred; but it is partly because there is no hatred in this poem that it is so assured a masterpiece.

In the *Epistle to Dr. Arbuthnot* Pope looks back at his own career and claims in his defense:

> That not in Fancy's Maze he wander'd long,
> But stoop'd to Truth, and moraliz'd his song,
>
> (340–341)

and earlier in the same poem he contrasts the "pure Description" of his early work with the "Sense" that is now his aim. The contrast between the two halves of his career would be more complete were it not for the perfect union of Fancy and Truth, Description and Sense, in *The Rape of the Lock*, which forms a sort of bridge between his early work and his late, but there is no gainsaying the fact that in the later years of his life he held his Fancy in strict subordination to the claims of Truth. Although many critics have regretted this, it was inevitable that Pope should have "moraliz'd his song." No poet has taken his art more seriously: it would not have occurred to him to be merely "the idle singer of an empty day": his was the dedicated life of Spenser, of Milton, and of Wordsworth, who told Lady Beaumont that he desired to be regarded as a teacher or as nothing.

It was fated to be principally in satire that Pope fulfilled his moral function, but this was not his original intention. The clue to much that is puzzling in his poetic career lies in a poem that was never completed—his epic, *Brutus*. The plan of this poem is printed in Ruffhead's *Life of Pope*, and it is there stated that the author has part of the manuscript, in blank verse, lying before him. Although it is difficult to believe that *Brutus* would have been a great poem—it seems unlikely that anyone could have written a successful epic at the middle of the eighteenth century—it is essential to an understanding of Pope to remember that he, like Dryden before him, shared the Renaissance ambition of writing a great heroic poem. The notion that the Augustans were content to disport themselves on the lower slopes of poetry, ridiculing the soaring ambitions of the more vigorous race of writers who had preceded them, is a travesty of literary history. It was because Pope had thought so much about heroic poetry that he was able, in a *pièce d'occasion* that chanced to become his masterpiece, to write the greatest of all mock heroic poems. From the age of twelve onward his object was to write an epic poem, and the great epics of the world, with the yet more intoxicating Idea of the Epic, were the constant subjects of his meditation. He knew Vergil and Milton almost by heart, and spent more than a decade producing his triumphant translations of Homer. This continual devotion to the greatest of all poetic forms confirmed him in his exacting estimate of the moral function of the poet.

There was one poetic kind that was felt to share

something of the dignity of the epic while sparing the poet the difficulty of finding an acceptable myth: didactic poetry. The suggestion that Pope should write a poem in this kind, justifying the ways of God to man, may have come from his friend Henry St. John, Viscount Bolingbroke: much of the philosophy in it certainly did. But the evidence of the poem itself suggests either that there was some conflict between the philosophy that Bolingbroke expounded to Pope and that which took form in the poet's own mind, or that Pope's understanding of his friend's philosophy was incomplete. It was the somber implications of Bolingbroke's philosophy that touched Pope's mind and heart most deeply. Like Jonathan Swift's, Pope's spiritual roots lay deep in the seventeenth century: he was accessible, to a degree in which Joseph Addison (for example) was not, to the terror and despair that lie beneath the surface of human life. In this Lucretian poem it is not when he is celebrating the power of man that he is at his greatest, but when he is emphasizing the paradoxes and perils of the human situation:

> Plac'd on this isthmus of a middle state,
> A being darkly wise, and rudely great:
> With too much knowledge for the Sceptic side,
> With too much weakness for the Stoic's pride,
> [Man] hangs between; in doubt to act, or rest,
> In doubt to deem himself a God, or Beast;
> In doubt his Mind or Body to prefer,
> Born but to die, and reas'ning but to err.
>
> (II. 3–10)

It is, indeed, as Paul Hazard has said, "déisme impur" that we find in the *Essay on Man*, "déisme où persistaient quelques-unes des données psychologiques que, précisement, on voulait proscrire: un effort de volonté, plus qu'une évidence rationelle; et une acceptation du mystère."[2]

The *Essay on Man* attracted a great deal of attention, becoming a center of religious controversy and making Pope a European celebrity. Yet, though the poem contains many brilliant passages, it might have been as well for his reputation if it had never been written. For no other of his poems—unless it be the *Essay on Criticism*, an early and successful

---

[2]"A modified deism in which there persisted some of the very psychological data which the deists wished to proscribe: an effort of the will rather than a rational demonstration; and an acceptance of mystery."

attempt at a humbler sort of didactic poetry—has done so much to lend credence to the notion that Pope was a gnomic versifier of genius, and that his work is "poetry of the surface" characterized by the directness of prose rather than the complex suggestiveness of great poetry. For all its brilliance, the *Essay* should not be taken as an example of his greatest work.

Heroic and didactic poetry are two of the forms in which a poet may embody his teaching: there remains the reverse of the medal, satire, in which he sets out to teach us what is good by painting evil in its true colors. To this form of writing, in which he had already shown himself a master, Pope devoted the best of his remaining energies.

One has only to remember Aristophanes, Miguel de Cervantes, Swift, and Jane Austen to acknowledge that the satiric impulse has been the inspiration of much of the world's greatest literature. Yet it remains true, perhaps because we are still in some respects the heirs of the romantics, that critics are apt to let intrusive biographical and ethical considerations confuse them in their attempt at assessing satiric writings. In its most naive form the objection to satire seems to be an objection to grumbling, and the only answer to it is that man has a great deal to grumble about. Before the Fall there was no satire, because there was no need of it; anyone who still feels that there is nothing to cry out against in life will find satire little to his taste. Satire is born of the impulse to protest: it is protest become art. If Voltaire and Swift had never lost their tempers, the world would be an immeasurably poorer place.

While the work of every satirist is liable to be misunderstood by those who dislike satire, even among satirists Pope has been particularly unfortunate. That critics during his lifetime should too often have discussed his character instead of his poetry is at least understandable; that this tendency should have continued for almost two centuries after his death is striking evidence of the difficulty, in literary criticism, of keeping to the point. The common reader of the late nineteenth century was too often content to read the hysterical condemnation of Pope's character in Thomas Macaulay's mendacious essay on Addison, and to reflect that only a very limited satisfaction could be derived from the work of a man as deformed in mind and body as Alexander Pope.

In the last thirty years various factors—including, no doubt, the increased sympathy for the unfortunate that psychology has brought with it, as well as a growing body of accurate information about his life and times—have combined to lead critics toward a more favorable estimate of Pope's personality. Edith Sitwell's enthusiastic biography was followed by George Sherburn's scholarly account of Pope's early life, and the researches of a number of scholars have now obscured the bogeyman of the Victorians, putting in his place a human being who is often attractive and always comprehensible. Pope had a great deal to contend with. As a Roman Catholic, he was debarred from the principal careers, as well as being liable to double taxation and other species of legal persecution; while his poor health and wretched physique—he was only four feet six inches tall and suffered from severe curvature of the spine, apparently due to a tubercular infection—made of his whole life one long disease. It is hardly surprising that he was touchy and liable to fits of moroseness and to unfounded suspicions. What is astonishing is that he was able to rise above his disabilities, to support his parents and himself by being a pioneer in the independent profession of a man of letters, and to behave (on occasion) with great forbearance and generosity, as well as becoming the greatest poet of his century.

The ultimate justification of Pope's satire lies in the sincerity of his purpose and the soundness of his code of values. He is a moral satirist in a sense in which Dryden is not. (Of Dryden's three main satires, two are essentially political pamphlets, while the third is an attack on a personal enemy.) But this central fact about Pope's satire has frequently been obscured by two things: his habit of centering much of his satire in attacks on individuals, often individuals who had given him personal offense (a method traditional to satirists, and wholly justifiable); and the fact that his longest satire, *The Dunciad*, is less securely based on moral premises than most of his work. In its original form, as a poem in three books, *The Dunciad* is essentially a satire on bad writing. Pope would have agreed with the later critic who said that "the number of books has increased—is increasing—and ought to be diminished." The poem is many times the length of its model, *MacFlecknoe*, and all the brilliance of individual passages cannot prevent the feeling that it is too long. No doubt it was because he felt this that Pope's friend William Warburton suggested he should widen the scope of the poem. The result was a new book, *The New Dunciad*, written more than a decade

later, in which the satire is of the widest possible sort—moral and political as well as literary. From the opening lines:

> Yet, yet a moment, one dim Ray of Light
> Indulge, dread Chaos, and eternal Night!
> Of darkness visible so much be lent,
> As half to shew, half veil the deep Intent

to the sublime conclusion:

> Lo! thy dread Empire, Chaos! is restor'd;
> Light dies before thy uncreating word;
> Thy hand, great Anarch! lets the curtain fall;
> And Universal Darkness buries All

this continuation far transcends the first three books, and it is not surprising that Pope himself considered it his masterpiece. Unfortunately, however, he was not content to leave *The New Dunciad* to stand by itself, but made an attempt to weld the four books into one poem. He substituted Colley Cibber for Lewis Theobald as his hero, introduced strokes of moral and political satire into the first three books, and endeavored to give Dullness a much wider connotation than it had had before, until (as Warburton explained) it did not stand for "mere Stupidity" but for "all Slowness of Apprehension, Shortness of Sight, or imperfect Sense of things." But a much more comprehensive revision would have been necessary to make a perfect unity of the four books (if indeed the feat was possible), and *The Dunciad* as it now stands is flawed by this uncertain direction.

It is fortunate for us that Pope completed the original *Dunciad* in 1728 and laid it aside, for it was in the years immediately following this that he wrote most of the poems that, with *The Rape of the Lock* and *The New Dunciad*, constitute the summit of his achievement. In these he left mock heroic poetry for satire in the Latin sense of the word. Instead of embodying his criticism of life in narrative form, he turned to the form of *satura* used by Horace and Juvenal, and in modern times by Boileau and Edward Young. In this he was doing something that Dryden had never done, although (characteristically) he is hardly less clearly Dryden's pupil in these poems than elsewhere. Perhaps because it was too personal a form for him, Dryden never made use of the classical form of satire on his own account, although he translated part of Juvenal and the whole of Persius.

Everything about this epistolary form of satire suited Pope. There was no need to find a plot: the poem could be long or short: the poet was free to move from one subject to another, as in conversation, so long as an underlying continuity was preserved: swift changes of tone and temper were expected: while the accommodating freedom of the form made it possible for him to find a home in these discursive poems for the detached passages that he was forever writing. In particular this sort of poem provided a perfect setting for the satiric "character." The creation of these was an art that Pope learned from Dryden, and if anyone has excelled the creator of Achitophel and Zimri it is he. He is extraordinarily skillful in adapting the scope and tone of his "character" to the nature and vulnerability of the person attacked. It is instructive, for example, to compare the direct loathing of the assault on Lord Hervey,

This painted Child of Dirt that stinks and stings,
(*An Epistle to Dr. Arbuthnot*, 310)

with the covert malice of the lines on Addison in the same poem. Remembering, perhaps, the touch of genius with which Dryden had rendered his attack on the earl of Shaftesbury yet more lethal by inserting a passage praising his integrity as a judge, and so giving the illusion of impartiality, Pope moves to the attack with a well-turned compliment to a man,

Blest with each Talent and each Art to please,
And born to write, converse, and live with ease,
(195–196)

before he brings the charge that Addison will

Damn with faint praise, assent with civil leer,
And without sneering, teach the rest to sneer;
Willing to wound, and yet afraid to strike,
Just hint a fault, and hesitate dislike.
(201–204)

From the narrow prison of such interlocking antitheses a man's reputation can hardly escape. It should be noted that when Pope revised these "characters" he often eliminated the merely particular in favor of the universal: Addison becomes Atticus, and what began as an attack on a personal enemy is transformed into an eternal type of the

petty jealousy of a man of letters. When Pope satirizes an individual it is as if he set fire to an effigy: the effigy crackles, blazes, and is burned up; but in the process it ignites a wider conflagration, and in the flames we see, brightly illumined, the hateful figure of Folly or Vice itself. Personal hatred often provides Pope's impetus, but it is the sanity of the position from which the attack is launched that gives his satire its penetration and permanence. We will not do justice to his fierce sincerity unless we understand that his feeling for order, "Nature," the sane norm of the good life, was as passionate and as personal as John Keats's love of Beauty or Wordsworth's love of a Nature very differently defined.

Satire in the modern sense of the word was not the only ingredient of the Latin *satura*, nor is it of Pope's satiric epistles. There are also eloquent passages in praise of his friends, such as the lines on John Gay:

Blest be the *Great*! for those they take away,
And those they left me—For they left me GAY,
Left me to see neglected Genius bloom,
Neglected die! and tell it on his Tomb;
Of all thy blameless Life the sole Return
My Verse, and QUEENSB'RY weeping o'er thy Urn!
(*Arbuthnot*, 255–260)

and the moving description of his father:

Unlearn'd, he knew no Schoolman's subtle Art,
No Language, but the Language of the Heart.
(*Arbuthnot*, 398–399)

Literary criticism is ubiquitous, as is an element of autobiography and self-justification:

Ask you what Provocation I have had?
The strong Antipathy of Good to Bad.
When Truth or Virtue an Affront endures,
Th' Affront is mine, my Friend, and should be yours.
Mine, as a Foe profess'd to false Pretence,
Who think a Coxcomb's Honour like his Sense;
Mine, as a Friend to ev'ry worthy Mind;
And mine as Man, who feels for all mankind.
(*Epilogue to the Satires*, dial. II, 197–204)

Whether one turns to the *Moral Essays*, which bear a close relation to the *Essay on Man* and are constructed comparatively systematically, or to the more loosely organized *Imitations of Horace*, one finds Pope in these epistolary poems writing at the top of his bent. Never did he handle words more surely, or with more extraordinary economy. Words are like people: you can get them to do almost anything, if only you understand them well enough. You get your way with them not by bullying but by studying their natures. This Pope did, and made words his slaves. He could take two sets of familiar substantives and arrange them in a couplet that says all about pedants that there is to say:

> Pains, reading, study, are their just pretence,
> And all they want is spirit, taste, and sense.
>
> (*Arbuthnot*, 159–160)

With five of the commonest words in the language he could conclude the most terrible of all epitaphs:

> See how the World its Veterans rewards!
> A Youth of frolicks, an old Age of Cards,
> Fair to no purpose, artful to no end,
> Young without Lovers, old without a Friend,
> A Fop their Passion, but their Prize a Sot,
> Alive, ridiculous, and dead, forgot!
>
> (*Moral Essays*, II, 243–248)

In considering Pope's poetry as a whole, one is struck by the fact that a remarkably high proportion of it is written in one meter—the heroic couplet. This was not a premeditated self-denial on his part, and he did not consider this meter the only satisfactory one for English verse. His epic was to be written in blank verse, he wrote a number of poems in stanzas of various sorts, while the squibs and occasional poems that he was forever throwing off were most often in ballad meter or tetrameters. Yet it remains true that no English poet of comparable stature is to the same degree a poet of one meter. Why is this?

To answer the question one must remember the revolution in English poetry that followed the Restoration. It is the function of poetic idiom to enable poets to express their own sensibility and that of their age with the greatest possible accuracy. As sensibility changes from one age to another, it follows that the need arises, from time to time, for a revolution in the idiom of poetry. When this takes place one usually finds that each of the main constituents of the new idiom—diction, imagery, syntax perhaps, rhythm and meter almost always—has undergone some alteration; but in any particular revolution the change in one of these constituents is often found to be of primary importance, to be in a sense the root from which the other changes are derived. In the Wordsworthian revolution a change in diction was the heart of the process; in the Augustan revolution it was the discovery of a new rhythm that was vital. The discovery of the rhythmical possibilities of the heroic couplet had an effect as electrical as the discovery of "sprung rhythm" by Gerard Manley Hopkins when his poems were published in 1918. When Pope began to write, the heroic couplet (as developed by Dryden) was still a recent discovery, and he was intoxicated by it.

One of the attractions of the new meter for Pope was its almost endless adaptability. When he aspired to rhythmical or syntactical effects that could better be achieved in some other measure, he was prepared to use another measure; but he found that he had so mastered the heroic couplet that he could compass in it an extraordinary variety of effect. Compare the description of the foolish man-about-town in *The Rape of the Lock*:

> With earnest Eyes, and round unthinking Face,
> He first the Snuff-box open'd, then the Case,
> And thus broke out—"My Lord, why, what the devil?
> Z—ds! Damn the Lock! 'fore Gad, you must be civil!
> Plague on't! 'tis past a Jest—nay prithee, Pox!
> Give her the Hair".—he spoke, and rapp'd his Box.
>
> (IV. 125–130)

with the translucent beauty of the lines that describe the sylphs:

> Soft o'er the Shrouds Aerial Whispers breathe,
> That seem'd but *Zephyrs* to the Train beneath,
> Some to the Sun their Insect-Wings unfold,
> Waft on the Breeze, or sink in Clouds of Gold.
> Transparent Forms, too fine for mortal Sight,
> Their fluid Bodies half dissolv'd in Light.
> Loose to the Wind their airy Garments flew,
> Thin glitt'ring Textures of the filmy Dew.
>
> (II. 57–64)

Compare the romantic melancholy of this passage from "Eloisa to Abelard":

> But o'er the twilight groves and dusky caves,
> Long-sounding aisles, and intermingled graves,
> Black Melancholy sits, and round her throws
> A death-like silence, and a dread repose:

> Her gloomy presence saddens all the scene,
> Shades ev'ry flower, and darkens ev'ry green,
> Deepens the murmur of the falling floods,
> And breathes a browner horror on the woods
>
> (163–170)

with the precise satiric observation of the Epistle to Miss Blount, "On Her Leaving Town after the Coronation":

> To part her time 'twixt reading and bohea,
> To muse, and spill her solitary tea,
> Or o'er cold coffee trifle with the spoon,
> Count the slow clock, and dine exact at noon.
>
> (15–18)

If one sets these passages beside the quotations already given from *The New Dunciad* and the *Epistle to Dr. Arbuthnot*, the absurdity of the notion that all poems in heroic couplets are monotonously similar becomes very evident. All that is necessary is to read Pope's verse aloud, taking care to find the correct tempo for each passage.

Great as is the variety of Pope's work in tone and style, there is one quality that may be found almost everywhere, and that is a remarkable conciseness. Another master of condensed expression, Swift, paid Pope the compliment of saying that he could

> . . . in one couplet fix
> As much sense as I can in six.

A Mr. Dobson who won a brief fame by translating Matthew Prior's *Solomon* into Latin verse was asked by Pope himself or by Lord Oxford to do the same for the *Essay on Man*, but he abandoned his attempt "on account of the impossibility of imitating its brevity in another language"—a remarkable testimony, in view of the habitual brevity of Latin. It is clear that this conciseness was the result of deliberate effort on Pope's part, and that he took pride in it. In the design prefixed to the *Essay on Man* he says that he chose to write this poem in verse instead of prose partly because "I found I could express them [his principles] more *shortly* this way than in prose." Reading his letters and other prose writings, we often come on confirmation of this claim; for we find numerous reflections and images that were later incorporated in a poem, and comparison of the prose and the verse always reveals the superior brevity of the latter—a

brevity that is often accompanied by an increase in point and wit. This conciseness provides a reason why Pope's poetry should usually be read slowly, and read more than once; only so will the full meaning (in his favorite phrase) "open" itself to the reader's mind.

And what of the end to which all this skill in words and rhythms was employed? If Pope was a serious poet as well as a poet of extraordinary technical accomplishment, what was his "message"? Of course a great writer does not offer us a message that can be detached from his work; the greater he is, perhaps, the less does he do so. It is for us to read what he has written, and so to see life as he sees it. But two generalizations may be made about Pope's vision of life. The first is that it is less personal and private than that (for example) of Wordsworth. Just as it would not have occurred to him to write a poem of epic length and seriousness about the development of his own mind, as Wordsworth did in *The Prelude*, so it would have seemed to him ridiculous to offer his readers a reading of life as idiosyncratic as that of the "Immortality Ode." The values on which his work is based, and that he regarded it as his poetic duty to promulgate, are values that have a longer history than those of Wordsworth: they would have been understood and accepted, in general terms, by Socrates, by Cicero, and by Jean Racine, as well as by civilized people in his own day and in ours. Secondly, the fallacy that Pope was a shallow optimist should be allowed to go into honorable retirement. Even in the *Essay on Man* he is an optimist only in a specialized and technical sense that makes the word highly misleading, while the greatest passage of the poem is a somber "diminishing" of man's estate reminiscent rather of a medieval *contemptus mundi* than of the thought of the more shallow among the thinkers of the Enlightenment. Hazlitt was right when on reading *The Rape of the Lock* he did not know whether to laugh or to cry. Pope often reminds one of Mozart: there is in his work the same depth of emotion, perfectly restrained by the strict patterning of art

> . . . since Life can little more supply
> Than just to look about us and to die.

Charles Augustin Sainte-Beuve said of Molière, "Il a au coeur la tristesse": the same words might form the epitaph of Pope.

SELECTED BIBLIOGRAPHY

I. BIBLIOGRAPHY. Detailed bibliographical information can also be found in the *New Cambridge Bibliography of English Literature*, vol. II. R. H. Griffith, *Alexander Pope: A Bibliography* (Austin, Tex., 1922; repr. London, 1962), vol. I, part i, *Pope's Own Writings, 1709–1734*; vol. I, part ii, *Pope's Own Writings, 1735–1751*; vol. II, intended to be "a record of books about Pope," has not appeared; additional bibliographical information may be found in the standard modern eds. of Pope's writings, notably in the Twickenham ed.; E. A. Abbott, *A Concordance to the Works of Alexander Pope* (London, 1875; facs. repr. New York, 1965).

II. COLLECTED EDITIONS. W. Warburton, ed., *The Works of Alexander Pope . . . with His Last Corrections*, 9 vols. (London, 1751); J. Warton, ed., *The Works of Alexander Pope with Notes and Illustrations*, 9 vols. (London, 1797); W. Elwin and W. J. Courthope, eds., *The Works of Alexander Pope, Including Several Hundred Unpublished Letters and Other New Materials*, 10 vols. (London, 1871–1889); J. Butt, gen. ed., *The Twickenham Edition of the Poems of Alexander Pope* (London, 1939–1969), an admirable ed. that is unlikely to be superseded for a long time; a less elaborate ed., based on the text of the Twickenham ed. and also edited by J. Butt, appeared in 1963 (paperback ed., 1965); vol. IV: J. Butt, ed., *Imitations of Horace, with an Epistle to Dr. Arbuthnot and the Epilogue to the Satires* (1939; 2nd ed.,1953), also includes the two adaptations from Donne and *One Thousand Seven Hundred and Thirty Eight*; vol. II: G. Tillotson, ed., *The Rape of the Lock and Other Poems* (1940; 2nd ed., 1954; 3rd ed., 1962), includes both texts of *The Rape of the Lock*, as well as translations, *The Temple of Fame*, "Eloisa to Abelard," and "An Elegy to the Memory of an Unfortunate Lady"; vol. V: J. Sutherland, ed., *The Dunciad* (1943; rev. ed., 1953), gives the texts of *The Dunciad Variorum* and *The Dunciad in Four Books*; vol. III, pt. i: M. Mack, ed., *An Essay on Man* (1950); vol. III, pt. ii: F. W. Bateson, ed., *Epistles to Several Persons (Moral Essays)* (1951; 2nd ed., with new material, 1961); vol. VI: N. Ault, ed., *Minor Poems* (1954), completed by J. Butt; vol. I: E. Audra and A. L. Williams, eds., *Pastoral Poetry and the Essay on Criticism* (1961), also includes "The Messiah," *Windsor Forest*, and Pope's translations from Ovid and Statius; vols. VII–X: M. Mack. et al., eds., *Homer's Iliad and Odyssey* (1967); vol. XI: M. Mack, ed., *Index* (1969); H. Davis, ed., *Pope: Poetical Works* (London, 1966), an admirable ed. in the Oxford Standard Authors series, includes everything except the Homer translations; with a new intro. by P. Rogers (paperback ed., 1978).

III. SELECTED WORKS. G. Sherburn, ed., *Selections . . .* (New York, 1929), reissued as *The Best of Pope* (1931); H. V. D. Dyson, ed., *Poetry and Prose* (Oxford, 1933), brief selections; W. K. Wimsatt, ed., *Alexander Pope: Selected Poetry and Prose* (New York, 1951); R. P. C. Mutter and M. Kinkead-Weekes, *Selected Poems and Letters of Alexander Pope* (London, 1962), a well-annotated volume that makes an excellent intro. to Pope.

IV. PROSE AND LETTERS. Various writings in prose, including prefaces to Shakespeare and Homer as well as numerous letters, appeared during Pope's lifetime. They are listed in the *New Cambridge Bibliography*; only a selection is listed here. N. Ault, ed., *Prose Works* (London, 1936), vol. I of an uncompleted collected ed., covering the years 1711–1720; C. Kerby-Miller, ed., *Memoirs of . . . Martinus Scriblerus*, written by Dr. Arbuthnot, Pope, Swift, Gay, Parnell, and Robert Harley (earl of Oxford) (New Haven, 1950); E. L. Steeves, ed., *The Art of Sinking in Poetry: Martinus Scriblerus'* ΠΕΡΙ ΒΑΘΟΥΣ (New York, 1952); G. Sherburn, ed., *The Correspondence of Alexander Pope*, 5 vols. (London, 1956), an admirable ed. that throws a good deal of new light on Pope's career; J. Butt, ed., *Letters of Alexander Pope* (London, 1960).

V. PRINCIPAL POEMS AND TRANSLATIONS. A much fuller and more detailed list may be found in Griffith and in the *New Cambridge Bibliography*. *Poetical Miscellanies, the Sixth Part* (London, 1709), vol. VI of Dryden's collection, *Miscellany Poems*, published by Tonson, which contains pastorals and other poems by Pope; *An Essay on Criticism* (London, 1711); *The Rape of the Lock and Other Poems*, in Lintott's *Miscellaneous Poems and Translations* (London, 1712), two cantos, 334 lines; see 1714 below; *Windsor Forest* (London, 1713); *The Rape of the Lock, in Five Cantos* (London, 1714), 794 lines. The sylphs, and much else, have now been added; this is the text usually reprinted; *The Temple of Fame: a Vision* (London, 1715); *The Works of Mr. Alexander Pope* (London, 1717–1735), contains "Verses to the Memory of an Unfortunate Lady," "Eloisa to Abelard," and other poems; *The Iliad of Homer*, vols. I–VI (London, 1715–1720); *The Odyssey of Homer*, vols. I–V (London, 1725–1726), books II, VI, VIII, XI, XII, XVI, XVIII, and XXIII were in fact by William Broome, and books I, IV, XIX, and XXII by Elijah Fenton; most reprints of these translations omit the footnotes and other interesting material; *The Dunciad* (London, 1728), in three books, with Theobald as hero, see 1729, 1742, and 1743; *The Dunciad Variorum* (London, 1729), an expanded text, with elaborate satirical prolegomena, footnotes, and other "scholarly" apparatus; *An Epistle to the . . . Earl of Burlington* (London, 1731), often called *Moral Essays, IV*; *Of the Use of Riches, an Epistle to . . . Bathurst* (London, 1732), often called *Moral Essays, III*; *The First Satire of the Second Book of Horace, Imitated* (London, 1733), other *Imitations of Horace* appeared between 1734 and 1738, but not separately listed here; *An Essay on Man* (London, 1733–1734), Epistles I–III appeared separately in

1733, Epistle IV appeared in 1734, followed by a collection of the four in the same year; *An Epistle to Cobham* (London, 1733), often called *Moral Essays, I*; *An Epistle . . . to Dr. Arbuthnot* (London, 1735), later called *Prologue to the Satires*; *Of the Characters of Women: An Epistle to a Lady* (London, 1735), often called *Moral Essays, II*; *Epilogue to the Satires, in Two Dialogues* (London, 1738), published separately in the same year, the first under the title *One Thousand Seven Hundred and Thirty Eight*; *The New Dunciad* (London, 1742); *The Dunciad in Four Books* (London, 1743).

VI. BIOGRAPHY. Throughout his life Pope was involved in controversy. The resultant "Popiana" have often little relevance to his poetry, and they are not listed here. J. V. Guerinot's *Pamphlet Attacks on Alexander Pope, 1711-1744: A Descriptive Bibliography* (London, 1969) gives an admirable account of them. W. Ayre, *Memoirs of the Life and Writings of Alexander Pope, Esq.*, 2 vols. (London, 1745); O. Ruffhead, *The Life of Alexander Pope* (London, 1769; repr. Hildesheim, 1968), the value of these and other early biographies is discussed by Sherburn in the preface to his *Early Career of Alexander Pope* (London, 1934); S. Johnson, *Prefaces, Biographical and Critical, to the Works of the English Poets*, 10 vols. (London, 1779-1781), often reprinted as *Lives of the English Poets*; the best ed. is that of G. Birkbeck Hill, 3 vols. (London, 1905), vol. III: "The Life of Pope"; the biographical part of the Life is sometimes inaccurate and inevitably out of date; but the assessment of Pope's character is shrewd and refreshingly free from the tendency to confuse a man's personality with his merit as a poet; the critical part is of the greatest interest to anyone who reads Pope's poetry; S. W. Singer, ed., *Anecdotes, Observations, and Characters of Books and Men Collected from the Conversation of Mr. Pope and Other Eminent Persons of His Time by the Rev. Joseph Spence* (London, 1820), indispensable; an admirable ed. in 2 vols. by J. M. Osborn, with full annotation, was published in 1966; C. W. Dilke, *The Papers of a Critic*, 2 vols. (London, 1875), most of vol. I consists of a series of scholarly investigations of Pope's writings; L. Stephen, *Alexander Pope* (London, 1880), in the English Men of Letters series; W. J. Courthope, *The Life of Alexander Pope* (London, 1889), in vol. V of the Elwin-Courthope ed.

E. Sitwell, *Alexander Pope* (London, 1930), unusual in its day for its sympathetic approach; G. Sherburn, *The Early Career of Alexander Pope* (Oxford, 1934), the standard biography "to about 1726 or 1727"; N. Ault, *New Light on Pope with Some Additions to His Poetry Hitherto Unknown* (London, 1949), a series of studies of Pope's life and the canon of his poems; some of the attributions are very uncertain; the chapter on Pope as a painter throws interesting light on the poems; W. K. Wimsatt, *The Portraits of Alexander Pope* (New Haven-London, 1965), a beautifully produced book that throws a great deal of light on Pope and his background; J. V. Guerinot, *Pamphlet Attacks on Alexander Pope 1711-1744: A Descriptive Bibliography* (London-New York, 1969).

VII. CRITICISM. J. Spence, *An Essay on Pope's Odyssey*, 2 parts (London, 1726; repr. Hildesheim, 1968), in the "Anglistica and Americana" series; J. Warton, *An Essay on the Writings and Genius of Pope*, vol. I (London, 1756), vol. II (London, 1782), this digressive study, in which each of Pope's principal poems is considered in turn, is still illuminating. Warton is often called a "pre-romantic," and his admiration of Pope was less wholehearted than Johnson's, but the extent of his reservations is often exaggerated; S. Johnson, *Prefaces . . . to . . . the English Poets* (London, 1779-1781), see "Biography" above; P. Stockdale, *An Inquiry into the Nature and Genuine Laws of Poetry, Including a Particular Defence of the Writings and Genius of Mr. Pope* (London, 1778); W. C. Hazlitt, *Lectures on the English Poets* (London, 1818); D. Masson, ed., *The Collected Writings of Thomas De Quincey* (London, 1889-1890), vols. IV and XI contain interesting criticism of Pope; much of this is reprinted in H. Darbishire, ed., *De Quincey's Literary Criticism* (London, 1900); L. Stephen, *Hours in a Library*, vol. I (London, 1874), contains the essay "Pope as a Moralist"; L. Stephen, *History of English Thought in the Eighteenth Century*, 2 vols. (London, 1876), a pioneering study that is still of great interest, see particularly vol. II, pp. 348-365; A. Beljame, *Le Public et les hommes de lettres en Angleterre au dix-huitième siècle, 1660-1744: Dryden, Addison, Pope* (Paris, 1881), translated by E. O. Lorimer as *Men of Letters and the English Public in the Eighteenth Century, 1660-1744: Dryden, Addison, Pope* (London, 1948), edited with an intro. and notes by B. Dobrée; L. Stephen, *English Literature and Society in the Eighteenth Century* (London, 1904), the Ford lectures, 1903; L. Strachey, *Pope* (Cambridge, 1925), the Leslie Stephen lecture, 1925, repr. in *Characters and Commentaries* (London, 1933), in *Literary Essays* (London, 1948), and in A. S. Cairncross, ed., *Modern Essays in Criticism* (London, 1938); an entertaining and stimulating lecture based on an imperfect understanding of Pope's character; A. Warren, *Alexander Pope as Critic and Humanist*, Princeton Studies in English, no. 1 (Princeton, N. J., 1929), a pioneering study, now inevitably out of date; E. Audra, *L'Influence française dans l'oeuvre de Pope* (Paris, 1931); F. R. Leavis, *Revaluation: Tradition and Development in English Poetry* (London, 1936), still of interest; A. O. Lovejoy, *The Great Chain of Being: A Study of the History of an Idea* (Cambridge, Mass., 1936), see particularly chap. 6; G. Tillotson, *On the Poetry of Pope* (Oxford, 1938), an enthusiastic and stimulating introduction; R. K. Root, *The Poetical Career of Alexander Pope* (Princeton, N. J., 1938); G. Wilson Knight, *The Burning Oracle: Studies in the Poetry of Action* (London, 1939), unusual and often suggestive, see chap. 5; H. Sykes Davies, *The Poets and Their Critics: Chaucer to Collins* (London, 1943; rev. ed., 1960), brief passages of criticism on Pope's poetry by critics from Pope's own time onward; *Essays on the Eighteenth Century Presented to David Nichol Smith* (Oxford, 1945), see particularly G. Sherburn's "Pope at Work"; C. Brooks, *The Well Wrought Urn; Studies in the Structure of Poetry* (New York, 1947), chap. 5 is an interesting study of *The Rape of the Lock*; J. Sutherland, *A Preface to Eighteenth Century Poetry* (Oxford, 1948), an excellent introduction to the period of Pope and that which followed it; J. L. Clifford and L. A. Landa, *Pope and His Contemporaries: Essays Presented to George Sherburn* (Oxford, 1949), see particularly M. Mack's "Wit and Poetry and Pope: Some Observations on His Imagery"; J. Butt, *The Augustan Age* (London, 1950), contains admirable brief introductions to Dryden, Addison, Swift, Pope, Johnson, and others; D. M. Knight, *Pope and the Heroic Tradition: A Critical Study of the Iliad* (New Haven, Conn., 1951); I. Jack, *Augustan Satire: Intention and Idiom in English Poetry, 1660-1750* (Oxford, 1952), chaps. 5-7 deal with Pope; R. W. Rogers, *The Major Satires of Alexander Pope*, Illinois Studies in Language and Literature: vol. XL (Urbana, Ill., 1955), makes some use of MS material; A. L. Williams, *Pope's "Dunciad": A Study of Its Meaning* (London, 1955); G. Tillotson, *Pope and Human Nature* (Oxford, 1958), deals with "the material Pope expresses" rather than with his manner of expressing it, the subject of Tillotson's earlier study; J. H. Hagstrum, *The Sister Arts: The Tradition of Literary Pictorialism and English Poetry from Dryden to Gray* (Chicago, 1958), a general study of great interest; R. Sühnel, *Homer und Die Englische Humanität: Chapmans und Popes Ubersetzungkunst im Rahmen der humanistischen Tradition* (Tübingen, 1958); R. A. Brower, *Alexander Pope: The Poetry of Allusion* (Oxford, 1959), illustrates the fact that an awareness of the allusions throughout Pope's poetry enriches our experience as we read it; J. L. Clifford, ed., *Eighteenth-Century English Literature: Modern Essays in Criticism* (New York, 1959), reprints three important articles in convenient form: M. Mack, "Wit and Poetry and Pope," E. Niles Hooker, "Pope on Wit: the Essays on Criticism," and J. Butt, "Pope Seen Through His Letters"; B. Dobrée, *English Literature in the Early Eighteenth Century, 1700-1740*, vol. VII: *Oxford History of English Literature* (Oxford, 1959), two long chaps. contain a full account of Pope's poetry; U. Amarasinghe, *Dryden and Pope in the Early Nineteenth Century* (Cambridge, 1962), the reputation of these two poets in the romantic period; T. R. Edwards, *This Dark Estate: A Reading of Pope* (Berkeley–Los Angeles, 1963); M. Mack, ed., *Essential Articles for the Study of Alexander Pope* (London, 1964), essential for the advanced student; M. Price, *To the Palace of Wisdom: Studies in Order and Energy from Dryden to Blake* (New York, 1964); R. Trickett, *The Honest Muse: A Study in Augustan Verse* (Oxford, 1967), an interesting account of "the underlying ethos of Augustan poetry" that has a long chapter on Pope; E. Jones, "Pope and Dulness," *Proceedings of the British Academy*, vol. LIV (1968), the Chatterton lecture delivered 13 November 1968, reprinted as an offprint (1970); P. Dixon, *The World of Pope's Satires* (London, 1968); M. H. Nicolson and G. S. Rousseau *"This Long Disease, My Life": Alexander Pope and the Sciences* (Princeton, N. J., 1968); G. S. Rousseau, ed., *Twentieth Century Interpretations of "The Rape of the Lock": A Collection of Critical Essays* (Englewood Cliffs, N. J., 1969); J. A. Jones, *Pope's Couplet Art* (Athens, Ohio, 1969); M. Mack, *The Garden and the City: Retirement and Politics in the Later Poetry of Pope, 1731-1743* (Toronto–London, 1969), the most important and interesting of recent books on Pope; D. H. White, *Pope and the Context of Controversy: The Manipulation of Ideas in "An Essay on Man"* (London, 1971); J. Barnard, ed., *Pope: The Critical Heritage* (London, 1973); P. Rogers, *An Introduction to Pope* (London, 1975); H. Erskine-Hill, *The Social Milieu of Alexander Pope* (New Haven, Conn., 1975); M. Leranbaum, *Alexander Pope's "Opus Magnum," 1729-1744* (London, 1977); M. R. Brownell, *Alexander Pope and the Arts of Georgian England* (London, 1978).

SAMUEL RICHARDSON

(1689-1761)

R. F. Brissenden

INTRODUCTION

FEW genuinely great novelists have been so extravagantly praised in their own day and so thoroughly neglected by succeeding generations as Samuel Richardson. During the eighteenth century he was probably more famous and more influential than any other novelist in Europe. His three novels, *Pamela. Or, Virtue Rewarded* (1740–1741), *Clarissa. Or, the History of a Young Lady* (1747–1748), and *The History of Sir Charles Grandison* (1753–1754), were translated into all the major European languages; they were read by people in every rank of society; and in some countries—notably France, Germany, and England itself—they had a profound effect on the development of the novel. In a famous pronouncement after Richardson's death on 4 July 1761, Denis Diderot, one of the major literary and intellectual figures of the age, declared that Richardson was fit company for the immortals, and that his works merited a place on the same shelf as those of Moses, Homer, Sophocles, and Euripides. Yet not much more than a hundred years later, the English scholar H. D. Traill was able to dismiss Richardson confidently with the remark that he was typical of "that class of writers who are . . . read by none but the critic, the connoisseur or the historian of literature."

In recent years the critical estimate of his novels has begun to rise again, but there are still many who would claim that Richardson's importance is mainly historical. It is understandable that this should be so, for his faults, both as a novelist and as a man, are obvious and unpleasant. The sheer size of his novels is enough to daunt the reader: he takes almost a million words to tell the story of *Sir Charles Grandison*, and *Clarissa* is even longer. But his "insupportable prolixity," as Clara Reeve, an eighteenth-century critic, called it, is not nearly so objectionable as the vein of prurience, hypocrisy, and sheer vulgarity that in

varying degrees runs through everything he wrote. In *Clarissa*, and to a certain extent in *Sir Charles Grandison*, this merges more or less completely into the general pattern of the work; but in *Pamela*, his first novel, its effect is extremely damaging: the structure of the whole book is seriously distorted.

Pamela is the story of a young, beautiful, and intelligent maidservant who staves off seduction so skillfully that she is able to convince her wicked master that he ought to reform and marry her. Unfortunately, Pamela's virtue is not quite so innocent as Richardson intended it to be, and the world is not likely to forget this easily. It is a commonplace of literary history that despite, or perhaps because of, its extraordinary popularity this novel inspired several parodies, including the aptly titled and amusing *Shamela*, and the opening chapters of *Joseph Andrews*. But it is a mistake to condemn *Clarissa* or even *Sir Charles Grandison* because of the notorious weaknesses of their elder sister. Even Henry Fielding, who was almost certainly the author of *Shamela* as well as of *Joseph Andrews*, paid unqualified tribute to *Clarissa*. "Such Simplicity, such Manners, such deep Penetration into Nature; such Power to raise and alarm the Passions few Writers, either ancient or modern, have been possessed of," he stated in his periodical, the *Jacobite's Journal*. And, in a personal letter to Richardson that has only recently come to light, Fielding speaks with an even more generous enthusiasm of Richardson's powers as a writer and freely admits that the sufferings of Clarissa have moved him to tears. The letter is typical of the warmth and honesty of Fielding's character. Richardson's response was typical too: when *Tom Jones* appeared, its success piqued his vanity, and he lost no time in abusing this "truly coarse-titled" book and its "low" and immoral author in private letters to his friends.

Yet Fielding's praise of *Clarissa* is entirely

justified; in many ways it is the greatest novel of its day. It has defects, it is true: it is too long; it is written in an epistolary convention that, especially to the modern reader, seems artificial and awkward; and it is pervaded with an air of moral solemnity that at times becomes oppressive. But the book has a naked realism, a moral and psychological insight, and a sustained and compelling dramatic force that set it above most of the other works of fiction produced in the eighteenth century. Narrow as Richardson's range may be, in *Clarissa* he strikes deeper into the heart of his own age than either of his two great contemporaries, Fielding and Laurence Sterne, ever do. One reason for this, perhaps, is that he strikes deeper into his own heart than do most novelists. It is painfully clear that he is, to an unusual extent, personally involved in the problems about which he is writing. As a result there is an air of urgency and suspense to his work that is lacking in *Tom Jones* or *Tristram Shandy*. *Clarissa*, in particular, once one has become immersed in the story, has an almost hypnotic effect. It is a book that unrelentingly engages both the heart and the mind to the full. Not only is it a work of considerable moral significance, but also, despite its length, it is extremely readable.

Pamela and *Sir Charles Grandison* are important books, and *Clarissa* is a great one. Yet it is impossible to regard Richardson himself as a great man. That this timid, sanctimonious, prudish businessman should somehow have been able to create the somber and powerful tragedy of *Clarissa* is one of those embarrassing paradoxes with which history occasionally presents us. The character of Richardson is an affront to every conception of what an artist should be; and indeed there can be no doubt that he was to a large extent an artist by accident and despite himself. When, as he put it, he "slid into the writing of *Pamela*," he was, to all outward appearances, nothing but a middle-aged London printer, respected and prosperous, but in no way distinguished. He was then fifty-one years old, having been born in Derbyshire in 1689, and in his career up to this point he had not deviated in the slightest from the conventional middle-class pattern of material advancement through virtue and hard work. It was not without pride that, in later life, he described his apprenticeship in a letter, dated 2 June 1753, to his Dutch translator, Johannes Stinstra:

I served a diligent Seven years to it, to a Master who grudged every Hour to me, that tended not to his Profit, even of those Times of Leisure & Diversion, which the Refractoriness of my Fellow Servants *obliged* him to allow them, and were usually allowed by other Masters to their Apprentices. I stole from the Hours of Rest & Relaxation my Reading Times for Improvement of my Mind. . . . But . . . I took Care, that even my Candle was of my own purchasing, that I might not in the most trifling Instance make my Master a Sufferer.

Like the virtuous apprentice in William Hogarth's *Industry and Idleness*, he married his master's daughter; and after she died, he prudently took for his second wife the sister of an eminent bookseller in Bath. By the time he was fifty, he had become an established figure in "the trade" in London, with a flourishing business and a house on the rural outskirts of the city at "agreeable suburban North End." He had also acquired the reputation of being a ready man with his pen, willing to oblige his fellow booksellers "with writing Indexes, Prefaces, & sometimes for their minor Authors, *honest* Dedications; abstracting, abridging, compiling, and giving his Opinion of Pieces offered them." Nobody, least of all Richardson himself, would ever have dreamed that he might one day add the writing of novels to this list of sober and useful activities. Yet it was his colleagues' opinion of his literary abilities that indirectly led to his becoming a novelist.

In 1739, Charles Rivington and Thomas Osborne, booksellers (or publishers, as they would now be called), asked Richardson to compile a small volume of model letters for use by people without much formal education or practice in correspondence. Such letter-writing manuals were not at all uncommon at this time, and in most respects Richardson's *Letters Written to and for Particular Friends*, or *Familiar Letters*, as it is more generally known, follows the conventional pattern fairly closely. Like all its fellows, it would be quite forgotten today were it not that while he was writing it, Richardson got the idea of using some of the model letters as the nucleus of a didactic story. He had intended from the beginning that his manual should not only teach people how to write letters but should also be morally instructive; and in the course of composing a group of letters designed to advise handsome servant girls "how to avoid the Snares that might be laid against their Virtue," he recalled a story he had heard of one maidservant who had avoided the snares and won the hand of her master into the bargain. In his own words, "hence sprung Pamela."

PAMELA

THERE has never been a literary success quite like that of *Pamela*. Certainly no previous work of fiction had ever attained such rapid, widespread, and enduring popularity, and few have since. *Pamela* seems to have appealed to every sort of potential reader, and, although judged by modern standards the reading public at this time formed only a small proportion of the general population, the book enjoyed a wide circulation. Fashionable ladies smiled at the heroine's "lowness," but wept in their chambers over her trials; her virtue was praised in the pulpit; and, according to one story, the villagers at Slough rang the church bells to celebrate her marriage. Within a year *Pamela* had run through six printings and had been translated into French. Translations into other languages soon followed, and the book eventually became more popular on the Continent—where it inspired not only other novels but also several plays and an opera—than in England. *Pamela* became the archetypal Cinderella story of the age—in Lady Mary Wortley Montagu's phrase, "the joy of the chambermaids of all nations." Probably no other novel was read by so many people in the eighteenth century. In the general imagination of the period, Pamela acquired something of the status of a mythical figure.

How are we to account for the extraordinary popularity of this novel? Part of the answer lies in its quality as a work of fiction. Although the book as a whole may be justly criticized for its unevenness, its crudity, and its sentimentality, the first portion of the novel, dealing with Mr. B.'s various attempts to seduce Pamela, is a lively and convincing piece of writing. Moreover, the situation is presented with a psychological realism and a moral seriousness that were new in English fiction. These things would not have been enough in themselves; what guaranteed the success of *Pamela* was that in so many respects it was the right book at the right time. Since the end of the seventeenth century, the demand for fiction had been growing steadily, largely as a result of an increase in the number of middle-class people, especially women, with enough leisure for reading. "The world is so taken up of late with novels and romances, that it will be hard for a private history to be taken for genuine," complained Daniel Defoe in 1722, in his preface to *Moll Flanders*; and in 1740, the year in which the first part of *Pamela* was published, there were enough works of fiction in

print and enough people wanting to read them for the first circulating library in London to be opened. But mere quantity was not enough to satisfy this developing appetite; the majority of the "novels and romances" published at this time were, as Richardson states on the title page of *Pamela*, "Pieces calculated for Amusement only." Whether they tended also to "inflame the Minds they should instruct" is doubtful. Though their plots and titles were often erotic enough, the stories themselves were for the most part shallow, insipid, and incredible. When something realistic, like Defoe's brilliant documentary narratives of contemporary life, was produced, it lacked psychological depth and subtlety.

Moreover, people wanted to be instructed as well as amused: it was their gentle didacticism as much as anything else that made the *Tatler* and the *Spectator* so popular; and even in this increasingly secular age, works on religious subjects still constituted the largest single category of books published each year. Allegories such as John Bunyan's *The Pilgrim's Progress*, works of practical piety such as Richard Allestree's *The Whole Duty of Man*, Jeremy Taylor's *Holy Living and Holy Dying*, and Defoe's various *Family Instructors* went through dozens of editions, and collections of sermons were bestsellers. And the practicality of these and innumerable similar works was often as important as their piety. They were concerned with the most pressing social problems of the day—the status of women, the rearing of children, the extent to which private convictions should be allowed to conflict with social responsibilities. Allestree spends more space discussing man's duty to his neighbors than in discussing his duty to God; and Defoe, in the dramatic dialogues in *Religious Courtship*, is more concerned with problems of marriage than with problems of religion.

This is the tradition in which *Pamela*, like the *Familiar Letters*, was initially conceived. When Richardson began to write *Pamela*, he probably had no intention of producing a novel at all. As the subtitle, *Virtue Rewarded*, indicates, his purpose was simply to use his story to demonstrate both that servant girls ought to resist the amorous advances of their masters and that Providence will look after them if they do so. But, in spite of his modest aim, the conduct-book parable came alive in his hands and developed into a novel.

Richardson became a novelist primarily because

he had the novelist's genius. But this genius needed something to release it. For Richardson the release was effected through his intense concern with certain moral issues, a concern that was the result of a profound conflict within his own personality between a strong and sympathetic sense of justice and an innate and almost pathological timidity. This conflict is reflected in all his writings; indeed, it was out of the attempt to resolve it that his novels were born.

In the preface to the *Familiar Letters*, Richardson, speaking of himself in the third person, states that it has been his purpose through the letters

to inculcate the Principles of *Virtue* and *Benevolence*; to describe *properly* and recommend *strongly*, the SOCIAL and RELATIVE DUTIES. . . .

Particularly, he has endeavoured to point out the Duty of a *Servant* not a *Slave*; the Duty of a *Master* not a *Tyrant*; that of a *Parent*, not as a Person morose and sour, and hard to be pleased; but mild, indulgent, kind, and such a one as would rather govern by *Persuasion* than *Force*.

This could serve as an introduction to everything Richardson wrote. The "SOCIAL and RELATIVE DUTIES" are, in some form or other, the theme of all his novels. He is preoccupied by the problem of the relation between the individual and the various social groups to which one belongs. What are the obligations owed to those who are socially either one's superiors or one's inferiors? What are the obligations that, in common humanity, one owes to others irrespective of class, sex, creed, or nationality? And what is one to do when these two sets of duties come into conflict? Stated in the most general terms, these are the questions that Richardson continually raises and seeks to answer in his novels.

In some form or other these are the questions with which all serious novelists are concerned. Richardson is particularly interesting because, to begin with, his attitude to these matters was not that of a novelist at all. He approached the whole problem of human conduct as a moral propagandist rather than an artist. But through the attempt to apply his dogmatic and relatively simple moral theory to the practical and untidy realities of life, he developed, by a process of forced and often painful growth, not only into a novelist but also into a moral and social thinker of some force and profundity.

The process can be observed very clearly in *Pamela*. At the superficial level it is a tract on the virtues of chastity and, more particularly, dutifulness. The heroine succeeds in getting Mr. B. to marry her because, no matter how sadistically he tries her, she endeavors to treat him still with that respect to which as her master and as a man he is "properly" entitled. The hypocritical twists and subterfuges through which Pamela goes—or is forced to go by Richardson—in order to keep up this facade of respect are among the more unpleasant and ridiculous features of the novel; and if Pamela's dutifulness were the only explanation for the eventual marriage of the hero and heroine, the book would have been forgotten long ago. But the situation is more complex than it seems at first. Pamela finally gets her man not because she is dutiful to him, but because she succeeds in convincing him that he owes a duty to her, not merely as a woman but simply as a human being. She does this by distinguishing with scrupulous thoroughness between the occasions on which he deserves to be respected and those on which he forfeits this right by trying to demand her obedience in an "improper" way. After his attempt on her virtue in the summer house, for instance, Pamela announces rebelliously that she won't stay:

You won't, hussy! said he: Do you know whom you speak to? I lost all fear and all respect, and said, Yes, I do, Sir, too well!—well may I forget that I am your servant, when you forget what belongs to a master.[1]

(letter 11)

The scene is typical: every encounter between the two follows the same pattern of angry, passionate, and frustrated argument. So long as the debate is verbal, Pamela always wins; and despite Mr. B.'s attempts to gain her affection by kidnapping and imprisoning her, she gradually achieves more and more real freedom. Whenever her exasperated master descends to more direct methods, she is always saved by her "happy knack of falling into fits."

But the book is much more than a debate about the rights of women. Although Mr. B.'s wooing of his beautiful servant girl is conducted in terms of rights and duties, it is infused with powerful feeling. Whenever the two lovers come into each other's presence, the emotional temperature rises im-

---

[1]All quotations from Richardson's novels are from the Shakespeare Head edition of *The Novels*, 18 vols. (Oxford, 1929–1931).

mediately. There is little affection between them—their meetings almost always end in impotent fury on one side and tears on the other—but their attraction for each other, distorted and frustrated though it may be, is undoubtedly there. In this first novel there is considerable crudeness and naiveté in Richardson's presentation of sexual passion, and his characterization of Mr. B. can scarcely be called successful. One anonymous contemporary critic remarked rather dryly that it is just as well that the author has informed us that Mr. B. "had been a great rake, and had debauch'd several women . . . for from his whole behaviour towards his Pamela, one should be apt to think him the meerest novice in the world." But despite the gaucheries both of Mr. B. and of Richardson himself, one cannot deny the strength and complexity of feeling that develop as the novel unfolds. Psychological realism such as this, though common enough in drama, was something new in English fiction, and it had an immediate appeal to the contemporary reading public. Even today the first section of *Pamela*, that in which the story of the courtship is told, can hold and excite the interest. Once the marriage has occurred, the tension disappears; and apart from one or two scenes the rest of the book, in which the preacher is allowed to take over almost completely from the novelist, is dull, worthless stuff.

Much of the power in the first part of *Pamela* arises from the suppressed and morbid sexual passion that burns like a slow fire beneath the surface of all of Richardson's work. But an equally important element in the complex of feelings that both inspired and were released by the writing of this and the other novels is Richardson's obsession with the moral and social problems of the rights of the individual. The two sets of feelings are, in fact, inextricably involved; the sexual conflict in his novels always reflects a social struggle of much wider significance. Pamela and Mr. B., like all of Richardson's lovers, express their "love" for each other in debates about rights and duties, and in one way the battle in which they are all involved is not sexual at all. Richardson's heroines are all democrats; their most fundamental desire is that their suitors should "respect" them—that is, should accord them their rights as individual human beings before beginning to treat them as women. As Pamela says to Mr. B.:

Whatever you have to propose, whatever you intend by me, let my assent be that of a free person, mean as I am,

and not of a sordid slave, who is to be threatened and frightened into a compliance.

(letter 32)

In a sense this is a denial of sex, and the way in which Pamela and Clarissa argue with their lovers and use tears and fits in an attempt to escape from the physical realities of the sexual situation is undoubtedly "sentimental." But from another point of view, there is nothing sentimental at all in their attitude: Richardson's heroines have no illusions about the disadvantages of belonging to the weaker sex. As Anna Howe, who represents the voice of common sense in *Clarissa*, remarks, there is nothing very glorious in being "cajoled, wire-drawn and ensnared, like silly birds into a state of bondage . . . courted as princesses for a few weeks, in order to be treated as slaves for the rest of our lives." In a society dominated by men, such ideas, especially when they are held by a mere maidservant such as Pamela, are socially rather embarrassing; and there can be no doubt that much of the ridicule that Richardson's first novel attracted was aroused by the brilliant insubordination of his heroine. Parody is, more often than not, just as much an attempt to laugh an uncomfortable truth out of existence as it is to ridicule error, hypocrisy, and dullness. *Shamela*'s most obvious target is the genuine sentimentality and hypocrisy of Richardson, but Fielding also wrote in it the effort to make Pamela conform, to force her into the more easily acceptable mold of the feminine fortune hunter. But Pamela is far too complicated to be forced into any pattern. Indeed, it is because she refuses to fit into the usual pattern, refuses to behave like Moll Flanders or Roxana, that she becomes the first real heroine in English fiction.

Pamela's complexity reflects the complexity of Richardson himself. As Brian Downs has so aptly put it, he wrote from "a divided heart." And the divisions, the inner conflicts in Richardson's heart, are significant not simply because they provided the impetus for writing the novels, and generated the complex feeling with which they are charged, but also because they symbolized in a personal and dramatic form some of the most fundamental problems of the society in which he lived. Richardson's guilts and fears were the guilts and fears of his age; and when he turned his unwitting eyes in upon the dark corners of his own soul, his readers felt that theirs were being exposed too. "C'est lui," wrote Diderot, "qui porte le flambeau au fond de la caverne."

Richardson was not a happy man. Craving affection, he had learned to mistrust it, and instead to pin all his hopes of emotional security on the exercise of power. "There can be no love without fear!" he maintained; children must learn to respect their parents, and wives their husbands, before they can love them. Timid, lonely, and socially diffident, he drew great satisfaction from the influence and respect that his position as a paterfamilias, a successful printer, and later a successful novelist brought him. Clearly he had a vested interest in trying to preserve those conventions of the social order in which his own small authority rested. Yet he was blessed (or cursed) with that primary innocence and honesty of vision that all great artists possess. If suffering and injustice existed, he could not blind himself to them nor, in the last resort, forgive himself for them, even when the suffering and injustice were the direct result of those aspects of the social structure that it was plainly in his own interest to leave undisturbed. Indeed, these were the things that seemed to fascinate him most. Although in real life he enjoyed exercising his rights as a man, a husband, a father, and a bourgeois snob, in his novels he subjected the question of the validity of these rights to a most painful and searching examination.

Richardson's attitude to women, to children, and to the family was essentially ambivalent, a compound of sympathy and hatred, arrogance and fear, pride and guilt. His sympathy for women, for instance, made him a passionate advocate of their rights; but at the same time his outraged and terrified male ego, in the nightmare figures of Mr. B., Lovelace, and the kind but implacable Grandison, ensured that the Pamelas and Clarissas of this world would be punished for their rebelliousness and the Charlotte Grandisons and Harriet Byrons kept firmly in their place.

It seems clear that when Richardson began to write *Pamela*, he had no great understanding or control of the conflicting inner forces he was about to release. In a very real sense he did not know what he was doing. Almost without his realizing it, his simple moral tract somehow turned into a novel. In the process he discovered his powers, but he did not discover how to organize and discipline them. Because of this the characterization and structure of his first novel are twisted out of shape, and the book as a whole displays bewildering contradictions in tone and intention. But in the successful sections of the novel, his ability, the promise of his genius, is clearly manifest. The source is obvious too; the most vital element in the book, the thing that made it so spectacularly successful in its own day, is its confused but angry concern with social injustice. And it is this rather than its psychological realism that makes it still readable. Pamela's arguments with Mr. B. are as lively and convincing today as when they were first written.

But the most impressive scene in *Pamela* is one in which Mr. B. does not appear; it is the quarrel between Pamela and Mr. B.'s sister, Lady Davers. By an almost theatrical, but no doubt unconscious, contrivance Richardson is able in this scene to forget all those conventional notions of duty and decorum that lay a film of sentimentality and hypocrisy over so much of the novel. Lady Davers not only does not know that Pamela is her brother's wife, but she is completely unprepared to believe it. Pamela, knowing that she is indeed married, and therefore Lady Davers' social equal, is entirely sure of her own position. Each of them is thus able to speak her mind with perfect honesty, without false condescension on the one hand or false humility on the other. The situation is electric; the dialogue, rapid and colloquial, crackles back and forth, Pamela's dignified but spirited defense of herself contrasting vividly with the passionate and spiteful raging of Lady Davers. It is an ugly and perhaps slightly hysterical scene, but it is savagely revealing. Its sheer dramatic power is undeniable: it is the most sustained piece of writing in *Pamela* and one of the least cluttered or involved. Richardson's literary genius here breaks free completely from the restrictive patterns of Puritan didactic literature; and it is patent that given the right material and the right opportunities to develop it, he should be able to produce a work of fiction of considerable force and stature. In *Clarissa* this is what he does. And if the title means anything, it is *Clarissa*, rather than *Pamela* or *Joseph Andrews*, that should be called the first English novel.

CLARISSA

CLARISSA, which was published in 1747–1748, a year or more before *Tom Jones*, is the first English novel to have been conceived and planned from the beginning as a unified piece of what Henry James delighted to call "fictive art." Inspired and encouraged by the success of *Pamela*, and with his imagination fired by a theme that suited his genius perfectly, Richardson was determined to produce a work of literature that could be measured by the highest standards of art as well as of morality. And he succeeded: *Clarissa* is a great novel. One of its most impressive features—especially when it is compared with *Pamela*—is its structural coherence, its formal unity. The length of the novel has been criticized since it first appeared, perhaps with justice, but one must agree with the author himself when he claims that

long as the Work is, there is not one Digression, not one Reflection, but what arises naturally from the Subject, and makes for it, and to carry it on.[2]

There is nothing accidental or haphazard about *Clarissa*; it is a triumph of craft. But the care with which it has been constructed has not in any way stifled the inner vitality of the story. Although the multitude of incidents dovetail in a way that could only be the result of scrupulous planning, the action seems to develop organically toward its inevitable climax and conclusion: Lovelace's physical violation of Clarissa and her spiritual triumph and glorification.

Richardson's determination to carry his story through to its preordained end was quite unshakable. Despite tearful pleas from his female admirers—and even requests from Colley Cibber, Fielding, and other men of letters—"to make what is called a Happy Ending," he never wavered from his tragic design. It is this inflexibility of purpose that makes *Clarissa* such a convincing and at times terrifying book. It moves forward as slowly and inexorably as a lava flow, and with this movement the characters are caught up and borne irresistibly along. It is "such a strange situation . . . we are in," writes Clarissa apprehensively to her friend Anna Howe on the eve of her abduction by Lovelace; "*strange* I may well call it . . . we seem all to be *impelled*, as it were, by a perverse fate, which none of us are able to resist."

No one reading *Pamela* could have predicted that its author would produce anything so comprehensive in scope and so formally satisfying as *Clarissa*. Richardson's attainment of artistic maturity was amazingly rapid. Moreover, it was consciously and intelligently directed; he knew what he was doing when he wrote his second novel. Like Fielding, whose discussions of the principles of his art are one of the pleasantest features of *Tom Jones*, Richardson evolved a theory of fiction to justify and explain his practice. Unfortunately, he lacked Fielding's knowledge of the traditions of literature and literary criticism. He had to turn to friends like Joseph Spence, and the poets Edward Young and Aaron Hill, for assistance in working out his ideas. His projected critical preface for *Clarissa* never got beyond the stage of a rough draft, although he did include some of his ideas, in a less trenchant form, in the postscript he added to the final version of the novel.

It is a pity that Richardson was not able to give a conclusive shape to his theory of the novel, for it is sophisticated and perceptive, and much closer to what we now believe to be the truth about the essential nature of this literary form than Fielding's theory of the comic epic poem in prose. He shared with Fielding the belief that the novel should be realistic and should concern itself with the lives of ordinary people; as one of his friends, Philip Skelton, put it, "the workings of private and domestic Passions" are his subject, not the "imaginary Adventures of Kings, Heroes, Heroines." But Richardson was also convinced—convinced as thoroughly as Henry James was a century and a half later—that the novel was at its best when it was most dramatic. His main concern in all his novels is not so much to tell a story as to present and explore particular situations that could conceivably occur "in a private Family," and that raised the moral issues and problems significant both for himself and for society as a whole. He aimed for the closest realism and the most thorough examination of the situation, and he felt that this could be obtained best "not in the narrative way"—that is, not by writing about the people involved—but by letting them speak for themselves:

by making them write their own thoughts to Friends, soon after each Incident happened; with all that Naturalness and Warmth, with which they felt them, at that Time, in their own Minds.[3]

Thus he justifies his use of the epistolary way of writing fiction, and he asserts that there is no need

[2] The quotation is reprinted in R. F. Brissenden, ed., *"Clarissa": Preface, Hints of Prefaces and Postscripts* (Los Angeles, 1964), for the Augustan Reprint Society.

[3] A comment on *Clarissa* by Joseph Spence, reprinted in *"Clarissa": Preface, Hints of Prefaces and Postscripts*.

to insist on "the evident Superiority of this Method to the dry Narrative."

The advantages of the epistolary method are indisputable. In *Clarissa* the reader is kept more continuously and intensely aware of the action and the people involved in it than in *Tom Jones*—"the characters," in Richardson's words, "sink deeper into the Mind of the Reader." Moreover, this technique enables the writer to present the moral and emotional problems with which his characters are faced in very fine detail. The slightest nuances of feeling, the subtlest shades of discrimination, can be captured; the web and texture of experience, of moment-to-moment living, can be suggested if not fully rendered. But although the epistolary method permits the writer to achieve all this, one cannot deny its inherent clumsiness and implausibility. Recent and contemporary novelists such as Henry James, Marcel Proust, James Joyce, and William Faulkner, to mention but a few, have learned how to attain similar effects in more realistic and less obviously artificial ways, and the technical apparatus used by Richardson seems primitive and awkward by comparison.

Nevertheless, his use of the letter form can, especially in *Clarissa*, be accepted as a convention no more essentially unrealistic than blank verse, the stream-of-consciousness technique, or the use of song in opera. And it can be accepted because it is something more than a mere literary device. For Richardson it is a technique that reflects perfectly the themes with which he is preoccupied. Indeed, it is doubtful whether any other contemporary fictional form would have enabled him to allow such full expression to his genius, for the epistolary novel gives the author a unique opportunity for presenting and examining the inner lives of his characters—and Richardson was preeminently concerned with the moral significance of the inner life.

His main characters are all placed in situations in which they are forced to defend their personal integrity. Richardson was a conventional man, but he also believed profoundly in the right of the individual to make up his or her own mind in matters of morality, to be like Sir Charles Grandison, his ideal hero, and live "to himself, and to his own heart, rather than to the opinion of the world." But the forces of convention often come into conflict with the free moral conscience; and it was just this aspect of life that Richardson, himself deeply committed to both sides of the struggle, found most

fascinating. Pamela and Clarissa, and to a smaller degree many of his other characters, have to fight for the privilege of being able to follow the dictates of their own consciences. Clarissa, in fact, sacrifices her life in the process.

At one level the battle is fought overtly between the individual and the members of the various social groups to whom he or she owes allegiance. Clarissa, for instance, has one struggle with her family, another with Lovelace and the world he represents, and a third with society as a whole. But the most bitter conflicts are those that go on at a deeper level, in the hearts of the characters themselves. Clarissa is torn between her love for and loyalty to her parents, her tormented and frustrated passion for Lovelace, and her profound conviction that she has every right to resist their efforts to make her own decisions for her. It is this "war of duties" within the individual personality, together with "the delineation of . . . subtlety of feeling . . . [and] entanglements of delicacy," that Henry Mackenzie, in 1785, pronounced to be the distinguishing feature of the sentimental novel.

Since the latter half of the eighteenth century, Richardson has been described as a sentimental novelist; and to those readers who are acquainted only with *Pamela*, the title may seem justified. But when Mackenzie described "that species [of novel] called the sentimental," the word "sentimental" carried little of that connotation of shallowness, excess, and insincerity that it bears today. When Richardson's reputation stood highest, a sentimental novel was understood to be one in which the moral sentiments of the characters were presented and analyzed with some care and seriousness. In this sense *Clarissa* certainly is sentimental; and except for the overlong conclusion, and perhaps for the fact that Clarissa has to die at all, it is marred by little of the false sentimentality that so disfigures *Pamela*. *Clarissa* is a mercilessly realistic and profoundly sad exposure of human behavior.

Indeed, one of its fundamental themes is the tragic ineffectiveness of any view of life that is sentimental in the sense of being foolishly optimistic. In the preface to the third edition of *Clarissa*, Richardson states that the first of his intentions in writing the novel is "to warn the inconsiderate and thoughtless of the one sex against the base arts and designs of specious contrivers of the other." And *Clarissa* is above everything else a warning: a warning to the credulous, the idealistic, and the trustful—a warning not only against putting one's trust in rakes, but also against putting one's trust in anyone or anything except, ultimately, one's own conscience and judgment. Clarissa is not destroyed by the libertine Lovelace; she is destroyed by the forces of convention—forces that work almost as strongly within her own heart as they do in the society in which she moves. Her family, who are ordinary, conventional people distorted into monsters of cruelty by their weakness and their lust for power and money, humiliate her and force her to elope with Lovelace because she refuses to submit to the hypocrisy of a marriage without love. But she also brings destruction on herself because, in her own heart, she cannot finally deny the authority of her family and because she refuses to face up to the realities of her relationship with Lovelace. It is Clarissa's determination not to recognize the suspicious aspects of the situation in which Lovelace involves her in London that compensates for, and in part explains, the apparent implausibility of this part of the novel. As Albrecht von Haller, one of the earliest critics of *Clarissa*, remarked, it is doubtful

whether probability has been preserved in the detestable audacity of Lovelace; to carry a lady of quality to a brothel, to confine her captive there against her will, to give her opium, and to violate her person.[4]

In one sense the situation is obviously incredible, but at the psychological level it is not. Clarissa is more securely enmeshed in the web of her own conventional illusions than in all of Lovelace's plots. As Samuel Johnson remarked, there is always something she prefers to truth. At one level the novel is an account of seduction and rape; at another it is the story of the pitiless awakening of a conventional young woman, a "nice girl," to the realities of life. Circumstances conspire against Clarissa to shatter, one by one, the illusions she cherishes—that parents "naturally" love their children; that no man with any human feeling can be utterly cruel; that love is always stronger than lust or greed. The final blow is struck when, after a long process of deception and subtle torture, Lovelace violates her.

There is a sense in which Clarissa, like all sentimental heroines, asks to be raped. Her prudery

(which Lovelace, in his perverted fashion, both flouts and encourages) forces her to deny the sexual facts of the situation in which she is involved, and the treatment she receives at his hands is in part a savage masculine retaliation for her prim coldness. ("Dear creature!" Lovelace exclaims in despairing admiration, "Did she never romp?") At another level it can be regarded as a punishment inflicted by society on an individual who has dared to be unconventional. Clarissa herself looks at it in this way, seeing in it the fulfillment of her father's curse, a reward for her filial impiety. But the significance of the rape and of the role Lovelace plays in it is more complex than this. Lovelace is one of the most remarkable characters in English fiction. In some ways he is an implausible monster, an unhappy blend of literature and life—a "fancy piece," as Anna Laetitia Barbauld (who edited Richardson's correspondence in 1804) calls him. But he is a fancy piece endowed by Richardson's imagination with a fierce, inextinguishable vitality; and it is clear that, like John Milton's Satan, he partly escaped from his creator's control and assumed a life of his own. He is not all villain; one of his most important functions in the novel is to act as the voice of reason and skepticism, and he is not an altogether unworthy representative of the intellectual side of aristocratic libertinism. He hates the Harlowes for their canting hypocrisy, and he despises them for their parvenu values and their crudely obvious attempts at social climbing. And Clarissa, by her refusal to admit that he is justified in his opinion of her family, puts herself in the position of defending the very attitudes and beliefs against which she herself has been struggling and that have, in effect, driven her into his arms. The rape is thus not merely a personal attack on Clarissa but also an attack on the conventional values that her family and, in part, she herself represent. It is the most violent expression of that hatred of middle-class hypocrisy and materialism by which so much of the novel is animated. It is also the physical culmination and symbol of that brutal process of awakening through which Clarissa has been made to go. Lovelace, the Hobbesian man of reason, forces her to acknowledge the truth about herself and other people.

But, paradoxically enough, in doing so he destroys himself. The rape, committed while Clarissa is drugged, is a token rape only; a confession of impotence, not a demonstration of power; an expression of rage at his failure to arouse in her the love he really craves. But Clarissa is spiritually lib-

---

[4]The quotation is from an article by Haller originally published in *Bibliothèque raisonnée des ouvrages des savans de l'Europe* (Paris, 1749) and reprinted in translation in *Gentleman's Magazine*, 19 (London, 1749).

erated by the event, even though it results, rather implausibly, in her death later in the novel. After this ultimate act of betrayal, she has no illusions left. The persons from whom she has had every right to expect kindness and loyalty—her family and her lover—have deserted and abused her; the ideals in which she has put her faith have all, save one, been destroyed. Her faith in her personal integrity is still unshaken; if anything, it is now stronger than ever. Few people have been compelled so cruelly to face the unpleasant facts of human nature as Clarissa; but when the last shreds of illusion have been torn away, she accepts the situation with honesty and courage. It is one of the great moments in English literature when, defying not only her seducer but also her family and the whole world of conventional respectability, she cries out to Lovelace, "The man who has been the villain to me you have been, shall never make me his wife!"

Lovelace is a terrifying enough figure, but he is a cardboard horror compared with the Harlowes. The opening scenes of the novel, in which the slowly deepening conflict between Clarissa and her family is presented, have an extraordinary power. As Clarissa's determination not to let herself be sacrificed to the ruthless ambition of her brother hardens, the motives of the rest of the family begin to stand out in their true colors. Shame at the knowledge that they are in the wrong only makes them act with gradually increasing cruelty and anger toward the girl they pretend to love. The characterization is masterly: the brother and sister, utterly vulgar and selfish, and the basically kind but pathetically weak mother are clearly imagined and most convincingly portrayed. The father is a figure of tremendous psychological force: incapacitated and embittered by illness, he has let the management of the family fall into the hands of his arrogant son, and Clarissa rarely sees him. But he is still a terrifying symbol of parental authority; she receives his commands like distant thunderings from Mount Sinai, and the curse he hurls after her as she flees with Lovelace haunts her to her deathbed.

As the action develops, the atmosphere slowly becomes more and more claustrophobic. Every door Clarissa turns to is locked; every member of her family whom she asks for help and sympathy rejects her. Even her attempts to state her case reasonably to her parents are continually frustrated. She knows before she begins that her arguments will be useless whatever happens. "I will hear what you have to say," says her mother in one of their tortured interviews, "but with this intimation, that say what you will, it will be of no avail elsewhere." Her words are continually twisted against her, and everything she does and says is interpreted as evidence, not of her dislike of the repulsive Solmes, but of her love for Lovelace. As the frustrating and agonizingly repetitive arguments go on, Clarissa becomes bewildered, angry, and finally terrified. She slowly realizes that, incredible as it may seem, there is not one person among her supposedly loving family who has either enough sympathy or enough courage to come to her defense. And even though she becomes more and more strongly convinced that her passive defiance of her parents is morally justified, she cannot allow herself to forget that she is technically guilty of filial impiety. This impasse in which she finds herself generates an atmosphere of bafflement, fear, and maddening frustration that becomes more and more nightmarish. And in true nightmare fashion, when she does try to escape, the sanctuary in which she seeks refuge turns out to be even more horrible than the terrors from which she flees: she places herself in the hands of a man who is much more ruthlessly determined to ruin her than her family ever was.

In the opening sections of *Clarissa*, there is an intensity that one finds hardly anywhere else in the English novel. Though he is a lesser writer than either of them, Richardson here reminds us most strongly of Feodor Dostoyevsky and Franz Kafka. In no other English writer of comparable stature do we find the same obsessive preoccupation with the problems of guilt and cruelty, or such a bleak and terrifying vision of the lonely battle that must be fought by the person who wishes to preserve the right to make his own moral decisions. "What a world is this!" cries Clarissa in despair and perplexity:

What is there in it desirable? The good one hopes for so strangely mixed, that one knows not what to wish for! And one half of mankind tormenting the other, and being tormented themselves in tormenting!

(letter 52)

The picture of suffering humanity that is presented in *Clarissa* is profoundly sad. It is also in some ways narrow and limited: there are qualities in life to which Richardson was completely insensitive. But the picture is unforgettable. *Clarissa* leaves its mark indelibly on the mind of the reader as only the greatest novels can.

SIR CHARLES GRANDISON

HAVING presented the world with the portrait of a good woman in *Clarissa*, Richardson was urged by his friends to produce a novel about a good man. He did not need a great deal of encouragement; in 1753–1754 he published *The History of Sir Charles Grandison*. It was respectfully received by the public and the critics, but in many ways it is the least successful of his three novels. The hero, Sir Charles Grandison, has become a byword for priggish and pompous virtue; and the book, huge, slack, and nerveless, lacks both the unity and the tension of *Clarissa*, and possesses little of the vigor and liveliness of the much cruder *Pamela*. Yet it contains some of Richardson's best writing, and in certain respects it played a more important part in the development of the novel than anything else he wrote.

The first portion of the novel is the best and was the most influential. It deals with a situation that was to become one of those most favored by the novelists, especially the women novelists, who followed Richardson—a situation that, in the hands of Jane Austen and Henry James, was to prove highly rewarding. Fanny Burney, the first important successor to Richardson, described the situation best, perhaps, when she gave the subtitle of *A Young Lady's Entrance into the World* to her first novel, *Evelina* (1778). It is a subject especially rich in satiric possibilities; and in the first part of *Sir Charles Grandison*, which deals with the introduction of Harriet Byron into London society, Richardson takes full advantage of them. This portion of the novel is written with a lightness of touch and a feeling for wit and comedy that are as admirable as they are unexpected. His presentation of Harriet's encounters with her various suitors, especially the villain of the piece, Sir Hargrave Pollexfen, is remarkably polished. Richardson's portraits of men from the women's standpoint are often astonishingly penetrating. From the outside, at least, his rakes are always convincing: arrogant, selfish, ignorant of love, amazed and incredulous at the spectacle of a woman's having a mind of her own, and altogether unable to comprehend that someone could dislike them. Sir Hargrave is no exception. Harriet describes one of his attempts at courtship thus:

Had not Sir Hargrave intended me an honour, and had he not a very high opinion of the efficacy of eight thousand pounds a year in an address of this kind, I dare say he would have supposed a little more prefacing necessary: But, after he had told me, in a few words, how much he was attracted by my character before he saw me, he thought fit to refer himself directly to the declaration he had made at Lady Betty Williams's . . . then talked of large settlements; boasted of his violent passion; and besought my favour with the utmost earnestness. . . . I thought it best to answer him with openness and unreserve.

To seem to question the sincerity of such professions as you make, Sir Hargrave, might appear to you as if I want to be assured: But, be pleased to know you are directing your discourse to one of the plainest-hearted women in England. . . . I thank you, Sir, for your good opinion of me; but I cannot encourage your addresses.

You *cannot*, madam, *encourage my addresses*! And express yourself so seriously! Good Heaven! . . . I have been assured, madam, recovering a little from his surprise, that your affections are not engaged. But, surely, it must be a mistake: Some happy man—

Is it, interrupted I, a necessary consequence, that the woman who cannot receive the addresses of Sir Hargrave Pollexfen, must be engaged?

Why, madam—as to that—I know not what to say—But a man of my fortune, and, I hope, not *absolutely* disagreeable either in person or temper; of *some* rank in life—He paused; then resuming—What, madam, if you are as much in earnest as you seem, can be your objection? . . .

We do not, we *cannot*, all like the same person. . . .

(letter 17)

Social comedy of this sort had not appeared in the English novel before; but once the vein had been opened, it was to be exploited with increasing frequency and success. *Sir Charles Grandison* is the direct ancestor of the novels of Jane Austen, and it is not surprising to learn that Richardson was one of Austen's favorite authors. According to her nephew J. E. Austen-Leigh in his *Memoir of Jane Austen*:

Her knowledge of Richardson's works was such as no-one is likely again to acquire, now that the multitudes and merits of our light literature have called off the attention of readers from that great master. Every circumstance narrated in Sir Charles Grandison, all that was ever said or done in the cedar parlour, was familiar to her; and the wedding days of Lady L. and Lady G. were as well remembered as if they had been living friends.

(ch. 5)

How are we to account for the unusual excellence of the opening sections of *Grandison*? There are, I think, two main reasons. One is that, in this part of the novel, Richardson has no particular moral ax to grind. The impossibly stiff and virtuous Sir Charles has not yet appeared, and the author's only concern is to paint a convincing picture of the life of a quiet but fashionable young woman. The atmosphere is light and—strange word to use in connection with Richardson—happy. But a more important reason is that Harriet Byron is a completely independent person, the type toward which all Richardson's heroines have been tending. As she tells Sir Hargrave:

If I do not meet with a man to whom I can give my whole heart, I never will marry at all. . . . You are angry, Sir Hargrave . . . but you have no right to be so. You address me as one who is her own mistress.

(letter 19)

If Pamela or Clarissa had been able to say this, there would have been no novels written about them—but how much happier they would have been! Harriet, a wealthy orphan, is free from the social obligations against which they have to struggle. She can be honest with herself where they cannot; and, being conveniently detached from society, she is able to criticize it with impunity. She is the only really likeable character Richardson ever created: she lacks the sentimentality of Pamela and the stiffness of Clarissa, and though she may be waspish, she is free alike from the hardness of Anna Howe and the vulgarity of Charlotte Grandison. It is obvious that she is the model on whom Fanny Burney's *Evelina* is based, and there are traces of her lineaments in Elizabeth Bennett (*Pride and Prejudice*) and Marianne Dashwood (*Sense and Sensibility*), not to mention the heroines of countless minor novels now deservedly forgotten.

The promise held out in the first two hundred pages of *Sir Charles Grandison* is not fulfilled. With the introduction of the hero, Richardson's moral earnestness reasserts itself. Yet the appearance of Sir Charles on the scene is very skillfully stage-managed: in his first brush with Sir Hargrave, he cuts a dashing and gallant figure. But although he saves Harriet from being ruined by Sir Hargrave, he quite effectively ruins her in another way. As soon as she begins to play heroine to Sir Charles's hero, Harriet loses her sparkle and becomes a dull girl indeed. The rest of the novel, though admirable in many ways, is on the whole insipid. Virtue triumphant is never as interesting as virtue in distress; and when, as in *Sir Charles Grandison*, it consistently triumphs through several volumes, it becomes positively boring.

Not only is *Sir Charles Grandison* boring; also it is often deliberately sentimental and sensational, as *Pamela* and *Clarissa* rarely are. In *Clarissa*, even though the emotional force of the novel arises naturally out of the basic theme and situation, Richardson had discovered that he possessed to a remarkable degree the power of playing on the feelings of his readers. And in his last novel he often obviously contrives effects that seem to have been previously achieved with unselfconscious spontaneity. Pathetic figures like Emily Jervois and Clementina della Poretta are used to bring tears to the reader's eyes; and Sir Hargrave Pollexfen, a pale shadow of Lovelace, exists mainly for the purpose of producing easy thrills. These characters, and the sentimental and violent situations in which they appeared, were to be imitated over and over again in the cheap and degenerate novels of sentiment that were produced in such numbers during the next thirty or forty years. But if Richardson is partly responsible for inspiring some of the most worthless fiction ever written in England, he also inspired some of the best; and the influence of *Sir Charles Grandison* on the technique of the novel is incalculable. It is surely one of the most naturalistic of all novels, and the exposition and resolution of its vast and complicated plot are conducted with unobtrusive skill. The only trouble is that the characters are very ordinary and uninteresting people, and the situations in which they are involved are not in general of sufficient significance to engage the full attention of the reader—especially the modern reader. Like its hero the novel is undoubtedly worthy; it is also unquestionably dull.

RICHARDSON'S RANGE

DULL but worthy: the verdict can certainly be applied with justice to *Sir Charles Grandison* and to long stretches of Richardson's other novels. But it can by no means be applied to his works as a whole. An artist deserves to be judged by his best achievement, and *Clarissa* is a masterpiece. It towers above most of the other novels of the century, and it exhibits, as neither *Pamela* nor *Sir Charles Grandison* does, Richardson's particular abilities consistently employed to their fullest advantage; for although he is a great novelist, he is very much a one-book novelist.

What are Richardson's talents? What are the qualities that give his work greatness and distinguish it from the work of other novelists? One of them certainly is his sentimentalism, his ability to analyze and present with subtlety, exactness, and sympathy the changing thoughts and feelings of his characters. Like Proust and James, he has the power of making the reader intensely and continuously aware of the myriad significances of apparently simple human situations and of suggesting, with innumerable delicate strokes, the variety and complexity of the human personality and the mystery that lies at its core. We are compelled to read *Clarissa* by curiosity as much as anything else. Richardson manages somehow simultaneously to excite and frustrate the reader's attention; for as long as possible, the situation is kept unresolved, the tension and suspense are maintained and intensified. In this atmosphere of quivering sensibilities, the lightest touch may be loaded with incalculable meanings and a whisper may break in with the violence of a thunderclap. Morbid, stifling, dreamlike—*Clarissa* has all these qualities, but it is undeniably fascinating.

It is also undeniably realistic. At the most superficial level there is the Hogarthian vigor of scenes like the death of Mrs. Sinclair (which the Abbé Prevost paid Richardson the compliment of omitting, together with several other passages, from his translation of the novel because he considered them too strong for French taste). Equally impressive, though sometimes tedious, is the exhaustive thoroughness with which he has traced out every thread in the complex relationship—financial and legal as well as emotional—by which the characters are bound to each other and on which so much of the plot depends. We know more about the people in Richardson's novels than we do about most people in real life, and there are few other novelists who attempt to present such a complete picture of a human situation.

Richardson's realism and his sentimentalism are at bottom the same. His preoccupation with the details, both psychological and material, of his characters' lives is the strongest expression of that desire for the truth, the urge to come to terms with himself and with human problems that were his concern, by which he was obsessed. The range of his vision is narrow, it is true, but in *Clarissa* he achieves an analytical rendering of a human situation that is at once extraordinarily comprehensive and profoundly moving. Clarissa perhaps lacks nobility —her virtue, after all, is of the passive kind—and after reading the novel we are left with a heightened awareness not of man's potentiality for good and great actions but of his capacity for meanness and his ability to inflict pain on others and on himself. We admire the courage of Clarissa, but our admiration is not so strong as our feeling of despair and outrage, our feeling that no one should be allowed to suffer as she has suffered, our realization that humanity needs protecting more strongly from itself than from anything else. *Clarissa* certainly has its limitations, but the vision of life it offers is a valid and necessary one. With all its faults it remains a great novel, and the only major work of fiction of tragic dimensions produced during the eighteenth century.

SELECTED BIBLIOGRAPHY

I. Bibliography. A. D. McKillop, *Samuel Richardson, Printer and Novelist* (Chapel Hill, N.C., 1936), includes a detailed bibliography; W. M. Sale, *Samuel Richardson: A Bibliographical Record of His Literary Career with Historical Notes* (New Haven, Conn., 1936), the standard bibliography; W. M. Sale, *Samuel Richardson: Master Printer* (New York, 1950).

II. Collected Works. *The Works*, 19 vols. (London, 1811), with a sketch of his life and writings by Rev. E. Mangin; *The Novels*, 3 vols. (London, 1824), with "A Memoir of the Life of the Author" by Sir W. Scott, in Ballantyne's Novelist's Library; *The Works*, 12 vols. (London, 1883–1884), with a prefatory ch. of biographical criticism by Sir L. Stephen; *The Novels*, 19 vols. (New York, 1901–1902), with a life of the author and intros. by W. L. Phelps; *The Novels*, 20 vols. (London, 1902), with an intro. by E. M. M. McKenna; *The Novels*, 18 vols. (Oxford, 1929–1931), the Shakespeare Head ed.

III. Separate Works. *Letters to and for Particular Friends, on the Most Important Occasions* (London, 1741), repr. as *Familiar Letters on Important Occasions* (London, 1928), with intro. by B. W. Downs; *Pamela. Or, Virtue Rewarded*, 2 pts. (London, 1740–1741), the text used in all modern reprs. is that of the 6th ed. (London, 1742), which Richardson had revised considerably; *Clarissa. Or, the History of a Young Lady* (London, 1747–1748), the standard text is that of the 4th ed. (London, 1751); *Meditations Collected from the Sacred Books—Being Those Mentioned in the History of Clarissa* (London, 1750); *Letters and Passages Restored from the Original Manuscript of the History of Clarissa* (London, 1751); *The History of Sir Charles Grandison* (London, 1753–1754), the usual text repr. is that of the 3rd ed. (London, 1754), although the most authoritative modern ed., J. Harris (Oxford, 1972), uses that of the 1st ed.; *A Collection of the Moral and Instructive Sentiments . . . Contained in . . . "Pamela," "Clarissa," and "Sir Charles Grandison"* (London, 1755); S. W. Baker, Jr., ed., *Samuel Richardson's Introduction to Pamela* (Los Angeles, 1954), with an intro., for the Augustan Reprint Society; R. F. Brissenden, ed., *"Clarissa": Preface, Hints of Prefaces and Postscripts* (Los Angeles, 1964), with an intro., for the Augustan Reprint Society.

IV. Letters. A. L. Barbauld, ed., *The Correspondence of Samuel Richardson*, 6 vols. (London, 1804); J. Carroll, ed., *Selected Letters of Samuel Richardson* (London, 1964). The bulk of Richardson's letters, still unprinted, are in the Forster Collection in the Victoria and Albert Museum.

V. Some Biographical and Critical Studies. Sarah Fielding [?], *Remarks on Clarissa* (London, 1749); ["A Lover of Virtue"], *Critical Remarks on Sir Charles Grandison, Clarissa, and Pamela* (London, 1754; facs. repr., Los Angeles, 1950); D. Diderot, "Éloge de Richardson," *Le Journal étranger* (January 1762), a famous tribute to Richardson's genius, containing some extravagant but illuminating criticism; A. L. Barbauld, "Richardson," the preface to *Clarissa* in the British Novelists ed. (London, 1802) and to her ed. of *The Correspondence of Samuel Richardson* (London, 1804); Sir L. Stephen, "Richardson's Novels," the intro. to *The Works of Samuel Richardson* (London, 1883–1884), repr. in *Hours in a Library* (London, 1892); A. Dobson, *Samuel Richardson* (London, 1902), in the English Men of Letters series; B. W. Downs, *Richardson* (London, 1928); P. Dottin, *Samuel Richardson 1689–1761, imprimeur de Londres, auteur de "Pamela," "Clarisse" et "Grandison"* (Paris, 1931); J. W. Krutch, *Five Masters: Boccaccio, Cervantes, Richardson, Stendhal, Proust* (London, 1931); F. S. Boas, *From Richardson to Pinero* (London, 1936), see "Richardson's Novels and Their Influence"; A. D. McKillop, *Samuel Richardson, Printer and Novelist* (Chapel Hill, N.C., 1936), for many years the standard work on Richardson, and still valuable; V. S. Pritchett, *The Living Novel* (London, 1946), contains a consideration of *Clarissa*; W. M.

Sale, "From Pamela to Clarissa," in F. W. Hilles, ed., *The Age of Johnson: Essays Presented to Chauncey Brewster Tinker* (New Haven, Conn., 1949); A. Kettle, "Richardson, Fielding, Sterne," in *An Introduction to the English Novel* (London, 1951; 1953); C. Hill, "Clarissa Harlowe and Her Times," *Essays in Criticism*, 5, no. 4 (October 1955); D. Daiches, *Literary Essays* (London, 1956), contains an essay on *Clarissa*; A. D. McKillop, *The Early Masters of English Fiction* (Lawrence, Kans., 1956), contains a ch. on Richardson; F. Bradbrook, "Samuel Richardson," in *Pelican Guide to English Literature*, vol. IV (London, 1957); I. Watt, *The Rise of the Novel: Studies in Defoe, Richardson and Fielding* (London, 1957); A. Kearney, *Samuel Richardson* (London, 1968); I. Konigsberg, *Richardson and the Dramatic Novel* (Lexington, Ky., 1968); R. Cowler, ed., *Twentieth-Century Interpretations of Pamela* (Englewood Cliffs, N.J., 1969); J. Carroll, ed., *Samuel Richardson: A Collection of Critical Essays* (London, 1969); T. C. D. Eaves and B. D. Kimpel, *Samuel Richardson: A Biography* (Oxford, 1970), the standard biography; M. A. Doody, *A Natural Passion: A Study of the Novels of Samuel Richardson* (Oxford, 1973); M. Kinkead-Weakes, *Samuel Richardson: Dramatic Novelist* (London, 1973); E. B. Brophy, *Samuel Richardson: The Triumph of Craft* (Knoxville, Tenn., 1974); R. F. Brissenden, *Virtue in Distress: Studies in the Novel of Sentiment from Richardson to Sade* (London, 1974), contains a ch. on *Clarissa* and an extended analysis of sentimentalism.

VI. Parodies, Anti-Pamelas, etc. H. Fielding [?], *An Apology for the Life of Mrs. Shamela Andrews* (London, 1741; facs. repr., Los Angeles, 1956), the facs. ed., for the Augustan Reprint Society, has an intro. by I. Watt; E. Haywood [?], *Anti-Pamela: or, Feign'd Innocence Detected* (London, 1741); C. Povey, *The Virgin in Eden: or, The State of Innocency* (London, 1741); H. Fielding, *The History of the Adventures of Joseph Andrews, and of His Friend Mr. Abraham Adams* (London, 1742), may be considered as in part a parody of *Pamela*; B. Kreissman, *Pamela-Shamela: A Study of the Criticisms, Burlesques, Parodies, and Adaptations of Richardson's "Pamela"* (Lincoln, Nebr., 1960).

HENRY FIELDING

(1707-1754)

John Butt

To say that the English novel began in the 1740's with the work of Samuel Richardson and Henry Fielding is to invite refinement, if not contradiction. The Elizabethans had plenty of novels to read, by Thomas Nashe, Robert Greene, Thomas Lodge, and Thomas Deloney; in the latter half of the seventeenth century, there were numerous translations and imitations of the French romance; and Aphra Behn, Daniel Defoe, and Mary Manley all have some claim upon the historian of the novel. Yet there is something in the broad contention that Richardson and Fielding, for all their differences, would have approved. Recalling the circumstances of his writing *Pamela* (1740), Richardson claimed, in a letter to a friend, that he had hit upon "a new species of writing," and Fielding was equally confident that *Joseph Andrews* (1742) was a "kind of writing, which I do not remember to have seen hitherto attempted in our language." At least some of their readers were prepared to acknowledge the claim. Samuel Johnson, writing in 1750, when *Clarissa*, *Tom Jones*, and Tobias Smollett's *Roderick Random* had been published, was able to distinguish one important difference between the new style of fiction and the old. In *Rambler* No. 4 he remarks:

The works of fiction, with which the present generation seems more particularly delighted, are such as exhibit life in its true state, diversified only by accidents that daily happen in the world, and influenced by passions and qualities which are really to be found in conversing with mankind. . . . Its province is to bring about natural events by easy means, and to keep up curiosity without the help of wonder: it is therefore precluded from the machines and expedients of the heroick romance, and can neither employ giants to snatch away a lady from the nuptial rites, nor knights to bring her back from captivity; it can neither bewilder its personages in deserts, nor lodge them in imaginary castles.

Such, Johnson would have us believe, were the themes and incidents of the older style of fiction. All the writer had to do was "let loose his invention, and heat his mind with incredibilities; a book was thus produced without fear of criticism, without the toil of study, without knowledge of nature, or acquaintance with life." Very different, in Johnson's opinion, was the equipment of the modern novelist. Besides "learning which is to be gained from books," he must have "experience which . . . must arise from general converse and accurate observation of the living world." His books will then be not merely "just copiers of human manners," but will also serve as "lectures of conduct, and introductions into life."

Perhaps Johnson was not altogether fair to the older style of fiction. Many novelists since the time of Sir Philip Sidney had been interested in providing "lectures of conduct," and many besides Defoe (whom Johnson seems to have overlooked) were acquainted with life. But one of the principal differences between the old and the new is made very clear in his emphasis upon "accidents that daily happen in the world." The men and women in the novels of Fielding—and Richardson—act "in such scenes of the universal drama as may be the lot of any other man" or woman. That is true of neither Sidney nor Defoe. A young man might imagine himself feeling like Sidney's Musidorus or acting like Robinson Crusoe, but he could never expect to share their experiences, as he might expect to share the experiences of Tom Jones. A young woman might well believe all that Moll Flanders reports had happened to her, but she could scarcely say of Moll, as she could say of Amelia or even of Clarissa, "there but for the grace of God go I."

But when Fielding, Richardson, and Johnson insisted that such accidents as "daily happen in the world" must be the staple of the new style of fiction, they were writing not at the beginning, but toward the end, of a critical tradition. The marvelous had long been losing esteem, and writers of romances in the previous century had been accustomed to discuss in their prefaces to what use historical incidents might be put. Thus Sir George Mackenzie, in the preface to his *Aretina* (1660), had censured those who have "stuffed their Books with things impracticable, which because they were above the reach of man's power, they should never have fallen within the circle of his observation"; and Robert Boyle took credit for having chosen an episode from history for his *Theodore* (1687), since:

True Examples do arm and fortify the mind far more efficaciously than Imaginary or Fictitious ones can do; and the fabulous labours of *Hercules*, and Exploits of *Arthur* of *Britain*, will never make men aspire to Heroick Vertue half so powerfully, as the real Examples of Courage and Gallantry afforded by *Jonathan*, *Caesar*, or the *Black Prince*.

These novelists were following in the steps of Georges de Scudéry, the most famous of the French romance writers, whose *Ibrahim* (1642) had been translated into English in 1652. In the preface to that work, Scudéry claimed that he had observed

the Manners, Customs, Religions, and Inclinations of People: and to give a more true resemblance to things, I have made the foundations of my work Historical, my principal Personages such as are marked out in the true History for illustrious persons.

Even though the practice of these writers did not always accord with their theory, it is easy to see how in time the desire for "a more true resemblance to things" could lead the author of *Robinson Crusoe* to declare that "the Editor believes the thing to be a just History of Fact; neither is there any Appearance of Fiction in it." The innocent deception of passing off fiction as history or biography is perpetrated on several title pages. Thus the reader is offered *The Life and Strange Surprising Adventures of Robinson Crusoe, of York, Mariner. Written by Himself* and *The Fortunes and Misfortunes of the Famous Moll Flanders. Who Was Born in Newgate, Was Twelve Year a Thief, Eight Year a Transported Felon in Virginia. Written from Her Memorandums.* Twenty years later the novelists were less concerned for the success of their deceptions. *Pamela. Or, Virtue Rewarded* (1740) is merely *A Narrative Which Has Its Foundations in Truth and Nature*, but the tradition of offering "a more true resemblance to things" is maintained in such titles as *The History of the Adventures of Joseph Andrews and of His Friend Mr. Abraham Adams* (1742); *Clarissa. Or, The History of a Young Lady* (1747–1748); and *The History of Tom Jones, a Foundling* (1749).

In choosing to let their novels pass as histories or biographies, these writers were aware of what they might adopt in structure and narrative technique from a well-established literary "kind," and it is not surprising that they should search for profitable analogies in other forms of narrative as well. It was certainly to be expected that they would have an eye to the epic in particular, since this was a form of paramount reputation and much critical thought had been given to the analysis of its constituent parts. Sidney had long ago declared that the *Theagenes and Chariclea* of Heliodorus was not prevented from exerting influence as a heroic poem though it was written in prose, and he had set an example when revising his *Arcadia* to make its structure conform more truly to epic principles. Scudéry again had emphasized what valuable lessons a novelist might learn from the epic, and possibly the most successful of modern epics, François Fénelon's *Les aventures de Télémaque*, had been written in prose. Thus, when Fielding told his readers that *Joseph Andrews* was to be regarded as "a comic epic poem in prose" and that, moreover, it was a "kind of writing which I do not remember to have seen hitherto attempted in our language," the novelty of his claim lay not so much in the notion of a prose epic, nor even of a comic epic poem—for this everyone recognized in Alexander Pope's *Dunciad*—but in a conflation of the two. The act of conflation required the spark of Fielding's genius, and the critical temper of the day was prepared to see such a spark fly.

II

FIELDING was well prepared for this new venture by his experience of men and books and by his previous career as a writer. Born near Glastonbury on 27 April 1707, he came of a family of small landowners in the West Country related to the earls of Denbigh. Among his immediate forebears were men who had risen to positions of some distinction in the learned professions. It might be suspected that the novelist derived his inclination toward the law from his mother's father, who was a justice of the Queen's Bench, and that to his paternal grandfather, an archdeacon of Salisbury, he owed both his love of learning and the strong bent toward Christian moral teaching that characterize his novels. Though we need not pay too much attention to such surmises nor inquire what traits of character were inherited from his somewhat feckless father, Lieutenant General Edmund Fielding, it is at least clear in what rank of society he was bred.

After a boyhood spent on his mother's Dorsetshire estates, Fielding joined his father in London. In 1728, at the age of twenty-one, he wrote his first play, *Love in Several Masques*, a comedy of manners. No doubt owing partly to the patronage of his cousin, Lady Mary Wortley Montagu, the play was performed at the Drury Lane Theatre, and ran for four nights. But though he was to lead a busy life as a dramatist and theater manager between 1730 and 1737, Fielding now decided not to pursue his moderate success but to enroll as a student in the Faculty of Letters at the University of Leiden under the redoubtable critic Peter Burmann. In later years he was to mock Burmann's editorial manner in the notes to his burlesque tragedy *Tom Thumb*, but it is probable that he now received his first instruction in critical theory and began to obtain his extensive knowledge of classical literature. Certainly he was later to own a remarkable library of classical and modern texts, and his novels show that he possessed what Dr. Johnson considered the primary equipment of the modern novelist: "learning which is to be gained from books."

At the age of thirty-five, when he began to write *Joseph Andrews*, Fielding had had sufficient opportunity to acquire the second item in Johnson's equipment, "experience which . . . must arise from general converse and accurate observation of the living world." If we did not know this from *Joseph Andrews* itself, we should know it from the plays written during the seven years following his return from Leiden in 1730 and from his journalistic essays. These serve to show something of the range

of that experience as well as to indicate how the experience might be used by the future novelist.

Writing for the stage had taught him how to manipulate dialogue and to devise speech rhythms for distinguishing a country squire from a man-about-town or a modish lady from a young miss. It had taught him to contrive a concatenation of incidents by which the principal characters are brought together in the final scene of play or novel for the unraveling of the knot. It seems also to have accustomed him to imagine some of his scenes in terms of a drawing room set on a stage of limited dimensions, and to offer in the novel scenes that experience told him would be effective in the theater. His plays abound in scenes where characters are interrupted by an unexpected entry that disturbs and perplexes their existing relationship. Thus in Act III of *The Temple Beau* (1730), an early play, young Wilding is pretending to make love to Lady Lucy Pedant and has just taken her in his arms when they are interrupted by the entry of her husband ("Hoity-toity? Hey-day! What's here to do? Have I caught you, gentlefolks. . . .") and, immediately after, of Wilding's father, who has lately discovered his son's deceptions. This use of the unexpected entry is more skillfully developed in *Tom Jones* (XV.5), in a scene where Lord Fellamar's unwanted attentions to Sophia in Lady Bellaston's house are interrupted by the entry of Squire Western, who has at last discovered where Sophia has taken refuge. Western is followed by Lady Bellaston, who joins him in representing to Sophia the advantages of agreeing to a proposal of marriage. Lord Fellamar, being assured that his suit was favored by Lady Bellaston and assuming that it must also be favored by Western, decides to take advantage of the new turn in the situation:

Coming up therefore to the squire, he said, "Though I have not the honour, sir, of being personally known to you; yet, as I find I have the happiness to have my proposals accepted, let me intercede, sir, in behalf of the young lady, that she may not be more solicited at this time."

"You intercede, sir!" said the squire; "why, who the devil are you?"

"Sir, I am Lord Fellamar," answered he, "and am the happy man, whom I hope you have done the honour of accepting for a son-in-law."

"You are the son of a b——," replied the squire, "for all

your laced coat. You my son-in-law, and be d——n'd to you!"

"I shall take more from you, sir, than from any man," answered the lord; "but I must inform you, that I am not used to hear such language without resentment."

"Resent my a——," quoth the squire. "Don't think I am afraid of such a fellow as thee art! because hast got a spit there dangling at thy side. Lay by your spit, and I'll give thee enough of meddling with what doth not belong to thee. I'll teach you to father-in-law me. I'll lick thy jacket."

"It's very well, sir," said my lord, "I shall make no disturbance before the ladies. I am very well satisfied. Your humble servant, sir; Lady Bellaston, your most obedient."[1]

There can be little doubt that in this episode Fielding has made use of his theatrical experience, as he has also done in scenes involving the use of stage properties, even though the number of these is meager. The most notable example in his plays is perhaps to be found in Act III of *The Letter Writers* (1731), where Mrs. Wisdom and her gallant Rakel are disturbed by the arrival of Mrs. Softly, and Rakel, wishing to protect Mrs. Wisdom's reputation, hides under the table. Mrs. Softly is followed by Mr. Wisdom and a nephew who, in a drunken fit, overturns the table and discovers Rakel. This is the prototype of more memorable discoveries: of Lady Bellaston discovering Mrs. Honour hiding behind the bed in Jones's room (XV.7), and of Jones discovering the philosopher Square behind a rug in Molly Seagrim's bedchamber (V.5). It is surprising that after his early experiment in *The Letter Writers*, Fielding should not have improved upon the device in a subsequent play. The hint was to be taken by Richard Brinsley Sheridan, who in *The School for Scandal* shows, in the scene of Sir Peter Teazle's discovery of his wife behind a screen in Joseph Surface's library, that he had learned something from each of the episodes in *Tom Jones*, for he there combined the embarrassment of Square's discovery and the reversal of fortune that sprang from Mrs. Honour's.

During his career as a dramatist, Fielding had attempted a considerable number of forms. He had written witty comedies of intrigue in the Restoration manner, farces, ballad operas with political im-

plications, burlesques, comedies reflecting upon modern manners, and satirical comedies on the pattern of the duke of Buckingham's *Rehearsal* (1671), in which an absurd play is rehearsed with comments from the author, a critical acquaintance, and the players. Two of the last of these, *Pasquin* (1736) and *The Historical Register* (1737), were among the most successful of his plays; and the device he there employed, accompanying the action with critical comment from the wings, may have suggested to him the "prolegomenous" chapters of *Tom Jones*, which, on a more serious level, serve the same purpose. Equally significant is his early experience of burlesque in *Tom Thumb* (1730) and *The Covent-Garden Tragedy* (1732) where, by burlesquing an old-fashioned "kind," he produced a new "kind," as it were, by mutation. Though the burlesque of epic is not so prominent in *Joseph Andrews* and its successors as the burlesque of tragedy in *Tom Thumb*, it is by a similar process of "mutation" that the novels arose.

Fielding's experience as a journalist was scarcely less useful to his future career than his experience in the theater. From 1739 to 1741 he was the leader of a group of writers responsible for conducting an opposition newspaper called *The Champion*. To this journal Fielding contributed a number of essays modeled on *The Spectator*. Just as Joseph Addison had invented a Spectator Club and had defined the persona of one member of the club who should write his lucubrations, aided and abetted by his fellow members, so Fielding assumed the persona of Captain Hercules Vinegar, whose business it was to write about the issues of the day, aided by his wife Joan and their two sons. Also like Addison he varied the form of his articles: now character sketches, now lay sermons or letters from imaginary correspondents, visions, critical papers, essays in installments, and Saturday papers on religious matters. These essays reveal a more serious-minded Fielding than one might suppose, judging from the plays alone. Here he is seen formulating his views on the moral problems that form the staple of his three novels and illustrating those problems by anecdotes and character sketches. He was also unwittingly practicing what was regarded as an important part of the novelist's duty. The novelist was expected to provide, in Johnson's phrase, "lectures of conduct." He was not merely to edify by the story he told, but to make sure that his

---

[1]Quotations are from the Everyman's Library edition of *Tom Jones* (London, 1963).

lesson was understood. Hence the pithy and summary comment upon manners, common both to the novelist and the essayist.

III

For much of his future work, Fielding was well prepared both in theory and in practice. It is not surprising, therefore, that from the beginning his command was assured, even though his approach was haphazard, even accidental. If it had not been for Richardson's *Pamela*, he might never have become a novelist. This story deals with a young woman's marriage outside her station in life. When a young man and a young woman of different social classes fell in love, it was generally assumed that their association could only be illegitimate. "Why, what is all this, my dear," says Sir Simon Darnford, one of Richardson's characters, to his wife, "but that our neighbour has a mind to his mother's waiting maid! And if he takes care she wants for nothing, I don't see any great injury will be done her. He hurts no *family* by this." And Parson Williams reports the opinion of Parson Peters that this was "too common and fashionable a case to be withstood by a private clergyman or two." What makes this particular case uncommon is that Pamela resists her would-be seducer, yet cannot help loving him in spite of his ill treatment; and that Mr. B. expects to be able to seduce Pamela, yet, in spite of favorable circumstances, is won by her behavior and, against the opinion of the world, offers her marriage.

Thus Pamela's virtue is rewarded. But though Richardson emphasizes that aspect of his story in his subtitle, there is much more to the novel. Had that been all, we might have expected that her virtue would be rewarded by marriage in the last chapter. But the ceremony takes place two-thirds of the way through, and yet we read on, since it is not merely Pamela's chastity but the integrity of her personality that is tested. She must also be shown preserving her humility, her thankfulness, her piety, and her intelligence in her new station. Hers is indeed a most difficult task. She is required to loathe Mr. B.'s behavior, yet to love him; to be content with her lowly position, yet to aspire to Mr. B.'s hand; to be humble, yet to reprobate aristocratic vice; to be meek, yet outspoken; to be simple, yet quick-witted; to be innocent, yet wide awake

and on her guard. It would seem almost impossible that Richardson should succeed in steering so intricate a path. But each incident is related with such careful attention to detail, Pamela's letters give so powerful a sense of immediacy, and Richardson himself preserves such an unhesitating belief in Pamela's word and in the truth of appearances, that he almost persuades us to believe too. Almost, but not quite. Many contemporaries were persuaded, but others saw that a different interpretation was possible. Among the latter was Fielding.

To convey this alternative interpretation, Fielding called upon his experience in burlesque and produced, pseudonymously, *An Apology for the Life of Mrs. Shamela Andrews. In Which, the Many Notorious Falshoods and Misrepresentations of a Book Called Pamela, Are Exposed and Refuted; and All the Matchless Arts of That Young Politician, Set in a True and Just Light. Together with a Full Account of All That Passed Between Her and Parson Arthur Williams; Whose Character is Represented in a Manner Something Different from That Which He Bears in Pamela. The Whole Being Exact Copies of Authentick Papers Delivered to the Editor.* It is a riotous travesty, in which Pamela is shown as a shameless and designing hussy, yet ready to talk for "a full Hour and a half, about my Vartue" or "of honourable Designs till Supper-time," and Mr. B.'s full name is discovered to be Booby. And just as the rehearsed plays in *Pasquin* and *The Historical Register* had been enclosed within a framework of commentary from the supposed author and his friend, so these authentic letters are sent by Parson Oliver, who knew the facts, to Parson Tickletext, who had taken *Pamela* at Richardson's valuation.

If any moral is to be drawn, it is that the distinction between being and seeming must be recognized. No exponent of the comedy of manners could fail to draw such a distinction, and Fielding's plays are especially rich in characters who are not what they seem, from Lady Gravely, the affected prude of *The Temple Beau*, to the false and grasping Valences of *The Fathers*. But Fielding had more than a professional dramatist's interest in unmasking appearances. He returned to the subject in an essay on the pursuit of reputation, published in *The Champion* on 4 March 1740. In it he showed that folly and vice "are continually industrious to disguise themselves," and wear the habits of virtue and wisdom, "which the world, always judging by the outside, easily suffers them to accomplish." The irony of *The Life of Mr. Jonathan Wild the Great* is sustained—tediously, it must be admitted—to prove that the Great Man, properly considered, is no better than a gangster.

The distinction between being and seeming is the guiding principle of *Joseph Andrews.* In the preface to his novel, Fielding explains that the ridiculous is his province, that the only source of the true ridiculous is affectation, and that affectation "proceeds from one of these two causes, Vanity or Hypocrisy." To display the ridiculous he has devised this new kind of writing, the comic epic poem in prose, observing the best epic practice in such matters as fable and characters. But whereas the epic fable is customarily grave and solemn, his will be light and ridiculous, and whereas epic characters are of the highest, his will mostly be of inferior rank and manners. The difficulty is to see how Fielding interprets the representation of the fable in action. Fortunately he is more explicit in the preface he wrote for his sister's novel, *David Simple* (1744). There, after referring to his preface to *Joseph Andrews*, he mentions the two great originals of all epic writing, the *Iliad* and the *Odyssey*, which

differ principally in the action, which in the *Iliad* is entire and uniform; in the *Odyssey*, is rather a series of actions, all tending to produce one great end.

The followers of Homer have observed this principal difference, whether their imitations were serious or comic. And so we see that just as Pope in *The Dunciad* fixed on one action, Samuel Butler and Miguel de Cervantes fixed on a series. Fielding's sister's work belongs to the latter category: "The fable consists of a series of separate adventures, detached from and independent of each other, yet all tending to one great end."

The same may be seen in *Joseph Andrews.* It too is an Odyssean epic, "consisting of a series of separate adventures, detached from and independent of each other, yet all tending to one great end." And it may be observed that just as the *Odyssey* relates the adventures of Odysseus in finding his way home and the hardships that befell him after incurring the wrath of Poseidon, so Fielding relates the adventures of Joseph Andrews and Parson Adams in finding their way home and the hardships that befell them after Joseph had incurred the wrath of Lady Booby. Perhaps contemporary readers might have noticed an even closer application of the

burlesque. The critic Andrew Ramsay had pointed out that in Fénelon's *Aventures de Télémaque* it is the hatred of Venus, rather than the wrath of Poseidon, that supplies the cause of the action, and in his *La Vie de Fénelon* that "the Hatred of *Venus* against a young Prince, that despises Pleasure for the Sake of Virtue, and subdues his Passions by the Assistance of Wisdom, is a Fable drawn from Nature, and at the same Time includes the sublimest Morality." No reader could fail to relish the notion of the lascivious Lady Booby in the role of Venus, whose desire for her handsome footman Joseph Andrews is turned to hatred when that young prince despises pleasure for the sake of virtue, and subdues his passions with the assistance of his sister Pamela's wisdom.

But what is the great end to which all the separate adventures are tending? Why, surely, the display of the ridiculous, of those affectations that arise from vanity and hypocrisy. This is the characteristic common to Lady Booby, Mrs. Slipslop, and Mrs. Grave-airs, all of them women who pretend to more modesty, more learning, or more gentility than they possess. And this is the characteristic of the innkeepers and their wives who can make a show of human kindness once they are satisfied of the standing of their guests, of the soldiers who pretend to valor, of the justices who pretend to a knowledge of the law, and of the parsons who pretend to godliness. Even Parson Trulliber can make a show of Methodism, when he is satisfied that Adams has not come to buy his pigs: "Get out of my doors," he cries, when Adams tells him that, in addition to faith, he must perform the good works of giving to the needy. "Fellow, dost thou speak against faith in my house? I will no longer remain under the same roof with a wretch who speaks wantonly of faith and the Scriptures."

The two interpolated stories fall into place in this pattern. The unfortunate jilt is a story of pretense to affection, and the story of Mr. Wilson is a tale of the pretenses practiced in London life. Vanity of vanities is Mr. Wilson's theme as he recalls his experiences of life in the Temple among smart fellows who drank with lords they did not know and intrigued with women they never saw, and of town coquettes animated solely by vanity who sometimes have a whim to affect wisdom, wit, good nature, politeness, and health, but are also affected to put on ugliness, folly, nonsense, ill nature, ill breeding, and sickness in their turns.

Such are Mr. Wilson's reflections. Far from being an idle digression, they are highly appropriate to Fielding's scheme and purpose; for his action, by confining him to the high road and the inn, precludes him from commenting upon London life; it is a sample of London society that Mr. Wilson's story exposes.

But these at worst are transient characters, and at best they are minor. What of Parson Adams himself? He too has his vanities—innocent vanities, indeed—his learning and his power as a preacher. His role is that of a modern Don Quixote, a man of good sense, good parts, and good nature, as Fielding declares, but "as entirely ignorant of the ways of this world as an infant just entered into it could possibly be." His book reading did not, like his illustrious prototype's, lead him to mistake windmills for giants or inns for castles; it led him instead to expect on every hand an honest, undesigning, Christian behavior. He is therefore constantly the victim of deceit. But he never loses our affection, partly because his expectations are noble and partly because (like Don Quixote) he hurls himself upon the oppressor, thinking only of the blows his fists or his crabstick will deliver, and nothing of those he will receive. It is not merely in such episodes as the fight at the inn, which interrupts the story of the unfortunate jilt, or the "roasting" of Adams by the fox-hunting squire (which recalls the treatment of Don Quixote at the hands of the duke and duchess), or the midnight tussle with Mrs. Slipslop, in which Adams believes himself bewitched, that the reader recognizes the justice of the assertion on the title page of *Joseph Andrews* that it is "Written in Imitation of the Manner of Cervantes."

But there are two sides to the relationship of being and seeming. While most of the men and women in *Joseph Andrews* are worse than they seem, others are better. And though the bedraggled appearance of the worthy Adams is the most prominent example, Fielding asks us to notice that the man who lends all but sixpence of the sum needed to pay the stranded travelers' bill is not the wealthy Parson Trulliber but "a fellow who had been formerly a drummer in an Irish regiment, and now travelled the country as a pedlar"; that when Joseph lies sick at the Tow-wouses' inn, it is not the surgeon or the parson or the innkeeper who looks after him, but Betty the chambermaid, whose morals are no better than they should be; and that when Joseph has been found wounded and naked in a ditch, it is not any of the fine ladies in a passing coach who takes pity on him, but the postilion:

(a lad who hath been since transported for robbing a hen-roost), [who] voluntarily stript off a greatcoat, his only garment, at the same time swearing a great oath (for which he was rebuked by the passengers), "that he would rather ride in his shirt all his life than suffer a fellow-creature to lie in so miserable a condition."[2]

To some extent this anatomy of the ridiculous is a counterblast to *Pamela*, and by recalling certain incidents in that novel and introducing one or two of its characters, Fielding made sure that we should keep *Pamela* in view. Richardson had placed an implicit trust in the truth of appearances. But that way lies self-deception. It is only by the most careful scrutiny that we can see beneath appearances and find the true springs of human action.

IV

YET appearances are important too. "It is not enough," Fielding writes, "that your designs, nay that your actions, are intrinsically good; you must take care that they shall appear so"; for "prudence and circumspection are necessary even to the best of men." The passage occurs in one of those chapters of *Tom Jones* (III.7) "in which the author himself makes his appearance on the stage," and it is close to the heart of the novel. The theme is in fact announced in similar terms in the dedication:

I have endeavoured strongly to inculcate, that virtue and innocence can scarce ever be injured but by indiscretion; and . . . it is this alone which often betrays them into the snares which deceit and villainy spread for them.

To illustrate this idea, Fielding chose a hero as typical of his own order of society as the epic hero was of his. We are asked to recognize that Tom, in spite of some lack of prudence and circumspection, and in spite of some contraventions of the moral code, is essentially a good man. It might be said of Tom, as Ramsay had said of Fénelon's Telemachus: "Our Poet does not lift *Telemachus* above Humanity; he makes him fall into such Weaknesses, as are

---

[2]Quotations are from the Everyman's Library edition of *Joseph Andrews* (London, 1962).

compatible with a sincere Love of Virtue." Young Mr. Blifil, on the other hand, with whom Tom is brought up in Mr. Allworthy's household, has more than enough of prudence and circumspection, but his love of virtue is on a par with the affectations that Fielding exposed in *Joseph Andrews*. The distinction is one that Sheridan was to make familiar when he contrasted the brothers Charles and Joseph Surface in *The School for Scandal.*

The best critical theory of the day stated that an epic should have a beginning, a middle, and an end; that the beginning should deal with the causes of the action; and that in the causes might be observed two opposite "designs," the hero's and the design of those who opposed him. In adopting these sensible precepts, Fielding provided an introductory section of six books in which numerous incidents open Tom's character and reveal the designs of Blifil and his two tutors, Thwackum and Square, who sought to prejudice Tom in the eyes of Mr. Allworthy and to prevent him from marrying Sophia and inheriting Squire Western's estate. Tom is shown (IV.6) to have "somewhat about him, which, though I think writers are not thoroughly agreed in its name" (the third earl of Shaftesbury had called it the "moral sense")

. . . doth certainly inhabit some human breasts; whose use is not so properly to distinguish right from wrong, as to prompt and incite them to the former, and to restrain and withhold them from the latter. . . . Though he did not always act rightly, yet he never did otherwise without feeling and suffering for it.

Thus the boy is incited to sell the little horse that Mr. Allworthy had given him so as to prevent the family of a dismissed servant from starving, and he is prompted to risk his neck in recovering Sophia's pet bird, which Blifil had maliciously allowed to escape. And if he is prompted to fornication with the gamekeeper's daughter, he is prepared to deal honorably with her until he discovers that he was not the first to seduce her; and if he was drunk and disorderly in Mr. Allworthy's house, it was because he had already been thrown into an "immoderate excess of rapture" on hearing that Mr. Allworthy was recovering from his dangerous illness. Allworthy summarizes (V.7) what Fielding wishes us to think of Tom when he says to him on his sickbed: "I am convinced, my child, that you have much goodness, generosity, and honour, in your temper: if you will add prudence and religion to these, you must be happy."

But in spite of his conviction, Allworthy allows his mind to be poisoned by the malicious insinuations of Blifil and turns Tom out of his house and into a series of adventures on the high road, corresponding to those of Joseph Andrews and Parson Adams. They fill the second six books of the novel and correspond, in epic terms, to "the Shipping off of *Aeneas*, his Voyages, his Battels, and all the Obstacles he met with," which (in the words of René Le Bossu, the chief authority on epic structure at that time) "compose a just Middle; [for] they are a Consequence of the Destruction of Troy . . . and these same Incidents require an End."

The high road leads to London, and on it are not only Tom and Partridge (his Sancho Panza) but also Sophia, who has fled from her father's house to escape being forced into marriage with Blifil. As in *Joseph Andrews*, the high road and the inn provide a suitable scene for the testing of character, the recognition of bad nature masquerading as good, and of good nature concealed or tainted by imprudence. Tom has something to learn even from the Man of the Hill, who, like Mr. Wilson and like many a character in epic, is permitted to interrupt the narrative with his story. The Man of the Hill provides further instances of imprudence, in particular of incautiousness in placing his affections, as a result of which he had become a misanthrope and a hermit. But, as Tom permits himself to comment (VIII.15), "What better could be expected in love derived from the stews, or in friendship first produced and nourished at the gaming table?" One must not think evil of the rest of mankind on that account, for, as Tom continues, enunciating Fielding's doctrines of the good-natured man and the deceptiveness of appearances:

If there was, indeed, much more wickedness in the world than there is, it would not prove such general assertions against human nature, since much of this arrives by mere accident, and many a man who commits evil is not totally bad and corrupt in his heart.

(VIII.15)

Sophia is learning as much as Tom, directly in such scenes as that at the inn at Upton, and by proxy as she listens to Mrs. Fitzpatrick's cautionary tale of her imprudent marriage, which is interrupted by appeals to Sophia to declare how she would have acted in like circumstances.

The lovers reach London independently, and the

final section of six further books begins. Tom's good nature is as clear as ever, notably in his generous treatment of the highwayman who is driven by penury to attack him and in his chivalrous championship of Mrs. Miller's daughter. His imprudence is clearer still in "the ignominious circumstance of being kept" by Lady Bellaston. Fielding never asks his readers to overlook Tom's misdemeanors. His worst offense is most severely punished, for his relations with Lady Bellaston cannot be forgiven by Sophia. We see him at the end of the sixteenth book at the nadir of his fortunes, rejected by Sophia, dismissed from Allworthy's favor, and imprisoned on a charge of murdering his opponent in a duel. "Such," Fielding muses (XVII.1), "are the calamities in which he is at present involved, owing to his imprudence . . . that we almost despair of bringing him to any good; and if our reader delights in seeing executions, I think he ought not to lose any time in taking a first row at Tyburn."

Readers of the epic will recognize that the time is ripe for a discovery or a reversal of fortune, perhaps even for both, and they will recall that it was not unusual for the author to invoke divine aid for rescuing a hero in distress. Fielding has prepared both for his discovery—that was allowed for in making Tom a foundling—and for his reversal of fortune, but he disdains to employ the marvelous. It is true that luck is on Tom's side when his victim in the duel recovers from his wound and when the facts of his parentage (concealed by Blifil) are discovered, but in other respects the reader is asked to recognize that Tom has worked his passage. He has cast his bread upon the waters in acts of abundant good nature, and by the assistance of Mrs. Miller's representations to Mr. Allworthy, he finds it after many days. His virtue is rewarded by restoration into the favor of Allworthy and the good graces of Sophia. Since he is now discovered to be Allworthy's nephew and heir, Squire Western has no further objections to bestowing his daughter upon him; they marry and "preserve the purest and tenderest affection for each other, an affection daily increased and confirmed by mutual endearments and mutual esteem."

This is a pious hope that the reader may find it difficult to share, for it rests upon the assumption that Tom has ceased to be indiscreet. He is at best a good-natured man, and though endowed with a well-developed moral sense, he must, on Allworthy's evidence, add religion as well as prudence to his good nature. Even if we allow that he has become prudent, there is nothing to show that he has become religious.

Some such reflections seem to have occurred to Fielding, for his next novel, *Amelia* (1751), begins where *Tom Jones* leaves off. Captain and Mrs. Booth also entertain the purest and tenderest affection for each other and confirm it by mutual endearments and mutual esteem, yet various accidents befall them, owing partly to Booth's character, and it is with these accidents and with their effect upon this worthy couple that the novel is concerned.

V

THE decision to deal with the accidents of domestic life set Fielding some new problems in structure. The high road and the inn could have no place here, since married folk are not usually nomadic. Consequently we miss the Odyssean-Quixotic episodes that in the earlier novels provided him with so many shining opportunities for unmasking affectation and testing character. He had also to decide how to relate the earlier history of his couple, a problem he had not been required to face before. But the comic adaptation of epic conventions was available here, as it had been at the beginning of *Joseph Andrews.* Just as Aeneas was stranded on the coast of Carthage, was succored there by Dido, related to her his story, and consummated his furtive love in a cave; so Captain Booth was stranded in Newgate Prison, was succored there by Miss Matthews, a high-class courtesan, related to her his story, and consummated his furtive love in a superior kind of cell. Nor is this merely an ingenious piece of burlesque. Booth's misdemeanor with Miss Matthews, which he is ashamed to confess to Amelia, dogs him throughout the novel, and the somberness of the opening scenes in Newgate sets the tone of the book. Fielding takes care to show us the squalor and oppression that were the lot of the penniless prisoner and the relative comfort to be had at the price of a bribe. He also describes the coarse and depraved ruffians, male and female, the tricksters and sharpers, who molest and prey upon the weak, the unfortunate, and even the innocent who have come there through a miscarriage of justice.

This is the scene in which we first discover Booth, whose previous history shows him to be imprudent, liable to deception, with "very slight and uncertain" notions of religion, yet essentially good-natured. He will not return to Newgate, but he will always be in danger of return. And when he escapes, the reader recognizes that Newgate was only a somewhat more lurid epitome of society outside, where merit counts for nothing, where civil and military places go by influence exerted for a bribe, where those in high places have rogues, pimps, and bawds in their pay, and where gallantry is a cover for fornication and adultery. Fielding had said as much in his play *The Modern Husband* (1731), and had repeated it in *Jonathan Wild*. And if *Joseph Andrews* and *Tom Jones* appear lighter in tone than *Amelia*, it is only because the scene is laid more frequently in the country. London is the breeding place for such creatures as Lord Fellamar and Lady Bellaston, and Mr. Wilson anticipated Booth in finding that in London "poverty and distress, with their horrid train of duns, attorneys, bailiffs, haunted me day and night. My clothes grew shabby, my credit bad, my friends and acquaintance of all kinds cold."

The scene is in fact so somber that a tragic conclusion seems inevitable. Even a stronger and a better man than Booth could scarcely escape that fate. In considering the conclusion to which he was leading his "worthy couple," Fielding is likely to have paid attention to the best critical teaching available. The consensus among commentators upon the epic pointed to a conclusion favorable to the hero. But Le Bossu could discover no reason why that should be so:

"Yet if any heed be given to Authority," he concluded, "I do not know any one Instance of a Poet, who finishes his Piece with the Misfortunes of his Heroe. . . . The *Epick Poem's* Action is of a larger Extent than that of the Theatre; [and] it would perhaps be less satisfactory to the Reader, if, after so much Pains and so long Troubles with which this kind of Poem is always fill'd, it should at last bring them to a doleful and unhappy End."

(Traité du poème épique)

The easiest way of bringing the Booths to a happy end might well have been to repeat the formula of *Tom Jones* and show the eventual reward of the hero's virtuous actions. But Fielding seems to have been no longer content with such teaching. It was Booth's mistake to believe that since men "act entirely from their passions, their actions can have neither merit or demerit." If a man's ruling passion happened to be benevolence, he would relieve the distress of others, but if it were avarice, ambition, or pride, other men's miseries would have no effect upon him. Booth is eventually corrected of an error, which to Amelia seems little better than atheism, by reading a volume of Isaac Barrow's sermons while detained in the bailiff's house, but in the meanwhile Fielding allows him little opportunity for charity. The reader notices instead how his imprudence in the use of what little money he has reduces Amelia to penury and how his ill-placed trust and his single act of fornication endanger her chastity. She, on the other hand, shows herself to be on all occasions a model of wifely prudence, constancy, obedience, forgiveness, and love.

"To retrieve the ill consequences of a foolish conduct, and by struggling manfully with distress to subdue it, is one of the noblest efforts of wisdom and virtue." That is all that Fielding asks of his worthy couple, and having displayed their struggles, he is not averse to rescuing them by an epic discovery (that Amelia is an heiress) and an epic reversal of fortune, which enables a now prudent and Christian Booth to retire to a country estate.

In *Amelia*, as in *Tom Jones*, Fielding implies that at the end of the book the hero is in some respects an altered man without persuading us of the fact. Charles Dickens was the first novelist to succeed in such persuasion and George Eliot the first to specialize in showing the modifying effect of incident upon character. These Victorian successes have made demands that the modern reader is inclined to impose upon earlier novelists and earlier dramatists without perhaps reflecting whether changes in character are necessary or always important. *Amelia*, like *Tom Jones*, deals with wider issues than the modification of character. It has to do not merely with Booth and his wife but also with miseries and distresses typical of mid-eighteenth-century London life. No other novel provides such a wide panorama of London society or better conveys what it was like to live in London in the 1750's.

VI

In a paper that he wrote for the last of his periodicals, *The Covent Garden Journal* (28 January 1752), Fielding declared that he would not trouble the world with any more novels. He had not been entirely committed to the profession of letters since the abrupt termination of his career as a dramatist. The severity of his attack upon Walpole's government in *Pasquin* had led directly to the Licensing Act of 1737 and to the closure of all theaters but Drury Lane and Covent Garden. Fielding's Little Theatre in the Haymarket was the principal victim, and his chief source of income was thus removed. He thereupon began a serious study of the law, was called to the bar in 1740, and practiced for some time on the Western Circuit. Shortly after completing *Tom Jones* in 1748 and before its publication, he had been appointed a police court magistrate at Bow Street, and his jurisdiction was soon extended to the whole of the county of Middlesex. He was also appointed justice of the peace for Westminster in the same year. As a magistrate he was exceptionally industrious and did much to break up the gangs of thieves that infested London. His *Enquiry into the Causes of the Late Increase of Robbers* (1751), dedicated to the lord chancellor, the earl of Hardwicke, shows both an extensive knowledge of the law and an intimate acquaintance with the evil and its origin. His energies might have been directed more and more to clearing up the criminal underworld if his health had not broken down. In the summer of 1754, he undertook a sea trip to Lisbon with his wife and daughter in a desperate search for health, and whiled away his time in keeping a diary. This he revised, and the manuscript was posthumously published as *The Journal of a Voyage to Lisbon* (1755). Not the least of its merits is the picture it gives us of the man himself, affectionately considerate to his family, patiently suffering from an incurable disease, yet observing with undiminished zest the oddities of human behavior and seizing such opportunities as incidents offered for social or political comment. The book is prefaced by a disquisition on travel literature comparable in kind with the disquisition on the comic epic poem in prose that prefaces *Joseph Andrews*. Once again Fielding declares that he is laying down the rules for a kind of writing that had not been properly undertaken before (except by Lord George Anson in the published account of his circumnavigation, 1740–1744), for travelers seem to have fallen either into the fault of "filling their pages with monsters which nobody hath ever seen, and with adventures which never have, nor could possi-

bly have happened to them," or, on the other hand, they

waste their time and paper with recording things and facts of so common a kind, that they challenge no other right of being remembered than as they had the honour of having happened to the author.[3]

This opportunity of reforming travel literature was as haphazard as the chance Fielding took of reforming the novel, but even if he had lived longer—he died at Lisbon on 8 October 1754, at the age of forty-seven—it was not likely that he would have had occasion to write more in this kind. It is easy, however, to see that his theories might have been profitably applied to biography and that he was well equipped by imagination, a reverence for truth, judgment, and a sense of proportion to succeed in that kindred form.

But this is idle speculation. Even though Fielding may have felt that he had outgrown the novel, it is there that his achievement lies, and it is an achievement typical of an age that relished the mock epics of Pope and the ballad operas of John Gay. Like those poets, Fielding brought literary experience gained in other writing and a wealth of critical learning to bear upon the production of a new form, but a form that constantly recalls older, well-tried forms and adapts them to the spirit and use of his own times. He showed himself, in Johnson's words, one of those "just copiers of human manners," who could offer "lectures of conduct and introductions into life."

SELECTED BIBLIOGRAPHY

I. COLLECTED WORKS. A. Murphy, ed., *The Works*, 4 vols. (London, 1762); *The Dramatic Works*, 4 vols. (London, 1783); A. Chalmers, ed., *The Works*, 10 vols. (London, 1806); Sir W. Scott, ed., *The Novels*, 10 vols. (London, 1821); T. Roscoe, ed., *The Novels* (London, 1831–1832); T. Roscoe, ed., *The Works* (London, 1840); L. Stephen, ed., *The Works*, 10 vols. (London, 1893); G. Saintsbury, ed., *The Works*, 12 vols. (London, 1893); E. Gosse, ed., *The Works*, 12 vols. (London, 1899); W. E. Henley et al., eds., *The Complete Works*, 16 vols. (London, 1903); *Fielding's Novels*, 10 vols. (Oxford, 1926). A new collected ed. is being published by the Wesleyan

[3]Quotation from the Everyman's Library edition of *The Journal of a Voyage to Lisbon* (New York-London, 1932).

University Press and the Oxford University Press. The first vol. to appear is M. C. Battestin, ed., *Joseph Andrews* (London–Middletown, Conn., 1967); H. K. Miller, ed., *Miscellanies* (London, 1972); F. Bowers, ed., *Tom Jones* (London, 1975); W. B. Coley, ed., *The Jacobite Journal and Related Writings* (London, 1975).

II. SELECTED WORKS. H. Fielding, *Miscellanies*, 3 vols. (London, 1743), vol. I: poems and essays, vol. II: *A Journey from This World to the Next* and plays, vol. III: *The Life of Mr. Jonathan Wild the Great*; H. Fielding, *The Beauties of Fielding* (London, 1782); J. P. Browne, ed., *Miscellanies and Poems* (London, 1872); G. H. Geroulde, ed., *Selected Essays* (New York, 1905); G. Saintsbury, ed., *Fielding* (London, 1909); L. Rice-Oxley, ed., *Fielding* (Oxford, 1923).

III. SEPARATE WORKS. *Love in Several Masques, a Comedy* (London, 1728); *The Temple Beau, a Comedy* (London, 1730); *The Author's Farce* (London, 1730); *Tom Thumb, a Tragedy* (London, 1730), rev. ed., with annotations, titled *The Tragedy of Tragedies; or, The Life and Death of Tom Thumb the Great* (London, 1731), both texts repr. in J. T. Hillhouse, ed. (New Haven, Conn., 1918); *Rape upon Rape; or, The Justice Caught in His Own Trap, a Comedy* (London, 1730); *The Letter-Writers: or, A New Way to Keep a Wife at Home, a Farce* (London, 1731); *The Welsh Opera: or, The Grey Mare the Better Horse* (London, 1731), drama; *The Lottery, a Farce* (London, 1732); *The Modern Husband, a Comedy* (London, 1732); *The Old Debauchees, a Comedy* (London, 1732); *The Covent-Garden Tragedy* (London, 1732); *The Mock Doctor; or, The Dumb Lady Cur'd. A Comedy, Done from Molière* (London, 1732); *The Miser. A Comedy, Taken from Plautus and Molière* (London, 1733); *The Intriguing Chambermaid, a Comedy* (London, 1734); *Don Quixote in England, a Comedy* (London, 1734), contains the famous songs "When Mighty Roast Beef Was the Englishman's Food" and "The Dusky Night Rides Down the Sky"; *An Old Man Taught Wisdom: or, The Virgin Unmask'd, a Farce* (London, 1735); *The Universal Gallant: or, The Different Husbands, a Comedy* (London, 1735); *Pasquin, a Dramatick Satire upon the Times* (London, 1736); *Tumble-down Dick: or, Phaeton in the Suds. A Dramatick Entertainment* (London, 1736); *Eurydice, a Farce* (London, 1737); *The Historical Register for the Year 1736* (London, 1737), drama, also contains *Eurydice Hiss'd*, "a very merry Tragedy."

The Champion (15 November 1739–19 June 1740), 2 vols. (London, 1741), essays, also edited by S. J. Sackett as *The Voyages of Mr. Job Vinegar* (Los Angeles, 1958); *Of True Greatness* (London, 1741), poem; *The Vernoniad* (London, 1741), poem; *An Apology for the Life of Mrs. Shamela Andrews* (London, 1741), repr. with essays by R. B. Johnson, ed. (London, 1926), also in B. W. Downs, ed. (London, 1930), S. W. Baker, Jr., ed. (Berkeley, Calif., 1953), and I. Watt, ed. (Los Angeles, 1956), the

Watt ed. being considered the most reliable; *The Crisis, a Sermon* (London, 1741); *The History of the Adventures of Joseph Andrews and of His Friend Mr. Abraham Adams*, 2 vols. (London, 1742), repr. in the World's Classics ed. with preface by L. Rice-Oxley (London, 1919), J. P. de Castro, ed. (London, 1929), Everyman's Library ed. with preface by A. R. Humphreys (London, 1962), and M. C. Battestin, ed. (London, 1965), the last being annotated and including *Shamela*; *Miss Lucy in Town, a Farce* (London, 1742); *Plutus, the God of Riches. A Comedy, Translated from the Original Greek of Aristophanes* (London, 1742); *Some Papers Proper to be Read Before the Royal Society* (London, 1743), satirical pamphlets; *The Wedding-Day, a Comedy* (London, 1743); *The Life of Mr. Jonathan Wild the Great* (London, 1743; new ed., with corrections and additions, 1754), also in the World's Classics ed., text of 1743 with variants of 1754 in appendix (London, 1951), first published in *Miscellanies*; *A Serious Address to the People of Great Britain* (London, 1745), political tract; *A Dialogue Between the Devil, the Pope, and the Pretender* (London, 1745), political tract; *The True Patriot* (5 November 1745–17 June 1746), essays; *Ovid's Art of Love Paraphrased* (London, 1747), reiss. as *The Lover's Assistant* (London, 1959), also in C. E. Jones, ed. (Los Angeles, 1961), a prose travesty; *The Jacobite's Journal* (5 December 1747–5 November 1748), essays; *The History of Tom Jones, a Foundling*, 6 vols. (London, 1749), repr. in Everyman's Library ed., with intro. by A. R. Humphreys, 2 vols. (London, 1963), R. P. C. Nutter, ed. (London, 1966), the last being considered the best annotated ed.; *A Charge Delivered to the Grand Jury* (London, 1749), legal work; *A True State of the Case of Bosavern Penlez* (London, 1749), legal work.

An Enquiry into the Causes of the Late Increase of Robbers (London, 1751), legal work; *Amelia*, 4 vols. (London, 1752), also in Everyman's Library ed., with intro. by A. R. Humphreys (London, 1962), Fielding's revised text first published in Murphy's ed. of *The Works*; *A Plan of the Universal Register Office* (London, 1752), essay; *Examples of the Interposition of Providence in the Detection and Punishment of Murder* (London, 1752), treatise; *A Proposal for Making an Effectual Provision for the Poor* (London, 1753), essay; *A Clear State of the Case of Elizabeth Canning* (London, 1753), legal work; *The Journal of a Voyage to Lisbon* (London, 1755), also in A. Dobson, ed. (London, 1892; 1907), J. H. Lobban, ed. (London, 1913), and H. E. Pagliaro, ed. (New York, 1963), a full ed. published in 1755 and suppressed, also repr. with *Jonathan Wild* in Everyman's Library (London–New York, 1932); *The Father's; or, The Good-Natur'd Man, a Comedy* (London, 1778); E. L. McAdam, "A New Letter from Fielding," in *Yale Review*, 28 (1949).

IV. BIOGRAPHICAL AND CRITICAL STUDIES. W. C. Hazlitt, *Lectures on the English Comic Writers* (London, 1819); Sir W. Scott, *Lives of the Novelists* (London, 1825); W. M. Thackeray, *The English Humourists of the Eighteenth Cen-*

tury (London, 1853); A. Dobson, *Fielding* (London, 1883), and *Eighteenth Century Vignettes* (1st ser., London, 1892; 2nd ser., 1896); Sir W. A. Raleigh, *The English Novel* (London, 1894); G. M. Godden, *Henry Fielding: A Memoir* (London, 1910); W. L. Cross, *The History of Henry Fielding*, 3 vols. (New Haven, Conn., 1910), the standard biography, with a valuable bibliography; A. Digeon, *Les Romans de Fielding* (Paris, 1923), also an English translation (London, 1925); F. T. Blanchard, *Fielding the Novelist* (New Haven, Conn., 1926), a study of Fielding's reputation; F. W. Bateson, *English Comic Drama 1700–50* (Oxford, 1929); E. M. Thornbury, *Henry Fielding's Theory of the Comic Prose Epic* (Madison, Wis., 1931); F. O. Bissell, *Fielding's Theory of the Novel* (Ithaca, N.Y., 1933); B. M. Jones, *Henry Fielding, Novelist and Magistrate* (London, 1933); G. Sherborn, "Fielding's *Amelia*: An Interpretation," in *Journal of English Literary History*, 3 (1936), an outstanding essay; K. C. Slagle, *The English Country Squire as Depicted in English Prose Fiction from 1740 to 1800* (Philadelphia, 1938).

W. R. Irwin, *The Making of Jonathan Wild* (New York, 1941); B. Willey, *The Eighteenth Century Background* (London, 1946); M. P. Willcocks, *A True Born Englishman: Being the Life of Henry Fielding* (London, 1947); E. Jenkins, *Henry Fielding* (London, 1947); J. A. Work, ed., "Henry Fielding, Christian Censor," in F. W. Hilles, ed., *The Age of Johnson: Essays Presented to Chauncey Brewster Tinker* (New Haven, Conn., 1949); F. H. Dudden, *Henry Fielding: His Life, Works, and Times*, 2 vols. (Oxford, 1952), useful on the social background; R. S. Crane, "The Concept of Plot and the Plot of *Tom Jones*," in Crane's *Critics and Criticism Ancient and Modern* (Chicago, 1952); A. R. Humphreys, *The Augustan World* (London, 1954); J. M. Murry, *Unprofessional Essays* (London, 1956), contains a masterly defense of Fielding against some modern denigrations; A. D. McKillop, *The Early Masters of English Fiction* (Lawrence, Kans., 1956); I. Watt, *The Rise of the Novel* (London, 1957); W. Empson, "Tom Jones," in *Kenyon Review*, 20 (1958); M. C. Battestin, *The Moral Basis of Fielding's Art: A Study of Joseph Andrews* (Middletown, Conn., 1959; repr., 1964); J. Loftis, *Comedy and Society from Congreve to Fielding* (Stanford, Calif., 1959).

W. C. Booth, *The Rhetoric of Fiction* (Chicago, 1961); M. Johnson, ed., *Fielding's Art of Fiction: Eleven Essays on "Shamela," "Joseph Andrews," and "Amelia"* (Philadelphia, 1961); H. K. Miller, *Essays on Fielding's Miscellanies* (Princeton, N.J., 1961); R. Paulson, ed., *Fielding: A Collection of Critical Essays* (Englewood Cliffs, N.J., 1962), an intro. followed by thirteen essays by modern critics, including those by Sherburn, Murry, and Empson mentioned above; S. Sacks, *Fiction and the Shape of Belief: A Study of Fielding* (Berkeley, Calif., 1964); A. E. Dyson, *The Crazy Fabric* (London, 1965); I. Ehrenpreis, *Fielding: Tom Jones* (London, 1965); A. Wright, *Henry Fielding: Mask and Feast* (London–Berkeley, Calif., 1965); R. D. Spector, ed., *Essays on the Eighteenth-Century Novel* (London, 1965); M. Golden, *Fielding's Moral Psychology* (Amherst, Mass., 1966); J. Preston, "The Ironic Mode: A Comparison of 'Jonathan Wild' and 'The Beggar's Opera,'" in *Essays in Criticism*, 16 (1966); M. Irwin, *Henry Fielding: The Tentative Realist* (Oxford, 1967); G. R. Levine, *Henry Fielding and The Dry Mock: A Study of the Techniques of Irony in His Early Works* (The Hague, 1967); R. Alter, *Fielding and the Nature of the Novel* (Cambridge, Mass., 1968); M. C. Battestin, ed., *Tom Jones: A Collection of Critical Essays* (Englewood Cliffs, N.J., 1968); G. W. Hatfield, *Henry Fielding and the Language of Irony* (Chicago, 1968); R. Paulson and T. Lockwood, eds., *Fielding: The Critical Heritage* (London, 1968); C. J. Rawson, *Henry Fielding* (London, 1968), contains short bibliography; H. Goldberg, *The Art of Joseph Andrews* (Chicago–London, 1969); J. Compton, ed., *Henry Fielding's "Tom Jones": A Casebook* (London, 1970); C. J. Rawson, *Henry Fielding and the Augustan Ideal Under Stress* (London, 1972).

SAMUEL JOHNSON
(1709-1784)

S. C. Roberts

I

"SAMUEL JOHNSON is more vivid to us in a book written by another man than in any of the books that he wrote himself." Such is the penalty of being the subject of the greatest biography in the language, with the further result that many readers tend to separate Johnson the writer from Johnson the man as displayed by James Boswell.

Fundamentally, the distinction is unsound. It was Johnson's writings that first attracted Boswell, and if the reader wishes to recapture the Boswellian aura, he must do as Boswell did and study the works of the man who became known as the Great Moralist and the Great Lexicographer while Boswell was still a schoolboy. This simple chronological reminder is the best critical antidote to the ancient fallacy that Johnson was made by Boswell. Of course, Boswell's ultimate triumph in "Johnsonizing the land" was supreme. But the old view that "it was the object of Boswell's life to connect his own name with that of Johnson" contains little more than a dangerous half-truth. Boswell wished his name to be associated with many other famous names besides that of Johnson, and his wish was fulfilled. But among all his schemes for the attainment of literary fame, there remained at the back of his mind the possibility of a magnum opus, and for the subject of his culminating work he chose Johnson. Why? The answer, or the foundation of an answer, can best be found in a contemplation of Johnson's early career and of his position in the world of letters at the time of Boswell's introduction to him in 1763.

II

WHEN Johnson came to try his fortune in London, he was twenty-eight years old. The son of a not very successful bookseller in Lichfield, he had left Oxford after four terms, without a degree. Poverty and ill health made his prospects poor. After an unhappy experience as an assistant teacher in a grammar school, he moved to Birmingham, where he chanced upon some hackwork (notably the translation of Jeronimo Lobo's[1] *Voyage to Abyssinia*) and also upon a wife, "a widow, the relict of Mr. Porter, a mercer," and Johnson's senior by twenty years. The bride brought a modest fortune with her, and near his old home at Lichfield Johnson determined to set up an academy where young gentlemen could be "boarded and taught the Latin and Greek languages." An elaborate classical curriculum was prepared, but the school failed and Johnson made his final choice of life—"to become an author by profession."

It was a profession that could be followed only in London, and so Johnson went there in 1737. He was, as he said, "an adventurer in literature," and he brought one of his pupils, David Garrick, with him:

The two fellow-travellers had the world before them, and each was to choose his road to fortune and to fame. They brought with them genius, and powers of mind, peculiarly formed by nature for the different vocations to which each of them felt himself inclined. They acted from the impulse of young minds, even then meditating great things, and with courage anticipating success. . . . In three or four years afterwards Garrick came forth with talents that astonished the publick . . . Johnson was left to toil in the humble walks of literature.

For many years the walks were humble indeed. A newly founded journal, the *Gentleman's Magazine*, edited by Edward Cave, was the medium of Johnson's first contributions to periodical literature.

[1]Portuguese Jesuit missionary (1593–1678) in India and Abyssinia whose manuscript account of his travels was translated into French: *Voyage Historique d'Abissinie* (1728).

Odes, epigrams, epitaphs, reviews, short biographies, and other pieces were accepted by Cave, who quickly recognized Johnson's quality as a journalist. In particular, he employed his new contributor to revise and embellish the reports of debates in Parliament that formed an important feature of his magazine. They were not the verbatim reports to which the modern reader of *Hansard's House of Commons Journal* is accustomed. They were written with a fervor that "bordered upon enthusiasm" and with a particular determination "that the Whig dogs should not have the best of it." In later years Johnson had some compunction in looking back upon these *Debates* and warned historians not to quote them. After listening to the praises poured upon a famous speech of William Pitt beginning "Sir, the atrocious crime of being a young man . . . " he broke in with "That speech I wrote in a garret in Exeter street."

But while he faced the necessity of "writing for bread" Johnson preserved also the legitimate ambition of a man of letters. As a young man, he had written of

> . . . the young author panting for a name
> And fir'd with pleasing hope of endless fame

and early in 1738 he submitted his poem "London" to Cave for publication. It was a poem of more substance than his customary contributions to the magazine and Cave arranged for its publication by Robert Dodsley. "London" is at once an illustration of the literary fashion of its time and an individual expression of Johnson's scholarship. It was written in imitation of Juvenal's third satire and *saeva indignatio* is turned against the lawlessness of the streets:

> Here malice, rapine, accident conspire,
> And now a rabble rages, now a fire;
> Their ambush here relentless ruffians lay,
> And here the fell attorney prowls for prey;
> Here falling houses thunder on your head,
> And here a female atheist talks you dead,[2]
> (13–18)

against the corruption and cowardice of the government:

[2]Quotations are from the Yale edition of *The Works of Samuel Johnson* (New Haven, 1958), still in progress.

> Here let those reign, whom pensions can incite
> To vote a patriot black, a courtier white;
> Explain their country's dear-bought rights away
> And plead for pirates in the face of day
> (51–54)

and, more personally, against the poor man's lot:

> Of all the griefs that harrass the distress'd,
> Sure the most bitter is a scornful jest;
> Fate never wounds more deep the gen'rous heart
> Than when a blockhead's insult points the dart. . . .
> This mournful truth is ev'ry where confess'd,
> SLOW RISES WORTH, BY POVERTY DEPRESS'D. . . .
> (165–168; 176–177)

In form, "London" may be regarded as a Latinist's exercise; in substance, it comes from the heart of Grub Street and from the heart of the writer. The poem was published anonymously, but its quality was recognized. "Here," people said, "is an unknown poet, greater even than Pope," and Pope himself, being informed that the author was an unknown man named Johnson, declared: "He will soon be *déterré*." Johnson's monetary reward was ten guineas.

So the hackwork continued and sometimes more than hackwork: the *Life* of his friend Richard Savage, for instance, of which he wrote forty-eight pages at a sitting, and the *Observations on Macbeth* (1745), to which were appended *Proposals* for an edition of Shakespeare. For his old pupil, David Garrick, he wrote a prologue for the opening of the Drury Lane Theatre in 1747, surveying in rapid review the history of the English stage since Shakespeare's time. His comment on the Restoration was essentially that of the moralist:

> The Wits of *Charles* found easier Ways to Fame,
> Nor wish'd for Jonson's Art or Shakespeare's Flame;
> Themselves they studied, as they felt, they writ,
> Intrigue was Plot, Obscenity was Wit.
> Vice always found a sympathetic Friend;
> They pleas'd their age and did not aim to mend.
> (17–22)

Two years later Johnson came forward himself as a playwright. In the early days of his marriage he had drafted a tragedy based on the story, as told by Richard Knolles in his *Generall Historie of the Turkes*, of Mahomet II and the beautiful Greek maiden, Irene, who was taken captive at the fall of

Constantinople. The play, *Irene: A Tragedy*, was finished soon after his arrival in London. For some years his efforts to have it either published or acted were fruitless; but when Garrick came into power at Drury Lane, he determined to do his best for his old schoolmaster. The play was produced "with a display of eastern magnificence" on 6 February 1749 and ran for nine nights. It has never been revived. One contemporary critic remarked that "to instance every moral which is inculcated in this performance would be to transcribe the whole." From Johnson's point of view, the heart of the matter is Irene's failure to resist the appeals of Mahomet and to hold fast to her religion. To her friend, Aspasia, she puts the question:

> Upbraid me not with fancy'd Wickedness
> I am not yet a Queen, or an Apostate.
> But should I sin beyond the Hope of Mercy,
> If, when Religion prompts me to refuse,
> The Dread of instant Death restrains my Tongue?
> (III. viii. 21–25)

to which Aspasia answers:

> Reflect that Life and Death, affecting Sounds,
> Are only varied Modes of endless Being:
> Reflect that Life, like ev'ry other Blessing,
> Derives its Value from its Use alone;
> Not for itself but for a nobler End
> Th' Eternal gave it, and that End is Virtue. . . .
> (III. viii. 26–31)

And when Irene hints at the benefit her own country might derive from her apostasy:

> O! did Irene shine the Queen of *Turkey*,
> No more should *Greece* lament those prayers rejected.
> Again should golden Splendour grace her Cities. . . .
> (III. viii. 51–53)

the reply is prompt and uncompromising:

> By virtuous Ends pursued by virtuous Means,
> Nor think th' Intention sanctifies the Deed:
> That Maxim publish'd in an Impious Age,
> Would loose the wild Enthusiast to destroy,
> And fix the fierce Usurper's bloody Title.
> The Bigotry might send her Slaves to War,
> And bid Success become the Test of Truth.
> (III. viii. 57–63)

As a dramatic production, *Irene*, in spite of Garrick's efforts, was not a success; but it is one of the many evidences of Johnson's preoccupation with the proper tests of truth. Primarily, it was the work of a "young author panting for a name," but in Johnson's hands the story of Irene quickly became a reflection of the continuing struggles in his own mind. A man at once of strong passions and of deep dependence upon an ultimate faith, he pointed the moral of Irene's apostasy with all the fervor of a Christian moralist. It would be idle to pretend that *Irene* left any permanent mark upon the history of English drama; but a few of its lines are preserved in footnotes to chapter 68 of Edward Gibbon's *Decline and Fall of the Roman Empire.*

Just before the production of his play, Johnson had, with greater success, published his second satire, "The Vanity of Human Wishes," the first work to be issued with the author's name on the title page. Like "London," the poem was written in imitation of Juvenal, but the treatment is much freer. The theme of the young author is developed, and the lot of the struggling scholar is presented in lines that have become part of the English literary tradition:

> Deign on the passing world to turn thine eyes
> And pause awhile from letters, to be wise;
> There mark what ills the scholar's life assail,
> Toil, envy, want, the patron and the gaol.
> (158–161)

But the poem is much more than a personal complaint. Thomas Cardinal Wolsey, Charles XII of Sweden, and others are cited to demonstrate the impermanence of human fame and the hollowness of martial triumph:

> The festal blazes, the triumphal show,
> The ravish'd standard, and the captive foe,
> The senate's thanks, the gazette's pompous tale.
> With force resistless o'er the brave prevail.
> Such bribes the rapid Greek o'er Asia whirl'd,
> For such the steady Romans shook the world;
> For such in distant lands the Britons shine,
> And stain with blood the Danube or the Rhine;
> This pow'r has praise, that virtue scarce can warm
> Till fame supplies the universal charm.
> Yet Reason frowns on War's unequal game,
> Where wasted nations raise a single name,
> And mortgag'd states their grand-sires' wreaths regret,
> From age to age in everlasting debt;

Wreaths which at last the dear-bought right convey
To rust on medals, or on stones decay.

(175–190)

Here is no transient satire upon current events, but "the high seriousness which comes from absolute sincerity," though Matthew Arnold would never have put this hallmark on the work of an Augustan poet.

Meanwhile, Johnson was too good a realist to imagine that satire in verse would enable him to make a living; but he was now coming to be recognized as a competent man of letters, and he sought for some more solid and more scholarly task than weekly journalism could provide. So, when a syndicate of booksellers approached him with a proposal for a dictionary of the English language, he accepted the offer and produced his plan in 1747. He was drawn forward, he said, by the prospect of employment that, though not splendid, would be useful. The plan was addressed to Lord Chesterfield, whose initial neglect and subsequent attempts to make amends provoked the most famous of all Johnson's letters. At the outset, even Johnson was "frighted" at the extent of the work he had undertaken. But on the top floor of his house in Gough Square he organized his six amanuenses (five of them from Scotland, as Boswell is careful to point out) and the "harmless drudgery" went forward.

Johnson made no complaint about the sum the booksellers paid him, but, even so, the prospective fame of lexicography would not keep the wolf from the door. Accordingly, he decided to embark upon a weekly paper, which he entitled the *Rambler*. In general form it followed the pattern of the *Spectator* and the *Tatler*, and Johnson had an especially high opinion of Joseph Addison's prose. The *Rambler* was not conceived as a series of papers to provide weekly entertainment. It was deliberately the work of a "majestic teacher of moral and religious wisdom" and Johnson embarked upon it with a prayer: "Grant, I beseech Thee, that in this undertaking thy Holy Spirit may not be withheld from me, but that I may promote Thy glory and the salvation of myself and others."

An appreciation of the nature and the circumstances of the production of the *Rambler* is fundamental to an understanding of Johnson's position in the world of letters. To later critics it has been a stumbling block. Thomas Macaulay grumbles at "Johnsonese"; Hippolyte Taine complains that the essays are no more and no less than sermons; Leslie Stephen notes that a moralist must not aim at originality in his precepts; and readers, as a whole, put the *Rambler* aside and go back to Boswell. But they do not always reflect upon Boswell's own attitude. In his early reading he had nowhere found "more bark and steel for the mind" than in the *Rambler*; in his early meetings with Johnson his culminating pride was in the fact that he had spent an evening not with the great clubman, not with the Great Lexicographer, but with the author of the *Rambler*. Unlike readers today, Boswell was primarily drawn to Johnson by the "amazing universality" of his genius as a writer. The highest compliment he could pay to his conversation was to put it on a level with his written works. Here it must be remembered that when Johnson took a pen in his hand, he deliberately adopted a style and a standard that were quite distinct from his tavern chair manner. Talking and writing were for him quite separate arts:

As many please [he wrote] by extempory talk, though utterly unacquainted with the more accurate method and more laboured beauties which composition requires; so it is very possible that men wholly accustomed to works of study may be without that readiness of conception and affluence of language always necessary to colloquial entertainment.

(*Rambler* No. 14)

If the *Times* (London), as we know it, had existed in Johnson's day, he would have made an admirable lead editorial writer; but he would not have been commissioned to write the light commentaries. Accordingly, the reader of the *Rambler* must not look for "colloquial entertainment"; but he will be a dull reader if he does not occasionally derive pleasure, as well as instruction, from its pages. Unlike his successors of today, Johnson never "complied with contemporary curiosity" and rarely "exemplified his assertions by living characters." Consequently, the *Rambler* is not a day-to-day commentary on the political, social, or literary events of the time. If, on occasion, Johnson had individual characters or particular events in mind, he was careful to generalize them. Yet, nowhere can a better picture of the journalist's lot be found than in the *Rambler* No. 145:

It has formerly been imagined that he who intends the entertainment or instruction of others must feel in himself some peculiar impulse of genius. . . . But the authors whom I am now endeavouring to recommend have been too long hackneyed in the ways of men to indulge the chimerical ambition of immortality; they have seldom any claim to the trade of writing, but that they have tried some other without success, they perceive no particular summons to composition, except the sound of the clock . . . and about the opinion of posterity they have little solicitude, for their productions are seldom intended to remain in the world longer than a week.

This is but one of several shrewd reflections on the profession of literature, and when Johnson wrote of Grub Street he wrote of what he knew. But in fact only a small proportion of the *Rambler* is devoted to literary topics. Many of the essays are character sketches; one of them, that of Suspirius, was used by Oliver Goldsmith for the making of Croaker in *The Good Natur'd Man*, and it was Croaker who made the play a success. Domestic relationships provided material for many essays, and it is legitimate to conjecture that in the *Rambler* No. 112 the description of the fussy housewife and the grumbling male may reflect some features of Johnson's own experience. Solemnity is by no means the pervading quality of the *Rambler*, but it is certainly evident in the treatment of such subjects as the death sentence for robbery. Here, and not only here, Johnson's opinions were in advance of his time:

Death is. . . . of dreadful things the most dreadful. . . . To equal robbery with murder is to reduce murder to robbery, to confound in common minds the gradations in iniquity and incite the commission of a greater crime to prevent the detection of a less.

(*Rambler* No. 114)

The *Rambler*, in short, abounds in passages that are an essential complement to Johnson's utterances as preserved in Boswell's record, and, let it be repeated, it was on the *Rambler* that Boswell's admiration was initially based.

Johnson's second series of periodical essays (the *Idler*) were contributed to the *Universal Chronicle*, a weekly publication, between 1758 and 1760, and to anyone who still protests that Johnson is unreadable, there is no better answer than to confront him with a selection of *Idler* papers. Boswell himself is curiously apologetic. The *Idler*, he says, has less body and more spirit than the *Rambler*, and he comes as near to censure as a hero worshiper can when he reflects upon Johnson's wantonness of disquisition and his failure to suppress his power of

sophistry—and all this because Johnson made fun of the opinion "that our mental facilities depend, in some degree, upon the weather," in an essay beginning:

It is commonly observed that when two Englishmen meet, their first talk is of the weather; they are in haste to tell each other, what each must already know, that it is hot or cold, bright or cloudy, windy or calm. . . .

(*Idler* No. 11)

Some of the *Idler* papers, as Boswell is pleased to remark, approximate in "profundity of thought" and "labour of language" to the *Rambler* standard; but others display a lighter touch and a remarkable freshness. On newswriters in wartime, for instance:

In a time of war . . . the task of news-writers is easy: they have nothing to do but to tell . . . that a battle has been fought, in which we and our friends, whether conquering or conquered, did all, and our enemies did nothing. Scarcely anything awakens attention like a tale of cruelty. . . .

(*Idler* No. 30)

Or this description of a bargain hunter:

I am the unfortunate husband of *a buyer of bargains* . . . whatever she thinks cheap, she holds it the duty of an economist to buy; in consequence of this maxim, we are encumbered on every side with useless lumber. The servants can scarcely creep to their beds through the chests and boxes that surround them. The carpenter is employed once a week in building closets, fixing cupboards and fastening shelves. . . .

(*Idler* No. 35)

But perhaps the most revealing essay is that in which Johnson purports to display the character of his old friend Sober:

Sober is a man of strong desires and quick imagination, so exactly balanced by the love of ease, that they can seldom stimulate him to any difficult undertaking; they have, however, so much power, that they will not suffer him to lie quite at rest; and though they do not make him sufficiently useful to others, they make him at least weary of himself.
Mr. Sober's chief pleasure is conversation; there is no end of his talk or his attention; to speak or to hear is equally pleasing. . . . But there is one time at night when he must go home, that his friends may sleep; and another

time in the morning, when all the world agrees to shut out interruption. These are the moments of which poor Sober trembles at the thought. . . .

(*Idler* No. 31)

It is Johnson's *apologia pro vita sua.*

III

BEFORE the series of *Idler* papers was completed, Johnson heard that his mother, now ninety years old, was gravely ill at Lichfield. On 13 January 1759 he contrived to send her twelve guineas. A week later he wrote in terms of deep affection and distress and on the same day he also wrote to William Strahan, the printer, telling him that he had written a new work for which he would need an immediate advance of £30. The work was *The History of Rasselas Prince of Abyssinia* and Johnson had written it in the evenings of a week. His mother died a few days after he had delivered the copy, but at least he had earned some money for the expenses of her funeral. Apart from the circumstances of its production, *Rasselas* is important in relation not only to Johnson's philosophy of life but also to eighteenth-century taste. Neither the *Rambler* nor the *Idler* had achieved more than a succès d'estime, but *Rasselas* was immediately welcomed and was, indeed, the one work of Johnson's that won solid popularity during the author's lifetime. As Boswell says, it was "extensively diffused over Europe" in a variety of translations, and readers of Elizabeth Gaskell's *Cranford* will remember that in the middle of the nineteenth century old-fashioned ladies still regarded it as a more reliable kind of fiction than the new-fangled and sensational stuff then being produced by Charles Dickens.

The eighteenth century loved a moral tale ("impressive truth, in splendid fiction drest") and *Rasselas* is Johnson's culminating work as a social and ethical philosopher. The setting of the tale, but little else, was no doubt taken from Lobo's *Voyage to Abyssinia.* Rasselas and his sister, "wearying of the soft vicissitudes of pleasure and repose," leave their happy valley with a determination to gain experience of the varying conditions of human existence and to make their choice of life. They meet and talk with young men and old, with professors, astronomers, shepherds, and poets. Their conclu-

sion ("in which nothing is concluded") is similar to that of the author of *Ecclesiastes,* and so they resolve to return to Abyssinia. No work of Johnson's is more relevant to the study of the author's temperament and outlook than *Rasselas.* It is addressed, at the outset, to those "who listen with credulity to the whispers of fancy and pursue with eagerness the phantoms of hope; who expect that age will perform the promises of youth and that the deficiencies of the present day will be supplied by the morrow," and the discussions between Rasselas and his companions range over many of the fundamental issues of art and life. Are the Europeans happier than we? Rasselas asks. Imlac, in reply, describes their many advantages and Rasselas feels that with all their conveniences and ease of communication they must surely be happy. Then comes Imlac's—and Johnson's—final verdict: "The Europeans are less unhappy than we, but they are not happy. Human life is every where a state in which much is to be endured, and little to be enjoyed."

In whatever context it is sought, happiness continues to be elusive. The poet sets himself so high a standard ("the interpreter of nature . . . the legislator of mankind . . . a being superior to time and place") that Rasselas protests himself convinced that no human being can ever be a poet. The hermit, after fifteen years of solitude, resolves to return to the world, convinced that "the life of a solitary man will be certainly miserable, but not certainly devout." The way to be happy, says the philosopher, is to live according to nature. What is life according to nature? asks Rasselas. "To live according to nature," is the reply, "is to act always with due regard to the fitness arising from the relations and qualities of causes and effects: to concur with the great and unchangeable scheme of universal felicity; to co-operate with the general disposition and tendency of the present system of things." Upon which Rasselas appropriately concluded that "this was one of the sages whom he should understand less as he heard him longer."

Similarly, after an earnest discussion of the problems of family life, the conclusion is reached that "marriage has many pains, but celibacy has no pleasures"; and a visit to the Great Pyramid leads Imlac to observe: "I consider this mighty structure as a monument of the insufficiency of human enjoyments."

From all this we may understand Boswell's feeling when he wrote: "The fund of thinking which this work contains is such that almost every sentence of it may furnish a subject of long meditation." Boswell did not comment on Johnson's conjecture that someday man might use "the swifter migration of wings"; but it may still provoke prolonged meditation:

What would be the security of the good, if the bad could at pleasure invade them from the sky? Against an army sailing through the clouds, neither walls, nor mountains, nor seas could afford any security. A flight of northern savages might hover in the wind, and light at once with irresistible violence upon the capital of a fruitful region that was rolling under them.

(*Rasselas*, ch. 6)

Meanwhile Johnson's work in another field had been going steadily forward. "This is a great work, William Sir," said Dr. Adams, master of Johnson's old college. "How can you do this in three years?" To which Johnson said, "Sir, I have no doubt that I can do it in three years." And when told that the forty members of the Académie Française had taken forty years to compile their dictionary, he replied, "Sir, thus it is. This is the proportion. Let me see; forty times forty is sixteen hundred. As three to sixteen hundred, so is the proportion of an Englishman to a Frenchman." This was Johnson talking for victory, and in fact he was engaged upon his task for eight years. In the plan of 1747 it is characteristic that, although the work was to bring him a degree, it was not undertaken merely as an academic thesis:

The value of a work must be estimated by its use; it is not enough that a dictionary delights the critick, unless, at the same time, it instructs the learner, as it is to little purpose that an engine amuses the philosopher by the subtilty of its mechanism, if it requires so much knowledge in its application as to be of no advantage to the common workman.

(*The Plan of a Dictionary of the English Language*)

The two massive folios that appeared in 1755 may well have seemed a formidable tool to be used by the common workman of literature. But Johnson was a pioneer in lexicography. Even the most rapid and casual comparison of Johnson's handling of a familiar English word with the scanty definitions given by his immediate predecessor, Nathaniel Bailey, is enough to demonstrate the quality and

magnitude of Johnson's achievement. Conscious alike of the "scholar's reverence for antiquity" and the "grammarian's regard to the genius of our tongue," he realized that words were not museum pieces to be cataloged, but symbols subject to continual change and adaptation. He realized also that if he followed every byway of research, he would never finish his work:

I saw one inquiry only gave occasion to another, that book referred to book, that to search was not always to find, and to find was not always to be informed. . . . I then contracted my design, determining to confide in myself.

(*ibid.*)

It was a confidence well placed. No one before Johnson had attempted to analyze the finer variations of meaning that a simple word might have acquired in different authors and in different contexts;[3] and the wealth of illustrative quotation was the fruit of his own wide reading and tenacious memory. That the work would contain "a few wild blunders and risible absurdities" Johnson was well aware. Even Boswell admits that his definition of "network" ("Anything reticulated or decussated, at equal distances, with interstices between the intersections") was quoted with sportive malignity; and today it is the grim little jokes in the definitions of "oats" and "excise" and "lexicographer" that are remembered by the ordinary reader. Such is the inevitable work of time, which "antiquates antiquities and hath an art to make dust of all things." But Johnson's *Dictionary* has not come to dust. The late editor in chief of the *Oxford English Dictionary*, Sir James Murray, described it as "a marvellous piece of work to accomplish in eight and a half years"; and it remains a battered, but enduring, milestone in the history of English lexicography.

So, in 1755, Johnson became the Great Lexicographer, and he had the further satisfaction of being able to add the letters A.M. (*Artium Magister*) after his name on the title page. But the ground on which he was recommended for an Oxford degree is significant: he had "very eminently distinguished himself by the publication of a series of essays, ex-

---

[3]The word "go," for instance, is defined by Bailey as "to walk, move about, etc." Johnson distinguishes sixty-seven senses of the word, with illustrations from the Bible, Shakespeare, Locke, Dryden, Swift, and many others.

cellently calculated to form the manners of the people, and in which the cause of religion and morality is everywhere maintained by the strongest powers of argument and language." In 1775 the University of Oxford awarded him the higher degree of Doctor of Civil Law. But ten years earlier he had been made LL.D. (*Legum Doctor*) by Trinity College, Dublin, and it should not be forgotten that it was an Irish university that first created "Doctor Johnson." In the preface to the *Dictionary* can be found some of the best examples of Johnson's prose:

In this work, when it shall be found that much is omitted, let it not be forgotten that much likewise is performed; and though no book was ever spared out of tenderness to the author, and the world is little solicitous to know whence proceeded the faults of that which it condemns; yet it may gratify curiosity to inform it, that the English Dictionary was written with little assistance of the learned, and without any patronage of the great; not in the soft obscurities of retirement, or under the shelter of academick bowers, but amidst inconvenience and distraction, in sickness and in sorrow.

One of Johnson's principal sorrows had been the death of his wife in 1752, just after the issue of the last *Rambler*. "Remember me in your prayers," Johnson wrote to his friend Dr. John Taylor, "for vain is the help of man," and while Mrs. Johnson in her lifetime may well have provoked a certain measure of domestic irritation by her "particular preference for cleanliness," there can be no doubt of Johnson's devotion to the memory of his dear Tetty. Although the scholastic triumph of the *Dictionary* in 1755 marked the final stage of Johnson's emergence from hackwork to literary eminence, it was not until 1762 that he was delivered from the labor and anxiety of "writing for bread." In that year, to his surprise, he was informed that His Majesty King George III was graciously pleased to award him a pension of three hundred pounds a year. Johnson was staggered. Had he not written in "London" of those "whom pensions can incite/To vote a patriot black, a courtier white"? Had he not defined "pension" as "pay given to a state hireling for treason to his country"? Conscious of all this, Johnson hesitated to accept the honor; but his friends reassured him and, in particular, Lord Bute, the prime minister, overcame his scruples by telling him: "It is not given you for any thing you are to do, but for what you have done."

IV

SUCH were a few of the events in Johnson's career before his first meeting with Boswell, but enough, perhaps, to indicate the celebrity he had achieved by 1763. In a diary of the previous year, Boswell had recorded how, after reading some *Rambler* papers to the company assembled in a country house, he delivered his opinion that Johnson was "a man of much philosophy, extensive reading and real knowledge of human life" and when, on 19 September 1762, he beheld the City of London from Highgate Hill, his soul "bounded forth to a certain prospect of happy futurity." On 18 December he was delighted to accept an invitation to meet Johnson at dinner with Tom Davies the bookseller, on Christmas Day. Unfortunately, Johnson decided to go to Oxford for Christmas, but Boswell had the pleasure of meeting Oliver Goldsmith and seized the opportunity of discussing the *Rambler* and *Idler* with him. The famous first meeting in Tom Davies' shop, on 16 May 1763, was in fact accidental, but it was the beginning of one of the most famous associations in history. Boswell had two principal ambitions: to be the friend of famous men and to be a famous author himself. Among the celebrities whom he wished to meet in London in 1763, Johnson stood very high, and when Boswell found himself supping on easy terms of intimacy with him and realized that the quality of Johnson's talk was equal to that of his writings, he rejoiced at his good fortune and immediately began to make notes of their conversations. ("We sat till between one and two and finished a couple of bottles of port. I went home in high exultation.")[4] But the *Life* was not an isolated achievement; it was, as has already been observed, the final triumph of a career of literary ambition and effort.

Johnson, for his part, was immediately captivated by Boswell's ingenuous charm. To the end of his life, he looked upon every day in which he did not make a new acquaintance as being lost. Boswell was a superb listener, and nothing could have been more flattering to a lonely scholar than to be eagerly admired by someone thirty years his junior. During the summer of 1763 the friendship developed. There were suppers at the Mitre Tavern and excursions on the Thames, but the most strik-

[4]Quotations of Boswell are from the Everyman's Library edition of his *Life of Samuel Johnson* (London, 1949).

ing proof of Johnson's attachment was his decision to accompany Boswell to Harwich at the end of his London visit. There Boswell received good advice on a variety of subjects. He was bound for Holland, where he was to continue his study of law, and Johnson bade him kneel in the church and commend himself to his Creator and Redeemer. When they came out of the church, Johnson demonstrated his contempt for the Berkeleian theory of matter by "striking his foot with mighty force against a large stone." He also warned Boswell of the folly of pretending indifference to food and of using big words for little matters. As they parted they promised to write to each other. Boswell expressed the hope that Johnson would not forget him. "Nay, Sir," Johnson replied, "it is more likely you should forget me than that I should forget you." It was the reply of one who loved the acquaintance of young people; young acquaintances, he said, lasted longest.

To Johnson a club was one of the first necessities of life. In his *Dictionary* he defined it as "an assembly of good fellows meeting under certain conditions." As early as 1749 he founded the Ivy Lane Club, where he would "pass those hours in a free and unrestrained interchange of sentiments, which otherwise had been spent at home in painful reflection." It was not a purely literary gathering; three members of the club were physicians (including Johnson's very dear friend Richard Bathurst, who could not tolerate fools or rogues or Whigs and was, in short, "a very good hater"). There were John Hawkesworth, editor of the *Adventurer*, John Payne, publisher of the *Rambler*, Samuel Salter, formerly archdeacon of Norfolk, and Sir John Hawkins, for whom Johnson was afterward driven to coin the word "unclubable."

More famous was the Club, founded in 1764. It was Sir Joshua Reynolds who first suggested its formation to Johnson, and among the original members were Edmund Burke, Topham Beauclerk, Bennet Langton, and Goldsmith. Boswell was admitted later, after some hesitation on the part of certain members. Johnson told Boswell the story of his election with characteristic candor: "Sir, they knew that if they refused you, they'd probably never have got in another. I'd have kept them all out." Posterity is heavily indebted to Johnson's dictatorship. Meetings of the Club provided Boswell with material for some of his most brilliant reporting. Good company, good food, and good conversation con-

stituted the primary solace of Johnson's life, and now that he was relieved of the necessity of earning his living by his pen, he wás free to take his pleasures—but not always with a good conscience. On Easter Eve 1764 he recorded:

My indolence, since my last reception of the Sacrament, has sunk into grosser sluggishness, and my dissipation spread into wilder negligence. . . . A kind of strange oblivion has overspread me, so that I know not what has become of the last year. . . . This is not the life to which heaven is promised.

(*Life of Johnson*, vol. I, p. 300)

On Easter Day, he went to church (coming in "at the first of the Psalms"), and in his prayers he recommended his dear Tetty as well as his father, mother, brother, and Bathurst, "so far as it might be lawful." As he received the Sacrament at the altar, he resolved to repel sinful thoughts, to study eight hours daily, to go to church every Sunday, and to read the Scriptures. After putting his shilling in the plate, he saw a poor girl at the Sacrament in a bedgown and gave her, privately, a crown. He then prayed earnestly for amendment and repeated his prayer at home. This account of Easter 1764 is no isolated record. It is typical of Johnson's self-examination at Easter, or on his birthday, or on New Year's Day, over a long period of years.

There was one delay that weighed with particular force on Johnson's mind. In 1756 he had published his *Proposals* for an edition of Shakespeare, hoping to complete the work by the end of the following year. It was a mark of editorial optimism not peculiar to Johnson or his period. But after six years it provoked some raillery:

He for subscribers baits his hook
And takes your cash; but where's the book?

When the eight volumes at length appeared in 1765, the subscribers' names were not included in them. For this omission Johnson gave what he described as two cogent reasons—he had lost the names and spent the money.

After the *Dictionary*, the edition of Shakespeare is the most valuable legacy of Johnson's scholarship. Every generation produces its quota of Shakespearean editors and critics and, in 1908, Walter Raleigh remarked that while Johnson had been neglected and depreciated in the nineteenth century he would probably be respected in the twentieth. This forecast has been fulfilled; and a modern editor of Shakespeare was not ashamed to entitle the first chapter of his book on Falstaff "Back to Johnson."[5]

Throughout his life Johnson had been a devoted student of Shakespeare; he began at so early an age that the speech of the Ghost in *Hamlet* terrified him when he was alone. His first work as an anonymous commentator (*Miscellaneous Observations on the Tragedy of Macbeth*) was published in 1745, with a postscript on the recent edition of Sir Thomas Hanmer, which was weighed in the balance and found wanting:

Its pomp recommends it more than its accuracy. There is no distinction made between the ancient reading and the innovations of the editor; there is no reason given for any of the alterations which are made; the emendations of former criticks are adopted without any acknowledgment, and few of the difficulties are removed which have hitherto embarrassed the readers of Shakespeare.

To this devastating summary of editorial failure Johnson appended proposals for an edition of his own; but copyright difficulties arose and it was not until after the publication of the *Dictionary*, which abounds in quotations from Shakespeare, that he issued his more elaborate *Proposals*. Here, the justification of a new edition and the primary obligations of an editor are set out in positive form: first, it is his business to correct what is corrupt, and the circumstances of the writing of Shakespeare's plays made this a difficult task, since the plays were "vitiated by the blunders of the penman . . . changed by the affectation of the player . . . and printed without the concurrence of the author"; secondly, Shakespeare presented many obscurities that it was the commentator's duty to elucidate, especially the obscurities inherent in Shakespeare's common colloquial language with its "allusive, elliptical and proverbial" phrases; finally, in order to appreciate Shakespeare's use of his sources, the editor must read the story "in the very book which Shakespeare consulted." As to the occurrence of obsolete diction in the plays, Johnson claimed, not immodestly, that he had had more motives to consider the whole extent of the English language than any other man.

Philology apart, Johnson was too honest a critic not to "confess the faults of our favourite to gain

[5] J. Dover Wilson, *The Fortunes of Falstaff* (London, 1943).

credit to our praise of his excellencies," and his fundamental criticism of Shakespeare was the criticism of the Christian moralist:

His precepts and axioms drop casually from him; he makes no just distribution of good and evil . . . he carries his persons indifferently through right and wrong and at the close dismisses them without further care, and leaves their examples to operate by chance. This fault the barbarity of his age cannot extenuate: for it is always a writer's duty to make the world better.

(*Preface to Shakespeare*, p. 71)

There speaks the Rambler, and by any argument for the artist's primary duty of self-expression he would have been unshaken.

Another characteristic mark of Johnson's approach was that he had a greater relish for the printed than the spoken word. Many of the plays, he thought, and particularly the tragedies, were the worse for being acted, and he was insensitive to dramatic illusion:

The truth is that the spectators are always in their senses and know, from the first act to the last, that the stage is only a stage and that the players are only players. They come to hear a certain number of lines recited with just gesture and elegant modulation.

(*ibid.* p. 77)

Here Johnson reveals his fundamentally bookish attitude to the drama. What good actor is content with recitation? What good playgoer with elegant modulation? And yet Johnson realized, as clearly as any modern critic, that it was for the playgoer that the plays were written:

Shakespeare regarded more the series of ideas, than of words; and his language not being designed for the reader's desk, was all that he desired it to be, if it conveyed his meaning to the audience.

(*ibid.* p. 97)

But it was at his reader's desk that Johnson absorbed, and was absorbed by, Shakespeare's series of ideas. By the great tragedies he was deeply moved. He was so shocked by Cordelia's death in *King Lear* that he could not bring himself to read again the last scenes of the play until he undertook to revise them as an editor; and on the murder of Desdemona in *Othello*, he wrote: "I am glad that I have ended my revisal of this dreadful scene. It is not to be endured."

In his treatment of the comedies Johnson shows clearly how the Rabelaisian and the moralist were constantly striving for mastery within them. Thus, the one great fault that he found in *The Merry Wives of Windsor* was the frequency of profane expressions; "there are laws of higher authority than those of criticism." At the end of *As You Like It*, Shakespeare had "lost an opportunity of exhibiting a moral lesson."

But to Falstaff, Johnson made a complete surrender. Despicable as he might be from the moralist's point of view, he was saved "by the most pleasing of all qualities, perpetual gaiety, by an unfailing power of exciting laughter." No one was more keenly aware than Johnson of the virtue of cheerfulness. His first observation on the characters of *The Tempest* is that Gonzalo, being the only good man who appears with the king, is the only man who preserves his cheerfulness in the wreck.

Like all critics, Johnson had his prejudices and his limitations; but he never forgot the stature of the poet whom he was editing: "The stream of time, which is continually washing the dissoluble fabricks of other poets, passes without injury by the adamant of Shakespeare." Johnson's criticism, too, has its adamantine qualities.

For the last twenty years of his life Johnson liked to regard himself as a professional writer who had won his discharge. "I wonder, Sir," said Boswell, "you have not more pleasure in writing than in not writing." "Sir," said Johnson, "you *may* wonder." Nevertheless, circumstances led him to produce two works of substance. In 1773 Boswell persuaded him to make a tour in Scotland. Starting from Edinburgh, the travelers followed the east road and turned westward through Banff and Inverness. At Anoch, Johnson found himself seated on a bank, "such as a writer of Romance might have delighted to feign":

I had indeed no trees to whisper over my head, but a clear rivulet streamed at my feet. The day was calm, the air soft, and all was rudeness, silence and solitude. Before me, and on either side, were high hills, which by hindering the eye from ranging, forced the mind to find entertainment for itself. Whether I spent the hour well I know not: for here I first conceived the thought of this narration.

(*A Journey to the Western Islands of Scotland*, p. 40)

The narration was published in 1775 and was entitled *A Journey to the Western Islands of Scotland*.

By all except professed students of Johnson it is commonly neglected in favor of Boswell's *Journal of a Tour to the Hebrides* (1785). The preference is natural. The *Tour* was, in fact, the first installment of the *Life*, and Boswell had Johnson's authority for saying that it was a very exact picture. It was not only exact but brilliant. "Let me not be censured," he wrote, "for mentioning minute particulars"; and it is this particularity, based upon acute observation and continuous industry, that has won the admiration and the affection of the great company of Boswellians. Johnson's own account was different. He was concerned primarily to describe a country and a society that were new to him. Himself fundamentally urban, he thought it worthwhile to record his impression of the religion, language, education, agriculture, and daily life of a society he had long desired to visit. At an early age he had read Martin Martin's *Description of the Western Islands* (1703) and in one respect he was disappointed. Since the second Jacobite rebellion of 1745, the Highlanders had been tamed:

We came hither too late to see what we expected, a people of peculiar appearance and a system of antiquated life. The clans retain little now of their original character, their ferocity of temper is softened, their military ardour is extinguished, their dignity of independence is depressed, their contempt of government subdued, and the reverence of their Chiefs abated.

(*ibid.* p. 57)

Nevertheless, he rejoiced to find a vigorous patriarchal life at Raasay:

Raasay has little that can detain a traveller, except the Laird and his family; but their power wants no auxiliaries. Such a seat of hospitality, amidst the winds and waters, fills the imagination with a delightful contrariety of images. Without is the rough ocean and the rocky land, the beating billows and the howling storm: within is plenty and elegance, beauty and gaiety, the song and the dance. In Raasay, if I could have found an Ulysses, I had fancied a Phaeacia.

(*ibid.* p. 66)

Not all of Johnson's comments are so favorable. He was interested in everything he saw and did not shrink from blunt criticism. But he realized clearly his limitations as a city dweller and modestly reflected that his thoughts on national manners were the thoughts of one who had seen but little.

Apart from his edition of Shakespeare, the other

major work of Johnson's later life is the one that is best known, or least neglected, today—*The Lives of the Poets*. Like the *Dictionary*, the scheme for the *Lives* originated with a group of booksellers who were planning an elegant and uniform edition on the English poets and invited Johnson to write a short life of each poet. For once Johnson undertook the work without hesitation. An introduction to a literary work was one of the things he felt confident he could do well, and he had at first no intention to give more than a short account of each poet. But the "honest desire of giving useful pleasure" led him to write more when he felt so disposed, and his essays on such poets as Abraham Cowley, John Dryden, and Alexander Pope have become classics of English criticism. For many less eminent writers Johnson felt that "little lives, and little criticism" would serve and appealed to his friends for biographical facts. He wrote, for instance, to Dr. Richard Farmer to inquire whether there might be useful material at Cambridge, and offered to inspect such material himself, "for who that has once experienced the civilities of Cambridge would not snatch the opportunity of another visit?" Similarly he wrote to William Sharp for information about Isaac Watts, whose name he had always held in veneration. "I wish to distinguish Watts," he wrote, "a man who never wrote but for a good purpose." When he came to write the *Life*, he counseled his readers to imitate Watts "in all but his nonconformity." For a short life of George Lyttelton, whom he did not like, Johnson applied to his brother, Lord Westcote: "My desire is to avoid offence, and to be totally out of danger." On the other hand, the help given by his old friend Gilbert Walmsley in the *Life* of Edmund Smith led Johnson to include a tribute to Walmsley himself, which is as splendid as it is irrelevant:

> He was a Whig, with all the virulence and malevolence of his party; yet difference of opinion did not keep us apart. I honoured him, and he endured me.
> He had mingled with the gay world, without exemption from its vices or its follies, but had never neglected the cultivation of his mind; his belief of Revelation was unshaken; his learning preserved his principles; he grew first regular, and then pious. . . . His acquaintance with books was great; and what he did not immediately know, he could at least tell where to find. Such was his amplitude of learning, and such his copiousness of communication, that it may be doubted whether a day now passes in which I have not some advantage from his friendship.

This paragraph sheds no additional light or luster on the poetry of Edmund Smith, but it is a good example of the obiter dicta that serve to enhance the charm of *The Lives of the Poets*. "Sir," said Johnson, "the biographical part of literature is what I love most," and in these *Lives* he was concerned at least as much with fact and anecdote as with theories of poetry. He made no attempt to separate the poetry from the personality of the poet, and if he disliked the personality, he frankly colored his criticism with his dislike. The two best-known instances of this are the *Lives* of John Milton and Thomas Gray.

About the greatness of the author of *Paradise Lost* Johnson had no doubts:

> The characteristic quality of his poem is sublimity. He sometimes descends to the elegant, but his element is the great. . . . He can please when pleasure is required; but it is his peculiar power to astonish.

As an epic poet, Milton displayed all the qualities that Johnson sought—knowledge, morality, piety, grandeur; and his confession that "we read Milton for instruction . . . and look elsewhere for recreation" is, in effect, a tribute to the intellectual and emotional effort that a proper appreciation of *Paradise Lost* demands. Even Johnson's notorious prejudice against blank verse is forgotten in the sublimity of Milton's subject: "I cannot prevail on myself to wish that Milton had been a rhymer; for I cannot wish his work to be other than it is." Such is Johnson's considered verdict on a poem that is "not the greatest of heroic poems only because it is not the first." They are the concluding words of a long essay, but much earlier the reader will, no doubt, have been astonished by the two devastating pages on "Lycidas." Why should Johnson have condemned the diction as harsh, the rhymes as uncertain, the numbers as unpleasing? Why should he have set his mind so stubbornly against an appreciation of such lines as:

> We drove a field and both together heard
> What time the Gray-fly winds her sultry horn,
> Battening our flocks with the fresh dews of night

and commented, like a fractious child: "We know that they never drove a field and that they had no flocks to batten"? Part of the answer must be sought in the biographical portion of the essay, in which Milton's religious and political opinions are ruthlessly denounced:

He has not associated himself with any denomination of Protestants; we know rather what he was not, than what he was. He was not of the Church of Rome; he was not of the Church of England. To be of no church is dangerous. . . . Milton, who appears to have had full conviction of the truth of Christianity . . . yet grew old without any visible worship.

To Johnson, a good Church of England man who preferred the papists to the Presbyterians because the latter body had no church or apostolical ordination, any kind of undenominationalism was exasperating. Similarly, in politics:

His political notions were those of an acrimonious and surly republican. . . . Milton's republicanism was, I am afraid, founded in an envious hatred of greatness and a sullen desire of independence. . . . He hated monarchs in the State and prelates in the Church; for he hated all whom he was required to obey.

"Lycidas" was in the form of a pastoral ("easy, vulgar and therefore disgusting"); but in spite of such epithets, Johnson could take pleasure in a pastoral poem, provided it was genuinely descriptive of country life. Years before, in a *Rambler* essay, he had declared it to be an improper medium of political or ecclesiastical criticism. Furthermore, "Lycidas" mingled "trifling fictions" with "the most awful and sacred truths" and so became the target of Johnson's exaggerated scorn. His criticism of the poem is distorted by his fundamental distrust of the anarchical temperament of the poet—but it did not weaken his belief in Milton's greatness.

Against Gray, Johnson was less violently prejudiced. Here again, he paid full tribute to the "Elegy," but he had little patience with the fastidious productions of the scholar who asked for leisure to be good and wrote only when the humor took him. He also disliked what he regarded as Gray's affectation in his tricks of inversion and in the use of antiquarian epithets. In the *Lives* of Milton and Gray it is possible to detect some slight bitterness on Johnson's part as he compared their academic careers with his own four terms at Oxford, followed by the long years in Grub Street. The mythological imagery of "Lycidas," he observes, "is such as a college easily supplies" and the even tenor of Milton's life appeared to be attainable only in colleges. Gray's plea, made from college rooms, that he could write only when he was in the right mood Johnson dismissed as "fantastick foppery."

The Rambler had produced his paper twice a week, whatever his mood.

There are some, perhaps, who feel about Johnson's writings as Johnson felt about Milton. They recognize the element of greatness in them and read them as a matter of duty; but for recreation and companionship they turn elsewhere—and most naturally to Boswell. They may recognize that Johnson's own works were, historically, the foundation of the *Life*, but the brilliance of Boswell's superstructure, with its superb record of conversation and its convincing picture of the social scene, has inevitably monopolized their interest. But for Boswell it was always the Rambler who argued and declaimed. Whether at the Mitre, the Club, or Mrs. Thrale's dining table, Boswell looked for instruction at least as much as for entertainment—indeed, he was slightly shocked whenever Johnson indulged his capacity for pure fun. At Corricatachin, for instance, Boswell found it "highly comick" to see the grave philosopher—the Rambler—toying with a Highland beauty (and a married woman, too) upon his knee; when Johnson "exulted in his own pleasantry" at the expense of Bennet Langton, Boswell felt that it was not such as might be expected from the author of the *Rambler*. But whether the evening's conversation had been grave or gay, there came, inevitably, "the one time at night when he must go home," and at home Johnson would be left to his reflections and his melancholy—the melancholy not merely of loneliness but of penitence. For to Johnson the doctrine of the sinfulness of man and of man's redemption by the passion of Jesus Christ was fundamental. Year after year he recited his sins of omission—his failure to read good books (and particularly the Bible); to rise early; to worship regularly; to keep a journal; to avoid idleness. On his birthday in 1764 he deplored that he had spent fifty-five years in resolving but had done nothing. It was his conscience as a scholar that especially troubled him. He knew that he had been endowed with a scholar's talents, but how had he used them? "O God," he prayed, "make me to remember that *the night cometh when no man can work.*"

At Easter 1779, he found little good of himself to report except the publication of the first part of the *Lives of the Poets* and "a little charity." The last phrase is significant. Johnson sought the companionship he needed to make life endurable not only in distinguished clubs and fashionable drawing rooms, but among the poor and the unfortunate, and to several of these he offered a refuge in his own house. Among them were Anna Williams, the blind lady to whose "variety of knowledge" he was indebted for thirty years; Mrs. Desmoulins, the daughter of his godfather (Dr. Swinfen), to whom he made an allowance of half a guinea a week; Francis Barber, his black servant, whom he sent to school at Bishop's Stortford; and Robert Levet, "an obscure practiser of physick amongst the lower people," who shared Johnson's penny loaf at breakfast. In the great panorama of Boswell's narrative there are many minor figures who have attained immortality by a single phrase or incident. Of these, the best known perhaps is Oliver Edwards, who remarked, "You are a philosopher, Dr. Johnson. I have tried too in my time to be a philosopher; but I don't know how, cheerfulness was always breaking in." But Robert Levet's immortality was conferred upon him by Johnson himself in a tribute that came straight from the heart of a man who had lost his friend:

> Condemn'd to hope's delusive mine,
> As on we toil from day to day,
> By sudden blasts, or slow decline,
> Our social comforts drop away.
>
> Well try'd, through many a varying year,
> See LEVET to the grave descend;
> Officious, innocent, sincere,
> Of ev'ry friendless name the friend.
>   . . .
> In misery's darkest cavern known,
> His useful care was ever nigh,
> Where hopeless anguish pour'd his groan
> And lonely want retir'd to die.
>
> No summons, mock'd by chill delay,
> No petty gain, disdain'd by pride;
> The modest wants of ev'ry day
> The toil of ev'ry day supply'd.
>
> His virtues walk'd their narrow round,
> Nor made a pause, nor left a void;
> And sure th' Eternal Master found
> The single talent well employ'd.
>   ("On the Death of Dr. Robert Levet,"
>   1–8; 16–28)

Here, as Walter Raleigh suggests, the reader may find at least a partial explanation of Johnson's failure to appreciate "Lycidas" as a lament for a friend.

Johnson's treatment of Francis Barber was prompted not only by personal affection but by his persistent hatred of the slave trade. How is it, he asked, that we hear the loudest yelps for liberty among the drivers of Negroes? Johnson disliked yelps for liberty wherever they came from, but when Macaulay described him as "a Tory . . . from mere passion such as inflamed the Capulets against the Montagues," he was seeking too easy an answer. It is true that Johnson was inflamed by passion; but it was a passion not for a party but for order in church and state and society. The first Whig was the Devil, who had upset the order of Heaven, and Whig talk about liberty in the abstract infuriated him, especially when it championed a man of the character of John Wilkes. As to the American colonists, Johnson regarded them simply as English subjects who had voluntarily crossed the ocean and left their voting rights behind them; they still enjoyed the protection of the armed forces of the crown, and for that protection it was right that they should pay. But, whatever his views on current controversy, Johnson was no supporter of absolute power:

> When I say that all governments are alike, I consider that in no government power can be abused long. Mankind will not bear it. If a sovereign oppresses his people to a great degree, they will rise and cut off his head.
>   (*Life of Johnson*, vol. I, p. 424)

So he regarded the Irish situation of his own time with profound misgiving. "The Irish," he said, "are in a most unnatural state; for we see there the minority prevailing over the majority." In France he deplored the lack of a healthy middle class between the magnificence of the rich and the misery of the poor. A decent provision for the poor was, he said, the true test of civilization—and by a decent provision he meant something more than the bare necessities. "What signifies," said someone, "giving halfpence to common beggars? they only lay it out in gin and tobacco." "And why," thundered Johnson, "should they be denied such sweeteners of their existence?"

V

THUS the study of Samuel Johnson is something more than the enjoyment of a great clubman and a great diner-out whose conversational exploits have been uniquely described by a great literary artist.

Johnson's personality presents many facets and many paradoxes. The man whose character and opinions have delighted, and continue to delight, great multitudes of readers was a man to whom life was something to be endured rather than enjoyed; and those against whom he displayed his most violent prejudices—Whigs, Americans, atheists, Scots—are among his most faithful worshipers. When Goldsmith proposed some additions to the Club, since the existing members had traveled over one another's minds, Johnson flashed out: "Sir, you have not travelled over *my* mind, I assure you."

Nor, perhaps, have we.

SELECTED BIBLIOGRAPHY

I. BIBLIOGRAPHY. W. P. Courtney and D. N. Smith, *A Bibliography of Samuel Johnson* (Oxford, 1915; reiss., 1968), supplement by R. W. Chapman and A. T. Hazen, Oxford Bibliographical Society (1938); *The R. B. Adam Library, Relating to Dr. Samuel Johnson and His Era*, 4 vols. (London, 1929–1930); J. L. Clifford, *Johnsonian Studies 1887–1950* (Minneapolis, 1951), supplement 1950–1960 by J. L. Clifford and D. J. Greene in M. Wahta, ed., *Johnsonian Studies* (Cairo, 1962); J. D. Freeman, *A Preliminary Handlist of Documents and Manuscripts of Samuel Johnson*, Oxford Bibliographical Society (Oxford, 1968).

II. COLLECTED WORKS. [G. Kearsley], ed., *The Poetical Works* (London, 1785; enl. ed., 1789); J. Hawkins, ed., *The Works*, 11 vols. (London, 1787), with two additional vols. by J. Stockdale, ed. (1787); A. Murphy, ed., *The Works*, 12 vols. (London, 1792), new ed. by A. Chalmers (1806); R. Anderson, ed., *The Poetical Works* (Edinburgh, 1795), vol. XI: *The Poets of Great Britain*; F. W. Blagdon, ed., *The Poems* (London, 1808); A. Chalmers, ed., *The Poems* (London, 1810), vol. XVI: *The Works of the English Poets*; *The Works*, 11 vols. (London, 1825), Oxford English Classics series; R. Lynam, ed., *The Works*, 6 vols. (London, 1825); G. Gilfillan, ed., *The Poetical Works of Johnson, Parnell, Gay, Etc.* (Edinburgh, 1855); T. M. Ward, ed., *Poems* (London, 1905), includes Goldsmith, Gray, and Collins; D. N. Smith and E. L. McAdam, eds., *The Poems* (Oxford, 1941); *Works*, the Yale ed., in progress, comprises: E. L. McAdam, Jr., and D. and M. Hyde, eds., vol. I, *Diaries, Prayers and Annals* (New Haven, 1958); W. J. Bate, J. M. Bullitt, and L. F. Powell, eds., vol. II, *The Idler and The Adventurer* (1963); E. L. McAdam, Jr., ed., vol. VI, *Poems* (1964); A. Sherbo, ed., vols. VII and VIII, *Johnson on Shakespeare* (1968).

III. SELECTED WORKS. *The Beauties of Johnson* (London, 1781), and later eds.; S. Howard, ed., *The Beauties of Johnson* (London, 1833); G. B. Hill, ed., *Wit and Wisdom of Samuel Johnson* (London, 1888); G. B. Hill, ed., *Select Essays*, 2 vols. (London, 1889); C. G. Osgood, ed., *Selections from Johnson* (New York, 1909); A. Meynell and G. K. Chesterton, eds., *Samuel Johnson* (London, 1911); R. W. Chapman, ed., *Johnson, Prose and Poetry* (Oxford, 1922); R. W. Chapman, ed., *Selected Letters* (Oxford, 1925), in the World's Classics ed.; S. C. Roberts, ed., *Samuel Johnson, Writer* (London, 1926); J. E. Brown, ed., *The Critical Opinions of Samuel Johnson* (Princeton, N. J., 1926); A. T. Hazen, ed., *Samuel Johnson's Prefaces and Dedications* (London, 1937); M. Wilson, ed., *Johnson, Prose and Poetry* (London, 1950); E. L. McAdam, Jr., and G. Milne, *Johnson's Dictionary: A Modern Selection* (London, 1963); R. T. Davies, ed., *Samuel Johnson: Selected Writings* (London, 1965); P. Cruttwell, ed., *Samuel Johnson: Selected Writings* (London, 1968), with intro. and notes.

IV. LETTERS. H. L. Piozzi, ed., *Letters to and from Samuel Johnson*, 2 vols. (London, 1788); G. B. Hill, ed., *Letters of Samuel Johnson*, 2 vols. (Oxford, 1892); Marquess of Lansdowne, ed., *Johnson and Queeney* (London, 1932), letters to Queeney Thrale; and *The Queeney Letters* (London, 1934); R. W. Chapman, ed., *The Letters of Samuel Johnson*, 3 vols. (Oxford, 1952), the standard ed.

V. SEPARATE WORKS. Lobo. *A Voyage to Abyssinia* (London, 1735), also in H. Morley, ed. (London, 1887); *London: A Poem* (London, 1738), also in T. S. Eliot, ed. (London, 1930); *Marmor Norfolciense* (London, 1739); *A Compleat Vindication of the Licensers of the Stage* (London, 1739); *Life of Mr. Richard Savage* (London, 1744), repr. in *Lives of the Poets*; *Miscellaneous Observations on Macbeth* (London, 1745); *The Plan of a Dictionary of the English Language* (London, 1747); *The Vanity of Human Wishes* (London, 1749), also in E. J. Payne, ed. (Oxford, 1876) and T. S. Eliot, ed. (London, 1930); *Irene: A Tragedy* (London, 1749); *Rambler* (London, 1750–1752), some selections in W. H. White, ed. (London, 1907); *A Dictionary of the English Language*, 2 vols. (London, 1755); *A Dictionary of the English Language*, 2 vols. (London, 1756), abstracted from the folio ed.; *The History of Rasselas Prince of Abyssinia*, 2 vols. (London, 1759), also in G. B. Hill, ed. (London, 1887) and R. W. Chapman, ed. (Oxford, 1927); *Idler*, 2 vols. (London, 1761), papers from *Idler* in S. C. Roberts, ed. (Cambridge, 1921); *The Plays of William Shakespeare*, 8 vols. (London, 1765; 10 vols., 1773), with notes by Johnson and Steevens; Johnson's proposals, preface, and notes are conveniently assembled in Sir W. A. Raleigh, *Johnson on Shakespeare* (London, 1908); *The False Alarm* (London, 1770); *Thoughts on the Late Transactions Respecting Falkland's Islands* (London, 1771); *Patriot* (London, 1774); *Taxation No Tyranny* (London, 1775); *A Journey to the Western Islands of Scotland* (London, 1775), also, with Boswell's *Tour*, in R. W. Chapman, ed. (Oxford, 1924); *Prefaces to the Works of the English Poets*, 10 vols.

(London, 1779–1781), reiss. as *The Lives of the English Poets*, 4 vols. (London, 1781), also in A. Napier, ed., 3 vols. (London, 1890), A. Waugh, ed., World's Classics ed., 6 vols. (London, 1896), G. B. Hill, ed., 3 vols. (London, 1905), L. A. Hind, ed., Everyman's Library ed., 2 vols. (London, 1925); the six chief lives—Milton, Dryden, Swift, Addison, Pope, Gray—edited by Matthew Arnold (London, 1878); a more recent selection is S. C. Roberts, ed. (London, 1963); G. Strahan, ed., *Prayers and Meditations* (London, 1785), also in G. B. Hill, ed., *Johnsonian Miscellanies* (London, 1897), and in H. Higgins, ed. (London, 1904) and H. E. Savage, ed. (Lichfield, 1927); *Debates in Parliament*, 2 vols. (London, 1787); R. Wright, ed., *An Account of the Life of Dr. Samuel Johnson from His Birth to His Eleventh Year, Written by Himself* (London, 1805); R. Duppa, ed., *A Diary of a Journey into North Wales in the Year 1744* (London, 1816), repr. in A. M. Broadley, *Dr. Johnson and Mrs. Thrale* (London, 1910); M. Tyson and H. Guppy, eds., *The French Journals of Mrs. Thrale and Dr. Johnson* (Manchester, 1932).

VI. BIOGRAPHICAL AND CRITICAL STUDIES. *The Life of Samuel Johnson, LLD* (London, 1785), attributed to William Cooke; *Memoirs of the Life and Writings of the Late Dr. Samuel Johnson* (London, 1785), attributed to William Shaw; J. Boswell, *The Journal of a Tour to the Hebrides with Samuel Johnson* (London, 1785), also in J. W. Croker, ed. (London, 1831), R. Carruthers, ed. (London, 1851), A. Napier, ed. (London, 1884), G. B. Hill, ed. (London, 1887), R. W. Chapman, ed. (London, 1924), with Johnson's *Journey*, F. A. Pottle and C. H. Bennett, eds. (London, 1936), from the MS; H. L. Piozzi, *Anecdotes of the Late Samuel Johnson* (London, 1786), also in S. C. Roberts, ed. (London, 1925); J. Hawkins, *The Life of Samuel Johnson* (London, 1787); J. Boswell, *The Life of Samuel Johnson* (London, 1791), also in J. W. Croker, ed., 5 vols. (London, 1831), R. Carruthers, ed., 4 vols. (London, 1851–1852), A. Napier, ed., 5 vols. (London, 1884), G. B. Hill, ed., 6 vols. (Oxford, 1887), includes the *Tour*, reedited by L. F. Powell (London, 1934–1940), the standard ed. for scholars, R. Ingpen, ed., 2 vols. (London, 1907), notable for its illustrations; other reprints by Oxford, Globe, and Everyman's Library; A. Murphy, *An Essay on the Life and Genius of Samuel Johnson* (London, 1792); R. Anderson, *The Life of Samuel Johnson* (London, 1795); T. B. Macaulay, "Croker's Edition of Boswell's *Life of Johnson*," in *Edinburgh Review* (Sept. 1831); T. Carlyle, "Boswell's *Life of Johnson*," in *Fraser's Magazine* (May 1832); Dr. T. Campbell, *A Diary of a Visit to England in 1775*, edited by S. Raymond (Sydney, 1854), also in J. L. Clifford, ed. (London, 1947), from the newly discovered MS; T. B. Macaulay, "Samuel Johnson," in *Encyclopaedia Britannica*, 8th ed., vol. XII (London, 1856); G. B. Hill, *Dr. Johnson: His Friends and His Critics* (London, 1870); L. Stephen, *Samuel Johnson* (London, 1878), in the English Men of Letters series; A. Napier, ed.,

Johnsoniana (London, 1884); F. Grant, *Life of Samuel Johnson* (London, 1887), with a bibliography by J. P. Anderson; G. B. Hill, ed., *Johnsonian Miscellanies* (Oxford, 1897; facs. ed., 2 vols., London, 1968); G. Whale and J. Sargeaunt, eds., *Johnson Club Papers* (London, 1899; 2nd ser., 1920); T. Seccombe, *The Age of Johnson* (London, 1889); J. A. H. Murray, *The Evolution of English Lexicography* (London, 1900); A. L. Reade, *The Reades of Blackwood Hill and Dr. Johnson's Ancestry* (London, 1906), and *Johnsonian Gleanings*, 11 vols. (London, 1909–1952), an encyclopedia of Johnson's family and of his early life; J. T. Raby, ed., *Bi-centenary of the Birth of Dr. Samuel Johnson* (London, 1909); Sir W. A. Raleigh, *Six Essays on Johnson* (London, 1910), an important restatement, correcting Macaulay's views; J. Bailey, *Dr. Johnson and His Circle* (London, 1913); S. C. Roberts, *The Story of Dr. Johnson* (London, 1919); P. H. Houston, *Dr. Johnson: A Study in Eighteenth-Century Humanism* (Cambridge, Mass., 1923); C. Hollis, *Doctor Johnson* (London, 1928); R. Lynd, *Doctor Johnson and Company* (London, 1928); D. N. Smith, R. W. Chapman, and L. F. Powell, *Johnson and Boswell Revisited* (Oxford, 1928); S. C. Roberts, *Doctor Johnson* (London, 1934); J. W. Krutch, *Samuel Johnson* (London, 1944); S. C. Roberts, *Samuel Johnson* (London, 1944), British Academy lecture; B. H. Bronson, *Johnson Agonistes and Other Essays* (London, 1944); R. W. Chapman, *Johnsonian and Other Essays and Reviews* (Oxford, 1953); W. J. Bate, *The Achievements of Samuel Johnson* (New York, 1955); J. L. Clifford, *The Young Samuel Johnson* (London, 1955); E. A. Bloom, *Samuel Johnson in Grub Street* (Providence, 1957); S. C. Roberts, *Doctor Johnson and Others* (London, 1958); F. W. Hilles, ed., *New Light on Dr. Johnson* (New Haven, 1959); D. J. Greene, *The Politics of Samuel Johnson* (New Haven, 1960); R. Voitle, *Samuel Johnson the Moralist* (Cambridge, Mass., 1961); M. J. C. Hodgart, *Samuel Johnson and His Time* (London, 1962); M. J. Quinlan, *Samuel Johnson, A Layman's Religion* (Madison, Wis., 1964); D. J. Greene, ed., *Samuel Johnson* (Englewood Cliffs, N. J., 1965), the Twentieth-Century Views series, *Johnson, Boswell and Their Circle* (Oxford, 1965), essays by various hands presented to L. F. Powell in honor of his eighty-fourth birthday; A. Sachs, *Passionate Intelligence: Imagination and Reason in the Works of Samuel Johnson* (Baltimore–London, 1967); F. E. Halliday, *Doctor Johnson and His World* (London, 1968), contains illustrations with accompanying text; J. P. Hardy, ed., *The Political Writings of Dr. Johnson* (London, 1968); J. T. Boulton, ed., *Samuel Johnson: The Critical Heritage* (London, 1971); F. Grant, *Time, Form and Style in Boswell's "Life of Johnson"* (New Haven, 1971); G. Irwin, *Samuel Johnson: A Personality in Conflict* (Wellington, New Zealand, 1972); A. Passler, *Life of Samuel Johnson* (London, 1972); R. B. Schwartz, *Samuel Johnson and the New Science* (Madison, Wis., 1972); D. J. Greene, *The Politics* of *Samuel Johnson* (Port Washington, N. Y., 1973); A. T. Hazen, *Samuel Johnson: Prefaces and Dedications* (Port Washington, N. Y., 1973); C. McIntosh, *Samuel Johnson and the World of Fiction* (New Haven, 1973); R. Stock, *Samuel Johnson and Neo-classical Dramatic Theory* (Lincoln, Nebr., 1973); J. Wain, ed., *Johnson as Critic* (London, 1973); J. H. Sledd and G. J. Kolb, *Dr. Johnson's Dictionary: Essays in the Biography of a Book* (Chicago, 1974); J. Wain, *Samuel Johnson* (London, 1974); M. Lane, *Samuel Johnson and His World* (London, 1975); R. B. Schwartz, *Samuel Johnson and the Problem of Evil* (Madison, Wis., 1975); J. Wain, ed., *Johnson on Johnson* (London, 1976), in the Everyman's Library; W. Edinger, *Samuel Johnson and Poetic Style* (Chicago, 1977); R. Folkenflik, *Samuel Johnson, Biographer* (Ithaca, N. Y., 1978); W. J. Bate, *Samuel Johnson* (London, 1978).

LAURENCE STERNE

(1713-1768)

D. W. Jefferson

I

In more than one place Laurence Sterne claims a medicinal value for his great comic masterpiece *The Life and Opinions of Tristram Shandy, Gentleman* (1759–1767):

—If 'tis wrote against anything,—'tis wrote, an' please your worships, against the spleen! in order, by a more frequent and a more convulsive elevation and depression of the diaphragm, and the succussations of the intercostal and abdominal muscles in laughter, to drive the *gall* and other *bitter juices* from the gall-bladder, liver, and sweetbread of his majesty's subjects, with all the inimicitious passions which belong to them, down into their duodenums.

(bk. 4, ch. 22)

In another passage he writes:

True *Shandeism*, think what you will against it, opens the heart and lungs, and like all those affections which partake of its nature, it forces the blood and other vital fluids of the body to run freely thro' its channels, and makes the wheel of life run long and chearfully round.

(bk. 4, ch. 32)

But turning from *Tristram Shandy* to a letter written about June 1791 to his amiable companion, John Hall-Stevenson, in which he complains of "a thin death-doing pestiferous north-east wind" blowing upon him, we see the virtues of the Shandean philosophy in another light:[1]

. . . and if God . . . had not poured forth the spirit of Shandeism into me, which will not suffer me to think two minutes upon any grave subject, I would else just now lay down and die. . . .

[1]Quotations from letters are from L. P. Curtis, ed., *Letters of Laurence Sterne* (Oxford, 1965).

Sterne was long a sick man, a victim of hemorrhages of the lungs, driven to travel abroad for his health. The gaiety of *Tristram Shandy* and also of *A Sentimental Journey Through France and Italy* (1768) takes on a different significance against this background.

Sterne's character is of a kind that needs, but also inspires, tender and careful handling. No reputation has suffered more than his from nineteenth-century moral prejudice and obtuseness. William Thackeray's account of him in *The English Humourists of the Eighteenth Century* is one of the disgraces of English criticism. Our own age can perhaps more easily accept simply as psychological fact some aspects of his life that gave scandal to the Victorians. He was emotionally unstable. His marriage with Elizabeth Lumley was not very successful: she has been described as a "fretful porcupine," and no doubt there were faults on his side. After eighteen years of married life she had a curious mental breakdown, following which Sterne's helpless susceptibility to women manifested itself in a series of sentimental relationships (they were not affairs of physical passion) that are not quite in keeping with the character of a clergyman. He was singularly unabashed about this side of his nature, as the following passage from a letter written about 23 August 1765, possibly to John Wodehouse, testifies:

. . . I am glad that you are in love—'twill cure you (at least) of the spleen, which has a bad effect on both man and woman—I myself must ever have some dulcinea in my head—it harmonizes the soul—and in those cases I first endeavour to make the lady believe so, or rather I begin first to make myself believe that I am in love—but I carry on my affairs quite in the French way, sentimentally—"l'amour" (they say) "n'est rien sans sentiment."

What the modern reader may find engaging here is Sterne's easy candor. Perhaps it is easier today to sympathize with an aspect of him that has tended in the past to alienate sympathy; namely, the elements of artifice that accompany his expressions of emotion. Even in the *Journal to Eliza* (1767), written to the woman who meant much more to him than any of the others, during a period of overwrought emotion combined with poor health, he shows an artist's awareness of the exquisite distress he is depicting:[2]

Ap. 28. I was not deceived, Eliza! by my presentiment that I should find thee out in my dreams; for I have been with thee almost the whole night, alternatively soothing Thee, or telling thee my sorrows—I have rose up comforted & strengthened,—& found myself so much better, that I ordered my Carriage, to carry me to our mutual friend—Tears ran down her cheeks when she saw how pale & wan I was—never gentle creature sympathized more tenderly—I beseech you, cried the good Soul, not to regard either difficulties or expenses, but to fly to Eliza directly—I see you will dye without her—save yourself for her—How shall I.look her in the face? What can I say to her, when on her return I have to tell her, That her Yorick is no more!—Tell her my dear friend, said I, that I will meet her in a better world—& that I have left this, because I could not live without her; tell Eliza, my dear friend, added I—That I died broken hearted—and that you were a witness to it—as I said this she burst into the most pathetick flood of Tears that ever kindly Nature shed—you never beheld so affecting a scene—'twas too much for Nature!

Our response to this depends very largely on our response to Sterne as a man. To some readers it is sheer wanton indulgence, self-conscious manipulation of the feelings, and fundamentally insincere. But perhaps it is wiser to recognize that everyone has his "style," in the emotions as in other things. To the present writer, at least, the *Journal to Eliza* is a moving document, the record of genuine suffering. If Sterne was, to use an unkind modern term, somewhat exhibitionist about his feelings, these outpourings, with all their elements of conscious heightening, are the expression of a need. There is, of course, pathological weakness here, and it must be related to his state of physical health. But it was Sterne's gift that he could make something out of his weaknesses. He expressed himself to the full, and somehow the result is humanly acceptable. Re-

cent scholarship has uncovered some much less attractive cases of emotional instability among the Victorian writers. Thackeray himself was somewhat frustrated and unfulfilled, which may help to explain his dislike of Sterne's freedom and fluency in matters of the heart.

We might feel less kindly about this side of Sterne's life were it not for the agreeable impression we get from his letters and from outside testimony of his efforts during these later years to make things as comfortable as possible for his wife. The solicitous interest he took in the details of her journey to France, when she decided to join him there with their daughter Lydia; his patience with her trying humors during their sojourn there; and his reasonable attitude to her financial demands, after he had returned to his Yorkshire parish and she had formed the project of living apart from him: all this testifies to good elements in him and to a sweetness of disposition in the face of vexation. How far he is to be blamed for the central fact of the failure of their marriage is a matter concerning which we have insufficient evidence.

Our own age is not only better equipped temperamentally to appreciate Sterne and his work; it also has the advantage of more information about his life, for which we are indebted partly to the nineteenth-century biographer Percy Fitzgerald, but more especially to the American scholar Wilbur L. Cross, whose monumental *Life and Times of Laurence Sterne* destroyed a number of malicious traditions that misled earlier critics. We now have more evidence, for example, about his treatment of his mother, whom he was alleged to have scandalously neglected.

Sterne's father was a poor ensign who made an unfortunate marriage in Flanders with the daughter of a sutler: he appears to have married her because he owed money to her father. Born in 1713, Laurence spent his infancy in barracks in Ireland, and was then sent to school in Yorkshire, where he came under the protection of his father's relatives, upon whom he was dependent for the expenses of his education (his father died penniless in 1731). During the period when Sterne was at Cambridge, and for some years after his ordination as a clergyman in the Church of England, his mother lived in Ireland on her pension, supplemented by what she earned from keeping an embroidery school; and there appears to have been little contact between them.

[2]Quotations are from Ian Jack, ed., *The Journal to Eliza* (with *A Sentimental Journey*) (Oxford, 1968).

In 1741, when Sterne was established as a prebendary of York, and was married to a woman whom his mother believed to have money, the elder Mrs. Sterne decided to come with her daughter to England to live at her son's expense. The story of the persecutions he suffered over a period of years, of the drain upon his income and his various financial anxieties, of her unreasonableness and dishonesty and his repeated efforts not to forget that he was a son, "though she forgot that she was a mother," is told in a letter by Sterne himself that was not published until 1892. We have only his word for its truth, but it is a circumstantial document and has the ring of genuineness. It was written in indignation to his uncle and old enemy, Dr. Jaques Sterne, who, after playing a not very helpful part in this affair, had caused Sterne's mother to be placed in a charitable institution in York (according to some, "the common gaol") apparently with no other motive than the wish to damage his nephew's reputation. Before the publication of this letter there were many, no doubt, who believed, with Lord George Byron, that Sterne "preferred whining over a dead ass to relieving a living mother." We do not know the whole story. It seems likely that Sterne's handling of this extremely difficult situation fell short of the heroic, but Cross's comment that "a man of finer grain would have taken in his mother and sister and made the best of it" is a lapse into insensitive moralizing. Not that moral principles do not apply to Sterne as much as to other men, but one of the effects of his elusive and sympathetic personality is to remind us of how little, even when we know the "facts," we can judge any human being's response to the strains and stresses of life.

What can be said of his character as a clergyman? It is difficult for us to appreciate the motives with which, in this period, men like Jonathan Swift and Sterne entered the church: they seem to have had no special insight into their religion, no overmastering sense of vocation. Both of these clergymen had a distinctly secular turn of wit. Part of the answer is that in an age when intense religious fervor was condemned by reasonable people as "enthusiasm," the tendency was for clergymen to behave outwardly as men of the world, so that it is not easy for us to tell how serious they were beneath the surface. Sterne's sermons have little doctrinal content, and show no feeling for the supernatural values of his religion; one has the impression that he takes all this

for granted. It is the human, moral aspects of the Bible stories that he dwells upon, often with sensitiveness and insight, though none of his sermons rises to great heights. As for his parochial activities, from the little evidence we have it is impossible to say how diligent he was. In a letter to the archbishop of York in 1743 replying to a questionnaire, he makes the remarkable statement: "I Catechise every Sunday in my Church during Lent, But explain our Religion to the Children and Servants of my Parishioners in my House every Sunday Night during Lent, from six o'clock till nine," which, according to Canon Ollard, who published the letter[3] and examined many other such returns, stands alone as an example of zeal. Sometimes the evidence points to a more easygoing attitude. Cross quotes a story to the effect that as Sterne "was going over the fields on a Sunday to preach at Stillington, it happened that his pointer dog sprung a covey of partridges, when he went directly home for his gun and left his flock that was waiting for him in the church in the lurch." On the whole Cross, whose knowledge of Sterne is unrivaled, gives him a good character for attention to his ecclesiastical duties and generosity to his curates, a class of men who in that age were not always well treated.

For nearly thirty years his associations were with York and the villages north of it: Sutton-in-the-Forest, Stillington, and finally Coxwold, the living of which he obtained in 1760. Like other parsons of his day, he farmed his own land, and it is not altogether agreeable to note that he used the practice of enclosure to build up a sizable property. That Sterne was attached in this way to his locality, with a countryman's feeling for it, is one of the things that contribute to the flavor of *Tristram Shandy*; and a love for Coxwold, his "land of plenty" and "delicious retreat," colors the pages of the *Journal to Eliza*, written in his last year. But in the last eight years of his life he was absent for long periods, partly because of bad health and the need to travel, partly because as a man of letters he was eagerly claimed by the society of the metropolis.

Sterne had an unholy taste for the company of Rabelaisian wits such as John Hall-Stevenson, who entertained his club of "Demoniacs" at Skelton Castle ("Crazy Castle," as he called it), which was near enough for Sterne to pay frequent visits. In the days of his fame the freedom of his conversation gave of-

[3]In the *Times Literary Supplement*, 18 March 1926.

fense to Samuel Johnson, who felt the disgrace to the cloth. Apropos of Johnson's disapproval, it is quite likely that Sterne's anarchic wit, stimulated by an uncontrolled eagerness of temperament, often went too far, so that he gave an unjust impression of his true worth.

Sterne developed late as a literary artist. His earliest writings, as far as we know, were political articles and letters written for local newspapers during a celebrated Yorkshire election of 1741. It was as an assistant to his uncle, who was a vigorous Whig and persecutor of Catholics and Jacobites, that he had this short spell as a political propagandist, but later he regretted it as "dirty work," and his refusal to write any more in such a cause earned him the undying ill will of Dr. Sterne, manifested, as we have seen, in the situation created by his mother. Apart from the occasional sermon that was printed, he wrote nothing more for nearly twenty years.[4] In 1759 a local squabble about ecclesiastical preferments provoked him to compose a witty allegory in the manner of Swift entitled *A Political Romance*, later known as *The History of a Good Warm Watch-Coat* (1759). About the turn of the new year in 1760 he published the first two volumes of *Tristram Shandy*. At the age of forty-six, Sterne, previously quite obscure, suddenly achieved a celebrity to which there can be few parallels in literary history.

Visiting London by chance a few months after *Tristram Shandy* made its debut, he discovered that copies of it "could not be had either for love or money"; and the news that the author was in town led to an astonishing sequence of social triumphs. Lord Rockingham, one of the great Yorkshire Whigs and a future prime minister, took the lead in welcoming Sterne into the world of fashion; he made the acquaintance of the duke of York; and he dined at Windsor Castle, on the occasion of the installation of Prince Ferdinand of Brunswick as Knight of the Garter. Among his new friends in the world of the arts was David Garrick, the manager of the Drury Lane Theatre. Those who are not well disposed toward Sterne may be inclined to regard this as a somewhat meretricious social success—he was an amusing companion and a fashionable novelty—but this is not the whole truth. Dr. John

Hill (a dubious figure, but there is no reason to question his good faith here) wrote in a contemporary periodical: "Everybody is curious to see the author; and, when they see him, everybody loves the man; there is a pleasantry in his conversation that always pleases; and a goodness in his heart, which adds the greater tribute of esteem."

Further volumes of *Tristram Shandy* appeared over the next seven years, the pace of composition being greatly reduced by periods of illness and the distractions of travel abroad. On his first journey to France, which lasted from 1762 to 1764, Sterne was given a flattering reception into Parisian society, and became an associate of Paul Thiry d'Holbach's circle. It is with his second visit to the Continent, in 1765 to 1766, that *A Sentimental Journey* appears to be mainly concerned, though some incidents from the earlier visit are incorporated; but after all it is not primarily as a factual record that we value this remarkable work of art, which was published in 1768, a few weeks before his death.

One of the more damaging of the legends that recent biographers have been able to correct concerns his death. It is not true that he died friendless and in mean lodgings. His last days were spent in comfortable apartments, where he had many visitors until he was too ill to receive any more; and there were friends to show him kindness until the end. It is true that when he died of pleurisy in 1768, he left large debts: the sale of his works, though considerable, was insufficient to offset the expenses of foreign travel and of a separate establishment for his wife and daughter.

II

Tristram Shandy is one of those works to which one can return again and again with increasing satisfaction; but let us begin by looking at it as it appears to the delighted but baffled reader who is approaching it for the first time. His impression is of a kind of rich chaos, an inspired disorder. First, there is the apparent lack of progression. The reader waits helplessly until the third book for the hero to be born; the christening occurs in the fourth; in the sixth there is talk of putting him into breeches; and this, apart from a freakish, wholly unrelated passage about his travels in the seventh book, is as far as his history is developed. Whatever the reader is getting, it is not what the title promised: the "Life

[4]Unless some literary articles in the *York Journal* of 1750–1751, referred to by L. P. Curtis in *The Politicks of Laurence Sterne* (Oxford, 1929), are by him, but we have no definite evidence.

and Opinions" of the hero. Meanwhile, there are digressions. No writer, it is safe to say, ever used the digression more often or, it would seem, more wantonly. It would be difficult to find digressions at a steeper angle from the main course than some of Sterne's. Yet Sterne is completely at home and at his ease amid this seeming anarchy; and if the reader loses all sense of movement and direction, something sustains him: an atmosphere so humanly satisfying and beguiling that the author, with all his vagaries, has him totally at his mercy.

Lying on the surface of *Tristram Shandy* are innumerable manifestations of Sterne's playfulness and delight in absurdity, which serve to accentuate the impression of artistic irresponsibility. For example, halfway through the third book, when Mr. Shandy falls asleep as he sits in the parlor waiting for his son to be born, and Uncle Toby follows him, and the other characters have also been conveniently disposed of for the time being, the narrator then decides that he has a moment or two to spare, so he writes his preface. When the moment arrives in the sixth book for a picture of the Widow Wadman, the narrator abdicates and invites the reader to supply it himself ("Sit down, Sir, paint her in your own mind—as like your mistress as you can—as unlike your wife as your conscience will let you—"), leaving a blank page for the purpose. And in the last book, when Uncle Toby is about to call on the Widow Wadman to pay court to her, and is in fact on the threshold, the chapter ends and the next two chapters (18 and 19) are left blank, to be supplied out of their order a few pages later. After the sketch of Parson Yorick in the first book—a Cervantic self-portrait, full of humor and Sterne's peculiar brand of pathos—a page is devoted to his tombstone. At the end of the sixth book, promising to mend his ways and tell his story "in a tolerable strait line," Sterne draws a number of irregular lines representing the tortuous paths taken in the earlier books. And if the reader, turning over the page from book 4, chapter 23, thinks that something has gone wrong at the printer's, he will soon see that it is just another of the author's jokes: there is no twenty-fourth chapter, and there is a gap in the pagination signifying the loss of ten pages.

But some readers will see, even on their first approach, that there is a good deal of method in Sterne's chaos. There is, for example, quite a good reason why the hero's birth should be so long delayed: it is not a beginning, it is a climax. The novel opens with his begetting, and no one can complain of lack of promptness in the treatment of it. In most autobiographical novels the birth and infancy of the hero are passed over fairly quickly, the main interest being attached to his later adventures; but Sterne's novel is different. Its theme, to reduce it to a simple formula, is "How the hero came into the world and how, owing to various mishaps pre-natal and post-natal, he came to be the unfortunate creature he is." It is as if a modern novelist wrote a Freudian romance dealing with the decisive traumatic experiences of the central character; as in *Tristram Shandy*, it would not be necessary to trace the hero's career beyond infancy. It is part of Sterne's comic purpose that we should be somewhat befogged as to his intention, yet from the beginning there are plenty of explicit indications as to what he is doing. His technique is to dangle the point in front of the reader's nose, but also to keep him so entertained and bewildered by other things that he will probably not see it. The present writer could not have identified the central plan of *Tristram Shandy* after the first reading, but there is no reason why an observant reader should not do so.

The first chapter begins with these words:

I wish either my father or my mother, or indeed both of them, as they were in duty both equally bound to it, had minded what they were about when they begot me.

And then follows a discourse on "the animal spirits, as how they are transferred from father to son etc. etc." and how much depends on their condition during this important journey; and we are told of the ill-timed question of his mother ("Pray, my dear, have you not forgot to wind up the clock?"—an example of John Locke's doctrine of association of ideas, in which Sterne was much interested), which, by interrupting Mr. Shandy, "scattered and dispersed the animal spirits, whose business it was to have escorted and gone hand in hand with the HOMUNCULUS, and conducted him safe to the place destined for his reception." This is the first of the series of catastrophes blighting the fortunes of the infant hero.

The second arises out of a clause in Mrs. Shandy's marriage settlement, the sense of which is that if she becomes pregnant her husband undertakes to pay the expenses of her journey to and confinement in London; but if on any occasion she puts him to this expense "upon false cries and tokens," she forfeits these rights the next time. Unluckily for the young hero, a fruitless journey to London was made in the year before his birth, under peculiarly annoying circumstances for Mr. Shandy, as it was toward the end of September, "when his wall-fruit and green-gages especially, in which he was very curious, were just ready for pulling." The terms are enforced, it is settled that the hero shall be born in the country, and "I was doom'd by marriage articles, to have my nose squeez'd as flat to my face, as if the destinies had spun me without one." But this is looking ahead.

Mr. Shandy is a man of theories, and he applies his speculative mind to the supreme parental task of ensuring that his child shall have the best start in life. One of his beliefs concerns noses; namely, that "the excellency of the nose is in a direct arithmetical proportion to the excellency of the wearer's fancy." The events culminating in Tristram's being brought into the world defective in this respect have to be traced, therefore, with some care; and, indeed, the narrator lavishes every circumstantial embellishment upon the various stages of the fatal sequence. In the first place, Mrs. Shandy is as obstinate in her own way as her husband: deprived of the best professional attention, she insists on having the most primitive—the local old woman, in preference to Dr. Slop, an operator with an impressive equipment of obstetric instruments. So, by way of compromise, she gets her own way, while Dr. Slop is to sit in the parlor and drink a bottle of wine with Mr. Shandy and Uncle Toby, for which he is to receive a fee of five guineas. But as they sit there Dr. Slop is called upon, in an emergency, to intervene: the old woman has fallen on the edge of the fender and bruised her hip; and he too has suffered a somewhat Shandean misadventure, having cut his thumb while trying to sever the knots in the strings with which Obadiah, the servant at Shandy Hall, has tied up his bag of instruments. The next thing we hear of Dr. Slop, after he has been suddenly summoned, imperfectly prepared, to his task, is that, having applied his "vile instruments" with disastrous effect, he is making "a bridge for master's nose . . . with a piece of cotton and a thin piece of whalebone out of Susannah's stays."

The dismal climax is led up to with touches of dramatic heightening. "Truce!—truce, good Dr. Slop: stay thy obstetrick hand. . . ." Thus begins an eloquent invocation to the operator as he approaches Shandy Hall. "Sport of small accidents, Tristram Shandy! that thou art, and ever will be!" are the bitter words provoked by Obadiah's tying of the knots.

Such is the story of the hero's birth, when the relevant details are abstracted and pieced together; but how unlike the effect of the novel, in which the fragments of the narrative have the appearance of interruptions to digressions.

One of Sterne's notable characteristics is an imaginative interest in the physiological aspects of human situations. It is no accident that the Shandean philosophy, stated at the beginning of this essay, should be expressed in physiological terms. An excursion into the history of science would be necessary to explain why it was possible for Sterne and his predecessors, François Rabelais and Robert Burton, to derive so much inspiration from a subject that in modern times has not had much to give to the literary artist. The fact is that the old speculative approach to knowledge, the prescientific approach, offered greater opportunities to the imagination, especially in the direction of comic travesty, than the specialized experimental disciplines of later periods. Mr. Shandy, with his doctrine of noses and other curious excursions into physiological theory, is a speculative philosopher of the old school. And in becoming more efficient, science has acquired a sterilized quality; the fusion of scientific ideas with a homely personal manner or a lively fancy has gone. There are certain passages in *Tristram Shandy*—for example, the last chapter of book 2, in which Mr. Shandy's mind, running on obstetrics, is excited by the advantages of the cesarean section (he mentions it to his wife "merely as a matter of fact; but seeing her turn pale as ashes" drops the subject), and the later chapters of book 3, in which he goes deeply into the philosophy of noses—where his curious pedantry takes on an extraordinary richness of flavor, one to which we are accustomed in Rabelais, who was immensely learned in medicine and imaginatively alive to the poetry of the bodily functions. Here, for example, is a passage dealing with the ideas of Ambrose Paroeus, "chief surgeon and nose-mender to Francis the ninth of France." His view is

. . . that the length and goodness of the nose was owing simply to the softness and flaccidity of the nurse's breast—as the flatness and shortness of *puisne* noses was to the firmness and elastic repulsion of the same organ of nutrition in the hale and lively—which, tho' happy for the woman, was the undoing of the child, inasmuch as his nose was so snubb'd, so rebuff'd, so rebated, and so refrigerated thereby, as never to arrive *ad mensuram suam legitimam;*—but that in case of the flaccidity and softness of the nurse or mother's breast—by sinking into it, quoth Paraeus, as into so much butter, the nose is comforted, nourish'd, plump'd up, refresh'd, refocillated, and set agrowing for ever.

(bk. 3, ch. 38)

The delight in strange words, and the play between learned and homely words, gives a piquancy to the diction reminiscent of the older writers to whom Sterne was indebted.

The atmosphere in which the drama of the hero's birth is enacted is charged, then, with obsessions: obsessions with obstetrics, with noses, and also with names. Thwarted over his son's nose, Mr. Shandy turns to his theory that a name has an important positive or negative influence on its owner's destiny. If his son can be christened Trismegistus he may still enter upon life handsomely endowed. But the child has a fit, the christening has to be conducted in a hurry, and while his father, who has been roused from his bed, looks around for his breeches, the name has been irretrievably reduced to Tristram, a name that ranks very low in Mr. Shandy's system. He is still not wholly discouraged in his attempts to apply his learning to the problems of parenthood: he composes a *Tristra-paedia*, a plan for Tristram's education, on the lines of Xenophon's *Cyropaedia*; he develops a curious theory about physical health; he discovers a shortcut to knowledge based on the use of auxiliary verbs.

One of Sterne's structural devices is to interrupt the history of the hero's birth by filling in the human background, so that the Shandy world is well peopled and familiar to us when the moment for his arrival comes. He preferred to do this in digressions, though if he had wished he could have contrived a more orthodox framework. Because the hero is not yet born, these sections have the appearance of being deviations from the matter in hand and, as we have seen, it is part of Sterne's purpose that the reader should never know quite where he is. Thus several chapters in the first book are devoted to Yorick, a digression for which the pretext is rather slender: he comes in apropos of the old midwife to whom he used to lend his horse. And there is a sequence of chapters about Uncle Toby, with an elaborate explanation of the origin of his "hobby-horse." In an extremely interesting chapter

(book 1, chapter 22), Sterne claims—playfully, but there is serious truth in it—that his work is digressive and progressive at the same time. The digression often has a central purpose, though it also has its independent life. There are some digressions in *Tristram Shandy* for which this excuse could hardly be offered. There is something to be said for the view that freedom to digress is an artistic advantage, provided the writer can control the tension set up between new sources of interest and the reader's anxiety to reach a promised goal; and ability to manipulate the reader in this way is certainly one of Sterne's gifts. His lyrical defense of digressions is worth remembering:

Digressions, incontestably, are the sunshine;—they are the life, the soul of reading!—take them out of this book, for instance,—you might as well take the book along with them;—one cold eternal winter would reign on every page of it; restore them to the writer;—he steps forth like a bridegroom,—bids All-hail; brings in variety, and forbids the appetite to fail.

There is another reason for his use of digressions. One of the features of the Shandy world is the intensity with which the characters are absorbed in their own ideas and fantasies. Both Mr. Shandy and Uncle Toby are, to use Sterne's expression, "hobby-horsical," and Sterne's greatness as an artist is nowhere more manifest than in his ability to give imaginative depth to their preoccupations; otherwise what would be more boring than Mr. Shandy's theories or more childish than Uncle Toby's toy fortifications? The two brothers, though continually together and full of brotherly affection, virtually inhabit different mental spheres, which collide sometimes though they can hardly be said to meet. Uncle Toby's "hobby-horse" has its origin in his attempts, while he is recovering from his wound obtained at the siege of Namur, to explain to visitors how it all happened. The complexity of the terrain confuses him, and the story breaks down, so in order to clarify it he resorts to military maps and textbooks, until his servant, Corporal Trim, has the inspired idea of building miniature fortifications on the bowling green, where they fight mock battles with improvised fieldpieces made from such materials as a melted-down pewter shaving basin and the lead weights from sash-windows. As Mr. Shandy expounds his philosophical views, Uncle Toby, smoking quietly in his corner and comprehending little, makes remarks of engaging simplicity; but when his brother speaks of a train of ideas, his mind turns readily to a train of artillery, and when it is reported that Dr. Slop is making a bridge, he is very gratified, thinking of the broken drawbridge on the bowling green that has given him some trouble; and the history of the drawbridge provides us with a digression at this point. Sterne enjoyed furnishing illustrations for Locke's theory of association of ideas. More perhaps than any other novelist before Virginia Woolf, who may have learned from him, he succeeds in capturing the atmosphere that is created when two or three people, ostensibly in conversation together, are in fact thinking their own thoughts and maintaining a rather tenuous contact with each other. "I wish, Dr. Slop, you had seen what prodigious armies we had in Flanders," is Uncle Toby's contribution to a conversation specifically directed toward obstetrics (book 3, chapter 1).

Sterne is nowhere greater than in his power to convey a sense of Uncle Toby's absorption in his own private world, of its remoteness and of the completeness of the spell. It is when he takes us into that world, more than at any other time, that he shows us what he has learned from Miguel de Cervantes, to whom he continually makes affectionate references. Just as Don Quixote's delusions are given a potency that challenges everyday reality, so that in each episode we see the events from two points of view, so Uncle Toby's curious game of make-believe is given an extraordinary inwardness. In certain passages describing his technical problems we visualize the objects as the toys they are, yet they are invested with some of the importance of the things they represent. The effect depends on the use of detail. One of Sterne's most pleasing artistic habits is that of entering delightedly into the particulars of a complicated situation: the details are felt, made real to the imagination. The following passage about the drawbridge (book 3, chapter 25) has something of this quality:

It turned, it seems, upon hinges at both ends of it, opening in the middle, one half of which turning to one side of the fosse, and the other to the other; the advantage of which was this, that by dividing the weight of the bridge into two equal portions, it impowered my uncle *Toby* to raise it up or let it down with the end of his crutch, and with one hand, which, as his garrison was weak, was as much as he could well spare—but the disadvantages of such a construction were insurmountable;——for by this

means, he would say, I leave one half of my bridge in my enemy's possession——and pray of what use is the other?

(pp. 133–134)

Although the element of the fantastic is generously developed in the Shandy brothers, it is characteristic of Sterne's art that the better we come to know them the more of everyday human nature we see in them. The Shandy world is very solidly built, in spite of the magic elements in the atmosphere. Uncle Toby is a more real person than the great Dickens creations. He is of Shakespearean quality. Sterne can afford, in his half-playful, half-tender way, to give him an almost ideal charm: there are sufficient touches of plain, earthy normality to prevent the effect from being spoiled. We can believe completely in Uncle Toby, whereas it is necessary with Mr. Pickwick not to probe too far. We need to forget, for example, that he was once a businessman.

A number of passages concerning Uncle Toby have always caught the fancy of Sterne's readers; for example, the too often quoted story (book 2, chapter 12) of the fly that he allowed to escape: "Go, says he, lifting up the sash, and opening his hand as he spoke, to let it escape;—go, poor devil, get thee gone, why should I hurt thee?—This world surely is wide enough to hold both thee and me." Some of these episodes are composed rather in the manner of set pieces, an element of humorous artifice leaving the reader a certain amount of "play" between different possible levels of emotional response. The following admirable passage occurs in the story of the poor dying soldier Le Fever (book 6, chapter 8), upon whom Uncle Toby and Trim lavished their generous care:

——In a fortnight or three weeks, added my uncle *Toby*, smiling,—he might march.——He will never march; an' please your honour, in this world, said the corporal:—He will march; said my uncle *Toby*, rising up, from the side of the bed, with one shoe off:——An' please your honour, said the corporal, he will never march but to his grave:——He shall march, cried my uncle *Toby*, marching the foot which had a shoe on, though without advancing an inch,—he shall march to his regiment. ——He cannot stand it, said the corporal;——He shall be supported, said my uncle *Toby*;——He'll drop at last, said the corporal, and what will become of his boy?——He shall not drop, said my uncle *Toby*, firmly.——A-well-'o-day,—do what we can for him, said *Trim*, maintaining his point,—the poor soul will die:——He shall not die, by G—, cried my uncle *Toby*.

——The ACCUSING SPIRIT, which flew up to heaven's chancery with the oath, blush'd as he gave it in;—and the RECORDING ANGEL, as he wrote it down, dropp'd a tear upon the word, and blotted it out for ever.

(pp. 40–42)

III

STERNE is a figure of European importance, but mainly as the author of *A Sentimental Journey*. The influence of this work was prodigious: volumes have been written on its vogue in France, in Germany, in Italy; and countless publications with the word "sentimental" in the title appeared during the generation or so after his death. It was from outside England, from such writers as Johann Wolfgang von Goethe and Heinrich Heine, that the highest tributes to his genius came.

If the Victorians misread him ungenerously, disliking his vein of sentiment, he was certainly misread in the opposite way by some of his admirers outside England. Heine attributes to him a kind of intensity that is not his: "He was the darling of the pale, tragic goddess. Once in an access of fierce tenderness, she kissed his young heart with such power, passion, and madness, that his heart began to bleed and suddenly understood all the sorrows of this world, and was filled with infinite compassion." Those who know Sterne will know what kind of weight—not too much nor too little—to attach to such words as the following, which occur in his letter of 12 November 1767 to Mrs. William James: "I told you my design in it [i.e., *A Sentimental Journey*] was to teach us to love the world and our fellow creatures better than we do." To extract too much moral value from Sterne's work, on the authority of sentences such as these, may do him a disservice by provoking the old objection that the sentiment he helped to make fashionable is largely of the self-indulgent and self-deceiving kind. The disservice lies in the fact that Sterne's art, properly understood, forestalls this criticism. He had more awareness of the nature of emotional self-indulgence and self-deception than most of his critics. He showed just the right degree of awareness of them in himself; to have shown more would have been a fault.

Sterne seems to have played a decisive part in helping to establish certain meanings of the word "sentimental" in English. There has been some debate as to whether the letter of about 1739–1740 to his future wife, in which the word occurs, seemingly for the first time, is authentic or not. The same passage with small verbal changes is found in the *Journal to Eliza* of nearly thirty years later, which means that either Sterne touched up an old letter or his daughter Lydia, in editing the letters, fabricated one out of materials from the then unpublished *Journal*. From what we know of Lydia's editorial morals, the latter seems highly likely; and this solution becomes doubly acceptable when we consider the history of the word. The passage runs: "I gave a thousand pensive, penetrating looks at the chair thou hadst so often graced, in those quiet and sentimental repasts." It has been shown that this meaning of the word ("tender," "full of emotion") does not come into vogue until the 1760's, and then mainly through the writings of Sterne himself, the earlier meanings being based on the definition of "sentiment" as "thought" or "moral reflection" rather than "feeling." Sterne, it is suggested, was influenced by the French meaning of "sentiment" and was responsible for attaching it to the English word "sentimental."

Chilly generalizations concerning Sterne's place in contemporary literary history, as an instrument in the creation of a vogue, have little bearing on the essential value or interest for us of *A Sentimental Journey*. It is very much a personal achievement, a miracle not to be repeated, though there were many attempts to imitate it. It is alive and significant for us while the fashions of the period seem peculiarly dead and unreal.

To appreciate *A Sentimental Journey* we must first accept the personality of the narrator. Sterne was supremely skilled in presenting himself to the reader, a matter requiring considerable tact and the right combination of naturalness and sophistication. From the outset we see him as a somewhat slender, though engaging, personality. He is sympathetically responsive, but the situations described are such as to exercise the sympathies agreeably rather than otherwise. From the *Journal to Eliza*, a more personal document, we know that he was capable of more poignant feelings, but this is not the side of his nature that he reveals here. Perhaps the most important need for us in approaching the pathetic passages is to see them in their right proportion. The most usual way of misreading them is to assume that they claim more than they do, and then to attack them for their inadequacy. It is quite permissible, quite within the range of the author's intention, that in the chapter "The Dead Ass" (volume I), for instance, we should note his fond cherishing of the little details of the story, and see in it an element of amiable affectation:

Everybody who stood about, heard the poor fellow with concern——La Fleur offer'd him money.——The mourner said, he did not want it—it was not the value of the ass,—but the loss of him.—The ass, he said, he was assured loved him—and upon this told them a long story of a mischance upon their passage over the Pyrenean mountains, which had separated them from each other three days; during which time the ass had sought for him as much as he had sought the ass, and that they had neither scarce ate or drank till they met.

Thou hast one comfort, friend, said I, at least, in the loss of thy poor beast; I'm sure thou hast been a merciful master to him.——Alas! said the mourner, I thought so, when he was alive—but now that he is dead, I think otherwise.——I fear the weight of myself and my afflictions together have been too much for him—they have shortened the poor creature's days, and I fear I have them to answer for.—Shame on the world! said I to myself—Did we love each other, as this poor soul but loved his ass—'twould be something.——

(pp. 127–128)

In a number of incidents, Sterne allows us to see the limits or fluctuations of his generous feelings. When the Franciscan calls on him to beg for his convent, an inexplicable perversity prompts him to give nothing, in spite of—or because of—the altruistic after-dinner mood in which he has been interrupted. (But later they are amusingly reconciled.) And what becomes of the caged starling, the plight of which provokes him to such an elaborate outburst on liberty? In the episode of the beggars he makes admirable play with the illusions that accompany charitable giving. On the strength of eight sous, which he has arbitrarily decided is all he has for this purpose, how much moral satisfaction he extracts from the scene that follows. How he delights in the refinements of courtesy with which the beggars accept what he gives. But when he realizes that he has given away "his last sou," and that a *pauvre honteux* must go without, "Good God! said I—and I have not one single sou to give him—But you have a thousand! cried all the powers of nature, stirring within me."

In the following passage from the first volume, Sterne shows a humorous awareness of the absurdity of an infatuation, without robbing it of its charm:

Then I will meet thee, said I, fair spirit! at Brussels—'tis only returning from Italy through Germany to Holland, by the rout of Flanders, home—'twill scarce be ten posts out of my way; but were it ten thousand! with what a moral delight will it crown my journey, in sharing in the sickening incidents of a tale of misery told to me by such a sufferer? to see her weep! and though I cannot dry up the fountain of her tears, what an exquisite sensation is there still left, in wiping them away from off the cheeks of the first and fairest of women, as I'm sitting with my handkerchief in my hand in silence the whole night beside her.

(pp. 134–135)

It is surprising that he has not been more valued for these corrective effects. There are two kinds of sophistication in him that our age might well find enjoyable: his recognition of foibles and vanities in the sphere of the affections and sympathies, and his uninhibited expression of the latter, notwithstanding this recognition.

How are we to take those episodes dealing with encounters with women? They are, as sexual adventures, rather slender: that he was not more passionate is, for some readers, a point against him. For other readers, the point against him is the philandering in itself. For still others, it is his lingering over the details, his cherishing of each vibration. If we like Sterne, what will please us in these incidents is their fragrance, which this lingering over the details never spoils, and his gaiety of conscience. The fact is that for him such experiences are good. A point that needs to be made is that Sterne really believes in "virtue," though he cannot resist a woman's charm, and the sweetness of the episodes in question lies in the amount he gets out of them without actual transgression. In "The Conquest" he conveys admirably a fact of experience that is normal enough; namely, that it can be pleasant to feel desire and also pleasant not to give full rein to it. After he has refrained from laying hands on the *fille de chambre*, and has raised her up by the hand, led her out of the room, locked the door and put the key in his pocket, then, "the victory being quite decisive," he kisses her on the cheek and takes her safe to the gate of the hotel. In the episode of the girl in the bookshop (volume II), there is as much subtle suspense and intimacy of atmosphere as if it had been the beginning of an amorous intrigue:

We stood still at the corner of the Rue de Nevers whilst this pass'd—We then stopp'd a moment whilst she disposed of her *Egarements de Coeur*, etc. more commodiously than carrying them in her hand—they were two volumes; so I held the second for her, whilst she put the first into her pocket; and then she held her pocket, and I put in the other after it.

'Tis sweet to feel by what fine-spun threads our affections are drawn together.

We set off afresh, and as she took her third step, the girl put her hand within my arm—I was just bidding her—but she did it of herself with that undeliberating simplicity, which shew'd it was out of her head that she had never seen me before. For my part, I felt the conviction of consanguinity so strongly, that I could not help turning half round to look in her face, and see if I could trace out any thing in it of a family likeness—Tut! said I, are we not all relations?

When we arrived at the turning up of the Rue de Guineygaude, I stopp'd to bid her adieu for good and all: the girl would thank me again for my company and kindness—She bid me adieu twice—I repeated it as often; and so cordial was the parting between us, that had it happen'd anywhere else, I'm not sure but I should have sign'd it with a kiss of charity, as warm and holy as an apostle.

But in Paris, as none kiss each other but the men—I did, what amounted to the same thing—

—I bid God bless her.

(pp. 9–11)

The delicacy of his narrative technique in episodes like these is one of his important contributions to the art of the novel. And with what piquancy and wit he describes the participants. Here is his description of Madame de L—— (volume I), the object of his fantasies in the early chapters of the book:

When the heart flies out before the understanding, it saves the judgment a world of pains—I was certain she was of a better order of beings—however, I thought no more of her, but went on and wrote my preface.

The impression returned, upon my encounter with her in the street; a guarded frankness with which she gave me her hand, shewed, I thought, her good education and her good sense; and as I led her on, I felt a pleasurable ductility about her, which spread a calmness over all my spirits—

Good God! how a man might lead such a creature as this round the world with him! . . .

When we had got to the door of the Remise, she withdrew her hand from across her forehead . . . it was a face of about six and twenty—of a clear transparent brown, simply set off without rouge or powder—it was not critically handsome, but there was that in it, which in the frame of mind I was in, attached me more to it—it was

interesting; I fancied it wore the characters of a widow'd look, and in that state of its declension, which had passed the two first paroxysms of sorrow, and was quietly beginning to reconcile itself to its loss. . . .

(pp. 46–48)

All these effects in Sterne may be examined in terms of technique in the handling of prose. Of all English novelists none had greater virtuosity in this respect. Sir Herbert Read, in an excellent introduction to *A Sentimental Journey*, has called attention to his range of styles, from the easy conversational manner of the opening chapter to the studied beauty of his description of "The Captive," in the starling episode. It would be possible, taking his work as a whole, to identify a considerable number of ways in which prose is exploited to give to particular types of passages their essential flavor and tone. He is highly individual, but with all his idiosyncrasies he has the great eighteenth-century virtues: order, proportion, and a regard for fineness of surface.

While *A Sentimental Journey* has the virtues of a novel, it is, with much allowance made for embellishment, an account of incidents that really occurred and people he really met. Monsieur Dessein, the Calais hotelkeeper, made his fortune out of his appearance in Sterne's masterpiece; the Franciscan turns up some years later in *Journey Through France*, by Hester Lynch Piozzi (best known as Samuel Johnson's friend Mrs. Thrale); rumor was active concerning the identity of Madame de L——. An absorbing interest in people, in all kinds of people, high and low, gives that quality to his work which, in the man himself, was perhaps the chief reason why he was so much sought after. That it should have been composed when he was in desperate health shows that, whatever his philosophy of life amounted to, it was not altogether a vain one.

SELECTED BIBLIOGRAPHY

I. BIBLIOGRAPHY, ETC. W. L. Cross, *Life and Times of Laurence Sterne* (rev. ed., New Haven, 1909; 3rd rev. ed., 1929), includes a detailed bibliography; C. Wibley, ed., *Catalogue of Sterne's Library* (London, 1930), a facs. of the rare sale catalog of Sterne's books; E. Cardasco, ed., *A List of Critical Studies, 1896–1946* (Brooklyn, 1948); J. M. Yoklavich, "Notes on the Early Editions of Tristram Shandy," *PMLA* 63 (1948); J. C. T. Oates, "On Collecting

Sterne," *The Book Collector* (Winter 1952); L. Hartley, *Laurence Sterne in the Twentieth Century* (Chapel Hill, N. C., 1966), with an intro.

II. COLLECTED EDITIONS. *The Sermons of Mr. Yorick*, 7 vols. (London, 1760–1769), various eighteenth-century reprints in 2 and 6 vols.; *Works*, 5 vols. (London, 1773–1774), the first collected ed., numerous eighteenth-century collections in 5, 7, 8, and 10 vols.; *Works* (London, 1869), the Globe ed.; G. Saintsbury, ed., *Works*, 6 vols. (London, 1894); W. L. Cross, ed., *Works*, 12 vols. (New York, 1904); *Works*, 7 vols. (Oxford, 1926), the Shakespeare Head Press ed.

III. LETTERS. *Letters from Yorick to Eliza* (London, 1775); *Letters to His Friends* (London, 1775); *Letters of the Late Mr. Laurence Sterne*, 3 vols. (London, 1775); W. D. Cooper, ed., *Seven Letters* (London, 1844); R. B. Johnson, ed., *Letters* (London, 1927); L. P. Curtis, ed., *Letters* (Oxford, 1935), the standard ed.

IV. SEPARATE WORKS. *The Case of Elijah* (York, 1747), sermon; *The Abuses of Conscience* (York, 1750), sermon; *A Political Romance* [*The History of a Good Warm Watch-Coat*] (York, 1759), polemics; *The Life and Opinions of Tristram Shandy, Gentleman*, 9 vols. (London, 1759–1767), novel, popular current eds. include the Everyman's Library, the World's Classics, and Macdonald's Illustrated Classics; *The Journal to Eliza* (London, 1767), in vol. X of W. L. Cross, ed., *The Works of Laurence Sterne* (New York, 1904), also in I. Jack, ed. (Oxford, 1968), with *A Sentimental Journey*; *A Sentimental Journey Through France and Italy*, 2 vols. (London, 1768), travel, popular current eds. include the Everyman's Library, with an intro. by G. Saintsbury (London, 1927), and the World's Classics ed. with intro. by V. Woolf (London, 1928), also an ed. with intro. by H. Read (London, 1929); M. R. B. Shaw, ed., *The Second Journal to Eliza* (London, 1929), the authenticity of this work is doubtful.

V. CRITICAL AND BIOGRAPHICAL STUDIES. J. Ferrier, *Illustrations of Sterne* (London, 1798); W. Scott, *Memoir of Sterne* (London, 1823); S. T. Coleridge, *Literary Remains*, vol. V (London, 1836); W. M. Thackeray, *The English Humourists* (London, 1853), includes an unfavorable study of Sterne; P. Fitzgerald, *Life*, 2 vols. (London, 1864); P. Stapfer, *Laurence Sterne, sa personne et ses ouvrages* (Paris, 1870); L. Stephen, *Hours in a Library*, vol. III (London, 1892), includes a critical study of Sterne; H. D. Traill, *Sterne* (London, 1882); W. Bagehot, *Estimations in Criticism*, ed., C. Lennox (London, 1909), includes the study "Sterne and Thackeray"; W. L. Cross, *Life and Times of Laurence Sterne* (New York, 1909), important additions, 2 vols. (New Haven, 1925; further rev., 1929), the standard work on Sterne; W. Sichel, *Sterne. A Study* (London, 1910); A. Wright and W. L. Sclater, *Sterne's Eliza* (London, 1923); A. Defroe, *Sterne and His Novels in the Light of Modern Psychology* (Groningen, 1925), despite its shortcomings an interesting analysis; J. B. Priestley, *The English Comic Characters* (London, 1925), includes "The Brothers Shandy"; L. P. Curtis, *The Politicks of Laurence Sterne* (Oxford, 1929); R. Read, *The Sense of Glory* (London, 1931), includes a study of Sterne; V. Woolf, *The Common Reader: Second Series* (London, 1932), contains an essay on *A Sentimental Journey*; "Sterne's Ghost" appears in V. Woolf, *The Moment* (London, 1947); A. C. Marshall, *The English Novelists* (London, 1936), includes a study of Sterne; J. Laird, *Philosophical Incursions into English Literature* (Cambridge, 1946), includes "Shandean Philosophy"; E. N. Dilworth, *The Unsentimental Journey of Laurence Sterne* (New York, 1948), a study of Sterne's attitude to sentimentalism; L. H. Hammond, *Sterne's Sermons of Mr. Yorick*, Yale Studies in English 108 (New Haven, 1948); F. W. Hilles, ed., *The Age of Johnson* (New Haven, 1949), includes R. D. F. Putney's "Sterne: Apostle of Laughter"; E. Erämetsä, *A Study of the Word "Sentimental"* (Helsinki, 1951), relevant to passages in the present essay; J. Traugott, *Tristram Shandy's World, Sterne's Philosophical Rhetoric* (Berkeley–Los Angeles, 1954); B. Ford, ed., *From Dryden to Johnson*, Pelican Guide to English Literature, vol. IV (London, 1957), includes D. W. Jefferson's "*Tristram Shandy* and Its Tradition"; M. R. B. Shaw, *Laurence Sterne, The Making of a Humourist, 1713–1762* (London, 1957); W. Connely, *Laurence Sterne as Yorick* (London, 1958); A. B. Howes, *Yorick and the Critics* (London, 1958); H. Fluchère, *Laurence Sterne: From Tristram to Yorick, An Interpretation of Tristram Shandy*, trans. and abr. by B. Bray (London, 1965); L. Hartley, *Laurence Sterne and the Twentieth Century* (Chapel Hill, N. C., 1966); J. M. Stedmond, *The Comic Art of Laurence Sterne. Convention and Innovation in "Tristram Shandy" and "A Sentimental Journey"* (Toronto, 1967); J. Preston, *The Created Self. The Reader's Role in Eighteenth Century Fiction* (London, 1970), includes two chaps. on Sterne; A. H. Cash and J. M. Stedmond, eds., *The Winged Skull. Papers for the Laurence Sterne Bicentenary Conference* (London, 1971); A. B. Howes, ed., *Sterne. The Critical Heritage* (London, 1974); A. H. Cash, *Laurence Sterne. The Early and Middle Years* (London, 1975); P. Conrad, *Shandyism. The Character of Romantic Irony* (Oxford, 1978).

THOMAS GRAY

(1716-1771)

R. W. Ketton-Cremer

I

THOMAS GRAY was born in the City of London on 26 December 1716, the son of a scrivener of comfortable means. He was a delicate child and the only one of a large family who survived infancy. His father was a morose and at times violent man who bullied his wife unmercifully and kept her so short of money that she was obliged to run a milliner's shop.

From this uneasy home life the boy was removed to Eton at an early age. He was extremely happy there, and the beauty and tradition of his surroundings made an ineffaceable impression upon him. His closest friends were Horace Walpole, a son of Prime Minister Robert Walpole, and Richard West, whose father was a distinguished lawyer. They were delicate, studious, and precocious boys like himself.

At the age of eighteen, Gray was sent to Peterhouse College, Cambridge, but left in 1738 without taking a degree. The next year he accompanied Walpole on the grand tour and spent the best part of two years in France and Italy. In 1741 he quarreled violently with Walpole and returned home alone. The next year he was deprived of his other intimate friend by the death of West.

At the end of 1742, Gray returned to Peterhouse and lived mainly at Cambridge for the rest of his life. He resided at the college, quietly pursuing his studies and taking advantage of the intellectual amenities of a university, but he was never a fellow and never took any part in tutoring, lecturing, or other academic duties. He spent considerable periods away from Cambridge, sometimes at Stoke Poges in Buckinghamshire, where his mother had settled, sometimes in modest social activities in London (he and Walpole were reconciled in 1744), sometimes in sightseeing tours in various parts of the country. It was a way of life that suited his limited income and his unadventurous disposition. He read and studied incessantly. Classical literature, medieval history, architecture, natural history, and botany were only a few of his interests. But he studied for himself alone, and scarcely anything remains, apart from a vast accumulation of notes, to attest to his profound and varied scholarship.

By nature Gray was retiring, fastidious, overly careful of his health, somewhat affected in manner and speech. He never married, and apart from a passing attraction to a young woman of fashion, Henrietta Speed, his emotions were deflected into channels of friendship. Toward the end of his life, he was disconcerted by the violence of his feelings for a young Swiss visitor to England, Charles-Victor de Bonstetten. Otherwise he seems to have accepted the mischance of his temperament with entire decorum.

In 1756, as a result of a practical joke based on his fear of fire, attempted by some undergraduates, he moved from Peterhouse to Pembroke College. In 1768 he was appointed professor of modern history; but he never delivered any lectures, and he treated the office, despite some occasional prickings of conscience, as a sinecure. He died after a short illness on 30 July 1771.

It had been a lifetime of reading, of reflection, of essentially uncreative study and research, diversified by little outward incident. But occasionally, at long and unpredictable intervals, Gray was impelled to write poetry. He was very conscious of the fitfulness of his inspiration and its brief duration. "Whenever the humour takes me," he wrote, "I will write, because I like it; and because I like myself better when I do. If I do not write much, it is because I cannot." No English poet of his stature has produced so small a body of work. The whole of the poetry that he published in his lifetime amounted to less than one thousand lines, and little more was found among his papers after his death. But this handful of poems exerted a powerful influence on his contemporaries and his immediate successors; and one of them, "Elegy Written in a Country Churchyard," ranks among the supreme poems not only of its century but of all English literature.

II

APART from a few translations, all of Gray's earliest poems were in Latin, a language that he handled with remarkable ease and grace. His first English poem, "Ode on the Spring," was written in May 1742. He had barely completed it when he heard the news of the death of Richard West. This bereavement only served to enhance the mood of creative activity that possessed him at this time and was so seldom to be repeated. During the next three months he wrote "Ode on a Distant Prospect of Eton College," "Hymn to Adversity," and a sonnet on the death of West. He also mourned West in some Latin lines, outstanding in their intensity of feeling and beauty of expression, that he proposed to include in his ambitious philosophical poem "De principiis cogitandi." But he never completed or even resumed this work and, indeed, never wrote in Latin again.

There was no trace of diffidence or inexperience in Gray's first English poems. From the outset his technical accomplishment was perfect. "Ode on the Spring" is primarily a descriptive poem, an evocation of the sights and sounds of the Buckinghamshire countryside. But the two closing stanzas bring a sudden change of mood. The poet, following a train of thought suggested by a half-remembered passage of Matthew Green's, points an unexpected moral and introduces a personal, indeed an autobiographical, note. He has been observing the insects, the bees and gnats and butterflies, as they revel in the sunshine, and pitying the brevity of their life and happiness. Thereupon the insects, in their turn, reply to the lonely, obscure, and uncompanioned poet:

> Methinks I hear in accents low
> The sportive kind reply:
> Poor moralist! and what art thou?
> A solitary fly!

> Thy Joys no glittering female meets,
> No hive hast thou of hoarded sweets,
> No painted plumage to display:
> On hasty wings thy youth is flown;
> Thy sun is set, thy spring is gone—
> We frolick, while 'tis May.

In the other poems of this memorable summer, written after the shock of West's death, an even stronger note of personal experience and of private emotion is everywhere noticeable. "Ode on a Distant Prospect of Eton College" ostensibly contrasts the carefree years of boyhood with the anxieties, passions, infirmities, frustrations, and disasters of mature life. But in fact Gray is recalling in every line the happiness of his own schooldays, secure in the friendship of Walpole and West, and lamenting his present state, with Walpole apparently hopelessly estranged and West lost to him forever. Four stanzas portray that vanished contentment, "the sunshine of the breast"; four describe the varied and tragic fates in store for the "little victims" as the pitiless years take their toll; and the final stanza reveals resignation and almost reconcilement:

> To each his suff'rings: all are men,
> Condemn'd alike to groan;
> The tender for another's pain,
> Th' unfeeling for his own.
> Yet ah! why should they know their fate?
> Since sorrow never comes too late,
> And happiness too swiftly flies.
> Thought would destroy their paradise.
> No more: where ignorance is bliss,
> 'Tis folly to be wise.

In "Hymn to Adversity" the same mood persists:

> The gen'rous spark extinct revive,
> Teach me to love and to forgive

is surely a reference to his estrangement from Walpole. But in this poem his fear of life, the dread of what the future might hold in store for him, the whole burden of what his age knew as melancholy and ours prefers to describe as angst, have almost overshadowed the anguish of his grief for West. In the "Sonnet on the Death of Richard West," on the other hand, that grief is expressed with intensity and concentration. "My lonely anguish melts no heart, but mine"—such was the measure of his sadness.

III

THESE months of creative inspiration and intense personal sorrow may also have seen the beginnings of the poem eventually known as "Elegy Written in a Country Churchyard." Some critics believe that a substantial portion of the "Elegy" was completed in 1742 and the years immediately following. There can be no doubt that the emotional mood of the poem was deeply influenced by West's death, but I am inclined to think that, except perhaps for some of the opening lines, it was written at a considerably later date and probably over a long stretch of time—that it was, in fact, an example of "emotion recollected in tranquillity."

At the end of 1742, Gray returned to Cambridge and embarked on the scheme of life that has already been described and that he did not substantially alter to the end of his days. Each summer he passed many weeks at his mother's house at Stoke Poges; and there, during his slow, contemplative walks about the fields and lanes, he stored in his memory those country sights and sounds, those sober musings upon the human lot, that were the material of the "Elegy." The progress of its composition will always remain uncertain. We know only that between 1742 and 1750 this quiet scholar, this academic and solitary man, achieved a poem that was to become an enduring part of the English heritage.

The opening stanzas conjure up the solemnity and mystery of evening, the slow advance of dusk over the countryside.

> The Curfew tolls the knell of parting day,
> The lowing herd wind slowly o'er the lea,
> The plowman homeward plods his weary way,
> And leaves the world to darkness and to me.
>
> Now fades the glimmering landscape on the sight,
> And all the air a solemn stillness holds,
> Save where the beetle wheels his droning flight,
> And drowsy tinklings lull the distant folds; . . .

This eloquence, this faultless music of words, is sustained throughout the poem. It sounds in every line of the succession of stanzas in which Gray meditates upon the fate of those who lie "beneath those rugged elms, that yew-tree's shade." He had watched the laborers of Stoke Poges at work in the fields and woods, had admired their skill in the

handling of plow and ax and scythe; and he contrasts their obscure destiny with the range of opportunity, for good or evil, that lay open to those whose lot was less restricted by circumstance.

> Let not Ambition mock their useful toil,
> Their homely joys, and destiny obscure;
> Nor Grandeur hear with a disdainful smile
> The short and simple annals of the poor.
>
> The boast of heraldry, the pomp of pow'r,
> And all that beauty, all that wealth e'er gave,
> Awaits alike th' inevitable hour.
> The paths of glory lead but to the grave.
>   . . .
> Perhaps in this neglected spot is laid
> Some heart once pregnant with celestial fire;
> Hands, that the rod of empire might have sway'd,
> Or wak'd to extasy the living lyre.
>
> But Knowledge to their eyes her ample page
> Rich with the spoils of time did ne'er unroll;
> Chill Penury repress'd their noble rage,
> And froze the genial current of the soul.
>   . . .
> Th' applause of list'ning senates to command,
> The threats of pain and ruin to despise,
> To scatter plenty o'er a smiling land,
> And read their hist'ry in a nation's eyes,
>
> Their lot forbad: nor circumscrib'd alone
> Their growing virtues, but their crimes confin'd;
> Forbad to wade through slaughter to a throne,
> And shut the gates of mercy on mankind,
>
> The struggling pangs of conscious truth to hide,
> To quench the blushes of ingenuous shame,
> Or heap the shrine of Luxury and Pride
> With incense kindled at the Muse's flame.

At one stage of its composition, the "Elegy" consisted of eighteen stanzas, of which this was the last, together with the following additional stanzas, which brought the poem to a climax and a close.

> The thoughtless World to Majesty may bow
> Exalt the brave, & idolize success
> But more to Innocence, their Safety owe
> Than Power & Genius e'er conspired to bless
>
> And thou, who mindful of the unhonour'd Dead
> Dost in these Notes their artless Tale relate
> By Night & lonely Contemplation led
> To linger in the gloomy Walks of Fate,

Hark how the sacred Calm that broods around
Bids ev'ry fierce tumultuous Passion cease
In still small accents whis'pring from the Ground
A grateful Earnest of eternal Peace

No more with Reason & thyself at Strife
Give anxious Cares & endless Wishes room
But thro' the cool sequester'd Vale of Life
Pursue the silent Tenour of thy Doom.[1]

Large was his bounty, and his soul sincere,
Heav'n did a recompence as largely send:
He gave to Mis'ry all he had, a tear,
He gain'd from Heav'n ('twas all he wish'd) a friend.

No farther seek his merits to disclose,
Or draw his frailties from their dread abode,
(There they alike in trembling hope repose),
The bosom of his Father and his God.

In this form the "Elegy" was a perfect artistic whole, its reasoning and emotion moving in unbroken harmony from the opening to the close. Some critics view Gray's subsequent recasting as a regrettable afterthought. Walter Savage Landor, for example, spoke of the new conclusion, the three stanzas of the epitaph, as a tin kettle tied to the poem's tail. The reader would do well to compare the earlier with the final version and form an independent judgment, for Gray in due course made some drastic alterations and additions. He canceled the four stanzas just quoted, preserving only a few fragments that he incorporated into his new work. In place of sober resignation, the comfort of "the sacred Calm that broods around," he introduced a sudden note of loneliness, almost of anguish:

> For who to dumb Forgetfulness a prey,
> This pleasing anxious being e'er resign'd,
> Left the warm precincts of the cheerful day,
> Nor cast one longing ling'ring look behind?

He sounded a still more personal note when he brought into the foreground

> . . . thee, who mindful of th' unhonour'd Dead
> Dost in these lines their artless tale relate—

the figure of the poet himself. He dies; he is buried beside those other dead whose humble lives he had described; and the poem closes now with his "Epitaph," which must also be regarded as Gray's summing up of his own life and his own beliefs:

> Here rests his head upon the lap of Earth
> A Youth to Fortune and to Fame unknown.
> Fair Science frown'd not on his humble birth,
> And Melancholy marked him for her own.

[1] These lines appear only in the manuscript of the "Elegy" in the library of Eton College, and are quoted here exactly as they appear in that manuscript.

Alfred Tennyson once spoke of the "Elegy's" "divine truisms that make us weep." Its reflections upon fame and obscurity, ambition and destiny, have indeed become truisms. But in the eighteenth century the poem burst upon the England of King George II, line after noble line, stanza after majestic stanza, with a novel and extraordinary impact. Of one passage Samuel Johnson wrote: "I have never seen the notions in any other place; yet he that reads them here, persuades himself that he has always felt them." Gray gave expression to thoughts that lay deep in the consciousness of all Englishmen—thoughts about their history and traditions, the religion in which they put their trust, the landscapes they knew and loved, the tranquil continuity of village life in an age when the majority of the nation were still country dwellers. And as the century advanced, a century of development and expansion that was to prove so momentous, the "Elegy" became the representative poem of its age. The fastidious and hypochondriacal recluse had spoken for the English people.

The "Elegy" was running in General James Wolfe's mind a few years later in Canada, on the day before his victory and his death. It has been present in the minds of countless other men and women from that time to this, at moments of crisis in their lives or during hours of quiet reflection. It is probably still the most popular and the best-loved poem in English, the poem that has most surely reached the heart of the ordinary man. As Johnson said—and it should be remembered that Johnson disliked Gray and persistently undervalued the rest of his poetry—the "Elegy" "abounds with images which find a mirrour in every mind, and with sentiments to which every bosom returns an echo."

IV

The "Elegy" was published in 1751, almost by accident. Manuscript copies had been circulated without Gray's sanction, and it was necessary to hurry it out at short notice in order to forestall its piratical printing in a magazine. Its enthusiastic reception somewhat disconcerted the author. His newfound celebrity brought no alteration to his way of life, and he made no attempt to derive advantage from his popular success. Its most important personal consequence, perhaps, was the friendship of two neighbors at Stoke, the Dowager Viscountess Cobham and her young relation Henrietta Speed. Gray described their first encounter in a delightful piece of burlesque poetry, "A Long Story." Walpole once said, with great truth, "Gray never wrote anything easily but things of humour: humour was his natural and original turn." "A Long Story" was all grace and lightheartedness, an entirely gay and happy poem, with its gentle self-mockery and its affectionate portrait of Miss Speed:

> To celebrate her eyes, her air——
> Coarse panegyricks would but teaze her.
> Melissa is her *nom de guerre*.
> Alas, who would not wish to please her?

"A Long Story" was a private joke, written for the amusement of Gray's friends. But his next productions were the two great Pindaric odes, "The Progress of Poesy" and "The Bard," which were very much intended for a public audience. Eminent writers are often apt to place unexpected and somewhat disconcerting values upon their own performances; and Gray regarded these two odes, rather than his masterpiece the "Elegy," as the works by which he hoped to be remembered. Youth was now behind him; the youthful sentiments, the personal longings and regrets that lingered in the "Elegy," were to have no place here. He intended the Pindaric odes to be the crown of his poetic maturity.

For almost a century English poets had been producing odes—Abraham Cowley's "Pindariques" are an example—modeled on the odes of Pindar, although no poet until Gray, William Congreve apart, had followed Pindar's structure with absolute fidelity. It was the content, not the form, of these two odes that bewildered his contemporaries. In the first, "The Progress of Poesy," Gray set himself to glorify the poet's calling; and he did so with an exaltation, an allusiveness, and at times an obscurity that render some of its passages difficult even to the instructed reader of today. The notes, which he refused to furnish for the first edition, explain the purport of each stanza and the more recondite of his allusions, but his contemporaries were not accustomed to this rhapsodical and almost incantatory poetry, and remained perplexed. Yet surely some prelude of the romantic revival, some foreshadowing of Samuel Taylor Coleridge and John Keats, is sounded in such a passage as

> In climes beyond the solar road,
> Where shaggy forms o'er ice-built mountains roam,
> The Muse has broke the twilight-gloom
> To chear the shiv'ring Native's dull abode.
> And oft, beneath the od'rous shade
> Of Chili's boundless forests laid,
> She deigns to hear the savage Youth repeat
> In loose numbers wildly sweet
> Their feather-cinctur'd Chiefs, and dusky Loves. . . .
>
> (II. 2)

The second ode, "The Bard," portrays a traditional episode during the final subjugation of Wales by the English forces. Gray was deeply versed in English history and had recently made some study of Welsh poetry and prosody. The conclusion of the poem, after hanging fire for some time, was inspired by the strains of a blind Welsh harper who happened to visit Cambridge. Most of the stanzas are supposed to be uttered by the bard, who cursed the invading English monarch and his posterity, and who foresaw the time when the prophecies of Merlin and Taliesin would be fulfilled and a Welsh dynasty, in the persons of the Tudor sovereigns, would rule once more over the whole island of Britain. At times during its composition, Gray was seized with a fervor of inspiration that seldom visited him, and during which, as he said later, "I felt myself the bard."

The poem is full of splendid rhetoric, of color and movement and pageantry. It is also heavy with obscurity. Gray lived so intimately in English history that he filled his stanzas with cryptic personifications, the She-wolf of France and the agonizing King, the meek Usurper and the bristled Boar, whose identity evaded—and, were it not for the footnotes, would still evade—the ordinary reader. Many critics, with Johnson at their head, have pointed out the faults of "The Bard" and its companion—incomprehensibility, overelaboration, "glittering accumulations of ungraceful ornaments." But no other writer of the eighteenth century could have achieved the force and eloquence of the penultimate stanza, with its radiant picture of the first Queen Elizabeth:

> Girt with many a Baron bold
>   Sublime their starry fronts they rear;
> And gorgeous Dames, and Statesmen old
>   In bearded majesty, appear.
> In the midst a Form divine!
> Her eye proclaims her of the Briton-Line;
> Her lyon-port, her awe-commanding face,
> Attemper'd sweet to virgin-grace.
> What strings symphonious tremble in the air,
> What strains of vocal transport round her play!
> Hear from the grave, great Taliesin, hear;
> They breathe a soul to animate thy clay.
> Bright Rapture calls, and soaring, as she sings,
> Waves in the eye of Heav'n her many-colour'd wings.
>
> (III. 2)

The Pindaric odes were written in the early 1750's, one of the periods during which, to quote Walpole's words, "Gray was in flower." During these same years he worked on a third poem, never completed, that might have held a very high place among his writings. William Mason gave it the title "Ode on the Pleasure Arising from Vicissitude." The surviving stanzas show that it was to be a poem in his earlier manner, with a strongly personal note, in contrast with the Pindaric odes, which were almost wholly objective. There is a similar contrast between the rhetorical splendor of the Pindarics and the limpid freshness, the almost Wordsworthian simplicity, of this unfinished work.

> New-born flocks in rustic dance
>   Frisking ply their feeble feet.
> Forgetful of their wintry trance
>   The birds his presence greet.
> But chief the Sky-lark warbles high
> His trembling thrilling ecstasy
> And, less'ning from the dazzled sight,
> Melts into air and liquid light.
>   . . .
> Yesterday the sullen year
>   Saw the snowy whirlwind fly;
> Mute was the musick of the air,
>   The Herd stood drooping by:
> Their raptures now that wildly flow,
> No yesterday, nor morrow know;
> 'Tis Man alone that Joy descries
> With forward and reverted eyes.
>
> (9–16; 21–28)

The Pindaric odes were published in 1757, as the firstfruits of Walpole's private press at Strawberry Hill. Gray looked upon them as the summit of his poetic achievement, and was deeply anxious that they should be well received. But he disregarded the warnings of his friends and printed them without notes or any form of explanation to help the reader. Largely as the result of this, their reception was by no means enthusiastic. A fire of criticism, both public and private, was directed against the obscurity of their content and the loftiness of their style. Their admirers, though influential, were few; and altogether Gray was bitterly disappointed. This sense of disappointment, and indeed of frustration, was permanent. Apart from a single poem—written primarily from a sense of duty—he never produced another major work. He withdrew from the contest and devoted his life ever more completely to scholarship and private study.

V

GRAY's youth had been steeped in classical learning, and his years in Italy had enhanced his love of ancient Greece and Rome. But in middle age he began to feel the lure of a very different world. The Norns, and not the Sirens, were calling him now. Instead of the sun-drenched Mediterranean landscape or the quiet scenes of the English countryside, he explored the haunted mists of the Celtic and Scandinavian past. His Welsh studies had already borne fruit in "The Bard." He read deeply in early Norse poetry, history, and legend; and in 1760 he was among the first to welcome "Ossian," the alleged translations from ancient Highland poetry produced by James Macpherson. He could never feel quite satisfied as to their genuineness, and he was no more impressed than anyone else by the shifty figure of Macpherson. But the Ossian poems held for him a mystery, a magic and wild romance that he had hitherto sought in vain. "I am gone mad about them," he wrote, "*extasié* with their infinite beauty."

One of Gray's projects, never fulfilled, was a history of English poetry, in the early chapters of which he proposed to include some renderings of the poetry of the Welsh and of the ancient Norse. His next productions were intended as a part of this scheme. "The Descent of Odin" and "The Fatal Sisters" were translations, by way of an intermediate Latin version, from Icelandic originals. He also translated four fragments of varying length from the Welsh, of which "The Triumphs of Owen" alone was published in his lifetime. This group of poems has little real significance today; but to those of Gray's contemporaries who had fallen, as he had, under the spell of northern romanticism, their appeal was profound. "Noble incantations," Walpole called them, and they played their part in the furtherance of the romantic revival not only in England, but throughout continental Europe, where Gray came to be widely read.

Apart from these translations and certain occasional verses, Gray wrote absolutely nothing between 1757 and 1769. His moods of inspiration had always been fitful and ill-sustained, but this prolonged silence was unquestionably due in great measure to his disappointment over the reception of the Pindaric odes. The occasional verses were mainly satirical in intent, those "things of humour" that he wrote so easily. Few of them have survived; there is good reason to think that others were suppressed by his own caution or by the discretion of his executor, William Mason. "The Candidate" was a savage and brilliant squib inspired by the circumstances of a disputed election for the high stewardship at Cambridge. Still more impressive is the poem that he wrote after visiting the eccentric villa built on the North Foreland by Henry Fox, first Lord Holland, a discredited politician whose career he had long watched with deep disapproval.

> Old, and abandon'd by each venal friend,
>   Here Holland took the pious resolution
> To smuggle some few years, and strive to mend
>   A broken character and constitution.
>
> On this congenial spot he fix'd his choice,
>   Earl Goodwin trembled for his neighbouring sand;
> Here seagulls scream and cormorants rejoice,
>   And mariners, though shipwreck'd, dread to land.
>
> Here reign the blust'ring North and blighting East,
>   No tree is heard to whisper, bird to sing,
> Yet Nature cannot furnish out the feast,
>   Art he invokes new horrors still to bring.
>
> Now mould'ring fanes and battlements arise,
>   Arches and turrets nodding to their fall,
> Unpeopled palaces delude his eyes,
>   And mimick desolation covers all.
>
> "Ah!" said the sighing peer, "had Bute been true,
>   Nor Shelburne's, Rigby's, Calcraft's friendship vain,

> Far other scenes than these had blest our view,
>   And realiz'd the ruins that we feign.
>
> Purg'd by the sword and beautified by fire,
>   Then had we seen proud London's hated walls;
> Owls might have hooted in St. Peter's choir,
>   And foxes stunk and litter'd in St. Paul's."

In 1768 the professorship of modern history was bestowed on Gray by the duke of Grafton, who had lately become chancellor of the university, and the grateful poet felt it his duty to write an ode to be performed at the ceremonial installation of the duke in the following year. Since the ode was to be set to music, it was designed in the irregular form of a cantata, with sections of uneven length allotted to various soloists and to the chorus. Gray had no personal acquaintance with Grafton and was much attacked and ridiculed for his praises of this highly unpopular figure. Nevertheless the "Installation Ode"[2] was a genuine rekindling of the flame of poetry that had lain so long dormant within him. It is full of striking passages and lines, and at times it is less a paean in praise of the new chancellor than an expression of Gray's gratitude and *pietas* toward the university itself. This was impressively shown when he conjured up the majestic procession of its founder and benefactors, in a passage comparable with the noblest in the Pindaric odes:

> But hark! the portals sound, and pacing forth
> With solemn steps and slow
> High Potentates and Dames of royal birth
> And mitred Fathers in long order go:
> Great *Edward* with the lillies on his brow
> From haughty *Gallia* torn,
> And sad *Chatillon*, on her bridal morn
> That wept her bleeding Love, and princely *Clare*,
> And *Anjou's* Heroine, and the paler Rose,
> The rival of her crown, and of her woes,
> And either *Henry* there,
> The murther'd Saint, and the majestick Lord,
> That broke the bonds of *Rome*.
> (Their tears, their little triumphs o'er,
> Their human passions now no more,
> Save Charity, that glows beyond the tomb).
> (35–50)

Such, in the last of his poems, was Gray's tribute of homage and farewell to Cambridge, where he had passed so many tranquil years.

[2]The title appears as "Ode for Music" in R. Lonsdale's edition of the *Poetical Works*, the standard.

THOMAS GRAY

GRAY was described after his death by an enthusiastic friend as "perhaps the most learned man in Europe." Such superlatives are, of course, futile. It is sufficient to say that he was a man of exceptionally wide culture and interests. But none of his major projects—the annotation of Plato, the edition of Strabo, the history of English poetry—came to anything at all. He read and annotated and filled huge notebooks with extracts; he drew up lists and catalogs and pedigrees; Walpole told a friend that "Mr. Gray often vexed me by finding him heaping notes on an interleaved Linnaeus, instead of pranking on his lyre." Such occupations were his barriers against melancholy, his refuge from the depression that so often weighed upon his spirits. "To be employed is to be happy," he wrote, and "to find oneself business is the great art of life."

But Gray has a second claim upon the attention of posterity. He was one of the supreme letter writers of his century, the peer of Horace Walpole and William Cowper. He may seldom have touched his lyre, and then with difficulty and reluctance; but throughout his life he was able to express himself in his private letters to his friends with unfailing ease, clarity, and grace. They begin during his undergraduate days at Cambridge and end only a week or two before his death. They can portray landscape and natural beauty in a manner almost unique in the eighteenth century; they contain some of the most intelligent literary criticism of the time; they are often gay and colloquial, irradiated with a humor usually gentle but occasionally angry and sardonic; they are full of perception and sympathy, and sometimes of deep emotion. In them the story of Gray's life is unfolded, for the comprehending reader, in a manner that makes nonsense of Matthew Arnold's celebrated contention that "Gray never spoke out."

The quality of Gray's letters can best be illustrated by a few brief examples. In nothing was he more original, more ahead of his time, than in his appreciation of the splendors of mountain scenery. When the ordinary traveler was still averting his eyes from the horrid spectacle of the Alps, Gray in his twenty-third year was anticipating Jean Jacques Rousseau and William Wordsworth. "In our little journey up to the Grande Chartreuse," he wrote in 1739, "I do not remember to have gone ten paces without an exclamation, that there was no restrain-ing: Not a precipice, not a torrent, not a cliff, but is pregnant with religion and poetry. There are certain scenes that would awe an atheist into belief, without the help of other argument." Thirty years later he was writing of English mountains:

In the evening walk'd alone down to the Lake by the side of *Crow Park* after sunset and saw the solemn colouring of night draw on, the last gleam of sunshine fading away on the hilltops, the deep serene of the water, and the long shadows of the mountains thrown across them, till they nearly touch'd the hithermost shore. At distance heard the murmur of many waterfalls not audible in the day-time. Wish'd for the moon, but she was *dark to me and silent, hid in her vacant interlunar cave.*

For his humor, directed so often against himself, a letter may be chosen in which Gray has been discussing his melancholy, his ennui, the spell of indolence that the life of Cambridge was casting over his soul. The prevailing spirit of the place, he wrote, was the spirit of laziness.

Time will settle my Conscience, Time will reconcile me to this languid Companion: we shall smoke, we shall tipple, we shall doze together. We shall have our little Jokes, like other People, and our long Stories; Brandy will finish what Port begun; and a month after the Time you will see in some Corner of a *London Evening Post*, "Yesterday, died the Revnd. Mr. John Grey, Senior-Fellow of Clare-Hall, a facetious Companion, and well-respected by all that knew him. His death is supposed to be occasion'd by a Fit of an Apoplexy, being found fall'n out of Bed with his Head in the Chamber-Pot."

Gray's understanding of the sorrows of others is revealed in the beautiful letter to William Mason at the time of his wife's death.

I break in upon you at a moment, when we least of all are permitted to disturb our Friends, only to say, that you are daily and hourly present to my thoughts. If the *worst* be not yet past: you will neglect and pardon me. But if the last struggle be over: if the poor subject of your long anxieties be no longer sensible to your kindness, or to her own sufferings: allow me (at least in idea, for what could I do, were I present, more than this?) to sit by you in silence, and pity from my heart, not her, who is at rest; but you, who lose her. May He, who made us, the Master of our pleasures, and of our pains, preserve and support you!

Finally, to show the depth of emotion in Gray's own nature, a passage may be quoted from one of his letters to Bonstetten, written a year before he died and shortly after that delightful, if not wholly deserving, young man had returned to his native Switzerland.

I am return'd, my dear Bonstetten, from the little journey I had made into Suffolk without answering the end proposed. The thought, that you might have been with me there, has embitter'd all my hours. Your letter has made me happy; as happy as so gloomy, so solitary a Being as I am is capable of being. I know and have too often felt the disadvantages I lay myself under, how much I hurt the little interest I have in you, by this air of sadness so contrary to your nature and present enjoyments; but sure you will forgive, tho' you can not sympathize with me. It is impossible for me to dissemble with you. Such as I am, I expose my heart to your view, nor wish to conceal a single thought from your penetrating eyes.—All that you say to me, especially on the subject of Switzerland, is infinitely acceptable. It feels too pleasing ever to be fulfill'd, and as often as I read over your truly kind letter, written long since from London, I stop at these words: *La mort qui peut glacer nos bras avant qu'ils soient entrelacés.*

VII

GRAY stands as the dominant poetic figure of the middle decades of the eighteenth century. It was a barren time, and he had few competitors. He wrote, moreover, to please himself, without the smallest notion of founding a school, or attracting a following, or achieving publicity of any kind. Nevertheless, although a poet of limited and fastidious output, he exerted a deep influence upon the age in which he lived.

Gray thus influenced his age, and at the same time he was in harmony with it. He was a good European, sensitive to the main trends of contemporary culture, at a time when that culture was becoming to some extent international, when educated people in France and England, Germany and Sweden and Russia, were beginning to think along much the same lines. He had seen the remains of classical antiquity with his own eyes. His travels had given him knowledge and appreciation of all that was best in music, painting, and sculpture. His poems were full of reminiscences of other languages and other literatures, living and dead—Homer and Vergil and Lucretius, Dante and Petrarch, William Shakespeare and John Milton. And in later life his interest in Scandinavian and Celtic legend, which consorted so well with his love of wild and rugged landscape, made him a precursor of the romantic revival that was to sweep across Europe like a flood.

But however great the admiration that was lavished upon Gray's other poems by his contemporaries, and whatever the degree of enjoyment that may be derived from them today, the "Elegy" remains a work apart. It stands as an extraordinary and isolated phenomenon, a poem that can move us today exactly as it moved our forefathers. That was Gray's achievement, and it is unique in English literature.

SELECTED BIBLIOGRAPHY

I. BIBLIOGRAPHY. C. S. Northup, *A Bibliography* (New Haven, 1917), the standard work, listing also all writings about Gray to 1917; F. G. Stokes, ed., *An Elegy Written in a Country Church Yard* (Oxford, 1929), contains detailed bibliographical descriptions of the early editions to 1771; H. W. Starr, *A Bibliography, 1917–1951* (Philadelphia, 1953), a continuation of Northup's *Bibliography* to 1951.

II. COLLECTED EDITIONS. *Poems* (London, 1768), supervised by the poet—R. Foulis' handsome ed. was published at Glasgow the same year; W. Mason, ed., *The Poems* (York, 1775); T. J. Mathias, ed., *The Works*, 2 vols. (London, 1814); J. Mitford, ed., *The Works*, 2 vols. (London, 1816); J. Mitford, ed., *The Works*, 4 vols. (London, 1835–1837), the Aldine ed., with a volume of correspondence added in 1843; E. Gosse, ed., *The Works*, 4 vols. (London, 1884); A. Lane Poole, ed., *The Poetical Works* (London, 1917), rev. by L. Whibley (London, 1937), with the poetical works of Collins, in the Oxford Standard Authors series; W. T. Williams and G. H. Vallins, eds., *Gray, Collins and Their Circle* (London, 1937); L. Whibley, ed., *Poems* (Oxford, 1939); H. W. Starr and J. R. Hendrickson, eds., *Complete Poems* (London, 1966), the Oxford English Texts series; A. Johnston, ed., *Selected Poems* (London, 1967), with poems of William Collins; R. Lonsdale, ed., *Poems* (London, 1969), the Annotated English Poets series; J. Crofts, ed., *Poetry and Prose* (Oxford, 1971), the Clarendon English series; *Poems* (London, 1973), facs. by Scolar Press of 1768 ed.; J. Reeves, ed., *Complete English Poems* (London, 1973), the Poetry Bookshelf series; R. Lonsdale, ed., *Poetical Works* (London, 1977), with poetical works of William Collins, the Oxford Standard Authors series.

III. SEPARATE WORKS. "Ode on a Distant Prospect of Eton College" (London, 1747); "An Elegy Wrote in a

Country Church Yard" (London, 1751), the text in the first quarto, with all the variants of the early ed., is given in Stokes's ed. (see above under "Bibliography"). The title was changed ("Wrote" to "Written") and the "Red-breast stanza" added in the third quarto, published 14 March 1751, a month after the first. (The stanza was dropped in 1753.) Facsimiles have been made of the three holograph MSS (British Museum; Eton College; Pembroke College, Cambridge), the latest being of the Eton by the Augustan Reprint Society, G. Sherburn, ed. (London, 1951); *Designs by Mr. R. Bentley for Six Poems by Mr. T. Gray* (London, 1753), a finely printed and illustrated folio ed. of some textual interest; *Odes* (Strawberry Hill, Middlesex, 1757); "Ode Performed in the Senate House at Cambridge" (Cambridge, 1769); L. Whibley, ed., "Ode on the Pleasure Arising from Vicissitude" (London, 1933).

IV. LETTERS. J. Mitford, ed., *The Correspondence of Thomas Gray and William Mason* (London, 1853); D. C. Tovey, ed., *Letters*, 3 vols. (London, 1900–1912); P. Toynbee, ed., *The Correspondence of Gray, Walpole, West and Ashton*, 2 vols. (Oxford, 1915); P. Toynbee and L. Whibley, eds., *Correspondence*, 3 vols. (Oxford, 1935; repr. 1971), in the Oxford Reprint series; W. S. Lewis, G. L. Lam, and C. H. Bennett, eds., *Walpole's Correspondence with Gray, West and Ashton* (New Haven, 1948), vols. XIII–XIV of the Yale ed. of Walpole's correspondence; J. W. Krutch, ed., *Selected Letters* (New York, 1952).

V. BIOGRAPHICAL AND CRITICAL STUDIES. W. Mason, "Memoirs of the Life and Writings of Mr. Gray" (York, 1775), prefixed to his ed. of the poems; S. Johnson, *Lives of the English Poets*, 4 vols. (London, 1781), vol. IV contains Johnson's account of Gray—the best modern ed. is by G. B. Hill, 3 vols. (Oxford, 1905); E. Gosse, *Gray* (London, 1882); M. Arnold, *Essays in Criticism: Second Series* (London, 1888), contains a discussion of Gray; D. C. Tovey, *Gray and His Friends: Letters and Relics* (Cambridge, 1890); C. E. Norton, *The Poet Gray as a Naturalist* (Boston, 1903); A. S. Cook, *A Concordance to the English Poems* (Boston, 1908); R. Martin, *Chronologie de la vie et de l'oeuvre de Thomas Gray* (Toulouse, 1931), and *Essai sur Thomas Gray* (Paris, 1934); W. Empson, *Some Versions of Pastoral* (London, 1935), contains an interesting interpretation of the "Elegy"; W. Powell Jones, *Thomas Gray, Scholar* (Cambridge, Mass., 1937); G. Tillotson, *Essays in Criticism and Research* (Cambridge, 1942), contains the essay "Gray's Letters"; Lord David Cecil, *Poets and Story-Tellers* (London, 1945), includes the Warton Lecture (1945) "The Poetry of Thomas Gray"; C. Brooks, *The Well Wrought Urn* (New York, 1948), contains the essay "Gray's Storied Urn"; Lord David Cecil, *Two Quiet Lives* (London, 1948); R. W. Ketton-Cremer, *Thomas Gray: A Biography* (Cambridge, 1955), the standard life; S. C. Roberts, *Doctor Johnson and Others* (Cambridge, 1958), includes the W. P. Ker Memorial Lecture (Glasgow, 1952) "Thomas Gray of Pembroke"; R. Fukuhara, *Essays on Thomas Gray* (Tokyo, 1960), mainly in Japanese but contains some useful essays in English; G. Tillotson, *Augustan Studies* (London, 1961), contains essays on "Ode on the Spring" and "Ode on the Death of a Favourite Cat"; *From Sensibility to Romanticism: Essays Presented to F. A. Pottle* (Oxford, 1965), contains I. Jack's "Gray's 'Elegy' Reconsidered."

TOBIAS SMOLLETT

(1721-1771)

Laurence Brander

I

THE story of Tobias Smollett is familiar. The young Scot, while still in his teens, traveled to London to make his way in the world with a tragedy in his baggage and a medical qualification to fall back on. He had a remarkable success, for by the time he was thirty, he had published two of the books that set the English novel on its way. He was much younger than Henry Fielding when he did so, and precocious compared with Samuel Richardson and Laurence Sterne. He was, in fact, little better than an angry young man. Since he is more than two hundred prose years away, it may help to meet him through others nearer his time.

Sir Walter Scott, for example, wrote from Abbotsford in 1821, just fifty years after Smollett died, summing up a sustained comparison with Fielding thus:

> It is, however, chiefly in his profusion, which amounts almost to prodigality, that we recognize the superior richness of Smollett's fancy. He never shows the least desire to make the most either of a character, or a situation, or an adventure, but throws them together with a carelessness which argues unlimited confidence in his own powers. . . .
> Smollett's sea-characters have been deservedly considered as inimitable; and the power with which he has diversified them, in so many instances, distinguishing the individual features of each honest tar, while each possesses a full proportion of professional manners and habits of thinking, is a most absolute proof of the richness of fancy with which the author was gifted, and which we have noticed as his chief advantage over Fielding. . . . The naval officers of the present day, the splendour of whose actions has thrown into shadow the exploits of a thousand years . . . when memory carries them back thirty or forty years, must remember many a weather-beaten veteran, whose appearance, language, and sentiments free Smollett from the charge of extravagance in his

characteristic sketches of British seamen of the last century.[1]

In 1851, William Thackeray celebrated Smollett the man of letters in a surprisingly benign way, with only sympathetic reference to the cantankerous anger that Smollett sustained into middle age in the peppery idiom of mid-eighteenth-century journalistic prose:

> Tobias Smollett, the manly, kindly, honest, and irascible; worn and battered, but still brave and full of heart, after a long struggle against a hard fortune. His brain had been busied with a hundred different schemes; he had been reviewer and historian, critic, medical writer, poet, pamphleteer. He had fought endless literary battles; and braved and wielded for years the cudgels of controversy. It was a hard and savage fight in those days, and a niggard pay. He was oppressed by illness, age, narrow fortune; but his spirit was still resolute, and his courage steady. . . . He is like one of those Scotch cadets, of whom history gives us so many examples, and whom, with a national fidelity, the great Scotch novelist has painted so charmingly.[2]

Those associated with the critical trade will note with amusement that it is not the Romantic who speaks so romantically of Smollett, then hasten on with some eagerness to meet a man who had the temerity ("his courage steady") to suggest to the English writing fraternity that they should organize themselves for the good of the language and of literature, and found an academy. One may be ready to show some affectionate attention to a man who ran a critical journal independently and honestly, which was so much against the fashion of

[1]*Lives of the Novelists* (London, 1821).
[2]*Lectures on the English Humourists of the Eighteenth Century* (London, 1911), the Centenary Biographical edition, pp. 292–295.

146

the times but, of course, so like the way things are done today. One can admire the business acumen of an author who was the first to publish a long historical work in weekly parts at a popular price, as well as the first to publish a full-length novel as a serial in a weekly journal. One may care to recall also that he was among the first, with Samuel Johnson, to run a writing factory as an independent and honorable alternative to the old system of patronage, and that, but for Johnson's famous letter of February 1755 to Lord Chesterfield ("Is not a Patron, my Lord, one who looks with unconcern on a man struggling for life in the water and, when he has reached ground, encumbers him with help?"), Smollett's words in *Humphry Clinker* might today be the common quotation when the end of patronage is mentioned:

I saw none of the usual signs of authorship, either in the house or in the landlord, who is one of the few writers of the age that stand upon their own foundation, without patronage and above dependence.
(letter of 10 June from Melford to Phillips, vol. II)

This extraordinarily active writer could write prose and could give a character life, color, and rich comic interest, and used both these gifts at the end of his life to produce *Humphry Clinker*.

II

TOBIAS SMOLLETT was a Scotsman, born of good family in Dumbartonshire in 1721. He studied medicine at Glasgow, and in 1739 he went to London. He joined the Royal Navy as a surgeon, and went on the Cartagena Expedition in 1741. This was part of the maritime war with Spain begun in 1739 over South American trade. The navy had not been on active service for a long time, and the expedition, badly organized, ended in disaster. Smollett wrote a pamphlet on the subject, one of his first attacks on muddleheaded stupidity. His experiences gave him copy for his novels, so that it might almost be said that the best things that came out of the expedition were the sailors in *Roderick Random* and *Peregrine Pickle* and the satirical treatment of it in *Roderick Random*.

Smollett found a wife in Jamaica and settled in London in 1744 to practice medicine from a house in Downing Street. He was living nearby in Mayfair in 1746 when the news of the battle of Culloden reached London and the citizens went mad with relief after being hysterical with fear of invasion by the Scots and their Stuart claimant to the throne. Two or three years later he settled in Chelsea, where he worked as a writer until his health broke in 1762. Chelsea was then a small town, and the road to the city of Westminster went across open country that was sometimes the hunting ground of footpads and highwaymen. The soft air of Chelsea seems to have been as congenial to authorship then as it is now.

From 1763 to 1765, Smollett lived in France and Italy, passing most of the time at Nice. He returned to England and spent much of his time traveling; and when he was not traveling, he lived in Bath, at that time a focus for English society. In 1768 he returned to northern Italy, for so many years an authors' annex for England, and settled in a house near Leghorn, where he died on 17 September 1771. He was buried in the English cemetery there, an old, neglected place now—very different from the English cemetery in Lisbon, bright with flowers, where Fielding lies.

III

THE forgotten mass of his work may be considered first, since it is relevant to the study of the four books that are read today.

Smollett seems to have begun his career as a journalist by working on the *Monthly Review* for Ralph Griffiths, the bookseller in St. Paul's Churchyard. It was after some experience at this kind of work that he wrote, in what became the first letter of *Travels Through France and Italy* (1766):

The miserable author must perform his daily task, in spite of cramp, colick, vapours, or vertigo; in spite of head-ach, heart-ach, and *Minerva's* frowns; other wise he will lose his character and livelihood, like a taylor who disappoints his customers in a birth-day suit.

In 1755 he broke away and projected a new journal that he called the *Critical Review*. From 1756 until his breakdown in 1762, he controlled its policy and no doubt used his factory for producing copy.

The proposals for this review, which Smollett called *Proposals for Publishing Monthly, The Progress or Annals of Literature and the Liberal Arts*, appeared in the last days of 1755. They indicate the position that the young man hoped to fill in the London literary world of the mid-eighteenth century.

This Work will not be patched up by obscure Hackney Writers, accidentally enlisted in the Service of an undistinguishing Bookseller [so much for Ralph Griffiths and his ilk], but executed by a Set of Gentlemen whose Characters and Capacities have been universally approved and acknowledged by the Public: Gentlemen, who have long observed with Indignation the Productions of Genius and Dullness; Wit and Impertinence; Learning and Ignorance, confounded in the Chaos of Publication; applauded without Taste and condemned without Distinction; and who have seen the noble Art of Criticism reduced to a contemptible Manufacture subservient to the most sordid Views of Avarice and Interest, and carried on by wretched Hirelings, without Talent, Candour, Spirit or Circumspection.[3]

The tone of the *Proposals* indicates the fervor of Smollett's campaigning in early maturity for a better literary London. His scheme for an Academy of Letters never got nearer to realization than in these proposals and in the conduct of the *Critical Review*.

Smollett's immense energies were absorbed at the same time in his *Complete History of England, Deduced from the Descent of Julius Caesar to the Treaty of Aix La Chapelle, 1748. Containing the Transactions of One Thousand Eight Hundred and Three Years*. He worked on it from 1755 to 1757, and it was published in four handsome quarto volumes in 1757–1758. His contract with James Rivington and James Fletcher seems to have been for the first three quartos, which were published together in April 1757, bringing the history up to the end of the reign of William and Mary. The fourth volume appeared nine months later. The idea appears to have come from the booksellers, who got it from David Hume's *History of England*, which began publication in 1754 and was completed in 1762. Hume published in Edinburgh, and the London booksellers probably hired Smollett so that they could exploit the idea for London sales. It was certainly not a Tory answer to Hume's skeptical and Whig approach, for Smollett began with Whig lean-

ings and only later, as he worked, did he discover a Tory outlook.

He revised the *History* in 1758 for publication in weekly parts at sixpence, showing good publishing sense in doing so and being the first writer in London who published a history in a popular format. He told Dr. John Moore that orders rose to ten thousand. There is a story that his publishers addressed an early part to every parish clerk in the country, enclosing half a crown and asking them to push sales by letting people see it.

In 1760, Smollett began publishing a continuation to his *History*, planning forty sixpenny parts covering the twelve years from the end of 1748. In a preface to the first number, he sees fit to stress again his independence as an author: "Guiltless of all connexions that might be supposed to affect his candour, and endanger his integrity, he is determined to proceed with that fearless spirit of independence, by which he flatters himself the former part of the work hath been remarkably distinguished." This contemporary survey was admirably written with an urbanity very different from the scratching and biting attacks so common in his journalism. The *Continuation* made amends for all that, and Smollett took the opportunity of the aloof approach of the historian to write of his contemporaries with detachment, good sense, and, often, magnificent compliment. One of the finest is to Fielding: "the genius of Cervantes was transfused into the mouth of Fielding, who painted the characters and ridiculed the follies of life with equal strength, humour and propriety." No eighteenth-century novelist could say better than that of another. Fielding had been dead for six years when these words sought to make amends for bitter things Smollett had said long before, during a paper quarrel. Happy the writer who lives long enough to atone for the angry words of his youth. The *Continuation* was used during the next eighty years at the end of Hume's *History*, often with title pages suggesting that Smollett had intended to continue Hume.

The labor of the *History* undermined Smollett's health. He wrote it in Chelsea, it is said in fourteen months, working with absurd concentration, refusing to see callers, worried by debt and by duns. With all of this he laid himself open to the tuberculosis that first attacked and eventually killed him.

During this intensive historical writing Smollett at least allowed himself the luxury of other kinds of

---

[3]*Public Advertiser*, 30 December 1755.

writing, for in 1756 he wrote *The Reprisal*, a brief play for performance after the main piece, which was produced by David Garrick in 1757 at the Theatre Royal in Drury Lane. This was generous of Garrick; and when Smollett revised *Peregrine Pickle* in 1758, the satire on Garrick's acting was removed.

At the beginning of 1760, Smollett launched the *British Magazine*, which ran until 1767. Much work for it had been prepared before the journal was launched, and it is distinguished by carrying some of the finest essays of Oliver Goldsmith. It was here that *Sir Launcelot Greaves* appeared in serial form.

Meanwhile, Smollett continued to be the life and soul of the *Critical Review*. On one occasion he cast doubts upon the courage of Admiral Sir Charles Knowles, who dealt with him in peremptory sailor fashion: in November 1760, Smollett disappeared for eleven weeks into the Marshalsea prison for having defamed the admiral's character. Prison conditions were made easy for him, and apparently his writing went on without interruption.

All this time Smollett was engaged in translation work and in the supervision of the immense compilations his literary factory produced. A thirty-eight-volume edition of Voltaire was among them; and Smollett, to demonstrate his appreciation of the greatest European writer of his time, wrote all the historical and critical notes for the volumes completed by May 1763. A few of them were resurrected in an American paperback of Voltaire's writings.

Finally, and unfortunately, Smollett was persuaded to edit the *Briton*, a political weekly that appeared from May 1762 to February 1763 in defense of the earl of Bute's ministry. Here he walked into real trouble, for his chief opponent was his old friend John Wilkes, who was easily the master of Smollett at this kind of work and scored off him with the greatest of ease. The *Briton* formed a focus for attacks on the Scots, at that time especially unpopular in London; and Wilkes, at the head of the local brigade of political journalists, smiled and smote in the *North Briton*. This was bad enough for anyone as sensitive as Smollett. What was worse was the corroding effect of an excursion into politics on an eager and spirited worker for the betterment of society. It ended as it was bound to end, in bitter disillusionment.

By the summer of 1762 Smollett was seriously ill, and eventually, in the summer of 1763, he cut himself away from all his burdens and went to France and Italy. This record of his writing up to his illness marks his extraordinary energy. He always worked well, and sometimes with genius. All the time he was urged on by the belief that if only man would think and organize, society would progress to happiness. He was especially haunted by a belief that the world of letters would exert its proper influence if it were organized.

All this journalism died with Smollett. It was popular at the time, apart from the political work, but it has not been read since; and his great efforts for improving literature and the arts, whether by academies or by bettering periodical criticism, have left no apparent result. None of it, except the *History* and its *Continuation*, has been reprinted.

The History and Adventures of an Atom (1769) must have been written during Smollett's last stay in Britain, some time after the period of his great activity just described. It is a vindictive satire of current affairs and public characters from 1754 to the date of publication, and it is Smollett's last fling at the politicians before he left them forever. It could hardly be further from the urbanity of his *Continuation*. The fiction under which the satire is maintained is that an atom moves from Japan to the brain of one Nathaniel Peacock, and dictates what he must write of its "Japonese" adventures. Any doubts about the true subject matter are dispelled in an early paragraph, which is an unmistakable portrait of the English people:

> The Japonese value themselves much upon their constitution, and are very clamorous about the words liberty and property; yet, in fact, the only liberty they enjoy is to get drunk when they please, to revile the government, and quarrel with one another. With respect to their property, they are the tamest animals in the world; and, if properly managed, undergo, without wincing, such impositions as no other nation in the world would bear.

Soon there follow the exceptionally disgusting descriptions that make all devout critics ignore the book or deny that Smollett wrote it. Yet immediately afterward the prose pictures of ministers are so good that they recall John Dryden's verse pictures. Pages of explosive virulence follow, directed against military and naval commanders, every statesman in the country, and, especially, the earl of Chatham. The common people, the political mob, are almost the most loathly of all. Indeed, the text of the book might be Swift's "I cannot but conclude the Bulk of your Natives, to be the most pernicious Race of little odious Vermin that Nature ever suffered to crawl upon the Surface of the Earth."

The Swiftian rancorous spleen is in Smollett's performance, but there is nothing of Swift's peculiar greatness, nothing of the ease—almost the magnanimity—of Swift's condemnation of the human race. Smollett has a smaller man's concentrated virulence, and eventually a weariness with the whole performance overtakes the reader. Perhaps Smollett did not write it. He never admitted authorship; and friendly critics have always either denied his authorship or left the question open. Yet so many of these characters are so well done, and so many of the sentences are quotable and memorable; and the main unpleasant theme, the sycophancy of public life, is so much Smollett's lifelong special hate that it is difficult to suggest he had nothing to do with it. If Smollett did not write it, what other tormented genius did?

IV

We come now to the three novels and the book of travels that are generally read today. Smollett was the third of the four writers who set the English novel on its way. *Roderick Random* was published in 1748, the same year that Richardson's *Clarissa* was completed, and within the decade that saw the great beginnings. *Pamela* (1740) begat Fielding's *Joseph Andrews* (1742), and *Tom Jones* followed in 1749. In 1751 came *Peregrine Pickle*, which obviously inspired Sterne's *Tristram Shandy* (1760–1767). *Humphry Clinker* (1771) completed the sequence.

According to the picaresque convention, Smollett claims a satirical and reforming intention in the preface to *Roderick Random*: "Of all kinds of satire, there is none so entertaining and universally improving, as that which is introduced, as it were, occasionally."[4]

The reader is a sensible and sober citizen who must have some excuse for enjoying a book in which the morals are those of a thieves' kitchen. The same convention is used in Alain René Le Sage's *Gil Blas*, which Smollett translated and

[4]Quotations are from the Everyman edition of *The Adventures of Roderick Random* (London, 1958).

published in 1749. It had been used, with much greater comic skill, by Fielding in the opening of *Jonathan Wild* (1743). Smollett blurs his comedy by breaking seriously into satire, especially in his descriptions of life in the navy. Indeed, he seems to have chosen picaresque, with the familiar gallery of odd characters, usually criminal types, strung together in a series of episodes, because he had a grudge against society. He had tried verse as a vehicle for his satire, and had failed; he would now try prose.

Roderick Random is the orphaned, unwanted grandson of a severe old Scots magistrate, exposed by his grandfather's known neglect to the malice of the community. His principal enemies are the schoolmaster and his grandfather's heir. It is not long before a deus ex machina appears in the form of a sailor uncle, Tom Bowling, and for the first time a British tar is portrayed in the English novel:

He was a strongly built man, somewhat bandy-legged, with a neck like that of a bull, and a face which (you might easily perceive) had withstood the most obstinate assaults of the weather. His dress consisted of a soldier's coat, altered for him by the ship's tailor, a striped flannel jacket, a pair of red breeches japanned with pitch, clean grey worsted stockings, large silver buckles that covered three-fourths of his shoes, a silver-laced hat whose crown overlooked the brim about an inch and a half, a black bob wig in buckle, a check shirt, a silk hankerchief, a hanger with a brass handle, girded to his thigh by a tarnished laced belt, and a good oak plant under his arm.

(ch. 3)

This excellent officer proceeds at once to discomfit the heir, interview the grandfather, and flog the schoolmaster. His speech is as good as his costume, and for the first time we hear the salt-spray accents in English fiction:

"Your servant, your servant. What cheer, father? What cheer? I suppose you don't know me; mayhap you don't. My name is Tom Bowling, and this here boy: you look as if you did not know him neither; 'tis like you mayn't. He's new rigg'd i' faith; his cloth don't shake in the wind so much as it wont to do. 'Tis my nephew, d'ye see, Roderick Random, your own flesh and blood, old gentleman. Don't lay astern you dog!" pulling me forward.

(ch. 3)

For a while all goes well with Roderick Random. But the sailor returns to sea, leaving the youngster settled with a Mr. Roger Potion, the apothecary in a neighboring town, who turns him away when misfortune overtakes Tom Bowling. Mr. Launcelot Crab, the surgeon, takes him in, because it will harm Potion, his rival. His school friends and relations melt away, and incident after incident reflects Smollett's cynicism as a young novelist.

His virtues as a writer are already apparent in these early chapters. He has the golden pen, the style that wraps the reader round. Characters and incidents follow one another in teeming plenty, and only a strong stomach is required to carry the reader forward, willing to follow Roderick Random anywhere. Indeed, there is some exertion in traveling, or there would be, but for the easy vehicle of this fine eighteenth-century prose. Character after character appears, sketched with the clear crudeness of an old woodcut, or designed, as it were, for the caricaturists like Thomas Rowlandson who were to spring from this English society as naturally as Smollett himself. Crab, the surgeon, is a good example of this prodigality; for here he is, and he lasts only for a part of a chapter:

This member of the faculty was aged fifty, about five feet high, and ten round the belly; his face was capacious as a full moon, and much of the complexion of a mulberry; his nose, resembling a powder-horn, was swelled to an enormous size, and studded all over with carbuncles; and his little grey eyes reflected the rays in such an oblique manner, that while he looked a person full in the face, one would have imagined he was admiring the buckle of his shoe.

(ch. 7)

Excellent average eighteenth century, matched later only by Charles Dickens, who profited by study of Smollett.

There is no resisting these characters and incidents unless they are perceived as being both too harsh and too gross for modern taste. One may find it difficult to realize, partly because of this harshness, partly because of the remoteness of eighteenth-century society, that for Smollett and his reader this was a picture of contemporary life in which many known characters were recognizable.

Roderick Random eventually joins the Royal Navy as a doctor, which gives Smollett his opportunity to describe with minuteness and trenchancy the inefficient methods of recruitment at that time. Eventually he puts to sea, and the first of the long series of stories of the Silent Service begins.

Smollett is concerned to describe the evil conditions on ships ("A man had better go to prison than go to sea," said Samuel Johnson) and to expose the incompetent management of the Cartagena Expedition. This celebration of the character of the navy and its sailors is the best part of the book. The ocean and the winds of the world form the background to many English stories of the little societies of men on ships; and the special atmosphere of these seafaring societies against their elemental background is caught in *Roderick Random* for the first time. While Smollett was writing, the British Empire was in the making and the formidable influences of vast spaces, both on land and at sea, so different from an island atmosphere, were beginning their work on the English character.

The indignation of the young doctor over conditions at sea finds trenchant expression:

I assisted Thomson in making up his prescriptions: but when I followed him with the medicines into the sickberth or hospital, and observed the situation of the patients, I was much less surprised that people should die on board, than that any sick person should recover. Here I saw about fifty miserable distempered wretches, suspended in rows, so huddled one upon another that not more than fourteen inches space was allotted for each with his bed and bedding: and deprived of the light of the day, as well as of fresh air; breathing nothing but a noisome atmosphere of the morbid steams exhaling from their own excrements and diseased bodies, devoured with vermin that hatched in the filth that surrounded them, and destitute of every convenience necessary for people in that helpless condition.

(ch. 25)

Smollett's descriptive comments on the Cartagena Expedition are of a kind to which we have grown accustomed after two world wars. Smollett's treatment is classical, for no expedition could exceed the Cartagenan in the stupidity of its conduct and no writer could surpass the happy gusto of contempt expressed by the young genius. Chapter 33 is a locus classicus for all war commentators. Smollett makes short shrift of the tactics of the commanders, writing, for example, of a particularly atrocious tactical blunder:

This piece of conduct afforded matter of speculation to all the wits either in the Army or Navy, who were at last fain to acknowledge it a stroke of policy above their comprehension.

He deals with the medical and quartermaster's arrangements with equal delight. Yet it is not for these things that *Roderick Random* is celebrated as the first naval novel, but for the descriptions of sailors and of storms at sea, and for the never-failing wonder at what common men can endure from their leaders and the elements.

Eventually Random returns to England and lands—not in any normal way, for this is a picaresque novel—by shipwreck and fights with his shipmates on shore. The normal adventures of a picaresque hero then follow. He becomes manservant to a local family and falls in love with the young lady of the house, the fair Narcissa. He goes abroad and serves as a common soldier in the French army, which gives an opportunity for discussing the battle of Dettingen.[5] His old friend Strap reappears to rescue him. The sudden reappearance of favorite characters to prove the truth of the adapted saying "cast your bread upon the waters and it will come back buttered after many days" is a piece of machinery frequently used. Thomson, who threw himself overboard in despair, survived to feed and outfit Random and set him on his way in Jamaica. In the end his father comes to life again and restores the family fortunes so that Random, now an undoubted gentleman, rent roll and all, can marry Narcissa. It is all engagingly simple, and supplies the only continuity the plot boasts.

The picaresque atmosphere is oppressive, principally because of the moral concepts the hero follows. He must never work honestly for his living. He may fight duels, gamble, try to marry for money, and accept whatever he needs from his equals and agents. He may not be cowardly or mean; rather, he must be foolishly brave and foolishly generous. His enemies may outwit him, but in the end picaresque justice demands that the hero or his good fortune overcomes them. It is never suggested that he is an enemy of society or that society has a case against him. The quarrels are all with individuals, and there is no hint that behind it all there may be a social structure that is damaged by his conduct. The sense of social structure comes only at the end, for he must be admitted again to honorable place (that is, position and money) so that he may marry and live happily ever after.

[5]Though nothing he has to say of it matches this note to his satire, *Advice* (1746): "This line relates to the behaviour of a General on a certain occasion: who discovered an extreme passion for the cool shade during the heat of the day: the Hanoverian General, in the battle of Dettingen."

The next novel, *Peregrine Pickle*, is equally offensive in these ways. It is rescued from being utterly sordid by the great character, Commodore Hawser Trunnion, and his shipmates, retired from the sea and settled on land as part of English village society. The hero rises out of English village society, which is to say average English society in the mid-eighteenth century. This brings the novel nearer to Fielding, who had an unfailing sense of social structure. Smollett usually preferred the shifting scene of London, where many societies have their own laws and customs.

Trunnion is much more real than any character in the first novel, a much more mature piece of work, although *Peregrine* was published only three years after *Roderick*, in 1751. It was heavily revised by Smollett and republished in 1758, about fifty pages shorter, the slanderous sketches of contemporaries being removed. It is invariably the revised edition that is reprinted today.

Commodore Trunnion is as lost ashore as a whale. He garrisons himself with old shipmates against all the perils of the land, of which the greatest are women and lawyers. When everyone, including the garrison, leagues against him to marry him off, he is lost. In a brief passage of high comedy, which is one of the most delicious things in the eighteenth-century novel, he makes his proposal of matrimony.

On the wedding day the groom sets out on horseback "at the head of all his male attendants, whom he had rigged with the white shirts and black caps formerly belonging to his barge's crew." But he does not arrive in time; indeed, the bridal party

waited a whole half hour for the commodore, at whose slowness they began to be under some apprehension, and accordingly dismissed a servant to quicken his pace. The valet, having rode something more than a mile, espied the whole troop disposed in a long file, crossing the road obliquely, and headed by the bridegroom and his friend Hatchway, who, finding himself hindered by a hedge from proceeding farther in the same direction, fired a pistol, and stood over to the other side, making an obtuse angle with the line of his former course; and the rest of the squadron followed his example, keeping always in the rear of each other like a flight of wild geese.

Surprised at this strange method of journeying, the messenger came up, and told the commodore that his lady and her company expected him in the church, where they had tarried a considerable time, and were beginning to be very uneasy at his delay; and therefore desired he would proceed with more expedition. To this message Mr. Trunnion replied, "Hark ye, brother, don't you see we make all possible speed? Go back, and tell those who sent you, that the wind has shifted since we weighed anchor, and that we are obliged to make very short trips in tacking, by reason of the narrowness of the channel; and that, as we lie within six points of the wind, they must make some allowance for variation and leeway." "Lord, sir!" said the valet, "what occasion have you to go zig-zag in that manner? Do but clap spurs to your horses, and ride straight forward, and I'll engage you shall be at the church porch in less than a quarter of an hour." "What! right in the wind's eye," answered the commander; "ahey! brother, where did you learn your navigation? Hawser Trunnion is not to be taught at this time of day how to lie his course, or keep his own reckoning. And as for you, brother, you best know the trim of your own frigate."[6]

(ch. 8)

Apart from the Trunnion group, which was so finely conceived that it inspired Sterne's Uncle Toby and his friends in *Tristram Shandy*, the old coarseness and sordid atmosphere remain. These qualities haunted Smollett in his next two novels, leaving him only in his last novel, his masterpiece. There was some quirk in his nature that drove him to expend his genius on descriptions of filth. And there is no doubt that Smollett's medical training gave added force to this idiosyncrasy. It may simply have been Scots realism in reaction to the English complacency around him. In the twentieth century George Orwell has shown a similar obsession in his early books.

Peregrine Pickle is essentially similar in kind to *Roderick Random*, but Commodore Trunnion, his counterpart Lieutenant Hatchway, and his retinue of sailors make it the greater book. They are more colorful and vivid in themselves and they acquire their full value by contrast with Peregrine's household and society in the village inn, which introduce, if only for a short space in the book's great length, good, normal eighteenth-century English country life. The poorest part of the book is the long interruption "The Memoirs of a Lady of Quality," which Smollett's publishing sense of good-selling exclusive scandal made him include, and certainly gave the book notoriety when it was published, but is now a deadly dull appendage.

His next novel, *Ferdinand Count Fathom* (1753), is plain picaresque and shows how poor the kind can be when no sailors or other bright characters come to relieve the tedium of repeated similar incident. *Sir Launcelot Greaves* (1760–1761) was a contemporary English Don Quixote, and the reader may get some amusement from it if he or she can ignore the fact that the hero would have been arrested after the first adventure.

Two books—the best Smollett wrote, and heartily to be commended to any reader—remain for consideration. In *Travels Through France and Italy*, Smollett is an early example of the personal travel writer, conforming to Norman Douglas' specification that it is the mind of the traveler that matters. Some of his comments are famous: his suggestion that a corniche along the French Mediterranean coast would pay dividends, his forecast of trouble for France as soon as there was a weak monarch, his remark on the natural use of the Borghese Palace as a gallery, his recommendation that the Roman Campania be drained and cultivated (which was carried out in the Pontine Marshes in 1932–1934), the commonplace that the entry to London from the south is a disgrace to any metropolis.

This is probably the first English book of travel that is interesting because it reflects a state of mind: the first of a kind for which English writers have displayed a special aptitude. Smollett describes the state of his mind when he set out:

> Traduced by malice, persecuted by fiction, abandoned by false patrons, and overwhelmed by the sense of a domestic calamity, which it was not in the power of fortune to repair.[7]

(letter 1)

Here are echoes of the *Briton*; of his service to Lord Bute, who discarded him; of Wilkes, who treated him so roughly in journalistic combat; and of the death of his fifteen-year-old daughter, from which he and his wife never properly recovered. The *Travels* were written as Smollett went along, in the form of letters addressed to the circle of Scots doctors in London who were his close friends. One may assume that these physicians had a talk among themselves before he left. They knew how ill Smollett was, and they knew that part of the cure would be for him to escape from the exertions of daily writing; but they also knew that it would be unwise for him to stop suddenly and altogether.

---

[6]Quotations are from the Everyman edition of *The Adventures of Peregrine Pickle* (London, 1956).

[7]Quotations are from the World's Classics edition of *Travels Through France and Italy* (London, 1907).

Therefore they proposed the letters or encouraged him when he made the suggestion, explaining how useful a record of inns, prices, and methods of transport would be to them if they wished to make the tour themselves. So Smollett tells them exactly what he thinks of the inns between London and Dover, and all the innkeepers he suffered from in France and Italy. He offers detailed and apparently sound advice on transport, and he tells them of the cost of living everywhere.

He discusses water supplies and food as one doctor to others. More personally he describes the state of his health, and in one letter (the only one that opens "Dear Doctor") he describes his exchange of letters with a French specialist on tuberculosis.

Two letters, the seventh and fifteenth, are addressed to the wife of one of the doctors (perhaps Mrs. Moore). The first is the famous attack on the French, and the second is an attack on dueling, a subject chosen carefully for his correspondent after her reproof about his harsh judgment of the French, to whom he makes amends in the opening of the latter letter.

In the other thirty-nine letters Smollett, one of the finest English journalists of his time, addresses a select audience over a period of two years. The first is dated Boulogne, June 1763, and he is delighted to have left England. In the last, dated Boulogne, June 1765, he is greatly recovered in body and spirit and records his pleasure at seeing again "the white cliffs of Dover."

Smollett is an honest travel critic. "I assure you, upon my word and honour, I have described nothing but what actually fell under my own observation." Moreover, he says what he thinks, and not what he should think. He is disappointed in Paris and Rome, and what honest traveler is not at first disappointed in places he has read about all his life and then sees?

The less-known places are different. The shock of surprise can be pure pleasure, as in Smollett's first sight of the Maison Carrée at Nîmes:

> The proportions of the building are so happily united, as to give it an air of majesty and grandeur, which the most indifferent spectator cannot behold without emotion. A man need not be a connoisseur in architecture, to enjoy these beauties. They are indeed so exquisite that you may return to them every day with a fresh appetite for seven years altogether. . . . Without all doubt it is ravishingly beautiful. The whole world cannot parallel it; and I am astonished to see it standing entire, like the ef-

fects of enchantment, after such a succession of ages, every one more barbarous than another.

> (letter 10)

That was written at Montpellier in November 1763. By September, Boulogne had become too cold. Smollett heard that Nice was an ideal wintering place. He reached it in December and stayed there until the autumn of the following year, when he went to Italy. The letters from Nice, as from Boulogne, are full of people and places and all the other things that would delight his correspondents.

In Italy, Smollett spent most of his time in Florence and Rome, and his letters are full of art criticism and a great deal of Latin learning. His taste in painting was very different from ours, and he enjoyed sculpture more, lingering with an anatomist's pleasure over the sculpture in the Pincio. But he always had space for what was present and lively. The English lived then in and around the Piazza di Spagna,[8] and he remarks:

> When you arrive at Rome, you receive cards from all your countryfolks in that city: they expect to have the visit returned next day: when they give orders not to be at home; and you never speak a word to one another in the sequel. This is a refinement in hospitality and politeness, which the English have invented by the strength of their own genius, without any assistance either from France, Italy or Lapland.

> (letter 29)

All through the *Travels* Smollett is at his best in the quick sketches of inns and innkeepers, postilions, and travelers. The worst of them, and so the best to read about, were between Nice and Genoa. At Noli:

> We ascended by a dark, narrow, steep stair, into a kind of public room, with a long table and benches, so dirty and miserable, that it would disgrace the worst hedge alehouse in England. . . . At length the landlord arrived, and gave us to understand, that he could accommodate us with chambers. In that where I lay, there was just room enough for two beds, without curtains or bedstead, an old rotten table covered with dried figs, and a couple of crazy chairs. The walls had once been white-washed: but were now hung with cobwebs, and speckled with dirt of all sorts, and I believe the brick-floor had not been swept for half a century.

> (letter 25)

[8]Where John Keats and Joseph Severn had rooms sixty years later.

A night or two later:

At the post-house in Lerici, the accommodation is intolerable. We were almost poisoned at supper. I found the place where I was to lie so close and confined, that I could not breathe in it, and lay all night in an outward room upon four chairs, with a leather portmanteau for my pillow.

(letter 26)

What happened on these occasions to poor Mrs. Smollett we are never told. No fellow traveler could be more dim. Only once, when Smollett flew into a rage at an inn outside Florence and insisted on defying innkeeper and coachman and walking through the night into the city, do we catch a glimpse of the poor woman:

Behold us then in this expedition; myself wrapped up in a very heavy greatcoat, and my cane in my hand. I did not imagine I could have walked a couple of miles in this equipage, had my life been depending; my wife a delicate creature, who had scarce ever walked a mile in her life; and the ragamuffin before us with our boxes under his arm. The night was dark and wet; the road slippery and dirty; not a soul was seen, nor a sound was heard: all was silent, dreary, and horrible. I laid my account with a violent fit of illness from the cold I should infallibly catch, if I escaped assassination, the fears of which were the more troublesome as I had no weapon to defend our lives. While I laboured under the weight of my greatcoat which made the streams of sweat flow down my face and shoulders, I was plunging in the mud, up to the mid-leg at every step, and at the same time obliged to support my wife, who wept in silence, half dead with terror and fatigue.

(letter 34)

Recollecting all these unequal struggles with rapacious innkeepers and cheating postilions as he wrote in the tranquillity of Nice, Smollett is obliged at last to admit that they were not worth the few sixpences he saved.

The *Travels* is a fine book, worthy to stand beside Fielding's *Voyage to Lisbon* (1755), Sterne's *Sentimental Journey* (1768), and Johnson's *A Journey to the Western Islands of Scotland* (1775). Sterne met Smollett in Rome and in Turin, and each time found him fulminating. He caricatures him as Smelfungus in the *Sentimental Journey* and lays his finger on Smollett's weakness for being miserable and angry. " 'I'll tell it,' cried Smelfungus, 'to the world.' 'You had better tell it,' I said, 'to your physician.' " Good common sense; and Smollett recognized it in the last letters, when he was a much fitter man. He was moving pleasantly toward the self-portrait in *Humphry Clinker*, "good humoured and civilized."

Something in Smollett's nature irritated him excessively when he saw the cruelty and craft of man to man. Examples occur again and again in the early novels like raw gashes in the comic body of his work. They are more controlled in the *Travels* because his greater power permitted restraint. In his last novel, the masterpiece, they are woven into the comic structure, becoming part of the caricature figures. *Humphry Clinker* is composed with the serenity of mastery. Smollett had at last come to terms with life, and expressed his views through the medium of a style that adorns a century of great prose stylists.

Humphry Clinker was published in June 1771, three months before his death. Once again he uses the letter form, and once again his characters travel. Once again he innovates, for the letters are not written by one character and a confidante, but by five characters, a device used only once before, and in verse, in Christopher Anstey's *New Bath Guide* (1766). The joy of this method is that episodes are seen through different eyes and the characters comment on one another as their story proceeds. Smollett cribbed shamelessly from Anstey's poem.

The chief character and chief letter writer is Matthew Bramble. He is Smollett's vehicle for comment on life and the kindly agent for good, exerting to that end his wealth, experience, and position. His nephew, Jeremy Melford, writes the other long letters, and these carry the main burden of the story. The other three writers are women, since the great novel readers were women and Smollett made few business errors.[9]

Miss Tabitha Bramble is Matthew's sister, a sourly aging spinster in search of a husband. Lydia Melford is the heroine, and a very pleasant one. Winifred Jenkins is the comic maid whose brief let-

---

[9]"Tim had made shift to live many years by writing novels, at the rate of five pounds a volume; but that branch of business is now engrossed by female authors, who publish merely for the propagation of virtue, with so much ease and spirit, and delicacy, and knowledge of the human heart, and all in the serene tranquillity of high life, that the reader is not only enchanted by their genius, but reformed by their morality" (*Humphry Clinker*, letter of 10 June from Melford to Phillips).

ters share with those of her mistress the old comedy confusion of misspellings and malapropisms.

For the three women there are three men: Lieutenant Lismahago, one of the great English comic characters, Mr. Wilson, and Humphry Clinker himself. In his letter of 10 July from Newcastle-upon-Tyne, Jeremy Melford describes Lismahago's true comedy entrance:

A tall, meagre figure, answering, with his horse, the description of Don Quixote mounted on Rozinante, appeared in the twilight at the inn door, while my aunt and Liddy stood at a window in the dining-room. He wore a coat, the cloth of which had once been scarlet, trimmed with Brandenburgs, now totally deprived of their metal; and he had holster-caps and housing of the same stuff and same antiquity. Perceiving ladies at the window above, he endeavoured to dismount with the most graceful air he could assume; but the ostler neglecting to hold the stirrup when he wheeled off his right foot, and stood with his whole weight on the other, the girth unfortunately gave way, the saddle turned, down came the cavalier to the ground, and his hat and periwig falling off, displayed a headpiece of various colours, patched and plastered in a woeful condition. . . .

He would have measured above six feet in height had he stood upright; but he stooped very much; was very narrow in the shoulders, and very thick in the calves of his legs, which were cased in black spatter-dashes. As for his thighs, they were long and slender, like those of a grasshopper; his face was at least half a yard in length, brown and shrivelled, with projecting cheek-bones, little grey eyes on the greenish hue, a large hook-nose, a pointed chin, a mouth from ear to ear, very ill furnished with teeth, and a high, narrow forehead, well furrowed with wrinkles. His horse was exactly in the style of its rider; a resurrection of dry bones which (as we afterwards learned) he valued exceedingly, as the only present he had ever received in his life.

Each of the five writers has a brief letter at the beginning that swiftly gives his or her character, so that in a very few pages they are outlined firmly and a love story is indicated that will no doubt end happily but is in a dreadfully unfortunate state when the story opens.

The action is mainly in Bath, London, Edinburgh, the Scottish Highlands, at the Welsh border, and on all the roads between these places. The story stands completely still (it is simple enough and waits easily) during the Scottish tour. It is generally agreed that Smollett wrote a good part of the book during his last stay in Britain, for many of the descriptions of places and of society have the air of recent observation. Matthew Bramble's letter from Bath on 23 April has comments on town planning and architecture that were surely written on the spot; and much of the Scottish tour bears the marks of recent observation. The final shape, color, and atmosphere were probably applied in Italy.

Smollett still does without a plot of any consequence, and relies instead upon letting his characters travel, meeting odd people and running into odd incidents on the road. The difference is that he is no longer writing picaresque. He is celebrating the England and the Scotland in which he has spent his life. He writes with an exile's love of his native land and people, and this changes and deepens the quality of his work. *Humphry Clinker* is one of the great pictures of eighteenth-century England, a picture of England at a great moment in its history, a record of a society that was setting out to change the appearance of half the world.

It stands with *Tom Jones* and *Tristram Shandy*, Edward Gibbon's *The Decline and Fall of the Roman Empire* and Edmund Burke's *Speeches on Conciliation*, Johnson's *Lives of the Poets* and Goldsmith's *The Vicar of Wakefield*; and the reader who has enjoyed them will enjoy *Humphry Clinker* the better. For these great pieces are centuries away now, and the society from which they grew seems very remote. Yet in a sense readers rely on the eighteenth century even more than they did a hundred years ago, because it developed the skeptical intelligence on which any progress will be based. It may also be because the technological revolution has brought so many people so close together in a clamor of communication that many return gladly to a century when solitude and silence were common experience, and writing and the society of books were sought as a source of strength. Those who are prepared to face the present problems of the human condition and not run easily away from thought and feeling still base themselves on the conclusions of men who wrote in what Matthew Arnold called the indispensable (eighteenth) century, and Smollett is of that company of writers.

In an extraordinary passage toward the end of *Humphry Clinker*, Smollett draws a picture of the ideal eighteenth-century society that, like Goldsmith's "The Deserted Village" and other pieces, records what might have been, as if in foreknowledge of the industrial revolution. Matthew Bramble, in his letters about Dennison and Baynard, expresses the eighteenth-century nostalgia for the ideal country life, the craving for a well-ordered society based on the perennial round of toil on the earth itself. The eighteenth century never failed to have a strong feeling of the need for good society in living the good life, and Smollett is at pains to show that the good and socially desirable life develops naturally in the country. The town author, then as now, has no doubts on the matter.

There is no warmer passage in the book than the letter from Matthew Bramble to his friend Baynard, recommending the ideal life of the country gentleman. Thus the Scots exile in Italy, who had nearly killed himself in his overworked life in London, came at the end to subscribe to the country ideals of eighteenth-century England.

Smollett, as one of the four writers who set the English novel on its way, is to be measured partly by the extent to which he inspired later novelists. Hawser Trunnion and his garrison inspired Sterne's Uncle Toby and Corporal Trim. Sir Walter Scott and Dickens acknowledge their debt. There are many others; and in general it may be claimed that all the novels about the sea and the English sailor descend from him. The student's judgment must be that Smollett stands well among the four. In assessing him one thinks in terms of the characters he created, so one looks back for comparisons over the centuries of character drawing in the novel. It is a large gallery, with many styles. The reader of George Eliot's *Middlemarch* catches the surprise of style difference when suddenly, during the rich enjoyment of the character play in that novel, someone mentions Smollett. George Eliot uses the rich potentiality of the novel for showing the principal characters developing and modifying by their contact with their environment and more fixed, older characters. The novel moves with the pace of life itself, the slow years and the sudden crises. At the moment of one of these crises in the life of Dorothea, the heroine, that stupid and sympathetic character, Mr. Brooke, recommends the reading of Smollett to her sick, pedantic husband:

. . . get Dorothea to read you light things, Smollett, *Roderick Random, Humphry Clinker*: they are a little broad, but she may read anything now she's married, you know. I remember they made me laugh uncommonly—there's a droll bit about a postilion's breeches. We have no such humour now.

(bk. I, ch. 30)

Indeed they hadn't. That simple, early-novel sort of humor after the quiet, pointed wit of George Eliot is like the guffawing of boys at play. There was an equal difference in the character drawing. Smollett never developed characters. He created them brilliantly, as has been shown, in a few sentences, then set them moving and talking among the other characters. He made them and was responsible for bringing them together so that the maximum amount of fun was extracted from them. They are comedy characters, created and used in Ben Jonson's way, by interplay without development.

In the guise of Matthew Bramble, Smollett carried his responsibility one stage further. Matthew Bramble concerns himself to help other people, and the novel becomes a more serious consideration of life than Smollett's earlier ones. It faces the simple and recurring human problem of living with other people and living one's own life at the same time. Therefore one still turns to Smollett, as one turns to Fielding and Sterne, for that humorous comment on life that is one of the great legacies from the eighteenth century.

Finally, Smollett was a good European. His novels derive from Miguel de Cervantes and Alain René Le Sage, whose works he translated; and it has already been noted that when he set his factory to translate Voltaire, he contributed the notes on the prose works himself. More generally, like so many of his English contemporaries, he derived from the literature of Rome. His comedy is like Latin comedy. His ideals—of gravity, of humanity, of disciplined industry and the proper organization of all human affairs—are Roman ideals. And his final belief, that man is at his best and happiest in a country society, reminds us of Cicero's words on the farmer's life: "nothing better, nothing more attractive, nothing more suitable for a free man."

SELECTED BIBLIOGRAPHY

I. Bibliography. D. Hannay, *The Life of T. G. Smollett* (London, 1887), contains a bibliography by J. P. Anderson; H. S. Buck, *A Study in Smollett* (New Haven, 1925), has a complete collation of the first and second eds. of *Peregrine Pickle*; E. Joliat, *Smollett et la France* (Paris, 1935), contains a bibliography of translations of Smollett's works; C. E. Jones, *Smollett Studies* (Los Angeles, 1942), includes a bibliography; F. W. Boege, *Smollett's Reputa-*

tion as a Novelist (Princeton, N. J., 1947), contains a bibliography; F. Cordaseo, ed., Letters (Madrid, 1949), has a bibliography of collected eds.

II. COLLECTED WORKS. Plays and Poems . . . with Memoirs of the Life and Writings of the Author (London, 1777); Miscellaneous Works, Containing Novels, Poems, Plays, and Travels, 6 vols. (Edinburgh, 1790); Miscellaneous Works, 6 vols. (Edinburgh, 1796), with memoirs of his life and writings by R. Anderson, repr. with enlarged memoir (Edinburgh, 1800); Works, 8 vols. (London, 1797), with memoirs of his life by J. Moore, repr. in J. P. Browne, ed. (London, 1872); Novels, 2 vols. (London, 1821), with a memoir by Sir Walter Scott, vols. II and III in Ballantyne's Novelist's Library; Miscellaneous Works, 12 vols. (London, 1824), with a life of the author; Miscellaneous Works (London, 1841), with a memoir of the author by T. Roscoe, frequently repr. throughout the nineteenth century; D. Herbert, sel. and ed., Works (Edinburgh, 1870), frequently repr. before the end of the nineteenth century; G. Saintsbury, ed., Works, 12 vols. (London, 1895; repr. 1899, 1902, 1925); W. E. Henley and T. Seccombe, eds., Works, 12 vols. (London, 1899-1901); G. H. Maynardier, ed., Works, 12 vols. (New York, 1902); Novels, 11 vols. (Oxford, 1925-1926), the Shakespeare Head ed.

III. SEPARATE WORKS. Advice: A Satire (London, 1746), verse; Reproof: A Satire (London, 1747), verse, repr. with Advice (London, 1748); The Adventures of Roderick Random, 2 vols. (London, 1748), in the Everyman ed. (London, 1958); The Regicide: or, James the First of Scotland (London, 1749), drama; The Adventures of Peregrine Pickle, 4 vols. (London, 1751), rev. ed. by Smollett (London, 1758), and in Everyman ed. (London, 1956); An Essay on the External Use of Water, with Particular Remarks upon the Mineral Waters at Bath (London, 1752), in C. E. Jones, ed. (Baltimore, 1935); A Faithful Narrative of the Base and Inhuman Arts That Were Lately Practised upon the Brain of Habbakkuk Hilding (London, 1752), an essay by Smollett under the pseudonym Drawcansir Alexander; The Adventures of Ferdinand Count Fathom, 2 vols. (London, 1753); T. G. Smollett, ed., A Compendium of Authentic and Entertaining Voyages, 7 vols. (London, 1756); The Reprisal: or, The Tars of Old England (London, 1757), a comedy; A Complete History of England, Deduced from the Descent of Julius Caesar to the Treaty of Aix la Chapelle, 4 vols. (London, 1757-1758; 2nd ed., 11 vols., London, 1758-1760); A Continuation of the Complete History, 4 vols. (London, 1760-1761; vol. V, London, 1765); The Adventures of Sir Launcelot Greaves, 2 vols. (London, 1762), first published in The British Magazine, 1 and 2 (1760-1761); Travels Through France and Italy, 2 vols. (London, 1766), repr. with Smollett's corrections in T. Seccombe, ed. (London, 1907), the World's Classics ed., the Chiltern Library ed. (London, 1949) has an intro. by Sir Osbert Sitwell; T. G. Smollett,

ed., The Present State of All Nations, 8 vols. (London, 1768-1769), an anthology; The History and Adventures of an Atom, 2 vols. (London, 1769), satire, some copies dated 1749; The Expedition of Humphry Clinker, 3 vols. (London, 1771), in the Everyman ed. (London, 1956), vol. I of the first ed. is misdated 1671; Ode to Independence (Glasgow, 1773), verse.

IV. LETTERS. Letters Hitherto Unpublished (Dumbarton, 1859), part of J. Irving's Some Account of the Family of Smollett of Bonhill; Letters 1721-1771 (London, 1926), part of Lewis Melville's The Life and Letters of Tobias Smollett, 1721-1771; E. S. Noyes, coll. and ed., Letters (Cambridge, Mass., 1926); F. Cordaseo, ed., Letters (Madrid, 1949), contains thirty-one unrecorded by Noyes.

V. PERIODICALS EDITED BY SMOLLETT. The Critical Review: or Annals of Literature (1756-1790), Smollett was editor in chief from 1756 to 1762 and an occasional contributor thereafter; The British Magazine: or Monthly Repository (1760-1767); The Briton (1762-1763); Smollett also contributed to The Monthly Review, see B. C. Nangle, The Monthly Review, Indexes of Contributors and Articles (Oxford, 1934).

VI. TRANSLATIONS BY SMOLLETT. A. R. Le Sage, The Adventures of Gil Blas, 4 vols. (London, 1749); Miguel de Cervantes Saavedra, Don Quixote, 2 vols. (London, 1755); The Works of Voltaire, translated with others, 36 vols. (London, 1761-1769), 3 vols. added later, Smollett had only a small part in the translation, but wrote all the historical and critical notes for the vols. completed by May 1763; François de Salignac de la Mothe Fénelon, The Adventures of Telemachus, 2 vols. (London, 1776).

VII. BIOGRAPHICAL AND CRITICAL STUDIES. W. C. Hazlitt, Lectures on the English Comic Writers (London, 1819); R. Anderson, "Life with Critical Observations on His Works," in vol. I of Smollett's Miscellaneous Works, 6 vols. (Edinburgh, 1820), the best of many memoirs by Anderson; Sir W. Scott, Lives of the Novelists (London, 1821); J. Irving, Some Account of the Family of Smollett of Bonhill: With a Series of Letters by T. Smollett Hitherto Unpublished (Dumbarton, 1859), repr. in Irving's The Book of Dumbartonshire, 3 vols. (Dumbarton, 1879); D. Hannay, Life (London, 1887), in the Great Writers series, with a bibliography by J. P. Anderson; W. H. O. Smeaton, Tobias Smollett (Edinburgh, 1897), in the Famous Scots series; C. H. Robinson, The British Tar in Fact and Fiction (London, 1909), valuable for its assessment of Smollett in relation to maritime fiction as a whole.

H. S. Buck, A Study in Smollett, Chiefly "Peregrine Pickle" (New Haven, 1925), includes a scrutiny of the 1758 ed.; A. Whitridge, Tobias Smollett. A Study of His Miscellaneous Works (London, 1925); L. Melville, Life and Letters 1721-1771 (London, 1926), L. Melville is the pseudonym of L. S. Benjamin; H. Read, Reason and Romanticism (London, 1926), contains an important chapter on Smollett; H. S. Buck, Smollett as Poet (New Haven, 1927);

E. A. Baker, *History of the English Novel* (London, 1930); E. Joliat, *Smollett et la France* (Paris, 1935); L. M. Knapp, "The Publication of Smollett's Complete History and Continuation," in *The Library*, 16 (1935); C. E. Jones, *Smollett Studies* (Los Angeles, 1942); L. L. Martz, *The Later Career of Tobias Smollett* (New Haven, 1942); G. M. Kahrl, *Tobias Smollett. Traveler–Novelist* (Chicago, 1945); V. S. Pritchett, *The Living Novel* (London, 1946); F. W. Boege, *Smollett's Reputation as a Novelist* (Princeton, N. J., 1947); L. M. Knapp, *Tobias Smollett, Doctor of Men and Manners* (Princeton, N. J., 1949; repr. 1963), the fullest modern study; A. D. McKillop, *The Early Masters of English Fiction* (Lawrence, Kans., 1956); A. B. Strauss, "On Smollett's Language: A Paragraph in *Ferdinand Count Fathom*," in H. C. Martin, ed., *Style in Prose Fiction: English Institute Essays, 1958* (New York, 1958); M. A. Goldberg, *Smollett and the Scottish School* (Albuquerque, N. M., 1959); R. Alter, *Rogue's Progress; Studies in the Picaresque Novel* (Cambridge, Mass., 1964); S. Baker, "*Humphry Clinker* as Comic Romance," in *Essays on the Eighteenth Century Novel*, R. D. Spector, ed. (Bloomington, Ind., 1965); D. Bruce, *Radical Doctor Smollett* (Boston, 1965); A. Parreaux, *Smollett's London* (Paris, 1965); P. -G. Boucé, "Les Procédés du comique dans *Humphry Clinker*," in *Études Anglaises* (Paris, 1966); R. Giddings, *The Tradition of Smollett* (London, 1967); R. Paulson, *Satire and the Novel in Eighteenth Century England* (New Haven, 1967); G. S. Rousseau and P. -G. Boucé, eds., *Tobias Smollett, Bicentennial Essays Presented to Lewis M. Knapp* (New York, 1971).

WILLIAM COLLINS

(1721-1759)

Oswald Doughty

I

WILLIAM COLLINS, biographically, is unsatisfactory. Too little is known about him to permit a convincing portrait. So slender is the material: two biographically disappointing letters, the few pages of his poetry, a brief memoir published four years after his death with some of his poems in an anthology, and two years later an edition of his poems with a biographical preface. Samuel Johnson's account of him in his *Lives of the Poets* appeared thirty years after his friendship with Collins, and for the rest there are but one or two allusions to him in contemporary letters by acquaintances and friends, with one or two short reminiscences of him by them long afterward. To this scanty gleaning may be added the few allusions to him in post-contemporary magazines and the very little of value produced by considerable modern research.

William Collins, mayor of Chichester, a somewhat pompous hatter who boasted of a friend of the great Alexander Pope among his customers, was forty-seven when, on Christmas Day 1721, his wife, seven years his junior, gave birth to a son at the family home and shop, 21 East Street. The only other members of the family were two sisters, Elizabeth and Anne, respectively seventeen and sixteen years old when William, the final addition to the family, arrived. Collins' mother, Elizabeth Martin, who came from a neighboring village, had a brother Edmund—a lieutenant colonel—and a clerical nephew, Dr. William Payne, a fellow of Magdalen College, Oxford. Both the brother and the nephew were destined to play a part in the little that is known of Collins' life.

The parents, ambitious for their son, early intended him for the church; and on 19 January 1733, Collins entered Winchester College as a "scholar," remaining there for the next seven years. Joseph Warton, destined to be a minor poet and headmaster of Winchester, was his schoolmate. Literary enthusiasm permeated the school, and before leaving, Collins composed four "Persian Eclogues."

On 21 March 1740 he entered Queen's College, Oxford, and in July 1741 was elected a demy of Magdalen. He disliked university life, feeling, as Gilbert White, an undergraduate friend, declared, "a sovereign contempt for all academic studies and discipline," and complaining of "the dulness of a college life." His father had died before Collins left Winchester, and his affectionate uncle, the lieutenant colonel, supported him throughout his university career.

At Oxford, Collins was soon noted for cleverness and indolence, but also as a scholarly and cultured man with, said White, "fine abilities, which properly improved, must have raised him to the top of any profession." Johnson later praised him as "a man of extensive literature, and of vigorous faculties, acquainted not only with the learned tongues, but with the Italian, French and Spanish languages," and also as "a man of uncommon learning and abilities."

At Oxford, Collins continued to write poetry, published his "Persian Eclogues" anonymously in 1742, and the following year received the bachelor of arts. A month later he published, also anonymously but as "By a Gentleman of Oxford," his "Verses to Sir Thomas Hanmer," a contemporary editor of Shakespeare's works. By this time restlessness and instability, as well as solitary and visionary tendencies, were appearing as deeply integrated elements in his nature. The "dulness" of academic life became intolerable; the attractions of the outer world, its amusements and excitements, irresistible. Oxford debts also were an anxiety. He would flee the university and "see life" in London.

There were other anxieties too. Collins had vexed

Dr. Payne by overspending his uncle's allowance, which Payne distributed, and had also appeared before that clerical doctor and fellow of Magdalen "gaily dressed, and with a feather in his hat." And when the outraged Payne told him "his appearance was by no means that of a young man who had not a single guinea he could call his own," Collins dared not answer the man who held the purse strings, though he spoke of him afterward as "a damned dull fellow." After this his failure to obtain a Magdalen fellowship may not have surprised, but it certainly disgusted, him, and increased his intention to leave Oxford. But above all other reasons, his friends declared, was his longing to "partake of the dissipation and gaiety" of London.

"The Manners," the most autobiographical of Collins' poems, which he was now writing, not only corroborates the evidence of his friends but also clearly illuminates his general mental and emotional state at this time:[1]

> Farewell, for clearer Ken design'd,
> The dim-discover'd Tracts of Mind:
> Truths which, from Action's Paths retir'd,
> My silent Search in vain requir'd!
> No more my Sail that Deep explores,
> No more I search those magic Shores,
> What regions part the World of Soul,
> Or when thy Streams, *Opinion*, roll:
> If e'er I round such Fairy Field,
> Some Pow'r impart the Spear and Shield,
> At which the Wizzard *Passions* fly,
> By which the Giant *Follies* die!
>
> (1–12)

On 6 July 1744 his mother died, leaving him a share of her fortune. Now an orphan with means, at this critical moment able to choose his way of life,

---

[1] If, as I suspect, the following passage from "The Manners" is a satire on Dr. Payne, lecturing in his ecclesiastical and academic garments at Magdalen, it is the only example of Collins' satirical wit (to which his friends testify):

> Farewell the Porch, whose Roof is seen,
> Arch'd with th'enlivening Olive's Green:
> Where *Science*, prank'd in tissued Vest,
> By *Reason*, *Pride*, and *Fancy* drest,
> Comes like a Bride so trim array'd,
> To wed with *Doubt* in *Plato's Shade*!

All quotations are from C. Stone and A. L. Poole, eds., *The Poetical Works of Gray and Collins* (Oxford, 1917), the Oxford Standard Authors edition.

Collins left Oxford for London, "to partake of its dissipation and gaiety," but also secretly spurred by literary ambitions.

The fog that descends at frequent intervals and for long periods upon Collins' life is all the more exasperating to the biographer because of the few intriguing glimpses one gains whenever it lifts for a moment. Shortly after arrival in London, Collins was worried about a friend, "Captn Hargrave," who "was quite abandoned" and "frequented night cellars." Three months later Collins' old school friend, John Mulso, his next-door neighbor in Soho, breakfasted with him while "Captn Hargrave played on the harpsichord; which," Mulso told Gilbert White, "he has not forgotten quite so much as he has himself." Whether the "Captn" was that "certain gentlewoman, properly called Nell Burnet but whose *nom de guerre* was 'Captn Hargraves,' in an officer's habit," thus described two years later by the Cambridge don and poet Thomas Gray, when a Pembroke College student, her cavalier, hid her in a cupboard, and the proctors and their men searched for her, is an unanswerable question.

But it is known that as "a man about Town" Collins haunted such pleasure resorts as Ranelagh and Vauxhall, theaters and coffeehouses, anxious to meet writers and actors, believing, said White, that "his superior abilities would draw the attention of the great world, by means of whom he was to make his fortune." Collins' geniality in such company soon won him distinguished friends, including David Garrick, James Quin, and Samuel Foote, who are said to have been "among the gentlemen who loved him for a genius," and who often asked his opinion upon plays before accepting them. Habitually indolent, though eager for pleasure and excitement, he idled his time away; but surely it was more than indolence that led him to lounge at the famous bookshop of the actor Tom Davies, where, long after Collins' death, Johnson was for the first time to meet James Boswell. "Passionately fond of music, good-natured and affable, warm in his friendships, and visionary in his pursuits; very temperate in his eating and drinking": thus White described Collins at this time. But one also learns of his keen, satiric observation of the men and manners he encountered, and of the amusement he provided for his intimate friends by his witty descriptions and comments.

His way of life was now evidently such as he had

anticipated in "The Manners": the rejection of mere study for the keen observation of real life. The poem reveals Collins the man of the world, for whom even Fancy turns but a cynical eye upon the crowd around him:

> Youth of the quick uncheated Sight,
> Thy Walks, *Observance*, more invite!
> O Thou, who lov'st that ampler Range,
> Where Life's wide Prospects round thee change,
> And with her mingling Sons ally'd,
> Throw'st the prattling Page aside:
> To me in Converse sweet impart,
> To read in Man the native Heart,
> To learn, where Science sure is found,
> From Nature as she lives around:
> And gazing oft her Mirror true,
> By turns each shifting Image view!
> Till meddling *Art's* officious Lore,
> Reverse the Lessons taught before,
> Alluring him from a safer Rule,
> To dream in her enchanted School.
>
>   . . .
>
> O Nature boon, from whom proceed
> Each forceful Thought, each prompted Deed;
> If but from Thee I hope to feel,
> On all my Heart imprint thy Seal!
> Let some retreating Cynic find,
> Those oft-turn'd Scrolls I leave behind,
> The *Sports* and I this Hour agree,
> To rove thy Scene-full World with Thee!
>
>   (19–34; 71–78)

With which intention the poem ends.

Literary ambitions still held Collins. He planned works to make him famous, works but seldom begun and never finished. Occasionally he would write an ode and read it to applauding friends; then, dissatisfied, and despite their protests, he would destroy it. His means dwindled, and poverty began to haunt him. "Entirely an author, and hardly speaks out of rule," the satiric Mulso described Collins in July 1744. "A literary adventurer, with many projects in his head and very little money in his pocket," wrote Johnson, now his friend. Another friend, John Ragsdale, similarly describing him at this time, added a significant comment: "In this manner he lived, with and upon his friends." Then for the next fourteen months the mists close in again.

Collins' next appearance—September 1745—is surprising: in London, seeking a bishop to make him a curate. He had visited his uncle, then fighting the French in Flanders; and the colonel, disappointed by his nephew's indifference to everything but intellectual interests, had sent him home to be a parson, as "too indolent even for the army." Mulso, meeting Collins as potential curate, informed White: "Don't laugh, . . . This will be the second acquaintance of mine who becomes the thing he most derides." But unlike Joseph Warton, the other acquaintance referred to, Collins was quickly persuaded by a London tobacconist to drop the plan. Shortly afterward she appeared at Guildford Races with Joseph Warton, both "in very high spirits," planning a joint volume of odes, for his share in which Collins would demand at least ten guineas from the publisher. Perhaps because of this exorbitant demand, when Warton's and Collins' odes appeared in December 1746, they were in separate volumes by different publishers.

Throughout the preceding spring and summer Collins was floundering in debt, demoralization, and illness. "The wandering Knight," one acquaintance sardonically named him, and a month later another saw him "in good clothes and a wretched carcass at all the gay places." Shortly before, he had been arrested for bilking his landlady; and it was probably about this time that Johnson saved him from a "prowling bailiff" by raising money from publishers on Collins' promise to translate Aristotle's *Poetics* for them, a promise quickly evaded when he could repay the loan. On 7 June his "Ode to a Lady on the Death of Colonel Ross" appeared in Robert Dodsley's *Museum.* The lady involved is said to have rejected Collins as a suitor. Pursuing creditors probably explain the poet's being abroad again as August opened. From Antwerp he sent Mulso a "rapturous" letter, as Mulso described it, about his journey through Holland. He was "in high spirits though near the French" as he made for the army, meeting "many wounded and sick countrymen as he travelled."

Collins found some compensation for the general neglect of his *Odes* in close friendship with James Thomson, the poet famous for his *Seasons* and now writing *The Castle of Indolence*, of which several stanzas were said (though not without question) to describe Collins. To be near a friend so akin to himself in temperament, Collins moved near Richmond, where he became a happy member of Thomson's distinguished circle. But the year in which *The Castle of Indolence* was published, 1748, was also that of Thomson's death. Collins then wrote his lovely "Ode on the Death of Mr. Thomson" and left Richmond forever.

In April 1749, Colonel Martin, who had been nursed for the last two years by Collins' sisters, died of war wounds. To the poet he left some two thousand pounds, "which," wrote Johnson, "Collins could scarcely think exhaustible, and which he did not live to exhaust." Thus rescued from poverty, Collins returned to Chichester and collected a distinguished library, including old and rare works. Angered by the neglect of his *Odes*, he bought all unsold copies and burned them. In October the *Gentleman's Magazine* published his charming "Song from Cymbeline," and before the year closed, he wrote his last known poem, "Ode on the Popular Superstitions of the Highlands of Scotland," addressed to the dramatist John Home, with whom, as a fellow guest, he then spent two or three weeks in a friend's house at Winchester.

On 2 July 1750 a musical performance of "The Passions: An Ode. Set to Music" was given in the Oxford theater. In November, Collins, who had only just heard of this performance, wrote one of his two surviving letters, offering the professor of music, who had composed the accompaniment, another ode: "On The Music of the Grecian Theatre"—"a nobler subject." If it ever existed, it has been lost. Thus, in the midyear of the century, Collins seemed about to enter upon a happy and poetically productive future, of greater promise than the past.

But the future was only "smiling to betray." "Man," wrote Johnson, "is not born for happiness. Collins, who, while he studied to live, felt no evil but poverty, no sooner lived to study than his life was assailed by more dreadful calamities, disease and insanity." The last eight years of Collins' life, from 1751 to the end, present a darkening scene in which at long intervals one gains a few harrowing glimpses of him as he deteriorates into melancholia and intermittent, sometimes violent, insanity. Visits to France and to Bath failed to arrest the disease. In 1754 he was removed from a London asylum to the care of his sister Ann, at Chichester. There, in September, Joseph and Thomas Warton found him "in high spirits at intervals" on the first day of their visit, but unable to see them on the second.

It was then that Collins showed them his "Ode on the Popular Superstitions of the Highlands" (not published until 1788), and another poem, now lost, "The Bell of Aragon." This was based on the Spanish legend that whenever a king of Spain was dying, the great bell of the cathedral of Saragossa tolled spontaneously. The only lines that Thomas Warton remembered and quoted are depressingly prophetic of Scott's romantic verse:

> The bell of Aragon, they say,
> Spontaneous speaks the fatal day.
> . . .
> Whatever dark aërial power
> Commissioned, haunts the gloomy tower. . . .

The poem ended, it is said, with "a moral transition to his own death and knell, which he called 'some simpler bell.'"

Near the close of 1754, Collins spent a month at Oxford, where Thomas Warton saw much of him, but found him too "weak and low" for conversation and once saw him attempt a short walk "supported by a servant." White "saw him under Merton wall, in a very affecting situation, struggling, and conveyed by force, in the arms of two or three men, towards the parish of St. Clement, in which was a house that took in such unhappy objects." That is the last glimpse of Collins. Johnson, who felt a sincere affection for the poet, followed his decline with a concern that was partly personal. "Poor dear Collins!" he wrote to Tom Warton on Christmas Eve that same year. "Let me know if you think it would give him pleasure if I should write to him. I have often been near his *state*, and therefore have it in great commiseration."

The poet lingered for five more years of living death, in the care of his difficult, eccentric, and miserly sister Ann, married to a lieutenant of marines. According to Johnson and others, Collins turned much to the Bible for consolation, though Johnson also says he found other sources of consolation as well, "eagerly snatching that temporary relief with which the table and the bottle flatter and seduce." He died on 12 June 1759, aged thirty-seven. After his death his sister, who had been angered by his habit during these last years of giving money to the cathedral choirboys in the cloisters, followed her brother's example (and unconsciously suggested that they had similar, hereditary temperaments) by burning whatever she could find of his poetic manuscripts.

The uncertainty that pervades so much of Collins' history, and even led his friends to misdate his death by several years, is equally obvious in the records of his physical appearance. "Decent," Johnson described it, probably meaning "comely." Another remembered or misremembered him as a "pockfretted man with keen black eyes" who "associated very little"; another, as "in stature somewhat above the middle size, of a brown [dark] complexion, keen expressive eyes, and a fixed sedate aspect, which from continual thinking had contracted an habitual frown." Gilbert White, however, remembered him as "of a moderate stature, of a light and clear complexion, with grey eyes, so very weak at times as hardly to bear a candle in the room."

The only estimate of Collins' character—Johnson's—suffers from an atmosphere of benevolent ambiguity:

His morals were pure, and his opinions pious: in a long continuance of poverty, and long habits of dissipation, it cannot be expected that any character should be exactly uniform. . . . That this man, wise and virtuous as he was, passed always unentangled through the snares of life, it would be prejudice and temerity to affirm; but it may be said that at least he preserved the source of action unpolluted, that his principles were never shaken, that his distinctions of right and wrong were never confounded, and that his faults had nothing of malignity or design, but proceeded from some unexpected pressure or casual temptation.

(*Life of Collins*)

Doubtless all true enough; but the realist must regret that Miss Bundy, the Soho landlady whom he bilked, has left no account of him.

Collins was buried in St. Andrew's Church, Chichester, where there is a memorial tablet to him and to other members of his family. In 1795 a monument by John Flaxman, with memorial verses by the poetaster William Hayley, was erected in Chichester Cathedral. It shows the poet seated, with his Bible open before him. Instead of Hayley's verbose epitaph a better one would have been Collins' own fatalistic lines in his "Ode to Pity," asking whether

CHANCE OR HARD INVOLVING FATE
O'ER MORTAL BLISS PREVAIL.

II

It is not surprising that Collins' four "Persian Eclogues," written when he was seventeen and published when he was twenty, have little merit as poetry. Their heroic couplets, weakly imitative of Pope's "Pastorals," are generally flat and monotonous. In only one line do they attain the verbal distinction that can turn verse into poetry, the description in the first eclogue of Chastity: "Cold is her breast, like Flow'rs that drink the Dew. . . . " Nevertheless, there are occasional passages of felicitous expression in these poems.

In the first eclogue the Persian poet, Selim, preaches virtue to the shepherds and shepherdesses: " 'Tis Virtue makes the Bliss, where'er we dwell."

In the second, Hassan, the camel driver, crossing the desert on a trade journey, and almost dead through hunger, thirst, and fear of wild animals, remembers (conveniently) the loving, weeping, and anxious Zara in Schiraz; feels (equally conveniently) a moral revulsion against the sacrifice of love and happiness to mere gold; and returns to Zara:

Curst be the Gold and Silver which persuade
Weak Men to follow far-fatiguing Trade!
The Lilly-Peace outshines the silver Store,
And Life is dearer than the golden Ore.

. . .

Thrice happy they, the wise contented Poor,
From Lust of Wealth, and Dread of Death secure!
They tempt no Desarts, and no Griefs they find;
Peace rules the Day, where Reason rules the Mind.

(31–34; 65–68)

The last line reminds one of the age in which Collins was born—the Age of Reason, by which he was influenced, but which he unconsciously assisted in its gradual transition toward romance. And in doing so he inevitably adapted "an Augustan style to an eighteenth-century sensibility," as T. S. Eliot said.

The third eclogue is a love romance in which the king of Persia, "Royal Abbas," out hunting, falls in love with, and marries, the shepherdess Abra. Although happy, and a queen, Abra so regrets absence from her former simple pastoral life and friends that every spring she rejoins them for a time; and "Royal Abbas," when able to escape from the cares of state, comes too. The description of Abra rises above the general level of the verse:

From early Dawn the live-long Hours she told,
'Till late at silent Eve she penn'd the Fold.
Deep in the Grove beneath the secret Shade,
A various Wreath of od'rous Flow'rs she made:
Gay-motley'd Pinks and sweet Junquils she chose,
The Violet-blue that on the Moss-bank grows;
All-sweet to Sense, the flaunting Rose was there;
The finish'd Chaplet well adorn'd her Hair.

. . .

Yet midst the Blaze of Courts she fix'd her Love,
On the cool Fountain, or the shady Grove;
Still with the Shepherd's Innocence her Mind
To the sweet Vale, and flow'ry Mead inclin'd,
And oft as Spring renew'd the Plains with Flow'rs,
Breath'd his soft Gales, and led the fragrant Hours,
With sure Return she sought the sylvan Scene,
The breezy Mountains, and the Forests green.
Her Maids around her mov'd, a duteous Band!
Each bore a Crook all-rural in her Hand:
Some simple Lay, of Flocks and Herds they sung;
With Joy the Mountain, and the Forest rung. . . .
(11–18; 37–48)

Near the close of the eclogue, a couplet states its democratic moral—already implied in the two preceding poems—the moral equality, if not superiority, of the poor, simple pastoral community to the highest in the land:

What if in Wealth the noble Maid excel;
The simple Shepherd Girl can love as well.
(61–62)

The fourth and last eclogue attempts the dramatic, as in a lesser degree the second had already done. In the second, fear and horror are caused by nature; but in the fourth, their cause is man. The effect is intensified in the fourth by the contrast of human misery with the peace, dignity, and indifference of the natural environment presented:

At that still Hour, when awful Midnight reigns,
And none, but Wretches, haunt the twilight Plains;
What Time the Moon had hung her Lamp on high,
And past in Radiance, thro' the cloudless Sky: . . .
(3–6)

two brothers, shepherds, fly from the marauding Tartars. For

. . . none so cruel as the *Tartar* Foe,
To Death inur'd, and nurst in Scenes of Woe.

He said; when loud along the Vale was heard
A shriller Shriek, and nearer Fires appear'd:
Th' affrighted Shepherds thro' the Dews of Night,
Wide o'er the Moon-light Hills, renew'd their Flight.
(69–74)

Such was the close of the last eclogue.

Even in these earliest poems Collins' romantic tendency is revealed in his attitude to "nature," to love, to human drama, to human emotion, however faintly expressed. But when reading Collins' later verse, so generally destitute of normal "human feeling," it is well to remember that in these earliest poems he expressed horror and fear of wildlife in nature, and a greater horror and fear of wild life in man. Scorned even beyond their deserts by most critics, the "Persian Eclogues" were equally overrated by Oliver Goldsmith, but were also found "admirable" "in parts" by no less a critic than William Hazlitt, who generally knew what he was talking about.

In 1743, the year following the publication of the "Eclogues," Collins published only a single poem. It was addressed to Sir Thomas Hanmer, whose sumptuous but badly edited Shakespeare was then appearing. Apart from some fatuous compliments to Hanmer, the poem is an expression of Collins' love and reverence for Shakespeare's works, and therefore illuminates Collins' personality. The poem thus has a value independent of its eighty plodding heroic couplets, many of them below the "Eclogues" in poetic quality. Collins reveals his ardent admiration for the poetic imagination of "th' unletter'd Bard," as he calls Shakespeare, and his own sense of poetic inadequacy, particularly of inadequate human feeling. His consciousness of this preyed upon him, as his later poems show. So now he praises Shakespeare above all his Elizabethan contemporaries:

But stronger *Shakespear* felt for *Man* alone:
Drawn by his Pen, our ruder Passions stand
Th' unrival'd Picture of his early Hand.
(76–78)

Like the "Eclogues" these verses to Hanmer attained a second edition in Collins' lifetime. This, when a little later his exquisite odes found no appreciation, was but an additional irritation to him.

Collins' next publication, the most important of his poetical works, *Odes on Several Descriptive and*

Allegorical Subjects, appeared in December 1746 (but dated 1747). It consisted of twelve short poems: odes to "Pity," "Fear," "Simplicity," "The Poetical Character," "Mercy," "Liberty," "Evening," "Peace," "The Manners," "The Passions"— ten abstract subjects—and two human ones: "How Sleep the Brave" and "To a Lady on the Death of Colonel Ross in the Action of Fontenoy."

Like "The Manners," though less explicitly, "Fear" and "The Poetical Character" reveal much of Collins' temperament. The intensity of a deeply personal experience, whether "real" or imaginative, vitalizes "Fear" almost in the manner of Blake, who was doubtless indebted to the poem, as to others by Collins:

> Thou, to whom the World unknown
> With all its shadowy Shapes is shown;
> Who see'st appall'd th' unreal Scene,
> While Fancy lifts the Veil between:
> Ah *Fear!* Ah frantic *Fear!*
> I see, I see Thee near.
> I know thy hurried Step, thy haggard Eye!
> Like Thee I start, like Thee disorder'd fly.
> For lo what *Monsters* in thy Train appear!
> *Danger* whose Limbs of Giant Mold
> What mortal Eye can fix'd behold?
> Who stalks his Round, an hideous Form
> Howling amidst the Midnight Storm,
> Or throws him on the ridgy Steep
> Of some loose hanging Rock to sleep:
> And with him thousand Phantoms join'd,
> Who prompt to Deeds accurs'd the Mind:
> And those, the Fiends, who near allied,
> O'er Nature's wounds, and Wrecks preside;
> While *Vengeance*, in the lurid Air,
> Lifts her red Arm, expos'd and bare:
> On whom the rav'ning Brood of Fate,
> Who lap the Blood of Sorrow, wait;
> Who, *Fear*, this ghastly Train can see,
> And look not madly wild, like Thee?
>   . . .
> O *Fear*, I know Thee by my throbbing Heart,
>   Thy with'ring Pow'r inspir'd each mournful Line,
> Tho' gentle *Pity* claim her mingled Part,
>   Yet all the Thunders of the Scene are thine!
>
>   (1–25; 42–45)

This is not the only passage in Collins' verse that unwittingly suggests his later insanity. His illness began as melancholia, and the following passage from "The Passions" probably owes something to

personal experience, as well as to John Milton's "Il Penseroso":

> With Eyes up-rais'd as one inspir'd,
> Pale *Melancholy* sate retir'd,
> And from her wild sequester'd Seat,
> In Notes by Distance made more sweet,
> Pour'd thro' the mellow *Horn* her pensive Soul:
>   And dashing soft from Rocks around,
>   Bubbling Runnels join'd the Sound;
> Thro' Glades and Glooms the mingled Measure stole,
>   Or o'er some haunted Stream with fond Delay,
>   Round an holy Calm diffusing,
>   Love of Peace, and lonely Musing,
>   In hollow Murmurs died away.
>
>   (57–68)

From the imaginative intensity of the opening of "Fear," Collins soon turns with relief to playing with fancies on the theme:

> Thou who such weary Lengths hast past,
> Where wilt thou rest, mad Nymph, at last?
> Say, wilt thou shroud in haunted Cell,
> Where gloomy *Rape* and *Murder* dwell?
>   Or, in some hollow'd Seat,
>   'Gainst which the big Waves beat,
> Hear drowning Sea-men's Cries in Tempests brought?
> Dark Pow'r, with shudd'ring, meek, submitted Thought
> Be mine, to read the Visions old,
> Which thy awak'ning Bards have told:
> And lest thou meet my blasted View,
> Hold each strange Tale devoutly true;
> Ne'er be I found, by Thee o'eraw'd,
> In that thrice-hallow'd Eve abroad,
> When Ghosts, as Cottage-Maids believe,
> Their pebbled Beds permitted leave,
> And *Gobblins* haunt from Fire, or Fen,
> Or Mine, or Flood, the Walks of Men!
>   O Thou, whose Spirit most possest
> The sacred Seat of *Shakespear's* Breast!
> By all that from thy Prophet broke,
> In thy Divine Emotions spoke:
> Hither again thy Fury deal,
> Teach me but once like Him to feel:
> His *Cypress Wreath* my Meed decree,
> And I, O *Fear*, will dwell with *Thee*!
>
>   (46–71)

The transition to Shakespeare, whose *Tempest* inspired the allusion to "drowning Sea-men," and whose *A Midsummer-Night's Dream* helped

Milton's "L'Allegro" to inspire the folklore passage, is therefore less irrelevant than it first appears.[2]

The poet's belief that poetic inspiration is a divine gift, conferred on few, is expressed in his "Ode on the Poetical Character." He chooses as a symbol Edmund Spenser's tale of Florimel's girdle, which refused to fasten when unchaste women tried to wear it. Then the poet continues:

> Young *Fancy* thus, to me Divinest Name,
>   To whom, prepar'd and bath'd in Heav'n,
>   The Cest of amplest Pow'r is giv'n:
>   To few the God-like Gift assigns,
>   To gird their blest prophetic Loins,
> And gaze her Visions wild, and feel unmix'd her Flame!
>
> The Band, as Fairy Legends say,
> Was wove on that creating Day,
> When He, who call'd with Thought to Birth
> Yon tented Sky, this laughing Earth,
> And drest with Springs, and Forests tall,
> And pour'd the Main engirting all,
> Long by the lov'd *Enthusiast* woo'd,
> Himself in some Diviner Mood,
> Retiring, sate with her alone,
> And plac'd her on his Saphire Throne,
> The whiles, the vaulted Shrine around,
> Seraphic Wires were heard to sound,
> Now sublimest Triumph swelling,

[2]Literary "influences" in the verse of Collins are so frequent that individual indication of them would require a large volume. Pope, the first, dominated the early "Eclogues" and "Verses to Hanmer," and occasionally appears in the later poems, though by then his heroic couplets were discarded and only occasional "echoes" remain.

About the time of Pope's death in 1744, two years before Collins' *Odes* appeared, he turned from Pope to the poetic ideal of his own, emerging generation: Milton. One might almost say that everything he wrote from this time to the end was Milton, and yet not Milton but essentially Collins. As a cow converts grass into cow—to take a crude but convenient illustration—so Collins assimilated Milton (as he did other sources after Pope). Milton's pastoral, folklore, remote, antiquarian, and classical interests, his verse forms, and his diction were appropriated and absorbed. The literary detective has listed 744 echoes and imitations from Milton in the small corpus of Collins' poetry, but the Miltonic influence is much greater and more important than that. (For instance, the Miltonic "denouncing" [prophesying] in the phrase "The War-denouncing Trumpet" in "The Passions.")

William Shakespeare's fairy lore, plays, lyrics, and diction were similarly but much less frequently employed, and are less obvious but not less important in general effect. The influence of Edmund Spenser is comparatively small. Only twice is he mentioned in the poems; but echoes and, more important, a general romantic quality of his can be detected, though seldom obvious.

> Now on Love and Mercy dwelling;
> And she, from out the veiling Cloud,
> Breath'd her magic Notes aloud: . . .

(17–38)

Thus Collins describes his fantasy of the birth of a poet: the offspring of Fancy (the 'lov'd *Enthusiast*") and of Creative Power—"God."

The next and final section of this ode, expressing the poet's devotion to Milton, alludes to his favorite oak (in "Il Penseroso"), and to Collins' rejection of the poet Edmund Waller, then still remembered for his smooth couplets and love verses. The conclusion laments the decline of poetry since Milton. As in the earlier parts of the poem, which include some of Collins' best verse of the semiacademic kind, there is occasional clumsiness of phrase and consequent obscurity. But this section begins with one of the best of the poet's romanticized landscapes:

> High on some Cliff, to Heav'n up-pil'd,
> Of rude Access, of Prospect wild,
> Where, tangled round the jealous Steep,
> Strange Shades o'erbrow the Valleys deep,
> And holy *Genii* guard the Rock,
> Its Gloomes embrown, its Springs unlock,
> While on its rich ambitious Head,
> An *Eden*, like his own, lies spread:
> I view that Oak, the fancied Glades among,
>   By which as *Milton* lay, His Ev'ning Ear,
> From many a Cloud that drop'd Ethereal Dew,
>   Nigh spher'd in Heav'n its native Strains could hear:
>
>   · · ·
>
> With many a Vow from Hope's aspiring Tongue,
> My trembling Feet his guiding Steps pursue;
>   In vain—Such Bliss to One alone,
>   Of all the Sons of Soul was known,
>   And Heav'n and *Fancy*, kindred Pow'rs,
>   Have now o'erturn'd th' inspiring Bow'rs,
> Or curtain'd close such Scene from ev'ry future View.

(55–66; 70–76)

So the poem ends, upon a pastoral note inspired by Milton.

This little volume of odes appeared at a critical moment in English history. One of the interminable wars of the eighteenth century was in progress (or rather regress, from the English point of view), for on 11 May 1745, England and its Continental allies had been defeated by the French at Fontenoy, Belgium, and two months later the Jacobite Scots began an invasion of England that ended only with their defeat at Culloden in April 1746. Several of the odes reflect these events more or less clearly, and so have been called the "patriotic" odes. Although patriotic, they are not jingoistic outbursts, but deeply humane utterances, clearly revealing the poet's pain at the miseries of war and his hatred of violence, as well as his admiration for those who make sacrifices in a noble cause such as freedom.

Unfortunately Collins adopted in these odes the clangorous style of John Dryden in his "Alexander's Feast," generally considered at that time to be the finest of all English lyrics. This extrovert bravura of Dryden's was so contrary to Collins' essentially introvert nature, given to "Love of Peace and lonely Musing," that when reading these odes one is reminded of Johnson's rebuke to Thomas Gray for a similar reason: "He has a kind of strutting dignity, and is tall by walking on tiptoe." It was this that led Collins to describe in "The Passions"—echoing Dryden—how

> *Revenge* impatient rose,
> He threw his blood-stain'd Sword in Thunder down,
> And with a with'ring Look,
> The War-denouncing Trumpet took,
> And blew a Blast so loud and dread,
> Were ne'er Prophetic Sounds so full of Woe.
> And ever and anon he beat
> The doubling Drum with furious Heat;
>
> And tho' sometimes each dreary Pause between,
> Dejected *Pity* at his Side
> Her Soul-subduing Voice applied,
> Yet still He kept his wild unalter'd Mien,
> While each strain'd Ball of Sight seem'd bursting from his Head.
> (40–52)

Thus it is with all these "patriotic" odes: Mercy, Pity, and Peace are ever at the side of the war gods, pleading, restraining, sorrowing, a complete contrast with their noisy, bellicose associates. In this way these odes proceed:

> Now sublimest Triumph swelling,
> Now on Love and Mercy dwelling,
> (35–36)

as he wrote in the "Ode on the Poetical Character." It is the same in his "Ode to Mercy," inspired by the Scottish revolt. There too Mercy overpowers the "Fiend of Nature"—evil influences over man—which has caused the conflict:

> When he whom ev'n our Joys provoke,
> The *Fiend of Nature* join'd his Yoke,
> And rush'd in Wrath to make our Isle his Prey;
> Thy Form, from out thy sweet Abode,
> O'ertook Him on his blasted Road,
> And stop'd his Wheels, and look'd his Rage away.
>
> I see recoil his sable Steeds,
> That bore Him swift to Salvage Deeds,
> Thy tender melting Eyes they own;
> O Maid, for all thy Love to *Britain* shown,
> Where *Justice* bars her Iron Tow'r,
> To Thee we build a roseate Bow'r,
> Thou, Thou shalt rule, our Queen, and share our Monarch's Throne!
> (14–26)

Liberty inspires Collins with warlike enthusiasm, and his ode to it begins and concludes its opening strophe with true Drydenian uproar, as it proceeds to trace the vicissitudes of liberty through history: "Who shall awake the Spartan Fife?" he begins, and after concluding the section with "many a barb'rous Yell," cries in the epode, "Strike, louder strike th' ennobling Strings" for freedom. Yet even here he looks forward, anxiously, to "Concord" at last:

> *Concord*, whose Myrtle Wand can steep
> Ev'n *Anger's* blood-shot Eyes in Sleep:
> Before whose breathing Bosom's Balm,
> *Rage* drops his Steel, and Storms grow calm.
> (133–136)

But it is in "Peace" (technically the worst of the odes) that Collins most fully voices his detestation of war, invokes Peace, and reassures her that war will be destroyed:

> Tir'd of his rude tyrannic Sway,
> Our Youth shall fix some festive Day,
> His sullen Shrines to burn:
> But Thou who hear'st the turning Spheres,
> What Sounds may charm thy partial Ears,
> And gain thy blest Return!
>
> O *Peace*, thy injur'd Robes up-bind,
> O rise, and leave not one behind
> Of all thy beamy Train . . . .
> (7–15)

When, from these generalizing "patriotic" odes (in which what I may call the "official" manner prevails), Collins turns to a personal situation—the consoling of a friend bereaved by war, and praise of the soldier dead—the "official" mood alternates with the personal; Dryden with Collins, as in the "Ode to a Lady on the Death of Colonel Ross":

> While, lost to all his former Mirth,
> *Britannia's* Genius bends to Earth,
>   And mourns the fatal Day:
> While stain'd with Blood he strives to tear
> Unseemly from his Sea-green Hair
>   The Wreaths of chearful *May*:
>
> The Thoughts which musing Pity pays,
> And fond Remembrance loves to raise,
>   Your faithful Hours attend:
> Still Fancy to Herself unkind,
> Awakes to Grief the soften'd Mind,
>   And points the bleeding Friend.
>   (1–12)

In the next two stanzas of the poem, Collins characteristically and skillfully (but somewhat incongruously, since the "Village Hind" is Dutch, and the river Scheldt slow) brings Shakespearean pastoralism and fairies into this lament for a soldier's death:

> By rapid *Scheld's* descending Wave
> His Country's Vows shall bless the Grave,
>   Where'er the Youth is laid:
> That sacred Spot the Village Hind
> With ev'ry sweetest Turf shall bind,
>   And Peace protect the Shade.
>
> Blest Youth, regardful of thy Doom,
> Aërial Hands shall build thy Tomb,
>   With shadowy Trophies crown'd:
> Whilst *Honor* bath'd in Tears shall rove,
> To sigh thy Name thro' ev'ry Grove,
>   And call his Heros round.
>   (13–24)

The remainder of the poem consists of two "official" stanzas calling on "The warlike Dead of every Age" to welcome the dead colonel to their company, while Freedom lies on the ground in disheveled garments, weeping until Victory comes. There are also two more stanzas, addressed to the bereaved lady, more impersonal and less emotional than the one, already quoted, to the "Blest youth," the dead soldier.

The poem, then, is far from being a masterpiece; but from the last two stanzas just quoted there sprang, when genuine inspiration came to the poet shortly afterward, not only one of Collins' two finest poems but a poem that has rightly taken its place among the finest lyrics of English poetry.

> How sleep the Brave, who sink to Rest,
> By all their Country's Wishes blest!
> When *Spring*, with dewy Fingers cold,
> Returns to deck their hallow'd Mold,
> She there shall dress a sweeter Sod,
> Than *Fancy's* Feet have ever trod.
>
> By Fairy Hands their Knell is rung,
> By Forms unseen their Dirge is sung;
> There *Honour* comes, a Pilgrim grey,
> To bless the Turf that wraps their Clay,
> And *Freedom* shall a-while repair,
> To dwell a weeping Hermit there!
>   ("Ode: Written at the Beginning of the Year 1746")

That is as near perfection as any lyricist may hope to attain. The achievement appears the more miraculous when one notes that at least ostensibly the ode is general, "official"—though in fact it is inspired by an exquisitely delicate sentimentality and a personal feeling, like William Wordsworth's, "too deep for tears." More remarkable still, it is made up of the stock eighteenth-century poetic images (such as the pilgrim and the hermit), stock personifications (Fancy, Honor, Freedom, Spring), and of Collins' Shakespearean pastoralism and fairies. But the miraculous moment brought a complete fusion of Collins' classicism and romanticism, one bringing a cold generality of statement and dignity of phrase and rhythm; the other, personal emotion, all the more effective for classical restraint in expression. And below all, deep in the unconscious of the poet, was the lyric power of Shakespeare that he had assimilated. It was no accident that Shakespeare admittedly inspired his "A Song from Cymbeline" ("Sung by Guiderius and Arviragus over Fidele, Supposed to be Dead")—the lyric closest to this ode of all Collins' poems, and with much of its charm, published two years before:

> To fair Fidele's grassy Tomb
> Soft Maids and Village Hinds shall bring

Each op'ning Sweet, of earliest Bloom,
  And rifle all the breathing Spring.

No wailing Ghost shall dare appear
  To vex with Shrieks this quiet Grove:
But Shepherd Lads assemble here,
  And melting Virgins own their Love.

No wither'd Witch shall here be seen,
  No Goblins lead their nightly Crew:
The Female Fays shall haunt the Green,
  And dress thy Grave with pearly Dew!

The Redbreast oft at Ev'ning Hours
  Shall kindly lend his little Aid:
With hoary Moss, and gather'd Flow'rs,
  To deck the Ground where thou art laid.

When howling Winds, and beating Rain,
  In Tempests shake the sylvan Cell,
Or 'midst the Chace on ev'ry Plain,
  The tender Thought on thee shall dwell.

Each lonely Scene shall thee restore,
  For thee the Tear be duly shed:
Belov'd till Life can charm no more,
  And mourn'd, till Pity's self be dead.

To another lyric of Shakespeare's—Ophelia's, in
Hamlet—

He is dead and gone, lady,
  He is dead and gone;
At his head a grass-green turf,
  At his heels a stone,

we owe Collins' "Song":

Young Damon of the vale is dead,
  Ye lowly hamlets, moan:
A dewy turf lies o'er his head,
  And at his feet a stone. . . .
                              (1–4)

This lovely dirge is an excellent and typical example of Collins' assimilation of "influences" and of
their conversion into essential Collins, by his own
rhythms and verbal music, and sometimes, as here,
by the introduction of his favored pastoral note.

Collins wrote one other threnody, a poem of
eleven stanzas on the death of Thomson, published
in 1749. It is one of his best poems, though uneven.
Space allows only a short quotation, but enough to
show the poet's usual imagery for these dirges and

his skill in transmitting emotion to his personifications:

In yonder Grove a Druid lies,[3]
  Where slowly winds the stealing Wave.
The *Year's* best Sweets shall duteous rise
  To deck *its* Poet's sylvan Grave.
                 . . .
Remembrance oft shall haunt the Shore
  When Thames in Summer-wreaths is drest,
And oft suspend the dashing Oar
  To bid his gentle Spirit rest!

And oft, as Ease and Health retire
  To breezy Lawn, or Forest deep,
The Friend shall view yon whit'ning Spire,
  And 'mid the varied Landscape weep.

But Thou, who own'st that Earthy bed,
  Ah! what will ev'ry Dirge avail?
Or Tears, which Love and Pity shed,
  That mourn beneath the gliding Sail?
                 . . .
And see the Fairy Valleys fade,
  Dun *Night* has veil'd the solemn View!
Yet once again, Dear parted Shade,
  Meek Nature's Child, again adieu!
                  (1–4; 13–24; 33–36)

Collins showed that "Fancy" (imagination) was
of supreme importance to him, as has been seen, in

[3] I read "grove" for "grave"; "grave" is the usual text, taken from
the 1749 edition of the poem. But in F. Fawkes and W. Woty's
Poetical Calendar (1763)—which H. W. Garrod rightly regards
as the first edition of the collected works, and in Pearch's *Collection of Poems* (1775) the word is "grove." My reasons for prefer-
ring "grove" are (1) "grave" occurs again three lines below,
which repetition Collins could not have tolerated; (2) that second
"grave" is "sylvan" (in a wood); (3) "grove" suits "Druid," for
"groves of oak and circles of stone were their places of worship";
(4) "grove" better fits the winding, "stealing wave" in the next
line of the poem. The result of this change of text is a complete
alteration and improvement in the poetical imagery that is the
background of the whole poem; a change from an ordinary
churchyard to the solitude and silence of a woodland grave.
Whether in fact it was so would not affect Collins. Compare
"grove" in "A Song from Cymbeline."
  "Druid": then a poetically "magic word"—both Gothic and
romantic. For Collins the literary order called bards were chiefly
men who sang their poems to the harp, and gave poetry a priest-
ly and mystical association. "I have frequently wondered that
our modern writers have made so little use of the Druidical
times, and the traditions of the old bards, which afford fruitful
subjects of the most genuine poetry, with respect to both imagery and sentiment" [Joseph Warton, *Essay on the Genius and
Writings of Pope* (London, 1756–1782), I, p. 355].

his "Ode on the Poetical Character." In his verses to Hanmer, he describes Fancy as the creator of fantasies:

> Where'er we turn, by Fancy charm'd, we find
> Some sweet illusion of the cheated Mind.
> Oft, wild of Wing, she calls the Soul to rove
> With humbler Nature, in the rural Grove;
> Where Swains contented own the quiet Scene,
> And twilight Fairies tread the circled Green:
> Drest by her Hand, the Woods and Vallies smile,
> And Spring diffusive decks th' *enchanted Isle.*
> (105–112)

Again Shakespeare's *Tempest.* In "The Manners" Collins speaks of Fancy's "potent spell"; and this "spell" was, as the word suggests, romantic. Johnson gives valuable insight into this aspect of the poet's nature, revealing his romanticism as more fantastic than his poetry suggests. But Johnson percipiently adds: "This was, however, the character rather of his inclination than of his genius." He continues:

He had employed his mind chiefly upon works of fiction and subjects of fancy; and, by indulging some peculiar habits of thought, was eminently delighted with those flights of imagination which pass the bounds of nature, and to which the mind is reconciled only by a passive acquiescence in popular traditions. He loved fairies, genii, giants and monsters; he delighted to rove through the meanders of inchantment, to gaze on the magnificence of golden palaces, to repose by the waterfalls of Elysian gardens.

(Life of Collins)

But Fancy's visions are not only pleasant. Fancy raises the veil that in "Fear" had hidden the terror-stricken world of anxieties and fears. And at times Fancy passes from mere fantasy to the deeper level of creative imagination. It is thus with Collins' two finest poems; Fancy appears only once by name in each, casually; but though invisible, it dominates, as poetic imagination.

Fancy at the lower level, fantasy, achieves its finest effects in the "Ode on the Popular Superstitions of the Highlands of Scotland," Collins' last poem. Home's tales of Highland folklore had appealed to the poet's love of the strange and fantastic, a taste recently developed by acquaintance with Torquato Tasso, whom in this same poem he praises:

> How have I trembled, when, at Tancred's stroke,
> Its gushing blood the gaping cypress pour'd;
> When each live plant with mortal accents spoke,
> And the wild blast up-heav'd the vanish'd sword!
> (192–195)

This appeal to the lower "romantic" taste for the merely marvelous (which Johnson had recognized in Collins, but as not of his "genius") has free play in this poem, and accounts for one's feeling of disappointment with it as a whole, despite fine passages.

Thomson, in a notable stanza of *The Castle of Indolence,* had touched upon this same theme of Scottish folklore:

> As when a shepherd of the Hebrid Isles,
> Placed far amid the melancholy main,
> (Whether it be lone fancy him beguiles,
> Or that aërial beings sometimes deign
> To stand embodied to our senses plain)
> Sees on the naked hill or valley low,
> The whilst in ocean Phoebus dips his wain,
> A vast assembly moving to and fro;
> Then all at once in air dissolves the wondrous show.
> (262–270)

It was in this mood of Thomson that Collins wrote his Scottish ode, delighting in his freedom to relapse from the romanticism of his adult mind into the merely fanciful romance of childhood, creating supernatural agencies that range from the merely mischievous to the intimidating and murderous.

> 'Tis Fancy's land to which thou sett'st thy feet;
> Where still, 'tis said, the fairy people meet
> Beneath each birken shade on mead or hill.
> There each trim lass that skims the milky store,
> To the swart tribes their creamy bowl allots;
> By night they sip it round the cottage-door,
> While airy minstrels warble jocund notes.
> There every herd, by sad experience, knows,
> How, wing'd with fate, their elf-shot arrows fly;
> When the sick ewe her summer food foregoes,
> Or, stretch'd on earth, the heart-smit heifers lie.
> (19–29)

But his attempts at the dramatic, at horror-history, or at fantasy are highly wrought—overwrought, indeed—and his wild, ancient Scots, whose "sturdy clans pour'd forth their bony swarms" amid "wat'ry strath" and "quaggy moss," along with a "kelpie" (a kind of Loch Ness monster that drowns people), are all very Hollywood. Yet just before drawing a lurid picture of the kelpie's victim's ghost visiting his wife, poetry suddenly reappears. Here, as often, literature is more inspiring to Collins than life or death or superstitions; the passage is inspired by a description in Lucretius, which Collins adapts to portray the dead man's wife and family, ignorant of his death, anxiously awaiting him:

> For him, in vain, his anxious wife shall wait,
> Or wander forth to meet him on his way;
> For him, in vain, at to-fall of the day,
> His babes shall linger at th' unclosing gate!
> (121–124)

Occasionally mere fancy takes fire, and raises the verse to a definitely imaginative level, as in the following lines, the best of this kind in Collins' verse, evidently influenced also by the passage quoted from *The Castle of Indolence*. For Collins' muse can now

> . . . extend her skirting wing
> Round the moist marge of each cold Hebrid isle,
> To that hoar pile which still its ruin shows:
> In whose small vaults a pigmy-folk is found,
> Whose bones the delver with his spade upthrows,
> And culls them, wond'ring, from the hallow'd ground!
> Or thither where, beneath the show'ry west
> The mighty kings of three fair realms are laid:
> Once foes, perhaps, together now they rest.
> No slaves revere them, and no wars invade:
> Yet frequent now, at midnight's solemn hour,
> The rifted mounds their yawning cells unfold,
> And forth the monarchs stalk with sov'reign pow'r
> In pageant robes, and wreath'd with sheeny gold,
> And on their twilight tombs aerial council hold.
> (140–154)

It is very good, and for such passages some have overpraised the poem. But good as they are, they are a tour de force, not the essential Collins.

"Nature" in Collins' verse means reality; and as such it includes both good and evil, just as "Fancy" does. "The Fiend of Nature" incites strife; creates bad psychological and moral influences and impulses, such as the

> thousand Phantoms join'd
> Who prompt to deeds accurs'd the Mind,

and

> the Fiends who near allied,
> O'er Nature's Wounds and Wrecks preside. . . .

In these and similar lines Collins shows his awareness of then obscure psychological realities, of "All the shad'wy Tribes of Mind," the wicked elements, that join their "murmurs" with "Heav'n's ambrosial Flow'rs," the good influences.

Collins also had a conception, unusual in his day, of vast geological changes in the earth, if not some vague foreshadowing of evolution.[4] The grandeur of these conceptions, his imaginative realization of the magnitude of stupendous changes over vast periods of time, aroused the romantic wonder that inspires the following fine passage in "Liberty," referring to a belief that at one time Britain was a part of the Continent:

> Beyond the Measure vast of Thought,
> The Works, the Wizzard *Time* has wrought!
> The *Gaul*, 'tis held of antique Story,
> Saw *Britain* link'd to his now adverse Strand,
> No Sea between, nor Cliff sublime and hoary,
> He pass'd with unwet Feet through all our Land.
> To the Blown *Baltic* then, they say,
> The wild Waves found another way,
> Where *Orcas* howls, his wolfish Mountains rounding;
> Till all the banded West at once 'gan rise,
> A wide wild Storm ev'n Nature's self confounding,
> With'ring her Giant Sons with strange uncouth Surprise.
>
> This pillar'd Earth so firm and wide,
> By Winds and inward Labors torn,
> In Thunders dread was push'd aside,
> And down the should'ring Billows born.
> (64–79)

Here Fancy, stimulated by Collins' sense of primeval power and mystery, successfully employs a

---

[4] Collins' note on this is interesting: "This tradition is mentioned by several of our old Historians. Some Naturalists too have endeavoured to support the probability of the Fact, by Arguments drawn from the correspondent Disposition of the two opposite Coasts." The note suggests an interest in scientific subjects, and that when Collins uses the word "science," he may sometimes mean not merely "knowledge," as was usual, but also "science" in the modern sense. Despite Edmund Spenser's allusion to this belief (*Faerie Queene*, II. x. 5), Collins adds: "I don't remember that any Poetical Use has been hitherto made of it." Stranger still, since Collins' "Liberty" is derived from Thomson's "Liberty," is Collins' apparent ignorance of Thomson's allusion to this same belief about Britain and France in "Liberty," IV. 460–463.

bravura that is in complete harmony with the vast-ness of the theme.

Nevertheless, it is an almost entirely contrary aspect of nature—contrary but for the presence of awe and wonder here also—that inspires Collins' only other poem comparable with "How Sleep the Brave"—if not, as some think, superior to it. The peace, the beauty, and the mystery of evening as it descends amid country solitude move the poet to an exquisite and entirely personal utterance, permeated though it is in both form and diction by the influence of Milton. "Ode to Evening" expresses the deepest harmonies of Collins' own nature, now for a moment finding satisfaction in those of the external world.

If aught of Oaten Stop, or Pastoral Song,
May hope, O pensive *Eve*, to sooth thine Ear,
    Like thy own brawling Springs,
    Thy Springs, and dying Gales,

O *Nymph* reserv'd, while now the bright-hair'd Sun
Sits in yon western Tent, whose cloudy Skirts,
    With Brede ethereal wove,
    O'erhang his wavy Bed:

Now Air is hush'd, save where the weak-ey'd Bat,
With short shrill Shriek, flits by on leathern Wing,
    Or where the Beetle winds
    His small but sullen Horn,

As oft he rises 'midst the twilight Path,
Against the Pilgrim born in heedless Hum:
    Now teach me, Maid compos'd,
    To breathe some soften'd Strain,

Whose Numbers stealing thro' thy dark'ning Vale,
May not unseemly with its Stillness suit,
    As musing slow, I hail
    Thy genial lov'd Return!

For when thy folding Star arising shews
His paly Circlet, at his warning Lamp
    The fragrant *Hours*, and *Elves*
    Who slept in Buds the Day,

And many a *Nymph* who wreathes her Brows with Sedge,
And sheds the fresh'ning Dew, and lovelier still,
    The *Pensive Pleasures* sweet
    Prepare thy shadowy Car.

Then let me rove some wild and heathy Scene,
Or find some Ruin 'midst its dreary Dells,

Whose Walls more awful nod
By thy religious Gleams.

Or if chill blust'ring Winds, or driving Rain,
Prevent my willing Feet, be mine the Hut
    That from the Mountain's Side
    Views Wilds, and swelling Floods,

And Hamlets brown, and dim-discovered Spires,
And hears their simple Bell, and marks o'er all
    Thy Dewy Fingers draw
    The gradual dusky Veil.

While *Spring* shall pour his Show'rs, as oft he wont,
And bathe thy breathing Tresses, meekest *Eve*!
    While *Summer* loves to sport,
    Beneath thy ling'ring Light:

While sallow *Autumn* fills thy Lap with Leaves,
Or *Winter*, yelling thro' the troublous Air,
    Affrights thy shrinking Train,
    And rudely rends thy Robes;

So long regardful of thy quiet Rule,
Shall *Fancy, Friendship, Science*, smiling *Peace*,
    Thy gentlest Influence own,
    And love thy fav'rite Name!

                     ("Ode to Evening")

So the poem ends: suddenly, as after the waxing and waning of a fitful sunset, night descends. It is a perfect transposition of natural beauty into an exquisite correspondence of both abstract and imitative imagery, verbal, metrical, and rhythmical harmonies akin to the art of the musician.

Space, unfortunately, allows but a fleeting glimpse of Collins' rise to posthumous fame. It is not surprising that one usually so remote in his verse from normal human interests and emotions, and so early silenced by disease and death, attracted little interest among his contemporaries, and even less appreciation. Gray said that despite many faults Collins "deserved to last some years but would not." Johnson, despite his affection for the man, harshly condemned his verse after his death. Goldsmith, his only appreciative contemporary of note, highly praised the "Eclogues" and "Evening," and denounced the neglect of the poet and his works.

Although William Cowper, a quarter of a century after Collins' death, first heard of him through reading Johnson's *Lives of the Poets*, and showed no appreciation of Collins' poetry, the years of neglect were already yielding to recognition in periodicals, anthologies, and such, while "echoes" of his verse gradually permeated the poetry of both major and minor poets as the romantic movement grew. Robert Burns praised; William Blake assimilated his influence; and romantic poetesses and women horror novelists took him to their sentimental and maternal hearts, chiefly because of "Fear" and of "neglect."

Samuel Taylor Coleridge in 1796 felt "inspired and whirled along with greater agitations of enthusiasm than the most impassioned scene in Schiller or Shakespeare" by part of "The Poet's Character." The next year Wordsworth's well-known verses to Collins' memory appeared in *Lyrical Ballads.* Robert Southey praised; Lord Byron, like Johnson, was interested in his illness on personal grounds; Percy Shelley thought him "a cold, artificial writer"; and John Keats's only mention of him in his letters is a casual remark, in February 1818, that he is attending William Hazlitt's lectures, and that the last one included Collins and Gray. At that lecture Keats must have heard Hazlitt's enthusiastic and detailed appreciation of Collins, in which he praised him for "that genuine inspiration, which alone can give birth to the highest efforts of poetry" and described him as "the only one of the minor poets of whom, if he had lived, it cannot be said that he might not have done the greatest things."

At the time of Hazlitt's lecture, Keats was revising his "Endymion"; and a comparison of a famous passage there, by Keats at his best in the style, with one in the same style by Collins, is interesting. The first, from "The Passions," is typically Collins—almost colorless, intellectual, unsensuous, marmoreal, but nevertheless living marble:

When *Chearfulness,* a Nymph of healthiest Hue,
  Her Bow a-cross her Shoulder flung,
  Her Buskins gem'd with Morning Dew,
Blew an inspiring Air, that Dale and Thicket rung,
  The Hunter's Call to *Faun* and *Dryad* known!
  The Oak-crown'd *Sisters,* and their chast-eyed *Queen,*
  Satyrs and sylvan Boys were seen,
  Peeping from forth their Alleys green:
Brown *Exercise* rejoic'd to hear,
  And *Sport* leapt up, and seiz'd his Beechen Spear.

          (70–79)

Whether he was consciously influenced by Collins cannot be said, but Keats continues the form of the preceding passage, with the addition of color and detail from Titian's famous painting *Bacchus and Ariadne.* This Collins would have appreciated, being attracted, as Keats was, by the romanticized classicism of the Renaissance. Indeed, I doubt, if the following extract from Keats were printed immediately after the preceding quotation from Collins, whether many persons would suspect that it was from a different poem by a poet writing more than half a century after Collins' death. But the fact shows how the poetic manner of Collins was already permeating English poetry. Nor was Keats's resemblance to Collins limited to this vital, processional form. In the marmoreal, coldly classical "Ode on a Grecian Urn," Keats comes, in spirit, close to the poet of "Evening" and of "How Sleep the Brave."

But to return to "Endymion":

Within his car, aloft, young Bacchus stood,
Trifling his ivy-dart, in dancing mood,
  With sidelong laughing;
And little rills of crimson wine imbrued
His plump white arms, and shoulders, enough white
  For Venus' pearly bite;
And near him rode Silenus on his ass,
Pelted with flowers as he on did pass
  Tipsily quaffing.

          (IV. 209–217)

In the last years of the eighteenth and the first years of the nineteenth century, Collins' popularity continued to increase. Charles Lamb, Thomas Campbell, John Keble, and John Clare, among many, praised or imitated, or did both; Collins became a fixed star in the poetic firmament as the Victorian age arrived. But as his influence merged more and more completely into the poetic stream, it lost identity and recognition, even by poets such as Matthew Arnold, who mentions Collins but once —with a respectful reference—in his essay on Gray, and not at all in 'The Study of Poetry.' Yet Arnold's own verse is permeated with obvious resemblances to various aspects of Collins, both as man and as poet. Algernon Swinburne praised Collins in characteristically hysterical terms, taking him, without reason, for an exponent of tyrannicide because of his "Ode to Liberty." But there is not room here to follow Collins among the Victorians. Certain poetic developments then militated against appreciation of him, particularly the passing of the love of abstractions and personifications, which like such "Gothic" terms as "pilgrim," "Druid," and "hermit" held poetic magic for the eighteenth century.

With the Victorians the arts, following political and social conditions, turned bourgeois, and poetry suffered bourgeois limitations. The great moral forces, such as pity, mercy, sorrow, and fear, the abstract contemplation of which moved Collins to such emotion as the mathematical Neoplatonists of Alexandria felt when contemplating the intellectual beauties of the circle, meant nothing to the average Victorian reader, unless apprehended through personal, individual, and preferably sentimental manifestations, as in Tennyson's "The May Queen." In this present age of abstract art and scientific abstractions that also are often tremendous and sometimes terrifying realities, one should be better able to appreciate the contrast between Tennyson's poem and Collins' "Evening" and "How Sleep the Brave." The contrast brings home to the reader that in the hands of such a poet as Collins, the typical eighteenth-century poetic attitude of emotional restraint, generalization, and personification is not necessarily inimical to the finest poetry.

Such was the poetry of Collins, the poet of an age of transition, of declining classicism and dawning romance. Reflected in his verse, it reminds one of his own design for the temple to liberty:

> In *Gothic* Pride it seems to rise,
> Yet Graecia's graceful Orders join,
> Majestic thro' the mix'd Design.

SELECTED BIBLIOGRAPHY

I. BIBLIOGRAPHY AND CONCORDANCE. W. C. Bronson, ed., *The Poems of William Collins* (Boston, 1898), bibliography on pp. lxxix–lxxxv; I. A. Williams, *Seven Eighteenth-Century Bibliographies* (London, 1924), covers first eds. only; B. A. Booth and C. E. Jones, *A Concordance of the Poetical Works of William Collins* (Berkeley, Calif., 1939); F. W. Bateson, ed., *The Cambridge Bibliography of English Literature*, 4 vols. (Cambridge, 1940), vol. II, 335–338; B. Ford, ed., *Pelican Guide to English Literature* (London, 1957), vol. IV, *From Dryden to Johnson*, includes a discussion of Collins.

II. COLLECTED POEMS. F. Fawkes and W. Woty, eds., *The Poetical Calendar* (London, 1763), vols. XI and XII contain an incomplete collection and erroneously include as Collins' "To Miss Aurelia C–R"—also includes a "Life"

by J. Hampton and a "Character" by Johnson; J. Langhorne, ed., *The Poetical Works* (London, 1765; repr. 1771, 1776, 1781), contents the same as in *Poetical Calendar*, but excludes "To Miss Aurelia C–R" and includes Langhorne's "Memoirs" of Collins and his "Observations on His Genius and Writings"; S. Johnson, ed., *The Works of the English Poets* (London, 1779), vol. XLIX includes Johnson's "Life" of Collins; *Poetical Works* (Glasgow, 1787), the Foulis Press ed. with preface and notes; A. Dyce, ed., *The Poetical Works* (London, 1827), includes Johnson's "Life," Langhorne's "Observations," and biographical and critical notes by Dyce; Sir S. E. Brydges, ed., *The Poetical Works* (London, 1830; repr. 1853), the Aldine ed., includes Sir Harris Nicholas' "Memoir" of Collins and Brydges' essay on the genius and poems of Collins; W. M. Thomas, ed., *Poetical Works* (London, 1858; repr. 1866, 1894, 1901), the Aldine ed., with an excellent biographical preface; C. Stone, ed., *Poems* (London, 1907); C. Stone and A. L. Poole, eds., *The Poetical Works of Gray and Collins* (Oxford, 1917; rev. eds. 1937, 1961), in the Oxford Standard Authors series; E. Blunden, ed., *The Poems* (London, 1929), with an introductory study by Blunden; W. T. Williams and G. H. Vallins, eds., *Gray, Collins, and Their Circle* (London [1937]); J. S. Cunningham, ed., *Drafts and Fragments of Verse* (Oxford, 1956), edited from the MSS; R. Lonsdale, ed., *The Poems of Thomas Gray, William Collins, Oliver Goldsmith* (London, 1969).

III. SEPARATE WORKS. "Persian Eclogues" (London, 1742), published anonymously, republished as "Oriental Eclogues" (London, 1757); "Verses Humbly Address'd to Sir Thomas Hanmer" (London, 1743), published anonymously, revised and republished as "An Epistle: Addrest to Sir Thomas Hanmer" (London, 1744), with the addition of "A Song from Cymbeline"; *Odes on Several Descriptive and Allegoric Subjects* (London, 1747), 1,000 copies published December 1746—facs. ed. by Noel Douglas Replicas (London, 1926) and Scolar Press (London, 1969); "Ode Occasion'd by the Death of Mr. Thomson" (London, 1749; facs. ed., London, 1927); "The Passions: An Ode. Set to Music" [Oxford, 1750], originally published in *Odes*, also a variant (undated) recorded with a Winchester (1750) imprint—both 1750 eds. have the last twenty-four lines rewritten (and spoiled) by the earl of Litchfield, vice-chancellor of Oxford University; "An Ode on the Popular Superstitions of the Highlands of Scotland, Considered as the Subject of Poetry," in *Transactions of the Royal Society of Edinburgh*, 1 (1788), 67–75.

IV. LETTERS. Manuscript letter from Collins to John Gilbert Cooper (author of *Letters Concerning Taste*, 1754), dated London, 10 November 1747 (BM Add. 41178.I), printed in full by H. O. White in his "Letters of William Collins," in *Review of English Studies*, 3, no. 9 (January 1927), 12–21; a letter from Collins to Dr. William Hayes (professor of music at Oxford), dated Chichester, Sussex, 8 November 1750, the original of which has disappeared—it was first printed in W. Seward's *Supplement to Anecdotes of Some Distinguished Persons* (London, 1797), p. 123, and reprinted in the preface to W. M. Thomas' ed. of the *Poems* (1901).

V. BIOGRAPHICAL AND CRITICAL STUDIES. S. E. Brydges, "On the Allegorical Style of the Poetry of Collins," in *Censura Literaria*, vol. VII (2d ed., 10 vols., London, 1815); A. C. Swinburne, *Miscellanies* (London, 1886), contains an essay on Collins that also appeared in T. H. Ward, ed., *The English Poets*, III (London, 1880); E. Montegut, *Heures de lecture d'un critique* (Paris, 1891); S. Johnson, *Lives of the English Poets*, G. Birkbeck Hill, ed., 3 vols. (Oxford, 1905), vol. III; A. Lang, ed., *Poet's Country* (London, 1907), has two good articles by J. C. Collins; J. C. Collins, *Greek Influence on English Poetry* (London, 1910); G. Saintsbury, *The Peace of the Augustans* (London, 1916); J. W. Mackail, "Collins and the English Lyric," in *Transactions of the Royal Society of Literature* (1921), also in Mackail's *Studies of English Poets* (London, 1926); O. Doughty, *English Lyric in the Age of Reason* (London, 1922); R. D. Havens, *The Influence of Milton on English Poetry* (Cambridge, Mass., 1922); J. M. Murry, *Countries of the Mind: Essays in Literary Criticism, First Series* (London, 1922); H. W. Garrod, *Collins* (Oxford, 1928); H. W. Garrod, *The Poetry of Collins* (Oxford, 1928), the Warton lecture, 1928; M. W. Walker, ed., *Studies in English* (Toronto, 1931), see A. S. P. Woodhouse, "Collins and the Creative Imagination"; E. G. Ainsworth, *Poor Collins: His Life, His Art, and His Influence* (Ithaca–London, 1937); O. F. Sigworth, *William Collins* (New York, 1965); P. L. Carver, *The Life of a Poet: A Biographical Sketch of William Collins* (London, 1967); P. M. Spacks, *The Poetry of Vision* (Cambridge, Mass., 1967).

OLIVER GOLDSMITH

(1728-1774)

A. Norman Jeffares

THE GOOD-NATURED LIFE

THE best way to find out why Oliver Goldsmith's writings are usually characterized as charming is to inquire into the nature of the man who wrote them; and the most rewarding way of doing this is to read his original writings, those pieces of self-expression that were accomplished in the midst of writing for the periodicals, of compiling for publishers, when "sheet after sheet was thrown off to oblivion." Though much of his hackwork is still readable for the ease of its style, for its characteristic delicacy of thought, and even for its occasional perspicacity, the real Goldsmith is to be found in the wise writings that drew largely upon his own experience, and in which his own generosity and gullibility are irradiated by a sense of sheer fun.

By the time he died on 4 April 1774, at the age of forty-five, Goldsmith had composed, out of a deep awareness of both the blessings and the sorrows of life, two of the best-known poems of the eighteenth century, *The Traveller* and *The Deserted Village*; he had written *The Vicar of Wakefield*, the novel upon which his fame has rested secure, strengthened throughout the nineteenth century by Johann Wolfgang von Goethe's intense approbation; he had created *She Stoops to Conquer*, a successful comedy that still delights audiences; and he had written many urbanely amusing yet subtly serious essays. Why, when he had written so well and with such versatility, and his friends had recognized the merits of his literary achievement, did he die obsessed with a sense of sadness and unease? When one of the doctors attending him in his last brief illness asked him if his mind was at ease, he answered poignantly, "No, it is not."

Samuel Johnson was the first to detect Goldsmith's ability as a writer, and in the Latin epitaph he wrote for the monument to his friend's memory, a joint work by Sir Joshua Reynolds and Joseph Nollekens set up in the Poets' Corner of Westminster Abbey, he roundly declared that there was almost no form of literature that Goldsmith had not put his hand to, and whatever he had attempted, he had made elegant. But even Johnson does not supply a completely satisfactory answer to the problem; he said that Goldsmith "died of a fever, exasperated, as I believe, by the fear of distress. He had raised money and squandered it, by artifice of acquisition and folly of expense." And he added a sentence that does provide a clue to the mystery: "But let not his frailties be remembered; he was a very great man."

The contrast between greatness and frailty is at the root of Goldsmith's growth. There was always a contradiction in his character between ambition and ability. He was kind and artless, good-humored and good-natured, gentle and generous; yet he was well aware of his failings, and no one satirized more effectively than he the elements of conceit and credulity that made up his fullness as a human being. Like George Primrose in *The Vicar of Wakefield* he had had his period of associating with disappointed authors, "who praised, deplored and despised each other," when no genius in another could please him. Yet his conceit was often apparent; it arose out of a mixture of shyness and awareness of his own merits, and was simply a desire to be taken seriously. The credulity was inborn; the unworldly, prodigal generosity was in part the result of his early upbringing; and, in a favorite phrase of his own, there was "no harm in him." There was, instead, an overpowering desire to give pleasure and create amusement.

Like most Irishmen, Goldsmith abhorred a conversational vacuum. If there was nothing else for the company to laugh at, he would laugh at himself. Such a method of creating laughter was less well appreciated in London society than it had been understood or accepted in Ireland. In one of his *Letters from a Citizen of the World*, he virtually describes this situation:

> The English in general seem fonder of gaining the esteem than the love of those they converse with: this gives a formality to their amusements; their gayest conversations have something too wise for innocent relaxation; though in company you are seldom disgusted with the absurdity of a fool, you are seldom lifted into rapture by those strokes of vivacity which give instant, though not permanent pleasure.[1]

(letter 4)

Goldsmith's idea of the function of conversation was different from that of Johnson. Talk, he once said, was something with which to conceal his thoughts—or, we might add, to discover them. Johnson realized something of this: "Goldsmith had no settled notions upon any subject; so he always talked at random. It seemed to be his intention to blurt out whatever was in his mind, and see what would become of it."

Goldsmith came from a worthy but feckless Anglo-Irish family. His father, a country rector at Pallas, near Ballymahon, was an unworldly man, something of whose character can be understood from the loving descriptions of Dr. Primrose in *The Vicar of Wakefield* or the more critical account given by the Man in Black of his father:

> His education was above his fortune, and his generosity greater than his education. Poor as he was, he had his flatterers still poorer than himself; for every dinner he gave them, they returned equivalent in praise; and this was all he wanted. The same ambition that actuates a monarch or the head of an army, influenced my father at the head of his table; he told the story of the ivy-tree, and that was laughed at: he repeated the jest of the two scholars and one pair of breeches, and the company laughed at that; but the story of Taffy and the sedan-chair was sure to set the table in a roar. Thus his pleasure increased in proportion to the pleasure he gave; he loved all the world, and he fancied all the world loved him.

(letter 27)

Having wound his children up to be "mere machines of pity," the rector showed his own con-

---

[1]All quotations, except those from *An History of the Earth, and Animated Nature*, are from A. Friedman, ed., *The Collected Works*, 5 vols. (London, 1965).

tempt for money by giving his land and tithes as a dowry to his daughter, who had clandestinely married the son of a wealthy local landowner. As a result there was not enough money to send Oliver to Trinity College, Dublin, as an undergraduate, as his elder brother Henry had been sent, so he was persuaded to sit for a sizarship examination, in which he was successful. Being a sizar meant that he would receive his education free at Trinity and would have virtually free rooms and commons (the main meal of the day), but in return would have to perform menial tasks such as sweeping the courts and waiting on the dons at high table. Goldsmith found this an indignity; he had the desire but not the means to become a college notability, and as a result he did not much enjoy his life as an undergraduate.

Goldsmith's "sensibility of contempt" was strong. He had feelings of inferiority about his appearance. He was considered plain if not downright ugly, and smallpox had scarred his face. The mockery of his bullying tutor in lectures did not aid an imagination and memory "more eager at seeking new objects than desirous of reasoning on those already known." Goldsmith was not assiduous, and he may well have been disturbed by passion. Like his hero Marlow in *She Stoops to Conquer*, he was probably not acquainted with a single modest woman, and, like him, "impudent enough among females of another class." He was poor, yet he could not be careful with his money, even with his possessions. There was "no harm in him," but in his unselfish generosity he was his own worst enemy.

His father died in 1747, leaving Goldsmith his blessing; luckily his uncle Thomas Contarine provided enough money to help him scrape through two more years as an undergraduate. What was he to do when he graduated with a B.A. in 1749? He spent nearly three years at home in the flat Irish midland country, which he was later to look back upon with pleasure and regret. He tried tutoring, returning home with a good horse and thirty pounds, both of which vanished on a trip to Cork begun with an idea of emigration. His uncle sent him to Dublin with fifty pounds, to become a lawyer; but cards claimed the money, and he was soon home again. Another clerical relative thought he might make a doctor, and Contarine again produced some money. This time Goldsmith did spend it on the destined object. He left Ireland for Edinburgh in 1752 and began an exile that never ended, having left behind in Ireland, he wrote to his uncle, everything he thought worth possessing: friends that he loved and a society that pleased while it instructed.

After attending medical lectures at Edinburgh in 1752 and 1753, and eventually achieving many friendships there, Goldsmith arrived in 1754 at Leiden, where he spent nearly a year attending lectures. Then he left with "a guinea in his pocket, one shirt to his back, and a flute in his hand." He walked through Flanders, France, Switzerland, Italy, and probably back through Germany. This was a year of philosophic vagabondage; we can see an aspect of it in a passage in *The Vicar of Wakefield*:

In all the foreign universities and convents there are upon certain days, philosophical theses maintained against every adventitious disputant; for which, if the champion opposes with any dexterity, he can claim a gratuity in money, a dinner, and a bed for one night. In this manner, therefore, I fought my way towards England; walked along from city to city; examined mankind more nearly; and, if I may so express it, saw both sides of the picture.

(ch.20)

Passages in *The Traveller* also tell us of his experiences. He played the flute; he begged; and surely he borrowed, for he was always a great borrower. He was also, when he was in funds, a great and generous lender, for to him money was always a means, never an end in itself.

Preparation was well and truly over when Goldsmith arrived in England in February 1756. He had passed the midpoint of his twenties; his tour, unorthodox but nonetheless grand, had to be followed by some means of getting a living. He had his degree in arts, some knowledge of medicine in an age when degrees were more the exception than the rule, and, being now at the bottom of fortune's wheel, a cheerful feeling that London was the mart where even his unusual qualities would meet some kind of reward. He tried working for an apothecary, proofreading for Samuel Richardson's printing works, and then teaching in a school directed by Dr. Milner, the father of a fellow student at Edinburgh. The occupation of usher (assistant teacher) he loathed.

It was at the Milners' that Goldsmith began his real career. There he met Ralph Griffiths the bookseller, owner and editor of the *Monthly Review*, who offered him a year's work on the *Review* in return for board, lodging, and a small salary, an arrangement that lasted nearly six months. Goldsmith found the work tiresome, quarreled with Griffiths, and then, "by a very little practice as a physician, and a very little reputation as a poet," he made a shift to live.

Goldsmith was driven back to teaching, the Milners once more readily receiving him. Then a solution presented itself: he got the promise of a medical appointment on the coast of Coromandel in 1758. But the French established their supremacy over virtually all of southern India, so the appointment was postponed. He found a chance of getting a post as surgeon on a naval vessel going to India. This would save fifty pounds for the passage, which he had decided to raise, with another seventy or so for an outfit, by writing *An Enquiry into the Present State of Polite Learning in Europe*. He applied to the Surgeons' Hall for a qualification but was found "not qualified."

But before appearing at Surgeons' Hall, Goldsmith had felt he ought to have a new suit. He had agreed to write four reviews for Griffiths in return for Griffiths' giving security to a tailor for a new suit, which was to be paid for or returned by a fixed time. He pawned the suit to get money to pay for it, but gave the money to Mrs. Martin, a future landlady, as the bailiffs were about to seize her husband for debt. Then he presumably pledged the four books he had reviewed, these belonging to Griffiths. Griffiths demanded the books and the money owed the tailor, but finally compounded for a life of Voltaire, whom Goldsmith alleged he had met in Geneva and always fervently admired. The financial crisis that begot this book was typical of a cycle repeated in varying forms during the rest of Goldsmith's life. He would overspend, overborrow, and overwork to try, unsuccessfully, to catch up. By the autumn of 1759, he was fully engaged in the life of a literary hack, editing for John Wilkie, another bookseller, a weekly magazine called the *Bee*, most of which he probably wrote himself.

In 1760, Goldsmith wrote for several magazines, among them the *Busy Body*, the *Lady's Magazine*, the *Critical Review*, and Tobias Smollett's *British Magazine*. John Newbery, one of the kindest of Goldsmith's publishers, started a daily journal called the *Public Ledger*, to which Goldsmith contributed a series of "Chinese Letters" (later reprinted as *The Citizen of the World*). These made a hit with their gay irony disguised as ignorance, and by the end of 1760 he was no longer in need, though still writing to order. He moved from Green Arbour Court, where Thomas Percy, later bishop of Dromore, had called on him and was given the only chair in the place; the visit was interrupted by a little girl who came to borrow "a chamber pot full of coals." Percy also came to his new and better lodgings in Wine Office Court, off Fleet Street, and brought Johnson there to dine with him in May 1761. This visit marks the beginning of Goldsmith's emergence into literary society, for Johnson became his friend and introduced him to Joshua Reynolds. When Johnson and Reynolds founded their famous Club, later known as the Literary Club, in 1763, they placed Goldsmith's name next to their own on the list of nine members they drew up.

Johnson saw the potential literary greatness underlying Goldsmith's essays and compilations, and firmly pronounced him "one of the first men we now have as an author." But Johnson did more than recognize his literary merits; he showed Goldsmith the way to express his genius, to use the admirably clear, unmannered, and effective style that his practice in writing had so developed. When he heard in 1762 that Goldsmith was in distress and had been arrested for his rent, he sent him a guinea (which Goldsmith quickly changed into a bottle of Madeira) and visited him, discovering during the visit that Goldsmith had written a novel that was ready for the press. Johnson quickly sold this to Newbery for sixty pounds, and Goldsmith was delighted: here was money, in cash—and, in his circumstances, a relatively large amount. This was the beginning of his ability to earn money for serious literary work and to earn it at a rate Johnson considered, in this case, "sufficient." Newbery made an arrangement by which he paid for Goldsmith's board and incidental expenses at Islington, then a village outside London, deducting the sum from what he paid him for his writing. Goldsmith stayed there in 1762 and 1764.

The first work published under his own name—and with the letters M.B. proudly added after it[2]—was *The Traveller*, a poem that Johnson had persuaded him to finish and polish up for publication, and then unselfishly praised as the finest poem written since Alexander Pope's death. This poem established Goldsmith's reputation among his contemporaries, though many of them found it hard at first to believe he could have written it. "The partiality of his friends," as Johnson remarked later, "was against him."

There was a brief interlude while he again attempted to practice medicine.[3] When a patient called in her apothecary in preference to Goldsmith, he swore he would leave off prescribing for his friends, to which his friend Topham Beauclerk remarked, "Do so, my dear Doctor. Whenever you undertake to kill, let it only be your enemies."

The Vicar of Wakefield was published in 1766 but did not at first greatly reinforce his reputation. The next year Goldsmith wrote *The Good Natur'd Man*, his first comedy; and after a depressing amount of to-and-froing between the rival theater managers, George Colman and David Garrick, Colman put it on at the beginning of 1768. Goldsmith leased a larger set of rooms in the Temple with the proceeds of the play, entertained generously, gave his money away freely to the inevitable horde of hangers-on, and so had to turn to work again. Writing *The Roman History* occupied him in 1768; he then undertook a *History of England* for Thomas Davies; and by 1769, he had agreed to write eight volumes of *An History of the Earth, and Animated Nature* for Griffiths, who had published his *Essays* some years before.

The Deserted Village took two years to write. Goldsmith dedicated the poem to Reynolds in these simple and moving words: "The only dedication I ever made was to my brother, because I loved him better than most other men. He is since dead. Permit me to inscribe this Poem to you." Through Reynolds, Goldsmith had met the Hornecks, a mother, her son in the Foot Guards, and two daughters of nineteen and seventeen, with the younger of whom, Mary, he became friendly and whom he named "The Jessamy Bride." He went to France for a holiday with them in 1770, and found the Continent less congenial than when he had been there in his twenties. The Hornecks traveled expensively, and consequently on his return Goldsmith had to recoup his finances by plunging immediately into more work: a life of Lord Bolingbroke and an

---

[2] A biographical puzzle is presented by this medical degree, for university records were not always well kept. It is now argued that Goldsmith probably obtained it not, as was previously supposed, on the Continent, but from the University of Dublin, possibly in 1762.

[3] See T. P. C. Kirkpatrick's article in the bibliography.

abridgment of his own *Roman History*. His *History of England* was published in 1771, and afterward, in the midst of writing *Animated Nature* in the summer of that year, he occupied time trying "to do something to make people laugh"—the delightful result being *She Stoops to Conquer*.

Colman shilly-shallied over producing this comedy; but finally Johnson, to whom the published version of the play is nobly and simply dedicated, entered the fray and prevailed upon him "by much solicitation, nay, a kind of force" to put the play on. Goldsmith was primarily a man of emotion rather than intellect, and gave way to his feelings when, some days after the successful first performance of the play, his works were attacked in the *London Packet* and Miss Horneck's name mentioned. He beat Thomas Evans, who published the paper (the offensive article was probably written by an old enemy, William Kenrick), with his cane, and had eventually to pay him fifty pounds as compensation.

Goldsmith entered upon more compilation, this time a *Grecian History*; but in the midst of convivial life, of running up tailors' bills, he was becoming noticeably more moody, less able to present his usual jester's mask to his friends. Indeed, he meditated adopting a more retired life, thinking two months in the year all he could stand of London. He had arrived in London too late in his development to shed a predilection, strengthened in his progress from Dublin to Edinburgh, Leiden, and the rest of Europe, for homeliness. He was not made for the stresses of intense metropolitan life, and the effort to keep his head above the troubled waters of debt and depression was increasingly hard to maintain. His sally at Johnson for sheltering behind the cover of a pension should make us realize the contrast between their positions. The amount of work Goldsmith had gotten through in fifteen years was enormous, and the strain imposed on him equally so. He seems to have reached a stage of wondering what the value of it all was; he was obviously, for the moment, worked-out and in need of rest. In his troubles his friends proved far from perceptive. Yet his return for their teasing, in particular for a competition in epitaph writing, was to invite them to dinner to hear the superb series of vignettes of them he had composed in the poem "Retaliation." His power of invention was reviving.

When Goldsmith came to town in March 1774 after a spell of illness in the country—he had been suffering from strangury—he continued to be feverish. On Friday, 25 March, he insisted on taking Dr. James's powders, a patent medicine, against the advice of his doctor, William Hawes, who called in two other doctors, George Fordyce and William Turton. The vomiting brought on by these powders left Goldsmith very feeble, and he continued thus for a week, unable to sleep, the doctors unable to diagnose any disease. Then, to the utter shock of his friends, and the particular desolation of Reynolds, Edmund Burke, and Johnson, who had not realized the seriousness of his situation, he died after a series of convulsions in the early hours of 4 April.

THE NOVEL

THAT Goldsmith wrote *The Vicar of Wakefield* out of deeper motives than those underlying his general work can be inferred from the curiously deprecatory tone of his advertisement, in which, having described his hero as uniting in himself the three greatest characters on earth—"a priest, an husbandman and the father of a family"—he asks:

> In this age of opulence and refinement whom can such a character please? Such as are fond of high life, will turn with disdain from the simplicity of his country fire-side; such as mistake ribaldry for humour, will find no wit in his harmless conversation, and such as have been taught to deride religion, will laugh at one, whose chief stores of comfort are drawn from futurity.

It is as though he were anticipating criticism. The novel is an unusual one, a moral and didactic tale made up of a series of appalling misfortunes suddenly redeemed by an abruptly contrived happy ending—on the face of it unpromising material for a novel, yet somehow in Goldsmith's hands it is successful. The vicar submits to adversity; we can share his gratitude for ultimate good fortune, but the reader's interest is successfully sustained through the book because Goldsmith provides an unusual element by freely indulging in his own brand of gently ironical humor in the midst of what might otherwise be scenes of overwhelming pathos or cloying domestic bliss.

The impressions of a contented, orderly, pastoral Christian life are given their classic simplicity by the use of traditional formulas, by a scaling down, as

D. W. Jefferson has pointed out, of conventional, archetypal features. The novel emphasizes the continuity of life. The following passage will illustrate the effectiveness of its technique: it is written as though Goldsmith were using a Claude glass, that ingenious device through which the eighteenth-century man of taste observed landscapes in order to get the picturesque into perspective, to see nature in terms of the picture he desired to achieve:

The little republic to which I gave laws was regulated in the following manner: by sunrise we all assembled in our common apartment, the fire being previously kindled by the servant; after we had saluted each other with proper ceremony, for I always thought fit to keep up some mechanical forms of good breeding, without which freedom ever destroys friendship, we all bent in gratitude to that Being who gave us another day. This duty being performed, my son and I went to pursue our usual industry abroad, while my wife and daughters employed themselves in providing breakfast, which was always ready at a certain time. I allowed half an hour for this meal, and an hour for dinner; which time was taken up in innocent mirth between my wife and daughters, and in philosophical arguments between my son and me.

(ch.4)

This ability to depict and cause the reader to accept a view of life in miniature allows Goldsmith to speed up his narration. Indeed, misfortunes occur in the baldest manner, comparable only with the speed with which the plot is sorted out at the end of the novel—all this because of the economy with which the background is built up. Goldsmith, in effect, creates a life of contentment for his characters that may suffer from sudden alteration. Though it is made clear that there is no need for novelty in scenes such as the following, they are obviously laid out to invite speedy disruption:

The place of our retreat was in a little neighbourhood, consisting of farmers who tilled their own grounds, and were equal strangers to opulence and poverty. As they had almost all the conveniences of life within themselves, they seldom visited towns or cities in search of superfluity. Remote from the polite, they still retained the primeval simplicity of manners; and, frugal by habit, they scarce knew that temperance was a virtue. They wrought with cheerfulness on days of labour; but observed festivals as intervals of idleness and pleasure. They kept up the Christmas carol, sent true love-knots on Valentine's morn-ing, ate pancakes on Shrovetide, showed their wit on the first of April, and religiously cracked nuts on Michaelmas eve.

(ch.4)

The continuity is evoked by an almost ritualistic calendar approach, and the binding link in this communal life is the church. Goldsmith was really in search of an English equivalent to the Gaelic present habitual tense, and had to achieve it by a subtle series of images and nuances in vocabulary:

Being apprised of our approach the whole neighbourhood came out to meet their Minister, dressed up in their finest clothes, and preceded by a pipe and tabor. A feast also was provided for reception, at which we sat cheerfully down; and what the conversation wanted in wit was made up in laughter.

(ch.4)

Another device Goldsmith used to give the story its liveliness was the solemn, deadpan narrative style placed in the mouth of the long-suffering vicar. Here is his description of the wicked squire, which avoids the melodramatic by its factual air, its objectivity:

This gentleman he described as one who desired to know little more of the world than its pleasures, being particularly remarkable for his attachment to the fair sex. He observed, that no virtue was able to resist his arts and assiduity, and that there was scarcely a farmer's daughter within ten miles round, but what had found him successful and faithless. Though this account gave me some pain, it had a very different effect upon my daughters, whose features seemed to brighten with the expectation of an approaching triumph; nor was my wife less pleased and confident of their allurements and virtue.

(ch.3)

This is ironic, but the irony is Goldsmith's, not the vicar's. The vicar is here a puppet; it is Goldsmith's benign humor that reaches us; and sometimes, when the novel moves nearer to events similar to those that happened in his own family, he is at his narrator's elbow. Here, for instance, is how Mrs. Primrose eggs on the flirtation, perhaps not unlike Mrs. Goldsmith in similar circumstances that occurred between her own daughter and the rich son of a rich neighbor:

It must be owned, that my wife laid a thousand schemes to entrap him; or, to speak it more tenderly, used every art to magnify the merit of her daughter. If the cakes at tea ate short and crisp, they were made by Olivia; if the gooseberry-wine was well knit, the gooseberries were of her gathering; it was her fingers which gave the pickles their peculiar green; and in the composition of a pudding it was her judgement that mixed the ingredients. Then the poor woman would sometimes tell the squire, that she thought him and Olivia extremely of a size, and would bid both to stand up to see which was the tallest.

(ch.16)

Goldsmith must have thought this an effective matchmaking device; he used it again in the comic scene in *She Stoops to Conquer* when Mrs. Hardcastle is encouraging her son and Miss Neville to form an attachment, and ironically appeals to Miss Neville's unsuspected lover, Hastings:

Don't you think they are like each other about the mouth, Mr. Hastings? The Blenkinsop mouth to a T. They're of a size too. Back to back, my pretties, that Mr. Hastings may see you. Come, Tony.

(II.i)

And, it being a comedy, Tony Lumpkin cracks his head against that of poor Constance Neville, partly out of rustic animal spirits, partly to irritate a mother typical of those whom Goldsmith deftly drew in all their vulgarity and would-be worldliness.

Goldsmith also makes use of older elements in the tradition of the novel: digressions that appear as the story of the gulling of Moses when he is persuaded to exchange a horse for the green spectacles, the picaresque adventures of the vicar's pilgrimages, the sermon, and the Tory oration. A pastoral element is also present in the rustic scenes of the Flamboroughs making merry over hunting the slipper. There is even the introduction of a misunderstood letter; and inevitably mistakes in identity occur, delightfully in the case of that brilliantly named pair, Miss Carolina Wilhelmina Amelia Skeggs and Lady Blarney. The hero is an archetypal eccentric, visiting his estates in the guise of a man of broken fortune. Literary parallels are there in plenty. Mr. Wilmot reminds the reader of the suitor used, and ruthlessly cast aside, by Richardson's Pamela; Sir William Thornhill, as D. W. Jefferson has noted, of the duke in *Measure for Measure*; and Dr. Primrose himself,

though he is more dignified, less a comic Cervantesque character, of Henry Fielding's Parson Adams. And there is, of course, the constantly welcome interruption of the smoothly flowing narrative with ripples of wit.

The Vicar of Wakefield is above all Goldsmith's apologia. It contains the wisdom he had extracted from trials at least as severe as those of Dr. Primrose; and in his own adult life he had none of the domestic blessings of the vicar to cushion hardship. Throughout the novel his own parts are acted by Moses, often driven to unhappy silence in an argument; by George, the philosophical wanderer; by Mr. Burchell, who carried benevolence to excess when young, who always brought gingerbread for the small boys whom he called "harmless little men," to whom he sang ballads and told stories. There are several delightful anecdotes of Goldsmith's own successful efforts to amuse children, who loved him for his treating them as equals and for sharing unsophisticated pleasures with them. He related of Mr. Burchell that though he was fondest of the company of children, he would at intervals "talk with great good sense." However little Goldsmith applied wisdom to his own life, his comment on Mr. Burchell's talk certainly applies to the general statements on life that he put forward in *The Vicar of Wakefield*.

Here are intelligent ideas about individual freedom; about reforming the criminal code, which filled up the wretched jails of his day; about the abuse of capital punishment for trivial offenses. Goldsmith shows his vicar busy at good works in the jail, with surprisingly quick results, be it admitted; but what is more important, he makes him preach his sermon in the midst of his own troubles. This is the test, and the vicar's noble answer to it is that the promise of happiness must be sought in heaven, for philosophy can bring the miserable no comfort:

As we grow older the days seem to grow shorter, and our intimacy with time ever lessens the perception of his stay. Then let us take comfort now, for we shall soon be at our journey's end.

(ch.29)

Here there is no question of puppetry. We must acknowledge the humanity; we recognize the vicar as a man. It is upon his ultimate faith—in humanity as well as in another world where things will be better—that the book at this point stands rock-steady. Dr. Primrose may be stuffy; he may be the kind of person whose utter niceness embarrasses the less uninhibited; but he is no moralizing prig like Richardson's Sir Charles Grandison, no benign Mr. Allworthy (in Henry Fielding's *Tom Jones*). Because we can smile at him, we can realize there is no harm in him. None at all.

What Goldsmith succeeded in doing was the most difficult of literary tasks, the creation of a genuine and yet likable good person. He did this partly through a superb command of style, partly through a sense of fun: something neither quite humor nor yet quite wit; something the vicar appreciated and almost expressed: "I can't say whether we had more wit among us now than usual, but I am certain we had more laughing, which answered the end as well."

The vicar is really, we observe as we get to know him, a dupe, akin to Parson Adams; and this aspect of his role is emphasized by the misfortunes that thrust themselves upon him with a touch of the ludicrous. In the midst of hymning his happiness he hears of his daughter's abduction:

"We are descended from ancestors that knew no stain, and we shall leave a good and virtuous race of children behind us. While we live they will be our support and our pleasure here, and when we die they will transmit our honour untainted to posterity. Come, my son, we wait for a song; let us have a chorus. But where is my darling Olivia? That little cherub's voice is always sweetest in the concert." Just as I spoke, Dick came running in—"O papa, papa, she is gone from us—she is gone from us; my sister Livy is gone from us for ever!"—"Gone, child!"—"Yes; she is gone off with two gentlemen in a postchaise, and one of them kissed her and said he would die for her; and she cried very much and was for coming back; but he persuaded her again, and she went into the chaise, and said, 'Oh! What will my poor papa do when he knows I am undone?'"—"Now, then," cried I, "my children, go and be miserable; for we shall never enjoy one hour more. . . ."
(ch.17)

This sudden bouleversement of fortune occurs elsewhere in the novel: in the occurrence of the fire, of the vicar's arrest and imprisonment, and the arrest of his son. In these Goldsmith was indulging his love of anticlimax, of the reduction of domestic heights of happiness to depths of absurdity. This reduction of the effect of calamity makes it tolerable, just as the comic element, which provides the sudden reversals in the family's fortunes, tests the vicar's moralizing and makes it, even if it occasionally appears unsound, the more convincing. Above all it moves the story from that tricky point where the moral tale can verge upon hypocrisy. But we should never underestimate Goldsmith's affection for the absurd in its own right. We should remember his habit of saying droll things with a perfectly serious face. This sense of fun wasn't always understood by his contemporaries, and he left not a few mines in his writings to be sprung by pompous critics in his own time—and afterward.

THE POEMS

LIKE William Butler Yeats, Goldsmith often drafted his poems in prose, in which, according to Cooke, he threw out his ideas as they occurred to him:

He then sat carefully down to versify them, correct them, and add such further ideas as he thought better fitted to the subject. He sometimes would exceed his prose design, by writing several verses impromptu, but these he would take uncommon pains afterwards to revise, lest they should be found unconnected with his main design.[4]

Yeats wrote that a line might take hours:

Yet if it does not seem a moment's thought,
Our stitching and unstitching has been naught.
("Adam's Curse," 5–6)

And this comment applies particularly well to the methods and effects of Goldsmith's work. He achieved an air of spontaneity throughout all his poetry, whether it be in the mock heroics of the "Description of an Author's Bedchamber,"

With beer and milk arrears the frieze was scored
And five crack'd tea cups dress'd the chimney board

in the epigrammatic ending of the "Elegy on the Death of a Mad Dog," or in the exquisite elegiac simplicity of the "Song" found in *The Vicar of Wakefield*:

When lovely woman stoops to folly,
And finds too late that men betray,

[4]From an unsigned artlcle by W. Cooke in *European Magazine*, vol. XXIV (1793), p. 172.

What charm can soothe her melancholy,
What art can wash her guilt away?

Goldsmith could write in many genres. He tried poetical epistles, prologues, and epilogues, as well as squibs of various kinds, and gave them all a light conversational touch, an apparent casualness. His early love for ballads came from hearing them sung at home; he wrote his own and sold them while he was an undergraduate; and his "Edwin and Angelina: A Ballad" was printed privately for the amusement of the countess of Northumberland in 1764 or 1765 and frequently reworked. This poem, which he included in *The Vicar of Wakefield*, he regarded as at best a trifle; both he and Percy had similar feelings about the ballads they wrote on this theme, which was taken from an old ballad entitled "Gentle Herdsman, Tell to Me: A Dialogue Between a Pilgrim and a Herdsman."

Goldsmith shrugged off seriousness when he could. Even his last poem, "Retaliation," is pervaded by humor, when he had every excuse for unleashing savage satire. He wrote this poem, which remained unfinished, upon the friends who were diverting themselves with writing extempore epitaphs upon him, celebrating his oddity. Among them was Garrick, who produced a couplet that cut near the bone:

Here lies Nolly Goldsmith, for shortness call'd Noll,
Who wrote like an angel, but talk'd like poor Poll.

Goldsmith's humor was always valiantly rushing to the rescue; it is in many ways a sign of his unhappiness that he released it in public paradoxically, to disguise his inner feelings of melancholy and loneliness. It is, however, a measure of the innate gentleness of his anomalous character, as Samuel Johnson's friend Hester Thrale called it, that his mildly mocking, ironic comments—perceptive in the extreme, for all that many of his contemporaries preferred to regard him as a kind of inspired idiot—inevitably concluded with a palliative. "There was no harm in him." There are excellent sketches in "Retaliation" of Garrick, Reynolds, and Burke, caught on the intellectual politician's rack. Alluding to Burke, Goldsmith wrote:

Though fraught with all learning, yet straining his throat
To persuade Tommy Townshend to lend him a vote.
(33–34)

But Goldsmith's self-portrait, achieved in one line, is no less fair, and its comments upon his character precise in its one adjective, "magnanimous."

His poetic power is to be judged at its best when he was allowing his thoughts to take their untrammeled, leisurely way through those two great and, in a sense, complementary poems, *The Traveller* and *The Deserted Village*. The first develops a thought he first put into print in letter 73 of the "Chinese Letters," that the farther he traveled, the stronger was the force with which he felt the pain of separation. Another idea, put forward in letter 103, was that his "fatigued wishes" recurred to home for tranquillity. He sketches in a picture of his brother's dwelling, an orthodox picture of domestic bliss and a foretaste of the brief descriptions of pastoral contentment achieved in miniature in *The Vicar of Wakefield*, and then draws his contrasting lot in life:

Impell'd, with steps unceasing, to pursue
Some fleeting good, that mocks me with the view;
That, like the circle bounding earth and skies,
Allures from far, yet, as I follow, flies;
My fortune leads to traverse realms alone,
And find no spot of all the world my own.
(*The Traveller*, 25–30)

This poem presents morality with such confidence and ease, with such simplicity and grace, that it must be recognized as one of the finer examples of the particular achievement of the eighteenth century in poetry, the art of stating known truths felicitously. The descriptions are vignettes executed with sureness and precision. Take, for example, the bodying forth of Holland:

Methinks her patient sons before me stand,
Where the broad ocean leans against the land,
And, sedulous to stop the coming tide,
Lift the tall rampire's artificial pride.
Onwards, methinks, and diligently slow,
The firm-connected bulwark seems to grow;
Spreads its long arms amidst the wat'ry roar,
Scoops out an empire, and usurps the shore;
While the pent ocean rising o'er the pile,
Sees an amphibious world beneath him smile;
The slow canal, the yellow-blossom'd vale,
The willow-tufted bank, the gliding sail,
The crowded mart, the cultivated plain,
A new creation rescu'd from his reign.
(283–296)

The Traveller contains more than masterly imaging of places and people. It is an experience of life felt through the pulses of the poet's being. His moods are there, from a gay and sprightly retrospective enjoyment not only of France's mirth and social ease but also of his own insouciantly tuneless piping for the dancing of the villagers young and old, to wry reflections burned into the fabric of his life:

> For praise too dearly lov'd, or warmly sought,
> Enfeebles all internal strength of thought. . . .
>
> (269–270)

Goldsmith's generalized reflections attained strength and dignity. They can become rhetorical and yet remain unsuspect of any affectation. The reason for this is probably that he was aiming at what he called, in his essay "Of Eloquence," true declamation, which "does not consist in flowering periods, delicate allusions or musical cadences but rather in a plain, open and loose style." The directness Goldsmith achieved by this declamation is extremely effective. The passage in which he addresses his brother and foretells the theme of *The Deserted Village* gains its effect by words in themselves plain, but in their context powerfully persuasive:

> Have we not seen, round Britain's peopled shore,
> Her useful sons exchang'd for useless ore?
> Seen all her triumphs but destruction haste,
> Like flaring tapers bright'ning as they waste;
> Seen Opulence, her grandeur to maintain,
> Lead stern Depopulation in her train,
> And over fields where scatter'd hamlets rose,
> In barren solitary pomp repose?
> Have we not seen, at Pleasure's lordly call,
> The smiling, long-frequented village fall?
> Behold the duteous son, the sire decay'd,
> The modest matron, and the blushing maid,
> Forc'd from their homes, a melancholy train,
> To traverse climes beyond the western main;
> Where wild Oswego spreads her swamps around,
> And Niagara stuns with thund'ring sound?
>
> (397–412)

The Traveller's success as a poem is due to the emotion that its theme engendered in Goldsmith. It is a prospect of society written by a man not only recollecting emotion without tranquillity, but also still emotionally involved in loneliness, still longing for his home.

This same longing informs *The Deserted Village*. It humanizes the general picture of depopulation,

lovingly blending into it character sketches of individuals who stand as types of their trade and calling: the smith, the village preacher, the village schoolmaster, the swain mistrustful of his smutted face. There is, of course, humor as well:

> Where village statesmen talk'd with looks profound,
> And news much older than their ale went round.
>
> (223–224)

Goldsmith can be at ease with his characters because he can treat them familiarly, with the naturalness that children appreciated in him and adults often did not. He is remembering, as he told Cooke, the depopulation of villages in his own country (which he had also seen in England), and yet remembering it against a context of happiness when he looked back on:

> Dear lovely bowers of innocence and ease,
> Seats of my youth, when every sport could please,
> How often have I loiter'd o'er thy green,
> Where humble happiness endear'd each scene.
> How often have I paus'd on every charm,
> The shelter'd cot, the cultivated farm,
> The never-failing brook, the busy mill,
> The decent church that topp'd the neighbouring hill,
> The hawthorn bush, with seats beneath the shade,
> For talking age and whisp'ring lovers made.
>
> (5–14)

Goldsmith manages to involve these homely memories with a delicately poignant air; he expresses a feeling for the continuity of life with a skill reminiscent of John Milton in "L'Allegro":

> The swain responsive as the milkmaid sung,
> The sober herd that low'd to meet their young;
> The noisy geese that gabbled o'er the pool,
> The playful children just let loose from school.
>
> (117–120)

Yet the contrast is there:

> But now the sounds of population fail,
> No cheerful murmurs fluctuate in the gale,
> No busy steps the grass-grown footway tread,
> For all the bloomy flush of life is fled.
>
> (125–128)

The pensive note is, ultimately, dominant. Goldsmith wove its plangency through the poem with skill; there is an underlying contrapuntal technique at work. The sonorous rhetoric of the famous passage beginning:

> Ill fares the land to hast'ning ills a prey,
> Where wealth accumulates and men decay
> (51–52)

gains from its position in the poem. Memory of what was, in particular of communal life, continues to crowd in upon the solitude of what is. Goldsmith, a solitary guest, was writing in England; the brother whom he had loved better than most men was dead in Ireland, and with his death there had vanished all prospect of any ultimate retreat from loneliness. There could be no prodigal hopes any more of any future in terms of what had been:

> In all my wand'rings round this world of care,
> In all my griefs—and God has given my share—
> I still had hopes, my latest hours to crown,
> Amidst these humble bowers to lay me down;
> To husband out life's taper at the close,
> And keep the flame from wasting by repose.
> I still had hopes, for pride attends us still,
> Amidst the swains to show my book-learn'd skill,
> Around my fire an evening group to draw,
> And tell of all I felt, and all I saw;
> And, as a hare whom hounds and horns pursue,
> Pants to the place from whence at first she flew,
> I still had hopes, my long vexations past,
> Here to return—and die at home at last.
> (83–96)

THE PLAYS

GOLDSMITH'S essay "On Sentimental Comedy" (1773) is well worth reading; it provides the theory that shaped both of his comedies. He thought the kind of sentimental comedy in vogue in his day inimical to humor, that if humor once vanished from the stage, it might be very difficult indeed to recreate. Sentimental comedy seemed to him a bastard tragedy; as a result of its successes, tragedy itself was being neglected. He decided to write a play that would exhibit nature and humor, and set about delineating character in order to do so.

The Good Natur'd Man has characters enough: Honeywood, the man "with no harm in him," who called his extravagance generosity, his trusting everybody, universal benevolence; Croaker, the perennial well-to-do pessimist oppressed by "taxes rising and trade falling; money flying out of the kingdom and Jesuits swarming into it"; Lofty, the poseur and bluffer, who boasts of his influence with people of power and position whom he has never met. These are new characters in English drama, and there was further novelty of invention in the scene where Honeywood pretends to Miss Richland that the bailiffs in his house are visiting acquaintances. This, however, was hissed as "low" by the audience at Covent Garden on the opening night; and Goldsmith, dressed for the occasion in "Tyrian bloom, satin grain garter blue silk breeches," had difficulty in hiding his disappointment. When he went to the Club that evening, he acted, of course, as though he hadn't a care in the world, singing his favorite song, breaking down only when all had left except Johnson. The play ran for ten nights, but Goldsmith and his friends took the lack of public enthusiasm for it the worse because Hugh Kelly's sentimental comedy *False Delicacy* was popularly successful in the rival theater, Drury Lane.

Goldsmith had not acquired sufficient experience in stagecraft, nor had *The Good Natur'd Man* enough comic force for this play to rival the sentimental strain successfully. There is irony in the handling of Honeywood, Lofty, and Croaker; the dialogue is witty; the scenes of satire and the speeches of self-exposure are effective enough. But after seeing or reading the play, there comes back into the mind a speech made by Jarvis the servant, when he discusses Honeywood's philosophizing:

> That same philosophy is a great horse in a stable, but an arrant jade on a journey. Whenever I hear him mention the name on't, I'm always sure he's going to play the fool.
> (I.i)

The trouble is that when Honeywood finally philosophizes, it is clear he has not played the fool to the best advantage. He is sinned against rather than sinning, and the comic humor is restricted largely to the cross-purposes of the plot. The characters are not fully drawn in the round, though the situations and speech are amusing. *The Good Natur'd Man* is usually read by those who have been led to it by the success of *She Stoops to Conquer*, in which Goldsmith did more than write good, witty lines, create new types, and invent new comic interrelationships—he gave his sense of fun and farce its head.

On receiving from a friend an equivocal comment about the merits of *She Stoops to Conquer*, Goldsmith further inquired, "Did it make you laugh?" and getting the answer "Exceedingly," said that was all he required. He had set about the creation of laughter by using for plot a reputed experience of his own as a schoolboy. It is said that he lost his way in Ardagh, asked to be directed to an inn, and was shown by a local fencing master, fond of a practical joke, the gateway to the local squire's house. The boy behaved somewhat like the play's hero Marlow, and was disabused in the morning when, on his calling for the reckoning, the identity of his supposed host, whom he had treated somewhat cavalierly the night before, was disclosed. The squire had been, according to tradition, at Trinity College with Goldsmith's father. Be that as it may, he utilized the comic possibilities of this situation to the full. Marlow is doomed to adore the female sex, yet to converse with the only part of it he despises. His stammer, his "awkward prepossessing visage" can never permit him to "soar above the reach of a milliner's prentice or one of the duchesses of Drury Lane." The situation is resolved for him by Miss Hardcastle, a sprightly girl who enjoys her role as supposed barmaid and plays it with verve.

The play's great creation is, of course, Tony Lumpkin, a squire's son who relishes the easy applause of a loutish audience, and later justifies our own applause when he enjoys the absurd situation of maintaining that the jewels in his mother's keeping have been stolen, in order to back up his mother's pretense that this has occurred, she not knowing that in fact they have been stolen by him. When she later bewails their loss, his delight in what he pretends is her excellent acting is superb, as is the farcical situation he brings about by pretending he has brought her to a deserted common when she is actually beside her own gate, the mulberry tree, and the horse pond, where Tony "with a circumbendibus" had lodged the coach, so as to act good fairy to one of the play's pair of lovers. And, incidentally, to make easier his own path to the affections of Bet Bouncer, that offstage country beauty immortalized as having "two eyes black as sloes and cheeks as broad and red as a pulpit cushion."

The pruning of excess is carried out in the tradition of great comedy; the audience has the pleasure of knowing more than the actors about their situation. Between the extremes of Molière's comic wit in *L'Avare* and the farcical antics of Hodge in *Gammer*

Gurton's Needle balances the equally laughter-producing invention, the equally timeless fun of *She Stoops to Conquer*.

Goldsmith gives the correct clue to comparison. When Mr. Hardcastle contributes to the irony of the plot by declaring to the young men, "This is Liberty Hall, you know," he is echoing Pleusicles in the *Miles gloriosus* when he says *"Liberae sunt aedes."* It is to Plautine comedy we must return to find, equally unencumbered by psychological profundities or sociological sermonizing, true gaiety.

ESSAYS AND OTHER WRITINGS

GEORGE PRIMROSE is made to remark in *The Vicar of Wakefield* that his little pieces came out in the midst of periodical publications, unnoticed and unknown, the public being "more importantly employed than to observe the easy simplicity of my style, or the harmony of my periods." So it happened with many of Goldsmith's own writings, turned out under pressure—tasks, as he called them, for he was a great procrastinator. Yet what he wrote to order was not all fugitive; what is remarkable is that his potboiling and compilation possess so much of lasting value for the reader who is not put off by versatility. Goldsmith, to survive, had to be versatile; he also husbanded his stock of experience carefully and, born conversationalist that he was, repeated himself in different contexts. But, as he once wrote to his brother, he had, while exposing himself to the insidious approaches of cunning, "contracted the habits and notions of a philosopher."

He began by writing criticism in the *Monthly Review* and the *Critical Review*; his essays appeared in many periodicals, among them the *British Magazine*, the *Busy Body*, and the *Public Ledger*. This last carried his *Letters from a Citizen of the World* (published in two volumes in 1762), a skillful, lively series of essays written as if by a Chinese visitor to England. The basic idea was not a new one, but the thoughts Goldsmith put forward are often profound and often original in their approach to political and social difficulties. He had learned from books to be disinterested and generous; his subsequent experience of life had only served to enrich his sympathies with the poor and the pitiable. And so his Chinese merchant had pertinent remarks upon the evils of capital punishment, the futility of revenge, the abuses of vote-catching by distribution of alcohol, absurdities in the marriage act, the Russian problem, cruelty to animals, excessive gambling, and many other problems. He understood the causes that were to lead to the French Revolution and the secession of the American colonies, and he dreaded the effect of luxury. There are passages in plenty on the literary world, as well as satiric descriptions of fashionable life.

Goldsmith contributed introductions and prefaces to the writings of others and wrote biographies to accompany various editions of authors' works, of which his "Life of Thomas Parnell" (1770) prompted Johnson to remark in his *Lives of the Poets* that it was seldom safe to contradict Goldsmith's criticism. The "Memoirs of M. de Voltaire" (1761) were full of good sense and advanced in biographical theory. The *Life of . . . Bolingbroke* (1770), though largely lifted from the *Biographia Britannica*, enabled Goldsmith to reveal some of his political feelings, while in writing the *Life of Richard Nash* (1762), the "open-hearted, generous and good-natured" dandy who was master of ceremonies at Bath, he had a subject who could not "stifle the natural impulse he had to do good but frequently borrowed to relieve the distressed." He was here able to pay a tribute of deep and sympathetic understanding in what is virtually an autobiographical biography of another and a pioneering work in the history of English biography.

Goldsmith constantly demonstrated his versatility by tackling whatever came his way, embarking gaily, for instance, on *A Survey of Experimental Philosophy* in 1764, the year his anonymous *History of England in a Series of Letters from a Nobleman to His Son* came out. It was as much the duty of the historian, he roundly asserted, to act the philosopher or politician in his narratives as to collect materials for narration; he demanded, as any man of his time would, as much exercise of judgment as of imagination. He despised abridgers, compilers, commentators, and critics; and his own compilations are not always remarkable for their historical sense, but, like everything else he wrote, they are easy to read and were used in schools for many years. Throughout his writings he put forward sensible ideas about children's education: play and other children often teach the child more than

anything else can. But work was not to be overlooked: "those masters who allege the incapacity of tender years, only tacitly reproach their own."

Of all Goldsmith's informative writings, that which preserves most interest for contemporary readers is his *History of the Earth, and Animated Nature*, which he wrote between 1769 and 1774, mainly at various lodgings on the outskirts of London. The earlier part of the book, dealing with quadrupeds (it ran to eight octavo volumes in all), he based upon Georges Buffon's writings, but for the rest he read widely—as well as being a compiler, he was a quick and efficient digester—and drew upon his own observation of nature. The result is a curious mixture of absurdity and accuracy. He is always at his best when relating what he has seen and reflecting upon it, as when he gazes at the rooks building their nests in the Temple garden, or recalls memories of decoying or bird-netting, or of partridges on the roads outside Paris, or even of the gander that is, though petulant and provoking, the most harmless thing alive.

The "hollow sounding bittern" of *The Deserted Village* may have come from Goldsmith's memories of the Irish midlands. The accurate language used in the following description makes nonsense of the critics who have too readily followed Johnson's jovial assertion that Goldsmith's knowledge of nature might not go beyond distinguishing a horse from a cow:

Those who have walked in an evening by the sedgy sides of unfrequented rivers, must remember a variety of notes from different water-fowl: the loud scream of the wild goose, the croaking of the mallard, the whining of the lap-wing, and the tremulous neighing of the jack-snipe. But of all those sounds, there is none so dismally hollow as the booming of the bittern. It is impossible for words to give those who have not heard this evening-call an adequate idea of its solemnity. It is like the interrupted bellowing of a bull, but hollower and louder, and is heard at a mile's distance, as if issuing from some formidable being that resided at the bottom of the waters.

The bird, however, that produces this terrifying sound is not so big as a heron, with a weaker bill, and not above four inches long. It differs from the heron chiefly in its colour, which is in general of a paleish yellow, spotted and barred with black. Its wind pipe is fitted to produce the sound for which it is remarkable; the lower part of it dividing into the lungs is supplied with a thin loose membrane that can be filled with a large body of air and exploded at pleasure. These bellowing explosions are chiefly heard from the beginning of spring to the end of the autumn, and, however awful they may seem to us, are calls to courtship, or of connubial felicity.

From the loudness and solemnity of the note, many have been led to suppose that the bird made use of external instruments to produce it, and that so small a body could never eject such a quantity of tone. The common people are of opinion, that it thrusts its bill in on a reed that serves as a pipe for swelling the note above its natural pitch; while others, and in this number we find Thomson the poet, imagine that the bittern puts its head under water, and then violently blowing produces its boomings. The fact is, that the bird is sufficiently provided by nature for this call; and it is often heard where there are neither reeds nor waters to assist its sonorous invitations. . . . I remember in the place where I was a boy with what terror this bird's note affected the whole village; they considered it as the presage of some sad event; and generally found or made one to succeed it. [5]

(vol. VI, ch.6)

The book contains much to justify Johnson's expectations that it would be as interesting as a Persian tale; it is written with all the ease and grace we expect from Goldsmith. It even includes passages tinged with his own brand of humor, as in this account of what happens when several polypi happen to fall upon the same worm, a mingling of moral reflection with a delicate appreciation of the absurd:

It often happens that while one is swallowing its respective end, the other is also employed in the same manner, and thus they continue swallowing each his part, until their mouths meet together; they then rest, each for some time in this situation, till the worm breaks between them, and each goes off with his share; but it often happens, that a seemingly more dangerous combat ensues, when the mouths of both are thus joined upon one common prey together: the largest polypus then gapes and swallows his antagonist; but what is very wonderful, the animal thus swallowed seems to be rather a gainer by the misfortune. After it has lain in the conqueror's body for about an hour, it issues unhurt, and often in the possession of the prey which had been the original cause of contention. How happy would it be for men, if they had as little to fear from each other!

(vol. VIII, ch.11)

Throughout *Animated Nature* Goldsmith's essential fairness of mind is at work; his gentleness is at its

[5]Quotations are from *An History of the Earth, and Animated Nature*, 8 vols. (London, 1774).

most charming when he can contemplate creatures that he believed "unlike men, never inflict a pain but when urged by necessity." His love of children and animals reminds us yet again that "there was no harm in him." He was very fond of quoting a passage from Sir William Temple's essay "Of Poetry," which explains him in his brave attempts to hide his loneliness behind a facade of fun:

When all is done, human life is, at the greatest and best, but like a froward child that must be played with and humoured a little to keep it quiet till it falls asleep, and then the care is over.

(*Works*, vol.II: *Miscellanea*, p.352)

SELECTED BIBLIOGRAPHY

I. Bibliography. I. A. Williams, *Seven XVIIIth-Century Bibliographies* (London, 1924), includes that of Goldsmith; K. C. Balderston, *A Census of the Manuscripts* (New York, 1926); T. Scott, *Oliver Goldsmith Bibliographically and Biographically Considered* (New York, 1928); W. D. Paden and C. K. Hyder, *A Concordance of the Poems* (Lawrence, Kans., 1940).

II. Collected Works. *Essays* (London, 1765; 1766), the latter contains two additional essays; *The Miscellaneous Works* (London, 1775); *Poems and Plays* (Dublin, 1777), contains a memoir by E. Malone; *The Poetical Works* (London, 1784); *The Miscellaneous Works*, 2 vols. (Edinburgh, 1791; 4 vols., 1792); *The Miscellaneous Works*, 7 vols. (Perth, 1792), the first uniformly collected ed.; *The Miscellaneous Works*, 4 vols. (London, 1801), the first vol. includes a memoir by T. Percy; W. Irving, ed., *The Miscellaneous Works*, 4 vols. (Paris, 1825); J. Mitford, ed., *The Poetical Works* (London, 1831), rev. by A. Dobson, ed. (London, 1895), the Aldine ed.; J. Prior, ed., *The Miscellaneous Works, Including a Variety of Pieces Now First Collected*, 4 vols. (London, 1837); H. G. Bohn, ed., *The Works, with a Life and Notes*, 4 vols. (London, 1848), some of the notes are useful; D. Masson, ed., *The Miscellaneous Works* (London, 1869), the Globe ed.; J. W. M. Gibbs, ed., *The Works: A New Edition, Containing Pieces Hitherto Uncollected*, 5 vols. (London, 1884–1886), a most useful ed.; A. Dobson, ed., *The Poems and Plays*, 2 vols. (London, 1889); A. Dobson, ed., *The Plays* (London, 1893), in the Temple Classics; A. Dobson, ed., *The Complete Poetical Works* (Oxford, 1906); C. E. Doble, ed., *The Plays* (London, 1909); *The Bee and Other Essays, with the Life of Nash* (London, 1914); R. S. Crane, ed., *New Essays* (Chicago, 1927), contains eighteen previously unidentified essays; A. Friedman, ed., *The Collected Works, 5 vols. (London, 1965), contains all works of literary interest, with good notes.

III. SELECTED WORKS. A. Dobson, ed., *Selected Poems* (Oxford, 1887); J. H. Lobban, ed., *Selected Essays* (London, 1910); R. Garnett, ed., *Selected Works* (London, 1950), in the Reynard Library; F. W. Hilles, ed., *The Vicar of Wakefield and Other Writings* (New York, 1955), in the Modern Library; A. N. Jeffares, ed., *A Goldsmith Selection* (London, 1963), in the English Classics, new series; *"The Traveller" with "The Deserted Village" and "The Prospect of Society"* (London, 1970).

IV. SEPARATE WORKS. Goldsmith contributed anonymously to various periodicals: *Monthly Review, Critical Review, Public Ledger, British Magazine, Lady's Magazine,* and others. For these and other occasional writings see R. S. Crane's list in the *Cambridge Bibliography of English Literature*, vol. II, 638–644. *The Memoirs of a Protestant, Condemned to the Galleys of France for His Religion*, 2 vols. (London, 1758), trans. by Goldsmith from the French, also in A. Dobson, ed. (London, 1895); *Bee*, 1–8 (1759); *An Enquiry into the Present State of Polite Learning in Europe* (London, 1759); *The Mystery Revealed: Containing a Series of Translations and Authentic Testimonials Respecting the Supposed Cock Lane Ghost* (London, 1762; repr. Westport, Conn., 1928); *The Citizen of the World; or Letters from a Chinese Philosopher, Residing in London, to His Friends in the East*, 2 vols. (London, 1762), in A. Dobson, ed. (London, 1891), repr. in Everyman's Library (London, 1970); *The Life of Richard Nash, of Bath, Esq.: Extracted Principally from His Original Papers* (London, 1762); *Plutarch's Lives*, 5 vols. (London, 1762), "abridged from the Original Greek, Illustrated with Notes and Reflections"; *An History of England in a Series of Letters from a Nobleman to His Son*, 2 vols. (London, 1764); *"Edwin and Angelina: A Ballad"* (London, 1765), privately "printed for the Amusement of the Countess of Northumberland," only one copy known; *The Traveller, or A Prospect of Society* (London, 1765), also in J. B. Hill, ed. (Oxford, 1888); *The Geography and History of England. In Two Parts. The Second Part Contains a Concise History of England: Or, the Revolutions of the British Constitution* (London, 1765); *The Vicar of Wakefield. A Tale*, 2 vols. (London, 1766), also in G. Saintsbury, ed. (London, 1886), O. Doughty, ed. (London, 1928), and A. Friedman, ed. (London, 1974), the Oxford English Novels series; *The Beauties of English Poesy, Selected by Oliver Goldsmith*, 2 vols. (London, 1767); *Poems for Young Ladies. In Three Parts: Devotional, Moral, and Entertaining* (London, 1767); *The Good Natur'd Man. A Comedy* (London, 1768); *The Roman History from the Foundation of the City of Rome to the Destruction of the Western Empire*, 2 vols. (London, 1769).

The Deserted Village (London, 1770), the first ed. was a quarto, the rare "trial" eds. have been shown to be later

piracies; see W. B. Todd in *Studies in Bibliography 1953–4*, vol. VI; *The Life of Henry St. John, Lord Viscount Bolingbroke* (London, 1770); *The History of England, from the Earliest Times to the Death of George II*, 4 vols. (London, 1771); *Dr. Goldsmith's Roman History Abridged by Himself for the Use of Schools* (London, 1772); *Threnodia Augustalis. Sacred to the Memory of Her Late Royal Highness, the Princess Dowager of Wales* (London, 1772); *She Stoops to Conquer: Or, the Mistakes of a Night. A Comedy* (London, 1773), also in G. G. Urwin, ed. (London, 1956), A. N. Jeffares, ed. (London, 1965), and A. Friedman, ed. (London, 1968); *An Abridgement of the History of England from the Invasion of Julius Caesar to the Death of George II* (London, 1774); *The Grecian History, from the Earliest State to the Death of Alexander the Great*, 2 vols. (London, 1774); *An History of the Earth, and Animated Nature*, 8 vols. (London, 1774); *"Retaliation. A Poem"* (London, 1774); *The Comic Romance of Monsieur Scarron*, 2 vols. (London, 1775), trans. by Goldsmith from the French; *The Haunch of Venison, a Poetical Epistle to Lord Clare* (London, 1776); *A Survey of Experimental Philosophy, Considered in Its Present State of Improvement*, 2 vols. (London, 1776).

V. CORRESPONDENCE. K. C. Balderston, ed., *The Collected Letters* (London, 1928), an admirable piece of scholarship.

VI. BIOGRAPHICAL AND CRITICAL STUDIES. E. Malone, "The Life of Oliver Goldsmith," in *Poems and Plays* (Dublin, 1777); T. Percy et al., "The Life of Oliver Goldsmith," in *Miscellaneous Works*, vol. I (London, 1801), personal knowledge of Goldsmith makes this very useful, though Percy's desire to present a certain view of him mars it; J. Prior, *The Life of Oliver Goldsmith*, 2 vols. (London, 1837), the first full-scale biography, upon which later writers have drawn heavily; W. Irving, *Oliver Goldsmith: A Biography* (London, 1850), adds some information to the biography of Prior, who accused Irving of plagiarism; W. M. Thackeray, "Oliver Goldsmith," in *The English Humourists of the Eighteenth Century* (London, 1853); J. Forster, *The Life and Times of Oliver Goldsmith*, 2 vols. (London, 1854), Forster added new information in his biography, but some of his conjectures are not now accepted; W. Black, *Goldsmith* (London, 1878), in the English Men of Letters series; A. Dobson, *The Life of Oliver Goldsmith* (London, 1888); J. J. Kelly, *The Early Haunts of Oliver Goldsmith* (Dublin, 1905); R. A. King, *Oliver Goldsmith* (London, 1910), a fighting defense of Goldsmith and the first to explain his difference from the literary society of his time on reasoned grounds; F. F. Moore, *The Life of Oliver Goldsmith* (London, 1910); K. C. Balderston, *The History and Sources of Percy's "Memoir of Goldsmith"* (Cambridge, 1926); T. P. C. Kirkpatrick, "Goldsmith in Trinity College and His Connection with Medicine," in *Irish Journal of Medical Science* (1929); S. Gwynn, *Oliver Goldsmith* (London,

1935), occasionally in error and untidy, a lively and sympathetic biography; D. C. Bryant, *Edmund Burke and His Literary Friends* (St. Louis, 1939); W. Freeman, *Oliver Goldsmith* (London, 1951); F. W. Hilles, ed., *Portraits by Sir Joshua Reynolds* (New York, 1952), then recently discovered, the account of Goldsmith is the fairest, most understanding contemporary view; R. M. Wardle, *Oliver Goldsmith* (Lawrence, Kans., 1957), scholarly and informative, in general a very sympathetic interpretation and well documented; F. L. Lucas, *The Search for Good Sense: Four Eighteenth-Century Characters* (London, 1958), stimulating and appreciative on Goldsmith; A. N. Jeffares, *A Critical Comment on She Stoops to Conquer* (London, 1965); R. Quintana, *Goldsmith: A Georgian Study* (London, 1967); R. H. Hopkins, *The True Genius of Oliver Goldsmith* (Baltimore, 1969); A. Friedman, "Aspects of Sentimentalism in Eighteenth Century Literature," in *The Augustan Milieu: Essays Presented to Louis Landa* (Oxford, 1970); R. Quintana, "Goldsmith: Ironist to the Georgians," in *Eighteenth Century Studies in Honour of Douglas Hyde* (New York, 1970); G. Winchcombe, *Oliver Goldsmith and the Moonrakers* (London, 1972); P. Murray, "The Riddle of Goldsmith's Ancestray," in *Studies* (Summer 1974); G. S. Rousseau, ed., *Goldsmith: The Critical Heritage* (London, 1974); A. L. Sells, *Oliver Goldsmith: His Life and Works* (London, 1974), seems based on a dislike of Goldsmith; J. Ginger, *The Notable Man: The Life and Times of Oliver Goldsmith* (London, 1977), the most interesting modern biography.

EDMUND BURKE

(1729-1797)

T. E. Utley

I

THE influence of Edmund Burke on the theory and practice of British politics since the end of the eighteenth century has been unique. No even approximate parallel to it can be found. It is impossible, for example, to think of any British statesman of whom it might be truthfully said that his mind had been formed by John Locke or Thomas Hobbes, yet it is equally impossible to think of any outstanding English parliamentarian during this period of whom it can be said that he altogether escaped the influence of Burke. Nevertheless, Burke was not merely a teacher of the techniques of political life; he was no mere Machiavelli of parliamentary government, taking its ends and origins for granted and confining himself to telling practical men how to achieve what they wanted to achieve. Burke's stature as a philosopher of politics has grown, though not steadily, since his death; and it has never seemed more impressive than it does today.

The key to Burke's influence as a political philosopher is that he has never appeared as the leader of a sect. On the contrary, he is the Aquinas of British political thought, from time to time claimed by all the sects but never entirely harnessed to any; a house of many mansions in which hospitality is generously given, on the strict understanding that guests will be mutually reconciled. In short, in British political thought Burke is the central point from which heresies diverge.

So little has a man's temperament to do with his convictions that, to judge from what is known of the life and character of Edmund Burke, it is almost incredible that he should have been an apostle of moderation in politics. The son of an Irish Protestant solicitor and his Roman Catholic wife, he was born in January 1729, educated at a Quaker school, and sent first to Trinity College, Dublin, and then to the Temple, where he alienated his father by neglecting his studies. He came to England as a penniless Irish adventurer, and for the rest of his life bore the stigma of those beginnings. Burke's candidature for admission to the English governing class was a thousand times bolder than Benjamin Disraeli's; he was from the first suspected of almost every vice and affiliation that could kill a man's reputation. He was known to be Irish and was suspected of being a Roman Catholic, a Jesuit in disguise trained at St.-Omer, a suspicion that was regarded as proved when in 1756 he married Jane Nugent, the daughter of a Roman Catholic doctor at Bath. He was suspected of being a crook, even within the broad definition of the term admitted by his contemporaries—and, what was worse, an unsuccessful and hypocritical crook, who lost what he had stolen on the Indian stock market while castigating his political opponents for corruption. Confronted with these suspicions, he was either secretive or angry, but resolutely refused to alter his conduct in any way likely to refute them. Indeed, the whole circumstances of his early life in England were such as to give bad impressions that nothing but several generations of exact scholarship could hope to eradicate.

Of these circumstances the most distressing were his cousin Will and his younger brother Richard. The fact that they joined him and treated his house as their home until the end of their lives made his own debut seem to be merely one act in a concerted campaign of social conquest. Will, who operated in Indian stock, was beyond doubt extremely dishonest; Richard was merely a wastrel and a cheat at cards. Both of them had an affection and a loyalty for Edmund that called forth a fervent and practical response from him; and he not only harbored them but rushed fanatically to their defense whenever —which was most of the time—they were in trouble. To help him with these encumbrances, Burke had only a miserable pittance inherited from his

193

father and, in his early years, the precarious and negligible rewards of literature, the most constant of which was the small sum he received from the printer Robert Dodsley for editing the *Annual Register*, which was founded in 1758 at Burke's initiative.

There were, of course, occasional and short-lived strokes of luck. In 1761, for example, Burke was invited to go to Ireland as an unofficial assistant to William Gerald Hamilton, who was secretary to Lord Halifax, the lord lieutenant. Hamilton benefited immensely from Burke's insight into the Irish question, which was then a compound of the discontents of Catholic tenants with Protestant landowners, and of Protestant traders with the commercial restrictions imposed by the home government. In 1763, Burke heard that his reward was to be a pension of £300 a year from the Irish treasury. Unfortunately, the offer was accompanied by the condition that he cease writing altogether: "To circumscribe my hopes," expostulated Burke, "to give up even the possibility of liberty, to annihilate myself for ever!" Burke's first patron was, accordingly, summarily discarded. Two years later there was again a fortunate turn: Lord Charles Rockingham became prime minister, and, overriding protests against Burke's alleged popery and generally shaky credentials, he made him his private secretary—chiefly, it seems, because he was impressed with the breadth of knowledge that Burke displayed in his annual survey of world affairs for Dodsley. On 26 December 1765, Burke was elected to Parliament for Wendover, partly as a result of the efforts of Will, who was at the time doing well and managed to procure another seat for himself.

One decisive part of the background of Burke's career had yet to be supplied. In 1769 he took a step that has caused unaccountable perplexity in all his biographers: in company with Will and Richard, he bought Gregories, near Beaconsfield, an enormous country estate in Buckinghamshire, for about £25,000, £14,000 of it on mortgage and the rest supplied in loans by friends. It is true that the estate cost well over £2,000 a year to keep up at a time when his annual income was in the hundreds, that it was accordingly a constant source of worry to him until his death, and that even this expenditure could not succeed in expelling an atmosphere of dirt and disorder that caused surprise to such critical guests as Hester Thrale, the great literary hostess of Samuel Johnson's circle. Burke knew, though, that the only test

that the English governing class imposes on parvenus is that they shall prove themselves capable of successfully living above their incomes for at least the first twenty years of their careers. He was not entirely wrong in his calculation that the best antidote to an obscure origin was a large country house. At the time his prospects seemed good, and in the nature of his circumstances it was on prospects that he must live. Besides, the idea of an establishment in the country had a strong appeal to his historical imagination; he enjoyed exercising those virtues and practicing that form of life that the English middle classes attribute to the aristocracy. At Gregories he could give alms to the poor, be a patron of letters (he saved George Crabbe from prison), and hold house parties for the eminent.

The fact that the imitation was not entirely successful, and in any case was an imitation of nothing real, merely gave it, in the eyes of all but the most complaining of guests, the charm of character. The family, indeed, was a trouble; it was not only the irregularities of Will and Richard, but also the necessity imposed by a generous disposition and adequate house space of entertaining unpresentable Irish relatives for long periods. To visit the Burkes in the summer was to get the impression of a rest home for Irish immigrants, and to invite Edmund and Jane to a party was to expose oneself to an invasion of unpredictable size from England's most troublesome colony. To the imperfections of his relatives, Burke remained throughout his life valiantly, ostentatiously, and most expensively indifferent.

It is necessary to fix Gregories clearly in mind because it was the solace as well as the plague of Burke's life, and, with the affection of his wife Jane, a woman of great tenderness, and later of his son Richard, it supplied, in spite of the mortgage, the most stabilizing influence on a mind otherwise so rent with public cares and passions that it often made an impression of lunacy even on friends. Burke said that when he crossed the threshold of Gregories, all worries left him. In the end it was a source of remorse, for not until after his son Richard's death at the age of thirty-six did he realize the full magnitude of the debts on which his domestic peace was founded, from the knowledge of which Jane and Richard had always shielded him. He began to think of himself as having exploited his wife and robbed his son of his youth, and as having been prevented by a harsh fate from doing anything to repay their sacrifice. In his last, miserable years he found the place full of unbearable associations with Richard's memory, yet he clung to it stubbornly. Indeed, it was eventually the only place where he could bear to be.

II

THE career that was built on Gregories would not have occupied much space in a contemporary *Who's Who*, that invaluable publication in which the offices and attainments of the eminent are listed. Burke was a member of Parliament from 1765 until 1794, most of the time representing rotten boroughs but also, for six memorable years, the freeholders of Bristol. In Lord Rockingham's brief administration in 1782, he occupied the post of paymaster-general, and he returned to that office in the ill-fated Charles Fox–Lord North coalition of 1783, after the death of Rockingham had deprived him of his only loyal patron. He never held office again. Thus, he was never more than a minor minister, and even that modest distinction never remained with him for more than a few months. The commoner prizes of political service in his day—sinecures, pensions on the civil list, and so on—eluded him until three years before his death, when William Pitt, in the face of considerable hostility, made a reasonable provision for him.

It is true that the list of Burke's publications would, by virtue of their variety as well as their number, have helped to redeem the impression of mediocrity left by the other entries under his name in the hypothetical *Who's Who* of the day. He would have appeared as the young author of a satire against Viscount Bolingbroke under the title of *A Vindication of Natural Society* (1756), a satire so telling as to lose its point entirely by convincing contemporaries that it was by Bolingbroke himself; as a writer of the essay *On the Sublime and the Beautiful*, which clarified the current, somewhat vague ideas of psychology as the proper basis for a theory of aesthetics; and as the composer of innumerable political pamphlets and tracts, including among them *Reflections on the French Revolution*, which was seen by contemporaries as the most eloquent and exhaustive expression of the faith for which England was fighting in the war against the French Revolution and Napoleon.

The bare account of Burke's offices and publications would convey nothing of the impact of his career. It would not show the part that Burke played until 1782 in welding the Rockinghamite Whigs into something resembling a modern political party, in transforming one of the innumerable splinter groups into which the eighteenth-century House of Commons was divided into an alliance based on mutual confidence and common principle, disciplined for action in the House of Commons and even, thanks to the literary qualities of Burke, capable of propaganda in the country. It would not reveal the unparalleled combination of fervor and detailed industry that Burke put into the campaign for reducing the royal influence in the House of Commons and over elections to it, by curtailing the patronage at the king's disposal. It would say nothing of the fierce and imperishable campaign that Burke led against the policy of trying to coerce the American colonies, and little of one of the greatest dramas in British parliamentary history: the impeachment of Warren Hastings for crimes and misdemeanors in the government of India, in which Burke was chief prosecuting counsel for the House of Lords; he was involved in the affair in one way or another for at least twelve years. Even the contemporary success of the *Reflections* gives no clue to Burke's importance, for, according to the judgment of his own age, that tract was chiefly a magnificent piece of wartime literature. Not until much later did it come to be acknowledged as the nearest approach to an accurate definition of whatever common political philosophy the English have.

Above all, no bare recital of the events of Burke's career can do justice to the impression he made on those who watched him. Here was this Irish parvenu, suddenly thrust, so to speak, into the royal enclosure of late eighteenth-century British politics, with a horde of doubtful or at the best scruffy relations in train, directing a series of political campaigns that cut to the foundations of government and empire, and thereby put an end to the preoccupation with minute particularities that had distinguished English public life ever since the Jacobite danger was expelled in 1745.

An Irishman about five feet ten inches in height and fifty years of age; wearing a tight brown coat and a little bob-wig with curls; near-sighted, so that as he spoke you might mark an occasional working of the brow, as you would also notice a beaky nose and a tight-pursed mouth; often harsh in tone and violent in gesticulation, and always speaking with much of the Irish accent and "an habitual undulating motion of the head . . . which had the appearance of indicating something of a self-confident or intractable spirit"; an Irishman you might have thought to be a schoolmaster if you had not known in advance that he was the Chrysostom of English politics. . . .

Thus vividly Sir Ernest Barker, in *Burke and Bristol, 1774–1780* (1931), recaptures Burke's effect on his Bristol constituents. It was not altogether appetizing. Among the eminent men of the day Burke had, indeed, fervent admirers, most notably Dr. Johnson. He was a conversational genius. His mind was shaped by the most valuable of all intellectual experiences, prolonged and undisciplined reading; he was grounded in history, in the classics, and in the Bible. What he took in was not merely stored, ready to be produced whenever the exigencies of debate or discussion required an epigram or an allusion; on the contrary, it supplied the material for a massive and powerful intellect, always under the sway of some consuming purpose, to weld into argument, and usually argument directed to some purpose no less comprehensive than the salvation of the state. Burke was equally capable, of course, of playing the part required of all his distinguished contemporaries, that of perpetual brain "trustee" to James Boswell and, in that capacity, of giving impromptu opinions on such matters as the relative merits of double and single beds in marriage. But though the vivacity and conviction with which Burke talked prevented him from ever being a bore, there is no evidence (for that cited by Boswell will not do) for the view that he had a sense of humor. He would wind himself into a subject, whether in the drawing room or on the floor of the House, thinking, worrying, qualifying as he went, until all this cautious, circuitous meditation yielded a conclusion exquisite in its balance and, because of the very patience with which it had been wrought, devastating in its effect. Women fainted when they heard him impeaching Hastings, and feared that, like William Pitt the elder, he would die from the force of his own eloquence. He had the sort of fanaticism that distinguishes men who are moderate not only by conviction but also from the subtlety of their minds and the sensibility of their hearts, and who cherish moderation so much that they are overpowered with anger, pity, and terror when it is assailed.

Add these qualities to the perpetual strain created by the suspicion of his origins, to the necessary unpopularity of many of his causes, to the defiant, unworldly magnanimity that made it impossible for him to betray a friend even when his friendship had become a taint in the eyes of others, and it is not hard to see why Burke never got cabinet office. The reason had nothing to do with the alleged defects of intellectuals—coldness, inability to get on with people, the reticence of pride. None of these qualities has ever prevented a man from being prime minister of England—the reasons for Burke's professional failure were totally different. Given the confidence of others, he could be a brilliant party manager, as he showed under Rockingham; but his prophetic anger was too great to make it easy for opponents to be reconciled with him. And since his course involved, without inconsistency, first the alienation of the Tories and then the alienation of the Whig admirers of the French Revolution, this was a serious defect. It was rendered fatal by the apparent doubtfulness of his credentials, which was always ready to the hands of his opponents. His response to their jeers and calumnies was of course often at fault, as in such cases it always must be; he was by turns haughtily indifferent and ferociously angry, but had he been by any ordinary standards a peevish and petulant character, he could never have remained at the heart of British politics for thirty-five years.

Only a little well-intentioned effort with some prospect of reward for compliance would have been needed in happier circumstances to contain his passion within the limits of what can be endured at Westminster. He had the misfortune of commanding an infinite and minute mastery of detail (exhibited particularly in his reports on India, his impeachment of Hastings, and his proposals for reforming the public economy) with an unrivaled grasp of principle. Mediocrity is disturbed by principle but humiliated by detail; Burke's talents could have been much more tactfully disposed. As it was, he had a prophet's reward, and his last years in Parliament were a period during which baiting Burke became one of the commonest diversions of the House. Gregories was the only refuge.

III

It is tolerable not to get office; it is not easy to bear the continual rejection of one's counsel. It is scarcely too much to say that each of the great practical aims of Burke's career appears to have been frustrated in his lifetime, a burden that cannot have been much lightened by the success of the *Reflections on the French Revolution* or even by a constant reputation among the best minds of the day for genius unequaled by anyone else in politics. To begin with, Burke set out to abolish the corruption of the constitution by royal patronage, a theme pursued in his pamphlet *Thoughts on the Cause of the Present Discontents* (1770). Burke gave the cause literary immortality, but his handling of it was a practical failure. The demand for a wider or more rational electoral franchise had already been heard; but Burke was against mechanical adjustments, believing that if the results of the Glorious Revolution settlement of 1688 could be defended against the encroachments of the crown that now bribed the Parliament it could no longer defy, the constitution would appear again in its historic perfection. Royal patronage was not abolished or substantially curtailed; instead the king gave the country a prime minister, the younger Pitt, whom it was possible until the middle of the twentieth century to describe without qualifying clauses as the greatest England has ever had; in the end the purification of the constitution, if so it must be deemed, was brought about by the very methods that Burke had rejected —that is, by widening the franchise and making it more uniform.

Burke sought to reform the government of India and to impeach Warren Hastings as the arch-representative of the cruelty and corruption that disfigured the government of India as then conducted by the chartered East India Company. The India Bill that he drafted for the Fox-North coalition merely led to the defeat of the coalition. The years spent in accusing Warren Hastings before the House of Lords according to the procedure known as impeachment (by which the House of Commons was empowered to bring servants of the crown before the House of Lords to answer for misconduct) ended in Hastings' acquittal. In one of the two greatest battles of his career, Burke tried to stop the government from driving the American colonies into rebellion by insisting to the full legal limit on the right to tax them, and then he tried to bring about conciliation with them; the War of Independence was not averted, but ended in the defeat of Britain and in a rupture between two English-speaking peoples, the full significance of which for the destiny of mankind intrigues and terrifies the imagination. It is true that the English eventually took up arms against the French Revolution, long after Burke had pleaded for intervention; but what drew them into the war was not the eloquence of Burke but the invasion of the Low Countries, to which British reaction was foreordained by history and geography. The impression of effort and passion spent without fruit that would have been left on any but a veritable knight of faith by this unmitigated record of rejected advice was crippling; and at the end, which came on 9 July 1797, Burke was almost crippled by it.

It would be satisfactory to add that on all these practical questions posterity had confirmed Burke's views; but judgments like this are usually superficial, and on many points the reverse may be said. There has been a reaction against what is commonly called "Whig history," against the view of English constitutional development that treats the crown as the invariable enemy and the Parliament as the constant friend of the people. Any undergraduate who has read Sir Lewis Namier now realizes that the institutions that Burke defended were as corrupt as the practices he assailed; that whereas he minded the king's giving sinecure posts, he did not mind the aristocracy's having rotten boroughs; that the effect of his reforms would not have been so much to purge the constitution as to destroy its inner balance by confirming the ascendancy of the aristocracy, which, freed from royal competition, would have been able to run Parliament to its own satisfaction. Everyone now knows that Lord North was not so feeble or foolish as the picture presented by Burke suggests, and that the arguments over American independence were not all on one side, a point that, it should be added, does not invalidate Burke's main contention that the attempt to tax the colonies by force was inexpedient. Certainly Burke's remedies for India, regarded as administrative proposals, had little influence on the slow development of an honorable British government there in the nineteenth century. It may be doubted whether earlier British interference in Europe against the French Revolution would have been wise, and it would certainly not have been in keeping with British diplomatic tradition.

It is clear, therefore, that the greatness of Burke is to be sought somewhere else than in the invariable correctness of his specific remedies for the discontents of the day. What has been claimed for him is that from all these speeches and writings there emerges a political philosophy, a complex philosophy incapable of being easily reduced to abstract expression, but nonetheless a coherent philosophy, and one that has had a unique part in shaping British political practice. Added to this is the incontestable claim that Burke was a great master of the written and spoken word, certainly a model for orators, but possibly also a master of elegant and exact writing.

IV

BEFORE Burke emerged into politics, he had written two books, one of which bears only indirectly on politics while the other has nothing to do with that subject; but both of them give some indication of the contribution he was to make to political philosophy. The satire on Bolingbroke, *A Vindication of Natural Society*, has all the appearance of a political tract even when its satirical intention is understood; but in reality it was an attack on Bolingbroke's religious opinions. Bolingbroke, a skeptic, had left for posthumous publication an assault on the whole idea of revealed religion and a defense for an alternative basis for moral judgment—that is, natural religion or the religion of reason. Burke's method of refuting him was to transfer the argument to the plane of politics and, posing as Bolingbroke, to take the artificial arrangements of society as the equivalent of revealed religion, and the political principles arising directly from reason as the equivalent of natural religion. If revealed religion, he argued, is a compound of traditions founded upon accident and hallowed by superstition and prejudice, so is the whole mechanism of civil society. If we are to embrace reason as the only guide to religious truth, so we must embrace reason as the only guide to political behavior. To do this is to condemn outright the arrangements of all known societies, to discredit all the methods by which society is kept together, to unleash universal chaos, and thus "to vindicate ourselves into perfect liberty."

It may be possible to have more than one opinion about the logic of this exercise of Burke's in reducing Bolingbroke to absurdity by transplanting his principles from religion to politics; the point is that Burke's purpose was not to vindicate artificial society by satirizing the notion of natural society, but to vindicate revealed religion by satirizing the notion of natural religion. The assumptions upon which the whole effect rests are that application of naked reason to the conduct of politics would produce disruption, and that this fact is in itself enough to refute the sovereignty of pure reason in politics. Burke took these propositions for granted; in them appears the germ of the great Burkian doctrine that prejudice, far from being the enemy of social good, provides the foundation and the motive power of every society; that without it social life would be as impossible as physical life would be if the act of breathing were always to require a conscious exercise of the rational will. In it also appears the germ of another idea that interpreters of Burke have often been apt to misunderstand: the idea that faith in tradition rests largely and legitimately on skepticism of the dependability of men's private reasoning. Later these doctrines will develop into something of massive intellectual power; at this time in Burke's career they are merely taken for granted.

The second of Burke's prepolitical treatises, *On the Sublime and Beautiful*, never deeply influenced aesthetic theory in England but had a profound influence on Immanuel Kant and much nineteenth-century German thought. Here it is characteristic of Burke that he should have followed the third earl of Shaftesbury, Joseph Addison, and others in deploring the habit of trying to discover the nature of beauty by studying beautiful objects, instead of by studying, with the aid of the best available psychological methods, the sentiments to which these objects appeal. Experience was the basis of his aesthetics, as it was to be of his politics.

Belief in the destructive effects of the application of pure reason to human affairs, in the utility of prejudice, in the importance of experiment and the observation of experience in the making of judgments, was the starting point of Burke's political thought. That thought was expressed in contributions to debates about matters that, far from being speculative, put in immediate question the survival of the country and the empire. The two greatest events of Burke's lifetime were also decisive for the whole course of modern history: the American War of Independence and the French Revolution. To use the jargon from which it is impossible altogether to free the discussion of politics, Burke's reaction to the first was liberal and to the second, conservative. These two contributions, though they may have occupied less of his time than did the affairs of India, contain the essence of Burke's political beliefs. The test of whether he had a consistent political philosophy depends largely on whether it is thought possible to reconcile them with each other.

V

THE controversies leading to the War of Independence give an extraordinarily clear picture of the main divisions over the principles of politics in late eighteenth-century England and America. The imposition of a stamp duty by the English government raised the purely legal question of whether the Parliament at Westminster was empowered to impose direct taxation on the colonies. This question was put shortly after the doctrine of parliamentary sovereignty, dating from the sixteenth century, had been given its most vigorous and systematic expression in the writing of Sir William Blackstone. When the stamp duty was withdrawn in deference to American protests, and an attempt made to raise the necessary revenue by new duties on American trade, the colonists shifted their ground, claiming that the home government had no right to impose even indirect taxation except for the purpose of regulating trade (as distinct from raising money). Soon the furies of fundamentalism were to be unleashed; the English government took its stand on the principle of sovereignty, not in the comparatively prosaic form in which that principle was later to be enunciated by the Benthamite jurist John Austin, but on the a priori grounds of Blackstone; soon the Americans were founding their case on the opposite dogma of natural rights. Constitutional Whigs like Pitt the elder and Charles Pratt, who derived their ideas from the conflicts of seventeenth-century England, took their stand on the doctrine of a historic fundamental law that limited, by custom and originally by divine ordinance, the spheres of the various organs of government, and therefore made sovereignty impossible. Burke's great contribution to this debate was a principle wholly different from that of any of these parties: utility based on historic empiricism.

It is worthwhile to analyze in detail the great speech that Burke delivered in the House of Commons on 22 March 1775, on moving his resolutions for conciliation with the colonies. He begins, after some formal courtesies designed to excuse his presumption in addressing the House at such length and at the same time to illustrate the superior consistency of his opinions, with an exposition of the nature and principles of the scheme he is proposing: "The proposition is peace." England must take the initiative in offering terms of reconciliation; this suggests two questions, the first of which is whether England ought to make concessions to the colonists, since reconciliation will be impossible without concession. Before this question is answered, Burke argues, "it may be necessary to consider distinctly the true nature and the peculiar circumstances of the object we have before us." England must govern America according to the circumstances that history and geography have created, "not according to our own imaginations, nor according to abstract ideas of right—by no means according to mere general themes of government, the resort to which appears to me, in our present situation, no better than arrant trifling."

Accordingly Burke sets out to give a detailed analysis of all the circumstances of the American colonies and their relationship to the mother country. The first thing, he mildly observes to a House now fully accustomed to debating the law and the metaphysics of the situation, is to consider how many people there are in the American colonies. He describes at length the growing size of the colonies, which increases so rapidly that while the House is "deliberating on the mode of governing two millions, we shall find we have millions more to manage." This is necessary in order to set the question in perspective, since the current assumption was that the American colonies were an unruly dependency; the mere contemplation of their size and potential power warned England, according to Burke, against trifling "with so large a mass of the interests and feelings of the human race." This is a theme that appeals strongly to Burke's imagination and evokes from him one of the most impressive passages in his work:

It is good for us to be here. We stand where we have an immense view of what is, and what is past. Clouds, indeed, and darkness rest upon the future. Let us, however, before we descend from this noble eminence reflect that this growth of our national prosperity has happened within the short period of the life of man. It has happened within 68 years. There are those alive whose memory might touch the two extremities. For instance, My Lord Bathurst might remember all the stages of the progress.[1]

(para. 25)

[1]All quotations are from W. Willis and F. W. Raffety, eds., *The Works*, 6 vols. (London, 1906–1907).

Burke goes on to imagine an angel unfolding to Bathurst as a child the future of the American colonies:

"Young man, there is America—which at this day serves for little more than to amuse you with stories of savage man, and uncouth manners; yet shall, before you taste of death, show itself equal to the whole of that commerce which now attracts the envy of the world. Whatever England has been growing to by a progressive increase of improvement, brought in by varieties of people, by succession of civilizing conquests and civilizing settlements in a series of seventeen hundred years, you shall see as much added to her by America in the course of a single life!"

(para. 25)

Burke reflects that for the child Bathurst to believe such a prophecy would have required "all the sanguine incredulity of youth, and all the fervid glow of enthusiasm." But "Fortunate man, he has lived to see it! Fortunate, indeed, if he lives to see nothing that shall vary the prospect, and cloud the setting of his day!"

There follows a digression on the general futility of force:

America, gentlemen say, is a noble object. It is an object well worth fighting for. Certainly it is, if fighting a people be the best way of gaining them. . . . my opinion is much more in favour of prudent management than of force; considering force not as an odious, but a feeble instrument for preserving a people so numerous, so active, so growing, so spirited as this, in a profitable and subordinate connexion with us. . . .

A further objection to force is, that you *impair the object* by your very endeavours to preserve it. The thing you fought for is not the thing which you recover; but depreciated, sunk, wasted, and consumed in the contest.

(paras. 31, 34)

Burke now resumes his analysis of the circumstances of America, turning to the American character. It has inherited an unusual devotion to liberty from the fact that the original settlers were Puritans fleeing from a hostile government. In the South, where the Episcopal church was strong, the submissiveness that this religious background might be expected to enjoy was entirely offset by the institution of slavery, for no one, Burke penetratingly observes, is harder to control than the master of a slave. Then he draws attention to the circumstance that the study of law was more popular in eighteenth-century America than in any other part of the world; and lawyers are by nature jealous of rights, not merely resenting oppression in fact but resenting it even in principle; finally, with a grand touch of contempt that must delight the heart of every political realist, he patiently reminds his colleagues in the House of Commons that "Three thousand miles of ocean lie between you and them. . . . Seas roll, and months pass, between the order and the execution; and the want of a speedy explanation of a single point is enough to defeat a whole system."

The analysis leads Burke to put the question, ignored by all the other participants in the debate, of how in fact one was to deal with such a people. There are three conceivable courses: First, to try to alter the conditions by restricting the growth of America; but if the government stopped its grants of land, what would the consequence be? "The people would occupy without grants." If the government tried to abate the high aristocratic state of Virginia, as some suggested it should, by declaring a general enfranchisement of their slaves, it would be necessary to induce the slaves to be freed—and "It is sometimes as hard to persuade slaves to be free, as it is to compel freemen to be slaves; and in this auspicious scheme we should have both these pleasing tasks on our hands at once." The second alternative, coercion, is again reviewed and dismissed for the reasons already implied in the analysis of the American character. There remains Burke's own policy, that of concession—or, as opponents of a later day would have dubbed it, "appeasement." The main objection leveled against it is that it would involve abandoning the right of taxation inherent in a sovereign. Then comes what to contemporaries was the most astonishing of all Burke's precepts:

Sir, I think you must perceive, that I am resolved this day to have nothing at all to do with the question of the right of taxation. Some gentlemen startle—but it is true; . . . I do not examine whether the giving away of a man's money be a power excepted and reserved out of the general trust of government, and how far all mankind, in all forms of polity, are entitled to an exercise of that right by the charter of nature; or, whether, on the contrary, a right of taxation is necessarily involved in the general principle of legislation, and inseparable from the ordinary supreme power. . . . high and reverend authorities lift up their heads on both sides, and there is no sure footing in the middle. . . . I do not intend to be overwhelmed in that bog, though in such respectable company. The question with me is, not whether you have a right to render your people miserable, but whether it is not your interest to make them happy.

(para. 66)

Burke goes on to ask what light English experience throws on the problem of the colonies. He takes the pacification of Ireland, or its relative pacification, that of Wales, and that of the palatinates of Chester and Durham as instances of the proven value of the policy of reconciliation. He concludes with six propositions that do no more than state the undisputed facts of the case, but that, without artifice, make the three resolutions embodying his plan of conciliation appear irresistible.

This ranks as the greatest speech of Burke's career. At the time it won unbounded admiration from his friends, particularly from Charles James Fox, and inspired respect among his foes. It was described by Lord Morley, the great liberal philosopher-statesman, who wrote Burke's life a century later, as an indispensable part of any man's instruction in statecraft, and as probably the greatest manifesto of the principles of liberal statesmanship ever produced. Lord Morley was a radical who, though the fact is scarcely remembered, resigned from Lord Asquith's administration on the eve of World War I rather than commit his country to what he regarded as the folly and futility of a modern war. It is remarkable that such a man as Morley should see in Edmund Burke, now commonly thought of as the philosopher of conservatism, the source of so much liberal wisdom. The explanation is that he was thinking of what used to be called the early Burke, on the assumption, though Morley was too percipient to make it consciously, that the French Revolution was a dividing line in Burke's life, as it was in William Wordsworth's. He could see Burke's speech on American conciliation, with some justice, as the charter of the self-governing empire. It was, in truth, the inspiration of the Quebec constitution of 1791, and the general principles of Burke's colonial policy may be said to have governed British policy toward its white subjects abroad ever afterward, a strange irony in view of the disproportionate time that Burke gave to the affairs of India and the elaboration of schemes for the welfare of that country that have had no discernible influence on its future.

What matters to a consideration of the consistency of Burke's thought is the political doctrine that emerges from the conciliation speech. It is not merely a guide to practical statesmanship; it contains at least some of the essentials of a philosophy of politics. Those who are determined to dissect can distinguish at least five major principles of general application in this magnificent exercise of the art of political analysis. There is, first and foremost, the principle of utility, the theory that no consideration of abstract right can be a sufficient basis for just authority and just obedience; that the proper end of government is the happiness of its subjects, and this should be the sovereign guide to its conduct, determining how far it shall press its authority in practice. Second, there is the principle that the character of a nation is the product of its history and geography, a principle to which systematic expression had been given by baron de Montesquieu in his *L'esprit des lois*, but so thoroughly assimilated by Burke that his elaborate enumeration of the circumstances that determine the American character would rank today as what is odiously called "geopolitics." Third, there is the germ, in a much modified form, of a doctrine very fashionable in eighteenth-century England, which took it from eighteenth-century France: the automatic harmony of interests. In Burke it assumes no more dogmatic form than the assertion that the view that force can accomplish everything is false and that, on the contrary, a country may often best promote its interests in the long run by curbing its ambitions in the short run. Fourth, there is the appeal to experience, the plea for a reverent consideration not of legal precedents but of the moral and political convictions of our ancestors. Last, and closely associated with it, the appeal to experiment, to the view that the consequences of action in politics are always so complex that every possible guide should be sought from history.

VI

Burke's *Reflections on the French Revolution* was first published in November 1790, while opinion in England was still divided on the merits of the revolutionary cause; it was repeatedly republished and, indeed, was largely responsible for rallying English opinion, though it was not the decisive step that Burke would have wished it to be toward converting England to the need for military intervention. It was subsequently much lengthened; and in its final form, though every sentence bears the mark of hav-

201

ing been deliberately forged for a purpose, it has not the economy and logical sequence of the speech on American conciliation. It is full of honest passion, and is inspired by Burke's characteristic conviction that it is the duty of a man not to be deaf to the counsels of the heart, but to submit them to the judgment of prudence. For these reasons it cannot be easily summarized. The form preserved throughout is that of a letter to a young Frenchman, which also gives Burke a latitude more fitting to his purpose of writing a political pamphlet than to that of scholars trying to distill a doctrine of politics from it. The argument starts with a comparison of the doctrines of the Glorious Revolution of 1688 with those of the French Revolution, a comparison arising from Burke's resentment of a sermon preached by Dr. Richard Price, the minister of the Old Jewry, in which the two were treated as parallels, and by the various pronouncements of the Constitutional Society and the Revolution Club in England. From this Burke proceeds to launch his attack on the French National Assembly, and to contrast the regime it is trying to establish with the established political and social order in England. The book contains an elaborate account of the various elements in the pre-Revolution constitution of France and in its social structure, and ends with a more detailed and full-scale denunciation of the National Assembly.

Burke, it must be remembered, is for the purposes of this study looking at the French Revolution with the eyes of a Frenchman—not, as he was looking at the American Revolution, with the eyes of an imperial statesman concerned to maintain a threatened link in the empire. In the case of America, the question is how authority should anticipate and react to a serious challenge; in the case of France, the question is the principles by which a state should be reformed. A precise parallel would be possible only if Burke had set out to advise Louis XVI in 1788 on how to cope with an impending revolution, and this he never did.

To those in search of Burke's political philosophy, certain passages in the *Reflections* stand out luminously. The starting point of the analysis must be the comparison of the proceedings of the English revolutionists in 1688 with those of the French revolutionaries of 1789. The English revolutionists set out to improve the state by correcting its corruptions, seeking diligently to preserve whatever they were not absolutely compelled to destroy in order to accomplish that reform; when they departed from

precedent, they did so with reluctance, and whenever they created something new, they tried to gain for it the respect due to age by absorbing it in their national tradition. The French might have followed their example:

> Your privileges, though discontinued, were not lost to memory. Your constitution, it is true, whilst you were out of possession, had suffered waste and dilapidation; but you possessed in some parts the walls, and, in all, the foundations, of a noble and venerable castle. You might have repaired those walls; you might have built on those old foundations.

Instead, the French had chosen to assert abstract principles professing to be universally valid, and to set up their own reason as superior to the reason of antiquity.

Burke, thus, is principally concerned to attack what later became known as rationalism in politics, and to oppose to it the method of gradual improvement based on the careful garnering of experience: "They wrought underground a mine that will blow up at one grand explosion all examples of antiquity, all precedents, charters, and acts of parliament. They have the 'rights of men' . . . against these no agreement is binding."

Burke then asks whether he is committed, by this enmity to rationalism in politics, to deny altogether the appeal to natural right; and he finds that he is not: "In denying their false claims of right, I do not mean to injure those which are real, and are such as their pretended rights would totally destroy. If civil society be made for the advantage of man, all the advantages for which it is made become his right." The test is always the same—that which conduces to the welfare of society is a human right: "Government is a contrivance of human wisdom to provide for human wants." To provide for human wants effectively, governments must bridle human passions, and "in this sense the restraints on men, as well as their liberties, are to be reckoned among their rights."

The necessary restraints, like the liberties, admit of infinite modifications: "They cannot be settled upon any abstract rule; and nothing is so foolish as to discuss them upon that principle."

This does not mean that reason has no part in determining human rights, or that human rights have no element of constancy in them but are merely makeshifts of convenience: "These metaphysic rights entering into common life, like rays of light which pierce into a dense medium, are, by the laws of nature, refracted from their straight line." Man's nature is infinitely complex and various, and his institutions must express this complexity and variety.

Burke returns to the English constitution founded upon church, crown, nobles, and commons; and from his analysis of it he draws two principles: that of organic growth reexpressed in terms of an adaptation of the theory of social contract, and that of balance between contending interests.

Society is indeed a contract. Subordinate contracts for objects of mere occasional interest may be dissolved at pleasure—but the State ought not to be considered nothing better than a partnership agreement in a trade of pepper and coffee, calico or tobacco, or some other such low concern, to be taken up for a little temporary interest and to be dissolved by the fancy of the parties. It is to be looked on with other reverence; because it is not a partnership in things subservient only to the gross animal existence of a temporary and perishable nature. It is a partnership in all science; a partnership in all art; a partnership in every virtue and in all perfection. . . . It becomes a partnership between not only those who are living, but between those who are living, those who are dead, and those who are yet to be born.

He defines the people as a sum total of all the separate orders and interests of society, when all these orders and interests act together in harmony (and this is only rarely so, because their natural condition is one of wholesome tension). "When great multitudes act together, under that discipline of nature, I recognize the people."

Even at the time of his bitterest enmity toward the Revolution, Burke never abandoned the view that great mass movements, however misguided, cannot be treated with mere contempt; his thoughts on the French constitution conclude with this passage:

The evil is stated, in my opinion, as it exists. The remedy must be where power, wisdom, and information, I hope, are more united with good intentions than they can be with me. I have done with this subject, I believe, for ever. It has given me many anxious moments for the two last years. If a great change is to be made in human affairs, the minds of men will be fitted to it, the general opinions and feelings will draw that way. Every fear, every hope, will forward it; and then they, who persist in opposing this mighty current in human affairs, will appear rather to resist the decrees of Providence itself, than the mere designs of men. They will not be resolute and firm but perverse and obstinate.

The real vice of the revolutionaries, Burke continually repeats, is the presumptuous demand for simplicity that leads them to renounce the past, to break all the solid links that hold society together, and to undermine the prejudices and conventions that are the basis of daily intercourse without examining the reasons behind them. He believes that one of the main danger points in this revolutionary process is the weakening of those lesser associations out of which society is formed and that are its cement.

To be attached to the subdivision, to love the little platoon we belong to in society, is the first principle (the germ as it were) of public affections. It is the first link in the series by which we proceed towards a love to our country, and to mankind. The interest of that portion of social arrangement is a trust in the hands of all those who compose it; and as none but bad men would justify it in abuse, none but traitors would barter it away for their own personal advantage.

The presumption of the revolutionaries is certain to fail, because it is a mere doctrine of naked force; this passion for abstract equality will end in tyranny. "The person who really commands the army is your master; the master . . . of your king, the master of your assembly, the master of your whole republic." In the career of Napoleon, Burke's prophecy was fulfilled to the letter.

VII

RECALL the different circumstances of the two pronouncements, and it is clear that Burke on America and Burke on France are essentially the same. The appeal to utility, the appeal to experiment, the appeal to experience, and the futility of force employed for any but limited and clearly defined ends are common to both. The difference is that in the *Reflections* they have received a more deliberate and majestic expression, at times so majestic as to give an impression of political mysticism that deluded many German admirers into believing that he anticipated Hegel. In reality Burke says in both pronouncements what he implied in everything else he wrote and said throughout his career: that sound political judgments are not to be made by employing only one faculty or appealing to only one intellectual authority; rather, they are complex, resting on an appeal to reason, checked by tradition and checked again by the carefully observed results of contemporary experience. He asks us to respect the past, not merely out of deference to the wisdom of our ancestors but also from doubt of our own private stock of wisdom; he asks us to respect tradition, not on the mystical ground that tradition is the voice of the people but largely on the practical ground that however bad a tradition may be, in proportion as it has shaped character, it has provided the material out of which alone reformed institutions can be forged. In *Reflections on the French Revolution* there is this lucid piece of common sense regarding the nature and function of prejudice in politics:

Many of our men of speculation, instead of exploding general prejudices, employ their sagacity to discover the latent wisdom which prevails in them. If they find what they seek, and they seldom fail, they think it more wise to continue the prejudice, with the reason involved, than to cast away the coat of prejudice, and to leave nothing but the naked reason; because prejudice, with its reason, has a motive to give action to that reason, and an affection which will give it permanence. Prejudice is of ready application in the emergency; it previously engages the mind in a steady course of wisdom and virtue, and does not leave the man hesitating in the moment of decision, sceptical, puzzled, and unresolved. Prejudice renders a man's virtue his habit; and not a series of unconnected acts. Through just prejudice, his duty becomes a part of his nature.

Burke is prevented from being a doctrinaire conservative by this English quality of doubt; he is the greatest of the English political philosophers of moderation in the line of Richard Hooker, the apologist of the English reformation; George Halifax, the Trimmer; and the great marquess of Salisbury. But he is not the possession of a political party. The British political system rests on the challenge and response of radicalism and conservatism; it is part of the essence of a radical that he uses the language of dogmatism in politics and sounds like the people whom Burke condemned; but it is also part of the essence of an English radical that he in practice recognizes that his utopia will not be fulfilled in the form in which he has conceived it, that he is contributing to a settlement of affairs that transcends the views of both Right and Left. Today this skeptical and empirical approach to politics is again being recognized by the English-speaking peoples as having the stature of a philosophy, and Burke has never enjoyed so prominent a place in the esteem of the academics.

In one outstanding respect Burke does not shed much direct light on contemporary politics: the politics of the late eighteenth century were not much preoccupied with the struggle between capital and labor, for industrial capitalism was scarcely born. Accordingly, Burke's views on the position of the poor in society are easy to dismiss as hypocrisy now:

They must labour to obtain what by labour can be obtained; and when they find, as they commonly do, the success disproportioned to the endeavour, they must be taught their consolation in the final proportions of eternal justice. Of this consolation whoever deprives them deadens their industry, and strikes at the root of all acquisition as of all conservation.

Yet even here Burke's teaching has its contemporary relevance: there is even in the atomic age a recurring gap between man's ambitions and his power to satisfy them; and the need for a principle that will reconcile him to his limitations is as great as ever.

"Ned," his cousin Will once remarked, using the measure of patriotism that occurred most easily to him, "works as hard as if he were getting twelve per cent from the Empire." Burke may have been disposed to ask on his deathbed what all the striving of this turbulent career had produced. The answer of posterity, at least in its present mood, must be "the nearest approach to an exact and comprehensive definition of the total contribution of the English-speaking peoples to the common stock of human wisdom about politics."

SELECTED BIBLIOGRAPHY

I. BIBLIOGRAPHY. Burke's papers, formerly at Wentworth Woodhouse, are now available for research at Sheffield University. W. B. Todd, *A Bibliography of Edmund Burke* (London, 1966), extends from the earliest printings of Burke in 1748 to the final issue of his collected works in 1827.

II. COLLECTED WORKS. F. Laurence and W. King, eds., *The Works*, 8 vols. (London, 1792–1827), later eds. published at London and Boston up to the end of the century in 16, 12, 9, and 8 vols. (the 16-volume text of 1803–1827 is the "definitive" ed.), the text, though often incorrect, has been used for all subsequent reprs. of Burke's writings; *The Speeches*, 4 vols. (London, 1816); R.

Laurence, ed., *The Epistolary Correspondence of Edmund Burke and French Laurence* (London, 1827); Earl Fitzwilliam and R. Bourke, eds., *Correspondence, 1744–97*, 4 vols. (London, 1844); W. Willis and F. W. Raffety, eds., *The Works*, 6 vols. (London, 1906–1907); *The Correspondence*: vol. I, *1744–68*, T. W. Copeland, ed. (Chicago–Cambridge, 1958); vol. II, *1768–74*, L. S. Sutherland, ed. (Chicago–Cambridge, 1960); vol. III, *1774–78*, G. H. Guttridge, ed. (Chicago–Cambridge, 1961); vol. IV, *1778–82*, J. A. Woods, ed. (Chicago–Cambridge, 1963); vol. V, *1782–89*, H. Furber, ed. (Chicago–Cambridge, 1965); vol. VI, *1789–91*, A. Cobban and R. A. Smith, eds. (Chicago–Cambridge, 1967); vol. VII, *1792–94*, P. J. Marshall and J. A. Woods, eds. (Chicago–Cambridge, 1968); vol. VIII, *1794–96*, R. B. McDowell, ed. (Chicago–Cambridge, 1970); vol. IX, *1796–97*, R. B. McDowell and J. A. Woods, eds. (Chicago–Cambridge, 1971), also contains additional letters; vol. X, *Index*, B. Lowe, ed. (Chicago–Cambridge, 1977), also contains additional letters.

III. Selected Works. E. J. Payne, ed., *Select Works*, 3 vols. (Oxford, 1874–1878); *Speeches and Letters on American Affairs* (London, 1908), with intro. by P. McKevitt; F. W. Raffety, ed., *Maxims and Reflections* (London, 1915); W. Morison, ed., *Select Speeches and Letters* (Cambridge, 1920); A. M. D. Hughes, ed., *Selections and Extracts* (London, 1921), contains essays by W. C. Hazlitt, M. Arnold et al.; H. Laski, ed., *Letters, Mainly Political* (London, 1922); L. N. Broughton, ed., *Selections* (New York, 1925); P. Magnus, ed., *Selected Prose* (London, 1948).

IV. Separate Works. *A Vindication of Natural Society* (London, 1756); *An Account of the European Settlements in America* (London, 1757), a collaboration by the Burke brothers, possibly with substantial contributions by Edmund; *A Philosophical Enquiry into the Origin of Our Ideas of the Sublime and Beautiful* (London, 1757), in J. T. Boulton, ed. (London, 1959), with intro.; *An Essay Towards an Abridgement of the English History* (London, 1757–1760), Burke contracted to finish the work by 25 December 1758 but apparently was still engaged on it in 1762—the portion now extant appears to have been printed in 1760 (see Todd); *Annual Register* (London, 1759–1766), Burke was principal ed. for those years but his contributions may have continued beyond 1766; *A Short Account of a Late Short Administration* (London, 1766), there may have been some collaboration with J. C. Roberts and W. Mellish, two officials in the "short" administration; *Observations on a Late State of the Nation* (London, 1769), written in answer to Knox's *Present State of the Nation*; *Thoughts on the Cause of the Present Discontents* (London, 1770); *Speech to the Electors of Bristol* (London, 1774); *Speech on American Taxation* (London, 1775); *Speech on Moving His Resolutions for Conciliation with the Colonies* (London, 1775).

Letter to the Sheriffs of Bristol on the Affairs of America (London, 1777); *Two Letters . . . to Gentlemen in the City of Bristol [on] the Trade of Ireland* (London, 1778); *Substance of the Speeches for the Retrenchment of Public Expenses* (London, 1779); *The Trial of the Honourable Augustus Keppel* (London, 1779), Burke made Keppel's formal defense and successfully refuted the charges against him; *A Letter . . . in Vindication of His Conduct with Regard to the Affairs of Ireland* (London, 1780); *Speech . . . for the Better Security of the Independence of Parliament* (London, 1780); *A Speech . . . in Bristol upon . . . His Parliamentary Conduct* (London, 1780); *Letter to a Peer of Ireland on the Penal Laws* (London, 1783); *Speech . . . on Mr. Fox's East India Bill* (London, 1784); *Speech Relative to the Nabob of Arcot's Debts* (London, 1785); *Articles of Charge Against Hastings* (London, 1786), these twenty-two charges later evolved into six articles of impeachment (1787); *Reflections on the Revolution in France and on the Proceedings in Certain Societies in London Relative to That Event* (London, 1790), rev. several times before publication, French trans. begun before publication of the English version and printed in November 1790; for the many printed observations and strictures on the *Reflections*, see *Cambridge Bibliography of English Literature*, vol. II, pp. 634–637; *Speech on the Army Estimates* (London, 1790); *An Appeal from the New to the Old Whigs* (London, 1791); *A Letter to a Member of the National Assembly* (London, 1791); *Two Letters on the French Revolution* (London, 1791).

A Letter to Sir Hercules Langrishe on the Subject of the Roman Catholics of Ireland (London, 1792); *Substance of the Speech . . . in Answer to Certain Observations in the Report of the Committee of Managers* [of the impeachment of Warren Hastings] (London, 1794); *A Letter to the Noble Lord on the Attacks Made upon Him and His Pension in the House of Lords* (London, 1796); *Two Letters . . . on the Proposals for Peace, with the Regicide Directory of France* (London, 1796); *A Letter . . . on the Conduct of the Minority in Parliament* (London, 1797); *Three Memorials on French Affairs . . .* (London, 1797); *Two Letters on the Conduct of Our Domestic Parties* (London, 1797); *Thoughts and Details on Scarcity Originally Presented to the Right Hon. William Pitt in the Month of November, 1795* (London, 1800); H. V. F. Somerset, ed., *Note-Book of Edmund Burke* (London, 1957).

V. Biographical and Critical Studies. C. M'Cormick, *Memoirs of Burke* (London, 1797); R. Bisset, *The Life*, 2 vols. (London, 1800); J. Prior, *Memoir of the Life and Character* (London, 1824); G. Groly, *A Memoir of the Political Life*, 2 vols. (London, 1840); F. H. Clark, *The Character of Edmund Burke* (London, 1845); P. Burke, *The Public and Domestic Life* (London, 1854); H. M. Butler, *The Character of Edmund Burke* (London, 1854); T. MacKnight, *History of the Life and Times*, 3 vols. (London, 1858–1860); J. Morley, *Burke* (London, 1879); E. A. Parkhurst, *Edmund Burke: A Study of His Life and Character* (London, 1886); T. S. Pillans, *Edmund Burke,*

Apostle of Justice and Liberty (London, 1905); N. Spinelli, *The Political Life* (London, 1908); J. McCunn, *The Political Philosophy* (London, 1913); A. P. I. Samuels, *The Early Life, Correspondence and Writings* (Cambridge, 1923), some of Burke's early writings are printed here for the first time; W. O'Brien, *Edmund Burke as an Irishman* (London, 1924); B. Newman, *Edmund Burke* (London, 1927); A. Cobban, *Edmund Burke and the Revolt Against the Eighteenth Century* (London, 1929).

E. Barker, *Burke and Bristol, 1774–1780* (Bristol, 1931); P. Magnus, *Burke* (London, 1939); A. M. Osborn, *Burke and Rousseau* (London, 1940); G. M. Young, *Burke* (London, 1943), the Annual Lecture on a Master Mind, presented to the British Academy; H. Laski, *Edmund Burke* (London, 1947), an address on the occasion of the bicentennial of the founding of the Club; E. E. Reynolds, *Edmund Burke, Christian Statesman* (London, 1948); T. W. Copeland, *Our Eminent Friend Edmund Burke* (New Haven, Conn., 1949); T. W. Copeland, *Edmund Burke, Six Essays* (London, 1950); L. Barry, *Our Legacy from Burke* (London, 1952); C. Parkin, *The Moral Basis of Burke's Political Thought* (London, 1956); F. L. Lucas, *The Art of Living. Four Eighteenth-Century Minds: Hume, Horace Walpole, Burke, Benjamin Franklin* (London, 1959); P. J. Stanlis, ed., *The Burke News Letter*, vols. I–VIII (Detroit, 1959–1967), a journal that was continued by *Studies in Burke and His Times* (see below); T. Mahoney, *Edmund Burke and Ireland* (Cambridge, Mass., 1960); F. D. Canavan, *The Political Reason of Edmund Burke* (London, 1960); T. H. D. Mahoney, *Edmund Burke and Ireland* (London, 1960); S. R. Graubard, *Burke, Disraeli, and Churchill: The Politics of Perseverance* (Cambridge, Mass., 1961); R. R. Fennessy, *Burke, Paine and the Rights of Man: A Difference of Political Opinion* (New York, 1963); C. P. Courtney, *Montesquieu and Burke* (London, 1963); an assessment of Burke's indebtedness to Montesquieu; C. B. Cone, *Burke and the Nature of Politics. The Age of the American Revolution*, 2 vols. (Lexington, Ky., 1965); H. Mansfield, *Statesmanship and Party Government: A Study of Burke and Bolingbroke* (Chicago, 1965); G. W. Chapman, *Edmund Burke: The Practical Imagination* (Cambridge, Mass., 1967); *Studies in Burke and His Time*, vols. IX–XIX (Detroit, 1967-1978), the continuation of *The Burke News Letter*, ceased publication after vol. XIX; F. O'Gorman, *Edmund Burke: His Political Philosophy* (Bloomington, Ind., 1973); D. Cameron, *The Social Thought of Rousseau and Burke: A Comparative Study* (Toronto, 1973); I. Kramnick, *Edmund Burke* (Englewood Cliffs, N.J., 1974), the Great Lives Observed series; I. Kramnick, *The Rage of Edmund Burke: Portrait of an Ambivalent Conservative* (New York, 1977).

WILLIAM COWPER
(1731-1800)

Norman Nicholson

I

FROM the end of the eighteenth century to nearly the middle of the nineteenth, William Cowper was probably the most widely read—at least in England—of any English poet. Even today a few of his hymns are sung throughout the English-speaking world. His place in literary history is secure; he brought a new kind of directness into descriptive poetry, showing the English country scene more as it really was and less as it was imagined to be. His place is secure, too, in the affection of all who know him from his correspondence.

The word "exciting" is perhaps the most overused cliché in modern criticism, and it is refreshing to be able to say of Cowper's poetry that it did not set out to be exciting. Excitement, indeed, was an experience he disliked and even feared, so that, instead of writing of the exciting, the strange, the rare, he celebrated the usual, the everyday, the humdrum. Though the world he depicted disappeared well over a century ago, it is one that, in some ways, is still close to us. His pleasures—the greenhouse, the garden, the fireside, the cup of tea—are still enjoyed. The landscape he described is surprisingly like that still to be seen on the edge of towns—a landscape not of mountains, torrents, and romantic wildness, but of hedges, walls, roads, ditches, puddles, plowland, and pigsties. Cowper, at first acquaintance, seems to be essentially the poet of the commonplace, the commonsensible, and the sane.

Yet throughout his life he was threatened by madness, and in this contrast lies much of the fascination of his personality and his poetry. For Cowper—the least paradoxical of poets in style—was a paradox in himself. His life was a sad one, yet his poetry is largely the poetry of pleasure. He was a recluse, an oddity, a refugee from the way of the world, yet he became a spokesman for the conscience of the middle class and a powerful voice among the forces of humanitarianism. He lived in an out-of-the-way village, meeting scarcely anyone but a few selected friends, yet he was able to exercise an immense influence on the society of his time. In his later years he believed himself to be damned and found no comfort in religion, yet his poems were treasured in thousands of houses that admitted no other books but the Bible and *The Pilgrim's Progress*. It is not surprising that the contradictions of his nature should have provoked the attention of many biographers, but it is a pity that interest in his psychology should have been allowed to obscure, to some extent, the fact that he is one of the most agreeable and companionable poets in the whole range of English literature.

II

COWPER was born on 15 November 1731 at Great Berkhamsted, in Hertfordshire, where his father, who was a nephew of the first earl Cowper, was the rector. His mother was related to the family of the poet John Donne, and she was the center of her son's life during his early years. She died when he was only six, but his memory of her and his love for her remained with him throughout his life. When, more than fifty years later, his cousin Mrs. Bodham sent him a copy of his mother's picture, he was able to recall, vividly and tenderly, the days at the rectory when she was still alive:

> Where once we dwelt our name is heard no more,
> Children not thine have trod my nurs'ry floor;
> And where the gard'ner Robin, day by day,
> Drew me to school along the public way,
> Delighted with my bauble coach, and wrapt
> In scarlet mantle warm, and velvet capt,
> 'Tis now become a history little known,
> That once we call'd the past'ral house our own. . . .
> Thy nightly visits to my chamber made,
> That thou might'st know me safe and warmly laid;

Thy morning bounties ere I left my home,
The biscuit, or confectionary plum;
The fragrant waters on my cheeks bestow'd
By thy own hand, till fresh they shone and glow'd.[1]
("On the Receipt of My Mother's Picture," 46–53; 58–63)

No modern poet would dare write such a poem for fear of what the psychologists would say. But there is no need to call in Sigmund Freud to see that his mother's death was the first, and perhaps the chief, tragedy of Cowper's life. When she had gone, he lost confidence in himself. In all his relations with women, he seems to have been seeking what would now be called a mother substitute; and it may well have been this, as much as anxiety about his mental condition, that made him avoid marriage.

Moreover, his mother's death destroyed Cowper's trust in the world. He felt cheated, and the well-meant efforts of the servants to protect him from the realization of his loss only emphasized this sense of having been deceived:

My mother! when I learn'd that thou wast dead,
Say, wast thou conscious of the tears I shed?
Hover'd thy spirit o'er thy sorrowing son,
Wretch even then, life's journey just begun?
. . .
Thy maidens griev'd themselves at my concern,
Oft gave me promise of a quick return.
What ardently I wish'd, I long believ'd,
And, disappointed still, was still deceiv'd;
By disappointment every day beguil'd,
Dupe of *to-morrow* even from a child.
(20–23; 35–40)

The loss of his mother was followed by what must have seemed like the loss of his home, for he was sent to a boarding school seven miles away, at a village called Market Street, where he was bullied and badgered until his nervous condition brought on a weakness of the eyes. Then, after treatment by Mrs. Disney, an oculist, he was moved to Westminster School in London. Westminster at that time ranked second only to Eton among public schools, but life there was harsh, frugal, and often brutal. Yet, oddly enough, Cowper seems to have been fairly happy. Later he attacked the educational system of his time for its lack of moral instruction, but his recorded memories of his school days are surprisingly cheerful:

[1]All quotations are from H. Milford, ed., *The Complete Poetical Works* (London, 1934).

We love the play-place of our early days
. . .
The wall on which we tried our graving skill,
The very name we carv'd, subsisting still;
The bench on which we sat while deep employ'd,
Tho' mangled, hack'd, and hew'd, not yet destroy'd;
The little ones, unbutton'd, glowing hot,
Playing our games, and on the very spot;
As happy as we once, to kneel and draw
The chalky ring, and knuckle down at taw.
("Tirocinium: or A Review of Schools,"
297; 300–307)

After leaving Westminster, Cowper decided—if that is not too strong a word—to study law. He lived for a time at the house of Mr. Chapman, an attorney, and was admitted to the Middle Temple and then the Inner Temple, in the latter of which he bought rooms in 1757. It is obvious that he was quite unfitted for the profession of the law, yet his days as a student were important to him because he enjoyed the company of his fellow students and, still more, because it was then that he met his cousins Harriet and Theodora, daughters of Ashley Cowper. Harriet, the elder, who married Sir Thomas Hesketh, was later the recipient of some of the most enchanting letters in the English language, but it was Theodora with whom Cowper fell in love. He was no more fitted to be a lover than a barrister, and though Theodora seems to have loved him deeply, it is doubtful that he would ever have faced the responsibility of marriage. But the choice was not left with him, for after an engagement had dragged on for a number of years, the girl's father insisted that it should be broken off. It was scarcely a harsh decision, for Cowper was not only without prospects but was also showing signs of depression and mental instability. He was assailed by strange fears that took a religious form. He began to think of himself as being singled out from among all men for ridicule and shame. Indeed, this sense of being "singled out" is most characteristic of Cowper. His melancholy was always essentially personal. Though he was often in despair about himself, he did not feel that the rest of mankind was involved in the same predicament. When, in a famous passage of *The Task*, he called himself "a stricken deer, that left the herd," he did not imply that there was anything wrong with the herd.

About the time of the breaking of the engagement, Cowper's father died, leaving no great fortune. The other members of his family, anxious that Cowper should start to earn his living, used their influence to obtain the offer of two administrative posts in the House of Lords—that of reading clerk and that of clerk of the committees. It was, on the face of it, exactly what he had been waiting for, but it forced on him the very thing he most wanted to avoid—the need to make up his mind. At once he began to imagine the most fantastic objections to the new posts. Cowper could not bring himself to undergo the formal examination that would be necessary, and he fancied that he was guilty by desire of the death of the man who held the positions before him. Finally, he tried to commit suicide, and his friends had to have him confined to an asylum.

Up to this time Cowper had had no special contact with the Evangelical movement, but now the religious fears of his boyhood returned, exaggerated and distorted. In a dream he saw himself shut out from a band of Christian worshippers. He began to brood over the Calvinist doctrine of predestination and to pervert it into the horrible idea that he alone, among all believers, was inevitably damned. But if religion suggested the form of his madness, it was also to provide, at least for a time, its antidote. Cowper passed from despair into resignation, and from resignation into hope; and then, reading a text in the Epistles of St. Paul (Rom. 3:25), he felt a sudden inrush of joy and grace. He was now able to leave the asylum. His friends and his relatives (Theodora among them) arranged to allow him a small pension, and his brother Jack, a don at Cambridge, found lodgings for him nearby at Huntingdon. Here he made friends with the Unwins, with whom he went to live at Huntingdon and then, after the death of Mr. Unwin, at Olney. With the Unwins he entered into the life of a typical Church of England Evangelical family, and at Olney he joined in the active work of a revivalist parish. For good or bad, these two experiences shaped the next stage of his life. At Huntingdon he was made happy; at Olney he was made a poet. From now on, his life, however secluded, was to be part of the most powerful popular social movement of the eighteenth century.

III

It may surprise some modern readers to hear of happiness being associated with the Evangelical revival, but this is because they confuse the Evangelicalism of the eighteenth century with the Puritanism of the sixteenth and seventeenth centuries. The two movements of course had some things in common. In both the emphasis was entirely on salvation. In both there was an acute awareness of a direct relationship between man and God; in both there was a distrust of certain kinds of pleasure. There were also many important differences. The Puritans were strongly political; they were in revolt against the liturgy and government of the Church of England; they were immensely interested in theology—none of which was true of the Evangelicals. More important still for an understanding of Cowper, the Puritans were by nature gloomy and austere, while the Evangelicals were bright and genial. The revival, in fact, was a romantic movement, one of feeling rather than of belief, for the Evangelicals were in revolt against the eighteenth-century ideal of reason and common sense, against a materialist society, and against a mechanistic view of nature that drained the mystery and wonder out of the world. A parallel revolt could be seen outside religious circles in the popularity of sentimental novels and medieval romances, in the cult of Gothic architecture and wild scenery. But such diversions meant nothing to the ordinary, often undereducated man of the time, who turned instead to the chapel and the prayer meeting, finding there a new exhilaration, a release of pent-up energies.

The violent manifestations that appeared at the gatherings of the more famous preachers—the swoonings, the fits, the hysterical sobbing—belonged to the two extremes of the movement—the Wesleyan Methodists, led by John and Charles Wesley, and the Calvinist Methodists, led by George Whitefield, both of which eventually broke away from the Church of England. The Evangelicals who remained within the church were of a quieter temper. In theology they were Calvinist, but their Calvinism had nothing of the intolerance and bigotry often found among the Dissenters who followed Whitefield. Temperamentally they had much more in common with the non-Calvinist branch of the revival, with John and Charles Wesley and their gospel of good news. But they were much more restrained than the Wesleys. They had less missionary zeal and more sense of propriety in religion. The impetuous fire that flared throughout Methodism was replaced in their case by a quiet, steady, decorous glow.

Yet there is no doubt about the warmth of that glow, nor that it thawed Cowper into a new life. In a letter of October 1766 to his cousin's wife, he gives a detailed picture of the daily round in the Unwin household at Huntingdon:

We breakfast commonly between eight and nine; till eleven, we read either the Scripture, or the sermons of some faithful preacher of those holy mysteries; at eleven we attend divine service, which is performed here twice every day; and from twelve to three we separate and amuse ourselves as we please. During the interval I either read in my own apartment, or walk, or ride, or work in the garden. We seldom sit an hour after dinner, but if the weather permits, adjourn to the garden, where with Mrs. Unwin and her son I have generally the pleasure of religious conversation till tea-time. If it rains, or is too windy for walking, we either converse within doors, or sing some hymns . . . and by the help of Mrs. Unwin's harpsichord make up a tolerable concert, in which our hearts, I hope, are the best and most musical performers. After tea we sally forth to walk in good earnest. Mrs. Unwin is a good walker, and we have generally travelled about four miles before we see home again. . . . At night we read and converse, as before, till supper, and commonly finish the evening either with hymns or a sermon; and last of all the family are called to prayers. I need not tell *you*, that such a life as this is consistent with the utmost cheerfulness; accordingly we are all happy, and dwell together in unity as brethren.

(letter to Mrs. Cowper, 20 October 1766)

There is no cause whatever to doubt this final assertion of Cowper's—such a life may seem dull and excessively pious, but it was certainly not inconsistent with cheerfulness. Cowper, in fact, was cheerful for almost the first time in his adult life. His days with the Unwins gave him all he ever knew of earthly felicity. For a few months, at least, his religious fervor charged his life with a new significance and, like a love affair, lifted him above the flats of day-to-day monotony. It set his senses trembling like wires and gave him a new awareness of the world around him. It did not—or not immediately—make him a poet, but it gave him the experience that eventually made poetry possible.

On the other hand, it may be argued that the religious tone of the Unwin house was pitched too high for Cowper's nerves. And the pitch was raised still higher when, after the death of Mr. Unwin, Cowper and the widowed Mary Unwin moved to the village of Olney, where they came into close contact with the Reverend John Newton, who was curate there. Newton was one of the most challenging personalities of the revival. His early life had been wild and blasphemous. He had been press-

ganged onto a naval ship, had been flogged, had worked as a slave in the American plantations, and had himself been captain of a slave ship. Then he was converted, took orders in the Church of England, and became a vigorous, strong-willed, uncompromising Evangelical, very different in temper from the mild-mannered Unwins. But Newton should not be thought of as a hardhearted religious fanatic—the man who wrote the hymn "How Sweet the Name of Jesus Sounds" certainly must have had some sweetness in his own character. His theology, indeed, was never extreme or narrow. Nor should he be blamed for infecting Cowper with the fear of damnation, for this was with the poet long before he went to Olney. But he undoubtedly led Cowper into a most exacting life of piety, prayer meetings, self-denial, and visiting the sick; and this, as anyone but Newton could surely have seen, was far too great a strain on the poet's nervous system. Before long he began to be discouraged, to feel flickerings of his former fears. Newton seems to have sensed something of this and, to distract him, suggested that the two of them collaborate in writing a volume of religious verse. The result of this suggestion was the *Olney Hymns*.

As might be expected, most of the hymns written by Cowper for this volume are lukewarm and uncertain, the forced and mechanical expression of a doctrine that was by then more of an anxiety than a comfort. Even at the height of his religious enthusiasm, he was not really a hymn singer. He had little experience of hymn singing as a corporate act in which the individual is carried away in the sweep and flood of a shared emotion. Yet in a handful of hymns, when the draft blows through the dying clinkers of faith, he was able to rekindle the fire of his early conversion and to write hymns that a congregation can take to its heart. "O! for a Closer Walk with God," "Hark, My Soul! It Is the Lord," and "God Moves in a Mysterious Way" have become part of the folk poetry of Protestant England.

The success of a hymn does not depend primarily on its poetry. A hymn is a poem written for a special purpose; and unless it fulfills this, it fails as a hymn. The purpose, of course, is to be sung by a congregation; and to make this practicable, it must be regular in structure, simple in language, broad in imagery, and unified in theme. Moreover, it must have that touch of the obvious that is found in all popular art.

The great English hymnists have generally belonged to one of two main traditions: that of Isaac Watts and that of Charles Wesley. Watts was the better poet. He filled his hymns with broad, universal images that could evoke a response in every singer:

> Time like an ever-rolling stream
> Bears all its sons away.

Wesley was the better craftsman. He relied less on poetic imagery and sought instead, by precise and often felicitous statement, to teach Christian doctrine and to communicate the exuberance of his own religious experience.

Cowper derives more from Watts than from Wesley. Like Watts, his favorite images are taken from nature, but as compared with the earlier poet, they are less generalized. One feels that his skies, seas, and storms, though known to everyone, are seen with a personal eye. They are common symbols, but symbols drawn in an individual style:

> God moves in a mysterious way,
>   His wonders to perform;
> He plants his footsteps in the sea,
>   And rides upon the storm.
>
> Deep in unfathomable mines
>   Of never-failing skill,
> He treasures up his bright designs,
>   And works his sovereign will.
>   ("Light Shining Out of Darkness")

These lines remind one of John Milton as well as of Isaac Watts, and the Miltonic ring is still louder in the hymn "Opening a Place of Social Prayer":

> Jesus, where'er thy people meet,
> There they behold thy mercy-seat;
> Where'er they seek thee thou art found,
> And ev'ry place is hallow'd ground.
>
> For thou, within no walls confin'd,
> Inhabitest the humble mind.
>   . . .
> Here may we prove the pow'r of pray'r,
> To strengthen faith, and sweeten care;
> To teach our faint desires to rise,
> And bring all heav'n before our eyes.[2]

Again, like Milton, Cowper's imagination was held and stirred by the Bible and especially by the

Old Testament. To English Protestants the Old Testament had become almost a national myth. They accepted it as the literal word of God and as a factual early history of mankind. But, at the same time, they saw it as a romance, a great roaring balladry of heroes, priests, and prophets, set in the dramatic landscape of the desert and the bare limestone uplands of Judea. It was not, of course, the kind of landscape in which Cowper could feel truly at home: he needed a softer, damper soil for his imagination to grow. Yet the myth, with its varied and ambiguous imagery, left its mark on his poetry and more particularly on the *Olney Hymns*, in one of which he penetrates very deeply into the substratum of meaning beneath the Old Testament symbols:

> There is a fountain fill'd with blood
>   Drawn from Emmanuel's veins;
> And sinners, plung'd beneath that flood,
>   Lose all their guilty stains.
>   ("Praise for the Fountain Opened")

This hymn, with its combination of sacramental and anatomical imagery, is not to the taste of the average modern congregation. But it is of immense interest to both the anthropologist and the psychologist, for in it one is aware of rituals even older than the Old Testament: of the dying god of the fertility cults and of primitive symbols that probe deeply into the subconscious.

Cowper's most characteristic hymns are his more personal ones. As a rule the personal devotional poem does not make a good hymn; it is too much like a private prayer to be sung in chorus. But with Cowper it is different. Take, for instance, one of his most famous hymns:

> Oh! for a closer walk with God,
>   A calm and heav'nly frame;
> A light to shine upon the road
>   That leads me to the Lamb!
>
> Where is the blessedness I knew
>   When first I saw the Lord?
> Where is the soul-refreshing view
>   Of Jesus, and his word?
>
> What peaceful hours I once enjoy'd!
>   How sweet their mem'ry still!
> But they have left an aching void,
>   The world can never fill.

[2]Compare Milton, "Il Penseroso":
>   Dissolve me into ecstasies
>   And bring all heav'n before mine eyes.

Return, O holy Dove, return,
  Sweet messenger of rest;
I hate the sins that made thee mourn,
  And drove thee from my breast.

The dearest idol I have known,
  Whate'er that idol be;
Help me to tear it from thy throne,
  And worship only thee.

So shall my walk be close with God,
  Calm and serene my frame;
So purer light shall mark the road
  That leads me to the Lamb.
              ("Walking with God")

That, surely, is essentially a private devotional poem rather than a congregational hymn. The second and third stanzas refer to Cowper's own life and have a delicacy of sentiment that could hardly be shared by the ordinary, hot-gospeling convert of the time. Yet the lines are astonishingly good for congregational singing, for the imagery is so simple, so clear and glowing, that everyone can recognize its truth. An intensely personal experience has become the expression of a universal longing; a backward look at those first days at Huntingdon has become an emblem of man's nostalgia for Eden, his regret for his lost innocence.

IV

NEWTON had hoped that the writing of the *Olney Hymns* would raise Cowper's spirits and distract him from his melancholy, but in this he was disappointed. In January 1773 the poet was afflicted with another bout of madness, and the next month came the terrible dream in which he thought he heard the voice of God pronouncing irrevocable damnation. For a year he lived at the vicarage under Newton's care; and when, eventually, he was well enough to return to his house, Orchard Side, he was greatly changed. Religion now seemed to offer him nothing but the threat of damnation, to distract himself from which he turned to his garden, his pets, and the countryside. Even the presence of Newton was now something of an embarrassment, and it was probably a relief when he left Olney in 1780 to become vicar of St. Mary Woolnoth in London.

But with Newton's departure Cowper had more time than ever on his hands, so that, at the age of forty-nine, he took up poetry as a kind of occupational therapy. He wrote, first of all, a few occasional verses, and then asked Mrs. Unwin to suggest a subject; she suggested "The Progress of Error." It was obviously not a very good choice, and led to a series of eight moral satires, with titles like "Truth," "Hope," and "Charity," that are merely dull and rather naive versifications of Calvinist doctrine. Nevertheless, the writing of these poems may have helped Cowper, for they enabled him to work the Evangelicalism out of his system. They also gave him a chance to exercise his muscles in the technique of verse, and above all they got him into the habit of composition—for poetry, with Cowper, was a matter more of routine than of inspiration.

Then, in the summer of 1781, Lady Austen, an attractive young widow, came to visit her sister, who was the wife of the vicar of the next parish. She at once took a fancy to the poet, who, in spite of his oddness and timidity, had a strong attraction for women. Almost before he knew what was happening, he was picnicking in Weston Woods, lunching out three days a week, and even composing a comic ballad ("John Gilpin"), which was soon sung all over London and is still widely known. It was a delightful experience, but it could not go on forever. Lady Austen was not the sort to be satisfied by an ambiguous, half-and-half relationship, yet anything else was impossible to Cowper, whose first emotional allegiance was to Mary Unwin. So, after a year or two, Lady Austen decided to break off the friendship and leave Olney; but before she left, she performed an immense service both to poetry and to the poet. One day, when Cowper was searching for a subject for a poem in blank verse, she playfully suggested that he should write on the sofa. And that was the beginning of *The Task*.

The Task is one of the happiest accidents in English literature. At first Cowper seems to have had little idea of the way in which the poem would develop. He begins, as requested, by writing about the sofa, but succeeds only in producing a hundred lines of the stiffest mock heroic, a parlor parody of Milton. Then, suddenly, with an ingenious trick maneuver, he twists out of the situation like a man escaping from a jail:

Oh may I live exempted (while I live
Guiltless of pamper'd appetite obscene)
From pangs arthritic, that infest the toe
Of libertine excess. The Sofa suits

The gouty limb, 'tis true; but gouty limb,
Though on a Sofa, may I never feel:
For I have lov'd the rural walk through lanes
Of grassy swarth, close cropt by nibbling sheep,
And skirted thick with intertexture firm
Of thorny boughs. . . .

(I. 103–112)

Sofa or no sofa, the reader is out in the open air, and will remain there for the better part of this poem.

It is doubtful that Cowper himself could have said what the poem was about without referring to the argument printed at the head of each section. In the first two books, in particular, he continually shifts his direction. Starting with the praise of country scenes, he manages to include gypsy life, slavery, and the duties of the clergy. But in the last four books he comes to see more clearly what his true aim should be: "to discountenance the modern enthusiasm after a London life, and to recommend ease and leisure, as friendly to the cause of piety and virtue." Or, to quote the most quoted line in the poem, "God made the country and man made the town."

Once Cowper had realized this, the poem took on a new unity. Book III deals largely with the greenhouse; book IV, with the winter evening, the tea urn, and pictures in the fire. Book V contains the wonderful description of the countryside under snow, while in book VI, Cowper depicts the spring world and goes on to his most eloquent defense of the rights of animals.

The Task is neither philosophical nor didactic, nor even autobiographical. It is discursive, a one-sided correspondence or a conversation between poet and reader. It is beautifully adapted to the tone of the poet's voice—a voice oddly personal, both pedantic and humorous, reserved and yet intimate. Except in rhetorical passages it has a curious slackness, an underpitching of the note that sets sounding gentle harmonics of poignancy. To those who love Cowper, his poetry is valued as much for what it reveals of the man as for its literary merits. He can be permitted faults that would be unpardonable in any other poet. His sometimes ponderous rhetoric, his milk-and-water Miltonisms, his pedantries, his platitudes—all these are forgiven not for the sake of the poetry but for the sake of the man. One might almost say that his style does not so much reveal him as give him away.

These delightful givings-away make up one of the chief pleasures to be gained from his verse. He can scarcely write two lines of what is intended to be purely factual description without showing his characteristic honesty and hesitation. At the beginning of book IV of *The Task*, he writes of the boy who delivered the mail:

Hark! 'tis the twanging horn o'er yonder bridge,
That with its wearisome but needful length
Bestrides the wintry flood, in which the moon
Sees her unwrinkled face reflected bright.

(IV. 1–4)

One notices, first, the clarity of the observation—the face of the moon is "unwrinkled" because the water is no longer flowing but is lying still, perhaps frozen, in the meadows. But when Cowper speaks of "wearisome" length, one is conscious that he has transposed to the bridge the physical tiredness he himself felt when he returned from a long walk through the muddy Midland lanes. And immediately, before he has finished his phrase, he realizes that he has been unfair, at once qualifies his statement, and, as it were, apologizes to the bridge. Its length may be wearisome, but it is needful. The word "needful" adds nothing to the picture. It is, by all rules, redundant, flat, and obvious. Yet it lets one look right into the hesitant, veering mind of the poet, and has the spontaneity of a half-rubbed-out pencil line in the sketchbook of a master.

When Cowper recommended country life as "friendly to the cause of piety and virtue," he was, of course, repeating a commonplace of Evangelical morality. But to him the sentiment was not commonplace; it was vital. To him country life was a physical necessity; it offered the only possible way of living. Away from the country he would have been in a madhouse in six months and probably in his grave in twelve. There are times when he indulges in a Rousseau-like longing for the lost age of the noble savage:

Oh for a lodge in some vast wilderness,
Some boundless contiguity of shade,
Where rumour of oppression and deceit,
Of unsuccessful or successful war,
Might never reach me more! . . .

(II. 1–5)

But Cowper did not always attain such broadness of gesture. More often he wrote of the country as if he were writing a doctor's prescription; indeed, his walks and his gardening were as much a rule of

213

health as a matter of personal choice. He turned to the country because he loved it, but he turned to it also because he was afraid to turn anywhere else:

> I was a stricken deer, that left the herd
> Long since; with many an arrow deep infixt
> My panting side was charg'd, when I withdrew
> To seek a tranquil death in distant shades.
> There was I found by one who had himself
> Been hurt by th' archers. In his side he bore,
> And in his hands and feet, the cruel scars.
> With gentle force soliciting the darts,
> He drew them forth, and heal'd, and bade me live.
> Since then, with few associates, in remote
> And silent woods I wander, far from those
> My former partners of the peopled scene;
> With few associates, and not wishing more.
>
> (III. 108–120)

The cult of the countryside as a retreat from the cares and vices of the world is older than the Evangelical movement and older even than Christianity, but many of the poets who have praised the excellence of rural peace probably knew very little about it. Cowper was not one of these. His approach to the country is never sentimental and usually strictly practical, though that may seem a strange word to apply to one who relied so much on the patience and charity of his friends. Yet, in his peculiar circumstances, could any man have been more practical? Faced with the fear of madness, he began to build a defensive wall of habit. He took regular walks; he planted and weeded and pruned; he made hutches for his tame hares and frames for his greenhouse. There was no place for idleness in his conception of the life of the solitary:

> The morning finds the self-sequester'd man
> Fresh for his task, intend what task he may.
>
> (III. 386–387)

Gradually Cowper became acutely conscious of his immediate physical environment. He took root like a cabbage. He felt that he belonged to Olney, and would have been incapable of writing anywhere else. To be in a familiar place and among familiar objects gave him a sense of stability in what was otherwise a tottering world:

The very stones in the garden-walls are my intimate acquaintances. I should miss almost the minutest object, and be disagreeably affected by its removal, and am persuaded that were it possible I could leave this incommodious nook for a twelvemonth, I should return to it again with rapture, and be transported with the sight of objects which to all the world beside would be at least indifferent.

(letter to John Newton, 27 July 1783)

Apart from his occasional melancholy, Cowper was never bored. The uneventful life at Olney was full of small adventures that he recounted with the greatest relish in his correspondence. There was the day the parliamentary candidate called, shook Cowper's hand, kissed the ladies and even the maid in the kitchen, "and seemed a most loving, kissing, kind-hearted gentleman." There was the day Puss (one of the tame hares) escaped from her box, and the day burglars tried to break into a neighbor's house, and the day a begging parson called and swindled Cowper out of five shillings.

And all this time he was getting to know the world of nature more intimately, perhaps, than any other poet of his time. Wild scenery had been popular with the literati for half a century and was now coming into fashion throughout genteel society. The poetry of James Thomson and the paintings of Claude Lorrain and Salvator Rosa had introduced the educated classes to the beauties of romantic landscape. Ruined abbeys, shaggy woods, jagged rocks, moonlight, sunset, storms, and snow—all the paraphernalia of the picturesque—had become the vogue. Everyone was learning to use the new vocabulary of landscape painting, speaking of "perspectives" and "foregrounds" and "sidescreens," and analyzing the view as if it were a picture. Cowper had little sympathy with this fashion, and got far closer to the reality behind the view than did the connoisseurs of the picturesque. In his small garden he caught a glimpse of the complex, organic life of nature. He learned to look on flowers and apple trees not just as ornaments to please the eye, but also as creatures with a life of their own.

He took a special pleasure in growing cucumbers, and describes their cultivation at length in *The Task*. The passage is a variation in miniature on a classical theme—that of the *Georgics* of Vergil. It moves at low pressure and at slow speed, and it is not free from a slightly embarrassed pedantry or from awkward circumlocutions like "pots of size diminutive." Yet prosy, unexciting, even humdrum as this verse may be, there is real life in it; and the vegetable it celebrates is a real vegetable and not just a subject for a still life. A few extracts will give an idea of its style:

... First he [i.e., the gardener] bids spread
Dry fern or litter'd hay, that may imbibe
Th' ascending damps; then leisurely impose,
And lightly, shaking it with agile hand
From the full fork, the saturated straw. . . .
Th' uplifted frame, compact at ev'ry joint,
And overlaid with clear translucent glass,
He settles next upon the sloping mount,
Whose sharp declivity shoots off secure
From the dash'd pane the deluge as it falls.
He shuts it close, and the first labour ends.
Thrice must the voluble and restless earth
Spin round upon her axle, ere the warmth,
Slow gathering in the midst, through the square mass
Diffus'd, attain the surface: when, behold!
A pestilent and most corrosive steam,
Like a gross fog Boeotian, rising fast,
And fast condens'd upon the dewy sash,
Asks egress; which obtain'd, the overcharg'd
And drench'd conservatory breathes abroad,
In volumes wheeling slow, the vapour dank; . . .
The seed, selected wisely, plump, and smooth,
And glossy, he commits to pots of size
Diminutive, well fill'd with well-prepar'd
And fruitful soil,

       . . .

These on the warm and genial earth, that hides
The smoking manure and o'erspreads it all,
He places lightly, and, as time subdues
The rage of fermentation, plunges deep
In the soft medium, till they stand immers'd. . . .
Two leaves produc'd, two rough indented leaves,
Cautious he pinches from the second stalk
A pimple, that portends a future sprout,
And interdicts its growth.
          . . . they soon supply
Large foliage, overshadowing golden flow'rs,
Blown on the summit of th' apparent fruit.
These have their sexes; and, when summer shines,
The bee transports the fertilizing meal
From flow'r to flow'r, . . .
Not so when winter scowls. Assistant art
Then acts in nature's office, brings to pass
The glad espousals, and ensures the crop.
(III. 475–479; 484–499; 511–514; 516–520; 526–529;
         534–539; 541–543)

V

THOSE lines may not show Cowper at his most ambitious, but they are full of the odd charm that rarely deserts him even at his worst. He adopts here the mock heroic manner, partly because he is thinking of the classical parallel, but more because he is afraid that he may be boring his listener. He is like a man who, realizing that he is riding his hobbyhorse, tries by a slight exaggeration, a mildly facetious overemphasis, to apologize for his enthusiasm. Yet behind the polite deprecation one can sense his real feelings: his almost comic seriousness, his solemn methodicalness, and above all his benign satisfaction at the final success. When, as here, Cowper tries to make a joke, it is nearly always, more than he realizes, a joke at his own expense.

The real importance of the cucumber georgic, though, is that it shows how the poet got to know the workings of nature by practical contact with leaf and soil, how he learned to look closely and intently, interpreting minute signs of development and decay. One might compile from his work an anthology of precise and vividly seen details. Of a shrub, for instance:

Hypericum, all bloom, so thick a swarm
Of flow'rs, like flies clothing her slender rods,
That scarce a leaf appears;
            (VI. 165–167)

or of shadows beneath trees:

The chequer'd earth seems restless as a flood
Brush'd by the wind;
            (I. 344–345)

or of a thresher:

          Wide flies the chaff.
The rustling straw sends up a frequent mist
Of atoms, sparkling in the noon-day beam.
          (I. 359–361)

Best of all are those small portraits or snapshots of living animals or birds, such as that of the robin in winter, in which the true personality of the bird is clearly caught in no more than a few strokes:

The redbreast warbles still, but is content
With slender notes, and more than half suppress'd:
Pleas'd with his solitude, and flitting light
From spray to spray, where'er he rests he shakes
From many a twig the pendent drops of ice,
That tinkle in the wither'd leaves below.
          (VI. 77–82)

So varied and so large a collection of observed felicities of nature could be made from few other English poets. Yet to collect them is to miss Cowper's unique contribution to the poetry of the countryside. For he was not just assembling details or carefully constructing a landscape. He was taking a walk. Thus the parts do not follow one another according to any design, but merely in the order in which he became aware of them. The focus shifts from the near to the middle distance, as the focus of the eye shifts when one is walking along a road. The scale changes with the focus, so that at one moment a few blades of grass fill the whole field of vision, and the next one is looking at a haystack fifty yards away. The poet, in fact, is not so much viewing the landscape as entering it, becoming almost part of it himself. As he looks around, there are continual variations in the intensity of his observation. Here, where his interest is aroused, it is keen and meticulous; there, it is comparatively casual. At any moment, too, the sight of some familiar object will lead to a comment or reminiscence. One is always aware not just of the thing seen but also of the one who sees, and yet each is kept detached. Here, to illustrate this intricate and varying vision, is a quotation of some length:

> 'Tis morning; and the sun, with ruddy orb
> Ascending, fires th' horizon; while the clouds,
> That crowd away before the driving wind,
> More ardent as the disk emerges more,
> Resemble most some city in a blaze,
> Seen through the leafless wood. His slanting ray
> Slides ineffectual down the snowy vale,
> And, tinging all with his own rosy hue,
> From ev'ry herb and ev'ry spiry blade
> Stretches a length of shadow o'er the field.
> Mine, spindling into longitude immense,
> In spite of gravity, and sage remark
> That I myself am but a fleeting shade,
> Provokes me to a smile. With eye askance
> I view the muscular proportion'd limb
> Transform'd to a lean shank. The shapeless pair,
> As they design'd to mock me, at my side
> Take step for step; and, as I near approach
> The cottage, walk along the plaster'd wall,
> Prepost'rous sight! the legs without the man.
> The verdure of the plain lies buried deep
> Beneath the dazzling deluge; and the bents,
> And coarser grass, upspearing o'er the rest,
> Of late unsightly and unseen, now shine
> Conspicuous, and, in bright apparel clad
> And fledg'd with icy feathers, nod superb.

> The cattle mourn in corners where the fence
> Screens them, and seem half petrified to sleep
> In unrecumbent sadness. There they wait
> Their wonted fodder; not like hung'ring man,
> Fretful if unsupply'd; but, silent, meek,
> And patient of the slow-pac'd swain's delay.
> He from the stack carves out th' accustom'd load,
> Deep-plunging, and again deep-plunging oft,
> His broad keen knife into the solid mass:
> Smooth as a wall the upright remnant stands,
> With such undeviating and even force
> He severs it away: no needless care,
> Lest storms should overset the leaning pile
> Deciduous, or its own unbalanc'd weight.
> Forth goes the woodman, leaving unconcern'd
> The cheerful haunts of man; to wield the axe
> And drive the wedge, in yonder forest drear,
> From morn to eve his solitary task.
> Shaggy and lean, and shrewd, with pointed ears
> And tail cropp'd short, half lurcher and half cur—
> His dog attends him. Close behind his heel
> Now creeps he slow; and now, with many a frisk
> Wide-scamp'ring, snatches up the drifted snow
> With iv'ry teeth, or ploughs it with his snout;
> Then shakes his powder'd coat, and barks for joy.
> Heedless of all his pranks, the sturdy churl
> Moves right toward the mark; nor stops for aught,
> But now and then with pressure of his thumb
> T' adjust the fragrant charge of a short tube
> That fumes beneath his nose: the trailing cloud
> Streams far behind him, scenting all the air.
> Now from the roost, or from the neighb'ring pale,
> Where, diligent to catch the first faint gleam
> Of smiling day, they gossip'd side by side,
> Come trooping at the housewife's well-known call
> The feather'd tribes domestic. Half on wing,
> And half on foot, they brush the fleecy flood,
> Conscious, and fearful of too deep a plunge.
> The sparrows peep, and quit the shelt'ring eaves
> To seize the fair occasion. Well they eye
> The scatter'd grain; and, thievishly resolv'd
> T' escape th' impending famine, often scar'd,
> As oft return—a pert voracious kind.
> Clean riddance quickly made, one only care
> Remains to each—the search for sunny nook,
> Or shed impervious to the blast.

> (V. 1–72)

Cowper's enjoyment of the physical world was not confined to the out-of-doors. The rooms at Orchard Side, the furniture, the deposition of odds and ends, made for him a personal landscape. They were known and real. He could rely on them to be there even if tomorrow brought madness again. Each article had its own associations, and in describing it he is almost writing his autobiography. He writes of a card table, for instance, in a letter to John Newton, describing it so affectionately that it takes on somewhat the same personal significance as Vincent Van Gogh's chair:

You will wonder [because Newton, being a strict Evangelical, disapproved of cards] when I tell you that I write upon a card-table; and will be still more surprised when I add, that we breakfast, dine, sup, upon a card-table. In short, it serves all purposes, except the only one for which it was originally designed. . . . The round table, which we formerly had in use, was unequal to the pressure of my superincumbent breast and elbows. . . . The fly-table was too slight and too small. . . . The card-table, therefore, which had for sixteen years been banished as mere lumber; the card-table, which is covered with green baize, and is, therefore, preferable to any other that has a slippery surface; the card-table, that stands firm and never totters—is advanced to the honour of assisting me upon my scribbling occasions; and, because we choose to avoid the trouble of making frequent changes in the position of our house-hold furniture, proves equally serviceable upon all others. It has cost us now and then the downfall of a glass: for, when covered with a tablecloth, the fish-ponds are not easily discerned; and not being seen, are sometimes as little thought of. But having numerous good qualities which abundantly compensate that single inconvenience, we spill upon it our coffee, our wine, and our ale, without murmuring, and resolve that it shall be our table still, to the exclusion of all others.

(letter to John Newton, 19 March 1785)

It was among such familiar and homely objects, rather than in the fields, that Cowper set his vision of earthly felicity. For he knew that the wildness of winter outside—the wind, the snow, the cold—was matched by the wildness in his own mind. He cherished the warmth and peace of his home, as he cherished his sanity while it lasted, so that, far from being smug or complacent, his picture of the winter fireside is both touching and moving, and has become the best-known in the whole range of his work:

> Now stir the fire, and close the shutters fast,
> Let fall the curtains, wheel the sofa round,
> And, while the bubbling and loud-hissing urn
> Throws up a steamy column, and the cups
> That cheer but not inebriate, wait on each,
> So let us welcome peaceful ev'ning in.
>
> (*The Task*, IV. 36–41)

VI

IN October 1784, when he had finished *The Task*, Cowper once again found himself lacking employment. He lacked company, too, now that Lady Austen had gone, and looking for some way to fill the time, he decided to translate Homer. It was a task—unlike the former—quite beyond his powers, for he could never catch even the faintest echo of the epic ring. The work began as a pleasant exercise, and ended as a long-drawn-out toil. For years he went on correcting, revising, badgering his friends for advice; and the work undoubtedly would have blocked the entire flow of his creative imagination had not a fortunate accident intervened once more. With the publication of *The Task* in 1785, Cowper had become the most famous poet of his day, and many friends of his former years were anxious to renew their acquaintance. Among these was Lady Hesketh, the Harriet Cowper of his Inner Temple days, now a widow. Before long she had become a regular correspondent and a fairly frequent visitor to Orchard Side, and later to the larger house at Weston, to which Cowper moved in 1786. She was in many ways an admirable companion, and though she failed to divert him from his Homeric labors, she did bring enough pleasure into his life to make his spirit burst out from time to time in the little splashes and flashes of his shorter poems.

In the picture of Cowper as the forerunner of the romantics or as a tragic poet haunted by madness, one often forgets that he was also a most accomplished writer of light verse. It was, moreover, verse that had nothing condescending about it, nothing that suggests the poet in shirt-sleeves, deliberately playing the fool. For even in the shortest poem Cowper always has something to tell, and the wish to tell it is the sole reason for the poem. He never wrote without thought of an audience, even when—as often—he wrote without thought of publishing. His poetry is always poetry to be listened to, not just poetry to be overheard. The incidents behind it are often very slight—the shutting up of a cat in a cupboard ("The Retired Cat") or the rescuing of three kittens from the threats of an adder ("The Colubriad")—but nearly always the tone is delicately adjusted between frivolity and seriousness. In "The Colubriad," for instance, he manages the pretended swagger of the mock heroic far better than in *The Task*:

On to the hall went I, with pace not slow,
But swift as lightning, for a long Dutch hoe;
With which well arm'd I hasten'd to the spot,
To find the viper. But I found him not,
And, turning up the leaves and shrubs around,
Found only, that he was not to be found.
But still the kittens, sitting as before,
Sat watching close the bottom of the door.
I hope—said I—the villain I would kill
Has slipt between the door and the door's sill;
And if I make despatch, and follow hard,
No doubt but I shall find him in the yard:—
For long ere now it should have been rehears'd,
'Twas in the garden that I found him first.
E'en there I found him; there the full-grown cat
His head with velvet paw did gently pat,
As curious as the kittens erst had been
To learn what this phenomenon might mean.
Fill'd with heroic ardour at the sight,
And fearing every moment he would bite,
And rob our household of our only cat
That was of age to combat with a rat,
With out-stretched hoe I slew him at the door,
And taught him never to come there no more.
(18–41)

In many of his shorter poems, Cowper demonstrates his strong humanitarian sympathies—his hatred of the slave trade and his great love of animals. In one or two he reveals a lyrical gift one might not divine from the rest of his work. The familiar "The Poplar Field" is perhaps the loveliest, welling up, in the first stanza, in bubbling rhythms and a liquid gurgle of *l*s:

The poplars are fell'd, farewell to the shade
And the whispering sound of the cool colonnade;
The winds play no longer, and sing in the leaves,
Nor Ouse on his bosom their image receives.
(1–4)

It is the rhythm of the country dance, and yet there is a poignancy about it, so that when the moral comes at the end, it seems neither unexpected nor forced. The sentiments were conventional enough in Cowper's day, but their sincerity here is quite beyond doubt; and the glimpse, in the next-to-last quatrain, of the now unshaded meadow with the stumps of the trees among the grass has the effect of placing the whole scene within the time perspective of the natural world:

My fugitive years are all hasting away,
And I must ere long lie as lowly as they,

With a turf on my breast, and a stone at my head,
Ere another such grove shall arise in its stead.
(13–16)

The terror that overhung Cowper like a storm, even in his most summerlike days, did not always express itself as gently as in "The Poplar Field" or in "Yardley Oak"—an ambitious, unfinished poem in blank verse that has been thought by some critics to anticipate William Wordsworth. At times, even when he is writing of his beloved countryside, his grief floods the poem even as the Ouse flooded the meadows in winter. There was one memorable instance toward the end of his life. For many months Cowper had been lost in melancholy: no light seemed able to pierce the gloom of depression. Then, one day, remembering the story of shipwreck that he had read in a book of voyages, he wrote "The Castaway":

Obscurest night involv'd the sky,
Th' Atlantic billows roar'd,
When such a destin'd wretch as I,
Wash'd headlong from on board,
Of friends, of hope, of all bereft,
His floating home for ever left.
(1–6)

It is stiff in form and language, yet the pent-up feeling breaks out of the eighteenth-century reserve like steam out of a boiler. Even the absurd inadequacy of a word like "billows" cannot disguise the emotion behind the lines. He goes on to describe the incident with a plenitude of detail worthy of Daniel Defoe's *Robinson Crusoe*:

He shouted: nor his friends had fail'd
To check the vessel's course,
But so the furious blast prevail'd,
That, pitiless perforce,
They left their outcast mate behind,
And scudded still before the wind.

Some succour yet they could afford;
And, such as storms allow,
The cask, the coop, the floated cord,
Delay'd not to bestow.
But he (they knew) nor ship, nor shore,
Whate'er they gave, should visit more.

. . .

At length, his transient respite past,
His comrades, who before
Had heard his voice in ev'ry blast,
Could catch the sound no more.

For then, by toil subdued, he drank
The stifling wave, and then he sank.

(19–30; 43–48)

Though scarcely a phrase or word is out of the ordinary in itself, the effect of the whole is direct, vivid, and original. And then, in the last stanza, Cowper draws the parallel that he has been implying since the beginning. Here again, the words are conventional enough, with perhaps a hint of a hymn, yet the identification of the poet with his own subject matter is so complete that the poem becomes passionate and compelling:

No voice divine the storm allay'd,
 No light propitious shone;
When, snatch'd from all effectual aid,
 We perish'd, each alone:
But I beneath a rougher sea,
And whelm'd in deeper gulphs than he.

(61–66)

VII

"THE Castaway" was Cowper's last poem, but its gloom need not be the last impression he leaves. For with the publication of his letters, spread over almost a century and a half, there gradually came to light more and more of the character that had roused so much affection and sympathy in so many friends. It is useless to try to decide who is the best of the English letter writers, but if it were not useless, Cowper would certainly be among those whose claims had to be considered. The circumstances of his life—so frustrating in other ways—favored him as a correspondent. Its solitude made him turn with pleasure to friends who, had they been nearer, would have tired him. Its uneventfulness made him turn to the trivia of his everyday existence, in the telling of which he revealed his own personality as completely as the most subjective of autobiographers. Not even Anton Chekhov, carefully selecting significant irrelevancies, can tell more of his characters than Cowper tells of himself in a passing remark about a visitor, a parson, or one of his tame hares. His style is colloquial and easy, and he has an enchanting way of blowing up a little incident like a soap bubble and watching it float away. And when he was in good spirits, his letters were full of a humor so spontaneous, so uncalculated, as to be—one suspects—partly unconscious:

My toothache is in a great measure, that is to say, almost entirely, removed; not by snipping my ears, nor by any other chirurgical operation, except such as I could perform myself. The manner of it was as follows: we dined last Thursday at the Hall; I sat down to table, trembling lest the tooth, of which I told you in my last, should not only refuse its own office, but hinder all the rest. Accordingly, in less than five minutes, by a hideous dislocation of it, I found myself not only in great pain, but under an absolute prohibition not only to eat, but to speak another word. Great emergencies sometimes meet with most effectual remedies. I resolved, if it were possible, then and there to draw it. This I effected so dexterously by a sudden twitch, and afterwards so dexterously conveyed it into my pocket, that no creature present, not even Mrs. Unwin, who sat facing me, was sensible either of my distress, or of the manner of my deliverance from it.

(letter to Lady Hesketh, 19 December 1787)

There is a cheerful sanity of tone about this civilized banter that contrasts very strangely with the madness that was always threatening Cowper, yet it was from just this contrast that his genius emerged. He cherished the trivial events of the small world of Olney because the events of the greater world held such terrors for him. He looked on his immediate surroundings with an eye made clear by his need to hold close to solid, safe, material things. The physical earth was a knife edge on which he walked between the heaven he believed he had lost and the hell he feared would gain him. In his precarious pilgrimage he looked on all around him—the grass, the lane, the wild creatures, and his own fireside—with the sharp tenderness of a good-bye.

Cowper's last years were spent in almost unrelieved melancholy. The work of translating Homer had tired him, and he made things worse for himself by taking on the still more troublesome task of editing Milton. In 1796 he was persuaded to move to Norfolk, in the hope that the change of scene would revive his spirits. But after the death of Mrs. Unwin, in December of that year, he gradually sank into a slough of lethargy and despair from which he never emerged. He died on 25 April 1800 at East Dereham, Norfolk, and was buried in the parish church.

SELECTED BIBLIOGRAPHY

I. BIBLIOGRAPHY. N. Nicholls, "Early Editions of Cowper," in *Bookman*, 80 (1931); L. C. Hartley, "Cowper: A List of Critical and Bibliographical Studies,

1895–1949," in *North Carolina State College Records*, 49 (1950); L. C. Hartley, *William Cowper: The Continuing Revaluation* (Chapel Hill, N. C.–London, 1960), an essay and a bibliography of Cowperian studies from 1895 to 1960; N. Russell, *A Bibliography of William Cowper to 1837* (Oxford, 1963).

II. Collected Works. *Poems*, 2 vols. (London, 1782–1785); W. Hayley, ed., *Life and Posthumous Writings*, 3 vols. (Chichester, 1803–1804); *Poems and Olney Hymns* (London, 1806); *Poems*, 3 vols. (London, 1815), vol. III contains posthumous poems and a biographical essay by Rev. J. Johnson; J. Newton, ed., *Works*, 10 vols. (London, 1817); J. Johnson, ed., *Private Correspondence Now First Published*, 2 vols. (London, 1824); J. S. Memes, ed., *Miscellaneous Works*, 3 vols. (Edinburgh, 1834); T. S. Grimshawe, ed., *Works: Life and Letters*, 8 vols. (London, 1835); R. Southey, ed., *Works*, 15 vols. (London, 1835–1837; repr., 8 vols., 1853–1855), the latter in Bohn's Standard Library; H. F. Cary, ed., *Poetical Works* (London, 1839; rev. ed., 1845); *Poetical Works*, 2 vols. (London, 1853), published by Pickering, with memoir; J. Wright, ed., *Unpublished and Uncollected Works* (London, 1900); T. Wright, ed., *Correspondence*, 4 vols. (London, 1904); J. C. Bailey, ed., *Poems* (London, 1905); H. S. Milford, ed., *Complete Poetical Works* (Oxford, 1905; enl. ed., 1913, 1926, and 1934 [the standard ed.; repr. with rev., 1967]); T. Wright, ed., *Unpublished and Uncollected Letters* (London, 1925); R. Inglefield, ed., *Poems* (London, 1973), a facs. of the 1782 ed.; R. Inglefield, ed., *The Task* (London, 1973), a facs. of the 1785 ed.; J. King and C. Ryskamp, eds., *The Letters and Prose Writings of William Cowper* (Oxford, 1979), the first vol. of a complete ed. of the letters.

III. Selected Works. W. Benham, ed., *Letters* (London, 1884); W. T. Webb, ed., *Selections from Cowper's Letters* (London, 1895); W. T. Webb, ed., *Cowper's Shorter Poems* (London, 1896); E. V. Lucas, ed., *Selections from Cowper's Letters* (London, 1908); M. L. Milford, ed., *Selections from Cowper's Letters* (London, 1911), in the World's Classics; J. G. Frazer, ed., *Letters*, 2 vols. (London, 1912); M. L. Milford, ed., *Poetry and Prose* (Oxford, 1921); W. Hadley, ed., *Selected Letters* (London, 1926), in Everyman's Library; D. Cecil, ed., *Selections* (London, 1933), M. Van Doren, ed., *Selected Letters* (New York, 1951); A. N. Jeffares, ed., *Selected Poems and Letters* (London, 1963); N. Nicholson, ed., *Cowper: A Choice of Verse* (London, 1972).

IV. Separate Works. *Olney Hymns* (London, 1779), with Rev. J. Newton; *Anti-Thelyphthora: A Tale, in Verse* (London, 1781), Cowper's retort to his cousin M. Madan's *Thelyphthora*, a treatise advocating polygamy; "The Journey of John Gilpin" (London, [1783]), first printed in the *Public Advertiser* (1782), the first separate printings (in chapbook form) are undated; *The Task* (London, 1785); *Poems* (London, 1798; type facs., 1926), includes "On the Receipt of My Mother's Picture" and "The Dog and the Waterlily"; *Table Talk, and Other Poems*, 2 vols. (London, 1817); M. J. Quinlan, ed., "Memoir of Cowper: An Autobiography," in *Proceedings of the American Philosophical Society*, 97 (1953), first published posthumously without authority in 1816 as *Memoir of the Early Life of William Cowper Written by Himself*, and repr. several times.

V. Translations. *The Iliad and Odyssey of Homer* (trans. into English blank verse), 2 vols. (London, 1791), Cowper's version of *The Odyssey* is in Everyman's Library; *The Power of Grace Illustrated; In Letters from a Minister of the Reformed Church (Van Lier) to John Newton* (London, 1792); *Poems Translated from the French of Madame de la Mothe Guion* (London, 1801); *Latin and Italian Poems of Milton* (London, 1808).

VI. Biographical and Critical Studies. S. Greathead, *Memoirs of William Cowper* (London, 1814); T. Taylor, *The Life Compiled from His Correspondence* (London, 1835); G. Smith, *Cowper* (London, 1880), in the English Men of Letters series; T. Wright, *The Tour of Cowper, or The Literary and Historical Associations of Olney* (London, 1886); T. Wright, *The Life of William Cowper* (London, 1892; rev. ed., 1921); H. Hesketh, ed., *Letters of Lady Hesketh to the Rev. John Johnson, Concerning William Cowper* (London, 1901); H. I'A. Fausset, *William Cowper* (London, 1928), an interesting and sympathetic study based on the theory—not held by the author of this study—that the cause of Cowper's madness was a conflict between poetry and religion in the poet's mind; D. Cecil, *The Stricken Deer: Or, the Life of Cowper* (London, 1929), based largely on the poet's letters; V. Woolf, "Cowper and Lady Austin," in her *Common Reader*, 2nd ser. (London, 1932); L. Strachey, "Gray and Cowper," in his *Characters and Commentaries* (London, 1933); G. Thomas, *William Cowper and the Eighteenth Century* (London, 1935; rev. ed., 1948); L. C. Hartley, *William Cowper, Humanitarian* (Chapel Hill, N. C., 1938); B. Martin, *John Newton* (London, 1950), throws some light on Newton's relations with Cowper at Olney; N. Nicholson, *William Cowper* (London, 1951); M. Quinlan, *Cowper: A Critical Life* (Minneapolis, 1953); C. Ryskamp, *William Cowper of the Inner Temple, Esquire* (London, 1959), a study of Cowper's early life, hitherto little known, with some newly discovered material.

Note: Orchard Side, Cowper's home at Olney, is now a museum, and both house and garden are open to the public. Exhibits include MSS, portraits, period furniture, and other items associated with Cowper or John Newton.

EDWARD GIBBON

(1737-1794)

C. V. Wedgwood

I

WHEN Edward Gibbon published the first volume of his *Decline and Fall of the Roman Empire* (1776), it was hailed by the most eminent critics of the time as "a truly classic work." In the more than two hundred years that have elapsed since then, that contemporary judgment has been confirmed. Gibbon's great book is still read for pleasure and information. The balance and lucidity of his presentation are as gratifying to the mind as a noble eighteenth-century building is to the eyes. The vigor of his narrative, the elegance of his prose, and the sharpness of his irony still have the power to enthrall and delight, and although seven generations of scholars have added to and modified knowledge of the events he describes, much of what Gibbon wrote, especially in the earlier volumes, is still useful as history.

Edward Gibbon was born at Putney, then a pretty suburban village a few miles from London, on 27 April 1737. His father was a gentleman of extravagant habits and comfortable means with interests in the City. In his youth the elder Gibbon and his family had come under the influence of William Law, and his two sisters are said to appear in Law's *Serious Call* as the frivolous Flavia and the devout Miranda. The devout Hester Gibbon continued to be Law's disciple and a pillar of his holy household until his death in 1761. It is strange that so close a link should exist between the great mystical writer and the highly rational historian.

As a child Gibbon was small and sickly, easily bullied by tougher boys at Richard Wooddeson's school, where he was sent at age nine to learn Latin. Of the seven children born to his parents, he alone survived. His delicate mother died when he was ten, and he was handed over to the care of her sister, Catherine Porten. Nothing more fortunate could have happened to him, for this excellent woman combined all the qualities most necessary to his health and happiness. She was resourceful, energetic, practical, deeply affectionate, imaginative in her understanding of his intellectual needs, and not unduly possessive. To ensure herself an independent income and to make a more cheerful home for her nephew, she set up a little boardinghouse in London for boys attending Westminster—the school that Gibbon himself attended on the rare occasions when he was well enough to do so. He gained his real education from the wide general reading in which she encouraged him. In the autobiography that he carefully composed in later life, he called her "the true mother of my mind as well as of my health" and left a grateful description of her personality:

Her natural good sense was improved by the perusal of the best books in the English language and if her reason was sometimes clouded by prejudice, her sentiments were never disguised by hypocrisy or affectation. Her indulgent tenderness, the frankness of her temper, and my innate rising curiosity, soon removed all distance between us: like friends of an equal age we freely conversed on every topic, familiar or abstruse, and it was her delight and reward to observe the first shoots of my young ideas.[1]

In his twelfth year Gibbon describes himself as having fully developed that "invincible love of reading, which I would not exchange for the treasures of India." During the brief time that he was well enough to attend Dr. Wooddeson's school at Kingston-on-Thames, he read Cornelius Nepos, whose elegant simplicity he later commended as an excellent model. More important was his discovery of Homer in Alexander Pope's translation, which, he says, "accustomed my ear to the sound of poetic harmony." In his mature style the influence of Pope's fluent precision in the use of words can still be traced. In the next two or three years he read

[1]The Everyman's Library edition of *The Memoirs of the Life of Edward Gibbon* . . . (London, 1911), pp. 28–29.

everything on which he could lay hands—poetry, history, travel, and romance—until, in his own phrase, his "indiscriminate appetite subsided by degrees in the *historic* line." He was fourteen when he came upon *An Universal History* while visiting friends, and he "was immersed in the passage of the Goths over the Danube when the summons of the dinner bell reluctantly dragged me from my intellectual feast."

When Gibbon was sixteen, his health suddenly improved. The prostrating headaches from which he had suffered as a child vanished, and he was sent to the university to complete his education. Owing to his irregular schooling and wide but unconventional reading, he arrived at Oxford in 1752 with "a stock of erudition that might have puzzled a doctor and a degree of ignorance of which a schoolboy might have been ashamed." But so slack was the instruction at Oxford at that time that no one took the least notice either of his erudition or of his ignorance. Teaching and discipline were equally lax, and Gibbon, who was ardent to acquire knowledge, was bored and disgusted. Thrown back on his own resources during what he was later to call "the most idle and unprofitable" months of his life, he began to examine the religious controversy recently caused by the publication of Conyers Middleton's *Free Enquiry into the Miraculous Powers . . .* (1749). The startling result of his researches into the early history of Christianity was his conversion to Catholicism, and he was privately received into the Church of Rome in June 1753.

As the law then stood in England, his conversion meant that he had to leave the university; and since Roman Catholics were excluded from public employment, it put a stop to any hope of a political or legal career. Gibbon's father, who was distressed at this unconventional turn in his son's life, packed him off to Lausanne to complete his studies and reconsider his religious views under the care of a Protestant pastor, Daniel Pavillard.

Gibbon stayed in Switzerland for nearly five years, and there he laid the solid foundations of his education. His conversion had not gone deep; at Christmas 1754 he was reconciled to the Protestant religion. During the ensuing year he perfected himself in Latin and French, and formed the habit of writing his copious diaries entirely in French. He read French and Latin historians, began to learn Greek, toured Switzerland, and for practice wrote "a very ample relation of my tour." But his most

valuable discovery was the important work on logic of the Abbé Jean Pierre de Crousaz, which, he records, "formed my mind to a habit of thinking and reasoning I had no idea of before." He now began to exercise his critical faculties by writing essays or, as he preferred to call them, "observations" on Plautus and Vergil. He corresponded with neighboring savants, saw the plays of Voltaire, and began to compose, in French, his *Essai sur l'étude de la littérature*. He knew that he wanted to be a man of learning and a writer, but he aimed at criticism or philosophy rather than history.

In June 1757, Gibbon met Suzanne Curchod, a pretty, intelligent, well-read young woman, the only child of a neighboring pastor. Suzanne had no fortune except her intellect and her charms, but she was greatly sought after. His entry in his diary is short and telling: "I saw Mademoiselle Curchod: Omnia vincit amor, et nos cedamus amori."[2] Gibbon himself was by no means unattractive. Although he was very small, his fresh color and lively expression gave him charm, and his conversation was fluent, witty, and erudite; also he appeared to be a young man with a future. But Mademoiselle Curchod, who had a good many admirers, was disposed to be coy. Gibbon pursued her. She held him off a little too long; and by the time she decided to relent, his own ardor was evidently cooling. But he could hardly admit that he had changed his mind, and when he left Switzerland in the spring of 1758, it was on the understanding that he would return to marry her. In his autobiography Gibbon gives a laconic and slightly disingenuous account of what occurred next. His father opposed the marriage, and Gibbon, in his famous phrase, "sighed as a lover, but obeyed as a son." He does not explain why—although he came home in May—he did not mention Suzanne to his father until August, nor does he tell of Suzanne's desperate letters, imploring him to be true to her.

Gibbon was not made for domestic life, and he probably knew it. He had the egoism of the natural scholar, and wrote of himself, "I was never less alone than when by myself." This is not the temperament that makes an ardent lover or a good husband. In a moment of youthful impulse, he had thought himself in love with an intelligent young woman; but it is clear that his love evaporated when he began to think about the responsibilities and

---

[2]Originally from Vergil's *Eclogues*: "Love conquers all things; let us too surrender to love."

commitments of marriage. The sigh that he heaved as a lover was a sigh of relief.

If Gibbon had the egoism natural to scholars, he also had an affectionate and grateful nature, and his treatment of Suzanne is the only example of blamable personal conduct in his life. He was a good son, although he had some cause for complaint against a father who never did much for him except squander his patrimony. The elder Gibbon had married again while his son was abroad, and it is much to Gibbon's credit that although naturally apprehensive at first, he soon became devoted to his stepmother and remained so to the end of his life. In all the ordinary exchanges of family and friendship, Gibbon was kind, reasonable, well behaved, and warmhearted. But when it came to the stronger passions, he failed, as scholars commonly do. Those whose first passion is knowledge justly fear the intrusion of any rival interest.

II

GIBBON was now twenty-one years old. He spoke and wrote French as fluently as—at this time more fluently than—he did English. He had fully determined to devote his life to scholarship and writing, though he had not yet settled on a subject. But for the next few years family interests and patriotic duty kept him in England. He had seen little of his father as a boy, and nothing at all since he left Oxford. An excellent relationship now sprang up between the two, for the elder Gibbon admired his son's erudition and enjoyed his company; and Dorothea Gibbon, the stepmother, who had no children of her own, was blessedly free from jealousy. In 1759 father and son volunteered for the Hampshire militia. The Seven Years' War was in progress, and there were rumors of a possible French invasion. Nothing of the kind happened, but Edward Gibbon spent the best part of two years marching about with the troops in Hampshire, living sometimes in billets and sometimes under canvas. Of this period he was later to say that "the Captain of Hampshire grenadiers . . . has not been useless to the historian of the Roman Empire." The part played by an English gentleman in local maneuvers hardly seems on a level with the exploits of the great Roman generals and the ferocious barbarian leaders whom Gibbon was later to describe.

But the good historian should be able to use his own experience to illuminate that of others, and however absurd the comparison between eighteenth-century Hampshire and the battlefields of the fifth century must appear, however wide the difference between Captain Edward Gibbon of the militia and the thundering chiefs of the Gothic hordes, there are certain unchanging elements in the soldier's experience that Gibbon learned to appreciate.

He found much of the life very boring, but he was young and strong enough to enjoy, in limited quantities, the rowdier amusements of his fellow officers. He did not neglect his studies, went on steadily with his reading in all his leisure hours, and completed the *Essai sur l'étude de la littérature* that he had begun at Lausanne. His proud father persuaded him to have this little work printed; and when the king's brother, the duke of York, came down to inspect the militia, Captain Edward Gibbon, again to satisfy his father's whim, presented him with a copy. The duke, sitting at breakfast in his tent, promised with conventional courtesy to read it as soon as he had time.

The little book is composed in elegant, uninspired French, imitated from Montesquieu. Gibbon himself, looking back on it from the eminence of his maturity, found it "marred by a kind of obscurity and abruptness," confused, and badly put together. It is indeed difficult to make out exactly what thesis Gibbon was trying to prove. "A number of remarks and examples, historical, critical, philosophical, are heaped on each other without method or connection," said Gibbon disparagingly, and the description is accurate. But the book contains one or two pages that reveal the writer's intelligence and his gift for history. In an admirable passage he compares Tacitus with Livy and praises the former as the ideal of the historian-philosopher. In another he considers the nature of historical evidence and the framework of historical cause and effect, within which all the other sciences are contained.

Irksome duty in the militia ended with the war, in 1763, and Gibbon, now twenty-five, set out on a second visit to the Continent. He passed through Paris, from which he wrote home that he had enjoyed better company and conversation in a fortnight than eighteen months in London could supply. Early in 1764 he was again in Lausanne, and was certainly taken aback when he encountered Suzanne Curchod during an entertainment at Voltaire's house. The unhappy business ended not too graciously. The girl, who was now an orphan and very poor, still hoped to marry him. She wrote him long letters, carefully and intelligently criticizing his *Essai sur l'étude de la littérature*. This was not perhaps the wisest way to win back a lover's heart, but even had she used more feminine wiles, she would not have succeeded. Gibbon was determined to escape her, and covering the shabbiness of his own conduct by an easy self-deception, he convinced himself that she was a shallow and calculating flirt. *"Fille dangereuse et artificielle,"* he wrote censoriously in his diary. Suzanne implored Jean Jacques Rousseau, then at Geneva, to see Gibbon and reason with him, but Rousseau replied that he liked nothing he had heard of Gibbon and thought him unworthy of her love. Suzanne gave up hope and shortly after married the elderly banker Jacques Necker.

She had done very well for herself, and soon she was inviting Gibbon to her house to prove to him that she no longer loved him and that she had made a better match. The procedure was natural; it was also, as Gibbon did not fail to note in his diary, rather vulgar. But time smoothed away all asperities. In later years these uneasy lovers enjoyed a pleasant middle-aged friendship, and the distinguished historian was once, to his amusement, the object of a proposal of marriage from Suzanne's precocious little daughter, the future Madame de Staël.

Gibbon was by no means occupied exclusively with Suzanne during his second visit to Lausanne. He renewed his friendship with the Swiss scholar Jacques Georges Deyverdun, who had been tutor to several distinguished young Englishmen, including Lord Chesterfield's heir, and he made the acquaintance of another traveling compatriot, John Holroyd, later Lord Sheffield; these two were to be his closest friends for many years. Meanwhile he went on with his studies and accumulated voluminous notes on the ancient monuments of Italy, in preparation for his journey there in a few months' time.

Gibbon was by now fairly sure that he intended to write history, but his mind still wavered among a number of topics. He had considered a history of the Third Crusade or of the Renaissance wars of France and Italy, or a life of Sir Walter Ralegh or of the marquess of Montrose. But by the summer of 1764, the principal subjects had reduced themselves to two: either the fall of the Roman Empire or the rise of the Swiss Republic.

About this time Gibbon visited the court of Savoy, an occasion of which he has left a characteristically vivid description. He got on so well with the princesses of Savoy and "grew so very free and easy that I drew out my snuff box, rapped it, took snuff twice (a crime never known before in the presence chamber) and continued my discourse in my usual attitude of my body bent forward and my forefinger stretched out." Gibbon was a mere twenty-seven, with only an obscure pamphlet to his name, but he already had the confidence and the tricks of speech and gesture of a much older and more established scholar. What made him different from other conceited young men was that he had something more than great erudition and a lively talent for conversation: he had genius, as almost everyone was able to see.

There was another difference. In spite of his assurance, in spite of the vanity that sometimes made him ridiculous, Gibbon had the inner humility of the scholar in the face of his material. He was more eager to learn than to teach.

In the autumn of 1764, he left Lausanne for Italy and by October had reached Rome, from which he wrote, in what for Gibbon is almost a bemused strain, to his stepmother:

I have already found such a fund of entertainment for a mind somewhat prepared for it by an acquaintance with the Romans, that I am really almost in a dream. Whatever ideas books may have given us of the greatness of that people, their accounts of the most flourishing state of Rome fall infinitely short of the picture of its ruins. . . . I was this morning upon the top of Trajan's pillar. I shall not attempt a description of it. Only figure to yourself a column of a hundred and forty feet high of the purest white marble . . . wrought into bas reliefs with as much taste and delicacy as any chimney piece at Up Park.

(letter of 9 October 1764)

The great conception already half-formed in Gibbon's mind was taking shape, but he was able—and that is one of the attractive things about Gibbon—to remember that he was writing to a lady with no conception at all of what he was trying to describe. He brings it within the scope of her imagination, in the most natural way in the world, by comparing it to the carved chimneypieces in a house she often visited.

Gibbon had thoroughly prepared himself for his visit to Rome by making careful notes of the topography of the classical city and the geography of Italy, and by mastering the science of medals, which is of paramount importance in the study of Roman history. But his first experience was one of an unfamiliar and inspiring emotion that he records in chapter 6 of his autobiography:

My temper is not very susceptible of enthusiasm, and the enthusiasm which I do not feel, I have ever scorned to affect. But at the distance of twenty five years, I can neither forget nor express the strong emotions which agitated my mind as I first approached and entered the eternal city. After a sleepless night, I trod, with a lofty step, the ruins of the Forum; each memorable spot where Romulus stood, or Tully spoke, or Caesar fell, was at once present to my eye; and several days of intoxication were lost or enjoyed before I could descend to a cool and minute investigation.

The crucial hour was now at hand, and Gibbon has recorded it with due solemnity:

It was at Rome, on the 15th of October, 1764, as I sat musing amidst the ruins of the Capitol, while the barefooted friars were singing vespers in the Temple of Jupiter, that the idea of writing the decline and fall of the city first started to my mind.

Gibbon slightly dramatizes this great moment, and it has been, perhaps pedantically, pointed out that his diaries show that the idea of writing something on the fall of Rome had been in his thoughts for some months. But there is a considerable difference between the first foreshadowings of an idea and the moment at which a book takes shape and quickens within the author's mind. It is that moment that Gibbon, with his natural sense of the dramatic, has fixed and recorded.

But other interests still competed with the "decline and fall," and on his return to England in 1765, Gibbon turned once again from the vices of the Roman Empire to the virtues of the Swiss Republic. He composed a long introductory section to a history of Switzerland, in French, and read it aloud to a literary society. By a rare stroke of good fortune, his listeners unanimously condemned it. "The momentary sensation," writes Gibbon, "was painful; but their condemnation was ratified by my cooler thoughts. I delivered my imperfect sheets to the flames and for ever after renounced a design in which some expense, much labour and more time had been so vainly consumed." He had another reason for changing his mind. He did not know German, and although his friend Deyverdun was gener-

ously willing to help in this part of the research, he saw that in order to study the growth of the Swiss Confederation, some personal knowledge of this "barbarous gothic dialect" would be essential. About the same time, fortunately, he was persuaded to drop the curious vanity of writing in French.

So at last, about his thirtieth year, the stage was set for Gibbon to begin his great book. He did not devote himself to it entirely, but, in the intervals of his study, lived the easy social life of a cultivated gentleman, dining and conversing among the distinguished men of his time. He was for twelve years an almost entirely silent member of Parliament, and he held a minor government post as a commissioner of trade and plantations, from which he derived a small additional income. This was welcome because his father, who had died in 1770, had not left him rich.

III

THE first volume of the *Decline and Fall* appeared in 1776. It carried the story of the Roman Empire from the ordered tranquillity of the Antonine epoch through the intrigues, revolutions, and disasters of the third century to the rehabilitation of the empire under Diocletian and the establishment of Christianity as the official religion under Constantine, a century and a half of rapidly succeeding events and changing ideas. The opening paragraph of the great book immediately wakens interest, creates a remarkable and comprehensive picture of the age described, and reveals that air of learned and untroubled candor and that sure and shapely style that were to be maintained throughout the gigantic undertaking:

In the second century of the Christian era, the Empire of Rome comprehended the fairest part of the earth, and the most civilized portion of mankind. The frontiers of that extensive monarchy were guarded by ancient renown and disciplined valour. The gentle but powerful influence of laws and manners had gradually cemented the union of the provinces. Their peaceful inhabitants enjoyed and abused the advantages of wealth and luxury. The image of a free constitution was preserved with decent reverence: the Roman senate appeared to possess the sovereign authority, and devolved on the emperors all the executive powers of government. During a happy period (A.D. 98-180) of more than fourscore years, the public administration was conducted by the virtue and abilities of Nerva, Trajan, Hadrian, and the two Antonines. It is the design of this, and of the two succeeding chapters, to describe the prosperous condition of their empire; and afterwards from the death of Marcus Antoninus, to deduce the most important circumstances of its decline and fall; a revolution which will ever be remembered, and is still felt by the nations of the earth.[3]

(I. 1)

Horace Walpole, prostrated by an attack of gout in the week of publication, sent a note congratulating Gibbon on "the style, manner, method, clearness and intelligence" of his first chapter, and added, "Mr. Walpole's impatience to proceed will give him such spirits that he flatters himself he shall owe part of his recovery to Mr. Gibbon." A few days later he wrote to the Reverend William Mason:

Lo, there is just appeared a truly classic work. . . . The style is as smooth as a Flemish picture, and the muscles are concealed and only for natural uses, not exaggerated like Michaelangelo's to show the painter's skill in anatomy. The book is Mr. Gibbon's *Decline and Fall of the Roman Empire.* . . . I know him a little, never suspected the extent of his talents for he is perfectly modest but I intend to know him a great deal more. . . .

(letter of 18 February 1776)

Walpole was wrong in imagining Gibbon to be modest, as he was later to discover. In every other respect his judgment has been fully confirmed by time.

The enthusiasm with which literary London received the book was not shared by the Anglican clergy. The first volume contained the famous chapters 15 and 16, devoted to the rise of Christianity and the treatment of Christians by the Roman Empire until the reign of Constantine the Great. It is a mistake to suppose that Gibbon was a militant anti-Christian; he was, rather, a typical product of the Age of Reason. He had acquired most of his philosophic ideas in the French-speaking part of Europe and had come to accept the easy cynicism of contemporary French intellectuals as though it were universal. Their way of thought appealed naturally to his exact, unemotional mind. When he described his subject as "the triumph of barbarism and Christianity," when in his autobiography he slyly drew attention to the same thing, in concrete form, with his striking tableau of the ruins of the Capitol and

the barefooted friars singing in the Temple of Jupiter, Gibbon was neither throwing out a challenge nor making propaganda against religion. He was stating what he felt to be the only accurate view of the matter: as the church had gained in power, so Roman civilization had declined. That was a simple, inescapable fact.

The violent attacks that were soon made on his treatment of Christianity astonished and distressed Gibbon. "I was startled," he writes, "at the first discharge of ecclesiastical ordnance." And well he might be, for not only were angry pamphlets written against him but he was twice made the object of special attack in a sermon. Most of the criticism was as trivial as it was passionate; but one cleric, the youthful Henry Davis of Balliol College, Oxford, accused him of misquoting his sources and of plagiarizing. These accusations were answered in a manner that exposed the presumption of his attacker. Gibbon was a thorough and careful scholar, and he had a deep and comprehensive knowledge of the available material. It is one of the minor ironies of history that he quarried so much of his book from the source materials laboriously assembled in the previous century by the great antiquarian and scholar Louis Le Nain de Tillemont, himself a devout believer, who, in his pertinacious gathering of the documents, had certainly never intended them to serve the purposes of a writer with so different an outlook on the church.

Gibbon's treatment of Christianity is in truth more offensive in manner than matter. Charles Sainte-Beuve, whose analysis of Gibbon in *Causeries du lundi* is particularly illuminating on this question, describes his writing as impregnated with a secret contempt for any feelings that he himself did not share. This contempt is all the more deadly for being cloaked in the guise of urbanity, as, for instance, in the famous paragraph in which he subtly discredits the initial miracles of Christianity:

But how shall we excuse the supine inattention of the Pagan and philosophic world to those evidences which were presented by the hand of Omnipotence, not to their reason but to their senses? During the age of Christ, of his Apostles, and of their first disciples, the doctrine which they preached was confirmed by innumerable prodigies. The lame walked, the blind saw, the sick were healed, the dead were raised, daemons were expelled, and the laws of nature were frequently suspended for the benefit of the Church. But the sages of Greece and Rome turned aside from the awful spectacle, and, pursuing the ordinary oc-

---

[3]All quotations are from J. B. Bury, ed., *The Decline and Fall of the Roman Empire*, 7 vols. (London, 1896–1900). References are to volume and page numbers.

cupations of life and study, appeared unconscious of any alterations in the moral or physical government of the world. Under the reign of Tiberius, the whole earth, or at least a celebrated province of the Roman Empire, was involved in a preternatural darkness of three hours. Even this miraculous event, which ought to have excited the wonder, the curiousity and the devotion of mankind, passed without notice in an age of science and history.

(I. 69–70)

This attitude of ironical superiority toward believers still has the power to exasperate and provoke the devout. But Gibbon was not so much an anti-Christian as an agnostic. It was not religion that he disliked, but exaggerated legends or meaningless rituals designed to captivate the multitude or make them amenable to the priest. Significant of this is his famous dictum: "The various modes of worship which prevailed in the Roman world were all considered by the people equally true, by the philosopher, equally false, and by the magistrates, as equally useful." This exact and careful statement, relating to a particular epoch, is frequently misquoted; and Gibbon is popularly credited with having said that "All religions seem to the people equally true, to the philosopher equally false, and to the magistrate equally useful." Whether or not he would have agreed to so general an assertion, he did not make it. He was too good a historian to generalize widely or wildly, and his comments were usually in strict relation to the epoch of which he was writing.

Nonetheless, Gibbon's inability or unwillingness to sympathize with other viewpoints is a blemish in his great work. It closed his understanding to the irrational forces that can inspire men to wisdom as well as to folly. Since the fourth century, which principally occupies his first and second volumes, was one of the most deeply and vehemently religious epochs of European history, his blindness on this point can be as irritating to the student of history as it is offensive to the Christian.

The failing is part of Gibbon's character and outlook, the very character and outlook that give to the whole history its air of classic mastery. To wish Gibbon different is to wish the masterpiece unmade; and even while one regrets the cynical pleasure that Gibbon evidently felt in demolishing the miracles and reducing the sufferings and the numbers of Christian martyrs in the persecution under Diocletian, one cannot but take pleasure in the sobriety of his argument and the poise of his style:

After the church had triumphed over all her enemies, the interest as well as the vanity of the captives prompted them to magnify the merit of their respective suffering. A convenient distance of time or place gave an ample scope to the progress of fiction; and the frequent instances which might be alleged of holy martyrs whose wounds had been instantly healed, whose strength had been renewed, and whose lost members had been miraculously restored, were extremely convenient for the purpose of removing every difficulty, and of silencing every objection. The most extravagant legends, as they conduced to the honour of the church, were applauded by the credulous multitude, countenanced by the power of the clergy, and attested by the suspicious evidence of ecclesiastical history.

(II. 136–137)

Gibbon goes on to investigate the statistics of the glorious army of the martyrs and to suggest that, after all, only a small number "sacrificed their lives for the important purpose of introducing Christianity into the world."

The arguments in this passage are unexceptionable. But the tone implies not only an unwillingness to accept false martyrs and invented sacrifices but also a disparagement of the emotions that inspired genuine martyrs to make real sacrifices.

This weakness in the book is also its greatness. It is Gibbon's capacity for writing of passionate and desperate times with a cool mind that enables him to write in general with such untroubled objectivity. It was not his gift to understand the hearts of men, but it was his duty and pleasure to understand their minds. He took great pains not only to read essential contemporary sources, but also to be fully acquainted with the literature and the other productions of the ages he studied. If he did not understand the heart of a Christian slave, he understood the mind of a Roman senator. If he did not greatly value the human passions, he set the highest possible value on the human intellect. His own mind had developed in the favorable atmosphere of a time that delighted to call itself the Age of Reason. As one of his most acute modern critics, Christopher Dawson, said: "he stood on the summit of the Renaissance achievement and looked back over the waste of history to ancient Rome, as from one mountain top to another."[4] The tragedy for him is the dethronement of a noble and intelligent civiliza-

---

[4]In his lecture *Edward Gibbon*, given at the British Academy in 1934 and published in *Proceedings of the British Academy* (London, 1934).

tion by force and ignorance. It is the triumph of the illiterate and the irrational that he records and deplores.

While he understood the minds and the calculations of the people about whom he wrote, Gibbon did not, like the romantic historians from Friedrich von Schiller to Thomas Carlyle, throw himself into their hearts and try to share their feelings. The historic present—Carlyle's favorite tense—is practically unknown to Gibbonian grammar, a point of language that forcibly illustrates the change that the romantic movement wrought in the literary treatment of history.

But if Gibbon is not conventionally religious, neither is he indifferent to moral standards. He assumes that it is the right and duty of the historian to have a clearly defined moral attitude, and he is exquisitely skillful in introducing judgment by way of implication. With what quiet contempt he deals, for instance, with the barbarian Ricimer, who in the fifth century elevated and destroyed puppet emperors at will. One of these, Majorian, was not only a man of strong and noble character but also an old companion in arms. Majorian strove to revive the ancient discipline of the Romans; this did not suit Ricimer, and he had to go. "It was not perhaps without some regret," writes Gibbon, "that Ricimer sacrificed his friend to the interest of his ambition." In fifteen words he more perfectly exposes the baseness of Ricimer than he could have done in a paragraph of rhetoric. He carries on the story in the same tone:

He resolved in a second choice to avoid the imprudent preference of superior virtue and merit. At his command the obsequious senate of Rome bestowed the Imperial title on Libius Severus, who ascended the throne of the West without emerging from the obscurity of a private condition. History has scarcely deigned to notice his birth, his elevation, his character or his death. Severus expired as soon as his life became inconvenient to his patron.

(IV. 24–25)

Gibbon's just and generous admiration is reserved for those who best display the classic virtues: justice, fortitude, perseverance, moderation. He greatly admires cleverness, but never for itself alone. His morality, classical again in this, did not permit him to respect success unless it was allied with the virtues. He admires Diocletian, the hardworking, self-made man who restored order to a distracted empire, more than Constantine, who succeeded to his work

and whose sly calculations and mercenary attitude to religion Gibbon found contemptible. He admires the men who failed nobly, such as Julian the Apostate or Majorian, who strove to save the tottering fabric; and he despises those who succeeded ignobly.

IV

GIBBON's reputation was established by the publication of his first volume, which ends with the triumph of Constantine. He was now something more than an erudite man and a good raconteur. He was an established historian equal in fame to David Hume and William Robertson, the two great figures whom he had admired in his youth. His vanity grew with his fame, or at least became more apparent; but since his erudition almost justified it and he had with it so much genuine good humor, his friends were disposed to regard it as an engaging foible. When he told an anecdote or illustrated an argument, he liked to be listened to, and the gesture he himself has described so well—the body bent forward and the forefinger extended—was no doubt designed to attract the attention that it commanded. But he was not a conversation killer; he did not wish to hold forth all the time; he knew how to take part in a general discussion; and one of his younger friends, Lord Sheffield's daughter, was to leave it on record that he had a great gift for drawing out the opinions and ideas of the young people he met. This capacity argues a genuine interest in the ideas of others and a benevolence that counteracted the effects of his vanity.

But he did not like to be put out of countenance. Once, at a dinner party, he had told a good story and "with his customary tap on the lid of his snuff box was looking round to receive our tribute of applause, when a deep toned but clear voice was heard from the bottom of the table very calmly and civilly impugning the correctness of the narrative." Gibbon defended his position, but the deep-toned, clear voice, which was that of the youngest guest present, would not be silenced. Seeing defeat imminent, Gibbon hurried from the table and was found by his host looking for his hat and cloak. "That young gentleman," said Gibbon, "is, I have no doubt, extremely ingenious and agreeable but I must acknowledge that his style of conversation is not exactly what I am accustomed to, so you must positively excuse me."

The young gentleman, twenty-one at the time, was William Pitt, who would be chancellor of the Exchequer at twenty-three and prime minister at twenty-four. In later life he came to value Gibbon's company, as Gibbon did his. Gibbon's vanity made him like the sensitive plant: he wilted for a moment at an aggressive touch, but he soon recovered and retained no malice against his offender.

In 1779, Gibbon brought out the second volume of the *Decline and Fall*, devoted to the invasions of the barbarians and the riotous mobs of Constantinople. The subject was not so much to the liking of the polite society of the eighteenth century as that of the earlier volume; and Horace Walpole, who had so deeply admired the first volume, was disposed to be critical, objecting that so much time and skill should be spent on so unrewarding a theme. Gibbon was highly offended. He seems to have taken with much more humor the reception he got from the king's brother, the duke of Gloucester, to whom he presented a copy. "Another damned thick book?" exclaimed the affable prince. "Always scribble, scribble, scribble, eh Mr. Gibbon?"

With the fall of Lord North's government in 1782, Gibbon lost the small post on which he had depended for part of his income. He decided that he would be able to live more peacefully and more cheaply in Lausanne; and by the autumn of 1783, he had transferred himself and his library to a delightful house that he planned to share with his old friend Deyverdun. The two scholars occupied separate parts of their pleasant mansion but met for dinner, over which they discussed the problems and pleasures of their work, and entertained their friends from time to time. Lausanne society still abounded, as it had in Gibbon's youth, with intelligent and well-behaved ladies, and the two middle-aged scholars sometimes wistfully thought that a wife between them would not be amiss: "Deyverdun and I have often agreed in jest and in earnest that a house like ours would be regulated, graced and enlivened by an agreeable female companion, but each of us seems desirous that his friend should sacrifice himself for the public good." Each of them feared the obligations more than he valued the advantages of taking so momentous a step, and they continued their bachelor existence. Gibbon knew how fortunate he was, and wrote with a full sense of his blessings to Lady Sheffield, describing his new library, which commanded from "three windows of plate glass, an unbounded prospect of many a league of vineyard, of fields, of

wood, of lake and of mountains." He concluded with satisfaction: "An excellent house, a good table, a pleasant garden, are no contemptible ingredients in human happiness."

Gibbon's admirable common sense and his freedom from any kind of self-deception are among his most attractive qualities. He did not want more than he had from life, and certainly by modern standards he had everything that a man could want. But comfortable means and ample leisure do not content everyone, and many writers have been as happily circumstanced as Gibbon without being so contentedly aware of the fact or so grateful for their blessings. Gibbon was firmly and rightly contemptuous of the delusion, shared by many eighteenth-century intellectuals, that the ignorant peasant, free from the anxieties and speculations of the educated and powerful, was much to be envied. Frederick the Great was reported to have said to Jean Le Rond d'Alembert, as they walked in the gardens of Sans Souci, that a poor old woman, whom they saw asleep on a sunny bank, was no doubt happier than they. "The King and the philosopher may speak for themselves," wrote Gibbon, "for my part I do not envy the old woman."

It was Gibbon's pleasant habit to work in a small pavilion at the end of his garden, and here he finished the last volume of his great work, a moment commemorated in a famous passage in his autobiography:

It was on the day, or rather the night, of the 27th June 1787, between the hours of eleven and twelve that I wrote the last lines of the last page in a summer house in my garden. After laying down my pen I took several turns in a *berceau* or covered walk of Acacias, which commands a prospect of the country, the lake, and the mountains. The air was temperate, the sky was serene, the silver orb of the moon was reflected from the waters, and all Nature was silent. I will not dissemble the first emotions of joy on the recovery of freedom, and perhaps the establishment of my fame. But my pride was soon humbled, and a sober melancholy was spread over my mind by the idea that I had taken my everlasting leave of an old and agreeable companion, and that whatsoever might be the future date of my history, the life of the historian must be short and precarious.[5]

The quietude and peace of that scene is illuminating. Gibbon is a very great writer, and his

[5]O. Smeaton, ed., *The Autobiography of Edward Gibbon* (London, 1911), p. 333.

book meant a great deal to him, but he never seems to have had—indeed, it is unthinkable that he should have had—that intense relationship—love, hate, exasperation—that many great writers have with their work. His attitude to it is well behaved and under control, like his writing: "an old and agreeable companion."

The *Decline and Fall* ends with a deliberately low-toned passage. Sainte-Beuve, with his usual perspicacity, said that Gibbon finishes "*cette longue carrière comme une promenade*," and at the moment of setting down his pen pauses to consider the view and to take his ease. The closing paragraph describes the gradual unearthing of imperial Rome from the rubble of the Middle Ages. There is a suggestion, but only a suggestion, of the new dawn after the six volumes that have discussed the long decay and the final collapse of anything resembling or carrying on the tradition of the Roman Empire:

Prostrate obelisks were raised from the ground, and erected in the most conspicuous places; of the eleven aqueducts of the Caesars and consuls, three were restored; the artificial rivers were conducted over a long series of old, or of new, arches, to discharge into marble basins a flood of salubrious and refreshing waters; and the spectator, impatient to ascend the steps of St. Peter's, is detained by a column of Egyptian granite, which rises between two lofty and perpetual fountains, to the height of one hundred and twenty feet. The map, the description, the monuments of ancient Rome, have been elucidated by the diligence of the antiquarian and the student; and the footsteps of heroes, the relics not of superstition, but of empire, are devoutly visited by a new race of pilgrims from the remote, and once savage, countries of the North.

(VII. 324–325)

That is the end of the book proper. Gibbon added a postscript, and after twenty years of work he could hardly have done less. He briefly summed up the story that he had tried to tell, and concluded: "It was among the ruins of the Capitol that I first conceived the idea of a work which has amused and exercised twenty years of my life, and which however inadequate to my own wishes I finally deliver to the curiosity and candour of the public." To anyone acquainted with the sufferings and struggles of the writer, the exhilarations and frustrations and fallacious triumphs—or, for that matter, with the labors and problems of historical research—the phrase "amused and exercised" must seem what perhaps it is: an understatement of Gibbon's ac-

tivities in relation to his great book. Yet it may not be. The judicious use of exact but unexaggerated terms produces exact and unexaggerated reactions. Gibbon's style reflects, and may partly have shaped, his character.

He came to England for the publication of his last three volumes, was given a splendid dinner by his publisher, attended the trial of Warren Hastings, and was made the object of a delicate compliment from Richard Brinsley Sheridan in his speech for the prosecution. "Nothing equal in criminality is to be found," said Sheridan, "either in ancient or modern history, in the correct periods of Tacitus or the luminous pages of Gibbon. . . ." Later he teased Gibbon by asserting that he had said not "luminous," but "voluminous."

V

IT was now 1788, a year before the fall of the Bastille. The political storms in which the century was to end were on the point of breaking, and literary fashions were moving fast away from the detached manner of Gibbon and toward the subjective and passionate manner of the romantics. During these years, Schiller's play *Don Carlos* (1787) and his passionate and vivid history of the revolt of the Netherlands—*Geschichte des Abfalls der Vereinigten Niederlande* (1788)—were published. Johann von Goethe's *Egmont* (1788) dates from the same time. The turbulent reaction against the logic and order of French thought and toward the exaltation of the passions and the ideal of a wild liberty was well under way. Count Honoré de Mirabeau, who had come to England shortly before the French Revolution, in search of radical inspiration in a country whose liberal institutions had been praised by Voltaire, looked about for English historians to translate into French. But for Gibbon, the greatest of them all, he felt only disapproval. At a large dinner party he fixed an indignant stare on a fat little man who had been pointed out to him as the author of the *Decline and Fall*, and spent the meal rehearsing what he would say to him.

You, an Englishman! . . . No, you cannot be. You, who admire an empire of more than two hundred millions of men not one of whom could call himself free. You who extol an effeminate philosophy which sets greater value on luxury and pleasures than on virtue; you who write in a style which is always elegant but never vigorous—you are not an Englishman but at most a slave of the Elector of Hanover.

His courage, perhaps fortunately, failed him, for the object of his angry glaring was guiltless of the *Decline and Fall*. Gibbon was in Lausanne at the time.

Mirabeau's view is unfair; like many other critics of Gibbon, he had not read the book. What Gibbon admired in the Roman Empire was not its expanse and power, still less its authority over the individual. What he admired was the spectacle of peaceful order that enabled the arts of civilization to be practiced. He did not admire effeminate philosophies and luxuries, and he deplored the decay of democratic institutions while appreciating the craft with which successive emperors had curtailed them. His admiration was reserved for the strong classical virtues, for reason and restraint.

If the rising romantics and the poor young *exaltés* of liberty who were soon to have such a rude awakening found much to criticize in Gibbon's book, its reception among the discriminating older generation surpassed even the author's by no means modest hopes. Adam Smith pronounced him "at the very head of the whole literary tribe at present existing in Europe." He was generally acclaimed as the greatest of English historians—a position from which he has not yet been dethroned.

On his return to Lausanne after his triumph in London, Gibbon found things were no longer what they had been. His friend Deyverdun was dead. The romantic movement had launched upon the country a quantity of staring tourists, come "to view the glaciers." Gibbon was also perturbed by the "furious spirit of democracy" that had been let loose by the French Revolution. His own political views are best summed up in his comment on the internal politics of Switzerland. Lausanne, long unwillingly subjected to the aristocratic government of Bern, was stirring uneasily. Gibbon had no patience with this nonsense: "While the aristocracy of Bern protects the happiness, it is superfluous to enquire whether it be founded on the rights of man," he wrote.

Fascinated by the politics of the past, he was resentful of the politics of the present because they threatened his calm retreat. Lausanne was now full of refugees from the French Revolution. "These noble fugitives," he wrote, "are entitled to our pity; they may claim our esteem, but they cannot, in their present state of mind and fortune, much contribute to our amusement. Instead of looking down as calm and idle spectators on the theatre of Europe, our domestic harmony is somewhat embittered by the infusion of party spirit." The comment is curiously insensitive, and Gibbon's public comments are indeed often out of key with the natural kindliness he showed in his personal life.

In 1793 his great friend Lord Sheffield was suddenly left a widower. His wife had fallen ill owing to long and strenuous hours of work on behalf of homeless French refugees in England. Gibbon, genuinely distressed at his friend's grief, hurried home to console him. He passed the summer between London and Lord Sheffield's country house, and was able both to give comfort and to receive much pleasure from the company of Lord Sheffield's daughters and their young friends. He was only fifty-six and at the height of his intellectual power. A great edition of English medieval documents, of which he was to be the editor, was projected; he looked forward to the new work, declaring with confidence that he was good for ten or twelve more years of valuable work. But his friends had grown alarmed at the state of his health. His vanity prevented him from admitting that the hydrocele from which he was suffering had reached embarrassingly large proportions. At length he agreed to an operation in the autumn of 1793. This was temporarily successful, but the condition worsened again in the winter, and he died on 16 January 1794.

English history lost a remarkable piece of editing when Gibbon died before he could begin work on the English medieval documents. But anything after the *Decline and Fall* would have been an anticlimax. His lifework is the one massive, incomparable book, and all the rest that he left behind him is interesting chiefly for the light it throws on the mind and the method behind the great history. Lord Sheffield piously edited Gibbon's autobiography, his occasional pieces, and some of his letters. In more recent years his journals and the earlier versions of the autobiography have been given to the world, with many more of his letters.

The *Decline and Fall* stands alone in English historical literature. Gibbon's unique quality—unique, that is, among English narrative historians—is his exact control. Most English historians of any literary sensibility are given to passion; the quality is inherent in the calling. They become involved in the events they describe, are moved, excited, carried away. This makes for vigorous writing and sometimes for a sharper insight into character, but it does not make for a steady, comprehensive vision or for clear presentation.

The English as writers have a false conception of themselves. They do not think of themselves as passionate, yet the great strength and almost all the faults of English writing arise from passion. The English are among the most passionate and impulsive writers in the modern world, and commonly set more value on something called "sincerity"—a word that often describes what happens when a writer loses control of his material—than on symmetry and order. They are the first to condemn a deliberate and perfected work of art as "dead." Sometimes this judgment may be right, but often it is no more than an angry prejudice arising from their own vehement and untidy minds. Consider, for instance, how few Englishmen are really capable of appreciating the flawless achievement of Jean Racine. William Shakespeare, the transcendent artist who broke all the rules, has left to his countrymen an unwritten charter to despise regulations.

Gibbon was not entirely without passion, for his love of learning and reverence for the intellect amount to passion. But he kept it within bounds, and when he wrote, his first thought was for the whole work of art. Each sentence performs its right function in relation to what goes before and after; each paragraph carries the narrative on at the necessary pace or establishes a point in the exposition. Because of this attention to detail, the massive volumes are always easy to read and never monotonous. The narrative passages are not clogged with intensive exposition, and the expository paragraphs and chapters stand out with a fine static clarity. Gibbon's control of his material was so sure, and his sense of form so strong, that he seems to have been able, at least in his later volumes, to achieve his effects without rewriting. His plan was clear in advance, and he would write his sentences in his head and commit them to paper only when he was satisfied of their completeness. In earlier times, when he still rewrote substantially, it seems to have been the form or order of each chapter rather than the shape of each sentence that gave him anxiety. Of his first volume he wrote to Lord Sheffield: "The first chapter has been composed *de nouveau*, three times, the second twice," and he spoke of an inten-

tion to *"refondre"* or recast other important parts of the book.

Gibbon's style is highly cultivated, and therefore artificial. It is also a dangerous style to copy, and he has suffered badly from imitators who aped his mannerisms without understanding their purpose and without having the sensitive ear and varied vocabulary that made it possible for him to use them with effect. He has, for instance, a trick of doubling words. Open anywhere, and you find phrases like "Gratian *loved* and *revered* him as a father," or *"The relaxation of discipline* and *the disuse of exercise* rendered the soldiers *less able* and *less willing* to support the fatigues of the service."

This is not done merely to add a spurious weightiness to simple statements. It is done, almost always, with the express purpose of slowing down the narrative at those points on which Gibbon wants the reader's mind to dwell. He thus detains the reader's attention by the simple device of making him or her read more slowly. But he never exactly duplicates his phrases; the additions are artistically correct, because they add to or modify the meaning. In the hands of less skillful writers, who duplicated without art and without apparent reason, the trick, which was widely copied, became intolerable.

The chance by which the *Decline and Fall* came to be written looks almost providential; here was an English mind with the romantic bent of the English —evident in his early reading and tastes—carefully cultivated in the French tradition and saturated with French culture. Gibbon produced, in consequence, in the most exact and expressive English, a history that is a model of lucid exposition and balanced form, yet never loses that undercurrent of feeling essential to great historical writing.

The Decline and Fall of the Roman Empire is an outstanding work of English scholarship and one of the great monuments of eighteenth-century English literature. This double achievement has had a profound influence on the whole tradition of English historical writing. The increasing complexity of techniques of historical research and the ever more exacting standards of scholarly accuracy that began to prevail in the later nineteenth century, thanks to the massive and precise scholarship of the Germans, inevitably divorced history from literature. But in England this divorce never became complete, thanks in great part to the influence of Gibbon. His method and manner and his splendid assurance may no longer be the models by which modern English historians work, but he remains the presiding genius of English historical literature. The union of erudition and style that he achieved is still the ideal of the English tradition.

SELECTED BIBLIOGRAPHY

I. BIBLIOGRAPHY. J. E. Norton, *A Bibliography of the Works* (London, 1940), a critical bibliography of outstanding interest; G. L. Keynes, ed., *The Library of Edward Gibbon* (London, 1940), an annotated catalog of Gibbon's books.

II. SEPARATE WORKS. *Essai sur l'étude de la littérature* (London, 1761), a hack translation of Gibbon's French original appeared in 1764; *Mémoires littéraires de la Grande Bretagne* (1768; 1769), an unsuccessful literary review produced by Gibbon and Deyverdun, the two annual vols. of which contain a number of anonymous contributions by Gibbon; *Critical Observations on the Sixth Book of the Aeneid* (London, 1770), published anonymously; *The Decline and Fall of the Roman Empire* (6 quarto vols., London, 1776–1788; 12 octavo vols., 1783–1790); further versions include J. B. Bury, ed., 7 vols. (London, 1896–1900), with critical apparatus; H. M. Beatty, ed., 7 vols. (London, 1909–1914), with bibliography; and abridged eds. by D. M. Low (London, 1960) and H. Trevor-Roper (New York, 1963); popular reprs. include the Everyman's Library ed., 6 vols. (London, 1910), frequently repr.; *Mémoire justificatif etc.* (London, 1779), written anonymously on the instructions of the government; *A Vindication of Some Passages in the Fifteenth and Sixteenth Chapters of the History of the Decline and Fall . . .* (London, 1779); Lord Sheffield, ed., *Miscellaneous Works . . . with Memoirs of His Life and Writings Composed by Himself* (2 quarto vols., London, 1796; 5 octavo vols., 1814), a third quarto vol. added in 1815 to complete Sheffield's ed. of 1796, with the additional material in the 1814 ed.; J. Murray, ed., *The Autobiography of Edward Gibbon* (London, 1896), the memoirs edited separately from the MSS used by Sheffield for his 1796 ed. of *Miscellaneous Works*; G. B. Hill, ed., *The Memoirs of the Life of Edward Gibbon* (London, 1900), an ed. with full critical apparatus—also note the intro. by J. B. Bury in his World's Classics ed. (London, 1907), and O. Smeaton, ed. (London, 1911), the Everyman's Library, both repr. several times.

III. LETTERS AND JOURNALS. M. et Mme. W. de Savery, *La Vie de société dans le pays de Vaud à la fin du 18e siècle*, 2 vols. (Lausanne, 1911–1912), the primary source for Gibbon's later years at Lausanne; D. M. Low, ed., *Gibbon's Journal to January 28th 1763. My Journal and Ephemerides I, II, and III* (London, 1929); G. Bonnard, ed., *Le Journal de Gibbon à Lausanne* (Lausanne, 1945); J. E. Norton, ed., *Letters of Edward Gibbon*, 3 vols. (London, 1955), the definitive ed.; G. Bonnard, ed., *Gibbon's Journey from Geneva to Rome* (Lausanne, 1961).

IV. SOME BIOGRAPHICAL AND CRITICAL STUDIES. W. Bagehot, *Estimates of Some Englishmen and Scotchmen* (London, 1858), includes a study of Gibbon; Royal Historical Society, *Proceedings of the Gibbon Commemoration, 1794–1894* (London, 1895), includes a catalog of an exhibition at the British Museum of MSS, notebooks, portraits, and other items; G. M. Young, *Gibbon* (London, 1932), a brilliant essay; S. T. McCloy, *Gibbon's Antagonism to Christianity* (London, 1933), contains a full list of the numerous contemporary works attacking Gibbon; C. Dawson, *Edward Gibbon* (London, 1934), a lecture at the British Academy; E. Blunden, *Edward Gibbon and His Age* (Bristol, 1935), a lecture at the University of Bristol; D. M. Low, *Edward Gibbon* (London, 1937), the standard biography, admirable in every respect; P. Quennell, *Four Portraits* (London, 1945), includes a study of Gibbon; M. Joyce, *Edward Gibbon* (London, 1953), in the Men and Books series; G. Giarrizzo, *Edward Gibbon e la cultura europea del settecento* (Naples, 1954); E. J. Oliver, *Gibbon and Rome* (London, 1958), a Roman Catholic approach; H. L. Bond, *The Literary Art of Edward Gibbon* (Oxford, 1960); J. W. Swain, *Edward Gibbon the Historian* (New York, 1966), a useful intro.; G. de Beer, *Gibbon and His World* (London, 1968), a perceptive and lively sketch of Gibbon and his times; D. P. Jordan, *Gibbon and His Roman Empire* (Urbana, Ill., 1971); G. W. Bowerstock, ed., *Edward Gibbon and The Decline and Fall of the Roman Empire* (Cambridge, Mass., 1977).

JAMES BOSWELL

(1740-1795)

P. A. W. Collins

My kindness for you has neither the merit of singular virtue, nor the reproach of singular prejudice. Whether to love you be right or wrong, I have many on my side.

(Samuel Johnson, letter to Boswell, 15 March 1772)

JAMES BOSWELL is a unique figure in English literature: a classic by virtue of the three masterpieces he published, he is also, in one sense, a contemporary. For much of his best work has been published only since the 1920's, and some still awaits publication, so that our ideas of the man and his art are being continuously modified. Boswell often referred to the journals and letters in "my Archives at Auchinleck," but initially only a few minor notebooks and manuscripts seemed to have survived. Since 1927, though, the Boswell papers have come to light in remarkable circumstances, and now more than four thousand items have been recovered, some of them hundreds of pages long.[1] For quantity, frankness, and literary merit these papers are unequaled among English diaries and correspondence. "My Wife," wrote Boswell, "who does not like journalising, said, 'It was leaving myself emboweled to Posterity', —a good strong figure; but I think it is rather leaving myself embalmed. It is certainly preserving myself."[2] It certainly was.

[1]See the bibliography for a note on the recovery and publication of the Boswell papers.

[2]Since some of the papers have been published only in modernized texts, all quotations in this essay will be modernized for the sake of uniformity. Quotations of Boswell's journal entries dated through 1778 are from the editions of the cited journals by F. A. Pottle et al. (see bibliography); journal entries after 1778 are from G. Scott and F. A. Pottle, eds., *The Private Papers of James Boswell from Malahide Castle in the Collection of Lt.-Colonel Ralph Heyward Isham*, 18 vols. (London, 1928-1934). The quotation from the letter to Margaret Stuart is from C. B. Tinker, ed., *Letters of James Boswell*, 2 vols. (Oxford, 1924). Quotations from the *Life of Johnson* and *A Journal of a Tour to the Hebrides* are from L. F. Powell's six-volume revisal of G. B. Hill's edition containing both texts (Oxford, 1934-1950; rev. ed., 1965).

Boswell, who had claimed that his *Life of Johnson* would exhibit Johnson "more completely than any man who has ever yet lived," can now be seen—as his editor notes—to have surpassed his own achievement. For if the *Life of Johnson* is the only English biography that is widely and constantly read, if many men, not primarily literate, could echo Leslie Stephen's deathbed remark that his enjoyment of books had begun and would end with it, the journals are the only biographical writing in English that can rival the *Life*. The greatest English biographer is also the most revealing English autobiographer. One of Boswell's favorite quotations, justly, was Alexander Pope's couplet from *The First Satire of the Second Book of Horace, Imitated*:

> I love to pour out all my self, as plain
> As downright Shippen, or as old Montaigne.
> (51–52)

Another of his favorite quotations is more surprising—Hamlet's

> How weary, stale, flat and unprofitable
> Seem to me all the uses of this world!

Here one notes the first of the many paradoxes in his "singular character"—"a character so composite," he informed a prospective father-in-law, "that you would need a great deal of time and many opportunities to study it." For Boswell's many friends regarded him not as a Hamlet but, rather, as a man of "goodhumour and perpetual cheerfulness," who had "so much good humour naturally, that it was scarcely a virtue" (to quote Samuel Johnson and Edmund Burke). Even his enemies praised him for this. Fanny Burney found her anger with him melting away, for "There is no resisting great good humour, be what will in the opposite scale." But Boswell wrote to a friend: "If you would think justly of me, you must ever remember that I have a melancholy mind. That is the great principle of my composition."

It was as "The Hypochondriack" that Boswell described himself when publishing a series of anonymous essays. Some of his friends—Johnson, for instance—thought this an affectation, but the journals show that his "mental disease" was actual enough. His melancholy, or "hypochondria," drove him sometimes to the edge of sanity and to thoughts of suicide. The gaiety and high spirits were the peaks, and the melancholy the troughs, of a manic-depressive curve. Hypochondria was the family complaint: one of Boswell's brothers was periodically insane, and one of his daughters extremely unbalanced.

Fortunately, hypochondria was not the only family inheritance. The Boswells were an old Scots family; "the blood of *Bruce* flows in my veins," Boswell told his readers—adding, typically, "who would not be glad to seize a fair opportunity to let it be known?" But the Boswells were not among the grandest of the Scottish landed gentry: Boswell's father enjoyed his style of Lord Auchinleck not by hereditary right but as one of the leading Scottish judges. Boswell and his father were different in almost every way—in politics and religion, in tastes and conduct, and in temperament. "If I am not so solid a man as my Father," he noted, "I am much livelier and of more extensive and varied views." But Lord Auchinleck had no admiration for "extensive views," and was neither subject nor sympathetic to the family melancholia or light-headedness. When Boswell justly remonstrated with him for treating his lunatic son John with "contemptuous disgust," he harshly replied, "If my sons are idiots, can I help it?" A month later Boswell stood by his deathbed and "wept; for, alas! there was not affection between us." Lord Auchinleck had been a dutiful, often a generous and long-suffering, father to his wayward eldest son, but he either felt no affection for him or could not show it. Many times Boswell vainly made overtures—"willing to talk with him, but as usual felt myself chilled."

This "niggardliness of fondness" and obvious contempt permanently undermined Boswell's self-confidence, and he was always seeking the approval and support his father had refused him. While still a youth he began the pursuit of great men that he prosecuted throughout his life with incomparable pertinacity and success. Simple hero worship and tuft hunting (seeking the acquaintance of the famous to achieve self-glorification) contributed to this passion, and so did his almost scientific interest in the more remarkable specimens of humankind; but the fundamental motive was to find an eminent elder from whom he could obtain, and to whom he could give, respect and affection. As an undergraduate at Edinburgh and Glasgow, he became acquainted with the learned doctors William Robertson, Hugh Blair, Adam Smith, prominent lawyers and judges, and the philosopher David Hume ("a very proper person for a young man to cultivate an acquaintance with," he announced at the age of seventeen). On a visit to London in 1760—he was then nineteen—he met Laurence Sterne, the actor David Garrick, various peers, and the young duke of York. Soon afterward another prominent actor, Thomas Sheridan, was "My Mentor! My Socrates! direct my heedless steps!" In 1762–1763, again in London, he added to his conquests Oliver Goldsmith, the wit and politician John Wilkes, and—on the momentous day, 16 May 1763—Samuel Johnson. "Upon my word," Boswell wrote a week later, "I am very fortunate. I shall cultivate this acquaintance"; and, a month later, "Finding him in a placid humour, . . . I opened my mind to him ingenuously, and gave him a little sketch of my life."

But in August 1763 he left England, to study law in Holland and then to make a grand tour—extended far beyond his father's wishes or knowledge—through the German courts, Switzerland, and Italy to Corsica and France. He met every great man within reach: the scholars Johannes Fredericus Gronovius and Johann Joachim Winckelmann, the philosopher Etienne Bonnot de Condillac, Lord Mountstuart, the prime minister's son, a dozen German princes, the pope, and—most important—Jean Jacques Rousseau, Voltaire, and General Pasquale di Paoli (the Corsican patriot, an eighteenth-century Garibaldi). Frederick the Great alone did not succumb to Boswell's skill and persistence; in vain did Boswell apostrophize him, "Ah, no, great King! . . . your soul shall be immortal . . . and I shall certainly speak to you in the other world, though I may not in this."

Many of these contacts were brief and perfunctory (Boswell's tuft hunting is apparent here), but to some of these great men, he laid bare his heart, with sincere and pathetic requests for advice. When no great men were in sight, a priest would do. He told one parson in Holland the whole story of my extraordinary life. My external changes have been pretty well, but for internal ones, I think I may enter the lists with any living being. [He] was struck with wonder. . . .

But of Rousseau he demanded more: "Will you, Sir, assume direction of me?" Rousseau declined, but Boswell sent him "a sketch of my life. . . . Oh, vouchsafe to preserve a true Scot!"[3] In later interviews with him, having previously prepared memoranda of topics for discussion, Boswell traversed all his most personal problems—hypochondria, Christianity and deism, moral relativism, the ethics of dueling, his political ambitions, his distaste for Scotland, his love affairs, his grosser desires ("I should like to have thirty women. Could I not satisfy that desire?"[4])—Rousseau gave him some good advice, and promised a lifelong correspondence. Boswell thereupon left Môtiers for Ferney, where "if ever two mortal men disputed with vehemence," he and Voltaire did so, over religion—a conversation "truly singular and solemn. I was quite in enthusiasm, quite agreeably mad to a certain degree. I asked his correspondence. He granted it. Is not this great?" Similarly, Paoli was informed "how much I had suffered from anxious speculations," and gave his advice on marriage, philosophy, and other urgent problems; with him Boswell struck up a warm friendship that lasted thirty years. On arriving back in London in 1766, Boswell discussed Corsican affairs with the statesman William Pitt; having found him abed at his first visit, he had said, "I'll call ten times." Not long afterward he was begging Pitt (now Lord Chatham) for a letter "now and then," for "To correspond with a Paoli and with a Chatham is enough to keep a young man ever ardent in the pursuit of virtuous fame."

Years later Boswell and his friend William Temple laughed at the awkward spectacle he presented in his teens, when they had first met—"the most puritanical being, and the most timid in society." Certainly by 1766 Boswell had acquired a confidence, if not brazenness, of manner. But it was largely the facade of a nature still fundamentally unsure of itself. All might appear to be well, Boswell acknowledged, "But I, who am conscious of changes and waverings

and weaknesses and horrors, can I look upon myself as a man of dignity?" He never acquired dignity or the restraint he so often, in his memoranda to himself, enjoined. "I am sensible," he noted in 1775, "that I am deficient in judgement, in good common sense"; his "vanity to be distinguished *for the day* makes me too often *splash* in life." It remained so to the end. But for several years after his return to Scotland, he was too busy to worry overmuch. He became an advocate in 1766, and for some years enjoyed a creditable practice, chiefly in Edinburgh, where he reluctantly lived. But his views of life were too "extensive and varied" for him to attain eminence in that drudging profession. He had wanted earlier to be a Guards officer—not to fight, but to escape from Scotland and the law—but that ambition was short-lived. His real ambition was, quite simply, to be a great man. When Garrick in 1763 had kindly said, "Sir, you will be a very great man," Boswell recorded that he could understand Garrick's thinking so. "For really, to speak seriously, I think there is a blossom about me of something more distinguished than the generality of mankind."

It was a vague adolescent desire, which Boswell never accomplished and never outgrew. "But what can be done," he wrote a few years before his death, "to deaden the ambition which has ever raged in my veins like a fever?" He was a man of great literary and social gifts, and extraordinary if spasmodic energy; but they were gifts that made him liked—or sometimes disliked—rather than honored. Literary success, which he achieved, did not satisfy him, and he lacked all the requisites for the success in political and public life that he craved. But in 1768 he made an excellent "splash," with his *Account of Corsica*. Corsica was in the news (partly through Boswell's own indefatigable activities as an anonymous contributor to the newspapers), and his book quickly went through several editions and was translated into German, Dutch, French, and Italian. At the age of twenty-seven, he was known all over Europe, and he was known as "Corsica Boswell" in English society for many years. At last he could write, with satisfaction, "I am really the *Great Man* now," for dozens of notabilities were seeking him out. Years later he remarked how far he had gotten in the world by having been to Corsica: "I had got upon a rock in Corsica and jumped into the middle of life."

The success of *Corsica* was not repeated until *A Tour to the Hebrides* nearly twenty years later. Meanwhile, and before, he had published a vast

[3]"Monsieur, voulez vous avoir soin de moi?. . .Je vous laisse une ébauche de ma vie. . . . O daignez de conserver un vraye Ecossais."

[4]"Je voudrois avoir trente femmes. Ne pourrois Je pas avoir cela?"

amount of anonymous journalism and various books and pamphlets, some anonymous and some not, but nothing that could increase his reputation; and he toyed with a score of literary projects, none of which proceeded far. His time was partly taken up with his legal work and with various good causes, which he espoused with great energy and remarkable success—but also largely with sundry pleasures, for which he had an extraordinary capacity. From his teens until his marriage to Margaret Montgomerie on 25 November 1769, he conducted a nonstop series of concurrent love affairs, ranging from casual flirtations to perplexed and hectic courtships. Luckily some of his love letters survive: "P.P.S. Read this letter with care. It contains very, very romantic sentiments."[5] "I charge you, once for all, be strictly honest with me. If you love me, own it. I can give you the best advice." "You ought to be flattered by my attachment. I know not if I ought to have been equally flattered by yours. A man who has a mind and a heart like mine is rare. A woman with many talents is not so rare."[6]

These samples must suffice to indicate the outrageous quality of these letters and the splendid comic effects that occur as Casanova finds himself playing Falstaff in *The Merry Wives*. There were also the experiments with keeping a mistress ("after all, can I do better than keep a dear infidel for my hours of Paphian bliss?"), and the more transitory and sordid conjunctions, not all as excusable as the debauch that resulted from "my getting drunk, because I would drink Miss Blair's health, every round, in a large bumper." Later in his life he was subject to bouts of drinking and gaming, habits that eighteenth-century Edinburgh did little to discourage. "I really love drams like a Savage," he confessed. Elsewhere, in verse:

> Extremely wretched sure all men must think
> A virtuous man who is inclin'd to drink;
> Who feels an inward suction in his breast
> A raging vortex which is ne'er at rest . . . .
> ("Ten Lines a Day," 30 May 1774)

And marriage did not cure him of his other major fault: "I have indeed the most veering amorous af-

---

[5]"Lisez avec soin cette lettre. Elle contient des sentiments bien, bien romanesques."
[6]"Vous devez être flatté [*sic*] de mon attachement. Je ne sais si J'ai dû être tant flatté du vôtre. Un Homme qui a de l'esprit et un Coeur comme le mien est rare. Une femme avec beaucoup des talents n'est pas si rare."

fections that I ever knew anybody have," he had early discovered. Though he loved and valued his wife as much as his capacities allowed, he was *"too many* for one woman"; he would try enclosing his wild mind with "moral fences," but too often "a storm of passion would blow them down." He tried to convince himself, though, that he could "unite little fondnesses with perfect conjugal love."

Boswell went through some sad and disgusting periods in this fashion, as well as some very comic ones, but it would be wrong to write him off as either a sensual sot or a foolish buffoon. He never became a complacent sinner. "My great object," he had written in 1763, "is to attain a proper conduct in life." He was repeatedly making good resolutions, fixing "eras" after which he would not drink or fornicate or gamble: "from henceforth [1768] I shall be a perfect man. At least I hope so." But it was with a sensible mixture of "benignant indulgence . . . and wise and salutary caution" that Dr. Johnson in 1781 received his declaration that "I would fain be a good man; and I am very good now." Boswell never acquired the habit of virtue, but few men's aspirations could have outlived so many catastrophic lapses. His pleasures, though, were not all sensual or illicit. In the essay "Intellectual Felicity" he wrote:

> Intellectual felicity affords a much higher delight to those who are capable of relishing it. Of this I am sure from what I have felt myself, and I should not say so, had I not also felt very exquisitely the pleasures of sense.
> (*The Hypochondriack*, no. 9)

Boswell was as sincere here as in his desire to be moral, pious, and respectable, despite all his lapses into degradation and his fantastic attempts to rationalize his failings into virtues. Intellectual felicity meant, above all, London and Johnson—though, as his wife suspected, his intellectual intercourse with Johnson and his pious fervor in St. Paul's were diversified by less exalted delights. These ranged from the innocent pleasure of playing cards on a Sunday ("hugging ourselves that we were out of the reach of presbyterian prejudice") and of embracing "a very desirable armful" on the coach home next morning ("Such incidents are marrow to my bones") to a thorough relapse into bad old habits ("After unpacking my trunk, I sallied forth like a roaring Lion after girls, blending philosophy and raking"). But the intellectual and social pleasures could excite him even more, to an indescribable ecstasy. He dined with General James Oglethorpe, one of the many distinguished men who—it is worth noting—retained a lifelong affection for him:

> Mr. Johnson and Dr. Goldsmith and nobody else were the company. I felt a completion of happiness. I just sat and hugged myself in my own mind. . . . Words cannot describe our feelings. The finer parts are lost, as the down upon a plum; the radiance of light cannot be painted.
>
> (journal, 10 April 1772)

So, despite his father's opposition and his wife's doubts, Boswell rarely missed his annual "jaunt" to London. He usually went during the Easter vacation, for about two months; only once did Johnson return the compliment, by making the famous Hebrides tour of 1773. Boswell had always felt "an almost enthusiastic fondness for the felicity of London," and long contemplated moving there and exchanging the Scottish bar for the English; but it was not until 1786, more than a year after Johnson's death, that he did so.

The move to London did not bring happiness —though if he had stayed in Edinburgh, the *Life* would certainly have remained unwritten. Boswell's hypochondria could not be cured by a permanent change of scene; a diurnal London became as tedious as Edinburgh. His wife was ailing and disliked London; she returned to Scotland and died there in 1789, while Boswell was away making an ignominious bid for political success. Mrs. Boswell had never shared his enthusiasms, and had suffered much from her volatile and fault-ridden husband; but neither she nor he seems to have regretted the marriage, and the loss of her companionship and restraining influence saddened and lessened his last years. The *Life* was completed in anguish and misery, and its success did not greatly cheer him; at a dinner to celebrate its profits, he "got into a pretty good state of joviality, though still dreary at bottom." The magnificent indiscretion of the *Life* and *Hebrides* made hostesses wary of inviting so noticing and communicative a guest, and Johnson was not the only good friend who was dead or gone. He sometimes had recourse to debauchery—"This is a wretched life for a man of talents, and a Christian"—and sometimes, left flat and lonely in the early evening, "just warmed with wine and having nobody on whom I could call, I thought the best thing I could do was to steal into bed, which I did a quarter before seven. Strange kind of life."

Boswell had inherited Auchinleck in 1782, and spent a month or so there most years; but the initial thrill of becoming laird soon palled, and though he remained a sensible, ambitious, and generous estate owner, he was never a devoted or happy one. No man, he decided, "of exuberant vivacity, keen sensations, and perpetual rage for variety," should attempt to live in the country. Nor could family life give him felicity, though he tried to be a good father to his five children. "It is a sad thing to have so *un*domestic a disposition."

Boswell's grasp on Scottish law had been uncertain, and he never mastered the entirely different English system. He could scarely keep up "the *appearance* of a lawyer. O Temple, Temple," he wrote to his friend in 1789, "is this realising any of the towering hopes which so often have been the subject of our conversations and letters?" Two years later his political ambitions also ended in disaster: "The embarrassed state of my affairs overwhelmed my spirits . . . the blasting of all my ambitious hopes was galling. I however still had glimpses of hope." Even the final journals, which are generally pitiful reading, are sometimes brightened by a gay period, a return of the youthful vitality, a generous act; but it was a sad and disappointed man who died on 19 May 1795, at the age of fifty-four.

THE JOURNALS AND CORRESPONDENCE

> [Dr. Johnson] read tonight . . . a great deal of this volume of my Journal, and said to me, "The more I read of this, I think the more highly of you." "Are you in earnest?" said I. Said he, "It is true, whether I am in earnest or no."
>
> (journal, 27 September 1773)

GEOFFREY SCOTT, the first editor of Boswell's papers, spoke of "the vast book-keeping operation of his life." Some of the papers had gone astray during Boswell's lifetime, and there are signs that others were destroyed, at random, after his death; but the quantity that has survived is fantastic. The central document is the journal, which is supplemented by various lesser daily writings—rough notes, memoranda, registers of correspondence, financial accounts, and so on. The other great group of papers is the correspondence, no less characteristic and sometimes no less frank than the journal. Boswell preserved hundreds of letters he received, and many copies or drafts of letters he sent; sometimes he also secured their return. In a written proposal of marriage, for instance, he includes the request that if he is rejected, the letter be returned; if he succeeds, he will collect or copy it when he calls—"for I shall always be curious to recall how I expressed myself in an affair of this consequence."[7] As F. A. Pottle remarks, in another connection, "If ever there was a man who intended to make work easy for his biographer, that man is Boswell." Pottle is referring here not to the papers, but to another specimen of Boswell's hoarding—his file of the *London Chronicle*, 1767–1768, in which he not only marks and indexes his ninety-five contributions to that newspaper within eighteen months but also distinguishes between those news items that are "facts" and the more numerous ones that are his own "inventions."

The first reference to the journal occurs in 1758. During an autumn tour with his father, "I kept an exact journal, at the particular request of my friend Mr. Love and sent it to him, in sheets, every post." (This journal is lost.) To keep such holiday journals was more common then than now; it was the equivalent of the snapshot album or home movies we show our friends. A similar jaunt in 1761 produced another (still unpublished) journal, and the next journal (which has been published) concerns "My Jaunt, Harvest 1762." Immediately after this, Boswell went to London—another extended jaunt, though he was also seeking the Guards commission—and his lengthy and brilliant *London Journal* was sent, like its predecessors, to admiring friends. These journals of 1762–1763, it would appear, gave Boswell the habit of journalizing, which he henceforth indulged in whether or not on a jaunt. There are gaps of as much as two years, when he ceased journalizing because he was too busy or too lazy, too happy or too sad; but of the time from autumn 1762 until his death in 1795, over one-third is recorded in fully written journals that have survived, and for the period when no fully written journal exists, there are less elaborate notes covering another quarter. This was a triumph of industry and willpower in so changeable and volatile a man.

The entries in the journal are not often merely mechanical records of the day's activities; Boswell is self-conscious about his states of mind and about

the artistic problems of recording them. Sometimes he congratulates himself:

How easily and cleverly do I write just now! I am really pleased with myself; words come skipping to me like lambs upon Moffat Hill; and I turn my periods smoothly and imperceptibly like a skilful wheelwright turning tops in a turning-loom.

(journal, 9 February 1763)

But more often he is graveled by the inadequacy of words, or his own skill, to describe the richness and clarity of his perceptions. Such expressions of chagrin recur: "It is impossible to clap the mind upon paper as one does an engraved plate, and to leave the full vivid impression." Or: "I find it is impossible to put upon paper an exact Journal of the life of Man. External circumstances may be marked. But the variations within, the workings of reason and passion, and what perhaps influence happiness most, the colourings of fancy, are too fleeting to be recorded." Boswell was a conscious artist long before he published his major works.

For whom, though, were the results of this careful art intended? The early holiday journals were read by friends, and some later journals of similar episodes—the Hebrides tour, for instance—were likewise circulated. So intimate a friend as Temple was shown some other later journals, but the bulk of those composed after Boswell's return to Scotland in 1766 were private documents written for himself. He rarely seems conscious of any other possible reader than himself or speculates about the fate of the journals after his death. Whether he intended them to be published, in part or in whole, during or after his lifetime, is a difficult and disputed question. He certainly realized that some passages could be adapted for publication. He decided quite early in their friendship to write Johnson's *Life*, and the journals—as he foresaw—provided much of his material. The better half of *Corsica* had been based on his journal and memories, and he hoped sometime to publish further striking episodes from the journals—his encounters with Rousseau, Voltaire, Hume, and others. But the journal did not exist for this purpose. Occasionally he speaks as if he had publication in mind: for instance, "My journal is ready; it is in the larder, only to be sent to the kitchen, or perhaps trussed and larded a little." The most plausible explanation is that unconsciously he hoped and expected that posterity—his own descendants, and possibly a wider public—would be inter-

---

[7]"Car Je serai toujour curieux de me rappeler comment J'ai écrit sur une affaire de cette conséquence."

ested in his archives, but that he never consciously and fully thought the matter out.[8] Certainly he ignored Johnson's advice to ensure that a friend would destroy the journals when he died. But if he did expect his papers to be read, he allowed this to influence him very little. He was a vain and histrionic man in his behavior and in many of his publications, but (as Geoffrey Scott remarks) in his journal "Candour can go no further. The Journal does not exist to show Boswell to advantage, but to objectify him in his own eyes."

The fundamental motives behind Boswell's journalizing were, indeed, moral and psychological. The *London Journal* opens with a sentiment he repeated twenty years later in a *Hypochondriack* essay on diaries (no. 66): "The ancient precept . . . 'Know thyself' . . . cannot be so perfectly obeyed without the assistance of a register of one's life." It was on similar grounds that Johnson, soon after meeting Boswell, had (unnecessarily) advised him to keep a journal, full, unreserved, and private. There is a famous conversation in the *Life* about diaries, in which Johnson recommends the publication of a candid one by Robert Sibbald as "an honest picture of human nature" (a motto, perhaps, for the Boswell papers?) and Boswell remarks that "As a lady adjusts her dress before a mirror, a man adjusts his character by looking at his journal." But Boswell's attempts to "know himself" were bedeviled by the complexities of his character; and when he consulted the mirror of his journal, the results were often disquieting—and not merely when he found the record of a conscienceless debauch: "This is an exact state of my mind at the time. It shocks me to review it." Even worse were the fundamental doubts about his own personality; as he confided to Temple, "Sometimes I think myself good for nothing, and sometimes the finest fellow in the world . . . Good heaven! what is Boswell?" We find him therefore addressing memoranda to himself, in answer to this daunting question: "This day (*Easter*) rouse. Be Johnson . . . Be *retenu*, &c. *What* am I? Oho, is it so? . . . At all events, be *manly*, and Sir David, &c."

This practice of addressing imperatives to himself is less odd than his use of the second person in describing his activities. At some periods his memoranda contain not only the orders for the day but also a review of the previous day's achievement: "Yesterday you did not at all keep to rules as you ought to do. You had sat up late and rose irregular. . . . Yesterday you did delightfully. You did not commit one fault in any respect the whole day." Such passages illustrate neatly the disjunction in Boswell's mind between the actor and the recorder, and may be regarded along with his famous declaration:

I should live no more than I can record, as one should not have more corn growing than one can get in. There is a waste of good if it be not preserved.

(journal, 17 March 1776)

The journal existed to perpetuate the moment and to give to Boswell's fluctuating character at least the permanence of the written word. This extraordinary faith in the written word led him to describe the pleasures of literary fame in unusual terms: "It is making another self, which can be present in many places, and is not subject to the inconstancies of Passion which the man himself is."[9]

The main motive, then, of Boswell's journalizing was the desire to understand, correct, and stabilize his character—aims in all of which he failed, though he attained many incidental successes in the first of them. Reluctantly he had to postpone until the future life not only his interview with Frederick the Great but also the lasting self-understanding and self-control that he sought with such assiduity:

The Great Power who made us will, I hope, in another period of our existence gratify us with an explanation of all the mysteries of our formation and progress through being which are now at all times so puzzling and sometimes so distressing.

(letter to Margaret Stuart, 23 March 1780)

Meanwhile, Boswell did his best, conscientiously recording the facts whether he understood them or not: "In whatever way it is to be explained, I have mentioned the fact." This is one of the fascinations of the journals. Boswell was not just a "singular character" and a skilled recorder of his actions and thoughts. His inability to understand himself pre-

---

[8] I owe much here to Pottle's admirable "History of the Boswell Papers," in the deluxe edition of the *London Journal 1762–1763*. Among other evidence he produces an important and hitherto unpublished codicil to Boswell's will. It is regrettable that this essay was printed in an edition not generally accessible.

[9] This remark of 1762 is echoed in the *Corsica* preface; the image of the diarist as farmer recurs in *The Hypochondriack* no. 66. Boswell was tenacious of and frugal with his ideas.

vented his noting only what seemed "significant" according to some psychological theory or some settled reading of his own personality. Continually perplexed and altogether candid and honest, he recorded both the significant and a rich sample of the seemingly inexplicable and irrelevant. The union of his egotistical preoccupation and scientific interest in "that favourite subject, Myself" is such that the reader rarely fails to respond.

There were, of course, other motives behind Boswell's journalizing. His urge to confess and exhibit himself, for instance, which was so conspicuous in his encounters with great men and with many lesser ones: "I have," he acknowledged, "a kind of strange feeling as if I wished nothing to be secret that concerns myself." Another motive is suggested by this remark, in 1765: "Could my feeble mind preserve but a faint impression of Johnson, it would be a glory to myself and a benefit to mankind." The journals recorded these impressions and many other "rich scenes," less for the possible delectation of mankind than for Boswell's own. He resembled William Wordsworth, who stored up in his memory and verses those crucial "spots of time," the recollection of which could later comfort and sustain him.

Thus, the journals are not confined to Boswell's anxious self-examinations and exhortations, though often he seems to himself, and to the reader, thoroughly introverted: "I think too closely. I am too concave a Being. My thoughts go inwards too much instead of being carried out to external objects." But there are at least as many pages of brilliant and "relished" observation of men and companies, and long buoyant periods when he "did not *think*, [but] leaped the ditches of life." One day he was expressing "in lively terms" his delight in a London scene, and his friend Bennet Langton thereupon

paid me the compliment of saying that it was agreeable to see such a scene with me. For I was not, like many people, in a state of dull amazement or illhumoured silence, but could talk of what pleased me.

(journal, 15 April 1779)

We can still experience Langton's pleasure, and Boswell's, through the journals.

A key to Boswell's character and to his success as a diarist is provided by his wife's observation that his spirits "required agitation, no matter by what."

He was a sensationalist, both in wanting to create a sensation and in needing strong and unhabitual sensations to keep him happy. He had "a rage for pleasure." When depressed, he "languished for . . . any state of animated exertion," and would "fly to every mode of agitation." His distaste for rural and domestic life has been mentioned; his distaste for Edinburgh, too, was largely the reaction against any regular existence, when "Such a day may be simply recorded *ditto* . . . I had no vivid enjoyment, but just moved along the tide of life." Too late he realized that he had accustomed himself "to expect too exquisite a relish of existence." His failure to grow up—so apparent in a dozen ways—is shown in his lifelong grudge against any day that was not exciting. The reason for his vices lies here; it was, for instance, "an inordinate desire of strong feelings which inclines me to [intoxication]."

This accounts, too, for his morbid interest in hangings and his romantic extravagance in seeking and creating situations that provided "a rich assemblage of ideas." His vanity also, the desire for "conspicuousness" that made him wish "rather to be conspicuous for faults than not to be conspicuous at all," was nourished by his feeling that there was no relish in a life of insignificance. Even sorrow was welcome, he noted: the news of a death or an illness provoked "a sort of agitation that rather gave a kind of pleasure."

The only places where the journal approaches dullness are in the quiet periods (usually in Edinburgh) when nothing excites Boswell; but soon his spirits are lifted by a jaunt to London, a cause célèbre, or some unusual visitor or occurrence. "My spirits were now," he writes after a mutiny in the Edinburgh garrison, "as good as when I am in London, such is the effect of agitation upon me." His worst periods of debauchery commonly occur when life seems "stale, flat and unprofitable" after a particularly stimulating period. Thus, the first great moral collapse after his marriage succeeded the exhilaration of his Hebrides tour with Johnson. "I am," he wrote in 1777, "for the most part either in too high spirits or too low. I am a grand wrestler with life. It is either above me, or I am above it."

Boswell's sensationalism is also the foundation of his literary genius. When he is on top of life, his zest for experience, his sharpness of perception, his curiosity about mankind, and his ability to recall and record his adventures are extraordinary. His skill developed early; the "Journal of My Jaunt,

Harvest 1762" is a completely Boswellian document. Already he is "strongly impelled to give a sketch of the characters" he meets, and is expert in handling the great men he seeks out. Having "got into an excellent method of taking down conversations," he gives a lengthy account of one with David Hume: "I showed away, started subjects and now and then spoke tolerably . . . I have remembered the heads and the very words of a great part of Mr. Hume's conversation." A few days later he exhibits another aspect of his powers of observation, memory, and reproduction—his skill as a mimic, which was acknowledged by all who heard him:

I began this night to take off Mr. David Hume which I did amazingly well. Indeed it was not an imitation but the very Man. I had not only his external address, but his sentiments and mode of expression.

(journal, 9 November 1762)

This short early journal exemplifies almost every trait of Boswell's character and literary skill—and his invaluable candor (recording, for instance, a friend's unkind but just remark on his penchant for philosophizing—"Boswell, you often dive for Pearls but you bring us up Cockleshells"). The *London Journal*, which follows, is perhaps the most brilliant narrative of them all.

Boswell knew his limitations as a journalist. "I have no pencil for visible objects," he confessed. "I am a very imperfect topographer." He did not care to visit the Lake District, having "little or no pleasure from seeing beautiful natural scenes"—a coolness he shared with Johnson. Mankind was his interest and specialty; but here too he had one great deficiency, as he realized. "I find it in vain to try to draw a portrait of a young lady. I cannot discriminate." He underestimated women and was markedly less interested in them (as individuals) than in men.[10] His love letters show this; they are often ludicrously maladroit when compared with his skillful approaches to his male quarries, which rarely failed. The journals, therefore, contain few vivid portraits of women. His records of Fanny Burney, for instance, are incomparably inferior to the maliciously comic picture of him that she draws in her diary.

With men he was much more successful. Telling Rousseau about his taste for mimicry, he explained, "When I espied any singular character I would say, 'It must be added to my collection!'" And so in the journals, though the characters are not all singular or great. "I am always studying human nature and making experiments on the lowest characters," he writes in France in 1765; and he records how this annoyed his servant Jacob, who found him both embarrassingly communicative and overcurious. "Your heart is too open," Jacob complained, ". . . And you force a servant to speak in a way he shouldn't, because you torment him with questions. You want to get to the bottom of things."[11] This propensity accounts for Boswell's fascination with criminals—for example, his interview with the beautiful forger Margaret Rudd, or his attempts to visit the gentleman murderer James Hackman (faute de mieux, he witnessed his execution and questioned the hangman), or this "curious scene" in a condemned man's cell, after the humble prisoner had smiled at one of Boswell's remarks:

I considered how amazing it would be if a man under sentence of death should really laugh, and, with the nicest care of a diligent Student of human nature, I as decently as possible first smiled as he did, and gradually cherished the risible exertion, till he and I together fairly laughed. How strange!

(journal, 21 February 1768)

The journals contain many such pictures of humble men (not always in circumstances so macabre), but Boswell's finest powers are called forth by the great. He realized the difficulty of verbal portraiture: "In description we omit insensibly many little touches which give life to objects. With how small a speck does a Painter give life to an eye." But the visual details are usually adequate—often perfect—and the subject is characterized more fully by his opinions and tone of voice. The finest interviews (apart from those included in his published books) are those with Rousseau and Voltaire. They are almost equaled by the deathbed interview with Hume, which has been called "the most sensational journalistic scoop of the eighteenth century," and the ecstatic audience with George III ("inclining

---

[10]Women have returned the compliment. Many of his most formidable social enemies were women; and in recent years, when female dons and critics have done so much for English studies, only one (Dr. Margery Bailey) has been conspicuous for her interest in Boswell.

[11]"[Monsieur] a le coeur trop ouvert . . . Et Monsieur force un Domestique de parler d'une manière qu'il ne doit pas faire, parce que Monsieur le tourmente en le questionnant. Il voudroit savoir tout au fond."

towards me with a benignant smile equal to that of any of Correggio's Angels, he said 'I think and I feel as you do'"). But one extended example of Boswell's skill and pertinacity in interviewing must be quoted. In 1774 the explorer James Bruce was in Edinburgh. He was an ill-tempered man; he detested Scotland; and he was smarting from a financial disappointment. "In this frame," Boswell reflected, "he seemed . . . impatient, harsh and uncommunicative."

My Curiosity and vanity united, were, however, sufficient to impel me, and, as he grew more rough, I grew more forward; so that I forced in a manner a good deal from him, while he looked big and stamped and took me short and held his head high and talked with a forcible loudness as if he had been trying whether the room had an echo. As this was a very remarkable scene with a very remarkable man, I shall as well as I can put it down in its very form as it passed.

(journal, 9 August 1774)

The record of this scene is full and vivid; Boswell concludes, "In this manner was information dug from him, as from a flinty rock with pickaxes." This interview furnished an article in the *London Magazine*, which offended Bruce; but Boswell did not worry: "No man can be agreeable to all kinds of people. And surely I am agreeable to as many as I could well expect."

THE PUBLISHED WORKS

"Miss Burney, [said the Queen] have you heard that Boswell is going to publish a life of your friend Dr. Johnson? . . . I can't tell what he will do. He is so extraordinary a man, that perhaps he will devise something extraordinary."

(*Diary of Fanny Burney* [*Madame D'Arblay*], 20 December 1785)

BOSWELL's journal, as well as having great intrinsic merits, is unique in having given birth to great independent literary works. His three major books, *An Account of Corsica* (1768), *The Journal of a Tour to the Hebrides* (1786), and *The Life of Johnson* (1791), are substantially the products of his daily records and phenomenal memory. The Corsica book consists of two parts: a historical and geographical account of the island, which is competent but not memorable, and "The Journal of a Tour to That Island; and Memoirs of Pascal Paoli," which

has the merits of the later books, though in less abundance. Boswell's visit to Corsica was shorter, and his acquaintance with Paoli less intimate, than his tour and friendship with Johnson, and Paoli was a much less interesting and complex subject. For Johnson, Boswell felt an "almost superstitious reverence," but he did not idealize or simplify his character; Paoli remains too much a heroic figure, despite the vivifying details. To depict a Paoli was a simpler task than Johnson would present him with, and it was well within Boswell's capacities in 1768; he produced a delightful book and acquired practice and confidence in the techniques that served him so well later. One notes particularly his skill in questioning Paoli, his pride in the perfect authenticity of his record of Paoli's sayings, his habitual self-exposure, and the unobtrusive efficiency of his prose, though it is short-winded and lacks resonance compared with that of his maturity.

Almost all the minor works written before and after *Corsica* have the merit of being manifestly Boswell's handiwork (and it is a rare man who can so stamp his personality on all he writes), but most of them have no other merit. "I have really," he noted in 1772, "a genius for particular history, for biography"—and, one would add, for autobiography; his genius was confined to these two genres. Of the minor works that have been reprinted, *The Hypochondriack*, though dull as a whole, contains the most interesting matter; some of these essays are almost as self-revealing as the journals and letters.

The two books on Johnson, though based on the journals, are not simple transcripts from them. Much irrelevant matter, concerned with Boswell or other people, is omitted; even the Hebrides journal, describing a period when Boswell was uninterruptedly with Johnson,[12] was cut by about a quarter. Boswell perforce, from "the peculiar plan of his biographical undertaking" (as he said), figured greatly in both books, but he suppressed much about himself, and not only when it recorded his discomfiture by Johnson. Thus he modestly passed over many evidences of Johnson's love for him, such as their reunion when Johnson received him with open arms and "hugged you to him like a sack."

[12]This was much their longest period together—101 days. Croker's calculation in 1831 that they only met on "about 276 days" during the whole of their friendship is still often quoted, but it is an underestimate. I have argued elsewhere that they met on about 425 days. See *Notes and Queries*, n.s. 3, no. 4 (April 1956), pp. 163–166.

Despite his self-confessed "egotism and vanity," Boswell seldom intrudes irrelevantly in these books. Over some passages reporting Johnson's words, too, he was reticent—aspersions on people or unrepeatably indelicate remarks ("mighty good stuff," he ruefully noted on canceling one)—and he tactfully omitted some details of Johnson's marital life and medical history.[13] A few excellent innocuous stories also were omitted, presumably because Boswell overlooked them; and many persons who might be offended by Johnson's remarks upon them were masked in anonymity.

Discretion was not Boswell's only concern in revising the journals. The more important alterations were made in the interests of clarity and vividness. The most obvious of these are his devices to heighten the dramatic quality of the "scenes" that provided his basic and characteristic material. Indirect speech becomes the typical—"JOHNSON. Why, No, Sir . . ."—and stage directions are continually added. Boswell also adds many connecting phrases and comments, and when he retains his original narrative, he dignifies and sophisticates its language (not always to advantage). What is of more concern is how he treats Johnson's language. "Authenticity is of the utmost consequence," he had written in the *Hebrides* dedication, and he publicly challenged Johnson's friends to demonstrate any errors in his reporting. Some people were offended by Boswell's printing of various remarks by Johnson, but no one seriously impugned their authenticity; Boswell had taken immense pains, during and after Johnson's life, to check the accuracy of his records and of the Johnsonian anecdotes he had obtained from other people. He had not, though, taken down Johnson's words on the spot in shorthand, as is sometimes imagined; the few recorded instances of his doing this are exceptional. His 1764 journal explains his usual practice:

My method is to make a memorandum every night of what I have seen during the day. By this means I have my materials always secured. Sometimes I am three, four, five days without journalising. When I have time and spirits, I bring up this my journal as well as I can in the hasty manner in which I write it.

(journal, 24 October 1764)

[13]J. L. Clifford's *Young Samuel Johnson* (London, 1955) draws on a file of Johnsonian matter in the Boswell papers, which Boswell labeled "Tacenda." Clifford's book is a useful supplement to Boswell, on the first half of Johnson's life.

Sometimes Boswell "brought up" his journal much more tardily. Some of the finest Johnsonian incidents were written up from notes or memory many years after the event; but Boswell had, as he claimed, "the best memory in the world for minutiae." Where he can be checked, one is amazed by his accuracy of recall.

During much of the Hebrides tour, he journalized more copiously and promptly than usual, having fewer distractions and being loath to leave unrecorded one moment of that unrepeatable jaunt—with the curious result that he was sometimes too busy journalizing to see much of Johnson. During hypochrondriac fits, he admits, "I did not exert myself to get Dr. Johnson to talk, that I might not have the labour of writing down his conversation." He always listened intently to Johnson ("one would think," Johnson wrote, "the man had been hired to be a spy upon me"), and he rapidly developed his capacity to record him:

when my mind was, as it were, *strongly impregnated with the Johnsonian aether*, I could, with much more facility and exactness, carry in my memory and commit to paper the exuberant variety of his wisdom and wit.

(*Life of Johnson*, 1 July 1763)

There are a few examples of his improving on Johnson's words, the best-known being his telescoping of these remarks on an implausible scheme—

Sir, it won't do. He cannot carry through his scheme. He is like a man attempting to stride the English Channel. Sir, the cause bears no proportion to the effect. It is setting up a candle at Whitechapel to give light at Westminster.

(*Life of Johnson*, 28 July 1763)

—into a single sentence: "Sir, it is burning a farthing candle at Dover, to shew light at Calais." Such liberties, though, are rare; a more typical instance of Boswell's re-creation of Johnson's words is his treatment of this dialogue, which Langton told him, recorded in *Boswell's Notebook, 1776–1777* under the heading "Bentley's Verses":

Smith. They are very well.
Johns. Yes Sir they are very well, but they are well in the manner of a man of ["strength of" deleted] a strong mind but not accustomed to write verses; for there is some uncouthness in the expression.

In the *Life* this is Johnsonized thus:

Johnson one day gave high praise to Dr. Bentley's verses in Dodsley's Collection, which he recited with his usual energy. Dr. Adam Smith, who was present, observed in his decisive professorial manner, "Very well—Very well." Johnson however added, "Yes, they *are* very well, Sir; but you may observe in what manner they are well. They are the forcible verses of a man of strong mind, but not accustomed to write verse; for there is some uncouthness in the expression."   (IV. 24–25)

"To see Dr. Johnson in any new situation is always an interesting object to me," Boswell writes in the *Tour to the Hebrides*, which recounts his most spectacular success in contriving to place Johnson in such situations. It was also the happiest; their letters and conversations in later years often reverted nostalgically to that blissful jaunt. "Shall we ever," Johnson wrote, "have another frolick like our journey to the Hebrides?" The journal is correspondingly buoyant. Boswell was elated to have conveyed Johnson to that remote region: "I compared myself to a dog who has got hold of a large piece of meat, and runs away with it to a corner, where he may devour it in peace, without any fear of others taking it from him."

He responded magnificently to his opportunities. The journal abounds in picturesque incidents: Johnson lying in Bonnie Prince Charlie's bed in Flora Macdonald's house; Johnson mounted on a wild heath pony, gravely led by a servant ("I wish, sir," said Boswell, "*the club*[14] saw you in this attitude"); or standing "with his ear close to the great drone" of a bagpipe; or strutting about the room, "a formidable appearance" with a broadsword and target; or solemnly embracing Boswell on the sacred ground of Iona. And even in London, among his intellectual compeers at the Club, Johnson had rarely spoken with such range and fluency as on many occasions here; even Boswell was astonished by the extent of knowledge he showed. "This man is just a *hogshead* of sense," said one admiring listener, and Boswell stood ready to keep Johnson talking (not always an easy task). He could justly claim

some merit in leading the conversation: I do not mean leading, as in an orchestra, by playing the first fiddle; but

leading as one does in examining a witness,—starting topics and making him pursue them. He appears to me like a great mill, into which a subject is thrown to be ground. It requires, indeed, fertile minds to furnish materials for this mill. I regret whenever I see it unemployed.

(*Journal of a Tour to the Hebrides*, 28 September 1773)

The journal, as Johnson acknowledged, presented "a very exact picture" of him during that period; it is, further, a wonderfully intimate and endearing picture.

Love is one source of the greatness of these books. As Walter Raleigh said, "Boswell made of biography a passionate science." He had gained Johnson's acquaintance, he often recalled, by perseverance; he kept it by love. Johnson returned this love, though his love was sometimes tempered by patronage and impatience, especially when Boswell, ever unsure of himself, kept demanding throughout their twenty-one-year friendship fresh testimonies of Johnson's affection. Johnson satisfied Boswell in every way—intellectual, spiritual, moral, emotional, and artistic. This wholehearted admiration accounts for Boswell's writing this alone, of his many biographical projects.[15] He notes at the beginning of the *Life* that Johnson's "extraordinary vigour and vivacity [of conversation] constituted one of the first features of his character." He could rightly add that few biographers had entered upon their task with more advantages, for Johnson was the perfect subject for Boswell's genius, with its conspicuous ability in recreating conversation. Moreover, the scientific Boswell, the "diligent Student of human nature," had great skill (mentioned above, and noted by all Johnson's friends) in coaxing Johnson out of silence and into admirable talk. Sometimes, he admits, Johnson "could not bear being teazed with questions . . . 'I will not be baited with *what*, and *why*; what is this? what is that? why is a cow's tail long? why is a fox's tail bushy?'"—but these are, after all, rather interesting questions, and even Boswell's notorious "If, Sir, you were shut up in a castle, and a new-born child with you, what would you do?" produced, like other foolish-sounding questions, an interesting re-

---

[14]The Club—later called the Literary Club—was founded by Sir Joshua Reynolds and met in London weekly or fortnightly. Its members included Johnson, Burke, Goldsmith, Charles Fox, Garrick, Sheridan, Edward Gibbon, Boswell, and many other illustrious writers and public men.

[15]Thus, he explained his decision not to write Joshua Reynolds' biography: "Sir Joshua was indeed a man of pleasing and various conversation, but he had not those prominent features which can be seized like Johnson's." Compare T. W. Copeland's essay (listed in the bibliography) on Boswell's failure in portraying Burke in the *Life*.

ply.[16] Where Boswell must be criticized, on both social and artistic grounds, is for his excessive delight in seeing Johnson in violent verbal combat with hated opponents. Johnson was combative enough, without Boswell's stimulating and exaggerating this tendency.

"Curiosity," wrote Hester Lynch Thrale, "carried Boswell farther than it ever carried any mortal breathing." He not only asked questions, risking rebuffs and insults so long as the great man spoke memorably, but also devised and stage-managed curious scenes. Without Boswell, Johnson would never have met his moral and political opposite Wilkes (Burke said there was nothing to equal Boswell's negotiation of this in the whole history of the diplomatic corps), and without Boswell's rapid contrivance "to be present at . . . so singular a conversation," we should never have heard the confession of Johnson's old college mate Oliver Edwards that he had tried to be a philosopher, "but, I don't know how, cheerfulness was always breaking in." Boswell did much to create his materials, as well as to re-create them on paper; he was anything but the patient stenographer that legend suggests. When he came to write up the *Life*, he was entirely aware of his originality. "The great Art of Biography," he had told one of his prospective subjects, Lord Kames, "is to keep the person whose life we are giving always in the Reader's view." He therefore wrote Johnson's life "in Scenes"; it was, he told his friends, "the best plan of biography that can be conceived," and this would be "*more* of a *Life* than any work that has ever yet appeared."

But Boswell did not rely solely on his own recollections of Johnson, or on this dramatic presentation; it was also his "design in writing the life of that great and good man, to put, as it were, into a mausoleum all of his precious remains that I can gather." He collected and printed many letters and manuscripts of Johnson's, and many anecdotes of him from dozens of friends; and he printed almost all of Johnson's excellent letters to him. One is grateful for this pious care to preserve all of Johnson, but the *Life* suffers from this intermixture, not always very adroit, of Johnson's written and spoken words. There are other disproportions in the

Life, notably (of course) the comparative brevity with which Boswell traverses the fifty-four years of Johnson's life before their meeting; and there is the famous episode of Boswell's begging Fanny Burney for anecdotes of the "gay Sam, agreeable Sam, pleasant Sam," which, as he realized, Johnson had displayed more adequately to her than to him, and in which his biography was therefore deficient. Nevertheless, there are few aspects of Johnson that the *Life* does not present vividly, and though other biographers have given us further facts about Johnson, there are few of Boswell's facts that need correction. And no other biographer has presented so vital a picture of *omnis vita senis*—the Horatian tag that Boswell used for the epigraph of the *Life*, having earlier intended to inscribe it "upon a chest containing my journal."

A picture, but not an interpretation: if one compares the *Life* with, say, J. W. Krutch's admirable *Samuel Johnson* (1948), one is struck by Boswell's disinclination to interpret. This was not owing to defect of mind (though there were aspects of Johnson he did not understand); when, at the end of the *Life*, he "collects into one view the capital and distinguishing features of this extraordinary man," he displays an impressive grasp upon his character, and the journals contain some perceptive remarks on Johnson that he did not reprint. He preferred, though, to give the evidence for an understanding of Johnson—thousands of "minute particulars"—rather than a distant view and generalizations. He presents with incomparable richness and immediacy all the qualities and the faults of a character as complex and paradoxical as his own; his discovery that he could not understand himself prevented his being hasty to explain Johnson.

Johnson lives, in Boswell's pages, through his inexhaustible and characteristic conversations; but Boswell does not record simply isolated sayings (as Hester Thrale [Mrs. Piozzi] did in her *Anecdotes of Johnson*). He gives them their context, in the conversation on such an occasion with such-and-such people, and points them with stage directions: "puffing hard with passion struggling for a vent" in an altercation; "blowing with high derision" at a fool; speaking of death "standing upon the hearth rolling about, with a serious, solemn, and somewhat gloomy air"; praising Fanny Burney "with an air of animated satisfaction"; or turning to Mrs. Thrale "with a leering smile." Similarly, he gives admirable descriptions of Johnson's appearance and manner-

[16]R. A. Leigh points out, moreover, that this question was a whimsical approach to an important topic—the educational problems raised by Rousseau. See his excellent essay, "Boswell and Rousseau" (1952).

isms: laughing like a rhinoceros, "in a kind of good humoured growl"; or "exhausted by violence and vociferation" after a dispute, "blowing out his breath like a Whale." Boswell has an eye for the picturesque and grotesque in Johnson's behavior, but succeeds in the task that Reynolds noted as crucial for Johnson's biographer—"to proportion the eccentric parts of his character to the proportion of his book." And, though the *Life* is conspicuous for its comedy, Boswell also has a surprising command of pathos; the scenes of his final meetings with Johnson are superbly restrained and moving.

When *Corsica* was published, the poet Thomas Gray noted that its success proved "what I have always maintained, that any fool may write a valuable book by chance, if he will only tell us what he heard and saw with veracity." This ludicrous dismissal of Boswell's art has been too often repeated by Thomas Macaulay, Lytton Strachey, and other patronizing persons. Manifestly, an extraordinary vigor and intelligence were required to perceive, record, and organize his memories so copiously as Boswell did; and this "fool" rarely missed the point of Johnson's omnifarious conversation. Johnson was the predestined subject for many biographies; a *Johnsoniana* had appeared nine years before his death, and Boswell's *Life* was the sixth to be published after his death. Several were good, but none approached Boswell's in range and vitality; and no biography of Johnson, or of anyone else, has since surpassed it. Those qualities and deficiencies of character that led Boswell to seek out great men and to write the immense journal, and the skills he acquired in doing so, led to the unique masterpiece of the *Life*. It was with characteristic accuracy, vanity, and enthusiasm that he told Fanny Burney of his forthcoming magnum opus: "There's nothing like it; there never was; and there never will be!"

SELECTED BIBLIOGRAPHY

I. BIBLIOGRAPHY. F. A. Pottle, *The Literary Career of James Boswell, Esq. Being the Bibliographical Materials for a Life of Boswell* (Oxford, 1929; 1966); F. A. Pottle and M. S. Pottle, *The Private Papers of James Boswell from Malahide Castle in the Collection of Lieutenant-Colonel Ralph Heyward Isham. A Catalogue* (Oxford, 1931); C. C. Abbott, *A Catalogue of Papers Relating to Boswell, Johnson and Sir William Forbes, Found at Fettercairn House, a Residence of the Rt. Hon. Lord Clinton, 1930–1931* (Oxford, 1936); L. Werkmeister, *Jemmie Boswell and the London Daily Press 1785–1795* (New York, 1963); W. H. Bond and D. E. Whitten, "Boswell's Court of Session Papers: A Preliminary Checklist," in W. H. Bond, ed., *Eighteenth Century Studies in Honor of Donald F. Hyde* (New York, 1970); F. A. Pottle, "James Boswell," in the *New Cambridge Bibliography of English Literature*, vol. II (Cambridge, 1971), the standard listing; A. E. Brown, *Boswellian Studies* (Hamden, Conn., 1972).

II. SEPARATE WORKS. *Observations, Good or Bad, Stupid or Clever, Serious or Jocular, on Squire Foote's Dramatic Entertainment, Intitled, The Minor. By a Genius* (Edinburgh, 1760), an essay published anonymously; *A View of the Edinburgh Theatre during the Summer Season 1759* (Edinburgh, 1760; repr. Los Angeles, 1976), the latter for the Augustan Reprint Society; *An Elegy on the Death of an Amiable Young Lady. With an Epistle from Menalcas to Lycidas* (Edinburgh, 1761), verse published anonymously and prefaced by three "Critical Commendatory Letters" by Boswell and his friends A. Erskine and G. Dempster; *An Ode to Tragedy. By a Gentleman of Scotland* (Edinburgh, 1761), published anonymously but dedicated "to James Boswell, Esq."; *A Collection of Original Poems. By Scotch Gentlemen*, vol. II (Edinburgh, 1762), Boswell contributed thirty-one poems and read the proofs; *The Cub, at Newmarket: A Tale* (London, 1762), an anonymous poem dedicated to Edward, duke of York; *Critical Strictures on the New Tragedy of Elvira, Written by Mr. David Malloch* (London, 1763; facs. ed., Los Angeles, 1952), the latter has an intro. by F. A. Pottle, essays published anonymously but written by Boswell, Erskine, and Dempster; *Letters between the Honourable Andrew Erskine, and James Boswell, Esq.* (London, 1763), repr. with *Tour to Corsica* in G. B. Hill, ed. (London, 1879), with omissions both indicated and otherwise, selections also in app. to [P. Francis], ed., *Letters to Temple* (London, 1857; 1908); *Disputatio judicia, ad tit. I. lib. XXXIII. Pand. De supellectile legata: . . . subjicit Jacobus Boswell, auct. et resp.* (Edinburgh, 1766), Boswell's thesis in civil law, upon which he was successfully examined 26 July 1766; *Dorando, A Spanish Tale* (London, 1767; 1930), anonymously published novel, later ed. lacks intro. and notes; *The Douglas Cause* (London, n.d. [1767]), a single-sheet ballad published anonymously on behalf of A. Douglas; *The Essence of the Douglas Cause* (London, 1767), anonymous pamphlet, a skillful resumé of this complicated case; *Letters of the Right Honourable Lady Jane Douglas* (London, 1767), Boswell assisted in editing this.

An Account of Corsica, the Journal of a Tour to That Island; and Memoirs of Pascal Paoli (London, 1768), in S. C. Roberts, ed. (London, 1923) and M. Bishop, ed. (London, 1951), and in F. Brady and F. A. Pottle, eds., *Boswell on the Grand Tour: Italy, Corsica and France, 1765–1766* (London, 1955); *Journal* repr. without *Account* in G. B. Hill, ed. (London, 1879), also many eighteenth-century reprs. and trans.; *British Essays in Favour of the Brave Corsicans: By Several Hands. Collected and Published by James Boswell, Esq.* (London, 1769), Boswell's share of this is uncertain; *Verses, in the Character of a Corsican at Shakespeare's Jubilee, at Stratford-upon-Avon, Sept. 6, 1769. By James Boswell, Esq.*, broadsheet repr. or repro. in many books on Boswell; "On the Profession of a Player," in *London Magazine* (August–October 1770; repr. London, 1929), three anonymous essays; Dedication to Garrick in *The Works of Shakespear* (Edinburgh, 1771); *Reflections on the Late Alarming Bankruptcies in Scotland* (Edinburgh, 1772), anonymous pamphlet; *The Decision of the Court of Session, upon the Question of Literary Property . . . Published by James Boswell, Esq: Advocate, One of the Counsel in the Cause* (Edinburgh, 1774); "The Hypochondriack," in *London Magazine* (1777–1783; repr., 2 vols., Stanford, Calif., 1928), the latter repr. under title *Boswell's Column*, with intro. and notes by M. Bailey (Stanford, Calif., 1951); *A Letter to Robert MacQueen Lord Braxfield, on His Promotion to Be One of the Judges of the High Court of Justiciary* (Edinburgh, 1780), a sensible and generous-minded anonymous essay on the dignity and office of a judge; *A Letter to the People of Scotland, on the Present State of the Nation* (Edinburgh, 1783), the first of Boswell's pamphlets to bear his name; *A Letter to the People of Scotland, on the Alarming Attempt to Infringe the Articles of the Union* (London, 1785), also published under his name, a garrulous, self-revealing, and absurd attempt to win political influence.

The Journal of a Tour to the Hebrides, with Samuel Johnson, LL.D. (London, 1785), in R. Carruthers, ed. (London, 1852), A. Napier, ed. (London, 1884), G. B. Hill, ed. (London, 1887), and L. F. Powell, ed. (London, 1950; rev. ed., 1958), also in J. W. Croker, ed., *Life of Johnson*, 5 vols. (London, 1831), and in R. W. Chapman, ed. (Oxford, 1924), with Johnson's *Journey to the Western Islands of Scotland; Ode by Dr. Samuel Johnson to Mrs. Thrale, upon Their Supposed Approaching Nuptials* (London, 1788), deliberately misdated 1784 on the title page, anonymous and scurrilous, quoted in *Life of Johnson*; *The Celebrated Letter from Samuel Johnson, LL.D., to Philip Dormer Stanhope, Earl of Chesterfield* (London, 1791), this and *A Conversation*, both misdated 1790 on their title pages, were published with notes by Boswell at an exorbitant price, apparently to safeguard his copyright in them for the *Life*; *William Pitt, the Grocer of London, an Excellent New Ballad, Written by James Boswell, Esq. and Sung by Him at Guildhall on Lord-Mayor's Day, 1790*, broadside, a fatuous but pathetic attempt by Boswell to secure Pitt's political patronage; *A Conversation between His Most Sacred Majesty George III and Samuel Johnson, LL.D.* (London, 1791); "Memoirs of James Boswell, Esq.," in *European Magazine* (May–June 1791), repr. in F. A.

Pottle, *The Literary Career of James Boswell* (Oxford, 1929), highly revealing anonymous self-portrait; *The Life of Samuel Johnson, LL.D.* (London, 1791), and *Corrections and Additions* (London, 1793; 2nd ed., with substantial changes, London, 1793; 3rd ed., with further new material, London, 1799), the most important later eds. are E. Malone, ed. (London, 1811); J. W. Croker, ed. (London, 1831; 1845; 1848); P. Fitzgerald, ed. (London, 1874; 1900); A. Napier (London, 1884); G. B. Hill, ed. (Oxford, 1887; repr. New York, 1889; 1891), rev. by L. F. Powell, ed. (Oxford, 1934–1950; 2nd ed., vols. V and VI, 1965), the standard scholarly text; R. Ingpen, ed. (London, 1907); C. B. Tinker, ed. (Oxford, 1933), rev. by R. W. Chapman, ed. (Oxford, 1953); E. G. Fletcher, ed. (London, 1938); S. C. Roberts, ed., 2 vols. (London, 1949); abridgments and selections include R. W. Chapman, ed., *Selections from Boswell's Life of Johnson* (Oxford, 1919); J. Bailey, ed., *A Shorter Boswell* (London, 1925); R. W. Postgate, ed., *The Conversations of Dr. Johnson* (London, 1930); *Everybody's Boswell* (London, 1930), illustrated by E. H. Shepherd; J. C. Dent, ed., *A Concise Boswell* (London, 1946); *No Abolition of Slavery; or, The Universal of Love: A Poem* (London, 1791), anonymous, "an exceedingly incongruous combination of a love letter with a political pamphlet" according to Pottle.

III. POSTHUMOUS PUBLICATIONS. This is a brief version of the complicated story of the discovery and publication of the Boswell papers. After Boswell's death most of his papers were returned to or remained in the Auchinleck archives, but some (about a third) were mixed with the papers of one of his executors, Sir William Forbes, and remained in the possession of Forbes's descendants, who apparently were unaware of the fact. A few other papers, detached from the main collection, came onto the market in 1825 and were later published (*Boswelliana, Notebook 1776-1777*, G. B. Hill's "Boswell's Proof-sheets"). Boswell's family, for obvious reasons, declined to give access to the Auchinleck archives, and did not discourage the rumor that all the papers had been destroyed. In 1905, Auchinleck was inherited by the Hon. J. B. Talbot (later Lord Talbot de Malahide), who moved the archives to Castle Malahide, near Dublin. In 1927 an American collector, Colonel Ralph Isham, having learned that the Boswell papers existed and were at Malahide, persuaded Lord Talbot to sell him the whole collection. Further important bundles of papers, of which Lord Talbot had been unaware, were discovered at Malahide in 1930, 1939, and 1949. Isham bought them also.

Meanwhile, the Forbes collection had been accidentally discovered at Fettercairn House, in Scotland, in 1930. After a protracted lawsuit this, too, came into Isham's possession. In 1949-1950, Isham sold all of his Boswell papers to Yale University. He had published a limited edition of the best of the papers then in his possession in 1928-1934, and in 1936 he had allowed publication of an unlimited edition of the Hebrides journal, which had been discovered at Malahide too late for inclusion in his own edition. In 1950, Yale University published—through Heinemann in London and McGraw-Hill in New York—the first of the Yale editions of the private papers of James Boswell; nine volumes have followed so far. This series is the trade edition, a reprint for the general public of the more interesting papers. There is also a limited deluxe issue of this edition, but only the first volume—the *London Journal*—differs markedly from the corresponding trade issue. Otherwise the difference is confined to a better format and more illustration. The early volumes of the Isham edition contain a few items not reprinted in the Yale editions, but more often the Yale editions are fuller. Yale has also begun to publish a research edition, reproducing more exactly a larger selection of the papers and containing appropriate annotation. For a full account see D. Buchanan, *The Treasure of Auchinleck*, listed below.

P. Francis, ed., *Letters of James Boswell, Addressed to the Rev. W. J. Temple* (London, 1857), repr. with new intro. by T. Seccombe (London, 1908), discovered at Boulogne in 1850, edited anonymously, bowdlerized and otherwise inaccurate, app. repr. some of the published Boswell-Erskine letters; *Boswelliana, The Commonplace Book of James Boswell. With a Memoir and Annotations by the Rev. Charles Rogers* (London, 1874), part of this previously published in *Miscellanies of the Philobiblion Society*, vol. II (London, 1856), Rogers' lengthy memoir is the first substantial attempt at a biography of Boswell; C. B. Tinker, ed., *Letters of James Boswell*, 2 vols. (Oxford, 1924), the most important collection of Boswelliana until the journals and other papers were published, over one hundred letters here printed for the first time; R. W. Chapman, ed., *Boswell's Notebook, 1776-1777* (London, 1925), an inaccurate transcript (1893) and a photographic facs. (1919) had been previously published in small lim. eds., Chapman printed the corresponding passages of the *Life of Johnson*, for which this notebook was compiled, on opposite pages; *Private Papers of James Boswell from Malahide Castle in the Collection of Lieutenant-Colonel Ralph Heyward Isham*, 18 vols. (London–Mt. Vernon, N.Y., 1928-1934), only 570 copies were printed; G. Scott, ed., vols. I–VI, the rest by F. A. Pottle; vol. VI, *The Making of the Life of Johnson as Shown in Boswell's First Notes, Original Diaries and Revised Drafts*, is highly important; F. A. Pottle et al., comp., *Index to the Private Papers of James Boswell from Malahide Castle* (London, 1937), was published separately as was the catalog (see "Bibliography"); F. A. Pottle and C. H. Bennett, eds., *Boswell's Journal of a Tour to the Hebrides with Samuel Johnson, LL.D. Now First Published from the Original Manuscript* (London, 1936; repr. London–New York, 1963; 1971), the latter with substantial app. of corrections and additions; F. A. Pottle, ed., *Boswell's London Journal 1762-1763. Now First Published from the Original*

Manuscript (London–New York, 1950), discovered at Fettercairn, contains the first meeting with Johnson, deluxe ed. contains the *Journal of My Jaunt, Harvest 1762* and F. A. Pottle, "The History of the Boswell Papers," the New York ed. has a preface by C. Morley; F. A. Pottle, ed., *Boswell in Holland 1763-1764, Including His Correspondence with Belle de Zuylen (Zélide)* (London–New York, 1952), Boswell's journal for this period having been lost in his lifetime, this consists of his notes, memoranda, letters, etc.; F. A. Pottle, ed., *Boswell on the Grand Tour: Germany and Switzerland 1764* (London–New York, 1953), includes the splendid interviews with Rousseau and Voltaire; F. Brady and F. A. Pottle, eds., *Boswell on the Grand Tour: Italy, Corsica and France 1765-1766* (London–New York, 1955), selections from Boswell's journals, notes, and correspondence during this period, repr. the published *Tour of Corsica* as no MS. journal exists for that episode; F. Brady and F. A. Pottle, eds., *Boswell in Search of a Wife 1766-1769* (London–New York, 1957), also includes his first years at the bar, his reaping the success of the *Tour to Corsica*, and two jaunts to London; M. K. Wimsatt, Jr., and F. A. Pottle, eds., *Boswell for the Defence 1769-1774* (London–New York, 1960), his strenuous efforts in the defense of John Reid, hanged for stealing sheep, and other legal activities, also contains two visits to London, on one of which he determines to write Johnson's biography; C. Ryskamp and F. A. Pottle, eds., *Boswell, the Ominous Years, 1774-1776* (London–New York, 1963), further meetings with Johnson, his matrimonial affairs, and some extramarital adventures; C. McC. Weis and F. A. Pottle, eds., *Boswell in Extremes 1776-1778* (New York, 1970; London, 1971), includes the famous deathbed interview with David Hume, and an important new journal for 1778; J. Werner, ed., *Boswell's Book of Bad Verse: A Verse Self-Portrait* (London, 1974); J. W. Reed and F. A. Pottle, eds., *Boswell: Lord of Auchinleck 1778-1782* (London–New York, 1977). Three vols. of correspondence have so far been published in the Yale Research ed.: R. S. Walker, ed., *Correspondence of James Boswell and John Johnston of Grange* (London–New York, 1966); M. Waingrow, ed., *The Correspondence and Other Papers of James Boswell Relating to the "Life of Johnson"* (London–New York, 1969); C. N. Fifer, ed., *The Correspondence of James Boswell with Certain Members of the Club* (London–New York, 1976).

IV. BIOGRAPHICAL AND CRITICAL STUDIES. P. Pindar (J. Wolcot), *A Poetical and Congratulatory Epistle to James Boswell, Esq., on His Journal of a Tour to the Hebrides* (London, 1786), this and the next item are examples of contemporary jocularity at Boswell's expense, also in *The Works of Peter Pindar*; *Picturesque Beauties of Boswell* (London, 1786), caricatures based on *Tour to the Hebrides* etched by T. Rowlandson from S. Collings' designs, repro. with annotation in J. Werner, ed., *Tour* (London, 1956); T. B. Macaulay, "Samuel Johnson," in *Edinburgh Review*

(September 1831), repr. in his *Critical and Historical Essays* (London, 1843), a review of Croker's ed. of the *Life*, a violent and very influential attack on Boswell and Croker; T. Carlyle, "Boswell's *Life of Johnson*," in *Fraser's Magazine* (May 1832), repr. in Carlyle's *Critical and Miscellaneous Essays* (Boston, 1838; London, 1839), praises Boswell, largely for his hero worship; G. B. Hill, *Dr. Johnson: His Friends and Critics* (London, 1870), contains chs. on Macaulay's and Carlyle's judgments on Boswell; P. Fitzgerald, *Croker's Boswell, and Boswell* (London, 1880), contains information on Boswell's revisions between eds.; G. B. Hill, *Footsteps of Dr. Johnson (Scotland)* (London, 1890), with twenty-five plates and many illustrations in the text, showing scenes on the Highland Hebrides tour; P. Fitzgerald, *Life of James Boswell (of Auchinleck)*, 2 vols. (London, 1891), neither accurate nor judicious; W. K. Leask, *James Boswell* (Edinburgh, n.d. [1896]), slight and unpretentious but generous and sensible in its judgments; G. B. Hill, ed., *Johnsonian Miscellanies* (Oxford, 1897), repr. accounts of Johnson by H. Thrale Piozzi, T. Campbell, Sir J. Reynolds, and others that can be usefully compared with Boswell's (also see the diaries of Fanny Burney for further matter on Boswell), much of this repr. in R. Napier, ed., *Johnsoniana* (London, 1884), and in Bohn's Library ed. (London, 1892); L. Stephen, *Studies of a Biographer*, vol. I (London, 1898), the essay "Johnsoniana" contains a useful comparison between Boswell and other biographers of Johnson (also see Stephen's life of Boswell in the *Dictionary of National Biography*); G. B. Hill, "Boswell's Proof-Sheets," in *Johnson Club Papers*, 1st ser. (London, 1899), describes Boswell at work on the final stages of preparing the *Life of Johnson*.

P. Fitzgerald, *Boswell's Autobiography* (London, 1912), hypothesizes that Boswell, not Johnson, is the subject of the *Life*; G. Mallory, *Boswell the Biographer* (London, 1912), the best comment on Boswell until then, now unduly neglected; J. Bailey, *Dr. Johnson and His Circle* (Oxford, 1913; rev. ed., London, 1944), the latter by L. F. Powell, a useful and sometimes acute book; C. B. Tinker, *Young Boswell* (London, 1922), admirably sympathetic, intelligent, and accurate, but unfortunately written before the discovery of the journals; F. A. Pottle, "Bozzy and Yorick," in *Blackwood's Magazine* (August 1925); C. B. Tinker and F. A. Pottle, *A New Portrait of James Boswell* (Cambridge, Mass., 1927), repro. of all the known portraits of Boswell, maintains that a portrait by G. Willison is of Boswell as a young man (the journals confirm this); *Johnson and Boswell by Themselves and Others* (Oxford, 1928), contains R. W. Chapman, "Boswell's Revises of the *Life of Johnson*" and L. F. Powell, "The Revision of Dr. Birkbeck Hill's *Boswell*"; R. W. Chapman, "Boswell's Archives," in *Essays and Studies* (1932); C. E. Vulliamy, *James Boswell* (London, 1932), concludes that Boswell was insane; J. L. Smith-Dampier, *Who's Who in Boswell?*

(Oxford, 1935), an eccentric companion vol. for readers of the *Life*; F. A. Pottle, *Boswell and the Girl from Botany Bay* (New York, 1937; London, 1938), recounts a very creditable episode from Boswell's last years; L. F. Powell, "Boswell's Original Journal of His Tour to the Hebrides and the Printed Version," in *Essays and Studies* (1938).

D. A. Stauffer, *The Art of Biography in Eighteenth-Century England* (Oxford, 1941), contains an excellent section on Boswell and comparisons with other biographers of this period; E. C. Mossner, *The Forgotten Hume: Le Bon David* (Oxford, 1943), a useful ch. on Boswell's relations with Hume; R. W. Chapman, *Two Centuries of Johnsonian Scholarship* (Glasgow, 1945); F. A. Pottle, "The Power of Memory in Boswell and Scott," in *Essays on the Eighteenth Century Presented to David Nichol Smith* (Oxford, 1945); P. Quennell, *Four Portraits: Studies of the Eighteenth Century* (London, 1945); C. C. Abbott, *Boswell* (Newcastle upon Tyne, 1946), a lecture by the discoverer of the Fettercairn papers; B. H. Bronson, *Johnson Agonistes and Other Essays* (Cambridge, 1946), published in the United States as *Johnson and Boswell: Three Essays* (Berkeley, Calif., 1945), the most penetrating study of Boswell's character; D. B. W. Lewis, *The Hooded Hawk or the Case of Mr. Boswell* (London, 1946; New York, 1949; 2nd ed., London, 1952), latter retitled *James Boswell; A Short Life*, an enthusiastic biography lessened in value by inaccuracies; F. A. Pottle, "The Life of Boswell," in *Yale Review* (September 1946); *The Age of Johnson: Essays Presented to Chauncey Brewster Tinker* (London, 1949), contains F. A. Pottle, "James Boswell, Journalist," T. W. Copeland, "Boswell's Portrait of Burke," and S. L. Gulick, "Johnson, Chesterfield, and Boswell," an expanded version of Copeland's essay appears in his *Edmund Burke: Six Essays* (New Haven, Conn., 1949; London, 1950); F. W. Hilles, ed., *Portraits, by Sir Joshua Reynolds* (London, 1952), in the Yale eds. of the private papers of Boswell, drawing on material about Reynolds discovered in the Fettercairn collection, includes chs. on Boswell and Reynolds, and Johnson and Reynolds; R. A. Leigh, "Boswell and Rousseau," in *Modern Language Review* (July 1952); R. W. Chapman, *Johnsonian and Other Essays and Reviews* (Oxford, 1953), see particularly "The Making of the *Life of Johnson*"; M. McLaren, *The Highland Jaunt: A Study of James Boswell and Samuel Johnson upon Their Highland and Hebridean Tour of 1773* (London, 1954), a delightful and perceptive book offering invaluable background information, well illustrated by contemporary landscapes and caricatures; L. Edel, *Literary Biography* (London, 1957), first ch. is of particular importance; F. L. Lucas, *The Search for Good Sense* (London, 1958), Boswell is one of the few eighteenth-century characters here studied, a depreciatory Macaulayan account; H. Pearson, *Johnson and Boswell: The Story of Their Lives* (London, 1958); W. K. Wimsatt,

Jr., "James Boswell, the Man and the Journal," in *Yale Review* (September 1959); F. R. Hart, "Boswell and the Romantics," in *ELH* (March 1960); P. F. Fussell, "The Force of Memory in Boswell's *London Journal*," in *Studies in English Literature* (June 1962); F. A. Pottle, "Boswell Revalued," in C. Camden, ed., *Literary Views: Critical and Historical Essays* (Chicago, 1964); F. Brady, *Boswell's Political Career* (New Haven, Conn., 1965); M. Lascelles et al., in *Johnson, Boswell and Their Circle: Essays Presented to L. F. Powell* (Oxford, 1965), including items on Boswell's travels, his university education and his reading, and a comparison between the *Life* and Lockhart's *Scott*; F. A. Pottle, *James Boswell: The Earlier Years 1740–1769* (London–New York, 1966), the first vol. of two, in the authoritative biography; J. Butt, *Biography in the Hands of Walton, Johnson, and Boswell* (Los Angeles, 1966); J. W. Reed, *English Biography in the Early 19th Century* (New Haven, Conn., 1966); M. McLaren, *Corsica Boswell: Paoli, Johnson and Freedom* (London, 1966); J. Kerslake, *Mr. Boswell* (London, 1967), catalog of a National Portrait Gallery exhibition; R. W. Rader, "Literary Form in Factual Narrative: Boswell's *Johnson*," in P. B. Daghlian, ed., *Essays in 18th Century Biography* (Bloomington, Ind., 1968); E. L. McAdam, *Johnson and Boswell: A Survey of Their Writings* (Boston, 1969); J. L. Clifford, ed., *Twentieth-Century Interpretations of Boswell's Life of Johnson* (Englewood Cliffs, N. J., 1970); A. R. Brooks, *James Boswell* (New York, 1971), in Twayne's English Authors series; D. C. Passler, *Time, Form and Style in Boswell's Life of Johnson* (New Haven, Conn., 1971); W. R. Siebenschuh, *Form and Purpose in Boswell's Biographical Works* (Los Angeles, 1972); F. Brady, "Boswell's Self-Presentation and His Critics," in *Studies in English Literature* (September 1972); C. Tracy, "Boswell: The Cautious Empiricist," in P. S. Fritz and D. Williams, eds., *The Triumph of Culture* (Toronto, 1972); M. Hyde, *The Impossible Friendship: Boswell and Mrs. Thrale* (Cambridge, Mass., 1972; London, 1973); D. Buchanan, *The Treasure of Auchinleck: The Story of the Boswell Papers* (London–New York, 1974), a detailed account of their rediscovery and subsequent history; D. Daiches, *James Boswell and His World* (London–New York, 1976), with numerous illustrations; M. Hyde, "Boswell's Ebony Cabinet," in R. F. Brissenden and J. C. Eade, eds., *Studies in the 18th Century III* (Toronto, 1976); W. R. Siebenschuh, "The Relationship between Factual Accuracy and Literary Art in the *Life of Johnson*," in *Modern Philology* (February 1977); R. B. Schwartz, *Boswell's Johnson: A Preface to The Life* (Madison, Wis., 1978); W. C. Dowling, "Boswell and the Problem of Biography," in D. Aaron, ed., *Studies in Biography* (Cambridge, Mass., 1978).

RICHARD BRINSLEY SHERIDAN

(1751-1816)

Arnold Hare

I

SHERIDAN (christened Thomas Brinsley, but always known as Richard) was born in Dublin in the autumn of 1751. His grandfather, Dr. Thomas Sheridan, a mildly eccentric clergyman, had been a friend of Jonathan Swift; his father, also Thomas, was an actor, a teacher of elocution, and later a writer on educational and linguistic matters; his mother, Frances, a minor novelist and playwright. For some years Thomas Sheridan managed the Smock Alley Theatre in Dublin until, in 1754, he was unwittingly caught in the cross fire of ultrasensitive Irish politics. A riot in the theater caused him to abandon management and migrate to England and an engagement as a leading actor under John Rich at Covent Garden. When this proved less successful than he had hoped, he returned to Dublin in 1756 for a second spell of management that, albeit for different reasons, ended in failure two years later. Thomas then returned to England and changed course into educational theory and practice and the compilation of a dictionary.

During this unsettled time Richard, the second surviving son, and his sisters were left behind in Dublin, first with relatives and then with a foster mother. Only after the second retreat from Dublin was the family brought together again, and then only briefly, since for about six years from 1762 Sheridan was sent to Harrow School. There, according to his own statement, he was very unhappy. He told Thomas Creevey that he "was a very low-spirited boy, much given to crying when alone"; and he attributed this very much to being neglected by his father, to his being left without money, and often not taken home at the regular holidays.

There are indications, too, that because of his father's precarious financial position—in 1764 the parents and the rest of the children had to take refuge from creditors by living in France—school fees were left unpaid and he was less than adequately clothed and shod. Nor was he particularly bright or hardworking as a scholar; while as a player's son at a time when the acting profession suffered under the legal stigma of "vagabondage," he seems to have been the recipient of much ill-natured persecution from his fellows. All in all, it would seem to have been a haphazard and unstable upbringing, which may well have affected the development of his character and attitudes in later life.

When the time came to leave school, the financial situation made it impossible for Richard to go on to university, so he rejoined the rest of his family (his mother had died in 1766) in Soho. There, exposed to his father's somewhat idiosyncratic educational theories and the social attractions of the town, the young man began to emerge into the larger world; but it was to the small yet highly concentrated world of Bath, to which his father moved in the autumn of 1770 to set up an academy of oratory, that Sheridan owed his real higher education.

In 1770, Bath was reaching the peak of its reputation as a fashionable resort. Exploiting the presence of hot springs, the curative properties of which might assist those suffering from the results of overeating, excessive drinking, and unsanitary habits, Bath since the late seventeenth century had, like many a modern watering place, laid itself out to cater to the whims of its visitors, and at the same time empty their pockets. Balls, assemblies, gaming, concerts, pleasure gardens, circulating libraries, and, of course, the theater in Orchard Street were designed to occupy the leisure time of which many of its visitors had too much. And the presence during the winter in concentrated form of the fashionables of the upper and upper middle classes meant that current attitudes and standards of social behavior were clearly demonstrated—presented for an alert young newcomer to adopt or criticize at will.

To publicize his new academy, Thomas Sheridan

presented a series of "Attic Entertainments" that included music as well as oratory, and to help with this he brought in one of the leading professional musicians of Bath, Thomas Linley. Linley had a musical family. His eldest daughter, Elizabeth Ann, aged sixteen, not only had a beautiful singing voice but also a beauty of face and form that can still be judged from Joshua Reynolds' paintings of her and that, inevitably, attracted suitors both desirable and undesirable. The wealthy but elderly Walter Long managed to persuade the Linley parents to a betrothal, which was eventually broken off with a financial settlement to Elizabeth and much titillation of the scandalmongers of Bath. (Samuel Foote turned the bare bones of the story into a satirical farce, *The Maid of Bath*, at the Little Theatre in the Haymarket in 1771.) Other undesirable attentions followed.

The young people of the Sheridan and Linley families had become friends, and could turn to each other for support against a sometimes intolerable adult outside world; so, in 1772, to help Elizabeth escape the unwelcome importunities of a married man, Thomas Mathews, Sheridan escorted her on a journey to France, where she was said, romantically, to have planned to enter a convent. There is some evidence, though not incontrovertible, that the young couple went through a form of marriage ceremony in France. Whether or not this was so, it need not have had any great force; since this would have been a clandestine marriage of minors without the knowledge of their parents, contemporary law would have made no difficulties about an annulment. Brought back to England and separated from Elizabeth, Sheridan fought two duels with the insufferable Mathews, in the second of which he was seriously hurt and reported, for a time, to be dying. He recovered, though, and was exiled by his infuriated father for some months to Farm Hill, near Waltham Abbey, with the intention that he should forget about Elizabeth and read for the bar. Parental opposition—Thomas Sheridan seems to have been reluctant to see his son marry, as he thought, into a lower social class, and Linley to have been concerned at losing a potential source of family income—was in due course overcome; in 1773 Sheridan and Elizabeth Linley were married, and settled in London.

Sheridan then made the understandable, if quixotic, decision that his position as a "gentleman" would be compromised as the husband of a professional singer, and that, therefore, Elizabeth henceforth would sing only in private. That being so, he had to begin to earn a living quickly; however much it might affect his gentlemanly instincts, the thing he knew something about by inheritance was the theater, and his own recent affairs had given him an unusual range of autobiographical experience to exploit. Covent Garden encouraged him, and in 1775 produced the first three of his plays, *The Rivals, St. Patrick's Day,* and *The Duenna*—the first, after a shaky start, to become one of the three of his works best known to posterity, and the last to be a runaway popular and commercial success in his own day.

At the other of the two major London theaters, Drury Lane, David Garrick was just coming to the end of his long reign as manager and leading actor. Since the long run of seventy-five performances of *The Duenna* at the rival theater provided the strongest competition, it must have seemed that its author's involvement at Drury Lane would be the best possible guarantee of a successful future there. Garrick happily agreed to Sheridan, in partnership with his father-in-law Linley, and a sleeping partner, Dr. James Ford, a court physician, taking over his share of the theater and entering into its management. (Though Linley and Ford could almost certainly have afforded to put up their share of the capital out of their own resources, Sheridan had to borrow, and thus began the long sequence of increasingly tangled financial arrangements that characterized his later working life.) For the next thirty-three years, no matter what other activities he undertook, Sheridan was to remain, for better or worse, manager at Drury Lane.

After a quiet start he began well. In 1777 he produced his own adaptation, adjusted to the taste of the time, of Sir John Vanbrugh's *The Relapse*, under the new title of *A Trip to Scarborough*, and followed that later in the year by what turned out to be his masterpiece, *The School for Scandal*. In 1778, Sheridan produced an effective piece of theatrical catering, exploiting the contemporary interest in the calling up of the militia, *The Camp*. This was an afterpiece, and in 1779 he wrote what was perhaps the greatest of all the Georgian afterpieces, *The Critic*. After that, apart from fragments of his own, and modifications of other people's work, there followed twenty years of silence as a playwright.

The reason was that in September 1780 Sheridan was elected member of Parliament for the borough of Stafford, and thus began his second, and to him much more important, career as a politician. Henceforth the theater was to be of secondary importance, to provide a source of income that enabled him to pursue—unsuccessfully, as it turned out—his dream of a great political reputation.

Again he began well. He held minor office in 1782 as one of the undersecretaries for foreign affairs, and in 1783 was secretary to the treasury; but his party (Whig) did not hold office for long, and the independence on which he prided himself endeared him to neither his friends nor his opponents. The fragility of Sheridan's financial affairs, complicated by his public and private extravagances, was no great help to his career, and his connection with the theater provided his political opponents with a perennial source of witticism and denigration. Nevertheless, he built up a reputation as an orator in the House of Commons, the high point of which was undoubtedly the attack he made on Warren Hastings and British colonial exploitation of India, when Hastings was impeached at Westminster Hall in 1788. Later that year, when the first regency crisis arose during George III's illness, Sheridan became one of the confidential advisers to the Prince of Wales; by now the player's son was accepted in high and fashionable society. But to be the friend of the prince was to be the enemy of Queen Charlotte and her circle; for as many friends as he acquired in society, he made an equal number of enemies.

In private, though his relationship with Elizabeth never completely broke down, it came under severe strain as a result of his free and easy attitude to the other sex; and though his was a society in which heavy drinking was commonplace, Sheridan's indulgence was at times more than sufficient to provoke comment. He spent less time on the affairs of the theater, but made greater financial demands upon it; after Elizabeth's death in 1792 he turned his attention for a time to its rebuilding and enlargement, and it was for the new theater that he wrote his final piece, an adaptation of August von Kotzebue's romantic tragedy *Die Spanier in Peru (The Spaniards in Peru)*, in 1799. By then he had married Esther Ogle, a daughter of the dean of Winchester, a marriage that the disparity in their ages did little to assist.

For a year Sheridan succeeded Charles James Fox as member of Parliament for Westminster, and after his defeat there became for five years member for Ilchester; but by now both his careers, as well as his private life, were dwindling into decline, so that the disastrous fire that destroyed Drury Lane in 1809 mirrored as a public symbol a private destruction almost as complete. Sheridan met both with a show of bravado. The story of his sitting over a bottle of wine in the Piazza Coffee House watching Drury Lane burn—"May not a man take a glass at his own fireside?"—may be apocryphal, but it represents the witty stoicism that by now was his only resource; and when finally, in 1812, he lost his seat in Parliament, he lost also his immunity from financial proceedings, and the interminable complications of his financial affairs led to arrest for debt. Since in the same year the theater in Drury Lane had been rebuilt, but only on the undertaking that Sheridan would take no further part in its affairs, and since by now his friendship with the Prince of Wales was a thing of the past, collapse had come on all fronts: political, theatrical, and social.

Sheridan's last four years were not happy ones. His financial affairs were somehow patched up, and he still had many friends whose help staved off those creditors who became too importunate (it is even possible that the prince regent, though their public estrangement remained, was in private one of these). But of the public honors he might have aspired to, all that had been achieved was a privy councillorship; he held for life the sinecure of the receivership of the duchy of Cornwall, a mark of former royal friendship; but his theater was in other hands, and the literary output of a lifetime amounted to six plays and two adaptations. In the last few weeks of his life, he reread some of his political speeches, then said to a visitor: "There are certain periods of a man's life when the horizon looks clear and beautiful, and the grass beneath him assumes a brighter green: at such a time I made use of five words which I will show you." Turning to his great speech of 13 June 1788 against Warren Hastings, he pointed to the final sentence: "My lords, I have done!" It is impossible not to sense on his part a feeling of waste and regret. The squalor of Sheridan's final illness may have been exaggerated by rumor; rumor and scandal dogged him all his life. But when at last he died on 7 July 1816, he was given a splendid funeral and a procession that included royal dukes as well as the servants at Drury Lane Theatre. He was buried in Westminster Abbey, in Poets' Corner, not far from David Garrick. The irony is that he had hoped to be buried among the politicians, near to Charles James Fox.

II

THE ambivalence of Sheridan's attitude to the theater is reflected on a larger scale in mid-Georgian society as a whole. The Licensing Act of 1737—the retort of the government of Robert Walpole to the strong political satire produced in the theater by John Gay, Henry Fielding, and others—not only firmly established political and social censorship by the lord chamberlain's department, but also, for all practical purposes, restricted licensing for public performance to the two royal patent theaters in London, with a summer license only for the Little Theatre in the Haymarket. It also confirmed that any other players were to be regarded legally as rogues and vagabonds, and, as such, subject, on arrest, to appropriate penalties laid down for them.

Yet during the second half of the eighteenth century, such was the demand for theatrical entertainment that, even though technically illegal, theaters were built in all the major—and many minor—provincial towns. (A legal fiction of charging for "concerts of music," and between the items performing a play gratis, was one among a number of ways of getting round the law.) Thus a network of touring circuits was built up, which by the end of the century linked more than 300 provincial playhouses. Popular pressure eventually forced changes in the law. Royal patents began to be granted in the major towns outside London—Bath had the first in 1768—and after 1788 limited licensing by quarter sessions for up to sixty days a year was allowed, putting an end at last to the embarrassing situation whereby the local legal officers, the justices of the peace, whose task it was to take action against the "vagabonds," were often, in their social capacity as the local gentry or the prosperous middle class, the strongest supporters of the theatrical companies.

Yet in spite of this public support, an element of social stigma remained. In part it may well have been historical. Many actors and actresses of the Restoration theater had acquired reputations that were hardly socially blameless; and the strolling players of the first half of the eighteenth century, before the circuit system developed, may not have been rogues but were certainly, many of them, poor vagabonds. This inheritance of social inferiority could be overcome, of course, by the leading actors, and especially in London. Garrick was eventually accepted in the highest of circles; the acquaintance of John Philip Kemble and Sarah Siddons in later years was sought after; stagestruck gentry preparing their private amateur performances could accept the help of some of the professional players on terms of reasonably easy friendship.

Nevertheless, well into the nineteenth century a certain element of social insecurity lingered even among the most established theatrical figures; both William Macready and Henry Irving felt it, and had to fight against it. And though to write for the theater was always a more respectable activity than to perform—clergymen, academics, even generals could do it—it is easy to understand why Sheridan, as the son of an actor-manager, and a not very successful one at that—made fun of, in consequence, at a sensitive age by his fellows—should approach a career in the theater with reservations. To justify the attempt, it was essential that he should be a success.

A young man setting out to write successful theatrical comedy in the 1770's had certain matters to take account of. The censorship meant that he had to avoid political affairs, and since the lord chamberlain's office was manned by members of the establishment of the day, he had to keep clear also of social attitudes that were too revolutionary, or that offended prevailing standards of taste in middle- and upper-class circles. Otherwise, performances would simply not have been allowed. His audiences would be for the most part affluent, familiar (or wanting to be thought familiar) with the metropolitan social round; and for him to be listened to, their preoccupations and assumptions would inevitably have to condition what he chose to write and how he wrote it. So the industrial developments that were beginning to change the face of England and the pattern of English society, or certain aspects of social or economic or political deprivation, were not material on which Sheridan could comment, whether or not he wished to do so. As John Loftis has pithily pointed out, "The distressed heroines of Georgian comedy may be poor, but they are rarely below the rank of gentry."

For the most part the affluent classes of the midcentury had a bland belief in acts of benevolence, and their associated feelings of goodwill, as a universal panacea. Natural affections were indigenous to uncorrupted man; sympathy for the joys and sorrows of others less fortunate than himself, even if he were unable or unwilling to do much to help, would be counted to him for virtue; the "man of feeling" was a model to be demonstrated and emulated. Hence that element of sentimentality in much eighteenth-century comedy that is so alien to twentieth-century taste. Artificially contrived distresses tidied away neatly in the last act, with whatever degree of improbability, by the discovery of an unknown family relationship and a consequent act of benevolence, became almost a trademark of the poorer eighteenth-century comedy. Somebody always had money to solve, eventually, whatever problems arose. As Charles Dickens' Harold Skimpole was later to say, "God Bless Somebody."

This was not a purely English phenomenon, of course. It can be seen in the European theater of the time, particularly in that of France; and the moral purpose of comedy had a long pedigree—Richard Cumberland maintained that his own theory of comedy, like that of Richard Steele, derived from Terence. Nevertheless, such an attitude was not conducive to biting satire or sharp contemporary social comment. It took the edge off the astringency of the best Restoration comedy.

But this should not be overstressed, as it sometimes has been, so as to devalue eighteenth-century comedy in relation to that of the late seventeenth century. The fact that many sentimental comedies were written and published has tended to make the nontheatrical assessor assume that these were primarily what Georgian audiences wanted. In fact, some of them were performed only briefly. One of the valuable results of the compilation of the monumental calendar of London stage performances during the eighteenth century has been to reveal that the most popular of Sheridan's predecessors were playwrights like Benjamin Hoadly, David Garrick, the elder George Colman, Arthur Murphy, and Oliver Goldsmith, all writers of the laughing and satiric comedy. Those plays most frequently performed were of precisely that kind: *The Suspicious Husband, The Jealous Wife, The Clandestine Marriage, The Way to Keep Him, Know Your Own Mind.* And even the writers of sentimental comedy like Richard Cumberland and Hugh Kelly do make considerable use of ludicrous characters and situations. They are by no means solemn all the time, the sentimentality being usually limited to a few scenes only.

It was fortunate for Sheridan, too, that in 1772, just before he began work in the theater, Goldsmith had written his *Essay on the Theatre: Or, A Comparison Between the Laughing and Sentimental Comedy*, in which he attacked the sentimental plays of his day; but perhaps even more important was the fact that in the following year, in *She Stoops to Conquer*, Goldsmith provided for a young aspiring writer an object lesson in what brilliant social comedy really could be. The decks, in a sense, were cleared for Sheridan.

What Goldsmith made clear, in practice, was the importance to comedy of structure, of the careful contrivance of situations in which the audience knows much more about what is happening than do the characters involved, so that the sequence of misunderstandings and mistaken identities that ensues can be fully relished. He showed, too, the equal importance of creating characters drawn from observation of real life, so that although they might be allowed to blunder into absurd situations, they were never so eccentric that they did not have some point to make about human beings and their relations in society. Since human folly is eternal, of course, some of the characters might properly come from the traditional stock and yet still be relevant; others could have something to say that was specifically of and for their own time. In drawing these characters, Goldsmith was demonstrating that the line from William Wycherley and Vanbrugh and George Farquhar and Gay was still open, and that there was still room for a successor.

Two other general points should perhaps be made before turning to examine Sheridan's remarkable five years of work in the 1770's. The first is the importance in the Georgian theater of music. That for a time there was a legal reason for the presence of music in the theater is only part of the story. The phenomenal popular success of Gay's *The Beggar's Opera* in 1728—in intent a political satire, and a burlesque of the current vogue for Italian opera, but later enjoyed for its own sake—helped to establish a vogue in the Georgian theater for ballad opera, comic opera, masque and pastoral, and other musical entertainments for which composers of the caliber of William Boyce and Maurice Greene, Thomas Arne, Charles Dibdin, and William Shield wrote or adapted the music. Some of these, like *The Duenna*, were main pieces. Others were afterpieces. The genre of the afterpiece, almost unknown to the twentieth-century theater, may also, therefore, require a brief comment.

The notion of a two-part program with a comedy or tragedy followed by a lighter piece of a different kind seems to have been established in France by the mid-seventeenth century and to have been copied occasionally in England in the last quarter of that century. Its regular use dates from John Rich's opening of the theater in Lincoln's Inn Fields in December 1714, when he used the double bill to tempt audiences from the rival Drury Lane Theatre, which in turn copied the idea, so that for the rest of the century and beyond, it became standard theatrical practice. There had already been precedent for charging half price to members of the audience coming in after the third act of a play; this was now transferred to half-price entry to the afterpiece. There were many types of afterpiece: harlequinade or pantomime, pastoral, comic opera, burlesque, and, by no means least in importance, farce and satire. Whether the cheaper entry fee helped to make the second-half audience proportionately less establishment in tone (in any case, the usual six o'clock start for performances could be inconveniently early for those engaged in business) can probably never be proven; but it is true that some of the sharpest satire and the broadest, most theatrically effective farce produced by eighteenth-century playwrights lie in the afterpiece form. Now, unfortunately, because of the pattern of contemporary playhouse programming, such pieces are hardly ever seen, and so remain virtually unknown. Sheridan in fact turned his hand successfully to all the popular forms of his day. It is therefore important to remember that, though scarcely known now, in his own time *The Duenna* was as popular as *The Rivals*, if not more so, and that in proposing Sheridan for membership in the Club, no less a critic than Samuel Johnson referred to *The Rivals* and *The Duenna* as "the two best comedies of the age."

III

ACCORDING to a letter written by Sheridan to his father-in-law in November 1774, his first comedy was begun with the encouragement of Thomas Harris, manager at Covent Garden and a major proprietor there for half a century. It had been written, he said, mostly within the previous two months, was about to go into rehearsal, and was sufficiently well liked by those who had read it for him to be assured of at least £600 profit. He must therefore have needed all his resilience after the first night of *The Rivals* on 17 January 1775, for it was little short of a disaster; too long, too wordy, too coarse, badly

performed were some of the initial reactions in the press. Yet Harris maintained his faith in the play, encouraged the young man to revise it, recast one of the major roles, and eleven days later remounted the piece, this time with success.

The changes made can be studied by comparing the original manuscript copy submitted to the lord chamberlain with the later printed editions. They show the apprentice writer learning fast the difference between what is effective on the page and on the stage, studying his audience's reactions, to take account of what it would and would not accept, and modifying his text accordingly.

Sheridan was aiming not for originality but for success, so he took care to weave a number of reliable stock characters and situations into a plot that, without being autobiographical, resembled at several points some of the incidents in his own recent life that gossip had made familiar, and that by now he could afford to stand back and laugh at. So Bob Acres is an eighteenth-century Cotswold version of the braggart-coward of the Roman comedy; and Mrs. Malaprop, though placed much further up the social scale, nevertheless, in her inspired mishandling of the English language, derives from the school of William Shakespeare's Dogberry. Sheridan's exploitation in Sir Lucius O'Trigger of stock Irish stereotype characteristics might well be thought to be in the tradition of Shakespeare's Welshman Fluellen. In fact the eighteenth-century theater made great use of "stage" Irish, Scots, and Welshmen, partly, perhaps, because of the number of them who had arrived in London in search of fortune or status; partly also, as Richard Cumberland made clear, rather smugly, in his preface to *The Fashionable Lover*, because of their apparent eccentricity:

The level manners of a polish'd country like this do not supply much matter for the comic muse which delights in variety and extravagance; wherever, therefore, I have made any attempts at novelty, I have found myself obliged either to dive into the lower class of men, or to betake myself to the outskirts of the empire; the centre is too equal and refined for such purposes.

In fact, in the first version of *The Rivals*, the "refined centre" found O'Trigger rather too outrageous, and he had to be toned down to be made acceptable.

Mistaken identities as a source of continuing

ludicrous situations have also been a staple source of comedy at least since Plautus, and again Sheridan contrived plenty of these. They lead, on the one hand, to the fine counterpoint of the two Jack Absolute/Sir Anthony scenes (II.i and III.i) in which Jack has first to reject an arranged marriage, since he is in love with Lydia, and then to recant on discovering the proposed betrothed to be Lydia herself; or to the even more superb centerpiece (III.iii) in which Jack, visiting Mrs. Malaprop as himself, is made to read out a scurrilous letter about her that he has written to Lydia in his character as Ensign Beverley; and later, when both Lydia and her aunt are present, he has to appear in both guises at the same time.

But the Ensign Beverley characterization is not only a source of that kind of near-farcical contrivance. It also enables Sheridan to point up and to satirize the romantic sensibility of Lydia, who, in her understandable desire to be herself and not a "Smithfield bargain" in an arranged marriage, goes to the other extreme and pines for wooings under difficulty, a romantic elopement, and an unrealistic paradise in Arcadian poverty, lived on nothing a year.

Using the formal structure of the seventeenth-century comedy of manners, Sheridan balances the realistic Jack and the romantic Lydia with the sentimental Faulkland and the sensible but sorely tried Julia. Faulkland's melancholy and "sensibility" (the "man of feeling") are perhaps the elements in the play that are most of their own time and alien to twentieth-century audiences. Yet, shorn of its period language and attitudes, the play is an exaggerated but recognizable comment on that adolescent hypersensitivity and self-torture that every generation knows to some degree, and that Sheridan must have observed either in himself or close at hand.

This pairing of the principal characters who complement or contrast with each other goes further as part of the formal structure of the comedy—Sir Anthony and Mrs. Malaprop, Sir Lucius and Bob Acres, for example—and their scenes together provide some of the most memorable of the play, the former on women's education and the evils of circulating libraries (I.ii) and the latter on honor and valor (III.iv and V.iii). But there is also an interesting hint of a duality, perhaps not sufficiently developed—though maybe it is surprising to find it there at all, in the social context already referred to—between the "high culture" of the main characters and the "subculture" of the servants and the

rustic Bob Acres, which parodies, and by implication satirizes, the former. It is planted particularly in the opening scene. When the newly arrived coachman, Thomas, asks what kind of place Bath is, he is told by Fag:

. . . 'tis a good lounge; in the morning we go to the pump-room (though neither my Master nor I drink the waters); after breakfast we saunter on the parades or play a game at billiards; at night we dance: but d—n the place. I'm tired of it: their regular hours stupify me—not a fiddle nor a card after eleven!—however Mr. Faulkland's gentleman and I keep it up a little in private parties;—I'll introduce you there, Thomas—you'll like him much. . . . But Thomas, you must polish a little—indeed you must: here now,—this wig!—what the devil do you do with a *wig*, Thomas? None of the London whips of any degree of Ton wear *wigs* now.

Coachman: More's the pity! more's the pity, I say.—Odd's life! when I heard how the lawyers and doctors had took to their own hair, I thought how 'twould go next.[1]

It is continued by Fag (end of II.i), Acres, and David (III.iv and IV.i); and the servant Lucy's reflections on the profitability of her "simplicity" (I.ii) underline the irony of the masters' and mistresses' exploitation of their servants being reflected by a clever exploitation in the other direction. In his rather between-class situation in Bath, Sheridan was perhaps in a better position to observe and be aware of this. But he does not develop the theme in the later plays, and it may not be without significance that an early nineteenth-century prompt copy from Dublin, now in the Bodleian Library in Oxford, refers to the opening scene, in which this element is strongest, as "generally left out."

The Rivals is a young man's play about young people, and about older people seen through a young man's eyes. The dialogue has more naturalism and less artifice than *The School for Scandal*, though wit is there in plenty. (Lydia's comment on Lady Slattern Lounger's reading habits when using the circulating library[I.ii]—"I always know when [she] has been before me.—She has a most observing thumb; and I believe cherishes her nails for the convenience of making marginal notes."—is genuine Sheridan.) Such mannered language as there is is often there for the purpose of ridicule:

---

[1]All quotations are from C. Price, ed., *The Dramatic Works of Richard Brinsley Sheridan*, 2 vols. (Oxford, 1973), which is now the standard.

Absolute (to Lydia): . . . By Heav'ns! I would fling all goods of fortune from me with a prodigal hand to enjoy the scene where I might clasp my Lydia to my bosom, and say, the world affords no smile to me—but here—

(Embracing her.)

If she holds out now the devil is in it.   *(Aside.)*

(III.iii)

For the most part the dialogue appears natural, though carefully shaped to be easily speakable; even Faulkland, the most guilty of artificiality, can be downright and forceful enough when the situation calls for it. When he thinks Julia has been enjoying herself too much in his absence:

. . . Country-dances! jiggs, and reels! am I to blame now? A Minuet I could have forgiven—I should not have minded that—I say I should not have regarded a Minuet—but *Country-dances!* Z——ds! had she made one in a *Cotillon*—I believe I could have forgiven even that—but to be monkey-led for a night!—to run the gauntlet thro' a string of amorous palming puppies!—to shew paces like a managed filly!—O Jack, there never can be but *one* man in the world, whom a truly modest and delicate woman ought to pair with in a *Country-dance*; and even then, the rest of the couples should be her great uncles and aunts!

(II.i)

And Mrs. Malaprop's inability to fit meaning and word together accurately has received the ultimate accolade of giving a name to the characteristic—a malapropism.

There, Sir! an attack upon my language! what do you think of that?—an aspersion upon my parts of speech! was ever such a brute! Sure if I reprehend any thing in this world, it is the use of my oracular tongue, and a nice derangement of epitaphs!

(III.iii)

She may, or may not, have been designed to satirize the new female intellectuals, the so-called blue-stockings; or Sheridan may simply have taken the idea of her from an unfinished manuscript of his mother's and developed it. It matters little. It is what he made of the idea that counts. Mrs. Malaprop has become one of the immortals.

After the revision of *The Rivals*, Sheridan turned to a two-act farce, *St. Patrick's Day: Or, The Scheming Lieutenant*, his first attempt at an after-piece (Covent Garden, 2 May 1775). He seems to have wanted in particular to write a good part for Lawrence Clinch, who had rescued *The Rivals* by

taking over the character of Sir Lucius O'Trigger and making a great success of him; so the central character is, as the subtitle implies, a young Irish officer, Lieutenant O'Connor, out to gain the hand of the daughter of the reluctant hypochondriac Justice Credulous, and prepared to go through a series of stratagems to outwit the old fellow. Disguised as a countryman, Humphrey, he becomes the justice's servant; in a recruiting scene he hears his own sergeant boasting of how he really controls his officer. Beating off an attempt to abduct Lauretta (the daughter) that is observed by the justice, he is then trusted to be left in charge of the girl; but when, in his own character, he begins to make love to her, the justice returns and the lieutenant is exposed. In a further twist of the plot, he poses as a German doctor and "cures" the justice, who believes himself to be dying, and so finally gains consent to the marriage.

It is all good knockabout farce, implausible (what good farce is not?) but theatrically effective. Again it contains many familiar characters and situations (Susannah Centlivre's *A Bold Stroke for a Wife* had its central character go through twice as many transfigurations to attain the same end); but there are good comic scenes written to exploit the strengths of the actors who played them originally—Lieutenant O'Connor (Clinch), Justice Credulous (Charles Lee Lewes), and Dr. Rosy (John Quick); and there is some sharp contemporary comment on, for example, women's fashions and army life, and on traditional butts like nagging women, Irishmen, and the recruiting of country bumpkins. Not a great comedy, but an efficient, workmanlike farce, it was steadily popular in its own day; occasionally now revived where the exigencies of modern program planning allow, in theatrical terms it can still hold its own.

Sheridan completed this remarkable year's work for Covent Garden on 21 November 1775, when his comic opera *The Duenna* was given its first performance. We can follow its genesis in part through Sheridan's correspondence with his father-in-law in Bath, who wrote or arranged some of the music, though about half—the best of it—was written by the younger Thomas Linley, now leading the orchestra at Drury Lane. Linley was now nineteen, and back from his Italian study tour, during which, in Florence in 1770, he had met and become friendly with his exact contemporary, Wolfgang Amadeus Mozart. Linley was already making a reputation as a promising composer, and it may well be, as Roger

Fiske has remarked, that his accidental death when only twenty-two changed for the worse the whole history of English music. With Tom as composer near at hand, and Elizabeth as an experienced singer available for advice and help (the original manuscript of the libretto survives mainly in her handwriting, an indication of her close involvement), Sheridan was in a good position to tackle the—for him—new form.

The plot is one of traditional intrigue, set in Spain and involving, like *The Rivals*, two pairs of young lovers destined by their parents for undesirable marriages. (Sheridan had still not worked this theme out of his system; though he was now reconciled with Linley, his own father had not yet accepted the situation.) Disguises and a series of contrived misunderstandings are involved, some of them concerning the heroine's rather unprepossessing governess, the duenna of the title; but all ends satisfactorily when Don Jerome, after two and a half acts of being a tyrannical parent, turns into a benevolent gentleman. There are elements of anti-Semitism in the handling of the character of the Portuguese Jew, Isaac Mendoza, that were more to the taste of Sheridan's contemporaries than to ours, and a drunken friars' scene that probably owes more to earlier farces than to any anti–Roman Catholic sentiment; Sheridan never worried too much about originality. Perhaps a more disturbing element is the rather sour comedy made, especially by Don Jerome, out of the duenna's ugliness. But to say this is perhaps to be hypersensitive; it bothered Leigh Hunt but not William Hazlitt. And certainly Margaret (the duenna) could give back as much as she was given. Her tricking of Mendoza into marriage (with her) is a reward in kind for his own intended duplicity over Louisa and her inheritance, and his rudeness to Margaret is thrown back in his face with interest.

> *Duenna*: Dares such a thing as you pretend to talk of beauty—a walking rouleau—a body that seems to owe all its consequence to the dropsy—a pair of eyes like two dead beetles in a wad of brown dough. A beard like an artichoke, with dry shrivell'd jaws that wou'd disgrace the mummy of a monkey.
> *Jerome*: Well done, Margaret.
>
> (III.vii)

If the dialogue is occasionally a little limp and rather obviously and unnaturalistically concerned with carrying on the incidents of the plot, it should be remembered that this is a musical piece; the recitatives of many of the finest of the opera seria are much more vapid. Much of the dialogue is as carefully shaped and laced with wit as in the best of the comedies of manners.

> *Enter DON JEROME and FERDINAND.*
> *Jerome*: What, I suppose you have been serenading too! Eh, disturbing some peaceable neighbourhood with villainous catgut and lascivious piping, out on't! you set your sister here a vile example—but I come to tell you, madam, that I'll suffer no more of these midnight incantations, these amorous orgies that steal the senses in the hearing, as they say Egyptian Embalmers serve mummies, extracting the brain thro' the ears; however, there's an end of your frolics—Isaac Mendoza will be here presently, and tomorrow you shall marry him.
> *Louisa*: Never while I have life.
> *Ferd*: Indeed, Sir, I wonder how you can think of such a man for a son-in-law.
> *Jerome*: Sir, you are very kind to favour me with your sentiments—and pray, what is your objection to him?
> *Ferd*: He is a Portugueze in the first place.
> *Jerome*: No such thing, boy, he has forsworn his country.
> *Louisa*: He is a Jew.
> *Jerome*: Another mistake: he has been a Christian these six weeks.
> *Ferd*: Ay, he left his old religion for an estate, and has not had time to get a new one.
> *Louisa*: But stands like a dead wall between church and synagogue, or like the blank leaves between the Old and New Testament.
> *Jerome*: Anything more?
> *Ferd*: But the most remarkable part of his character, is his passion for deceit, and tricks of cunning.
> *Louisa*: Tho' at the same time, the fool predominates so much over the knave, that I am told he is generally the dupe of his own art.
> *Ferd*: True, like an unskilful gunner, he usually misses his aim, and is hurt by the recoil of his own piece.
> *Jerome*: Anything more?
> *Louisa*: To sum up all, he has the worst fault a husband can have—he's not my choice.
> *Jerome*: But you are his; and choice on one side is sufficient—two lovers should never meet in marriage. . . .
>
> (I.iii)

The Duenna is, of course, in modern terms, musical comedy, a genre in which any connection between the plot and the real world can be very tenuous; but Sheridan does allow realism to creep in from time to time. Clara's romantic dreams of escaping from the toils of love into a nunnery are brought firmly down to earth by the more practical Louisa:

Why, to be sure, the character of a nun is a very becoming one—at a masquerade—but no pretty woman in her senses ever thought of taking the veil for above a night.

(III.iii)

And a few moments later the hero Antonio is firmly reminded by the same lady:

. . . I do not doubt your sincerity, Antonio: but there is a chilling air around poverty that often kills affection, that was not nurs'd in it—If we would make love our household god, we had best secure him a comfortable roof.

But to judge *The Duenna* solely by its text is as foolish as to assess an opera by its libretto. Unlike some of the lesser contemporary examples of the form, the songs are all in character and relevant to the plot, and the music is tuneful, attractive, and well orchestrated. Antonio's quiet opening serenade, with its lutelike accompaniment of pizzicato strings, and his display aria, "Friendship is the bond of reason" (I.ii—by Tom Linley), show some of its wide range. The first trio, by the elder Linley, involving hero, heroine, and tyrannical father, is dramatically shaped, with each character coming through clearly; Don Jerome's comic "If a daughter you have she's the plague of your life" (I.iii) contrasts effectively in style with Clara's "When sable night" (I.v) and "By him we love offended"(III.iii). *The Duenna* was, understandably, a runaway success. Its original sequence of seventy-five performances was longer than that of *The Beggar's Opera*, and it was constantly revived until the middle of the nineteenth century. It then fell out of fashion, but recent professional revivals suggest that the tide may, rightly, be turning back in its favor.

IV

SHERIDAN began his first season in management at Drury Lane in September 1776, and one of his early tasks was to revise Vanbrugh's *The Relapse* for presentation. The eighteenth century had no scruples about altering or rewriting earlier plays in the repertory, from Shakespeare downward, and the ways in which the plays were changed are often revealing about contemporary attitudes and assumptions. In turning *The Relapse* into *A Trip to Scarborough* (Drury Lane, 24 February 1777), Sheridan left a good deal of the original intact, though in cer-

tain places he cut heavily. The major changes were designed to bring the play into line with what was felt to be a more refined taste. So Coupler, Vanbrugh's homosexual pimp, is toned down considerably into a female matchmaker. The ends of Acts IV and V are rewritten to emphasize moral scruples on behalf of Amanda, Berinthia, and Loveless; and Vanbrugh's Act IV, scene iii, is altered to prevent Loveless from taking Berinthia to bed. In Vanbrugh this helps to point up the difference between the relaxed attitude of society to male sexual freedom and its disapproval of it in the female; in Sheridan, neither lady transgresses. Structurally Sheridan was concerned with tightening up the plot, so in the last act he cut the whole episode of Sir John Friendly and he rewrote other scenes for the same purpose (for example, IV. ii). He totally removed Vanbrugh's rather ponderous verse opening scene, which was probably a good thing; but equally, he often removed or maimed the artificial patterning of much of Vanbrugh's prose dialogue, which was not. (Compare, for example, the second acts of both plays.)

The play was not received with any great enthusiasm (some of the audience seem to have been expecting a completely new piece, and were irritated to find an old one refurbished), and it never gained a steady place in the repertory. The exercise was probably more important to Sheridan as a preparation for the writing of his next comedy, *The School for Scandal*, which opened on 8 May of the same year.

It would seem that he had been brooding over the twin themes of this play—scandalmongering and hypocrisy— for some time. On 31 December 1775 he had mentioned in a letter to his father-in-law that he was finishing a two-act comedy for Covent Garden that would be in rehearsal within a week. This work has never been identified and may never, in fact, have been completed; since that and later letters make clear that negotiations for the move to Drury Lane had already begun, Sheridan may well have decided to hold the play back for the other theater should the move prove successful. If so, what he had in mind may have been an earlier and shorter version of what eventually became *The School for Scandal*. The fragmentary but fascinating notes and drafts that Cecil Price has assembled in his two-volume edition of the plays show clearly that Sheridan had been brooding over the two elements of the plot. One scenario is called "The Slanderers, a Pump Room Scene," and another draft involves early versions of some of the Teazle scenes—the old man with the young wife. Thomas Moore, who first printed them, believed them to have been originally intended for two different plays. Price is not so sure.

It is easy to see why Sheridan should have been interested in both. Elizabeth's early projected marriage to Walter Long, had it transpired, would have produced something like the Teazle situation; and both it and the later matters of the elopement and the duels had exposed Elizabeth and Richard to the effects of rumor and slander, which were rife within the small, closed world of Georgian society. Indeed, Sheridan himself had written lampoons in the *Bath Chronicle*, and while recovering from the second duel had been amused to hear his death reported by local rumor—an incident he uses in Act V, scene ii. He must have seen plenty of examples of the contrast between the lip service paid to the approved sentiments of benevolence and the greed and self-seeking actually practiced; and to highlight it by contrasting two brothers, the one hypocritical in this way, the other appearing on the surface irresponsible and profligate, but underneath good-hearted and benevolent, was a typical example of Sheridan's structural method, as we have seen. He may also have taken a hint for it from the two brothers in Henry Fielding's popular novel, *Tom Jones*; Sheridan was always prepared to make use of the literary tradition he inherited. Even so, he always gave it something specifically his own. Thus the argument between the young, country-bred wife, intoxicated by the fashionable splendors of the town into extravagances that anger her older, more staid and responsible husband, might have come from any seventeenth-century comedy of manners, but not with the vividness of the vignette of the life of the midcentury lesser country gentry.

Sir Peter: . . . you forget what your situation was when I married you.

Lady Teazle: No—no—I don't—'twas a very disagreeable one or I should never have married you—

Sir Peter: Yes—yes, madam you were then in somewhat an humbler Style—the Daughter of a plain country Squire—recollect Lady Teazle when I saw you first—sitting at your tambour in a pretty figured Linnen gown—with a Bunch of Keys by your side, your hair comb'd smooth over a Roll, and your apartment hung round with Fruits in worsted of your own working—

Lady Teazle: O Yes, I remember it very well, and a Curious life I led! My daily occupation to inspect the Dairy, superintend the Poultry, make extracts from the Family Receipt book and Comb my aunt Deborah's Lap-Dog.

Sir Peter: Yes, yes, Ma'am, 'twas so indeed.

Lady Teazle: And then you know my evening amusements—to draw Patterns for Ruffles which I had not the Materials to make—to play Pope Joan with the Curate—to read a Novel to my Aunt—or to be stuck down to an old Spinnet—to strum my Father to sleep after a Fox chase.

Sir Peter: I am glad you have so good a Memory,—Yes—Madam—These were the Recreations I took you from.—But now you must have your Coach, Vis-à-Vis, and three powder'd Footmen before your Chair—and in summer a pair of white Cats to draw you to Kensington gardens—no Recollection I suppose when you were content to ride double behind the Butler on a dock'd Coach Horse.

Lady Teazle: No—I swear I never did that—I deny the Butler, and the Coach Horse.

Sir Peter: This madam was your Situation—and what have I not done for you?—I have made you a woman of Fashion, of Fortune, of Rank—in short I have made you my Wife—

Lady Teazle: Well then and there is but one thing more you can make me to add to the obligation—and that is—

Sir Peter: My widow, I suppose?

(II.i)

Early reactions to the play, like those of the *Morning Chronicle*, emphasized the attraction of the witty dialogue, even though some felt that it was too obviously set up in the scandal scenes. Ridicule like that of Lady Sneerwell and Sir Benjamin Backbite—

Lady Sneerwell: Well—well—if Mrs. Evergreen does take some pains to repair the Ravages of Time—you must allow she effects it with great ingenuity—and surely that's better than the careless manner in which the Widow Ocre—caulks her wrinkles.

Sir Benj: Nay now Lady Sneerwell—you are severe upon the Widow—come—come it is not that she paints so ill—but when she has finish'd her Face she joins it on so badly to her Neck that she looks like a mended Statue in which the Connoisseur sees at once that the Head's modern tho' the Trunk's antique.—

(II.ii)

is more contrived and less subtle than Mrs. Candour's:

Mrs. Candour: Positively you shall not be so very severe. Miss Sallow is a Relation of mine by marriage and as for her Person great allowance is to be made—for let me tell you a woman labours under many disadvantages who tries to pass for a girl at six and thirty.

(II.ii)

Yet all three are in character. Occasionally Sheridan was guilty of giving more wit to the speech of a personage than the characterization justified (Rowley, for instance, and sometimes Sir Peter Teazle), but the natural exuberance of a young playwright at the top of his form is understandable. And for the most part his contrivances are superbly relevant. The hackneyed device of Sir Oliver's disguisings leads not just to a sequence of comic misunderstandings but also to the climax of the auction scene (IV.i), so fully revelatory of Charles's character. The brilliant exploitation of the audience's superior knowledge in the screen scene (IV.iii) not only produces a series of comic confrontations and revelations, but also makes clear to the characters themselves the hypocrisy of Joseph, and enables Lady Teazle to overhear and understand Sir Peter's benevolence, which leads to her repentance. No wonder it became—and remains—the classic scene of the play.

Nevertheless, Sheridan's reliance on benevolence as the solution to all problems leads him into some difficulties and moral contradictions. When Charles, at the end of the auction scene, decides to send £100 of the £530 he has made to the mythical relative Stanley who has fallen on hard times, thereby almost certainly ensuring that some of his genuine creditors (tradesmen who are waiting downstairs) will remain unpaid, he may have a charitable motive, but he is showing a curious sense of values; and Sir Oliver's "...well—I'll pay his debts—and his Benevolences too" (IV.ii) is too easy a way out. Sheridan was making a deliberate statement here: to sell the inanimate members of his family (the portraits) to benefit the live (himself and Old Stanley) is showing, for Sheridan, a right sense of values, and clearly he approves; but there is no implication that Charles might try paying his legitimate debts and living within his means. "If Charles has done nothing false or mean, I shall compound for his extravagance," says Sir Oliver on another occasion (II.iii). This is not the world of "a fair day's work for a fair day's pay."

Just over a century later George Bernard Shaw in *Candida* could make a character say: "We have no more right to consume happiness without producing it than to consume wealth without producing it";

and the assumptions behind that statement are those of a totally different society and outlook. Sheridan's complete acceptance of the limited view of life of his own small social world goes far to explain the difference between himself and a contemporary like Pierre de Beaumarchais. Beaumarchais could criticize the accepted structure of society and thus be an influence for change. Sheridan could not. But to be fair to him, he was making the judgment of his class at the time (like the writer in the *Salisbury Journal* only a little later, who commented favorably on William Beckford's building extravagances at Fonthill Abbey as providing work for the unemployed laboring classes).

So also Sheridan, though wishing to show up the hollowness and hypocrisy of Joseph's sentiments, does not seem to notice that there is very little difference between the shallowness of Joseph's "... the Man who can break through the Laws of Hospitality—and attempt the Wife—of his Friend deserves to be branded as the Pest of Society"(IV.iii) and Charles's "... if I do not appear mortified—at the exposure of my Follies—it is because I feel at this moment the warmest satisfaction—in seeing you—my *liberal* Benefactor" (V.iii).

These matters did not pass unnoticed at the time. A percipient review in the *London Magazine* in 1777 sees Charles as "a dangerous character to be held out to the youth of the present age,"[2] and the *Thespian Magazine* in 1792 could write: "The moral of this play is also bad—dissipation and extravagance being rewarded and thereby encouraged."[3] But both had to admit that the wit, the pointed observation, the admirably drawn characters, and the comic situations made, for contemporary audiences, "ample amends for the fable." They have continued to do so ever since.

There is a curious little connection between *The School for Scandal* and Sheridan's next and last major comedy, *The Critic*. In the final moments of the former, Mr. Snake is being tidied out of the plot. Having been paid by Lady Sneerwell to lie, and double from another source to tell the truth, he has done so, but asks that it should never be made known.

Sir Peter: Hey! what the Plague—are you ashamed of having done a right thing once in your life?

Snake: Ah! Sir—consider I live by the Badness of my

[2]*London Magazine*, 46 (1777).
[3]*Thespian Magazine*, 1 (1792), p.42.

Character!—I have nothing but my Infamy to depend on! and if it were once known that I had been betray'd into an honest Action I should lose every Friend I have in the world.

Sir Oliver: Well—well we'll not traduce you by saying anything in your Praise never fear.

(*Exit* Snake.)

Sir Peter's comment after he goes out is prophetic: "There's a precious Rogue—yet that Fellow is a Writer and a Critic!" Germination, it would seem, had already begun, though before it could be completed another afterpiece had to be put together, a musical entertainment in two acts called *The Camp* (Drury Lane, 15 October 1778).

This is a slight piece—indeed, it has been attributed to various other writers since Tate Wilkinson threw doubt on Sheridan's authorship in 1795—among them General John Burgoyne and Sheridan's brother-in-law Richard Tickell; but the fact that a manuscript copy exists in Tickell's handwriting is no more evidence of authorship than Elizabeth Sheridan's manuscript of *The Rivals*. Cecil Price, who has studied the evidence more closely than most, feels sure that Sheridan was mainly responsible, his associates providing "only ideas or minor assistance."

In any case it is a trifle, designed to exploit a topical situation. In the summer of 1778 there had been much excitement about the possibility of invasion by the French and Spanish, who had allied with the Americans in their War of Independence; the militia was called out for training, and various camps were set up for this purpose. That at Coxheath, near Maidstone, became a fashionable attraction, so the Drury Lane painter, Philippe de Loutherbourg, was sent down to design some scenes, and Sheridan concocted a short piece to make use of them, with Tom Linley arranging the music. It must have been put together very quickly for the autumn season, and the fact shows. There are a few songs, a very thin plot line, some marching, drilling, and spectacle; some mild satire on fraudulent contractors, military mania, and camp fashions; some country bumpkins reminiscent of the recruits in *St. Patrick's Day*; and comedy scenes involving the characters of Bluard, Gauge, and O'Daub that the actors Robert Baddeley, William Parsons, and John Moody were skilled enough to exploit. But it is little more than a clever piece of theatrical catering, with the spectacular scenic devices providing much of the

interest and entertainment—one of the growing tendencies in the theater that Sheridan was to satirize a year later in his next afterpiece, *The Critic: Or, A Tragedy Rehearsed* (Drury Lane, 30 October 1779).

The Critic is part farce, part burlesque, part satire. The burlesque tradition in the theater goes back as far as the Greeks, but it was especially popular in the late seventeenth and eighteenth centuries; *The Rehearsal*, by George Villiers, duke of Buckingham; *Tom Thumb the Great*, by Fielding; and *A Peep Behind the Curtain*, by Garrick, are three only in a long line of which *The Critic* is probably the finest example. There is an element of political satire in it—there had been further invasion scares in the summer of 1779, so the adoption of *The Defeat of the Spanish Armada* for the parodied tragedy has its point in that context—but it may also reflect an absurd musical entertainment that the little theater at Sadler's Wells had mounted with enormous success in the summer, *The Prophecy: or, Queen Elizabeth at Tilbury*. In the same dual-purpose way Mr. Puff is satirized as an early practitioner of the excesses of advertising, but is also brought into the theatrical orbit as the author of the play to be rehearsed. A quick perusal of a few issues of any eighteenth-century newspaper will put into perspective Puff's vivid description of his art (I.ii). There will be found the auctioneers' exaggerations:

. . . 'twas I first taught them to crowd their advertisements with panegyrical superlatives, each epithet rising above the other. . . . by ME they were instructed to clothe ideal walls with gratuitous fruits—to insinuate obsequious rivulets into visionary groves—to teach courteous shrubs to nod their approbation of the grateful soil! or on emergencies to raise upstart oaks, where there never had been an acorn. . . .

And the advertisements "To the charitable and humane!" and "To those whom Providence hath blessed with affluence!" were not a Sheridan invention. Some of the real ones may have been genuine, but for Puff

. . . I suppose never man went thro such a series of calamities in the same space of time!—Sir, I was five times made a bankrupt, and reduced from a state of affluence, by a train of unavoidable misfortunes! then, Sir, tho' a very industrious tradesman, I was twice burnt out, and lost my little all, both times! I lived upon those fires a month.—I soon after was confined by a most excruciating disorder, and lost the use of my limbs!—That told very well, for I had the case strongly attested, and went about to collect the subscriptions myself.

Dangle: Egad, I believe that was when you first called on me.—

Puff: —In November last?—O no!—I was at that time, a close prisoner in the Marshalsea, for a debt benevolently contracted to serve a friend! I was afterwards, twice tapped for a dropsy, which declined into a very profitable consumption!—I was then reduced to—O no—then, I became a widow with six helpless children,—after having had eleven husbands pressed, and being left every time eight months gone with child, and without money to get me into an hospital!

(I.ii)

No wonder he was able to support himself for two years entirely on his misfortunes.

The devious forms of the theatrical puff are still the bane of the historian, who can never be quite certain whether what he is reading is an objective, independent comment or a disguised advertisement. Puff's extended analysis of his technique (and Sheridan had written many a puff for his own theater) is too long for the playhouse, though splendid fun in reading. But it is the theatrical satire that is the real joy of the piece. Sentimentalism comes under the lash in the opening scene:

Dangle (reading): "Bursts into tears, and exit." What, is this a tragedy!

Sneer: No, that's a genteel comedy, not a translation—only *taken from the French*; it is written in a stile which they have lately tried to run down; the true sentimental, and nothing ridiculous in it from the beginning to the end.

Mrs. Dangle: Well, if they had kept to that, I should not have been such an enemy to the stage, there was some edification to be got from those pieces, Mr. Sneer!

Sneer: I am quite of your opinion, Mrs. Dangle; the theatre in proper hands, might certainly be made the school of morality; but now, I am sorry to say it, people seem to go there principally for their entertainment!

Mrs. Dangle: It would have been more to the credit of the Managers to have kept it in the other line.

Sneer: Undoubtedly, Madam, and hereafter perhaps to have had it recorded, that in the midst of a luxurious and dissipated age, they preserved *two* houses in the capital, where the conversation was always moral at least, if not entertaining!

Dangle: Now, egad, I think the worst alteration is in the nicety of the audience.—No double entendre, no smart innuendo admitted; even Vanbrugh and Congreve obliged to undergo a bungling reformation!

(I.i)

But, as in the last speech and elsewhere, Sheridan cannot resist laughing at himself; and at other times he makes the actors do the same (in the first performance several of them made recognizable parodies of each other's mannerisms). So when Puff, in his imaginary theatrical puff (I.ii), says, "Mr. DODD was astonishingly great in the character of SIR HARRY! That universal and judicious actor Mr. PALMER, perhaps never appeared to more advantage than in the COLONEL;—but it is not in the power of language to do justice to Mr. KING! . . ." the three actors named were themselves playing that scene on the first night, James Dodd as Dangle, John Palmer as Sneer, and Thomas King as Puff himself.

When he turns to the rehearsal of the parody tragedy, Sheridan lays about him with gusto. Improbability of plot and construction, cutting that makes nonsense of the action, bombastic dialogue, artificial conventions, the deliberate contriving of tableaux (III.i), the discovery scene beloved of the sentimentalists in which an improbable long-lost relationship emerges (only seven years later Mozart and Lorenzo da Ponte were to have similar fun in the sextet in the third act of *The Marriage of Figaro*—"Sua madre? Sua padre?"), the domination of the action by the needs of the scene shifters, and the spectacular effects all come under the lash. And after even only a year or two of management, and reading the inanities submitted by amateur playwrights with no theatrical sense, Sheridan must have had an enormous delight in creating Burleigh.

Enter BURLEIGH, goes slowly to a chair and sits.

Sneer: Mr. Puff!

Puff: Hush!—vastly well, Sir! vastly well! a most interesting gravity!

Dangle: What, isn't he to speak at all?

Puff: Egad, I thought you'd ask me that—yes it is a very likely thing—that a Minister in his situation, with the whole affairs of the nation on his head, should have time to talk!—but hush! or you'll put him out.

Sneer: Put him out! how the plague can that be, if he's not going to say anything?

Puff: There's a reason!—why, his part is to *think*, and how the plague! do you imagine he can *think* if you keep talking?

Dangle: That's very true upon my word!

(BURLEIGH comes forward, shakes his head and exits.)

Sneer: He is very perfect indeed—Now, pray what did he mean by that?

Puff: You don't take it?

Sneer: No; I don't upon my soul.

Puff: Why, by that shake of the head, he gave you to understand that even tho' they had more justice in their cause and wisdom in their measures—yet, if there was not a greater spirit shown on the part of the people—the country would at last fall a sacrifice to the hostile ambition of the Spanish monarchy.

Sneer: The devil!—did he mean all that by shaking his head?

Puff: Every word of it—If he shook his head as I taught him.

(III.i)

The final scene, with Tilburina and her confidant "mad, according to custom," one in white satin, the other in white linen, and the parody masque of the Thames between his banks, the procession of all the English rivers and their tributaries with their emblems, getting entangled with the battle of the Armada, to music by George Frederick Handel, builds into a wild and zany climax of spectacular nonsense.

Sheridan undoubtedly tried to pack too much into *The Critic*, and the text benefits in performance now by cutting, as it did after that two-and-a-half-hour first performance, but it is full of theatrical point and comic incident, consistently high-spirited and enjoyable; and though some of the contemporary allusions are now lost, it is still uproarious when well performed. It was the culmination of five years of splendid achievement in the theater. And it was the last comedy Sheridan was ever to write.

V

HE continued to revise other people's work from time to time; he wrote the occasional prologue or ode; and he seems to have collaborated to some extent in a one-act musical entertainment, *The Glorious First of June*, which was cobbled together in three days in 1794 to celebrate the naval battle of the title. But once elected to Parliament, his main creative energy was channeled into his oratory.

Except perhaps to the political historian, there is nothing so dead as an old political speech. Once the immediate reason for it has passed, it is difficult to get excited about the Defence Amendment Bill, or the Bill for Regulating the Royal Scotch Burghs, or the Duties on Post Horses and Tobacco, or the "Motion by Mr. Mainwaring for leave to bring in a Bill

to explain and amend the Act of 6 Geo III cap 36, relative to Trees, Shrubs, Plants &c," on all of which—and many similar bills—Sheridan spoke.

Oratory, of its very nature, is designed to have an immediate impact, and though the arguments used can be assessed later from the printed page, their effect on auditors at the time of delivery cannot. Moreover, the Sheridan speeches as published are for the most part summaries, not verbatim reports. In this respect we can only accept the testimony of contemporaries, and here it is clear that in an age in which rhetoric was cultivated and admired, Sheridan was judged among the best. The editor of his collected speeches wrote:

It has been remarked, that Mr. Sheridan, in flow of diction, yielded not to Mr. Pitt; in force and acuteness he might be compared to Mr. Fox; while, in splendour of imagination, he equalled Mr. Burke, and in its use and management, far excelled him. His sarcasms were finer, but less severe, than those by which Mr. Pitt indulged his anger, and the wit displayed by Mr. Sheridan in Parliament was, perhaps, from the suavity of his temper, much less sharp than brilliant. But the quality which predominated over all its companions in the mind of Mr. Sheridan, was his exquisite and highly finished taste. In this rare talent he had no competitor; and that it was that gave such inimitable grace to his expressions; and which, in arguing or declaiming, in eulogy or invective, disposed his thoughts with an effect so full and admirable.

(vol. I, p.xxviii)

His great achievements, according to his contemporaries, were the series of speeches he made on English administration in India, first in Parliament, and then in Westminster Hall on the impeachment of Warren Hastings in 1788. It is unnecessary here to go into the arguments as to whether Sheridan, Fox, and Edmund Burke (for the prosecution) were right, whether Hastings was properly or unjustly accused of maladministration, oppression, and financial corruption (he was eventually acquitted, though not until 1795). Sheridan argued his case in detail and at length from sources and documents—one speech in the House of Commons lasted five and a half hours; that in Westminster Hall, four days. He poured satire and scorn on Sir Elijah Impey, he attacked Warren Hastings with the fervor of an Old Testament prophet, he painted a pathetic picture of the Begums of Oude as victims of rapacity and injustice, and he supported his theme from time to time with passionate appeals to the eternal verities.

Great God of Justice! canst thou from thy eternal throne look down upon such premeditated turpitude of heart, and not fix some mark of dreadful vengeance upon the perpetrators?

(I, pp.292–293)

This was British justice! this was British humanity! Mr. Hastings ensures to the allies of the company, in the strongest terms, their prosperity and his protection; the former he secures by sending an army to plunder them of their wealth and to desolate their soil! His protection is fraught with a similar security; like that of a vulture to a lamb; grappling in its vitals! thirsting for its blood! scaring off each petty kite that hovers round; and then, with an insulting perversion of terms, calling sacrifice, *protection!*—an object for which history seeks for any similarity in vain. The deep searching annals of Tacitus;—the luminous philosophy of Gibbon;—all the records of man's transgressing, from original sin to the present period, dwindle into comparative insignificance of enormity; both in aggravation of vile principles, and extent of their consequential ruin!

(II, pp.112–113)

The reported behavior of the Nabob to his mother brought forth another purple passage, like the last, to echo through *Pizarro* ten years later.

FILIAL PIETY! It is the primal bond of society—it is that instinctive principle, which, panting for its proper good, soothes, unbidden, each sense and sensibility of man!—it now quivers on every lip!—it now beams from every eye!—it is an emanation of that gratitude, which softening under the sense of recollected good, is eager to own the vast countless debt it ne'er, alas! can pay, for so many long years of unceasing solicitudes, honorable self-denials, life-preserving cares!—it is that part of our practice, where duty drops its awe!—where reverence refines into love!—it asks no aid of memory!—it needs not the deductions of reason!—pre-existing, paramount over all, whether law, or human rule, few arguments can increase and none diminish it!—it is the sacrament of our nature!—not only the duty, but the indulgence of man—it is his first great privilege—it is amongst his last most endearing delights!—it causes the bosom to glow with reverberated love!—it requites the visitations of nature, and returns the blessings that have been received!—it fires emotion into vital principle—it renders habituated instinct into a master-passion—sways all the sweetest energies of man—hangs over each vicissitude of all that must pass away—aids the melancholy virtues in their last sad tasks of life, to cheer the languors of decrepitude and age—explores the thought—elucidates the aching eye!—and breathes sweet consolation even in the awful moment of dissolution.

(II, p. 117)

And his peroration in Westminster Hall on 13 June 1788 returned once more to the great theme of British justice.

Justice I have now before me, *august* and *pure*; the abstract idea of all that would be perfect in the spirits and the aspirings of men!—where the mind arises, where the heart expands;—where the countenance is ever placid and benign;—where her favorite attitude is to stoop to the unfortunate—to hear their cry, and to help them,—to rescue and relieve, to succour and save:—majestic from its mercy; venerable from its utility:—uplifted without pride,—firm without obduracy:—beneficent in each preference:—lovely, though in her frown!

On *that justice I rely*; deliberate and sure, abstracted from all party purpose and political speculations! not in words, but on facts!—You, my lords, who hear me, I conjure by those *rights* it is your best privilege to preserve; by that fame it is your best pleasure to inherit; by all those *feelings* which refer to the first term in the series of existence, the *original compact* of our nature—our *controlling rank* in the creation—This is the call on all, to administer to truth and equity, as they would satisfy the laws and satisfy themselves, with the most exalted bliss, possible or conceivable for our nature.—The *self-approving consciousness of virtue*, when the condemnation we look for will be one of the most ample mercies accomplished for mankind since the creation of the world!

My lords, I have done!

(II, pp.126–127)

That speech in Westminster Hall had a powerful effect. Experienced men of affairs collapsed, and society ladies had to be taken out, suffering from nervous exhaustion. Burke spoke afterward of the

. . . wonderful eloquence of his honourable friend, Mr. Sheridan, who had that day again surprised the thousands who hung with rapture on his accents, by such a display of talents as were unparalleled in the annals of oratory, and as did the highest honour to himself, to that house, and to his country.

(I, p. xxv)

Sheridan's speeches are undoubtedly little read now; but aside from their content they still have an interest for the theater historian—they go a long way to explain why his last play, *Pizarro*, is so astonishingly different from all that he had done before.

In 1799 the finances of Drury Lane were once again in a parlous state, so Sheridan needed a popular success, and one that would give full scope to the talents of his two leading players, John Philip Kemble and his sister Sarah Siddons. In the previous year they had excelled in a version of *The Stranger*, by the German romantic playwright Kotzebue, in the revision of which Sheridan had had a considerable share, so he decided to turn to another play by the same author, *Die Spanier in Peru*. Knowing no German himself, Sheridan had a literal translation prepared, and then began to work on that. He kept to the main line of Kotzebue's plot, though with one or two developments for added theatrical effect, in particular making actual several incidents only narrated in the original; but he allowed himself freedom to expand the dialogue into declamation at points that seemed to him important. (Cecil Price prints examples of Sheridan's amplifications, and J. W. Donohue discusses the play interestingly in the context of the English romantic theater.[4]) Sheridan also, by adding songs, choruses, ritual, and processions, and making provision for elaborate scenic effects in the new and enlarged Drury Lane Theatre, turned the play into a semioperatic spectacular.

The two major protagonists are the Spaniard Pizarro, a product of so-called civilization but ruthless and violent, and Rolla, the chieftain of the Inca's troops, a noble savage, generous and self-sacrificing, the product of uncorrupted nature. John Philip Kemble played Rolla, for which his declamatory style and formal gestures and attitudes were admirably suited (indeed, Sheridan may well have had them in mind as he built up the rhetoric of the part). Sarah Siddons played Elvira, the mistress with a heart of gold; Charles Kemble and Dorothea Jordan, the young leading roles of Alonzo and Cora.

There were topical and political overtones that the audiences of the day were not slow to pick up; the "noble savage" element and the humanitarian sympathies of the play had a clear relationship to the current debate on the slave trade, and brought William Wilberforce to the theater for the first time in twenty years. Moreover, in the middle of the French Revolutionary Wars, English audiences were not slow to interpret Rolla's impassioned speech about the Spanish invaders in a sense much closer to hand.

> *Rolla:* . . . Your generous spirit has compared, as mine has, the motives which, in a war like this, can animate *their* minds, and OURS.—THEY, by a strange frenzy

driven, fight for power, for plunder, and extended rule—WE, for our country, our altars, and our homes.—THEY follow an Adventurer whom they fear—and obey a power which they hate—WE serve a Monarch whom we love—a God whom we adore.—Whene'er they move in anger, desolation tracks their progress!—Where'er they pause in amity, affliction mourns their friendship!—They boast, they come but to improve our state, enlarge our thoughts, and free us from the yoke of error!—Yes—THEY will give enlightened freedom to *our* minds, who are themselves the slaves of passion, avarice, and pride.—They offer us their protection—Yes, such protection as vultures give to lambs—covering and devouring them!—They call on us to barter all of good we have inherited and proved, for the desperate chance of something better which they promise.—Be our plain answer this: The throne WE honour is the PEOPLE'S CHOICE—the laws we reverence are our brave Fathers' legacy—the faith we follow teaches us to live in bonds of charity with all mankind, and die with hope of bliss beyond the grave. Tell your invaders this, and tell them too, we seek no change; and least of all, such change as they would bring us.

> *(Trumpets sound.)*

> *Ata (embracing ROLLA):* Now, holy friends, ever mindful of these sacred truths, begin the sacrifice. (*A solemn Procession commences from the recess of the Temple above the Altar—The Priests and Virgins of the Sun arrange themselves on either side—The High-Priest approaches the Altar, and the solemnity begins—The Invocation of the High-Priest is followed by the Chorusses of the Priests and Virgins—Fire from above lights upon the Altar.—The whole assembly rise, and join in the Thanksgiving.*)

> (II.ii)

This became one of the famous scenes in the play, and it is Sheridan the orator speaking. (Indeed, William Pitt, having visited the theater, felt that there was nothing new in the play—he had heard it all long ago in the speeches at Hastings' trial.) The ritual in the Temple of the Sun is just one example of the operatic and spectacular elements that made such an impresssion in the theater, though the great climax came in Act V, scene ii, with Rolla's escape, bearing in his arms the kidnapped child of Cora and Alonzo, crossing under fire a wooden bridge over a deep chasm and cataract, and eventually eluding his pursuers by tearing up by the roots the tree that supported one side of the bridge. Samson in Gaza could do no more. The powerful impression left by this scene is witnessed by the records made of it; Sir Thomas Lawrence painted Kemble in his famous attitude bearing the child, and there is a print of a command performance at Covent Garden in 1804

[4]J. W. Donohue, *Dramatic Character in the English Romantic Age* (Princeton, N. J., 1970); see bibliography.

depicting the whole scene—gorge, bridge, pursuers, and all. It is not, of course, tragedy in any traditional sense; it is the nineteenth-century spectacular melodrama already upon us, and Rolla's death a few moments later is of a banality that, divorced from the powerful personality of the actor, it is difficult to believe could ever be taken seriously. But it was.

> Enter ROLLA, bleeding, with the CHILD, follow'd by Peruvian SOLDIERS.
>
> *Rol:* Thy child! (*Gives the CHILD into CORA's arms, and falls.*)
> *Cora:* Oh God!—there's blood upon him!
> *Rol:* 'Tis my blood, Cora!
> *Alonzo:* Rolla, thou diest!
> *Rol:* For thee, and Cora—(*Dies.*)
>
> (V.iii)

It is perhaps not the least of the curiosities that surround *Pizarro* that again and again Sheridan writes seriously in the style of the parody in *The Critic* twenty years before, and does not appear to be aware of it.

> *Valverde:* But the hour of revenge is come.
> *Pizarro:* It is; I am returned—my force is strengthened, and the audacious Boy shall soon know that Pizarro lives, and has—a grateful recognition of the thanks he owes him.
> *Val:* 'Tis doubted whether still Alonzo lives.
> *Piz:* 'Tis certain that he does; one of his armour-bearers is just made prisoner: twelve thousand is their force, as he reports, led by Alonzo and Peruvian Rolla. This day they make a solemn sacrifice on their ungodly altars. We must profit by their security, and attack them unprepared—the sacrificers shall become the victims.
> *Elvira: (Aside.)* Wretched innocents! And their own blood shall bedew their altars!
> *Piz:* Right! (*Trumpets without.*) Elvira, retire!
> *Elv:* Why should I retire?
> *Piz:* Because men are to meet here, and on manly business.
> *Elv:* O, men! men! ungrateful and perverse! O, woman! still affectionate, though wrong'd! The Beings to whose eyes you turn for animation, hope, and rapture, through the days of mirth and revelry; and on whose bosoms in the hour of sore calamity you seek for rest and consolation; THEM, when the pompous follies of your mean ambition are the question, you treat as playthings or as slaves!—I shall not retire.
> *Piz:* Remain then—and, if thou canst, be silent.
> *Elv:* They only babble who practise not reflection. I shall think—and thought is silence.
>
> (I.i)

It all brings back ribald memories of Sir Christopher Hatton, Sir Walter Ralegh, the earl of Leicester, the governor of Tilbury Fort, and all, to say nothing of the silent, thoughtful Burleigh. And Alonzo and Cora, drooling over their baby at the beginning of Act II, are even more embarrassing than Sheridan discoursing on filial piety in Westminster Hall.

That this kind of thing could be taken seriously is an indication of the great change in the cultural climate that was taking place. To their credit, not everyone who saw it did accept it, though many did. *The Oracle* wrote satirically about "Kotzebue-mania," and Thomas Moore affirmed roundly that the dialogue of this play was "unworthy of its author, and ought never, from either motives of profit or the vanity of success, to have been coupled with his name. The style in which it is written belongs neither to verse or prose, but is a sort of amphibious native of both."

But the *Morning Post* of 25 May 1799 saw it very differently.

> The sentiment is derived from the very bosom of domestic and public duties: the tender and pathetic scenes are finely wrought up from the conjugal and parental virtues; those of sublimer cast from the energies of a free, brave, and generous people, fighting for liberty against oppression. They are laid in nature, and as such, are as applicable to the present day, as the age for which they are written. . . . If any part can be particularly called Mr. Sheridan's, it is the language; and here we trace no fault. There are no quaint conceits, no meretricious glare, no parade of words, no specious phraseology. It is nature attired by the Graces, in true expression with all the beauties of polished style and classical purity. The piece was listened to with the deepest interest, and received the warmest applause throughout.

Sheridan was aiming at the sublime. Clearly, for many of his audience he achieved it.

As with most of Sheridan's first nights, things went wrong—particularly with the machinery and the spectacle—and cutting and reshaping had to be done. But once it had settled down, the play became a great success. Whether the play was empty, sentimental rhetoric or not, Sheridan's instinct as to what the bulk of his audience would accept had once more proved impeccable.

Nevertheless, *Pizarro* remains a strange ending to the career that began with *The Rivals* and reached its peak with *The School for Scandal* and *The Critic*;

yet in the light of Sheridan's character and the choices he made in his life, it was logical, and perhaps inevitable. In the world of the theater there may well be feelings of regret that Sheridan did not remain there, and keep out of politics. But there is no guarantee that he would have continued to write as he did in *The School for Scandal*. He kept that play unpublished for years, saying he wanted to improve it; but he never did so. And as *Pizarro* dramatically shows, the cultural and theatrical climate in the last two decades of the eighteenth century was changing radically. A Sheridan writing like Thomas Holcroft or Elizabeth Inchbald would be an equal disappointment. In the last analysis one can only be grateful for those remarkable five years in the 1770's, in which all his best work was done. Without them the repertory of the Georgian theater—and the English theater today—would be without some of its luster.

SELECTED BIBLIOGRAPHY

I. BIBLIOGRAPHY. Detailed bibliographical information can also be found in the appropriate volume of the *Cambridge Bibliography of English Literature*. L. A. Williams, *Seven XVIIIth Century Bibliographies* (London, 1924), the Sheridan bibliography is a standard work of reference for first eds.; R. C. Rhodes, ed., *The Plays and Poems*, 3 vols. (Oxford, 1928), bibliographies of separate works are included.

II. COLLECTED WORKS. *The Dramatic Works, Together with a Life of the Author* (London, 1798), the first ed. (1797) does not contain the "Life"; "A Constitutional Friend," ed., *Speeches of the Late Right Honourable Richard Brinsley Sheridan (Several Corrected by Himself)*, 5 vols. (London, 1816); *The Works*, 2 vols. (London, 1821), the first authorized collection, with a preface by T. Moore; *The Dramatic Works* (London, 1840), with a biographical and critical sketch by L. Hunt; A. W. Pollard, ed., *The Plays* (London, 1900); W. F. Rae, ed., *The Plays, Prepared Partly from MS Drafts* (London, 1902), with an intro. by the marquess of Dufferin and Ava, Sheridan's great-grandson; R. C. Rhodes, ed., *The Plays and Poems*, 3 vols. (Oxford, 1928); *Plays* (London, 1955), with an intro. by T. Guthrie; C. Price, ed., *The Letters of Richard Brinsley Sheridan*, 3 vols. (Oxford, 1966), a comprehensive collection, devotedly edited; C. Price, ed., *The Dramatic Works of Richard Brinsley Sheridan*, 2 vols. (Oxford, 1973), now the standard ed.; C. Price, ed., *Sheridan—Plays* (London, 1975), based on the 1973 ed., without textual detail but with a valuable critical intro.—the best text for general reading.

III. SEPARATE WORKS. *The Duenna, or The Double Elopement* (London, 1775), comic opera; *The Rivals* (Dublin, 1775), the most accurate version of this comedy is the parallel text ed. (Oxford, 1935) prepared by R. L. Purdy from collations of the Larpent MS and the earliest published versions; *The School for Scandal* (Dublin, 1780), the first of several textually corrupt eds., the first genuine text being published at Dublin in 1799—Sheridan's final revision was printed in the collected ed. of 1821; *The Critic: Or, A Tragedy Rehearsed* (London, 1781), a burlesque; *A Trip to Scarborough* (London, 1781), an adaptation of Vanbrugh's *The Relapse* (1697); *Speech . . . Against Warren Hastings* (London, 1787), a report of Sheridan's most celebrated speech in the House of Commons; *St. Patrick's Day: Or, The Scheming Lieutenant* (Dublin, 1788), a farce; *Pizarro, a Tragedy in Five Acts . . .* (London, 1799).

Sheridan also collaborated in a number of theatrical entertainments, such as *The Forty Thieves* (London, 1808), and contributed several prologues and epilogues to plays by other writers. His most important piece of occasional verse is *Verses to the Memory of Garrick, Spoken as a Monody* (London, 1779).

IV. BIOGRAPHIES. There is no completely satisfactory biography of Sheridan; most have their qualities and their flaws. Moore, for example, had access to much contemporary knowledge, but was hampered by current conventions of what might be said; Sichel is long and detailed, but often tedious; Rhodes has valuable new information but too many gaps, particularly in the early years; Bingham is readable and better on the early years, but gives little indication of sources. Some biographies that may be consulted are T. Moore, *Memoirs of the Life of the Right Honourable Richard Brinsley Sheridan*, 2nd ed., 2 vols. (London, 1825); W. F. Rae, *Sheridan: A Biography*, 2 vols. (London, 1896), documented, and with an intro. by the marquess of Dufferin and Ava; W. Sichel, *Sheridan*, 2 vols. (London, 1909); M. T. H. Sadler (M. Sadleir), *The Political Career of Sheridan* (Oxford, 1912); W. A. Darlington, *Sheridan* (London, 1933), a drama critic's estimate; R. C. Rhodes, *Harlequin Sheridan: The Man and the Legends* (Oxford, 1933); L. Gibbs, *Sheridan* (London, 1947); M. Bingham, *Sheridan: The Track of a Comet* (London, 1972).

Early memoirs or journals containing useful information about Sheridan are A. Lefanu, *Memoirs of the Life and Writings of Mrs. Frances Sheridan* (London, 1824); J. Boaden, *Memoirs of the Life of John Philip Kemble Esq.*, 2 vols. (London, 1825); M. Kelly, *Reminiscences* (London, 1826), repr. in R. Fiske, ed. (London, 1975); W. Lefanu, ed., *Betsy Sheridan's Journal* (London, 1960).

V. BACKGROUND, CRITICAL, AND FACTUAL STUDIES. M. T. H. Sadler, *The Political Career of Sheridan* (Oxford, 1912); C. Black, *The Linleys of Bath*, rev. ed. (London, 1926); C. H. Gray, *Theatrical Criticism in London to 1795* (New York, 1931); J. J. Lynch, *Box, Pit* and Gallery (Berkeley, Calif., 1953); F. S. Boas, *Introduction to Eighteenth Century Drama* (London, 1955); A. Nicoll, *A History of English Drama 1660–1900*, vol. III, *1750–1800* (Cambridge, 1955); *The London Stage, 1660–1800: A Calendar of Plays, Entertainments and Afterpieces, Together with Casts, Box-receipts and Contemporary Comment*, 5 pts. (Carbondale, Ill., 1960–1969)—see pt. IV, G. W. Stone, ed., *1747–1776*, 3 vols., and pt. V, C. B. Hogan, ed., *1776–1800*, 3 vols.; J. Dulck, *Les comédies de R. B. Sheridan* (Paris, 1962), the first book to deal entirely with Sheridan's work as a dramatist; J. W. Donohue, *Dramatic Character in the English Romantic Age* (Princeton, N.J., 1970); R. Fiske, *English Theatre Music in the Eighteenth Century* (London, 1973); C. Price, *Theatre in the Age of Garrick* (Oxford, 1973); J. Loftis, *Sheridan and the Drama of Georgian England* (Oxford, 1976); A. Hare, ed., *Theatre Royal Bath: The Orchard Street Calendar 1750–1805* (Bath, 1977); M. S. Auburn, *Sheridan's Comedies* (Lincoln, Nebr., 1977).

VI. RECORDINGS. *The Rivals*: Edith Evans, Michael MacLiammoir, Pamela Brown, James Donald, Vanessa Redgrave, John Laurie, Robert Eddison, Alec McCowen, Alan Bates, Gerald James, Laurence Hardy, directed by Howard Sackler—Caedmon TC 2020/1,2 (1963); *The School for Scandal*: Cecil Parker, Baliol Holloway, Harry Andrews, Alec Clunes, Claire Bloom, Edith Evans, Athene Seyler, George Howe, William Squire, Anne Leon, Peter Williams, Peter Halliday, Michael Gough—E.M.I. TC-LFP 7028 (1978).

GEORGE CRABBE

(1754-1832)

R. L. Brett

THE MAN

GEORGE CRABBE was born on Christmas Eve 1754, in the Suffolk town of Aldeburgh. Aldeburgh changed greatly in Crabbe's lifetime. On a visit to his birthplace when he was sixty-eight, he wrote:

Thus once again, my native place, I come
Thee to salute—my earliest, latest home;
Much are we alter'd both, but I behold
In thee a youth renew'd—whilst I am old.
The works of man from dying we may save,
But man himself moves onward to the grave.
(Aldborough, October 1823)[1]

But the change that would greet him now, were he able to renew his visit, would surprise him even more. For towns, like individuals, can go up or down in the world. Aldeburgh today, though it is still little more than a huddle of buildings along a shingle beach, surrounded by mud flats and marshlands, is more than a fishing village. Though it provides a holiday place for those who dislike the communal hilarity of the holiday camp or the commercial vulgarity of many larger places, it is more than a seaside resort. Since Victorian times a discriminating if sober few had favored Aldeburgh as a watering place, but today the town has achieved an eminence beyond the expectations of even this select minority. For Aldeburgh, with the encouragement of a distinguished citizen, Benjamin Britten (whose opera *Peter Grimes* was inspired by Crabbe), has its deservedly famous music festival. Even so, the adjective "elegant," which Crabbe's son employs to describe Aldeburgh in his father's time, is hardly one that would be used today:

Aldborough [or, as it is more correctly written, Aldeburgh] was, in those days, a poor and wretched place, with nothing of the elegance and gaiety which have since sprung up about it, in consequence of the resort of watering parties. The town lies between a low hill or cliff, on which only the old church and a few better houses were then situated, and the beach of the German Ocean. It consisted of two parallel and unpaved streets, running between mean and scrambling houses, the abodes of seafaring men, pilots and fishers. The range of houses nearest to the sea had suffered so much from repeated invasions of the waves, that only a few scattered tenements appeared erect among the desolation.[2]

The image of Crabbe that has filled many people's minds has been one of good-tempered mediocrity: a middle-of-the-road man in theology, in his social and political views, and in his personal relations; not liable to extremes of passion or extravagant flights of fancy. The implication behind this account, of course, is that his poetry is dull and rather prosaic, the work of a "Pope in worsted stockings." We will leave the poetry on one side for the moment, but inquiry will show that Crabbe as a person was not like this at all. If the child is father of the man, one should expect Crabbe to be anything but dull. He was a sensitive child who reacted strongly to his environment. One is reminded of Alfred Tennyson's childhood at Somersby, further north on the Lincolnshire wolds, a countryside not unlike that around Aldeburgh, the same windswept coastline with the perpetual boom of the North Sea accentuating its sadness.

The struggle for existence had made its mark on the villagers of Aldeburgh, a population of longshoremen almost as much at home afloat as ashore:

---

[1] All quotations are from A. J. and R. M. Carlyle, eds., *The Poetical Works of George Crabbe* (Oxford, 1908).

[2] *Life of Crabbe* by his son, George Crabbe, vol. I of the *Collected Works* (London, 1834), p. 9.

—a wild, amphibious race,
With sullen woe display'd in every face;
Who far from civil arts and social fly
And scowl at strangers with suspicious eye.
                        (*The Village*, bk. I, 85–88)

Crabbe's home life, too, was the sort to make a high-strung child even more sensitive. He was the eldest of six children. His father (also named George) was the collector of salt duties at Aldeburgh, a minor customs official, whose meager salary of £10 a year obliged him to turn fisherman for part of the time. But his father was clearly superior in intelligence and education to most of his fellows. He had kept the village school at nearby Orford, and took pleasure in mathematics and in reading the poetry of John Milton and Edward Young to his family; both, one may guess, fairly rare accomplishments in Aldeburgh at that time. And yet in spite of his abilities—or perhaps because of them and the sense of frustration they brought him in such an environment—Crabbe's father was a man of uncertain temper. As a small boy the poet was terrified by his father's outbursts of passion, and his lifelong hatred of drunkenness sprang from the violence he witnessed at home when his father had been drinking.

Early experiences of this sort work themselves into the fabric of one's thought and haunt the imagination with a force denied to things that come later. Just as William Cowper, looking at his mother's portrait nearly fifty years after her death, was still filled with a sense of loss, so Crabbe carried through life the fears of his early years. In a manuscript fragment entitled "Infancy," which his son found among his papers, and which belongs to the year 1816, he writes of the death of a baby sister when he was seven years old. It was not simply the loss of his sister that desolated him,[3] but the spectacle of his parents' grief, the tears of his mother, and worse, the "terrors" of his father, who sought relief in drink.

Yes! looking back as early as I can,
I see the griefs that seize their subject Man;
That in the weeping child their early reign began

. . .

[3]There are good grounds for saying that it was not a sister but a brother (William) who died at this time. See René Huchon, *George Crabbe and His Times* (London, 1907), p. 7, n. 3.

But it was misery stung me in the day
Death of an infant sister made his prey;
For then first met and moved by early fears
A father's terrors and a mother's tears.
Though greater anguish I have since endured,
Some heal'd in part, some never to be cured,
Yet there was something in that first-born ill
So new, so strange, that memory feels it still.
                        (40–42; 57–64)

But it was not all misery for Crabbe as a child. His mother was a gentle and patient woman with great affection for her children. There were picnic parties and other excursions by land, by sea, and on the river Ald; and the life of the town itself, with the quay and the beach, provided enough amusement and distraction for any boy. He developed a keen interest in botany and knew the surrounding countryside and its walks as only a naturalist can. Though never a sailor by inclination or skill, he had watched the sea in all its moods; no poet has given so many or so fine descriptions of it. It formed part of everyone's life in Aldeburgh and provided the backdrop for many dramas.

Various and vast, sublime in all its forms,
When lull'd by zephyrs, or when roused by storms;
Its colours changing, when from clouds and sun
Shades after shades upon the surface run.
                        (*The Borough*, letter 1, 165–168)

Crabbe describes the sea as it lies peaceful in the sunshine. The tide comes in almost imperceptibly:

Then the broad bosom of the ocean keeps
An equal motion, swelling as it sleeps,
Then slowly sinking; curling to the strand,
Faint, lazy waves o'ercreep the ridgy sand,
Or tap the tarry boat with gentle blow,
And back return in silence, smooth and slow.
Ships in the calm seem anchor'd, for they glide
On the still sea, urged solely by the tide.
                        (179–186)

In contrast with this he presents the scene in winter:

All where the eye delights, yet dreads, to roam,
The breaking billows cast the flying foam
Upon the billows rising—all the deep
Is restless change; the waves so swell'd and steep,
Breaking and sinking, and the sunken swells,
Nor one, one moment, in its station dwells.

But nearer land, you may the billows trace,
As if contending in their watery chase;
May watch the mightiest till the shoal they reach,
Then break and hurry to their utmost stretch;
Curl'd as they come, they strike with furious force,
And then, re-flowing, take their grating course,
Raking the rounded flints, which ages past
Roll'd by their rage, and shall to ages last.

(200–213)

Crabbe left these scenes of his native place for considerable periods, even when young. He attended the dame school at Aldeburgh, but his father was ambitious for him and sent him away to school, first to Bungay on the borders of Norfolk, and then to Stowmarket. He was only eleven years old when he went to Stowmarket and must have been a good deal younger when he went to Bungay, for his son says that he could not even dress himself on his first day there. In his fourteenth year Crabbe left school and became apprenticed to a surgeon. A medical education then was often strictly practical; a doctor's assistant picked up his knowledge just as a plumber's would, by watching and helping his master. His first master, who practiced as an apothecary near Bury St. Edmunds, found farming a lucrative sideline to medicine, and Crabbe was expected to help on the farm and to share the bed of the plowboy. After three years he moved to Woodbridge, where he found a better master and more congenial society. Woodbridge, in fact, compared with Aldeburgh, was a center of urbane and literary society. Here he met Sarah Elmy, the "Mira" of his poems, who after a long engagement was to become his wife. Here he began seriously to write poetry, and it was while staying at Woodbridge that he persuaded an Ipswich printer to publish, in 1775, his youthful poem *Inebriety*.

In the same year, his apprenticeship ended, Crabbe returned to Aldeburgh, where he practiced medicine. With a conscientiousness all too rare at the time, he decided to spend a period in London, where he could visit the hospitals and gain the skill he lacked in surgery and (a sine qua non in a rural community) in obstetrics. Within the year he returned to Aldeburgh with this additional experience. But his practice never flourished. His rivals were unscrupulous, his patients were poor, and no one had much confidence in a youth who had grown up among them and whose background was the same as their own. Even worse, Crabbe's home life had become intolerable. His mother's

health was failing, but this seemed only to weaken the self-control of his father, who would return from the tavern in fits of drunken rage and hurl his food about the room if it was not to his taste. No wonder Crabbe recalled the gaiety of Woodbridge society and longed for the day when he could marry Sarah Elmy and set up his own home. From this conflict of hopes and fears emerged the conviction that he no longer wished to be a doctor, and the decision to go to London to try his fortune as a writer. The road from the provinces to the capital had already seen a dismal procession of young writers who had met defeat. Nevertheless, he left Aldeburgh as a man leaves prison. The famous lines in *The Village* describe his sense of liberation:

As on their neighbouring beach yon swallows stand,
And wait for favouring winds to leave the land;
While still for flight the ready wing is spread:
So waited I the favouring hour, and fled—
Fled from these shores where guilt and famine reign,
And cried, "Ah! hapless they who still remain; . . ."

(bk. I, 119–124)

Crabbe's second stay in London brought him close to disaster. His medical instruments in the hands of the pawnbroker proved more substantial pledges to fortune than the manuscript poems he sent to potential patrons. A year passed in disappointment and disillusionment. He approached Lord North, Lord Shelburne, and Edward Thurlow, the lord chancellor, but received only rebuffs. As a last resort he wrote to Edmund Burke and enclosed with his letter some specimens of his poetry that included parts of *The Library* and of *The Village*. Burke was member of Parliament for Bristol, and his magnanimity was perhaps stirred by the memory of Thomas Chatterton, "the marvellous boy" who, not long before, had left that city, only to perish as a suicide in a Grub Street attic. But nothing can detract from either Burke's goodness as a man or his perception as a literary critic. He gave immediate and effective assistance. Crabbe was received into his home and introduced to the literary celebrities of the day. In the words of his son, the incident "entirely, and for ever, changed the nature of his worldly fortunes."

The first effect of Burke's help was the publication by James Dodsley of *The Library*. The second was Crabbe's ordination by the bishop of Norwich. To some there might seem an element of worldliness in Crabbe's decision to enter holy orders at this juncture, a certain convenience in choosing a vocation that would provide him at one and the same time with a living and the chance to write. But this is unjust to Crabbe. He was a sincere and hardworking parish priest, who forsook writing for more than twenty years once he became an incumbent. But before this happened, he had to serve in two positions, in both of which he was unhappy. The first of these was as curate in Aldeburgh, where his parishioners found it difficult to forgive the good fortune that had come to him. The second was as chaplain to the duke of Rutland at Belvoir Castle. Thurlow, the lord chancellor (with a recollection of that delightful but gauche character in Henry Fielding's *Joseph Andrews*), once told Crabbe that he was "as like Parson Adams as twelve to a dozen," and his proud but naive honesty made him ill at ease in the role of domestic chaplain. It was while at Belvoir Castle that he completed *The Village*. Samuel Johnson read and approved of it, and even contributed some small revisions. Justly, but in his most headmasterly style, Johnson wrote to Joshua Reynolds: "I do not doubt of Mr. Crabbe's success."

The Village appeared in May 1783. In December of the same year, Crabbe married Sarah Elmy. The duke of Rutland was shortly afterward appointed to Ireland as lord lieutenant, but Crabbe preferred not to accompany him. Instead, he and his wife moved to Stathern in Lincolnshire, the first of many country livings they were to occupy. In 1785, *The Newspaper* was published; but that, apart from a few incursions into journalism, was the last of Crabbe's writings until, in 1807, *The Parish Register* appeared. This long period of silence was taken up not only with ministering to the souls of his flock but also with the application of his medical training to the healing of their bodies, with family responsibilities, and with his botanical interests. The account his son gives is of a quiet, self-contained, and busy domesticity.

Crabbe had much sadness to bear. Of his seven children only two survived. Under this succession of bereavements his wife became permanently manic-depressive, plunged in gloom for several months of the year and victim of an equally disturbing excitability for the remainder. The picture of Crabbe that one gets from his son's biography is of a devoted father and husband; a latitudinarian churchman without much sympathy for the evangelical fervor of Methodism; generous and sympathetic in his personal relationships, yet reserved in showing emotion. But though he showed his feelings to few, he was very far from being insensitive or uncomplicated. He was frequently seized by nervous fears and depression, and for the last forty years of his life he regularly took opium. His sleep was often disturbed by recurrent dreams, one of which was well known to his family. In this dream he was followed and taunted by a group of boys; he tried to frighten them away with a stick, but his blows were unavailing because the boys were made of leather. Sometimes when he came to the breakfast table after a poor night, he would say, "The leather-lads have been at me again."

It was family responsibilities that characteristically gave the impulse for Crabbe's reemergence as a poet. The publication of *The Parish Register* was intended to provide for the education of his second son. In spite of the new literary taste that the Lake poets had tried to establish a few years previously, the critics, and especially the *Edinburgh Review*, hailed Crabbe's reappearance with an enthusiasm that was perhaps surprising. Inspired by his newfound success, Crabbe produced *The Borough* in 1810 and *Tales in Verse* in 1812. Letters of congratulation showered upon him, and the fashionable literary circles that centered on Holland House welcomed him to London.

But in the midst of his triumphs there was sorrow. His wife died in the autumn of 1813. Crabbe himself had been in low spirits and poor health, and was exhausted both physically and emotionally by her illness and death. The grave, in fact, was kept open in case he too should die. But he survived this crisis, and there followed a period of serenity and happiness that lasted until his death on 3 February 1832. This Indian summer was spent at Trowbridge in Wiltshire, where Crabbe remained as vicar for the rest of his life. At one moment he came perilously near marrying for the second time, to a lady very much his junior, but prudence prevailed and he withdrew. With his son John as curate of Trowbridge and his elder son George established as incumbent of Pucklechurch, near Bath, he felt it was wiser, perhaps, to look to his own family for a bulwark against loneliness.

Certainly his last years brought Crabbe fame as well as happiness. He met William Wordsworth at Hampstead, visited Walter Scott in Edinburgh, was a celebrity in the literary society of Bath and a welcome visitor at the great houses of the county. Yet in all this he never overlooked his duties or forgot his humble beginning. Unlike many memorial tablets, the one erected by his parishioners at Trowbridge pays a genuine tribute to Crabbe's character.

He broke through the obscurity of his birth yet never ceased to feel for the less fortunate; entering (as his works can testify) into the sorrows and deprivations of the poorest of his parishioners; and so discharging the duties of his station as a minister and a magistrate as to acquire the respect and esteem of all his neighbours.

Of his merit as a poet the tablet is brief; it simply records Lord Byron's description of him as "Nature's sternest painter, yet her best."[4] But is this the most suitable or the only thing that can be said of Crabbe as a poet?

THE POET

CRABBE's life has all the makings of a success story that belongs to fiction, and his son's account of his life is a minor classic. These facts have often meant that his poetry has stood in the shadow of his life and been interpreted by reference to the changing fortunes of its author. This habit is a long-established one. As early as 1808 Robert Southey wrote to a friend:

Crabbe's [poems] have a gloom which is also not in nature, . . . the . . . shadows of one who paints by lamplight—whose very lights have a gloominess. In part this is explained by his history.

(To J. N. White, 30 September 1808)

There is truth in what Southey says. But to approach Crabbe's work only from the biographical standpoint is to give less than its due to the objectivity of the world that Crabbe created in his poetry.

For many readers Crabbe's poetry is interesting only because of Crabbe the man. For others even this cannot make it acceptable. And yet in his own lifetime he was a favorite with the public. William Hazlitt, who did not admire him and who (to use

Keats's phrase) "gave Crabbe an unmerciful licking" in *The Spirit of the Age*, had to admit that "Mr. Crabbe is one of the most popular and admired of our living authors." Readers today find no difficulty in a catholicity large enough to embrace both Wordsworth and Crabbe, but for a long time public taste, which had been bred upon romanticism, almost automatically excluded him from consideration. His admirers show how wrong public taste can be, for they include Wordsworth himself, Byron, Tennyson, John Henry Newman, Edward Fitz-Gerald, and E. M. Forster.

Crabbe was unfortunate in incurring the dislike of a powerful critic like Hazlitt. But a man's friends, as well as his enemies, can be a handicap. The support Crabbe received from the *Edinburgh Review* and its editor, Francis Jeffrey, was no recommendation in certain quarters. Yet Jeffrey remains one of his best critics. He recognized the uneven quality of Crabbe's writing and realized that this would be a stumbling block to many. As he wrote:

Mr. Crabbe is so unequal a writer, and at times so unattractive, as to require, more than any other of his degree, some explanation of his system, and some specimens of his powers.

(*Edinburgh Review*, July 1819)

The aim of this essay is to try to meet these requirements: to lay bare his "system," the rationale of his work, and to illustrate from its vast bulk those qualities that give his poetry literary distinction.

Crabbe's admirers as well as his detractors all too often assume that the core of his poetry is accurate and faithful description. Whether they like or dislike what he describes, both parties unite in thinking he describes it well. At the center of Hazlitt's criticism of Crabbe lies a twofold assumption: that Crabbe's descriptions are accurate and painstaking, but so unpleasant that his poetry amounts to little more than misplaced ingenuity. In "Mr. Crabbe–Mr. Campbell," an essay first published in *London Magazine* and later collected in *The Spirit of the Age* (1825), he contrasts Crabbe with Alexander Pope, and declares that in Pope "There is an appeal to the imagination; you see what is passing in a poetical point of view."

The implication, as Hazlitt develops his theme, is that Crabbe has no imagination. Hazlitt is clearly using the term "imagination" here in a very

---

[4]The quotation should be "Nature's sternest painter, yet the best."

restricted sense, as the ability to picture something absent. He continues his criticism: "Crabbe describes ugly things; his descriptions are true because they are facsimiles: because they are facsimiles they are ugly." The argument is that Crabbe is a realist who caught and held on his poetic retina a clear and accurate impression of everything around him.

Certainly Crabbe's descriptions are accurate, but one might have thought the critics of the nineteenth century would have welcomed this. After all, in "Thomas Gray" in his *Essays in Criticism* Matthew Arnold alleged that "The poetic language of our eighteenth century in general is the language of men composing *without their eye on the object.*"

But Hazlitt obviously has something else in mind. He objects not so much to the accuracy as to the ugliness. According to him:

> Mr. Crabbe's great fault is certainly that he is a sickly, a querulous, a uniformly dissatisfied poet. He sings the country; and he sings it in a pitiful tone. He chooses this subject only to take the charm out of it, and to dispel the illusion, the glory, and the dream, which had hovered over it in golden verse from Theocritus to Cowper.

It is true that Crabbe's poetry is deliberately antipastoral; he rebelled against what he considered to be the false and sentimental pictures of country life given by poets like Thomas Gray, Cowper, and Oliver Goldsmith. In the first book of *The Village* he asks:

> Then shall I dare these real ills to hide
> In tinsel trappings of poetic pride?
> (47–48)

and answers his question almost angrily:

> No; cast by Fortune on a frowning coast,
> Which neither groves nor happy valleys boast;
> Where other cares than those the Muse relates,
> And other shepherds dwell with other mates;
> By such examples taught, I paint the Cot,
> As Truth will paint it, and as Bards will not.
> (49–54)

In the same book he ironically contrasts the sporting young parson of *The Village* with his counterpart in *The Deserted Village*. Summoned to the deathbed of an inmate of the poorhouse, he comes reluctantly and as a stranger to his dying parishioner.

> And doth not he, the pious man, appear,
> He, "passing rich with forty pounds a year"?
> Ah! no; a shepherd of a different stock,
> And far unlike him, feeds this little flock;
> A jovial youth, who thinks his Sunday's task
> As much as God or man can fairly ask;
> The rest he gives to loves, and labours light,
> To fields the morning, and to feasts the night.
> (302–309)

But by being out of sympathy with his antipastoralism, Hazlitt has missed Crabbe's positive purpose. According to him, all that Crabbe does is to give

> . . . discoloured paintings of life; helpless, repining, unprofitable, unedifying distress. He is not a philosopher but a sophist, a misanthrope in verse; a *namby-pamby* Mandeville, a Malthus turned metrical romancer.

But there is more behind the irony at Goldsmith's expense than either misanthropy or painstaking realism.

Crabbe's descriptions of nature are wonderfully accurate. He had the trained eye of a botanist, and few poets give a more accurate picture of flowers and plants, as witness the following:

> Rank weeds, that every art and care defy,
> Reign o'er the land, and rob the blighted rye:
> There thistles stretch their prickly arms afar,
> And to the ragged infant threaten war;
> There poppies, nodding, mock the hope of toil;
> There the blue bugloss paints the sterile soil;
> Hardy and high above the slender sheaf,
> The slimy mallow waves her silky leaf;
> O'er the young shoot the charlock throws a shade,
> And clasping tares cling round the sickly blade;
> With mingled tints the rocky coasts abound,
> And a sad splendour vainly shines around.
> (*The Village*, bk. I, 67–78)

Even when Crabbe's subject matter would repel one in real life, it may still please as poetry, for the ugly as well as the beautiful may provide aesthetic delight. But there is a more important point to note about this and other descriptive passages in Crabbe's poetry. Rarely, if ever, does he write descriptive poetry for its own sake. His is not landscape poetry, and Hazlitt is wrong to regard him merely as a painter in words. In the above passage, for instance, he is not simply painting a scene, but contrasting the beauty of nature with its insensitivity to a man's struggle. The force of it depends upon irony as well as upon description. The image of warfare, with its threat of famine to the children of the poor, and the vanity and sadness that qualify nature's splendor in the last line, are the instruments of this irony and the real point of the description. There are few of Crabbe's landscapes into which man does not enter. There are few, if any, that do not serve to evoke an atmosphere appropriate to the story. And yet Crabbe, in the preface to his *Tales*, in comparing his own poetry with Pope's, speaks of their common pursuit of ". . . actuality of relation, . . . nudity of description, . . . poetry without an atmosphere."

In one sense he is right. Crabbe is anxious to be objective, to let his material speak for itself. But the work of every true artist carries the stamp of its creator's mind, and Crabbe's poetry is no exception. His poetry has a very real atmosphere, though one that is difficult to describe or define. Part of it derives from the scene in which the stories are set. The Suffolk coast has a peculiar and subtle beauty that owes much to the flat country and the wide expanse of sky that invests the landscape with a clear and delicate light. Crabbe's poetry catches this strange quality of light and reproduces natural objects with a wonderfully detailed and visual accuracy.

Nor is this all. Just as in Thomas Hardy's novels the heaths and woodlands of Wessex provide a setting of eternity in which the drama is played, so in Crabbe's poems the endless restlessness of the sea, and the sand dunes, ever-changing and yet always the same, provide a fitting background for the transitoriness of human life. In Hardy the sublimity of man's tragic situation is colored by recollections of man's vanity; in Crabbe the vanity of human affairs rises at times into a brief but tragic splendor that is more often implied than stated. The emphasis may be put in different places, but it should not surprise one that Hardy found inspiration for his novels in Crabbe, for the story that each tells is in many respects the same.

What is the story that Crabbe has to tell, and is it true to life? These are the questions one must answer. The failure to do so has led to much misunderstanding about his work. Many critics, for instance, tend to speak of Crabbe as a social reformer and of his poetry as part of a revolutionary campaign to alter the material conditions of the rural poor. Crabbe, no doubt, would have welcomed

such an improvement and would have been glad if his work had contributed to it. But this was not his aim, nor very present to him when he wrote. It is true, of course, that social change affected the temper of his poetry. Like Goldsmith, Crabbe was concerned with a countryside that had fallen upon bad times. Goldsmith drew attention to it by an idealized picture of the past; and it is the imaginary village of Auburn before the rot began, the simple community with its simple virtues, that catches the reader's imagination in his poem. Crabbe, on the other hand, idealized nothing. The figures he draws of the prosperous farmers are no more exaggerated than those of the village poor, kept from destitution by the niggardly hand of parish relief. The contemporary accounts and the researches of the social historian confirm the truth of what he relates of the increasing wealth of the East Anglian farmer and the corresponding poverty of the laboring classes. All this forms the framework within which Crabbe sets his story, but it would be wrong to mistake the framework for the story itself.

For most people who think of Crabbe as primarily a social reformer, he is the poet of *The Village*. But though *The Village* may be his best-known poem, it is not his most representative. His genius, as it matured, turned more and more to narrative poetry, and narrative poetry of a particular kind. More than anything else the main body of his poetry is concerned with character; the interaction of characters; the development of the individual character itself; and especially the response of the individual to challenge, whether from outside itself or within. The *Tales*—there were *Tales in Verse* (1812), *Tales of the Hall* (1819), and *Posthumous Tales* (1834)—not only account for the bulk of his verse, but also represent his most characteristic achievement.

But even the earlier poems reveal the same gift of acute psychological perception, the same interest in motive and insight into the mainsprings of human behavior. In such an early and immature work as *Inebriety*, for instance, one can discern a power of observing people that saves the poem from being merely a mechanical imitation of Pope. The drunken vicar in that poem is only the forerunner of a host of characters created by Crabbe. The picture is drawn conventionally enough to start with:

The reverend Wig, in sideway order plac'd,
The reverend Band, by rubric stains disgrac'd,

The leering Eye, in wayward circles roll'd,
Mark him the Pastor of a jovial Fold,
Whose various texts excite a loud applause,
Favouring the Bottle, and the good old Cause.

(part II, 51–56)

Though he bears with ordinary indecencies in his cups, there are limits:

Rather than hear his God blasphem'd he takes
The last lov'd Glass, and then the board forsakes.

(65–66)

But—and here is the twist that Crabbe often gives to his narrative—it is not religion that "prompts the sober thought." The vicar is anxious for promotion, and must be circumspect.

Vicars must with discretion go astray,
Whilst Bishops may be damn'd the nearest way.

(71–72)

By the time of *The Parish Register*, Crabbe had turned toward a poetic form that would allow his gift for characterization greater scope. The whole poem is no more than a series of loosely connected stories about the people who make up the village of his day. It surveys the entire community, from the aristocracy down through the farmers, the small shopkeepers and their kind, to the poorest agricultural laborers and the poachers, smugglers, and "failures" of the village. But it is not simply *The Village* on a larger scale and with greater detail. Some of the stories have little to do with what the nineteenth century called "the condition of the people question." The ruin of poor Robin Dingley by the scoundrel of a lawyer—

I give thee joy, good fellow! on thy name;
The rich old Dingley's dead, no child has he,
Nor wife, nor will; his ALL is left for thee:
To be his fortune's heir thy claim is good;
Thou hast the name, and we will prove the blood.

(part III, 522–526)

—has no "social message" in the narrower sense of that term. Poor Dingley, on the strength of his great expectations, sends his daughters to school, rents harpsichords for them, and plunges into reckless expenditure. But he loses his case at law, and with a mind overturned by this catastrophe, he leaves the village. Years later he returns, still crazed in mind,

and destitute. The parish allows him to enter the poorhouse, but as soon as he recovers his strength, he returns to his wandering. Finally he is brought back, his deathbed a heap of straw in a farm cart.

One can call this social documentation and can regard the story as an attack upon the corruption of a society that allows such abuses of legal administration. But the poem is more than part of a humanitarian struggle to relieve the needs of the poor. To regard it as this and no more is to fail to appreciate the nature of Crabbe's artistic vision; it is to fail to realize that Crabbe makes his own world out of this material. Nor should one mistake verisimilitude for lack of art. The truth to life of his scenes and characters is a tribute to his art. Crabbe has a clear notion of what he is doing when he writes in the preface to the *Tales in Verse*:

I must allow that the effect of poetry should be to lift the mind from the painful realities of actual existence, from its every-day concerns, and its perpetually-occurring vexations, and to give it repose by substituting objects in their place which it may contemplate with some degree of interest and satisfaction: but, what is there in all this, which may not be effected by a fair representation of existing character?

What is the nature of this artistic vision that can be claimed for Crabbe? Some have argued that there is no greater positive conviction behind his satire than the belief in a morality founded upon prudence, in honesty as the best policy. It is true, of course, that the virtues of self-help, thrift, and independence run like a refrain through the poems. They are found in *The Parish Register* in the advice given by Surly John when the supposedly penniless Roger asks him for food:

Give! am I rich? This hatchet take, and try
Thy proper strength, nor give those limbs the lie;
Work, feed thyself, to thine own powers appeal,
Nor whine out woes thine own right hand can heal,
And while that hand is thine, and thine a leg,
Scorn of the proud or of the base to beg.

(part III, 781–786)

Crabbe's theology, like his own later material circumstances, was comfortable without being ostentatious; and his morality owed more to utility than to the austerity of any categorical imperative. But one must recognize that he speaks with a wealth of practical experience. For people like his poorer characters, prudence was a very real virtue; the margin between a modest competence and ruin, a narrow one that could be maintained only by the exercise of thrift and self-discipline. Nor is Crabbe's satire at the expense of any one class; his preaching is not directed only at the poor. By keeping in the main to people whom he describes as no higher than middle life, he was wise. These were those he knew best: the people he had shepherded in his ministry, whose minds and characters he could enter with the greatest understanding. But he was interested in them as people, not merely as members of a social or economic class. The low, just as well as the high who were the objects of Pope's or Johnson's satire, could serve to illustrate the universality of the moral law. Their lot would do equally well to reveal the human predicament. Through them he could teach the lesson of Pope's *Moral Essays*: that to break the moral law is folly because retribution awaits the evildoer. Their lives would show, just as well as those of the great figures of Johnson's *Vanity of Human Wishes*, the truth Crabbe expressed in *The Library*:

> Some drops of comfort on the favour'd fall,
> But showers of sorrow are the lot of all.
> (645–646)

It is in the tradition of Pope and Johnson that Crabbe must be set as a moralist. His artistic vision is that of the Augustan poets of the eighteenth century.

One may reject the Christian-Stoic doctrines of these writers, but one can hardly consider them ignoble. Behind Crabbe's satire there lies a deep and comprehending charity. There is not the slightest hint of sentimentality in the pity he displays, nor any false idealization of the people he draws; but he shows a sensitive reluctance to judge the wrongdoer, however much he may condemn the crime. This is well illustrated in the story of Jachin, the parish clerk, in *The Borough*. Jachin is a man of great moral rectitude. His fellows, almost affronted by such virtue, have tried to seduce him, but without success. Invitations to the village tavern, to give a ruling on some theological dispute, fail to have the expected effect:

> In vain they tried; he took the question up,
> Clear'd every doubt, and barely touch'd the cup;

By many a text he proved his doctrine sound,
And look'd in triumph on the tempters round.
(letter 19, 94–97)

The next maneuver is to send a pretty girl to consult him "with tender tremblings and seducing tears." Again without avail:

> . . . he calmly heard her case,
> And plainly told her 'twas a want of grace;
> Bade her "such fancies and affections check,
> And wear a thicker muslin on her neck."
> (106–109)

But this apparently invulnerable citadel has its foundations on the sands of spiritual pride. Beyond everything else Jachin wants the respect of his fellow men, and he realizes that he can never command this while his clothes remain so shabby. And so, the most unlikely person, he is betrayed into the mean dishonesty of robbing the collection plate at Holy Communion, money that was always given to the poor. Crabbe's account of the tortuous casuistry and self-deception by which Jachin excuses his conduct is a brilliant piece of psychological analysis. But the pathos is reserved for the end. The squire, the vicar, and the villagers are all ready to condemn him; he is outlawed and disgraced; and, worst of all, he is stripped of his office and the respect that goes with it. But Crabbe himself speaks no word of judgment. The language he uses to describe Jachin's end and the setting he provides for it give the character a dignity in dying that he failed to secure in living.

> In each lone place, dejected and dismay'd,
> Shrinking from view, his wasting form he laid;
> Or to the restless sea and roaring wind
> Gave the strong yearnings of a ruin'd mind.
> On the broad beach, the silent summer-day,
> Stretch'd on some wreck, he wore his life away;
> Or where the river mingles with the sea,
> Or on the mud-bank by the elder-tree.
> Or by the bounding marsh-dyke, there was he.
> (270–278)

Finally he is drawn to the church, and then:

> To a lone loft he went, his dying place,
> And, as the vicar of his state inquired,
> Turn'd to the wall and silently expired.
> (298–300)

Crabbe goes to great lengths to deny any claim to imagination. He is content, he writes in the preface to the *Tales in Verse* (1812), to address himself to "the plain sense and sober judgement" of his readers, "rather than to their fancy and imagination." He claims the title of poetry for his work, but he makes no comparisons between it and other kinds of poetry. He is content to wait upon the verdict of public opinion, and finds consolation in the thought that

. . . an author will find comfort in his expulsion from the rank and society of poets, by reflecting that men much his superiors were likewise shut out, and . . . men not much his superiors are entitled to admission.

Most frequently the idiom he chooses for his narrative is the rhymed poetic couplet. For many, Crabbe's use of this metrical form is deplorable. They see in it a lazy and uninspired following of a tradition already bankrupt. Probably by the time Crabbe was writing, the rhymed couplet had begun to outlive its usefulness. Its success, in the long run, proved its worst enemy. And yet its popularity was more than accidental. The basis of the rhymed couplet is antithesis, and antithesis for many Augustan writers was a natural mode of expression. For Pope the couplet was the most appropriate measure in which to state man's equivocal position in the scheme of things:

Plac'd on this isthmus of a middle state,
A being darkly wise, and rudely great.
(*Essay on Man*, epistle II, I, 3–4)

Equally for Johnson the question

Must helpless man, in ignorance sedate,
Roll darkling down the torrent of his fate?
(*Vanity of Human Wishes*, 343–344)

finds an apt formulation in the antinomy of the couplet form. Crabbe's moral experience similarly suggested to him that rarely is there anything in this life that is perfect or without qualification, and the couplet again expresses this most succinctly. Crabbe's spectacle of the village maiden, wronged and then abandoned by the wealthy lover, was one that subsequently became the stock figure of Victorian melodrama, a fact that bears witness to the universality of its truth. Generalizations of the sort that Crabbe deduces from his observation of simple life find their most fitting form in couplets like the following from "Ellen Orford":

Happy the lovers class'd alike in life,
Or happier yet the rich endowing wife;
But most aggrieved the fond believing maid,
Of her rich lover tenderly afraid.
You judge th'event; for grievous was my fate,
Painful to tell, and shameful to relate;
Ah! sad it was my burthen to sustain,
When the least misery was the dread of pain;
When I have grieving told him my disgrace,
And plainly mark'd indifference in his face.
(*The Borough*, letter 20, 161–170)

From Pope, Crabbe learned how to achieve variety and flexibility in his use of the couplet. Especially did he acquire the trick of moving the position of the caesura to break up the monotony of the line and to approximate the rhythm of natural speech. In lines such as

For, married, soon at will he comes and goes
("Infancy," 37)

and

She knew that mothers grieved and widows wept,
And she was sorry, said her prayers and slept.
("Procrastination," 140–141)

there is the same ease that one encounters in Pope's manipulation of the couplet in the *Epistle to Arbuthnot*.

It is true that Crabbe, like many other eighteenth-century followers of Pope, imitated his master's epic style on occasions when it was inappropriate. Samuel Taylor Coleridge quite rightly pointed out that Pope's influence upon eighteenth-century poets was a bad one because, though his verse generally provided a good model, his translation of Homer foisted a false poetic diction upon his successors. The result of this epic influence on Crabbe's poetry is admittedly not a happy one. It produced a rather ponderous humor, a predilection for word inversion, apostrophes to mythical and lifeless deities, and all the other paraphernalia of a false style.

But Pope's influence was not the only one. Crabbe belongs to that tradition of English poetry that descends from Geoffrey Chaucer, that is found in John Donne's "The Calme" and "The Storme," that flowered in John Dryden, and that crops up again in Jonathan Swift's "City Shower": the tradition of being able to talk in verse. It was not from Pope but from Johnson, and even more, perhaps, from Cowper, that he learned how to make the rhymed couplet subserve this end. He knows how to tell a story, and boredom is a feeling rarely experienced in reading Crabbe. He keeps the vehicle of his verse moving all the time, carrying one forward with the interest in a journey into new country. It was a wise appreciation of his own gifts, and even more of the task he had set himself, not indolence or mere conservatism, that kept him mainly to the rhymed couplet. But he did not confine himself to this form. A brilliant example of his experimenting with a different meter can be seen in "Sir Eustace Grey."

Crabbe's interest in dreams and abnormal mental states probably derived, as with Coleridge and Thomas De Quincey, from opium taking. His wife's illness and his own medical and pastoral experience must also have introduced him to madness in its varied forms. Many of his poems reflect his psychological knowledge, but none more graphically than this poem. "Sir Eustace Grey" is the story of an inmate of a madhouse whose mind had been overturned by his wife's infidelity and his murder of the wife's lover. He is the victim of religious mania and a tormenting sense of guilt, a prey to hallucinatory visions in which his mind flees from reality to a timeless world:

> There was I fix'd, I know not how,
> Condemn'd for untold years to stay:
> Yet years were not;—one dreadful NOW
> Endured no change of night or day;
> The same mild evening's sleeping ray
> Shone softly solemn and serene,
> And all that time I gazed away,
> The setting sun's sad rays were seen.
>
> (204–211)

"Sir Eustace Grey" creates a landscape that is at once the product and the symbolization of a mental state. It is not description in the sense of depicting something physically present. Here one finds in an extreme form a characteristic feature of Crabbe's work, the gift he was loath to claim for himself: being able to create atmosphere, to give a mood or state of mind a local habitation and a name. Even when a descriptive purpose is there, when the landscape he describes is a physical one, the same power is evident. For Crabbe, as for Wordsworth, there is a reciprocity between nature and the mind of man. In "The Lover's Journey" he exploits quite lightheartedly an idealist account of perception. The poem begins by telling the reader that

> It is the soul that sees; the outward eyes
> Present the object, but the mind descries;
> And thence delight, disgust, or cool indiff'rence rise.
>
> (1–3)

It then proceeds to illustrate in a journey made by a lover how

> Our feelings still upon our views attend,
> And their own natures to the objects lend.
>
> (10–11)

At first one sees the lover as he sets off to meet his mistress; everything on the heath he rides across seems to him gay and colorful. Even the rough and sparse vegetation that fights for its life against the sand of the seashore has a beauty of its own. The people who live in the nearby houses seem to him happy peasants leading a life of virtuous simplicity. When he comes to the marshy and muddy banks that descend in slime to the distant seas, the prospect is still pleasing, and Crabbe's verse brings out the peculiar beauty that can invest such a scene.

> Here on its wiry stem, in rigid bloom,
> Grows the salt lavender that lacks perfume;
> Here the dwarf sallows creep, the septfoil harsh,
> And the soft slimy mallow of the marsh;
> Low on the ear the distant billows sound,
> And just in view appears their stony bound;
> Nor hedge nor tree conceals the glowing sun,
> Birds, save a wat'ry tribe, the district shun,
> Nor chirp among the reeds where bitter waters run.
> "Various as beauteous, Nature, is thy face,"
> Exclaimed Orlando: "all that grows has grace;
> All are appropriate—bog, and marsh, and fen,
> Are only poor to undiscerning men."
>
> (120–132)

On he goes to his destination. There he finds his mistress has gone to visit a friend, leaving instructions for him to follow. Disappointment, suspicion, and jealousy jostle each other in his mind as he resentfully continues his journey. The landscape now seems dull and barren. Heath and moor have given way to meadow, park, and market town, yet these all fail to please. The journey ends in reconciliation, and as they return the next day, engrossed in their own affairs, the lovers gain a different impression of the same places.

All this is little more than a jeu d'esprit, but the evocation of mood through landscape, allied to the notion that character and disposition are influenced by natural surroundings, is used with powerful effect in a poem like "Peter Grimes." When Grimes is banished by his fellows and lies all day in his boat, the description of the mud flats of the estuary catches exactly his mood of sullen depression and forms the perfect prelude for the account of violent madness that overtakes him. There is a power here that belongs to few poets, whether romantic or classical.

> When tides were neap, and, in the sultry day,
> Through the tall bounding mud-banks made their way,
> Which on each side rose swelling, and below
> The dark warm flood ran silently and slow;
> There anchoring, Peter chose from man to hide,
> There hang his head, and view the lazy tide—
> In its hot slimy channel slowly glide,
> Where the small eels that left the deeper way
> For the warm shore, within the shallows play;
> Where gaping muscles, left upon the mud,
> Slope their slow passage to the fallen flood—
> Here dull and hopeless he'd lie down and trace
> How sidelong crabs had scrawl'd their crooked race;
> Or sadly listen to the tuneless cry
> Of fishing gull or clanging golden-eye;
> What time the sea-birds to the marsh would come,
> And the loud bittern, from the bull-rush home,
> Gave from the salt-ditch side the bellowing boom.
> . . .
> Where all presented to the eye or ear
> Oppress'd the soul with misery, grief, and fear.
> (*The Borough*, letter 22, 181–198, 203–204)

Passages such as these are not landscape poetry in the manner of eighteenth-century poets such as James Thomson or Cowper, and the description has a directness and clarity not often found in those writers. Such passages have a dramatic narrative as well as a descriptive purpose. They set the scene for action or match a mounting tension in the story, for Crabbe is above all a narrative poet. But he is a narrative poet of a special kind; there is more in his work than the ability to tell a good story. I have already spoken of his psychological acumen and his interest in character. Crabbe is, in these respects, a child of the new age rather than of the eighteenth century. For romanticism was nothing if not introspective. One sees this in the morbid self-dramatization of Lord Byron; in the interest Wordsworth had in the growth of his own poetic powers; and in the subtle speculations about the mind that Coleridge pursued for the greater part of his life. But what specifically occupied Crabbe's attention and came to be its main interest can best be described as the psychology of moral experience. This, since morals can rarely, if ever, concern the really solitary man, necessarily leads him into a realm where characters are related in a common situation.

If one had to compare Crabbe with other writers, one would think not so much of his fellow poets as of the novelists of the nineteenth century. Crabbe was Jane Austen's favorite poet, and she was known among her family as "Mrs. Crabbe." It is easy to see likenesses between them, but perhaps Crabbe approaches in spirit even closer to George Eliot.

After the great wave of romanticism had passed, the literary energy of a new generation seemed to find a more natural outlet in the novel than in poetry. Crabbe's genius was too much identified with his own poetic idiom for him to wish to break away (though he did write three novels that he destroyed on his wife's advice), but the subject matter of his later verse approximates very closely to prose fiction and might easily have appeared as such if he had been born later. This is not to detract from his merit as a poet or to suggest that he might have written better as a novelist. Such conjectures are too hypothetical to pursue with any advantage. The only point of the comparison is to throw light on the kind of narrative poetry that was peculiarly Crabbe's.

Although early in his life Crabbe had given some indications of where his real gifts lay, in *The Village* and *The Parish Register* the characters show few signs of life or development. They are vividly drawn, but often, like a flash photograph, they catch their subject in one short moment. For all their intensity they are static figures, portraits hung in a gallery past which one perambulates with the poet as a guide. But in *The Borough* the figures have become animated; one sees them in action, shares their hopes and fears, and enters into the motives of their conduct. In letter 23, for instance, who can fail to be moved by the story of the highwayman on the night before his execution? In uneasy sleep he escapes for the moment from his present troubles in a dream about

> Life's early prospects and his Fanny's smile.
> (290)

In the dream the two lovers walk upon the beach

> Now arm in arm, now parted, they behold
> The glitt'ring waters on the shingles roll'd.
> (317–318)

They pick up shells that, as tokens of their love, they plan to place on their parlor mantelpiece. At this point in the dream, reality breaks in. At first the interruption is absorbed into and becomes part of the dream; a wave threatens to engulf Fanny. Then, with consciousness, there returns a realization of the truth.

> . . ."Oh! horrible! a wave
> Roars as it rises—save me, Edward! save!"
> She cries—Alas! the watchman on his way
> Calls and lets in—truth, terror, and the day!
> (329–332)

Similarly in *The Borough* (letter 9) one sees human nature in a moment of crisis. This time it is not an individual but a group of people; a party that sets off on a day's boating excursion is marooned on a sandbank. Their boat has drifted away; the mist has risen and hidden them from the shore. Some are silent in their misfortune:

> While fiercer minds, impatient, angry, loud,
> Force their vain grief on the reluctant crowd.
>   . . .
> A few assay'd the troubled soul to calm;
> But dread prevail'd, and anguish and alarm.
> (265–266; 271–272)

Their situation is serious and, as darkness comes, almost hopeless. Crabbe catches superbly the quiet that descends upon the angry brawlers as they fall mute in a common recognition of the danger.

> Now rose the water through the lessening sand,
> And they seem'd sinking while they yet could stand;

> The sun went down, they look'd from side to side,
> Nor aught except the gathering sea descried;
> Dark and more dark, more wet, more cold it grew,
> And the most lively bade to hope adieu;
> Children, by love then lifted from the seas,
> Felt not the waters at the parents' knees,
> But wept aloud; the wind increased the sound,
> And the cold billows as they broke around.
> (273–282)

At the last moment they are rescued, but not before Crabbe has caught the reader's attention in a mounting and dramatic suspense. Few narrative poets in English have such an ability to keep the reader with them right through the course of the story.

The reader has seen already, in the story of Jachin, the parish clerk in *The Borough*, something of Crabbe's developing sense of characterization, but the story that illustrates this best is "Peter Grimes" (letter 22). In both stories there is a penetrating awareness of how the human mind works and an understanding of the principles that govern what at first sight seems unpredictable behavior. Modern psychology could add little to the study of delinquency in "Peter Grimes." Peter is an independent-minded youth, strictly brought up by a father who believes in a repressive discipline. At length he rebels against the old man and knocks him to the ground. But the act sows seeds of guilt that eventually bring about Peter's destruction. When his father dies, he gets drunk and weeps, but more than maudlin sentimentality moves him. Beneath his contempt for filial piety there lies a deep sense of shame.

> Yes! then he wept, and to his mind there came
> Much of his conduct, and he felt the shame;—
> How he had oft the good old man reviled,
> And never paid the duty of a child;
> How when the father in his Bible read,
> He in contempt and anger left the shed;
> "It is the word of life," the parent cried;
> "This is the life itself," the boy replied.
> (12–19)

The poem is a moving working out of the retribution that Peter makes for his sin, a retribution that operates through the self-destructive forces he unleashes in his own personality. At the climax of the story, when Grimes goes mad, the hallucinatory figures of the apprentices he has murdered appear to him, and significantly they bring with them his father.

> In one fierce summer-day, when my poor brain
> Was burning hot and cruel was my pain,
> Then came this father-foe, and there he stood
> With his two boys again upon the flood;
> There was more mischief in their eyes, more glee
> In their pale faces when they glared at me.
> Still did they force me on the oar to rest,
> And when they saw me fainting and oppress'd,
> He, with his hand, the old man, scoop'd the flood,
> And there came flame about him, mix'd with blood,
> He bade me stoop and look upon the place,
> Then flung the red-hot liquor in my face.
>
> (348–359)

The series of *Tales*, which were to appear later, do not always rise to the heights of "Peter Grimes," but the general level of achievement is higher. The versification has more sinew. It is more compact, and yet at the same time has greater flexibility. Dialogue is fitted more neatly into the structure of the verse and rarely descends to the pantomime effect that Crabbe falls into at his worst. In "Resentment," which describes the implacable anger of a woman against her husband, the news of his pauper's death is broken to her by her servant in brief yet effective lines:

> Thus fix'd, she heard not her Attendant glide
> With soft low step—till, standing by her side,
> The trembling Servant gasp'd for breath, and shed
> Relieving tears, then utter'd—"He is dead!"
> "Dead!" said the startled Lady. "Yes, he fell
> Close at the door where he was wont to dwell."
>
> (469–474)

This increase of technical dexterity enabled Crabbe to deal with a more complex material. In the *Tales* the moral order that governs his imaginative world not only stands more clearly revealed but also is extended in time and over a larger field of human action. Two of these poems that exemplify his ability at its highest are "Procrastination" and "Delay Has Danger."

In "Delay Has Danger" the hero, Henry, is virtually engaged to one young lady, but through separation and lack of resolution becomes attracted to Fanny, a young and innocent girl who is the ward of her uncle and aunt. Without realizing the trap that is being laid for him by the uncle and aunt, Henry becomes entangled with Fanny to the point

where he is unable to extricate himself. At this stage the uncle and aunt strike. The uncle is steward to a nobleman:

> He was a man of riches, bluff and big,
> With clean brown broad-cloth and with white cut wig;
> He bore a cane of price, with riband tied,
> And a fat spaniel waddled at his side.
>
> (513–516)

Henry is terrified of him, and after an interview at which his intentions are willfully misunderstood, is confronted by the steward's wife. She takes immediate advantage of his demoralization. Crabbe presents her, as he does the husband, with a sly humor that is comic rather than satirical. There is no visual description of her, as of the husband, and this itself has some significance. For the steward, although an impressive personage, is only a figurehead behind whom his wife, the real brains of the partnership, carries out her plan. She reveals herself characteristically by her speech, through which one gains a clear impression of the sort of woman she is: loquacious, arch, and with a playfulness that barely conceals her purposefulness.

> Hurrying she came—"Now, what has he confess'd,
> Ere I should come to set your heart at rest?
> What! he has grieved you! Yet he, too, approves
> The thing! but man will tease you, if he loves.
> But now for business: tell me, did you think
> That we should always at your meetings wink?
> Think you, you walk'd unseen? There are who bring
> To me all secrets—O, you wicked thing!"
>
> (570–577)

Both characterization and dialogue are at their highest level here.

In general the *Tales* exhibit both a greater range and a more intensive probing of character. They are not always concerned simply with one central figure, but often with a group of characters. And yet, at the same time Crabbe's analytical powers have grown even sharper. Jeffrey wrote in July 1819 of the *Tales of the Hall* in the *Edinburgh Review*:

It seems, therefore, almost as if he had caught up the first dozen or two of persons that came across him in the ordinary walks of life, and then fitting in his little window in their breasts, and applying his tests and instruments of observation, had set about such a minute and curious scrutiny of their whole habits, history, adventures, and dispositions, as he thought must ultimately create not only a familiarity, but an interest, which the first aspect of the subject was far enough from leading any one to expect.

The only weakness of the three series of *Tales* is their lack of unity. The various letters that make up *The Borough* are linked only tenuously, but the poem itself demands no more. But in the *Tales* there should have been some central principle that would bind them together and that each in its turn should illustrate. The *Tales of the Hall* are, indeed, held together by some sort of plan. They are told by two brothers who are united after a long absence; they start from and return to this point. But this unity, if it deserves such a name, is imposed from the outside; it is not inherent in the stories themselves. It may be that there is a central principle implicit in the individual *Tales*; that they exhibit, in different ways, the imaginative vision for which a claim has been made on Crabbe's behalf. But even so, before they could rank with the highest achievements of poetry, they would need to show this principle not only individually but also in some sort of unified organization that embraced them all; and this is lacking. This is the only thing that denies them the greatness of novels like *Middlemarch* or *The Mayor of Casterbridge*. Perhaps Coleridge had something of the sort in mind when he said that though "no doubt, he has much power of a certain kind, there is in Crabbe an absolute defect of the high imagination."

Yet it would be silly not to enjoy Crabbe's poetry because he cannot join on equal terms with William Shakespeare, John Milton, and Wordsworth. His imagination, even if it is not creative on the largest scale, is genuine; on occasion it rises to a sublimity that belongs only to the greatest of tragic artists. It sees behind the manifold appearances of experience a reality that it embodies in forms that no other poet gives. His moods may not be many, but they are sincere; and he holds the reader's attention as very few narrative poets can. He shows the misery of the poor and the frustration of the rich. He is ready to lay bare the wickedness of both, the improvidences of the one and the pretensions of the other. But his satire is tempered by humor and is always the servant of a benevolence that, though it expects little from human nature, is ready to forgive much and believes in the ultimate salvation of mankind. His poetry is marked by the plain and simple beauty and the quiet sadness of his own Suf-

folk coast. But never far distant are vigor, movement, depth, and terror, the same qualities that the sea brings to this scene. These are the forces that mold his poetry just as they molded the man.

SELECTED BIBLIOGRAPHY

Detailed bibliographical information can also be found in the appropriate volumes of *The New Cambridge Bibliography of English Literature* and *The Oxford History of English Literature.*

I. BIBLIOGRAPHY. T. E. Kebbel, *Life of George Crabbe*, 2 vols. (London, 1888), contains a bibliography by J. P. Anderson; A. W. Ward, ed., *Poems*, 3 vols. (Cambridge, 1905–1907), contains a bibliography by A. T. Bartholomew; R. Huchon, *George Crabbe and His Times* (London, 1907), translated from the French by F. Clarke, contains an excellent bibliography; *Bibliography of Modern Studies for Philological Quarterly* (Princeton, 1950), contains useful supplementary information and references; T. Bareham and S. Gatrell, *A Bibliography of George Crabbe* (Folkestone, 1978).

II. COLLECTED EDITIONS. *The Entire Works*, 4 vols. (London, 1816); *The Poetical Works*, edited by Crabbe, 7 vols. (London, 1822); *The Poetical Works* (Paris, 1829); *The Works of the Rev. George Crabbe, with a Life by His Son*, 8 vols. (London, 1834), the *Posthumous Tales* first appeared here; A. W. Ward, ed., *Poems*, 3 vols. (Cambridge, 1905–1907); A. J. Carlyle and R. M. Carlyle, eds., *The Poetical Works* (Oxford, 1908); A. Pollard, ed., *New Poems* (Liverpool, 1960), a collection of previously unpublished poems; H. Mills, ed., *Tales 1812, and Other Selected Poems* (Cambridge, 1967).

III. SEPARATE WORKS. *Inebriety, a Poem in Three Parts* (Ipswich, 1775), published unsigned; *The Candidate, a Poetical Epistle to the Authors of the Monthly Review* (London, 1780), published unsigned; *The Library: A Poem* (London, 1781; 1783), the earlier version published unsigned; *The Village: A Poem in Two Books* (London, 1783); *The Newspaper: A Poem* (London, 1785); *A Discourse on 2 Corinthians, i, 9, Read in the Chapel at Belvoir Castle After the Funeral of the Duke of Rutland* (London, 1788); *Poems, by the Rev. George Crabbe, LLB* (London, 1807); *The Borough: A Poem in Twenty Four Letters* (London, 1810), in H. Williams, ed. (London, 1903); *Tales in Verse* (London, 1812); *The Variation of Public Opinion and Feelings Considered as It Respects Religion: A Sermon Preached Before the Rt. Rev. the Lord Bishop of Sarum on His Visitation Held at Devizes on Friday 15th Day of August* (London, 1817); *Tales of the Hall*, 2 vols. (London, 1819); J. D. Hastings, ed., *Posthumous Sermons* (London, 1850).

IV. CRITICAL AND BIOGRAPHICAL STUDIES. W. Hazlitt,

The Spirit of the Age (London, 1825), contains the essay "Mr. Campbell–Mr. Crabbe"; J. G. Lockhart, "The Life and Poems of Crabbe," in *Quarterly Review*, 50 (1834), 468–508; F. Jeffrey, *Contributions to the Edinburgh Review*, 4 vols. (London, 1844), contains reviews of several of Crabbe's poems; L. Stephen, *Hours in a Library*, 2nd ser. (London, 1876), contains an essay on Crabbe reprinted from *Cornhill Magazine*, 30 (1874); E. FitzGerald, ed., *Readings in Crabbe. Tales of the Hall* (London, 1882), contains introductory essay by Fitz-Gerald, reprinted in vol. I of *Works of Edward FitzGerald* (New York, 1882); T. E. Kebbel, *The Life of George Crabbe* (London, 1888); G. Saintsbury, *Essays in English Literature, 1780–1860* (London, 1895); A. C. Ainger, *Crabbe* (London, 1903); *Shelburne Essays*, 2nd ser. (New York, 1905), contains P. E. More, "A Plea for Crabbe," reprinted from *Atlantic Monthly*, 88 (1901), 850–857; R. Huchon, *George Crabbe and His Times, 1754–1832* (London, 1907), translated from the French; J. Bailey, *Poets and Poetry* (Oxford, 1911); A. M. Broadley and W. Jerrold, *The Romance of an Elderly Poet: A Hitherto Unknown Chapter in the Life of George Crabbe* (London, 1913; W. Strang, *George Crabbe* (London, 1913), the Quain Essay for 1913, University College, London; E. Thomas, *A Literary Pilgrim in England* (London, 1917), contains an essay on Crabbe.

F. L. Lucas, *Life and Letters*, VI (London, 1931), contains the essay "The Poet of Prose"; E. M. Forster, "George Crabbe," in *Spectator*, 147 (February 1932), 243–245; J. H. Evans, *The Poems of George Crabbe: A Literary and Historical Study* (London, 1933); D. Wecter, "Four Letters from George Crabbe to Edmund Burke," in *Review of English Studies*, 14 (1938), 298–309; E. M. Forster, "George Crabbe: The Poet and the Man," in *The Listener* (29 May 1941), 769–770; *Peter Grimes: Essays by Benjamin Britten, E. M. Forster, Montagu Slater, Edward Sackville-West* (London, 1946), see E. M. Forster, "George Crabbe: The Poet and the Man"; W. C. Brown, *Crabbe: Neo-Classic Narrative, the Triumph of Form: A Study of the Later Masters of the Heroic Couplet* (Chapel Hill, N.C., 1948); E. M. Forster, "George Crabbe and Peter Grimes," in his *Two Cheers for Democracy* (London, 1951); A. Sale, "The Development of Crabbe's Narrative Art," in *Cambridge Journal* (May 1952), 480–498; P. Cruttwell, "The Last Augustan," in *Hudson Review*, 7 (1954); R. Unwin, *The Rural Muse* (London, 1954); I. Gregor, "The Last Augustan: George Crabbe," in *Dublin Review* (First Quarter 1955), 37–50; L. Haddakin, *The Poetry of Crabbe* (London, 1955), the best and most comprehensive study of Crabbe's poetry; W. P. Ker, *On Modern Literature: Lectures and Addresses*, T. Spencer and J. Sutherland, eds. (London, 1955); R. L. Chamberlain, *George Crabbe* (New York, 1965); O. Sigworth, *Nature's Sternest Painter: Five Essays on the Poetry of George Crabbe* (Tucson, Ariz., 1965); A. Pollard, ed., *Crabbe: The Critical Heritage* (London, 1972); R. B. Hatch, *George Crabbe's Arabesque: Social Drama in the Poetry of George Crabbe* (Montreal, 1976); P. New, *George Crabbe's Poetry* (London, 1976); T. Bareham, *George Crabbe* (London, 1977).

WILLIAM BLAKE

(1757-1827)

J. B. Beer

SINCE we remember ages by their positive achievements, we tend to think of the eighteenth century as a time of elegant furniture and well-proportioned buildings in the midst of highly cultivated landscapes, a time of moderation and decency in the home, but also of uproarious life and broad humor in the streets: the age of Thomas Gainsborough and William Hogarth, of Alexander Pope and Henry Fielding. So indeed it was, but there was another side to the picture. Poverty was rife in town and country, with little to cushion the deprived against starvation and death, while disease could strike at all levels in society, cutting down the children of the well-to-do as well as of the poor. The law took its course, often oppressively and mercilessly, mirroring the popular religious conception of a God who, while favoring those who kept his commandments, would have no pity on those who resolutely disobeyed them.

When we look at this harsher side to the century, the dominating images are of imprisonment. Eighteenth-century prisons were notoriously grim: it was a time when even the modest reforms instigated by John Howard were only just beginning, and criminals could hope for little remission. The most notorious prison of the age, the Bastille in Paris, moved William Cowper (a poet not given to very radical sentiments) to declare that there was not an Englishman who would not be delighted if it were to be torn down.

It was not only the harshness of physical incarceration that fostered this atmosphere of oppressive enclosure. John Locke's view of the human mind, which inspired the dominant philosophy of the time, likened the understanding to "a closet, wholly shut from light, with only some little opening left, to let in external visible resemblance, or *ideas* of things without." The image of the mind itself was thus transformed into something dangerously resembling a prison cell. The guilt-ridden religious teaching of the time, similarly, would make any sensitive listener think of the body as a containing power, imprisoning the will, which tried to overcome its urges. Pope, a central spokesman for the contemporary intellectual view, could write:

> Most souls, 'tis true, but peep out once an age,
> Dull sullen pris'ners in the body's cage . . .
> ("Elegy to the Memory of an Unfortunate Lady")

Isaac Watts, the hymn writer, similarly, could count it a blessing that

> Shortly this prison of my Clay
> Must be dissolv'd and fall.
> ("There Is a House Not Made with Hands")

William Blake, born on 28 November 1757, the son of a successful London hosier, was a man who might have found it difficult to fit into any human society, but whose nature rebelled particularly against accepting one such as this. Endowed with unusually strong imaginative powers, he found the darker side of eighteenth-century life more oppressive than did most of his fellows. When he was only four years old, he said later, God "put his head to the window" and set him screaming. All his life he was haunted by images of prisons: images of human beings in gloomy, confined places appear throughout his designs, and he illustrated Dante's account of Count Ugolino and his sons in the Tower of Hunger several times over. Blake also had direct experience of the prisons of his time: during the Gordon riots in 1780 he was carried along at the front of the mob, and so saw the storming of the Newgate jail and the release of three hundred prisoners; more than once in his later life he was in danger of imprisonment when he fell under suspicion of treason. But he was also aware that imprisonment did not stop with buildings: most of the men and women he saw as he walked the streets of London had to him the air of captives, held by invisible bonds. Jean Jacques Rousseau's memorable saying, "Man is born free, and everywhere he is in chains," only deepened the mystery. Could it be that the chains were manufactured not by "society" but by human beings themselves?

Reflections such as this were intensified by an imaginative power that all too easily found fuel for its nightmares. Blake once said that he could look at a knot in a piece of wood until he felt frightened by it. Yet this capacity for fear was matched by an equally strong power of ecstatic vision that could transform the world into a place of joy and beauty. As a child he once saw a tree full of angels, spangling every bough, and on another occasion saw angelic figures walking among haymakers. On the first of these occasions he just escaped a thrashing from his father for telling a lie, being saved only by his mother's intercession. Blake evidently enjoyed the power of eidetic vision, a condition in which human perception projects physical images so powerfully that the projector cannot easily tell the difference between them and images of the natural world. Such a power is occasionally found among children, but it seldom persists beyond the age of twelve; in Blake it lasted all his life. In older age he would often sketch visionary heads "from the life," sitting at his table and looking at his sitters as if they were actually in the room.

The strong visionary capacity thus manifested resulted also in a proneness to states of enthusiasm and fear: later Blake was to tell how the great events of his time (particularly the American and French revolutions) took the form for him of visions so powerful that he felt he could hardly "subsist on the earth." Those who met him sometimes had an impression of mental abnormality. Joseph Farington said in 1796 that Blake had something of madness about him; a decade later William Hayley, speaking of a "nervous Irritation, & a too vehement desire to excel," said that Blake had often appeared to him to be on the verge of insanity. To those who knew only his works, the impression of madness could be even stronger, but those who had the opportunity of more intimate acquaintance denied such an implication indignantly. "I saw nothing but sanity," said Edward Calvert. "He was not mad, but perverse and wilful; he reasoned correctly from arbitrary, and often false premises," said Francis Oliver Finch. Another friend (perhaps Frederick Tatham) declared that his extravagance was "only the struggle of an ardent mind to deliver itself of the bigness and sublimity of its own

conceptions." The time when Blake came closest to insanity was in the first decade of the nineteenth century, when he was most deeply at odds with those around him. Some of the writings produced then hint at paranoia. But most often what we witness is a vehement energy that refuses to be bound by the demands of convention. In *The Marriage of Heaven and Hell* (ca. 1790) he spoke of himself as "walking among the fires of hell, delighted with the enjoyments of Genius, which to Angels look like torment and insanity."

In youth Blake's independence of mind was nurtured by the fact that he did not go to a conventional school, being first sent to Henry Pars's drawing school in the Strand and then apprenticed to James Basire, an engraver. But he was drawn not only to the visual arts; he loved music and poetry as well. To a person of his imaginative powers, the arts of the time seemed impoverished by comparison with their flourishing condition in, say, the Elizabethan period. His first book of poems, *Poetical Sketches* (1783), contained a lament for the current state of things:

> Whether on Ida's shady brow,
>   Or in the chambers of the East,
> The chambers of the sun, that now
>   From antient melody have ceas'd;
>
> Whether in Heav'n ye wander fair,
>   Or the green corners of the earth,
> Or the blue regions of the air,
>   Where the melodious winds have birth;
>
> Whether on chrystal rocks ye rove,
>   Beneath the bosom of the sea
> Wand'ring in many a coral grove,
>   Fair Nine, forsaking Poetry!
>
> How have you left the antient love
>   That bards of old enjoy'd in you!
> The languid strings do scarcely move!
>   The sound is forc'd, the notes are few![1]
>   ("To the Muses," 10–11)

Blake not only honored but also practiced all the arts. Apart from his progress in drawing and engrav-

[1]All quotations from Blake are taken from G. Keynes, ed., *The Complete Writings* (London, 1966–   ), the Oxford Standard Authors series; references are to page numbers. For Blake's original punctuation D. V. Erdman, ed., with commentary by H. Bloom (New York, 1965) should be consulted. Sources for most of the biographical statements will be found in G. E. Bentley, Jr., ed., *Blake Records* (London, 1969); see bibliography.

ing, he wrote poems such as "To the Muses" and accompanied them on the harp to airs of his own composing. So impressed was the company at the home of the Reverend Anthony Mathew, where he sometimes performed, that he was encouraged to publish a collection of his poems; some people there took down the tunes to which he had set them. Blake evidently won favor at this time for an air of inspiration; yet there was also a side to his nature that resisted any kind of adulation, particularly when it might impinge on his independence. He did not take easily to patronage at any time of his life; at the Mathews' he was after a time discouraged from continuing his attendance because of his "unbending deportment."

This alternation between visionary ardor and firm independence corresponds to a feature of Blake's personality that shows itself again and again. Not only was he unusually subject to contrary moods, he seems to have cultivated them actively, believing (in the words of his favorite advice to others) that "Truth is always in the extremes—keep them." The maxim, however unwelcome in a century that valued the "golden mean" and sought to dissuade people from extremes of any kind, was one to which he firmly adhered. Even in his earliest lyrics Blake tended to proceed by evoking contrary states of mind: two consecutive poems in *Poetical Sketches*, for example, each entitled "Song," give opposing versions of a village love. The first describes the pleasures of going to visit his beloved ("Each village seems the haunt of holy feet") and concludes:

> But that sweet village, where my black-ey'd maid
> Closes her eyes in sleep beneath night's shade,
> Whene'er I enter, more than mortal fire
> Burns in my soul, and does my song inspire.

The second song describes the torments of jealousy, culminating in a fear lest some other youth should walk with his love and concluding:

> O should she e'er prove false, his limbs I'd tear,
> And throw all pity on the burning air;
> I'd curse bright fortune for my mixed lot,
> And then I'd die in peace, and be forgot.

Blake's ability to see the same situation from varying points of view, his recognition that in different moods all the lights of a scene could be changed, was to come into its own in his later writing, notably in the *Songs of Innocence and of Experience* (1794).

Already in *Poetical Sketches*, though, there was much that looked to the future, including an image of winter ("O Winter! bar thine adamantine doors") that had the lineaments of his cold deity Urizen, and a characteristic image of imprisonment, wrought unexpectedly into what might appear at first sight to be a pleasant little love poem:

> How sweet I roam'd from field to field,
>   And tasted all the summer's pride,
> 'Til I the prince of love beheld,
>   Who in the sunny beams did glide!
>
> He shew'd me lilies for my hair,
>   And blushing roses for my brow;
> He led me through his gardens fair,
>   Where all his golden pleasures grow.
>
> With sweet May dews my wings were wet,
>   And Phoebus fir'd my vocal rage;
> He caught me in his silken net,
>   And shut me in his golden cage.
>
> He loves to sit and hear me sing,
>   Then, laughing, sports and plays with me;
> Then stretches out my golden wing,
>   And mocks my loss of liberty.
>
>   ("Song," 6)

So far as one can trace Blake's intellectual life as a young man (the evidence is mostly indirect), he read intensely in certain books, including both the most imaginative English poets, such as Edmund Spenser and William Shakespeare, and works of imaginative philosophy ranging from occult writers such as Paracelsus and Jakob Boehme to the writings of Plato and the Neoplatonists, which were being rediscovered and translated in his time by Thomas Taylor. The Bible and John Milton, which were especial favorites, he read by the light of his own intuition, valuing their passages of imaginative vision or fiery prophecy, while turning aside from those that represented God as a lawgiver bound by his own conception of justice.

At the same time his feeling for works of strong imagination made Blake impatient at the dominating thought of his time, which for all its progress in the applied sciences struck him as often trifling and uninspired. His attitude emerges briefly in *An Island in the Moon* (1787), in which he presents a group of cultured individuals, each wrapped in his or her own pursuits. Joseph Priestley, a man notable for the range of his intellectual interests, is probably the original of the character Inflammable Gas, while

Thomas Taylor the Platonist seems to be satirized as Sipsop the Pythagorean. But it should not be thought that such caricatures were altogether intended to belittle the originals. These were some of the leading thinkers of the time, discussing issues and making discoveries that were exciting in their implications. Blake's satire seems, rather, to poke fun at an ultimate ineffectuality, an unwillingness to think even more boldly. They remained in confinement, though on a pleasant enough island.

An Island in the Moon is an amusing piece of satire, but it has an unfinished quality that seems to betray Blake's uneasiness at the time he was writing it. Was there really any point in satirizing his contemporaries in this way? Was it not more important to find a bold line of his own and lead the way to a more genuine art? Some such reasoning would seem to lie behind the change from the inspired pastiches of *Poetical Sketches* and the gentle, probing satires of *An Island in the Moon* to the clear, incisive line of his subsequent work. From now on, he would follow a particular line with energy and determination at any one time—even if he might strike out in a quite new direction immediately afterward.

By 1787, Blake was in an unusual state of mind. In February his favorite brother, Robert, died, appearing to him as he did so to pass through the ceiling of his bedroom, clappping his hands for joy. It was a vision that Blake, who had been watching over him, and who then collapsed, exhausted, into sleep for three days and three nights, was never to forget. It led him to believe more firmly in the existence of a spiritual world surrounding and infusing the world of nature, not to be identified with it but not to be ignored either.

This was no simple "spiritualism" of the kind that was to become popular in the middle of the nineteenth century. So far as one can reconstruct Blake's state of mind during these years, he was moved by the discovery that his own psyche was not a simple entity, but changed according to his physical state. He was not the same man when he was exercising himself in energy as when occupied in rational study; he was a different man again when surrounded by affection, especially sexual love. It is necessary to grasp this triple distinction if one is to understand the distinctive features of his work, since it gave him an uncommon view of the world and even an unusual vocabulary.

When he speaks at this time of science and reason, Blake is thinking of the state of nature as it presents itself when contemplated and studied passively; when he speaks of wisdom, intellect, and the "spiritual," on the other hand, he is thinking primarily of the mind and imagination in a state of energy; and when he speaks of love and innocence, he is thinking of the state of affection. (In later years the distinctions are less clear, but are still touched by this early ferment of thought.) From such distinctions he developed his idea of the man of spirit as a "mental traveler," who in walking through the world of experience or laboring at his creative work develops "intellect," thus discovering true wisdom. His own ideal of passivity, similarly, submits him not to the world of sense perception but to the inner illuminations of innocent vision mediated by affection.

As he developed these ideas, Blake was assisted by a number of contemporary developments. In 1787, Thomas Taylor published "Concerning the Beautiful," a short translation from Plotinus that was the harbinger of many further translations from the Neoplatonist writers. In that pamphlet a number of unusual words occur with a charge of particular meaning: the "study" of "particulars," "non-entity," "indefinite." In particular Taylor distinguishes between "the corporeal eye" and "the intellectual eye"—a distinction that Blake was to take over in his own way. His "intellectual eye" belongs to the energetic human being who is a mental traveler and a maker.

Plotinus' philosophy was not simply a quietist or passive one, since he regarded matter as being "neither soul nor intellect, nor life, nor form, nor reason nor bound, but a certain indefiniteness"; this left the way open for an artist such as Blake to assert that his true activity lay in creating definite outlines and living forms. From this time forward, one of his most distinctive features as artist and poet—his love of the distinct and vibrant image, visual or verbal—is to be traced. Good as some of Blake's previous works are, they do not have quite this decisive line or dramatic directness of statement.

His move in this direction was assisted by his friendship with Henry Fuseli, an Anglo-Swiss painter noted for his flamboyant behavior and vehemence of expression. Blake, though a quieter man in demeanor, was attracted by such qualities in a man who must often have seemed to him to have "all the fury of a spiritual existence." A further stimulus, though of a quite different kind, was the establishing of the Swedenborgian Church in Britain. To those who were oppressed by a sense of gloomy imprisonment in the teachings of the eighteenth-century dissenting sects, the writings of Emanuel Swedenborg opened new windows by reasserting the power of visionary knowledge and insisting on a reading of the Bible according to its "internal sense." Nature was seen not as the intricately wrought machine of eighteenth-century rationalism, but as a world in which were to be traced correspondences with a God who was most himself when most human.

Blake was at first deeply drawn to teachings that ran in such close parallel with his own visionary leanings, and when the New Church was established by a general conference in London in 1789, he and his wife, Catherine, were among those who put their signatures to its manifesto. The influence of Swedenborg's ideas can be found here and there in the *Songs of Innocence* (1789) where, in exploring the new world that opened for him after the death of his brother, Blake subdues the more satirical and sardonic side of his personality to an art that is the medium of direct, light-filled vision. In particular he draws on his belief that childhood is the time when the imaginative powers are at their most intense.

From this account of Blake's progress it will be seen that the idea, still sometimes to be found in criticism, that the succession from *Songs of Innocence* to *Songs of Experience* (1794) corresponds to a dramatic change in Blake's view of the world as he passed from the innocence of youth to the bitterness of maturity, will hardly bear serious examination. It ignores, among other things, the fact that Blake was more than thirty when he put together the *Songs of Innocence*. The case seems, rather, to be that Blake felt drawn to press a particular point of view to its extreme, allowing its contrary then to emerge and shape a new way of writing. Some of the *Songs of Innocence*, such as "The Little Boy Lost" and "Nurse's Song," first appeared, in fact, in *An Island in the Moon*. In their new setting, though, they are not subdued to a general tone of amusement, but are free to transmit their vision in a pure form. No doubt there were shifts in Blake's attitudes, corresponding to the dominant tone of the work he was producing at any given time, but his personality cannot be contained within them. As with many great artists, he had the gift of concentrating himself into one point of view at a time while leaving much in reserve, ready to generate further changes when they were ready to emerge.

By the time he put together *Songs of Innocence*, Blake was already deeply read in many authors and points of view. The indications are that in the wake of his early enthusiasms, he had embarked on a long study of the significance of human nature in the light of his own experiences, turning particularly to authors (usually flourishing before the eighteenth century) who had explored the relationship between nature and the imagination. The fruits of his thought can be found, before *Songs of Innocence*, in the little collections of aphorisms entitled *There Is No Natural Religion* and *All Religions Are One* (both ca. 1788), in which he launched his first open attacks on contemporary intellectual attitudes.

For many eighteenth-century philosophers, following in the wake of Francis Bacon, John Locke, and Isaac Newton, the human body seemed to be a highly appropriate instrument for dealing with nature, the five senses being finely attuned to all that it had to offer. The task of the intellectual was simply to investigate the relationships between man and nature until they were brought into harmony. Blake could not agree. For him the idea that there was nothing in the universe that could not be perceived by the five senses was imprisoning. He would have agreed with Andrew Baxter, who argued that "the body, in its present constitution, *limits* and *confines* the perceptions of the soul, but no way effects them." Locke had, as we have seen, suggested that there might be other faculties locked up in man for want of an organ by which they could be perceived, likening the understanding to "a closet, wholly shut from light, with only some little opening left."

Blake took over from both Locke and Baxter the point that if we had only three senses, we should not have the means to know of the sense experiences we lacked, and used it in *There Is No Natural Religion*, concluding with the reflection: "If it were not for the Poetic or Prophetic character the Philosophic & Experimental would soon be at the ratio of all things, & stand still, unable to do other than repeat the same dull round over again." For him such a vision of science was nightmarish, since the necessary limits to knowledge that it implied must abandon human beings to the dull fate of continually contemplating the same limited mechanism. The "Poetic or Prophetic character," on the other hand, liberated them by invoking a vision that transcended the sum of sense experiences. They no longer need feel themselves trapped within the confines of their own physical bodies, but could know a sense of true freedom. That sense of freedom is implicit in the vision that informs *Songs of Innocence*.

But to paint such a state in vivid colors was to invoke (almost automatically, perhaps, in so spirited a man) a complementary sense of ways in which children were oppressed from their earliest years and subtly assisted to grow into practices of deceit and submission to secret, self-enclosed pleasures.

Blake's movement toward a collection of poems based on this alternative, more cynical vision no doubt gained impetus from the current political situation. A few months after the meeting that established the Swedenborgian New Church, the French Revolution had broken out: an event that, following so soon after the American War of Independence, appeared to mark a decisive movement forward in human affairs. For a time Blake was a fervent supporter, and is said to have worn the emblem of the revolutionaries openly in the streets of London. The sense that a new era was opening in human affairs, already prophesied in the writings of Swedenborg, must for a time have been compelling. At this time Blake was also producing engravings for the publisher Joseph Johnson, who brought out books by a number of forward-looking writers, including Richard Price, Joseph Priestley, Henry Fuseli, William Godwin, Thomas Paine, and Mary Wollstonecraft. Blake, who is said to have met some of these figures at Johnson's weekly dinners, would have heard much talk of new ideas, not only in politics but also in social affairs. His enthusiasm for the French Revolution is said to have come to an abrupt end at the time of the September massacres in 1792, when he tore off his white cockade and never wore it again.

It is to this event, the disappointing culmination—at least in political terms—to the intellectual ferment that he had known over the previous few years, that the increasing bitterness of his writings around 1793 may be attributed. Blake could not renege on the excitement and enthusiasm he had felt during the previous years; he was forced to admit, on the other hand, that his fellow citizens showed few signs of allowing themselves to be possessed by new ideals in the future shaping of their society. On the contrary, since they remained largely at the command of those who wished to manipulate them, the future looked bleak. Early in 1795 his friend George Cumberland wrote of fears that England would soon be living under an absolute government or be plunged into a civil war. Neither prospect would be inviting to Blake; either would intensify the imprisoned state from which his fellows seemed powerless to escape.

The poems written into his notebook a short time before, many of which were to find a place in his

Songs of Experience, are redolent of his mood at this time. Among other things Blake was haunted by a sense of sexual failure and restriction, of potentialities of fulfillment that were thwarted, almost inexplicably, among his fellows:

> Thou hast a lap full of seed,
> And this is a fine country.
> Why dost thou not cast thy seed
> And live in it merrily?

The reply is hopeless:

> Shall I cast it on the sand
> And turn it into fruitful land?
> For on no other ground
> Can I sow my seed
> Without tearing up
> Some stinking weed.
> (untitled, 168)

Yet Blake could not believe that human beings fully assented to this situation: "What is it men in women do require?" he asked in "Several Questions Answered," and went on to answer his own question: "The lineaments of Gratified Desire." He then put the same question and answer in relation to women. His thoughts on the matter often look forward to those associated with Sigmund Freud's conclusions:

> Abstinence sows sand all over
> The ruddy limbs & flaming hair,
> But Desire Gratified
> Plants fruits of life & beauty there.
> (verse fragment, 168)

In opposition to this vision of a free and happy gratification of sexual desire, Blake saw about him the secret indulgence of a lust that had no pleasure. The chapels in which abstinence was preached were caricatures of the true dwelling of sexual desire, and their adherents reaped a cruel crop:

> I saw a chapel all of gold
> That none did dare to enter in,
> And many weeping stood without,
> Weeping, mourning, worshipping.
>
> I saw a serpent rise between
> The white pillars of the door,
> And he forc'd & forc'd & forc'd,
> Down the golden hinges tore.

293

And along the pavement sweet,
Set with pearls & rubies bright,
All his slimy length he drew,
Till upon the altar white

Vomiting his poison out
On the bread & on the wine.
So I turn'd into a sty
And laid me down among the swine.
                    (verse fragment, 163)

Blake did not include this or some of the other, more bitter poems in *Songs of Experience*. Since it was still intended, evidently, as a book that might be read by children, he perhaps wished to omit poems that presented too dispiriting a view of the world that awaited them. Among the poems that remain, though, a similar trend is to be traced: a despair when he looked about him in society, coupled with a belief that the ultimate truth behind things was not what his fellows might suppose it to be as they listened to the preachings in their chapels and followed the discussions of contemporary scientists and philosophers.

The modern reader coming to these poems for the first time will soon pick up the underlying bitterness, but is likely to be seized even more immediately by the extraordinary simplicity and directness of the writing. This is all the more striking if one reads Blake's verses alongside others that were being written in his time. "London," one of his best poems, has been compared with one of Isaac Watts's poems for children, which begins:

Whene'er I take my Walks abroad,
    How many Poor I see?
What shall I render to my God
    For all his Gifts to me?
("Praise for Mercies, Spiritual and Temporal")

"London" opens:

I wander thro' each charter'd street,
Near where the charter'd Thames does flow,
And mark in every face I meet
Marks of weakness, marks of woe.
                    (216)

Despite their obvious similarity the difference between the two poems is revealed immediately as that between formally "taking a walk" and informally "wandering." Watts's stanza consists primarily of two exclamations, the first dominated by the second. We hardly have time to see the poor before the speaker is counting his blessings in not being of their number. Blake, by contrast, makes a single factual statement. We have an immediate impression of a man walking the streets, reflecting on the civilization about him, peering intently into the faces of all whom he meets to see what is to be read there, and finding primarily two bleak qualities: weakness and woe.

The purposes of the two poets are different, of course. Watts is writing a hymn for children: like all hymn writers his first aim is to lead those who sing it into suitable sentiments that all can share. He is the spokesman for a society of shared beliefs. Blake is a lonely figure, offering to speak for no one but himself. His is an adult poem: we are not sure whether even the speaker of the poem knows of a more positive vision, or whether he too does not bear the marks of weakness and woe.

The directness of "London" carries on into the remaining stanzas:

In every cry of every Man,
In every Infant's cry of fear,
In every voice, in every ban,
The mind-forg'd manacles I hear.

How the Chimney-sweeper's cry
Every black'ning Church appalls;
And the hapless Soldier's sigh
Runs in blood down Palace walls.

But most thro' midnight streets I hear
How the youthful Harlot's curse
Blasts the new born Infant's tear,
And blights with plagues the Marriage hearse.
                    (216)

This is one of Blake's greatest poems; it has the quality, which shapes his most characteristic utterances, of describing the world as if one were looking at it for the first time. There is nothing naive about the vision, moreover; we need only turn back to the first stanza to see two very complex effects at work. "And mark in every face I meet / Marks of weakness, marks of woe": there is something awkward in the repetition of the word "mark." The observer "marks," but he marks "marks." Yet the awkwardness is in no way inept; by that dulling repetition Blake reinforces the effect of being dragged into an imprisoned world, where nothing radiates from the faces he sees: he marks them, but they do not seem to mark him in return. The arrow of his perception finds its mark, but finds itself fixed there, no longer at liberty.

The word "charter'd," repeated in the second line, also draws the reader's attention by its suggestion of irony. The word "charter" was originally associated with liberty. Magna Charta, signed by King John in 1215, was traditionally one of the foundations of British liberty, and was one of many such charters over the centuries. But these charters were freedoms granted to particular classes of people: they automatically involved a loss of liberty for those who did not belong; and by Blake's time it was hard to walk around London without feeling that the whole city had been parceled out among different groups of this kind, leaving no freedom for the human beings they excluded. "It is a perversion of terms to say that a charter gives rights," wrote Thomas Paine in *The Rights of Man* (1791–1792); "it operates by a contrary effect—that of taking rights away." Even the Thames, which might be thought by definition to be free, was so given over to the uses of commerce as to lose all identity except as a trade route. One of Shakespeare's characters describes the air as a "chartered libertine"; used in connection with the Thames, the word reads more like "shackled," looking forward to the "mind-forg'd manacles" of the second stanza.

Not all Blake's poems are as straightforward in their effect as this one. In "London" there is a sense of accumulating power gathering strength from the dramatic use of certain words, such as "appalls" (which draws into itself the sense of "pall"), and culminating in the final stanza. In many of his most typical poems, on the other hand, there is something that resists interpretation. It is a feature all the more unexpected in view of the directness of the language, which carries the reader along in assent. Only when one tries to make out and paraphrase the sense of what has just been read may it be discovered that the poem is less simple than was thought. A good example is one of his most simple lyrics, "The Fly":

> Little Fly,
> Thy summer's play
> My thoughtless hand
> Has brush'd away.
>
> Am not I
> A fly like thee?
> Or art not thou
> A man like me?

> For I dance,
> And drink, & sing,
> Till some blind hand
> Shall brush my wing.
>
> If thought is life
> And strength & breath,
> And the want
> Of thought is death;
>
> Then am I
> A happy fly,
> If I live
> Or if I die.
>
> (213)

The poem has some clear antecedents in eighteenth-century poetry, notably in Thomas Gray's "Ode on the Spring":

> Methinks I hear in accents low
> The sportive kind reply:
> Poor moralist! and what art thou?
> A solitary fly!
> Thy Joys no glittering female meets,
> No hive hast thou of hoarded sweets,
> No painted plumage to display:
> On hasty wings thy youth is flown;
> Thy sun is set, thy spring is gone—
> We frolick, while 'tis May.

Whereas Gray's point is simple enough, Blake's "Fly" involves a strange shift of subject: the poem does not end as we might have expected. In the conclusion we discover that we can be happy whether we live or die—which might suggest, logically, that it does not matter very much whether we treat flies kindly. Yet there is a clear moral, connected with the lines in *King Lear*: "As flies to wanton boys, are we to the gods;/They kill us for their sport." We should not like to be treated in the way that boys treat flies, and this might be thought a good reason for being kind to insects. There is also an implication that those who show cruelty to living things are more likely to be cruel to their fellow human beings. To encourage kindness to animals and insects is to encourage habits of mind that may be beneficial to human society generally.

All this is in the vein of late eighteenth-century humanitarianism; there is little to criticize—apart, perhaps, from a veiled anthropocentrism. But Blake's interest in such closed systems of amoral approbation is limited. Their basis is ultimately an enlightened self-interest that has more to do with in-terest than with light. And behind this scene of moral instruction there remains a disturbing further im-plication from the *Lear* quotation: that however we treat flies or each other, we must eventually die in circumstances over which we shall have no control. Across the questions of kindness to others or other-wise there falls the shadow of a recognition that nature certainly entertains no such feeling for human beings.

It is this further shadow that seems to be responsi-ble for a shift in "The Fly" after the third stanza (ac-curately signaled in the illuminated version by the existence of branches and a tendril that discreetly cut off the last two stanzas from the rest). The effect is of a strange conjuring, whereby we find ourselves, at the end of the poem, in an unexpected place, having passed through a subterranean transformation of meaning that cannot easily be unraveled into or-dered sense, but that has changed the terms of the discussion from the question of kindness to that of life and its significance.

In these years Blake's poetic and literary powers reached their peak. The quality of his writing at this time is all the clearer when one looks at the notebook drafts and sees the process by which he reached his final versions. The ruthless parings and bendings in-to place are undeniably improvements. In "The Tyger," for instance, the early draft ran:

> And what shoulder & what art
> Could twist the sinews of thy heart?
> And when thy heart began to beat
> What dread hand & what dread feet
>
> Could fetch it from the furnace deep
> And thy horrid ribs dare steep
> In the well of sanguine woe?
> In what clay & in what mould
> Were thy eyes of fury roll'd?
>
> (172)

In the final version the second stanza is omitted, so that the last line of the first turns into a more in-definite, but at once more vivid, question:

> What dread hand? & what dread feet?
> (214)

Blake's revisions do not work only by way of dramatic contractions. An instructive example of another kind may be found in the notebook poem

that begins "I heard an Angel singing." The angel's theme, "Mercy, Pity, Peace/Is the world's release," is followed by another:

> I heard a Devil curse
> Over the heath & the furze,
> "Mercy could be no more,
> If there was nobody poor,
>
> And pity no more could be
> If all were as happy as we."
> At his curse the sun went down,
> And the heavens gave a frown.
>
> Down pour'd the heavy rain
> Over the new reap'd grain,
> And Mercy & Pity & Peace descended
> The Farmers were ruin'd & harvest ended.
>
> (164)

The swift and sardonic conclusion of the last stan-za was deleted by Blake; and when he came to draw upon the draft for "The Human Abstract," he took nothing but the four lines of the Devil's song, which formed, with slight changes, the opening stanzas of his new poem. He then moved from this piece of so-phistic logic to further examples ("mutual fear brings Peace," for instance). The result of the process emerges in the growth of a Tree of Mystery, nurtured by cruelty with the aid of humility. He concludes:

> The Gods of the Earth & Sea
> Sought thro' Nature to find this Tree;
> But their search was all in vain:
> There grows one in the Human Brain.
>
> (217)

This brilliant use of the eighteenth-century image of the upas tree (the tree that in contemporary mythology was said to poison the atmosphere for miles around) exemplifies a characteristic working of Blake's mind during these years. When faced with the effects and processes of social injustice, his first impulse was to speak out in indignation, sullen re-sentment, or simple sardonic statement; in the longer term, though, he was looking for deeper causes. If his society allowed itself to build great mills in which human beings were imprisoned most of the day, that must be because dark satanic mills in their own minds screened from them the incongruity and in-humanity involved. If they swallowed the spurious logic of contemporary spokesmen for the status quo, similarly it must be because their minds were so overshadowed by self-imprisonment that they could not detect the false reasonings that they would be only too swift to spot in a matter affecting their own material interests.

It is germane to Blake's own mental honesty, as well as to his desire to rouse his fellows to think for themselves, that he does not try totally to refute the writers with whom he disagrees. If there is a positive energy or illumination to which he can respond, he will respect that, while subtly subverting those elements he believes false. A good example is found in his dealings with Swedenborg, who interpolated into his writings passages that he called "Memorable Relations." One of these, as Kathleen Raine has pointed out, throws a direct light on the chimney sweep of *Songs of Innocence*: "There are also Spirits among those from the Earth Jupiter, whom they call Sweepers of Chimnies, because they appear in like Garments, and likewise with sooty Faces . . ."(*Earths in Our Solar System*, sect. 79). Swedenborg is informed that these figures will later, when they form part of the Grand Man, or Heaven, "constitute the province of the Seminal Vessels." This implication that the chimney sweep is a symbol of sexual activity can draw also upon popular traditions, such as that of the chimney sweep kissing the bride to give her good luck. Heather Glen has given a number of such instances. But for Blake the chief importance of the symbolism might well lie in the suggestion that the practice of forcing boys to climb chimneys to sweep them was tolerated as part of the social system because sexual activity itself was thought of as secret and dirty; he would also have liked Swedenborg's further assertion that it was the burning intensity of the sweeper's desire to be in heaven that led to his being called upon to cast off his clothes with a promise of new and shining raiment—an incident that resembles the dream of Tom Dacre in Blake's first "Chimney Sweeper" poem.

But although Blake could draw directly upon Swedenborg's visions, he must have found the "Memorable Relations" in general to be long and rambling, just as he found Swedenborg's philosophy, for all its imaginative promise, to be simply another way of presenting conventional teachings. So in *The Marriage of Heaven and Hell* he presents several "Memorable Fancies," the second of which is of a more quizzical kind and begins:

The Prophets Isaiah and Ezekiel dined with me, and I asked them how they dared so roundly to assert that God spake to them; and whether they did not think at the time that they would be misunderstood, & so be the cause of imposition.

Isaiah answer'd: "I saw no God, nor heard any, in a finite organical perception; but my senses discover'd the infinite in every thing, and as I was then perswaded, & remain confirm'd, that the voice of honest indignation is the voice of God, I cared not for consequences, but wrote."

Then I asked: "Does a firm perswasion that a thing is so, make it so?"

He replied: "All poets believe that it does, & in ages of imagination this firm perswasion removed mountains; but many are not capable of a firm perswasion of any thing."

(153)

It is well to bear this narrative in mind when reading some of the anecdotes that are told about Blake himself, since it has a strong bearing on his own practice. Even while Blake is asking whether Isaiah and Ezekiel thought they might be misunderstood when they said that God spoke to them, he knows perfectly well that he is in danger of being misunderstood for saying that Isaiah and Ezekiel dined with him. The defense they offer is also his own: the poet can be effective through the statement of firmly held convictions, which will also, if asserted powerfully enough, carry conviction back into his own mind.

The Marriage of Heaven and Hell provides the best example of Blake's dramatic power—a power that also emerges at times in *Songs of Experience*. "The Voice of the Devil" is not to be taken as Blake's own in more than a limited sense, as a reader with an ear for self-contradictions will soon detect. To say that "everything that lives is holy" is one thing; but when we read elsewhere in the book that "As the caterpiller chooses the fairest leaves to lay her eggs on, so the priest lays his curse on the fairest joys," we may find ourselves asking whether the life of caterpillars, then, is not, after all, holy. Blake's purpose in the book is not to proclaim the holiness of life or the gospel of energy as such but rather to allow room for voices not commonly heard in his society: to look at the world through the eyes of a human being exalted by the exercise of energy, for example, and to ask whether the resulting picture is not more attractive than the view projected by the eye of a containing and self-contained reason.

In one sense the enterprise was successful almost beyond Blake's expectations. His wit found room for full play in his little sketches of life in hell, and his assertion that Milton "wrote in fetters when he wrote of Angels & God, and at liberty when of Devils & Hell, is because he was a true Poet and of the Devil's party without knowing it" turned out to be true of himself in ways that he would hardly have acknowledged. Indeed, as he begins to enumerate the "Proverbs of Hell," they turn into a rhapsodic poetry on their own account:

> The pride of the peacock is the glory of God.
> The lust of the goat is the bounty of God.
> The wrath of the lion is the wisdom of God.
> The nakedness of woman is the work of God.
> Excess of sorrow laughs. Excess of joy weeps.
> The roaring of lions, the howling of wolves, the raging of the stormy sea, and the destructive sword, are portions of eternity, too great for the eye of man.
>
> (151)

The change of line length at the end is one that no poet of his time could easily have tolerated, yet it works triumphantly, looking forward to the large rhythm shifts of later writers.

Although much in *The Marriage of Heaven and Hell* is to be ascribed to Blake's dramatic invention, there are places where it is possible to misread him because of a failure of communication that he seems not to have foreseen. If it is the price he pays for not having submitted himself to a formal education, it is a small price, in view of his liberation from the constraints imposed by an overly formal grammar and syntax; it needs to be recognized, nevertheless. Some years ago a well-known American critic declared that in spite of his admiration for Blake, he must invite his readers to consider soberly the injunction in *The Marriage of Heaven and Hell*: "Sooner murder an infant in its cradle than nurse unacted desires." Vigorous and positive this might be, but was it not also a highly immoral statement? How would they defend it if asked to do so?

It is inconceivable that the Blake of *Songs of Innocence and of Experience* could ever have thought that the murder of a child was justifiable. On the contrary, he probably felt so sure that his readers would share his revulsion against such acts that he felt free to ignore such a possible reading of his remark. What he was urging, rather, was that desires are like infants: if you allow them to remain unacted, the action is like murdering an infant in its cradle. Instead of being repressed in this way, desires should be treated with the respect and delight that are equally appropriate to children: in that way they will grow up humanized. Unacted desires, on the other hand, like children stunted through lack of affection, are likely to turn to destruction: it is indeed (and ironically) such desires that might end in a crime so inhuman as child murder.

Possibilities of self-contradiction are bound to exist in such a philosophy, nevertheless, and Blake seems sometimes to have been conscious of them. Reading once about a meanness of mind that he disliked, he wrote in the margin, "To hell till he behaves better!" then added hastily, "Mark that I do not believe there is such a thing litterally, but hell is the being shut up in the possession of corporeal desires which shortly weary the man, *for* ALL LIFE IS HOLY" (annotation to J. C. Lavater, *Aphorisms on Man*, 74). He is not calling for a transvaluation of values, but for recognition of a dialectic between different views of the world—a dialectic that may in turn point back to a hidden harmony that could contain what are now warring elements. When he asserts that the Devil's version of events is that the Messiah fell, not himself, he is not saying that the Devil is right, but simply pointing to the impoverishment of reason once it is deprived of connection with energy. His book is not called *The Supremacy of Hell*, but *The Marriage of Heaven and Hell*; and it is that marriage, in the form of a reconciliation between reason and energy within a larger human vision, that he seeks to promote.

It was because he was dissatisfied with simple versions of the world and unwilling to proceed simply by inverting them that the quest for a viable mythology came to play such an important part in Blake's developing thought. Already in his youth, as we have seen, he seems to have engaged himself with mythologies and allegories of all kinds, ranging from alchemy and Greek tragedy to Shakespeare, Milton, and symbolic interpretations of the Bible, in order to discover a reading of human nature more optimistic than the conventional one. The first results are found in the rather turgid manuscript poem "Tiriel," in which the sources are comparatively near the surface of the poem and where many of the names of the characters can be traced to actual sources.

Later, though, Blake evolved his own mythology, in which the names (while still reflecting traditional themes) are purely his own, bearing the stamp of his distinctive thought. At some point the reader has to decide whether to follow Blake into this idiosyncratic world—and if not, where to stop. There is one figure so dominant in the writings and so absorbing in significance, however, that most readers find him fascinating. This is Urizen, best known from the design in which he leans down with compasses into darkness from a blank disk of a sun. When Blake looked at the behavior of human beings in his world and asked himself what kind of God they really worshiped, this was the answer he found. They believed themselves to be in a world where their fate was to be overwhelmed by the darkness and death that surrounded all human existence; the only possible course, therefore, seemed to be to build an ordered world that might protect them from the vision of such a dire end. Urizen, in Blake's designs, is not an ugly figure, but graceful, and even majestic; he is often depicted with his eyes closed, on the other hand, to suggest his lack of true vision.

When Blake is confronting the effects of such a rule in his own society, he is moved to indignation and even abuse, calling its originator by the belittling name of "Nobodaddy." His favorite form then is the pithy rhyme or epigram:

> Why art thou silent & invisible,
> Father of Jealousy?
> Why dost thou hide thyself in clouds
> From every searching Eye?
>
> Why darkness & obscurity
> In all thy words & laws,
> That none dare eat the fruit but from
> The wily serpent's jaws?
> Or is it because Secresy gains
>   females' loud applause?
>   ("To Nobodaddy," 171)

Elsewhere Nobodaddy enters some of Blake's more powerful political poems, as when he attacks the French monarch's tyranny in the poem that begins "Let the Brothels of Paris be opened":

> Then old Nobodaddy aloft
> Farted & belch'd & cough'd,
> And said, "I love hanging & drawing & quartering
> Every bit as well as war & slaughtering.
> Damn praying & singing,
> Unless they will bring in
> The blood of ten thousand by fighting or swinging."
>   (185)

Although Blake's indignation against the effects of social oppression found natural vent in such language, the object of his more sustained effort was an inquiry into why Urizen achieved such dominance if, as he believed, the ultimate reality in the universe was one of light and energy, color and music. In the long run, he concluded, Urizen was enabled to stay in power through some deep failure in human beings themselves.

Seen in these terms, the story of Urizen is one of tragedy rather than of evil; he could, indeed, be seen as a rather noble figure, pioneering a means of survival for all human beings who shared his dark sense of the world, rather in the way that Milton's Satan set out on his heroic journey when the other fallen angels had refused. This view of Urizen dominates *The First Book of Urizen* (1794), one of the darkest of the prophetic books and written as a conscious pastiche of the biblical book of Genesis. Creation here is seen not as a sublime creation out of darkness and chaos, but as the result of a withdrawal from the true state of eternity.

In creating Urizen, Blake evidently had in mind some of the more lurid portraits of God the Father that were current in his time. "Thinking as I do that the Creator of this World is a very Cruel Being," he once said, "& being a Worshipper of Christ, I cannot help saying: 'the Son, O how unlike the Father!' First God Almighty comes with a Thump on the Head. Then Jesus Christ comes with a balm to heal it" ("A Vision of the Last Judgment," 617). Such a portrait was recognizable in the teachings of some Christian denominations, particularly the gloomier ones; and it may be relevant that although the Blake children were baptized in an Anglican church (St. James's in Piccadilly), their father seems to have joined the Baptists, at least for a time. It is possible, therefore, that Blake was forced to read their hymns while attending chapel services with his father.

In any case, he could hardly have escaped acquaintance with the work of Isaac Watts, one of the most popular hymn writers of the eighteenth century. As we have seen, the *Songs of Innocence and of Experience* read in places like satirical versions of Watts's *Divine and Moral Songs for Children*. The God whom Watts paints likewise is a recognizable version of the "Cruel Being" whom Blake disliked. The fact that Watts was not a very subtle poet should not blind us to the impact that his descriptions of divine justice would have on an imagination so vivid as Blake's. It is easy to imagine him turning Watts's pages and reacting indignantly to the idea of the universe conveyed there, a universe in which men are invited to pursue their pleasures if they wish, but in which nevertheless a day of judgment awaits them. One of the hymns begins

> Adore and tremble, for our GOD
> Is a *Consuming Fire.*
> His jealous Eyes his Wrath inflame
> And raise his Vengeance higher.
> ("Divine Wrath and Mercy")

This is a prototype of the "jealous god" whom Blake conveys in Urizen; another of Watts's portraits comes even closer to the cold power that is stored in Blake's figure:

> God has a Thousand Terrors in his Name,
> A thousand Armies at Command,
> Waiting the signal of his Hand,
> And Magazines of Frost, and Magazines of Flame.
> Dress thee in Steel to meet his Wrath,
> His sharp Artillery of the *North*
> Shall pierce thee to the Soul, and shake thy mortal Frame.
> ("Divine Judgments")

Imagery such as this, along with that of a God with "Stores of Lightning," seems to have been at the back of Blake's mind as he depicted Urizen in *The Four Zoas* as basing himself in the north, or in *America* (1793) described how

> . . . his jealous wings wav'd over the deep;
> Weeping in dismal howling woe, he dark descended, howling
> Around the smitten bands, clothed in tears & trembling, shudd'ring cold.
> His stored snows he poured forth, and his icy magazines
> He opened on the deep, and on the Atlantic sea white shiv'ring
> Leprous his limbs, all over white, and hoary was his visage. . . .
>
> (203)

In Blake's work Urizen is always a cold god, working through snow, ice, and cold plagues. The fire and lightning are reserved for his opponent Orc, the uprising spirit of energy that cannot find humanized form.

There are many other places in which Watts's images can be discerned in Blake's writings, particularly during the early period, betraying his horror at the workings of such a God.

> Long ere the lofty Skies were spread,
> Jehovah fill'd his Throne,

> Or Adam form'd, or Angels made,
> The Maker liv'd alone . . .
> ("GOD's Eternity")

wrote Watts, who also painted a vivid picture of God making the human body, heart, brains, and lungs, in turn, and writing out his promise of redemption for men:

> . . . His Hand has writ the sacred Word
> With an immortal Pen.
> Engraved as in eternal Brass
> The mighty promise shines . . .
> ("The Faithfulness of GOD in the Promises")

Blake, translating this language into its visual imagery, could have gained some strong hints toward his depiction of Urizen, who turned aside from the light, color, and harmony of the Eternals to brood in solitude, "A self-contemplating shadow,/In enormous labours occupied," and wrote out his laws with an iron pen. When he eventually reports on his activities, it is in the words

> Lo! I unfold my darkness, and on
> This rock place with strong hand the Book
> Of eternal brass, written in my solitude.
> (*The First Book of Urizen*, 224)

That "Book" contains all the Christian virtues, but reduced to laws: "Laws of peace, of love, of unity,/Of pity, compassion, forgiveness." Everything is reduced to standardization, in the hope of imposing permanence.

Blake, by contrast, believes the human quest for permanence to be mistaken. In a world of life, fixity is impossible to achieve; the task of human beings is to learn how to live in a world where changes, shifts, and transformations are part of the essential process. "We are born to Cares and Woes," writes Watts gloomily in one of his hymns; Blake's version sees the human condition as one of necessary alternations:

> Man was made for Joy & Woe;
> And when this we rightly know
> Thro' the world we safely go.
> Joy & Woe are woven fine,
> A Clothing for the Soul divine;
> Under every grief & pine
> Runs a joy with silken twine.
> ("Auguries of Innocence," 432)

He did not wish to deny the existence of griefs and

sorrows, but believed that a view of the world that made them central was at once mistaken and dangerous, fostering a defensive attitude in individuals and a desire for permanence that was Urizen's great mistake, reflected in the mental captivity of his eighteenth-century subjects.

Looking closely at Urizen's activities, we see that, as elsewhere, Blake's purpose was not simply to attack his predecessor. In one sense he was on the side of Watts, whose work possessed a grandeur, and even visionary power, that he could respect deeply. The questions that were agitating him, on the other hand, deeper than any faced by Watts, related to his own vision. How was it that the beauty and delight that he discovered everywhere in the world seemed not to be noticed at all by his fellows? Why did they persist in disregarding not only their own imaginative faculties but also the psychic experiences induced by terror or the free exercise of energy?

At one level Blake found it easy to locate humanity's enemies. They formed the alliance of church and state attacked by eighteenth-century radicals such as Jean Messelier, who in his will, published by Voltaire, desired to see the last king strangled with the guts of the last priest. Looked at from a hostile point of view, the eighteenth-century church could be seen as lending supernatural backing to the authority of a law that was in fact no more than the will of an entrenched ruling class needing to secure its power more firmly.

Some of Blake's most memorable writings were spurred on by his sense of the social iniquities resulting from such an imposition. But, as has been said, he seems to have suspected also that there was something in the human psyche that allowed complicity in such conspiracies. It was hard to believe that the whole human race would have allowed itself to be hoodwinked for so long if some power in the mind were not assenting to the enforcement of law. From another point of view, it was hard to see how the rule of a solid law had come to be established against the setting of an eternity that consisted of "visionary forms dramatic." In such terms it was possible to take a much more sympathetic view of the ruling powers, seeing them as representatives of a blinded humanity that sought security in a world it did not understand and in which it felt constantly threatened by dangers of all kinds. So he moved toward the development of a mythology of his own that might help resolve some of these puzzles.

Urizen, in this larger view, is not just a "jealous god" whose purposes are inexplicably malignant, but a being who is bewildered, having lost his way in eternity and turned away from its light and energy to become wrapped in dark ruminations of his own. This view entails a total retelling of the Creation story as found in the Hebrew and Christian Scriptures. The creative "brooding" of the Spirit on the face of the waters in Genesis is replaced by the self-enclosed "brooding" of Urizen; the biblical Creation, a positive making on a firm basis in the midst of darkness and nonentity, by a work of desperation in the face of loss. Urizen begins to create the world we know, but in the hope of establishing ramparts against chaos in a universe where he has lost his bearings. Because he has turned away from eternity, where vision and energy are harmonized, he must continue to suffer the despair of a darkened imagination and the fears of a thwarted energy that returns to threaten his standing.

It was his interest in these questions that led Blake away from the short lyrics in which he excelled to the longer enterprise that we now think of as the prophetic books. A comment is needed on the word "prophetic." Blake's use of it did not mean that he claimed to be foretelling the future in any detailed sense. A better guide to his attitude is found in one of his own statements on the subject:

Prophets, in the modern sense of the word, have never existed. Jonah was no prophet in the modern sense, for his prophecy of Nineveh failed. Every honest man is a Prophet; he utters his opinion both of private & public matters. Thus: If you go on So, the result is So. He never says, such a thing shall happen let you do what you will. A Prophet is a Seer, not an Arbitrary Dictator. . . .
(annotation to Richard Watson's *Apology for the Bible*, 392)

He was looking, in other words, for the patterns of significance underlying human events. By comparison with the Bible, where the common assumption was that human ills were due to transgression of the divine law and that the God behind the universe was a great and gloomy lawmaker, Blake believed many of the ills of the world to result from a loss of imagination and an unwillingness to cultivate human energies in freedom. A mythology conceived in those terms provided, he thought, a more convincing interpretation of human existence than those normally derived from the Bible; if universally accepted, moreover, it would offer greater possibilities of human amelioration.

The resulting enterprise began with two poems, "Tiriel" and *The Book of Thel*, where Blake reorders well-known mythical narratives such as that of the Garden of Eden; it proceeded with the Lambeth books, such as *America* and *Europe* (1794), in which he offered his own interpretations of recent history; and it came to a climax in *Vala, Or the Four Zoas* (1797), in which he attempted to set out a total mythical pattern that could be applied to the whole of human history as well as to every individual human life.

The poem that resulted is one of the most interesting and extraordinary in English literature. It takes its form from Edward Young's *Night Thoughts* (1742–1745), which is, like this poem, organized in "nights" rather than "books"; but it is in most respects different from Young's poem, which has a very recognizable figure, that of the narrator, at the center of its reflections. It resembles *Night Thoughts* further only at the deepest level: its serious concern with life, death, and immortality. Since Blake rejects the normal Christian expectation of an immortality after death in favor of an eternity that lies about us all the time if we could only see it, he adopts a different approach, which takes some coloring from *Paradise Lost*. In Milton's poem we are made to feel not only that Satan has fallen from heaven but also that he is gradually forgetting what it was like, to be reminded only when he glimpses light in the distance or meets one of its inhabitants again. The characters of Blake's poem are in a similar state, moving about in a world they resent, yet haunted by the sense that things were once otherwise. From time to time one of the characters will have a dream in which some part of the story of their disruption is recaptured, so that the reader can gradually build up, through these flashbacks, a full picture of what that state was like.

These characters are not fully formed human beings, since it is a part of Blake's contention that what has been lost is the presence of an integrating power that should work in the human psyche and harmonize its various functions. Each Zoa embodies one of these conflicting functions, Urizen being associated with the head, Luvah with the heart, Tharmas with the genitals, and Urthona with the shaping powers generally. At times it may seem that Urizen is to blame for the disruption, with his substitution of eighteenth-century mathematical rationality for a more creative and imaginative kind of reasoning. At times it is the lost genital innocence of Tharmas that seems responsible. At times the other two Zoas are frightened by the unbridled energy of the figure Orc, a burning boy who threatens them with destruction from the region of the heart. In the course of the work, though, it becomes clear that these three are diminished by some deeper catastrophe: that Urizen's rationality, Tharmas' lost innocence, and Orc's uprising are the result of a deeper failure, to be localized, if anywhere, in the heart, Orc's bursting out there being the result of Luvah's impotence.

Gradually, moreover, the flashbacks make it clear that the failure does not rest even there, but with the Eternal Man, who allowed himself to be deluded by an illusion of impossible purity and holiness, and so failed in the noonday sun, sinking into a sleep within which all these events are nightmares. The implication is that if the Eternal Man awakens again, his self-recall will be felt first and foremost in the heart, and then almost simultaneously in a revival of vision in the reasoning powers and a regaining of sexual innocence.

One power has not been discussed so far. Urthona, associated with the earth forces, has been rendered even more impotent than the others by the failure of the Eternal Man. His powers can be expressed only by his representative Los, who lives primarily in his hands and feet, and can use them either to express his rage and frustration in a mad dance or to create into form anything that comes within reach. His is a visionless creativity, to be valued for its positive energy but powerless by itself to redeem the situation.

Eventually, in the last Night, an apocalypse takes place. In a rending of the universe, the Zoas find themselves pitched into a turmoil through which they recover a sense of their lost significance. Subsequent scenes of reconciliation are followed by a conclusion in which they are all seen and heard working in their ancient harmony, for the service of a restored humanity.

In certain respects this has the makings of a successful modern epic. It substitutes for the idea of a fall of man into states of sin and guilt the sense of a lost integration of the personality that many psychoanalysts, particularly those of the Jungian school, would later see as a valid account of the human condition. It is also unique in its time for the honesty of its representations of behavior, regarding sexual deviation (a theme still more evident in the illustrations) and sexual fulfillment as important factors when considering psychic health.

Blake's decision not to publish the poem suggests

that he was not fully satisfied with it—a feeling that may be associated with the form he had chosen. What he had not seen in advance, perhaps, was that any attempt at a mythical interpretation for the whole of experience might in itself be a work of Urizen. In any case, such a form was bound to run into difficulties. To have main characters who were not full human beings was to make for shadowy forms of action; even more difficult was the task of writing in terms of a mythology that the reader needed to discover (or even invent) as he went along. By comparison with Milton, who could take it for granted that his reader would know the basic story of the Creation and the Fall of man from the Bible and other accounts, Blake tells a story that is founded largely in his own ideas about the meaning of human existence. The central conception—that of finding an interpretation of human civilization that would also interpret the history of every individual human being—is a brilliant one, but the structural difficulties turn out to be immense. As the poem proceeds, Blake seems to become steadily more confined within the terms he has set himself.

But if there is in one sense a failure here, it is the kind of failure that reaches above most poetic successes. One cannot read *The Four Zoas* without a sense of a strong intelligence and imagination at play. In the early Nights the depiction of Urizen trying to construct a permanent world in the midst of a desolate space and time that he does not comprehend is particularly brilliant. For the general reader the most memorable passages of all are likely to be the cries of the main victims as they describe their deprivations. Blake knew well that to those who are comfortably situated the world looks very different from the way it looks to those who are suffering from injustice and need. In the early Nights of the poem the victim's view is expressed in several passages of unforgettable poignancy:

"What is the price of Experience? do men buy it for a song?
Or wisdom for a dance in the street? No, it is bought with
  the price
Of all that a man hath, his house, his wife, his children.
Wisdom is sold in the desolate market where none come to
  buy,
And in the wither'd field where the farmer plows for bread
  in vain.

"It is an easy thing to triumph in the summer's sun
And in the vintage & to sing on the waggon loaded with
  corn.

It is an easy thing to talk of patience to the afflicted,
To speak the laws of prudence to the houseless wanderer,
To listen to the hungry raven's cry in wintry season
When the red blood is fill'd with wine & with the marrow
  of lambs.

"It is an easy thing to laugh at wrathful elements,
To hear the dog howl at the wintry door, the ox in the
  slaughter house moan;
To see a god on every wind & a blessing on every blast;
To hear sounds of love in the thunder storm that destroys
  our enemy's house;
To rejoice in the blight that covers his field, & the sickness
  that cuts off his children,
While our olive & vine sing & laugh round our door, &
  our children bring fruits & flowers.

"Then the groan & the dolor are quite forgotten, & the
  slave grinding at the mill,
And the captive in chains, & the poor in the prison, & the
  soldier in the field
When the shatter'd bone hath laid him groaning among
  the happier dead.

"It is an easy thing to rejoice in the tents of prosperity:
Thus could I sing & thus rejoice: but it is not so with me."
                              ("Night the Second," 290)

Leaving behind the much revised *Four Zoas*, Blake went on to engrave two poems of looser structure, *Milton* (1804–1808) and *Jerusalem* (1804–1820). Each of these develops themes inherent in the earlier poem but without attempting a fully coherent narrative. *Milton* is primarily about inspiration, a manifesto for the role of the poetic genius in his time. The Milton who is Blake's model is a Milton appropriate to the new age, subduing the spectrous Puritan morals and rational devotion to law that rendered poems such as *Paradise Lost* inadequate for the future, and so releasing himself into the full vigor and self-giving illumination that Blake regards as his underlying qualities. The eighteenth-century world is seen as dominated by thinkers who wish to reduce it finally to quantitative measurement and the rule of law; it is the work of the poetic genius, by contrast, to explore the moment of illumination that can never be organized into any time scheme, to enter into the timelessness of certain sensuous experiences (the lark pouring out its song as it ascends the sky, the flower with its power to overwhelm the senses with its scent) and find in them the true significance of the world.

This is the point of some of the more mysterious sayings in *Milton*:

There is a Moment in each Day that Satan cannot find,
Nor can his Watch Fiends find it; but the industrious find
This Moment & it multiply, & when it once is found
It renovates every Moment of the Day if rightly placed.
(526)

We may compare William Wordsworth's "There are in our existence spots of time/That with distinct pre-eminence retain/A renovating virtue. . . ." Or, again:

Every Time less than a pulsation of the artery
Is equal in its period & value to Six Thousand Years,

For in this Period the Poet's Work is Done; and all the Great
Events of Time start forth & are conceiv'd in such a Period,
Within a Moment, a Pulsation of the Artery.
(516)

The poem, though not easy reading, is full of brilliant ideas and images of this kind, reordering the world in the image of a nature full of momentary inspirations. *Jerusalem*, by comparison, is a more patient work, devoted to Blake's belief that the long-term work of the artist is to continue making, giving forms to things, since this is the only true work of redemption that is possible in the world. Los is now the hero.

In these later prophetic books there are many references to Christianity—so many that at first sight Blake might appear to have been converted back to the established religion of his fellow Englishmen. Many of his paintings, similarly, are devoted to biblical subjects, and there was certainly a shift in his attitude somewhere about the turn of the century. He seems to have decided that for all its short-comings Christianity was the religion by which the forces of imagination had been most successfully nurtured. For the rest of his life, therefore, he supported it, though still very much on his own terms. The Bible was to be read not, as was common in his time, for its promulgation of the moral law, but for its dreams and visions and for its accounts of visionaries and prophets who had suffered for their beliefs. Like many religions, Christianity was to be seen as constantly dominated by priests intent on maintaining the existing order; it was also, on the other hand, founded in the life of a supreme visionary, Jesus of Nazareth, who had had little respect for either priests or conventions.

Blake's mature attitude to the Christian religion is set out in a poem entitled "The Everlasting Gospel," a fragmentary piece devoted to the theme that Jesus fulfilled the law by destroying it: he was not particularly humble, he forgave the woman taken in adultery—indeed, as the Devil in *The Marriage of Heaven and Hell* had pointed out, he broke most of the Ten Commandments at one time or another, because he "acted from impulse, not from rules." In many respects he could be seen as proclaiming Blake's own religion, which, in contradistinction to that preached by the church, set man at the center of things—but man interpreted through his powers of energy and imagination:

Thou art a Man, God is no more,
Thine own Humanity learn to adore. . . .
(750)

Jerusalem belongs to the same strain of thought, and the references to Christianity there must be read with that in mind. When Blake uses names and places from the Bible, it is not in order to refer the reader back to Christianity as commonly accepted, but to encourage a new interpretation. (He may also have hoped to make his poem more readily comprehensible by using familiar names and terms, though such names, when not used with their normal connotations, can be more, rather than less, bewildering at first sight.)

The reader should not expect to find a single, coherent narrative. The indications are that various of the single plates and sequences of plates were engraved over many years and then assembled into the four chapters of the final version. There is a general theme, the sleep and ultimate awakening of the Eternal Man; there is also some special motif for each chapter, announced in the preface. But there are many other themes and ideas at work; the reader will do best not to worry about unusual names and terms in the first instance, but to read the poem steadily with a sense of Blake's general themes and his loftiness of approach. If there is a list of English counties, with their equivalents among the tribes of Israel, this may be not an attempt to make a series of detailed parallels but a hint to the reader that if the poets and prophets of Israel could find splendor and sublimity in the provinces and landscapes of their native land, there is no reason why an English reader should not find similar qualities in the landscapes and cities of the British Isles. The more radical ideas at work in the poem are subtly deployed, sometimes surfacing in a particular name or unusual word. Readers who choose to ignore them and read at a more general level will find much to admire, but investigation of them will increase their respect for Blake's intelligence and imaginative power still further.

Looking at the high visionary intent of such a poem, we may well ask what had happened to the more satirical and dramatizing Blake of earlier years. There are touches of wit in *Jerusalem*, and some good dramatic moments, but the work as a whole is not pitched for an audience that would put such qualities in the forefront. During the 1790's Blake had shifted from his ingenious advocacy of extremism in *The Marriage of Heaven and Hell* to an extremist practice of his own, offering suggestions of illuminations and inspiration that his readers were free to follow or not, as they chose:

> I give you the end of a golden string,
> Only wind it into a ball,
> It will lead you in at Heaven's gate,
> Built in Jerusalem's wall.
> (*Jerusalem*, 716)

Despite his self-dedication in carrying forward his enterprise, Blake was too human not to feel the effects of opposition and neglect. On the one hand he pressed firmly on, asserting in private the lasting quality of his work:

> Still admir'd by Noble minds,
> Follow'd by Envy on the winds,
> Re-engrav'd Time after Time,
> Ever in their youthful prime,
> My designs unchang'd remain.
> Time may rage but rage in vain.
> For above Time's troubled Fountains
> On the Great Atlantic Mountains,
> In my Golden House on high,
> There they Shine Eternally.
> ("The Caverns of the Grave I've Seen," 558)

When he felt himself driven too far by the patronizing attitudes of others, he could set down his feelings—again in private: the sardonic power of the early writings would then reemerge in a more virulent form. William Hayley, who befriended him and gave him commissions, was unappreciative of his individual genius. Blake in turn considered him passive and basically uninspired. His feelings found vent in pithy epigrams:

> Thus Hayley on his Toilette seeing the sope,
> Cries, "Homer is very much improv'd by Pope."
> (556)

> Of Hayley's birth this was the happy lot
> His Mother on his Father him begot.
> (539)

T. S. Eliot praised Blake for his "terrifying honesty," and Samuel Palmer called him "a man without a mask." Neither of these characterizations ought to be taken too literally, as the private notebooks make clear. William Hayley can hardly have known some of the things that Blake thought of him, or he would not have continued to refer to him (with continuing patronization) as "our good Blake." What is being referred to is, rather, the sincerity of his major art, resulting from a determination to say what he feels, when he chooses to say it, without curtainings of Augustan decorum or concessions to the demands of propriety.

When Blake did make more public statements of his bitterness, they were often in aid of the depressed arts of his time, as in his *Public Address* and *Descriptive Catalogue*, where he campaigned for his own kind of visionary art. In private marginal comments on Sir Joshua Reynolds' first *Discourse*, he attacked the rich men of England, who, he said, "form themselves into a Society to Sell and Not to Buy Pictures":

> When Nations grow Old, The Arts grow Cold
> And Commerce settles on every Tree,
> And the Poor & the Old can live upon Gold,
> For all are Born Poor, Aged Sixty three.
> (452)

The social criticism inherent in *Songs of Experience* evidently remained very much alive in his mind, and from one point of view it is to be regretted that his former free-playing intelligence, ready to direct itself toward satire or vision in alternate breaths, did not survive more vigorously in his later works.

It is impossible not to honor the single-mindedness and determination with which Blake pursued his unusual view of the world, on the other hand, and the reader who engages with them will discover their peculiar rewards—particularly if one or two guidelines are followed. The first is that when one is puzzled by a piece of the text or by an unusual design, it is often helpful to look both for the point of imaginative illumination and for the moment of energy. These can take innumerable forms. Sometimes they may be simply stylized, as when a figure with long, flowing locks of hair is connected with imagination, while one with closely coiled curls has to do with energy (a bald figure being, by the same token, devoid of both). Or vision and energy may work through alternating poems, as with those lyrics in *Songs of Innocence* that find their counterparts in *Songs of Experience*. It is in the interplay of the two qualities that a central key to Blake's complexities is most often found. Second, it is always important to keep in mind Blake's most vivid statements, whether in his poetry or in his designs. Obscure passages sometimes reveal their significance when considered in the light of his powerful positive images, whether of enthrallment (as in the illustrations to *The Book of Urizen*) or of human potentiality—figures running through fire, angels singing for joy, faces bearing the lineaments of desire. These are the images and statements by which he lived and for which he was content to work in isolation and obscurity.

From 1818, Blake enjoyed a time of increasing serenity. This was partly due to his friendship with John Linnell, who introduced him to a wider circle of friends. His chief influence was now upon the young painters of the time, including Samuel Palmer, Frederick Tatham, Edward Calvert, and George Richmond, who formed a group called the Ancients. Another young disciple, Francis Finch, declared that Blake "struck him as *a new kind of man*, wholly original, and in all things." He was widely respected; but except for one or two grants from benevolent funds, little was done to assist his poverty.

In these years Blake could still be mercilessly satirical and teasing when in the company of devotees of rationalism, but was equally noted for his kindness and consideration to the young. Little poetry was written, but he occupied himself with further illustrations, including the well-known Job designs and a beautiful series of watercolors to illustrate Dante's *Divine Comedy*. The old alternation between vision and vehemence continued to move him, as may be seen from the memories of people who met him at this time. One, a lady, was taken to him as a young girl:

. . . he looked at her very kindly for a long while without speaking, and then stroking her head and long ringlets said "May God make this world to you, my child, as beautiful as it has been to me." She thought it strange at the time, she said, that such a poor old man, dressed in such shabby clothes, could imagine the world had ever been so beautiful to him as it must be to her, nursed in all the elegancies and luxury of wealth; but in after years she understood well enough what he meant. . . .

(*Blake Records*, 274–275)

This reminiscence may be set in contiguity with one by the young Samuel Palmer, who found Blake at work on his Dante drawings: "He said he began them with fear and trembling. I said 'O! I have enough of fear and trembling.' 'Then,' said he, 'you'll do' " (ibid., 291). Whether he was opening himself to the beauties of the world about him or working in the realm of energy that stretched from states of fear and trembling to states of ecstatic freedom, Blake retained his sturdy independence to the last. In one of his final letters, he can be seen facing death with equanimity, and with a sense that he is at last to be released from the body's cage. The images of the prison that haunted his early work have gradually been exorcised, but Blake still looks forward to death for a final release:

Flaxman is Gone & we must All soon follow, every one to his Own Eternal House, Leaving the Delusive Goddess Nature & her Laws to get into Freedom from all Law of the Members into The Mind, in which every one is King & Priest in his own House. God send it so on Earth as it is in Heaven.

(letter to George Cumberland, 12 April 1827)

Earlier in the letter he inveighs against his fellow countrymen who, since the French Revolution,

. . . are all Intermeasurable by One Another, Certainly a happy state of Agreement to which I for One do not Agree. God keep me from the Divinity of Yes & No too, The Yea Nay Creeping Jesus, from supposing Up & Down to be the same Thing as all Experimentalists must suppose.

Because he had remained so firmly independent of his fellows, Blake had cut himself off from some of the resources of communication that would have facilitated reception of his work. To this day a full appreciation of it calls for unusual efforts—not simply an empathizing with Blake's various states of vision, but a willingness to enter into the strenuous dialectic of mind involved. We need to understand both the moods in which he could remain passive to the visitations of imaginative experience and those in which he committed himself to the harmonies and energies of creative work. Yet in all his works there are taproots to the vividness of the works to which the general reader responds first of all.

Blake might seem in his later years to have shut himself off deliberately from the world about him. But as one penetrates further into his life and work, one comes to see that his firm independence, baffling at first sight to the aspiring reader, was really the defense for his belief in a bounding line of freedom and a capacity for illumination that he believed to be the inner condition of all human beings, if they could only find their way back to it. Stubborn and self-assertive he might be, but he was still serving the cause of human freedom.

SELECTED BIBLIOGRAPHY

I. BIBLIOGRAPHIES. G. Keynes, *A Bibliography of William Blake* (New York, 1921; rev. ed., 1953), originally a lim. ed. printed for the Grolier Club and since extended, by the first major biographer of Blake; G. E. Bentley, Jr., *Blake Books: Annotated Catalogues of Blake's Writings, Designs, Engravings, Books He Owned and Critical Works About Him* (Oxford, 1977).

II. COLLECTED WORKS. E. J. Ellis and W. B. Yeats, *The Works, Poetic, Symbolic, and Critical, Edited with Lithographs of the Illustrated "Prophetic Books" and a Memoir and Interpretation*, 3 vols. (London, 1893), largely of historical interest; G. Keynes, ed., *Writings (in Verse and Prose)*, 3 vols. (London, 1925), with reproductions and a portrait; G. Keynes, *The Complete Writings* (London, 1957), a new ed. of that of 1925, with variant readings; rev. continually and repr. from 1966 onward in the Oxford Standard Authors series, the best plain text for the general reader; D. V. Erdman, ed., *The Poetry and Prose of William Blake* (New York, 1965), commentary by H. Bloom, less complete than Keynes but reproduces Blake's idiosyncratic punctuation more precisely; W. H. Stevenson, ed., *The Poems of William Blake* (London, 1971), the only fully annotated ed., uses Erdman's text; D. V. Erdman, ed., *The Illuminated Blake* (London, 1975), reproduces in monochrome all the works in illuminated printing; G. E. Bentley, Jr., *William Blake's Writings*, 2 vols. (Oxford, 1977), the most fully edited text in bibliographical terms, illuminations to the text reproduced in line.

III. SEPARATE WORKS. *Note:* Entries marked * were engraved, printed, and published in small eds. by Blake himself as specimens of "illuminated printing"; those marked + have since been reproduced in facs. eds. by the Trianon Press. Additional facs. eds. are N. Bogen, ed., *The Book of Thel* (Providence, 1971), and K. P. Easson and R. R. Easson, eds., *The Book of Urizen* and *Milton* (both Boulder, Colo., 1978).

Poetical Sketches (London, 1783), verse; * + *All Religions Are One* (London, ca. 1788), prose, 10 plates, only one copy recorded; * + *There Is No Natural Religion* (London, ca. 1788), prose, 19 plates, no complete copy recorded; * + *Songs of Innocence* (London, 1789), verse, 31

plates; * + *The Book of Thel* (London, 1789), verse, 8 plates; *Tiriel* (London, ca. 1789), verse, not printed in Blake's lifetime, first complete and accurate text, from the MS in the British Museum, in the Nonesuch eds. of 1925 and 1927; facs. and transcript of the MS, reproductions of the drawings, and a commentary on the poem by G. E. Bentley, Jr. (Oxford, 1967); * + *The Marriage of Heaven and Hell* and *A Song of Liberty* (London, ca. 1790), prose, 27 plates; *The French Revolution. A Poem in Seven Books* (London, 1791), verse, the first book not published in Blake's lifetime, the only recorded copy is probably a proof; Blake completed only the first book; * + *Visions of the Daughters of Albion* (London, 1793), verse, 11 plates; * + *America. A Prophecy* (London, 1793), verse, 18 plates; * + *Songs of Innocence and of Experience, Showing the Two Contrary States of the Human Soul* (London, 1794), verse, 54 plates, facs. ed. reproduced from the original first ed. by G. Keynes (London, 1967); * + *Europe. A Prophecy* (London, 1794), verse, 18 plates; * + *The First Book of Urizen* (London, 1794), verse, 28 plates; + *The Song of Los* (London, 1795), verse, 8 plates; + *The Book of Los* (London, 1795), verse, 5 plates; *Vala, Or the Four Zoas* (London, 1795–1804), verse, not printed in Blake's lifetime, first complete and accurate text, from the MS in the British Museum, in the Nonesuch eds. of 1925 and 1927; also by H. M. Margoliouth, ed. (London, 1956), an attempted reconstruction of one of its early states, and the facs. by G. E. Bentley, Jr., ed. (Oxford, 1963) includes all illustrations; * + *The Book of Ahania* (London, 1795), verse, 6 plates, only one copy recorded; * + *Milton* (London, 1804–1808), verse, 45 plates; * +*Jerusalem. The Emanation of the Giant Albion* (London, 1804–1820), verse, 100 plates, not completed until 1820; *Blake's Chaucer: The Canterbury Pilgrims* (London, 1809), a prospectus by Blake for an engraving of his fresco of the Canterbury pilgrims; *A Descriptive Catalogue of Pictures, Poetical and Historical Inventions. Painted in Water Colours, Being the Ancient Method of Fresco Painting Restored: and Drawings for Public Inspection* (London, 1809), comp. by Blake for an exhibition of his works; + *For the Sexes: The Gates of Paradise* (London, ca. 1818), emblems, 21 plates, a rev. ed. of *For Children: The Gates of Paradise* (London, 1793) with text added.

Blake also designed and engraved illustrations for a number of books. The most important of these are Edward Young's *Night Thoughts* (London, 1797), Robert Blair's *The Grave* (London, 1808), and Robert Thornton's *The Pastorals of Virgil* (London, 1821) and *The Book of Job* (London, 1825).

IV. LETTERS AND NOTEBOOKS. *Letters from William Blake to Thomas Butts, 1800–1803*, printed in facs. with an intro. note by G. Keynes (Oxford, 1926); G. Keynes, ed., *The Note Book of William Blake Called The Rossetti Manuscript* (London, 1935), with a facs. of the *Note Book*, the verbal contents of this sketchbook and commonplace book used by Blake in 1793–1818 are included in the Nonesuch eds. of 1925 and 1927; D. V. Erdman and D. Moore, eds., *The Notebook of William Blake; A Photographic and Typographic Facsimile* (Oxford, 1973), more fully edited than Keynes's ed.

V. CRITICAL STUDIES. A. C. Swinburne, *William Blake: A Critical Essay* (London, 1868); W. B. Yeats, *Ideas of Good and Evil* (London, 1903), contains "William Blake and His Illustrations to the Divine Comedy"; J. H. Wicksteed, *Blake's Vision of the Book of Job* (London, 1910; rev. ed., 1924), see also his *Blake's Innocence and Experience* (London, 1928); D. Saurat, *Blake and Milton* (Bordeaux, 1920; rev. ed., 1935), see also his *Blake and Modern Thought* (London, 1929); S. F. Damon, *William Blake: His Philosophy and Symbols* (Boston, 1924); M. Plowman, *An Introduction to the Study of Blake* (London, 1927; new ed., 1967); J. M. Murry, *William Blake* (London, 1933); M. O. Percival, *William Blake's Circle of Destiny* (New York, 1938); M. R. Lowery, *Windows of the Morning. A Critical Study of "Poetical Sketches," 1783* (New Haven, Conn., 1940); J. Bronowski, *A Man Without A Mask: William Blake, 1757–1827* (London, 1944), reiss. as *William Blake and the Age of Revolution* (New York, 1965); K. Preston, *Blake and Rossetti* (London, 1944); M. Schorer, *William Blake: The Politics of Vision* (New York, 1946); R. Todd, *Tracks in the Snow. Studies in English Science and Art* (London, 1946), contains a study of Blake and the eighteenth-century mythologists; N. Frye, *Fearful Symmetry. A Study of William Blake* (Princeton, N. J., 1947); J. G. Davies, *The Theology of William Blake* (Oxford, 1948); G. Keynes, *Blake Studies. Notes on His Life and Works* (London, 1949), contains a bibliography of Keynes's writings on Blake; B. Blackstone, *English Blake* (London, 1949); H. M. Margoliouth, *William Blake* (London, 1951); J. H. Wicksteed, ed., *William Blake's "Jerusalem"* (London, 1953), a commentary on the facs. published by the William Blake Trust; S. Gardner, *Infinity or the Anvil: A Critical Study of Blake's Poetry* (Oxford, 1954); D. V. Erdman, *Blake—Prophet Against Empire* (London, 1954; rev. eds., 1969, 1977); H. Adams, *Blake and Yeats. The Contrary Vision* (Ithaca, N. Y., 1955); V. de Sola Pinto, ed., *The Divine Vision* (London, 1957), contains essays on Blake by various hands; A. L. Morton, *The Everlasting Gospel: A Study in the Sources of William Blake* (London, 1958); R. F. Glechner, *The Piper and the Road: A Study of William Blake* (Detroit, 1959); C. M. Bowra, *The Prophetic Element* (London, 1960), presidential address to the English Association; P. F. Fisher, *The Valley of Vision: Blake as Prophet and Revolutionary*, N. Frye, ed. (London, 1961); G. M. Harper, *The Neo-Platonism of William Blake* (Chapel Hill, N. C., 1961); H. Bloom, *Blake's Apocalypse: A Study in Poetic Argument* (New Haven, Conn., 1963); W. R. Hughes, ed., *Jerusalem* (London, 1964), with commentary and notes by Hughes, a simplified ed.; E. D. Hirsch, Jr., *Innocence and Experience: An Introduction to Blake* (New

Haven, Conn., 1964); A. Ostriker, *Vision and Verse in William Blake* (Madison–Milwaukee, 1965); D. G. Gillham, *Blake's Contrary States: The "Songs of Innocence and of Experience" as Dramatic Poems* (Cambridge, 1966); T. J. J. Altizer, *The New Apocalypse: The Radical Christian Vision of William Blake* (Ann Arbor, Mich., 1967); J. Holloway, *Blake: The Lyric Poetry* (London, 1968); J. B. Beer, *Blake's Humanism* (Manchester, 1968); R. Lister, *William Blake: An Introduction to the Man and to His Work* (London, 1968); K. Raine, *Blake and Tradition*, 2 vols. (New York, 1968; London, 1969), Andrew Mellon Lectures, 1962, reiss. in shorter form as *Blake and Antiquity* (London, 1970); A. H. Rosenfeld, ed., *William Blake: Essays for S. Foster Damon* (Providence, 1969); J. B. Beer, *Blake's Visionary Universe* (Manchester, 1969); D. Dorfman, *Blake in the Nineteenth Century: His Reputation as a Poet from Gilchrist to Yeats* (New Haven, Conn., 1969); M. D. Paley, *Energy and the Imagination: A Study of the Development of Blake's Thought* (Oxford, 1970); M. D. Paley and M. Phillips, *William Blake: Essays in Honour of Sir Geoffrey Keynes* (Oxford, 1973); D. Wagenknecht, *Blake's Night: William Blake and the Idea of Pastoral* (Cambridge, Mass., 1973); S. Curran and J. A. Wittreich, Jr., eds., *Blake's Sublime Allegory: Essays on The Four Zoas, Milton, and Jerusalem* (Madison, Wis., 1973); M. K. Nurmi, *William Blake* (London, 1974); T. Frosch, *The Awakening of Albion* (Ithaca, N. Y., 1974); D. D. Ault, *Visionary Physics: Blake's Response to Newton* (Chicago, 1974); S. Fox, *Poetic Form in Blake's "Milton"* (Princeton, N. J., 1976); R. N. Essick and D. Pearce, eds., *Blake in His Time* (Bloomington, Ind., 1978); M. Phillips, ed., *Interpreting Blake* (Cambridge, 1978); K. Raine, *Blake and the New Age* (London, 1979).

VI. COLLECTIONS OF CRITICAL ESSAYS. J. E. Grant, *Discussions of William Blake* (Boston, 1961); N. Frye, *Blake: A Collection of Critical Essays* (Englewood Cliffs, N. J., 1966); M. D. Paley, *Twentieth Century Interpretations of Songs of Innocence and Experience* (Englewood Cliffs, N. J., 1969); J. O'Neill, *Critics on Blake: Readings in Literary Criticism* (London, 1970); M. Bottrall, *William Blake: Songs of Innocence and Experience: A Casebook* (London, 1970).

VII. BIOGRAPHICAL STUDIES. A. H. Palmer, *The Life and Letters of Samuel Palmer* (London, 1802); B. H. Malkin, *An Account of Blake's Early Life*, preface to *A Father's Memoir of His Child* (London, 1806); A. Gilchrist, *The Life of William Blake*, 2 vols. (rev. ed., London, 1863), the best ed. of this classic biography is by R. Todd, ed., in the Everyman's Library; A. C. Swinburne, *William Blake: A Critical Essay* (London, 1868); F. Tatham, *Life* (London, 1906), preface to A. G. B. Russell, ed., *The Letters of William Blake* (London, 1906); M. Wilson, *The Life of William Blake* (London, 1927), rev. ed. with additional notes (London, 1948), the standard biography; G. E. Bentley, Jr., ed., *Blake Records* (London, 1969), an invaluable collection of the biographical records upon which other biographies are based, including lengthy reproduction of the nineteenth-century records.

VIII. VISUAL WORKS: REPRODUCTIONS AND DISCUSSIONS. *William Blake* (facs. ed., London, 1902), intro. by L. Binyon, all of Blake's woodcuts are photographically reproduced; G. Holme, ed., *The Drawings and Engravings of William Blake* (London, 1922), intro. text by L. Binyon; *William Blake's Designs for Gray's Poems* (London, 1922), intro. by H. J. C. Grierson; D. Figgis, *The Paintings of William Blake* (London, 1925); L. Binyon, *The Engraved Designs of William Blake* (London, 1926); *Illustrations to Young's "Night Thoughts"* (Cambridge, Mass., 1927), intro. essay by G. Keynes; G. Keynes, ed., *Pencil Drawings* (London, 1927); *Illustrations of the Book of Job* (facs. ed., New York, 1935), intro. by L. Binyon and G. Keynes; *Illustrations of the Book of Job* (facs. ed., New York, 1937), notes by P. Hofer; *Blake's Grave: A Prophetic Book* (Providence, 1953), with a commentary by F. S. Damon; A. S. Roe, *Blake's Illustrations to "The Divine Comedy"* (Princeton, N. J., 1954); G. Keynes, ed., *Blake's Pencil Drawings*, 2nd ser. (London, 1956); G. Keynes., ed., *William Blake's Illustrations to the Bible* (London, 1957); G. W. Digby, *Symbol and Image in William Blake* (Oxford, 1957); A. Blunt, *The Art of William Blake* (Oxford, 1960); J. H. Hagstrun, *William Blake, Poet and Painter: An Introduction to the Illuminated Verse* (Chicago, 1964); G. Keynes, *A Study of the Illuminated Books of William Blake, Poet, Printer and Prophet* (London, 1965); *The Book of Urizen* (Miami, 1966), intro. by C. Emery; *Blake's Job* (Providence, 1966), with a commentary and intro. by S. F. Damon; M. Butlin, *William Blake* (London, 1966), 32 plates, some in color, of paintings in the Tate Gallery; D. V. Erdman and J. T. Grant, eds., *Blake's Visionary Forms Dramatic* (Princeton, N. J., 1970); R. R. Easson and R. N. Essick, *William Blake: Book Illustrator* (Normal, Ill., 1972); G. Keynes, ed., *William Blake's Water-colour Designs for the Poems of Thomas Gray* (London, 1972), facs. of Blake's illustrated copy of "Poems by Mr. Gray" (London, 1790); B. Lindberg, *William Blake's Illustrations to the Book of Job* (Abo, 1973), the fullest study of these designs; R. N. Essick, *The Visionary Hand: Essays for the Study of William Blake's Art and Aesthetics* (Los Angeles, 1973); A. K. Mellor, *Blake's Human Form Divine* (Berkeley, 1974), discusses form in both the visual and verbal art of Blake; R. Lister, *Infernal Methods: A Study of William Blake's Art Techniques* (London, 1975); G. Keynes, ed., *The Complete Portraiture of William and Catherine Blake* (London, 1977); D. Bindman, *Blake as an Artist* (Oxford, 1977); R. N. Essick and D. Pearce, eds., *Blake in His Time* (Bloomington, Ind., 1978); W. J. T. Mitchell, *Blake's Composite Art* (Princeton, N. J., 1978); D. Bindman, *The Complete Graphic Works of William Blake* (London, 1978). *Note*: Studies of the visual art of Blake can also be found in many books listed under CRITICAL STUDIES.

IX. CATALOGS OF WORKS IN PUBLIC COLLECTIONS. M. Butlin, ed., *William Blake (1757-1827): A Catalogue of the Works of William Blake in the Tate Gallery* (London, 1957); H. D. Willard, *William Blake: Water-color Drawings* (Boston, 1957), the collection at the Boston Museum of Fine Arts; *William Blake: Catalogue of the Preston Blake Library* (Westminster, 1969); W. Wells, *William Blake's "Heads of the Poets"* (Manchester, 1969), the collection at the Manchester City Art Gallery; D. Bindman, *William Blake: Catalogue of the Collection in the Fitzwilliam Museum* (Cambridge, 1970); R. Morgan and G. E. Bentley, Jr., "A Handlist of Works by William Blake in the . . . British Museum," in *Blake Newsletter*, V (1972), pp. 223–258.

X. FINDING LIST. R. N. Essick, "Finding List of Reproductions of Blake's Art," in *Blake Newsletter*, V (1971), pp. 1–160.

XI. PERIODICALS. *Blake Newsletter* (1967–1977), continued as *Blake: An Illustrated Quarterly* (1977–   ); *Blake Studies* (1967–   ).

XII. REFERENCE WORKS. S. F. Damon, *A Blake Dictionary: The Ideas and Symbols of William Blake* (Providence, 1965); D. V. Erdman, ed., *A Concordance to the Writings of William Blake*, 2 vols. (New York, 1967); G. E. Bentley, Jr., *William Blake: The Critical Heritage* (London, 1975), repr. all the early reviews and essays.

A variety of audiovisual material is also available on Blake. See G. E. Bentley, Jr., *Blake Books: Annotated Catalogues . . .* , under BIBLIOGRAPHIES.

ROBERT BURNS

(1759-1796)

David Daiches

I

ROBERT BURNS is the national poet of Scotland. Every year on the anniversary of his birth thousands of Scotsmen at home and abroad attend celebratory "Burns suppers" and indulge in sentimental oratory extolling his poems, of which they often know only a few of the most hackneyed. Books about his life and loves are still written and read; every relic that has been associated with him is passionately treasured; and any odd piece of information that can be connected with Burns is eagerly sought by a host of amateur antiquarians. In this national worship of Burns there is a great deal that offends the literary critic, who complains that the Burns cult, as it is often called, obscures the true nature of Burns's literary achievement and perpetuates a quite unreal and preposterously sentimentalized picture of the man and the poet. The modern Scottish poet Hugh MacDiarmid has complained that the Burns cult "has denied his poetry to laud his amours. It has preserved his furniture and repelled his message."

Yet, however much we may agree that this sort of national worship of a poet is not conducive to the discriminating appreciation of his poetry, the fact remains that the cult developed spontaneously, soon after Burns's death, and there must be something about his poetic achievement that accounts for it. Scotland has no other national figure to compare with Burns. Not even Robert the Bruce, who led Scotland in the successful Wars of Independence against the English, holds a place in the hearts of Scotsmen that can begin to compare with that held by Burns. There is a universal feeling that Burns was a "real" person, that he understood men and their weaknesses, that he really knew what life was about, that he spoke for his fellow men in a unique way and to a unique degree. The English worship of William Shakespeare is a wholly different sort of thing; it reflects wonder and admiration before the almost godlike achievement of Shakespeare's genius. Shakespeare is not the great popular hero in England that Burns is in Scotland. Indeed, no country has made a poet into a national hero in quite the same way that Scotland has with Burns.

There are two principal reasons for the special place Burns has achieved in the affections of the ordinary folk of Scotland. The first is his humble origin. He was the son of a small tenant farmer and was a working farmer for most of his life. The second reason is the way in which Burns in his songs identified himself with the Scottish folk tradition and, by rescuing, completing, refurbishing, rewriting, or recreating hundreds of items from the vast but fragmentary mass of Scottish popular songs, came to symbolize the popular voice of Scotland. There are other reasons, too—social and economic as much as literary—why a rustic poet should have maintained a special appeal in an industrialized urban Scotland nostalgic for a lost pastoral rhythm of life. There is also the fact that Burns was, in a remarkable way, the poet of humanity's "unofficial self" (to borrow a phrase from George Orwell), the poet of realized experience in the individual instance. Many of his songs represent an abandonment to the emotional moment, a passionate acceptance of the reality and validity of the given situation:[1]

> As fair art thou, my bonie lass,
>   So deep in luve am I;
> And I will luve thee still, my Dear,
>   Till a' the seas gang[2] dry.

This kind of poetry is never reflective, but always isolates the individual experience to make it, for the moment, the sum of all life:

[1]All quotations are taken from James Kinsley, ed., *The Poems and Songs* (Oxford, 1968).
[2]Go.

310

But a' the pleasures e'er I saw,
  Tho' three times doubled fairly,
That happy night was worth them a',
  Amang the rigs o' barley.

Or again:

Green grow the rashes O,
  Green grow the rashes O;
The sweetest hours that e'er I spend,
  Are spent amang the lasses O!

I am not claiming that this represents the greatest kind of poetry—in any case, these are parts of songs, which must be sung to their proper tunes to be properly appreciated. But such verse does illustrate a strain in Burns that accounts for his special kind of appeal.

In this respect Burns is the opposite of a poet such as Percy Bysshe Shelley. He does not try to find in his individual emotional experiences or moments of physical passion any symbol of the Platonic idea of love or any proof of anything except the reality and zest of the experience. His love songs are not, for the most part, about "Love"; they are about two people (or one person) in a state of physical and emotional excitement. There is something refreshing and appealing about this. And popular instinct turns readily toward the unromantic love poetry of the folk tradition.

Popular instinct also turns to the kind of sentimental glorifications of rustic poverty that we find in that very unequal poem, "The Cotter's Saturday Night." Burns, who was much influenced by the sentimental tradition in late eighteenth-century English and Scottish literature, sometimes postured deliberately in order to attract the attention of the genteel sentimentalists of his day. He paraded himself before them as a "Heaven-taught ploughman," pretending that he was much less educated than he in fact was and playing the part of the simple "natural man" that philosophers of the period were fond of discussing in their theoretical works. It is on this side of Burns, unfortunately, that the orators at Burns suppers prefer to concentrate, with the result that they often present a picture of a rustic philosopher turning out edifying genteel platitudes about the life of the peasant.

There is yet another Burns, besides the unromantic love poet and the posturing sentimentalist, and that Burns, though largely ignored by the Burns cult, has a strength and a subtlety that the others wholly lack. This is the satirical poet, the ironic observer of contemporary men and manners, the shrewd and humorous critic of religion and politics, of human character, of the Scotland of his day. This is the Burns who wrote "Holy Willie's Prayer," "The Ordination," "The Twa Herds," "The Holy Fair," and other satirical poems in which he worked with assurance, technical brilliance, and originality in a Scottish literary tradition that goes back to the Middle Ages.

To understand how Burns's achievement was split in this way, and indeed how his character both as man and as poet was torn in different directions, we must have some appreciation of the nature of the Scottish literary tradition and of Burns's relation to it. Burns's relation to the Scottish literary past and to the situation of Scottish culture in his own day accounts for his split personality. The latter half of the eighteenth century was not a propitious time for a Scottish poet, and Burns's achievement becomes all the greater when one realizes the conditions, both personal and national, under which he worked.

II

In the Middle Ages, Scotland was an independent country with a vigorous culture of its own. The literary language of the medieval Scottish poets was what is known as "Middle Scots," originally a northern form of English but, as a result of independent development and of its use in a flourishing Scottish literature, now a language in its own right, though closely akin to English and in large measure intelligible to Englishmen. The great fifteenth-century Scottish poets, Robert Henryson and William Dunbar, had exercised and enriched the Scottish literary language, and their successors in the sixteenth century worked largely in the tradition they did so much to establish. The fifteenth- and early sixteenth-century Scottish poets had not only a national literary tradition and a literary language of their own, they were also European in their perspective, with close cultural links with the Continent, especially France. They drew in their own way on the common European storehouse of literary themes and modes, and they made their own use, too, of material drawn from the Latin and Greek classics. Gavin Douglas' translation of Vergil's *Aeneid* into Middle Scots verse early in the sixteenth century is the earliest rendering of Vergil into any branch of the English language. Unfortunately, the stability and integrity of Scottish culture was threatened by a series of events beginning in the latter part of the sixteenth century. The Reformation came to Scotland more violently than it came to England and precipitated more than a century of bitter controversy and sometimes sharp civil conflict. The Puritan suspicion of secular literature blighted Scottish drama and drove much folk literature underground. Further, once Scotland had officially become a Protestant country (though there remained a considerable Roman Catholic area in the Highlands), its destiny became more closely linked with Protestant England and separated from Catholic France, Scotland's traditional ally. English translations of the Bible were read by Scottish Protestants, and more and more English forms came into the Scottish literary language. Then, in 1603, King James VI of Scotland inherited the English throne and moved his court to London to become James I of England. This "Union of the Crowns," by removing the court—which had been the focus of Scottish culture—from Edinburgh and encouraging many of the Scottish poets to go south and write English courtly poetry, was a damaging blow to Scottish arts and letters. And when, in 1707, the Union of Crowns was succeeded by the Union of Parliaments and Scotland lost its own parliament to become simply the northern part of "Great Britain," the Scottish cultural situation became even more confused.

What happened was that standard southern English became more and more the language used by Scotsmen in writing, although they continued to speak their native Scots in daily conversation. Thus Scots as a living literary language disintegrated, for the literary language was now generally English. But if the Scotsman's ordinary language was conducted in Scots and his formal utterances were made in English, this meant that he spoke what was becoming more and more a provincial dialect no longer capable of use in complex literary works, while he wrote a somewhat stilted artificial language that he learned at school. Neither Scots nor English was therefore capable of being employed as a medium in which the whole man could express himself in Scotland. Once there ceased to be a living Scots literary language, drawing nourishment from spoken Scots but transcending it in richness of vocabulary, and there was no longer a literary norm

against which written Scots could be set, Scots degenerated into a series of local dialects, to be transcribed phonetically by antiquaries or regional humorists as interesting or amusing variations of standard English.

Frustrated Scottish national feeling manifested itself about the time of the Union of Parliaments in a deliberate attempt on the part of certain poets, editors, and publishers to preserve what could be collected of older Scottish poetry and to use Scots (in the form either of regional dialects or of deliberate imitations of the older literary language) in new verse of their own. This work was highly successful on the editorial side, and collections such as Allan Ramsay's *Tea-Table Miscellany* (1724) achieved great popularity. But the success was mostly with folk song and imitation folk song, much less with reprints of the complex and artful poetry of the medieval Scottish poets. As for Allan Ramsay's original work, though he occasionally captured the mood and tone of earlier Scottish poetry and sometimes produced a poem of considerable colloquial vigor and vitality, the greater part of his poetry in Scots shows clearly the dilemma of a Scottish poet working with one eye turned to a genteel London audience and the other to the rustic vulgarities of his own country. Scots verse became a dialect verse used for humorous or sentimental purposes, in a patronizing or an exhibitionist manner. Most serious poets turned to English, and left their country behind, often physically and literally as well as metaphorically. Thus James Thomson, author of *The Seasons*, is not generally thought of as a Scottish poet: he wrote in English for an English audience. And the prose writers all wrote in English. David Hume, Adam Smith, William Robertson, and other Scottish philosophers, historians, and men of letters whose work was known all over Europe, wrote in English, though their speech was often a broad Scots. David Hume was not the only eighteenth-century Scotsman to have his manuscripts carefully corrected by an English friend in order to make sure that all "Scotticisms" would be removed.

One eighteenth-century Scottish poet before Burns made a notable effort to produce a native Scottish poetry that was something more than merely rustic or bacchanalian or humorous, that was both fully Scottish and fully contemporary. This was Robert Fergusson, whose descriptive poems of Edinburgh life have a quality that most of Ramsay's verse lacks. Fergusson wove together the spoken dialects of Edinburgh, where he was born and lived, Aberdeenshire, where his parents came from, and Fife, where he attended St. Andrews University, with elements from Scotland's literary past to produce a richer Scots poetic idiom than had been seen for some time; but he died at the age of twenty-four, leaving only a handful of promising Scots poems. Burns, whose ambitions as a poet in Scots were nourished by his reading of Ramsay and, to a greater extent, of Fergusson (he wrote in one of his letters of "the excellent Ramsay and the still more excellent Fergusson") imitated the latter frequently. Indeed, it was emulation of Fergusson that sent him back to Scots poetry after his first youthful impulse had flagged. As he later put it, "Meeting with Fergusson's Scotch Poems, I strung anew my wildly-sounding rustic lyre with emulating vigour."

Meanwhile Scottish folk music was enjoying a revival. Collections of folk airs appeared in large numbers, sometimes with words, sometimes as dance tunes. It became a fashionable pastime among ladies and gentlemen to write new words to old folk airs—the words were generally English and sentimental, but sometimes they were in a rather self-conscious Scots dialect. Antiquarians such as David Herd collected every fragment of older Scottish song poetry that they could lay hands on. The combination of interest in Scottish music and antiquarian interest in Scottish folk poetry did something to keep Scottish national feeling alive, but it must be remembered that the arbiters of literary taste in Edinburgh in the middle and late eighteenth century—the "literati," as they liked to call themselves—had no use for Scottish verse and believed that Scottish literary culture could vindicate itself only by producing literature in English as good as the English themselves could produce. They looked for "elegance" and "sensibility." They had in large measure adopted the cult of feeling represented by that archsentimental novel, Henry Mackenzie's *The Man of Feeling*. They liked to reflect how "a cultivated taste increases sensibility to all the tender and humane passions." James Macpherson's *Ossian* had prepared them to find the tenderest sensibilities in primitive poets. They were also for the most part genteel, highly respectable, moralistic, optimistic, and inclined to confuse poetry with rhetoric. It is not in the least surprising that they approved Burns's "Cotter's Saturday Night" and "To a Mountain Daisy," but not "Holy Willie's Prayer" or the more abandoned of the

songs. What is surprising is that a plowman poet from Ayrshire should have had the independence of mind and the confidence in his own judgment to reject in large measure the advice of the Edinburgh literati and turn to more genuine Scottish traditions for inspiration, thus saving himself from turning into a minor English sentimental poet and achieving single-handed a remarkable Indian summer for Scottish poetry.

III

BURNS was born in 1759 in the village of Alloway, Ayrshire, in a clay cottage that his father had built with his own hands. His father had come to Ayrshire from the other side of Scotland, in an endeavor to improve his fortunes, but though he worked immensely hard, first on the farm of Mount Oliphant, which he leased in 1766, and then on that of Lochlie, which he took in 1777, ill luck dogged him continuously, and he died in 1784, worn out and bankrupt. It was watching his father being beaten down by overwork and economic misfortune that helped to make Burns both a rebel against the social order of his day and a bitter satirist of all forms of religious and political thought that condoned or perpetuated inhumanity. Like so many Scottish peasants, the elder Burns was ambitious for his children, and Robert received a certain amount of formal schooling from a teacher hired cooperatively by the farmers of the district, as well as sporadic education from other sources. He learned to read French and acquired a smattering of Latin, and he read most of the important eighteenth-century English writers as well as Shakespeare, John Milton, and John Dryden. Indeed, his formal education was oriented entirely toward England. His knowledge of Scottish literature was, in his childhood, confined to orally transmitted folk songs and folktales together with a modernization of the late fifteenth-century poem *Wallace*, which dealt rather naively with the life of Sir William Wallace, the Scottish hero in the Wars of Independence against Edward I of England. This last work, one of the first he ever read by himself, "poured a Scottish prejudice in my veins which will boil along there till the floodgates of life shut in eternal rest." Burns also studied biblical history, world geography, and English grammar, and he learned some physics, astronomy, and botany from such books as William Derham's *Astro-Theology* and John Ray's *Wisdom of God Manifested in the Works of the Creation*, which presented scientific facts as arguments for the existence of God as benevolent designer. Burns's religion throughout his adult life seems to have been a humanitarian deism.

Proud, restless, and full of a nameless ambition, the young Burns did his share of hard work on the family farm, while bitterly resenting the fact that others whom he met in town and country were born to higher destinies than his. "I formed many connections," he wrote later, looking back on his youth, "with younkers who possessed superior advantages, the youngling actors who were busy with the rehearsal of parts in which they were shortly to appear on that stage where, alas, I was destined to drudge behind the scenes." After his father's death, Burns, the oldest of seven children, was left head of the household and tenant of the farm of Mossgiel, to which the family moved. But he had already started writing poetry, in which the tone of Scottish folk song and that of eighteenth-century sentimental and meditative poetry were strangely mingled. Early in 1783 he began to keep a commonplace book, which began grandiosely, "Observations, Hints, Songs, Scraps of Poetry &c., by Robert Burness [the old spelling of his name, which he later dropped], a man who had little art in making money, a great deal of honesty, and unbounded good-will to every creature rational or irrational." In April 1783 he entered his first poem (a song, written for a specific folk tune), preceded by the comment, "There is certainly some connection between Love and Music and Poetry . . . I never had the least thought or inclination of turning Poet till I once got heartily in love, and then rhyme and song were, in a manner, the spontaneous language of my heart." The poem is an unpretentious, lilting piece, written in an English tipped with Scots, but it becomes pure neoclassic English in the final stanza. Shortly afterward he entered in the commonplace book sentimental, melodramatic, or melancholy pieces whose thought reflected the family misfortunes of the time and whose vocabulary and manner derived from minor eighteenth-century English poets. He was reading Thomas Gray, William Shenstone, Thomson, Mackenzie's *The Man of Feeling*, Sterne's *Tristram Shandy*, and Macpherson's *Ossian* and cultivating, in a heavily self-conscious way, a gloomy sensibility. But suddenly we come across a

lively, swinging piece deriving from the Scottish folk tradition rather than from contemporary English sentimentalists:

> My father was a Farmer upon the Carrick border O,
> And carefully he bred me in decency and order O. . . .

This was entered in the commonplace book in 1784, with an apologetic note that it was "miserably deficient in versification." Meanwhile his father's death freed him to seek male and female companionship where he would. He took sides against the dominant extreme Calvinist wing of the church in Ayrshire and championed a local gentleman, Gavin Hamilton, who had got into trouble with the Kirk Session (the local ecclesiastical authority) for sabbath breaking and other evidences of contempt for the strict observances demanded by the orthodox. Burns had an affair with a servant girl at the farm, Elizabeth Paton, who bore his first illegitimate child, and on the child's birth, he welcomed her with a lively poem that was part swagger and part the expression of genuine paternal affection and delight:

> Thou's welcome, wean[3]! mishanter[4] fa' me,
> If aught o' thee, or of thy mammy,
> Shall ever daunton[5] me or awe me,
>   My sweet wee lady,
> Or if I blush when thou shalt ca' me
>   Tit-ta or daddy. . . .

His eye was not on Gray or Shenstone here. The stanza form is one that had had a long history in Scottish—indeed, in European—poetry and had been used by Ramsay and Fergusson, while the language is the spoken language of Ayrshire, enlarged by words from southern English and by others from the older Scots literary tradition. Even more purely in the Scottish literary tradition is "The Death and Dying Words of Poor Mailie," entered in his commonplace book in June 1785. This is a "mock testament" put into the mouth of a dying sheep, done with shrewd ironical humor and considerable technical adroitness. By now Burns had available to him not only the Scottish folk tradition but also some of the traditions of Scottish "art" poetry, both as they came to him through Fergusson and as he found them for himself in collections of older Scottish poetry. Though some signifi-

[3]Child.   [4]Mishap.   [5]Discourage.

314

cant areas of earlier Scottish poetry had not been made available by eighteenth-century editors, Burns was nevertheless in contact with the main tradition, and his development as a poet clearly shows how the eighteenth-century antiquarian movement fed the creative impulse.

Burns developed rapidly throughout 1784 and 1785 as an "occasional" poet who more and more turned to verse to express his emotions of love, friendship, or amusement, or his ironic contemplation of the social scene. But these were not spontaneous effusions by an almost illiterate poet. Burns was a very conscious craftsman; his entries in the commonplace book reveal that, from the beginning of his activity as a poet, he was interested in the technical problems of versification. If he never learned to distinguish emotional control from emotional self-indulgence in eighteenth-century English poetry (his critical sense remained uncertain in this area of literature), he did learn to appreciate economy, cogency, and variety in the work of Alexander Pope and others. Most important of all, he learned from older Scots literature to handle traditional Scottish literary forms and stanza patterns, particularly in descriptive and satirical verse, with assurance and cunning. From the oral folk tradition he learned a great deal about song rhythms and the fitting of words to music. And out of his own Ayrshire speech, his knowledge of older Scots, and his reading in standard English, he fashioned a flexible Scots-English idiom, which, though hardly a literary language in the sense that Henryson's or Dunbar's language was, proved time and time again to be an effective medium for at least one man's kind of Scottish poetry.

Though he wrote poetry for his own amusement and that of his friends, Burns remained restless and dissatisfied. He won the reputation throughout the countryside of being a dangerous rebel against orthodox religion, and when in 1786 he fell in love with Jean Armour, her father refused to allow her to marry Burns, even though a child was on the way and, under Scots law, mutual consent followed by consummation constituted a legal marriage. Jean was persuaded by her father to go back on her promise, and Robert, hurt and enraged, took up with another girl, Mary Campbell, who died shortly afterward, while Jean bore him twins out of wedlock. Meanwhile, the farm was not prospering, and Burns, harassed by insoluble emotional and economic problems, thought of emigrating to Jamaica. But he first wanted to show his country what he could do. In the midst of his troubles with the Armours (and they were serious, for Mr. Armour threatened to sue him to provide for the upkeep of the twins), he went ahead with his plans for publishing a volume of his poems at the nearby town of Kilmarnock. It was entitled *Poems Chiefly in the Scottish Dialect*, and appeared on 31 July 1786. Its success was immediate and overwhelming. Simple country folk and sophisticated Edinburgh critics alike hailed it, and the upshot was that Burns, leaving his native county for the first time two months before his twenty-eighth birthday, set out for Edinburgh on 27 November 1786, to be lionized, patronized, and showered with well-meant but dangerous advice.

IV

THE Kilmarnock volume was an extraordinary mixture. It included a handful of first-rate Scots poems—"The Twa Dogs," "Scotch Drink," "The Holy Fair," "Address to the Deil," "The Death and Dying Words of Poor Mailie," "To a Mouse," "To a Louse," and some others, including a number of verse letters addressed to various friends. There were also a few Scots poems in which Burns was unable to sustain his inspiration, or that were spoiled by a confused purpose (such as "The Vision"); and one ("Hallowe'en") that was too self-consciously rustic in its dogged descriptions of country customs and rituals and its almost exhibitionist use of archaic rural terms. There were also six gloomy and histrionic poems in English with such titles as "Despondency, an Ode" and "Man was Made to Mourn, a Dirge." There were four songs: "It Was Upon a Lammas Night" (to the tune of "Corn Rigs Are Bonie"); two insipid love songs in English, to Scottish tunes; and a farewell to his fellow Freemasons of Tarbolton, Ayrshire, to the tune of "Goodnight and Joy Be Wi' You A'" (the traditional Scottish song at parting until Burns's "Auld Lang Syne" replaced it), an unsuccessful combination of familiar Scots and pretentious English. The final pages were padded out with a handful of poor epigrams and epitaphs. There were also what seemed to contemporary reviewers the stars of the volume, "The Cotter's Saturday Night" and "To a Mountain Daisy."

"The Twa Dogs" is a cunningly wrought dialogue between a gentleman's dog and a humbler example of the species. Its immediate inspiration was probably a poem of Fergusson's, but the dialogue is in fact in an old Scottish tradition, which Burns handles with complete assurance. Caesar, the aristocratic dog, begins by pitying the life of a poor dog such as his companion Luath, and Luath replies that poverty has its drawbacks, but there are compensations. Caesar, anxious to maintain his superiority, answers this by pointing out how contemptuously the poor are treated by the rich (a favorite theme of Burns's) and gives a brief but vivid description of the insults to be endured by "poor tenant bodies" at the hands of landlords. Luath replies with a sharply etched picture of the bright side of rustic life, wholly unsentimental and quite free from the synthetic pieties of "The Cotter's Saturday Night." The real turn in the poem comes when Luath, admitting that after all the poor are often ill-treated by the rich, talks about a member of Parliament giving up his time "for Britain's gude." Caesar interrupts him:

> Haith,[6] lad, ye little ken about it;
> For Britain's gude—guid faith! I doubt it!
> Say rather, gaun[7] as Premiers lead him,
> And saying *ay* or *no's* they bid him!
> At operas and plays parading,
> Mortgaging, gambling, masquerading.
> Or maybe, in a frolic daft,
> To Hague or Calais taks a waft,
> To mak a tour, an' tak a whirl,
> To learn *bon ton* an' see the worl'.
>   There, at Vienna or Versailles,
> He rives his father's auld entails;
> Or by Madrid he taks the rout,
> To thrum guitars an' fecht wi' nowt;[8]
> Or down Italian vista startles,
> Whore-hunting amang groves o' myrtles; . . .
> For Britain's gude!—for her destruction!
> Wi' dissipation, feud, and faction!

This is adroitly done. Caesar, the defender of the rich, is so anxious to display his knowledge of them to the ignorant Luath that the bitter truth about them comes from his mouth, not from Luath's. It is now Luath's turn to express pained surprise, and he goes on to ask demurely:

[6]Faith.   [7]Going.   [8]Fight with cattle.

> But will ye tell me, Master Caesar
> Sure great folk's life's a life o' pleasure?

In order to show how foolish Luath is in making this presumption, Caesar is led into a vivid picture of the bored and hypochondriac rich that by insensible degrees turns into a bitter denunciation of their wickedness. This is not mere abuse; it is successfully controlled satire. The tone of contempt for the amusements of the idle rich is brilliantly conveyed in such a phrase as "To thrum guitars an' fecht wi' nowt," where the homely Scots word for cattle reduces at once the ritual splendor of bullfighting to a meaningless brawl with a beast. Further, putting the dialogue into the mouths of dogs is not simply a humorous trick; the dog's-eye view of man is carefully manipulated so as to enhance the satire without in the least idealizing or sentimentalizing the dogs. They go off at the end, "rejoic'd they were na *men* but *dogs*."

"The Twa Dogs" is not by any means Burns's greatest poem, but it is a good example of his technical competence in a traditional Scottish mode. Burns here knows exactly what he is doing; he is absorbed in his job as he writes, and does not look up at intervals to see whether Henry Mackenzie or some other member of the Edinburgh literati approves of his sentiments. In the "Epistle to Davie," on the other hand, which opens magnificently with a vivid description of the January scene in a complex traditional Scottish stanza, the poet suddenly remembers the genteel audience he is hoping for, and we get this:

> All hail, ye tender feelings dear!
> The smile of love, the friendly tear,
>   The sympathetic glow!
> Long since, this world's thorny ways
> Had number'd out my weary days,
>   Had it not been for you!
> Fate still has blest me with a friend,
>   In every care and ill,
> And oft a more endearing band,
>   A tie more tender still.
>   It lightens, it brightens
>   The tenebrific scene,
>   To meet with, and greet with
>   My Davie or my Jean.

Burns found the word "tenebrific" in Edward Young's *Night Thoughts* and adopted it in this exhibitionist piece of rhetorical sentimentality. It is as well to bear in mind the temptation Burns was constantly under to cater to the educated taste of his day.

"The Holy Fair" is one of the finest poems in the collection. Written in the old Scottish tradition of poems describing popular festivities and adopting an old Scottish stanza form that came down to Burns through Fergusson (whose "Leith Races" is his model here), "The Holy Fair" describes with ironic humor the goings-on at one of the great outdoor "tent preachings" that were held annually in connection with the communion service. The poet describes himself as sauntering forth on a summer Sunday morning and meeting three young women, one of them Fun and the other two Superstition and Hypocrisy. Fun explains that she is off to Mauchline Holy Fair and asks the poet to accompany her. The tone is thus humorous rather than bitter, and Burns's Brueghelesque account of the noisy, bustling, many-colored scene, with rival preachers thundering to indifferent or drunken audiences, and drinking, roistering, lovemaking, and other profane activities going on all around, emphasizes the human weaknesses, follies, passions, and appetites that indulge themselves at the Holy Fair. There is no moral indignation in the poem, only an ironical amusement at the thought that human nature will have its way even in the midst of Calvinist thunderings on the one hand and less orthodox "moderate" pleading for good works on the other. The concluding stanza, with its deliberate confusion of theological, biblical, and amorous imagery, sums up the meaning of the poem:

> How mony hearts this day converts
>   O' Sinners and o' lasses!
> Their hearts o' stane, gin night[9], are gane[10]
>   As saft ony flesh is.
> There's some are fou[11] o' love divine,
>   There's some are fou o' brandy;
> An' mony jobs that day begin,
>   May end in houghmagandie[12]
>   Some ither day.

The notion of converted hearts is applied equally to sinners and to lasses, and the biblical image of replacing a heart of stone by one of flesh (signifying turning to God in repentance) is employed with mischievous ambiguity. Again, the conjunction of "fou o' love divine" and "fou o' brandy" further emphasizes the theme, while the popular Scots word describing the probable end of it all is a calculated shock to those who, following the religious images in the stanza, expect the word to be either "Heaven" or (more likely) "Hell." This is not satire on religion, but observation, both comic and ironic, of the way in which the claims of the flesh assert themselves in the midst of all the paraphernalia of religious celebration.

The "Address to the Deil," drawing on the devil of folklore rather than of Calvinist theology, uses a tone of amused familiarity in order to diminish the devil's stature from that of the terrifying father of evil to that of a mischievous practical joker. The poem is a fine example of Burns's technique of implicitly criticizing theological dogmas by translating them into the daily realities of ordinary experience. The ending is masterly:

> An' now, auld Cloots, I ken ye're thinkin',
> A certain Bardie's rantin,[13] drinkin',
> Some luckless hour will send him linkin'[14]
>   To your black pit;
> But faith! he'll turn a corner jinkin',[15]
>   An' cheat you yet.
> But fare you weel, auld Nickie-ben!
> O wad ye tak a thought an' men'!
> Ye aiblins[16] might—I dinna ken—
>   Still hae a stake:
> I'm wae[17] to think upo' yon den,
>   Ev'n for your sake!

The familiar titles of "auld Cloots" and "auld Nickie-ben" successfully reduce the devil's stature; the poet's genially penitent reference to himself includes the conventional religious reproof in a context of casual cheerfulness; and the concluding suggestion, that perhaps the devil himself might repent (again made with deliberate casualness), implicitly includes the devil among weak and sinful humanity, the final step in his dethronement and dismissal.

Some notion of the different degrees of skill and integrity displayed by Burns in the Kilmarnock volume can be obtained by setting side by side "To a Louse," "To a Mouse," and "To a Mountain Daisy." The first is easily the best, a bright, lively, humorous poem moving adroitly toward a conclusion expressed with the gnomic pithiness of a coun-

---

[9]By nightfall. [10]Gone. [11]Full. [12]Fornication.

[13]Roistering. [14]Hurrying. [15]Dodging. [16]Perhaps. [17]Sad.

try proverb. It begins with a sudden projection into the heart of the situation, as Burns addresses the louse he sees crawling on a lady's bonnet in church:

> Ha! wh'are ye gaun, ye crowlin'[18] ferlie[19]!

The lady, unconscious of the "ugly, creepin', blastit wonner" crawling on the back of her bonnet, is full of airs and graces, and the poet chides the louse for daring to set foot on her:

> How dare ye set your fit upon her,
> Sae fine a lady?

The contrast between the vulgarity of the insect and the social pretentiousness of the lady is developed with humorous irony until suddenly Burns drops his pose of outraged observer and addresses the lady herself:

> O Jenny, dinna toss your head,
> An' set your beauties a' abread[20]!
> Ye little ken what cursed speed
> The blastie's makin'!

At once, in calling her by the simple country name Jenny, the poet has changed her from a proud beauty to an ordinary girl whom he is warning, in friendly fashion, about an accident that might happen to anybody. Her airs and graces are stripped away, but not in the least savagely; the note of amusement is still there, but it is kindly now. The lady is restored to common humanity from whom she was distinguished earlier in the poem. And the conclusion has a simple proverbial note:

> O wad some Pow'r the giftie gie us
> To see oursels as others see us!
> It wad frae mony a blunder free us,
> And foolish notion:
> What airs in dress an' gait wad lea'e us,
> And ev'n devotion!

"To a Mouse," one of Burns's most charming and best-known poems, nevertheless lacks the tautness and the skillful manipulation of irony and humor that we get in "To a Louse." The poet expresses his regret to the "wee, sleekit, cow'rin', tim'rous beastie," on turning her up in her nest with the plow, and goes on to reflect that, just as the mouse's

provision for winter has been brought to nothing by this accident, so

> The best laid schemes o' mice an' men
> Gang aft a-gley.[21]

and he himself is in an even worse situation. The fellow feeling for the little creature is spontaneous and engaging and conveyed in a cleverly controlled verse, and the introduction of the proverbial note, as in "To a Louse," is most effective, but the emergence of self-pity at the end as the real theme seems somewhat forced, and there is a touch of attitudinizing about the poem. This attitudinizing runs right through "To a Mountain Daisy," a forced and sentimental poem, in which he laments the fate of the crushed flower (also turned down with the plow) and compares it to that of a betrayed maiden. Burns was here posturing as a man of feeling. It is significant that he wrote to a friend, enclosing the poem, as follows: "I am a good deal pleased with some sentiments myself, as they are just the native querulous feelings of a heart which, as the elegantly melting Gray says, 'Melancholy has marked for her own.'" A similar fault mars "The Cotter's Saturday Night," a grave descriptive poem in Spenserian stanzas evoking with pious approval an evening in the life of a Scottish peasant family. The poem is modeled on Fergusson's "The Farmer's Ingle,"[22] but Burns is more pretentious than Fergusson and displays too clearly his object of showing off the Scottish peasantry for the approval and edification of men of feeling in Edinburgh. The poem contains some admirable descriptive passages and shows considerable technical accomplishment in the handling of the stanza, but the introduction of hollow sentimentalities and rhetorical exclamations at critical moments spoils the work as a whole.

V

BURNS selected the Kilmarnock poems with care—he was anxious to impress a genteel Edinburgh audience. In his preface he played up to contemporary sentimental views about the natural man and the noble peasant, exaggerated his lack of education, pretended to a lack of technical re-

---

[18]Crawling.   [19]Wonder.   [20]Abroad.

[21]Go often awry.   [22]Fireside.

sources, which was ridiculous in the light of the careful craftsmanship his poetry displays, and in general acted a part. The trouble is, he was only half acting. He was uncertain enough about the genteel tradition to accept much of it at its face value, and though, to his ultimate glory, he kept returning to what his own instincts told him was the true path for him to follow, far too many of his poems are marred by a naive and sentimental moralizing.

The real Burns is revealed in his satiric and humorous poems and in the abandonment to the moment of experience that we find celebrated in many of his best songs. Burns the songwriter was hardly represented in the Kilmarnock edition. Most of his songs were still unwritten, but in any case the Edinburgh literati did not consider songs as one of the higher kinds of poetry. Burns the satirist was revealed in some degree, but the greatest of his satiric poems he deliberately omitted from the Kilmarnock volume in order not to shock his genteel audience. He omitted "The Ordination," a brilliant satire on Ayrshire church politics composed in the same stanza as "The Holy Fair" and done with greater verve and dexterity. He omitted the "Address to the Unco Guid," a somewhat pedestrian attack on Puritan hypocrisy that might have been included without offense. He omitted the amusing and skillful "Death and Doctor Hornbook" and the rollicking satire "The Twa Herds," an early poem that Burns himself described as a "burlesque lamentation on a quarrel between two reverend Calvinists." And he omitted "Holy Willie's Prayer," the greatest of all his satiric poems and one of the great verse satires of all time. Burns is here concerned to attack the Calvinist view of predestination and of salvation by predestined grace regardless of "good works" (for, according to this view, no works of fallen man can possibly be good in God's sight), and he makes the attack by putting a prayer in the mouth of a strict Calvinist who is convinced that he is predestined to salvation by God's grace. A solemn, liturgical note is maintained throughout the poem, and the creed damns itself in the process of its expression. It opens with a calmly expressive statement of the view that man's salvation or damnation is decreed by God without any reference to man's behavior; it is the very quietness and assurance of the statement that conceals at first its preposterousness and then suddenly reveals it when we least expect it:

O thou wha in the Heavens does dwell,
Wha, as it pleases best Thysel',
Sends ane to heaven and ten to hell,
    A' for thy glory,
And no for ony guid or ill
    They've done afore Thee!

I bless and praise Thy matchless might,
Whan thousands Thou has left in night,
That I am here before Thy sight,
    For gifts an' grace
A burnin' an' a shinin' light,
    To a' this place.

As the poem proceeds in this stately liturgical manner, the speaker's appalling complacency and egotism, disguised, even to the speaker himself, as humility, are cumulatively revealed. Holy Willie is not a conscious hypocrite. When he attributes his lust to God's protective desire to remind him that, however gifted and elect, he is still a man, he is revealing the moral horrors that, for Burns, lay beneath any claim by any individual that he had inner assurance of predestined salvation. When he asks God's vengeance on his personal enemies, he really believes that his will and God's cause are one. And when he asks for economic prosperity in this world in addition to his assured reward in the next, it is in order to demonstrate to the heathen that God protects and favors those whom he has elected. As the poem proceeds it becomes increasingly impossible to disentangle godliness from the most abandoned self-indulgence, and in the confusion the creed of election and predestination becomes monstrous. The poem ends in the same stately organ tones with which it began:

But, Lord, remember me and mine
Wi' mercies temp'ral and divine,
That I for gear[23] and grace may shine
    Excell'd by nane,
And a' the glory shall be thine,
    Amen, Amen!

Burns also omitted from the Kilmarnock volume his remarkable anarchist cantata, "The Jolly Beggars," in which he assembled a group of social outcasts and put into their mouths roaring songs of social defiance and swaggering independence. There was always a streak of pure anarchism in

[23]Wealth.

Burns, and here he associates it with conviviality in a characteristic way. All institutions, all conventions, anything that limits the freely chosen association of friends and lovers with one another, are hence abandoned in roaring professions of antisocial independence. It is not a mature or a complex attitude, but it does touch a fundamental human drive, and "The Jolly Beggars" gives brilliant expression to man as outcast and vagabond. Complete independence of social order implies poverty, squalor, and vice, but Burns does not shrink from that. He is not romanticizing independence from society, but simply bodying it forth, motivated less by doctrinaire anarchism than by sheer high spirits.

VI

EDINBURGH unsettled Burns, and after a number of amorous and other adventures there and several trips to other parts of Scotland, he settled at a farm in Ellisland, Dumfriesshire, leased to him by an admirer who was nevertheless a shrewd landlord. At Edinburgh he had arranged for a new and enlarged edition of his poems, but little of significance was added to the Kilmarnock selection. Substantially, it was by the Kilmarnock poems that Burns was known in his lifetime. He found farming at Ellisland difficult, though he was helped by Jean Armour, with whom he had been reconciled and whom he had finally married; she remained loyal to him throughout. At Edinburgh he had met James Johnson, a keen collector of Scottish songs who was bringing out a series of volumes of songs with music and enlisted Burns's help in finding, editing, improving, and rewriting items for his collection. Burns was enthusiastic about the project and soon became virtual editor of Johnson's *Scots Musical Museum*. Later he became involved with a similar project for George Thomson, but Thomson was a more consciously genteel person than Johnson, and Burns had to fight with him continuously to prevent him from "refining" words and music and so ruining their character. He did not always succeed. The latter part of Burns's life was spent largely in assiduous collecting and writing of songs, to provide words for traditional Scottish airs and to keep Johnson and Thomson going. He regarded this work as service to Scotland and quixotically refused

any payment. The only poem he wrote after his Edinburgh visit that showed a yet unsuspected side of his poetic genius was "Tam o' Shanter," a magnificently spirited narrative poem based on a folk legend associated with Alloway Kirk. The poem is in octosyllabic couplets, and in variations of speed and tone, in unfolding the details of the story and in creating the proper atmosphere for each part, Burns showed himself a master of a form that, unfortunately, he never attempted again.

Meanwhile, Burns corresponded with and visited on terms of equality a great variety of literary and other people who were considerably "above" him socially. He was an admirable letter writer and a brilliant talker, and he could hold his own in any company. At the same time, he was still a struggling tenant farmer, and the attempt to keep himself going in two different social and intellectual capacities was wearing him down. After trying for a long time, he finally obtained a post in the excise service in 1789, and in 1791 he moved to Dumfries, where he lived until July 1796, when he died of rheumatic heart disease, contracted in his youth as a result of too much physical exertion on an inadequate diet. (The myth that Burns died of drink has long since been exploded. Burns liked his glass, but he was not a heavy drinker for the time, and drink had nothing to do with his death.) His life at Dumfries was active until the end. He wrote numerous "occasional" poems on contemporary political and other events and did an immense amount of work for the two song collections, in addition to carrying out conscientiously his duties as exciseman. He remained defensive and sensitive about his social position, for the slightest suggestion of condescension on the part of a social "superior" infuriated him. He never found a way of life that really solved his social and intellectual problems.

Burns was the greatest songwriter Britain has produced. In refurbishing old songs, making new ones out of fragmentary remains, using an old chorus as a foundation for a new song, and sometimes simply touching up a set of characterless old words, as well as providing entirely new words to traditional airs and dance tunes, he was of course going far beyond the editorial and improving tasks he undertook for Johnson and Thomson. If he had not been an original poet himself and uncannily in tune with the folk tradition, he would have been execrated by later scholars for spoiling original material with false improvements. His work as a songwriter was a unique blend of the antiquarian and the creative. He took the whole body of Scottish folk song and, in a passion of enthusiasm for his native culture, brought it together, preserved it, reshaped it, gave it new life and spirit, speaking with the great anonymous voice of the Scottish people and uttering that voice with an assurance, a technical skill, and a poetic splendor that cannot be matched in the literature of any other country. And he not only rescued and preserved the words; he also took the mass of song tunes and dance tunes and saw to it that they each had words properly fitted, if necessary altering the pace and movement of a melody in order to bring out a quality that had been lost in speeding it up for dance purposes. He could sing the songs of either sex. No other man has ever captured the feminine delight in prospective motherhood combined with the feminine joy in sexual surrender as Burns did in the song he wrote for Jean when she was about to bear his child:

> O wha my babie-clouts[24] will buy?
> O wha will tent[25] me when I cry?
> Wha will kiss me whare I lie?
>   The rantin' dog the daddie o't . . . .

Nor has any other poet so powerfully and simply expressed the combination of tenderness and swagger, which is a purely male attitude toward love, as Burns did in "A Red, Red Rose." Nor has the note of male protectiveness sounded so poignantly as in the poem that Burns wrote for Jessie Leward, the girl who helped to nurse him in his final illness. With a supreme effort of the imagination, Burns, as he lay dying, reversed their roles and wrote, to one of Jessie's favorite old Scottish airs,

> O, wert thou in the cauld blast,
>   On yonder lea, on yonder lea,
> My plaidie to the angry airt,[26]
>   I'd shelter thee, I'd shelter thee . . . .

Nor has the note of remembered friendship ever been so movingly expressed as in "Auld Lang Syne," Burns's rewriting of an older song, which he never claimed as his own. It must always be remembered that these are songs and should never be judged without their tunes, for Burns thought of words and music as part of a single whole.

[24]Clothes.   [25]Look after.   [26]Direction.

VII

BURNS's influence on Scottish poetry has not been happy, for he was canonized partly for the wrong reasons and had his weaknesses imitated and his great strength ignored. That was not his fault but his posthumous misfortune. Thus modern Scottish poets have preferred to go back to Dunbar rather than to Burns, for they object not to Burns but to what has become of the Burns tradition. A coyly self-conscious emphasis on sensibility as such, a cloying coziness of tone, a false sugaring over of the realities of experience with stock sentimental situations, all done in a vernacular whose main feature is the adding of diminutive endings in "-ie" to as many words as possible—this is what later generations too often made of Burns. His faults rather than his virtues were praised and imitated. This was all the easier because Burns was a rustic poet who wrote when Scotland was on the verge of the Industrial Revolution, after which the temptation to sentimentalize over an idealized country life was irresistible. Burns did not—and could not have been expected to—help Scottish literature to come to terms with the Industrial Revolution.

But the real Burns is coming back. Modern readers recognize more and more that he is neither a minor figure in the English "romantic movement" nor a heaven-taught plowman artlessly warbling under the stress of his simple emotions, nor a naive idealizer of rustic life, nor a harmless rhetorical exhibitionist whose works are a storehouse of pious platitudes to be quoted from platform and pulpit. The real Burns—Burns using his full strength and genius as a poet—was the heir of Henryson in his humorous tenderness and of Dunbar in his technical brilliance, the heir of the sixteenth-century Scottish poet Alexander Montgomerie in his feeling for the shape and movement of a stanza, of Ramsay in his relish of humanity caught in the act, of Fergusson in his ability to render the color and absurdity of human behavior. And he was also the heir of the people, of the lost authors of Scotland's folk songs, whose fragments he gathered in, like a god gathering the remnants of a shattered world to recreate them and send them abroad again with new life and meaning. Songwriter, satirist, narrative poet, celebrator of friendship, of love, and of hate, Burns was also a brilliant talker, an intelligent observer, and a fascinating and sometimes dangerous personality. It was his fate to be born into a Scotland suffering from national schizophrenia, torn between a superficial genteel tradition and a deeper but frustrated national culture. It was not his fault that he was caught in the midst of these crosscurrents and sometimes carried off his true course. The remarkable fact is that he never left his true course for long, in spite of the many pressures on him, and that he spoke so often with an authentic voice.

SELECTED BIBLIOGRAPHY

I. BIBLIOGRAPHY. J. C. Ewing, *Bibliography* (London, 1909), privately printed; *Cambridge Bibliography of English Literature*, vol. II (London, 1940), the most complete short-title list of books, etc., by and about Burns; J. W. Egerer, *A Bibliography* (Edinburgh, 1964), the most complete listing of Burns's poetical and prose works between 1786 and 1802 and of all "formal" eds. after 1802, includes a list of translations and a section of "original material first published in periodicals."

II. COLLECTED AND SELECTED WORKS. The following list contains only the most important of the very large number of eds. of Burns's works published from 1800 onward. *Poems Chiefly in the Scottish Dialect* (Kilmarnock, 1786; Edinburgh, 1787; 2 vols., 1793), the latter being the last ed. with which Burns himself was directly concerned; J. Currie, ed., *The Works*, 4 vols. (London, 1800), with an account of his life in which the editor overemphasizes Burns's proneness to drink and paints a melodramatic picture of his last years; 8th ed. contains some new material by Gilbert Burns, the poet's brother; an explanation and defense of Currie's attitude is presented in R. D. Thornton, *James Currie "The Entire Stranger" and Robert Burns* (Edinburgh, 1963); J. Walker, ed., *Poems*, 2 vols. (Edinburgh, 1811), with an account of Burns's life that is largely dependent on Currie's biography, also includes "The Jolly Beggars," "Holy Willie's Prayer," and other poems omitted in earlier eds.; A. Peterkin, ed., *The Life and Works*, 4 vols. (Edinburgh, 1815), a revision of Currie's ed., with an attempt to free Burns from the misrepresentations of earlier biographers, includes letters; A. Cunningham, ed., *The Works [and] Life*, 8 vols. (London, 1834), the editor was a notorious inventor of biographical "facts" and the life is quite unreliable, but his account of Burns had great influence, includes letters; J. Hogg and W. Motherwell, eds., *The Works*, 5 vols. (Glasgow, 1834–1836), vol. V contains Hogg's life of Burns, much of which is the sheerest invention; R. Chambers, ed., *The Life and Works*, 4 vols. (Edinburgh, 1856–1857; rev. ed., W. Wallace, 1896), the library ed., based on careful research, this remained the standard ed. and life until its revision; poems and letters in chronological order, in-terspersed with biographical material, the monumental Chambers-Wallace ed. of 1896 is still the most comprehensive of all works on Burns; W. S. Douglas, ed., *The Works*, 6 vols. (Edinburgh, 1877–1879), a variorum ed. of the poems and letters with important notes and other apparatus; A. Lang and W. A. Craigie, eds., *Poems and Songs* (London, 1896), with intro., notes, and glossary, a useful ed. with the poems arranged in chronological order and biographical and explanatory notes at the foot of the page; W. E. Henley and T. F. Henderson, eds., *The Poetry*, 4 vols. (Edinburgh, 1896–1897), the centenary ed., a carefully edited text of the poems with important notes giving for the first time evidence of how Burns rewrote old songs, until 1968 the standard ed. of the poems; the biography, though full of brilliant insights, perpetuates the old errors about Burns's debauchery and degeneration; now out of print; J. L. Robertson, ed., *The Poetical Works* (London, 1904), in the Oxford Standard Authors series; L. Brander, ed. and sel., *Poems of Robert Burns* (London, 1950), in the World's Classics series, this and the World's Classics selection of Burns's letters described below together provide an admirable intro. to Burns as man and poet; J. Barke, ed., *Poems and Songs* (London, 1955), contains a number of uncollected poems and a few previously unpublished ones; G. S. Fraser, ed., *Selected Poems of Robert Burns* (London, 1960); J. Kinsley, ed., *The Poems and Songs*, 3 vols. (Oxford, 1968), the authoritative modern ed., vols. I and II contain the text together with all the identifiable airs for the songs in their eighteenth-century form, vol. III contains the commentary.

III. SONGS. The bulk of Burns's songs first appeared, often anonymously, in the five vols. of James Johnson's *Scots Musical Museum* (Edinburgh, 1787–1797), and in the four vols. of George Thomson's *Select Collection of Original Scottish Airs* (Edinburgh, [1793]–1805); *The Songs* (Glasgow, 1896), with symphonies and accompaniments by J. K. Lees and intro. and historical notes by H. C. Shelley, the historical account of Scottish music is quite out of date; J. C. Dick, ed., *The Songs* (London, 1903; repr., Hatboro, Pa., 1962), with bibliography, an important scholarly ed. of the songs, with the airs to which they were originally set, with historical and critical notes on both the words and the music, repr. together with the same editor's *Notes on Scottish Song* (London, 1908) and D. Cook, *Annotations of Scottish Songs by Burns* (London, 1922).

IV. LETTERS. J. De L. Ferguson, ed., *The Letters*, 2 vols. (Oxford, 1931), edited on modern scholarly principles from the original MSS, the standard ed.; J. De L. Ferguson, ed., *Selected Letters* (London, 1953), in the World's Classics series, text based on Ferguson's complete ed. but a few letters have original texts from MSS that had not been recovered at the time of the complete ed.

V. SOME BIOGRAPHICAL AND CRITICAL STUDIES. There is much biography and criticism in the collected eds. listed above. There is also a mass of miscellaneous material in the *Burns Chronicle*, published annually since 1892. The biographies listed below are the most important that have appeared independently of eds. of the works. R. H. Cromek, *Reliques of Robert Burns* (London, 1808), not strictly a biography but contains some important biographical material; J. G. Lockhart, *Life of Robert Burns* (London, 1828), long popular but very inaccurate; Thomas Carlyle's famous review that first appeared in *Edinburgh Review*, 48 (December 1828) is an important study of the man and his work, though it accepts Lockhart's misinformation about the man; A. Angellier, *Robert Burns: La Vie, les oeuvres*, 2 vols. (Paris, 1893), an important work of original scholarship and criticism, with a comprehensive bibliography; H. Hecht, *Robert Burns: Leben und Wirken des Schottischen Volksdichters* (Heidelberg, 1919; trans., Edinburgh, 1936; 2nd ed., 1950), translated by J. Lymburn; C. Carswell, *The Life of Robert Burns* (London, 1930), a lively and sympathetic study by a writer who knew all the relevant facts but interpreted them sometimes rather arbitrarily; F. B. Snyder, *The Life of Robert Burns* (New York, 1932), a scholarly study scrupulously documented; J. De L. Ferguson, *Pride and Passion: Robert Burns* (London, 1939), an excellent study of Burns the man by a sound scholar and perceptive critic; D. Daiches, *Robert Burns* (New York, 1950; London, 1952; rev. ed., 1966), primarily a detailed critical study of the poems but includes an intro. chapter on the Scottish literary tradition and considerable biographical material; M. Lindsay, *Robert Burns: The Man, His Work, the Legend* (London, 1954); M. Lindsay, *The Burns Encyclopaedia* (London, 1959), contains articles about people whom Burns met or referred to in his letters and his poems and descriptions of many of the places he visited; W. L. Renwick, ed., *Burns as Others Saw Him* (Edinburgh, 1959), compiled for the Saltire Society, a useful collection of accounts of Burns by twelve people who met him; T. Crawford, *Burns: A Study of the Poems and Songs* (Edinburgh, 1960), a critical and scholarly study; A. H. Dent, *Burns in His Time* (London, 1966); L. M. A. Butterworth, *Robert Burns and the Eighteenth Century Revival in Scottish Vernacular Poetry* (Aberdeen, 1969); D. Low, ed., *Robert Burns: The Critical Heritage* (London, 1974).

THE GOTHIC NOVEL

Brendan Hennessy

INTRODUCTION

THE desire to be terrified is as much part of human nature as the need to laugh. This has been recognized for as long as stories have been told, and today thriller writers and makers of horror movies depend on it. Popular novels devoted in predictable and artless ways to curdling the blood of the greatest number are understandably neglected or dismissed by literary critics. But one genre among them, the Gothic novel, which was originated in England by Horace Walpole's *The Castle of Otranto* in 1765 and flourished until the 1820's, has received much less attention than it deserves.

The term "Gothic" has three main connotations: barbarous, like the Gothic tribes of the Middle Ages—which is what the Renaissance meant by the word; medieval, with all the associations of castles, knights in armor, and chivalry; and the supernatural, with the associations of the fearful, the unknown, and the mysterious.

The Gothic novel was one aspect of a general movement away from classical order in the literature of the eighteenth century, and toward imagination and feeling, a development that ran parallel to the romantic movement and presents many points of contact with it.

There is justification for the view held by some critics that the Gothic novel was a wrong turning, in the sense that it left the mainstream of the tradition developed by Samuel Richardson, Henry Fielding, Tobias Smollett, and Laurence Sterne, and did not find its way back when that tradition continued with Jane Austen, Sir Walter Scott, and Charles Dickens. Characterization tended to be sacrificed to the demands of complicated, hair-raising plots; and the settings, elements, and machinery associated with fear were overexploited until they became monotonous. The weaker writers also overworked the emotionalism of "the novel of sentiment" developed by Richardson, to which the Gothic novel was a natural successor. Saintly heroines gushed tears by the bucketful.

No one can deny that it is against the stock, or cliché, responses that, as the critic I. A. Richards put it, "the artist's internal and external conflicts are fought," and that with them "the popular writer's triumphs are made." On the other hand, it is narrow-minded automatically to equate "popular" with "hackneyed" or "bad." The popular William Shakespeare, Feodor Dostoyevsky, and Dickens possessed the kind of energy that spilled over into excesses; it is at least doubtful whether their geniuses could have been expressed in a more selective way. The best Gothic novelists deserved their popularity, and some still demand to be read. Some were highly individual artists who added much to the scope of the novel. Some exerted a seminal influence on other literary genres.

The Gothic novel, in satisfying the hunger for mystery to replace the certainties of the eighteenth century, for awe and fear to replace rationalism, plundered the Middle Ages for its settings, content, and machinery. The characters, though they may look medieval, are generally contemporary in thought and speech. Gothic architecture, though in a vague rather than a realistic way, was part of most novelists' settings—in the form of a half-ruined castle or abbey—and was used to create "Gothic gloom" and sublimity, attributes that evoked awe. A castle had fairy-tale as well as medieval associations.

Such buildings displayed all the paraphernalia of fear: dark corridors, secret underground passages, huge clanging doors, dungeons with grilled windows. Nature was picturesque—ivy growing over the ruins and wild flowers in the cracks—and turbulently romantic—dense forests on mountainsides, thunderstorms. The scene that hauntingly recurs is of large, black, mysterious birds encircling a castle on a stormy, moonlit night in which owls screech and bats flit about. There are evil doings in the vaults, terrified fugitives stumbling through passages with candles, a weird, white-clothed figure glimpsed in a beam of moonlight that is fitfully cast across the ruin of a wall or a cell window as it shines through the gaps in the thunderclouds.

Various manifestations of the supernatural and of witchcraft recall those found in the ancient classics and in the Icelandic sagas. The *Iliad* has ghosts, and the Icelandic sagas of the thirteenth century contain many supernatural elements; the medieval romances, Dante, and Thomas Malory's *Morte d'Arthur* (1485) also exerted a powerful influence. But the immediate sources for the supernatural content, elements, and machinery of the Gothic novel are to be found in Elizabethan literature, from Edmund Spenser's fairyland to the portentous visitations depicted in Shakespeare. During the Gothic period the Elizabethan and Jacobean drama was revived, and the more bloodcurdling the better—John Webster, John Ford, John Marston, and Cyril Tourneur were performed and acclaimed, as was Shakespeare.

Terror and horror as main ingredients had been plentiful in poetry and drama since the *Oedipus* of Sophocles, but not in the novel. Though terror is used effectively in Smollett's *Ferdinand Count Fathom* (1753), it provides only one or two episodes among many. Witchcraft had been prominent in much literature since Apuleius' *The Golden Ass* (about A.D. 170), and there were many Elizabethan books on the subject, as well as a treatise on demonology written by James I.

The novels to which particular attention is paid in this essay are those that possess either a seminal importance, notably *Otranto*, or a raw, bleeding vitality and originality that gave them enormous popularity in their time and have kept them alive today—those of Matthew Lewis and Charles Maturin, for example—in defiance of critics whose palates are perhaps overdelicate.

HORACE WALPOLE:
THE CASTLE OF OTRANTO

HORACE WALPOLE, the fourth earl of Orford, the youngest son of the statesman Robert Walpole, had a long and productive life as member of Parliament for twenty-six years; as writer of essays, voluminous correspondence, and memoirs; and as an antiquarian with a taste for Gothic architecture. He died in 1797 at the age of eighty. Walpole suffered some ridicule in his own time for the eccentricity of turning his home at Strawberry Hill, Twickenham, near London, into "a little Gothic castle" and for the extravagances of his novel *The Castle of Otranto* (1765). He had his champions, but today he and his novel are regarded as curiosities. Here is a widely talented dilettante who through an accident of literary history created one of the most influential novels ever written. A greatly flawed work, it is hardly readable today for its own sake, but it contains innovations that have inspired numerous imitations and developments.

The ideas of Walpole (and the eighteenth century) about architecture were strongly influenced by the remarkable etchings of the Venetian architect Giovanni Battista Piranesi (1720–1778), with their "sublime visions" and dramatic contrasts of light and shade, exemplified in the series of imaginary prisons, *Carceri d'invenzione*, and in the views of ancient and modern Rome.

The rooms at Strawberry Hill were, in Walpole's words, "more the work of fancy than imitation," more rococo than Gothic. There was a monastic hall with statues of saints in arched windows and a staircase with suits of armor, but much of the decoration was sentimental or quaint. The Gothic Revival, as the architectural and antiquarian movement that was launched in the early eighteenth century came to be known, had been separate from the revival of the Gothic in the "graveyard" verse of the preromantic poets. But in midcentury there were writers of importance known both in the field of literature and as students of Gothic architecture, such as Thomas Gray. Kenneth Clark maintains in *The Gothic Revival* that Gray has undeservedly been overshadowed by the attention given to Walpole, and that it was literary taste that influenced the new Gothic architecture rather than the other way round.

However that may be, Walpole's importance in both movements derives from combining extensive antiquarian interests, a desire to revive Gothic architecture, and his liking for the medieval tales of chivalry. All these elements came together in the novel, inspired by a dream in which the author found himself in a castle and saw a gigantic hand in armor at the top of a staircase; the story was then written in a two-month rush.

Even the basic plot, quite apart from the supernatural elaborations and difficulties in method, cannot be taken seriously today. One has to make a great effort to see it from the standpoint of the age, hungry for magic and mystery after many decades of rationalism.

The setting is Italy. Manfred, the prince of Otranto, is the grandson of a usurper of the realm, who poisoned Alfonso, the rightful ruler. He has arranged the marriage of his son Conrad to Isabella, the daughter of the marquess of Vicenza. The evening before the wedding a huge helmet falls on Conrad, killing him; it is discovered by a peasant, Theodore, that the helmet is like one now missing from a black marble statue of Alfonso the Good, a former prince, in the Church of St. Nicholas. (A Piranesi etching shows an enormous plumed helmet hanging over tiny men.) There is a prophecy that the line of the usurper will continue to reign until the rightful ruler has grown too large to inhabit the castle, and so long as male issue of the usurper survives. Fearful that he will be left without male descendants, Manfred decides to divorce his wife and marry Isabella himself. At this, the plumes of the helmet shake, the portrait of Manfred's grandfather in the gallery comes to life, sighs, and goes into a chamber.

Isabella escapes from Manfred through an underground passage and is given refuge by Father Jerome at the Church of St. Nicholas. On the way she has met and fallen in love with Theodore. Matilda, Manfred's daughter, has noticed that Theodore, with his jet-black hair, is like the portrait of Alfonso in the gallery, and is also in love with him. Manfred is told by garrulous servants that a giant's leg in armor has been seen in the chamber at the end of the gallery.

Father Jerome is ordered by Manfred to give up Isabella and to behead Theodore, but when the monk discovers that Theodore is his son, the young man is spared. Isabella's father, Frederic, arrives. He is the nearest relative to the last rightful prince of Otranto, Alfonso. An enormous sword, carried by one hundred knights, is let fall near the helmet; it cannot be moved. Manfred tries to persuade Frederic that there should be a double wedding—he with Isabella, Frederic with Matilda, Manfred's daughter. Three drops of blood fall from the nose of the statue of Alfonso in protest.

Manfred confesses that his grandfather poisoned Alfonso in the Holy Land, and by a fictitious will the grandfather was declared the prince's heir. Jerome turns out to be Count Falconara. In an insane fit of jealousy Manfred kills his daughter Matilda, mistaking her for Isabella, whom he suspects of being in love with Theodore, and the castle is shaken by thunder. The giant Alfonso appears in the middle of the ruins, shouting, "Behold in Theodore the true heir of Alfonso." The new prince, Theodore, marries Isabella. Manfred and his wife will spend the rest of their lives in a convent, repenting.

Walpole's aim was to make the supernatural appear natural, especially through the portrayal of characters placed in unusual circumstances. He wanted to evoke all the magic, the marvels, and the chivalry of the Middle Ages without losing the reality of his own time. The characters, therefore, although contemporary in thought and speech, were as fully credulous about the supernatural machinery as if they were people of the eleventh or twelfth century. Sir Walter Scott, strongly influenced by Walpole, pointed out that this was the first "modern" novel to attempt such an effect, and that by calling his work Gothic, Walpole rescued the term from its previous derogatory sense of anything that offended true taste.

Appreciating that his effort could lead to bathos, if not disaster, Walpole treated his work as a half-joke in his first edition, pretending that it was a translation from an old Italian manuscript.

Original as Walpole's concoction was, it was in the peculiar combination of the elements in a new kind of novel that the originality lay, rather than in the elements per se. The laws of chivalry, and the saintly hero and heroine, came from the old romances, and there are incidents that show Walpole's acquaintance with fairy tales and Oriental tales—for example, the servant Bianca rubbing a ring before the giant Alfonso appears is reminiscent of stories in *The Arabian Nights*. There was a restless ghost, Patroclus, in Homer's *Iliad*. The talkative servants derive from Shakespeare's use of them as comic relief in his tragedies.

If not original in detail, Walpole was remarkably inventive. There were three significant innovations in his novel. First, there was the use of the Gothic castle of romance with all its appurtenances as the pivot for the work. All the Gothic machinery is there—vaults, passages, dungeons, convent, gusts of wind, moonlight, groans, and clanking of chains —and Walpole in his matter-of-fact way demonstrated its potential. He showed how it could be used in combination with old romance elements, and how ghosts could be given a definite function in the plot. The device of the portrait coming to life is found in many subsequent Gothic novels, notably Maturin's *Melmoth the Wanderer.* So are the devices of feigning translation from an old manuscript, and such borrowings from old romance as prophecies, dreams, and Theodore's birthmark, by which his father recognizes him. Ann Radcliffe and others favored the restoring of the hereditary rights of their protagonists after they had been cheated, as they were restored to Theodore; and Walpole's use of Italy as a setting was copied by many for the monks and the horrors of the Inquisition—if they did not prefer to use Spain.

Second, Walpole was innovative in the way he used the forces of nature to produce an atmosphere, to indicate the mystery of life, the possibility of evil forces shaping man's fate. As Isabella hurries through the underground passages, her lamp is blown out by a gust of wind, and the same wind will relentlessly blow out heroines' candles and lamps for many years to come. Moonlight is supposed to add to the awesomeness of the giant Alfonso's appearance, and it will more effectively accompany future ghosts.

Third, Theodore, in his appearance, provides one of the sources of the famed Byronic hero: dark-haired, handsome, melancholy, and mysterious. The other characters became the stock characters of Gothic fiction, and once again Walpole pointed to the way they would generally develop, though he did not provide more than sketches: the tyrant, the heroine, the challenger, the monk (there were to be both saintly and evil varieties), and the peasant who turns out to be noble.

The most evident shortcoming in the eyes of the modern reader is that Walpole fails to create an atmosphere of mystery. The pace and clarity that propel the story work against mystery, since what is required is some vagueness or obscurity that would stimulate the reader's imagination. The plot is too convoluted and the machinery appears too quickly, one episode crowding upon another before each has time to take effect. Since the characters lack individuality, the reader is not sufficiently involved. They twist and turn like puppets, bewilderingly gushing tears one moment and declaiming stoic

sentiments the next, with Prince Manfred ("his virtues were always ready to operate, when his passions did not obscure his reason," Walpole says jejunely) adding sudden bouts of callous cruelty. Amusement or irritation is too often the reader's reaction to a scene that is aimed at producing a shudder, so that the illusion rarely displays any power. From Walpole's shortcomings in this sphere Mrs. Radcliffe was to learn how to create eeriness and grandeur by setting a slower pace in which the atmosphere has time to build up.

The association of *Otranto* with a dream, and the author's readiness to draw upon the unconscious, together with such magic happenings as the flow of blood from the statue have led to talk of Walpole as "the first Surrealist novelist." But it hardly seems necessary to protest so much; absurd as he appears today, sufficient claims have already been made for giving him attention.

WILLIAM BECKFORD: VATHEK

THE influence of the Oriental upon *Otranto* has been noted. *The Arabian Nights,* which dates from about 800, was translated into French by Antoine Galland in 1704–1717, and other Oriental tales appeared in English at about the same time; more recently there had been such works as Voltaire's *Eastern Tales.* Most of these had been read by the scholarly William Beckford (1759–1844), the author of *Vathek* (1786), an Oriental-Gothic production of great originality. It is about a caliph who in his hunger for knowledge and power becomes a disciple of Eblis (the Arabic version of Satan), commits many horrible crimes, and undergoes numerous grotesque adventures before finding eternal torment. Beckford also translated Oriental tales and wrote satires and travel diaries. In these last he testifies to being strongly affected by Piranesi's etchings, and his descriptions of the ruins of Istakhr, below which lie the infernal regions of Eblis, are undoubtedly a tribute to the Italian architect.

Vathek, being exotic and poetic, on the surface a burlesque of the Oriental tale, with an elegant humor and irony that keep the terror of its incidents at a distance, was not at first considered Gothic. But subsequent Gothic novels and tales incorporated the fairy-tale exotic as well as terror, and Beckford's combination was highly influential in both Gothic and romantic fields.

Like many Gothic writers, Beckford was eccentric. He was set apart both by the great wealth he inherited from his father and by his homosexuality. There was a scandal over his relationship with William Courtenay, the young son of Louisa Beckford. She was married to a cousin of Beckford's, but was in love with the writer and encouraged the relationship with her son as a kind of sacrificial offering. Beckford was virtually coerced by his family to travel abroad for several years, and he was ostracized by society when he returned. Later he indulged his taste for the grandiose by building Fonthill Abbey, a gigantic Gothic structure with a central tower three hundred feet high, which collapsed in 1800.

Vathek was written very rapidly in French when Beckford was twenty-two, translated by his tutor Samuel Henley, and finally revised by the author. Its composition seems to have been directly inspired by the week of Christmas 1781, which Beckford spent at his luxurious country seat with Louisa, William Courtenay, and the painter Alexander Cozens, who has been suspected of having initiated the writer into magical practices. Beckford never forgot this visit, and nearly sixty years later described it in ecstatic terms on the flyleaves of Gustav Friedrich Waagen's *Works of Art and Artists in England* (1838):

Immured we were . . . for three days following—doors and windows so strictly closed that neither common daylight nor commonplace visitors could get in or even peep in. . . . It was the realisation of romance in all its fervours, in all its extravagance. The delirium into which our young and fervent bosoms were cast by such a combination of seductive influences may be conceived only too easily.

It is the last part of the novel that indelibly impresses itself upon the imagination. Spurred on by the sorceress Carathis, his mother, Vathek has arrived at the subterranean palace of Eblis, where the promise to regale him with the sight of the pre-Adamite sultans' stupendous treasures is to be fulfilled. He is accompanied by four princes and Nouronihar, the daughter of one of his emirs, whom he has abducted on the way. The splendor of the scene is evoked by the use of exact and sensuous detail. There are

. . . rows of columns and arcades, which gradually diminished, till they terminated in a point radiant as the sun when he darts his last beams athwart the ocean. The pavement, strewed over with gold dust and saffron, exhaled so subtle an odour as almost overpowered them. They, however, went on, and observed an infinity of censers, in which ambergris and the wood of aloes were continually burning.[1]

The horror is just as stylishly described. A multitude roams through these luxurious surroundings with "the livid paleness of death," their right hands not leaving their hearts, some in a trance, some "shrieking with agony," each avoiding the others. Further on, through halls lit by torches and braziers, in a place with long curtains brocaded with crimson and gold, they enter "a vast tabernacle hung round with the skins of leopards" in which Eblis is sitting on a globe of fire, being adored by multitudes. He is "a young man, whose noble and regular features seemed to have been tarnished by malignant vapours." In the gloom of a huge, domed hall are the wasted forms of the pre-Adamite kings, lying with hands covering their hearts; through the transparent chest of the most renowned Vathek sees the heart in flames. The guide says that after a few days, during which they enjoy the sights and are permitted to demand access to all the treasures, Vathek and his companions will suffer the same fate.

They wander in increasing despair through the halls, without appetite for the magnificent banquet laid out, and without curiosity. There is more power here than in most Gothic writers, and it has accumulated in the more lighthearted, earlier scenes in which Vathek prepares for and accomplishes the journey; here Beckford takes one so urbanely into the fantasy that one accepts it just as one accepts any fairy tale. One smiles when people collapse or even die under a darting glance from Vathek's eye, but it is a smile of complicity.

Thus one accepts the fate of the fifty boys sacrificed to the Giaour, the Indian who guides Vathek to Eblis. Vathek pushes them one by one over a cliff, at the bottom of which the Giaour is waiting to eat them. (One is glad to learn, much later, that a good genius saved them.) Carathis makes a sacrifice to the subterranean genii, piling serpents' oil, mummies, rhinoceroses' horns, strong-smelling woods, and "a thousand other horrible rarities" on top of a tower and setting it alight. One almost admires her

[1]Quotation taken from the Penguin edition of *Vathek* (London, 1968), p. 245.

expediency when 140 inhabitants of Samarah, the capital city, bring water to the top of the tower. Carathis has them strangled by her servants—a band of mutes and black women—and thrown on top of the pile to make an even bigger sacrifice.

Yet when Carathis arrives, as planned, at the Hall of Eblis, the atmosphere of profound dejection makes her crimes appear monstrous abominations rather than absurd exaggerations in Voltaire's *Candide* style. One shudders when she explains to Vathek how she has buried his wives alive with the help of her black women, "who thus spent their last moments greatly to their satisfaction," before setting fire to the tower and destroying them too, together with mutes and serpents. We leave them, together with Nouronihar and the four princes, with hearts on fire, all hating one another, screaming "in ghastly convulsions."

The tragic mood of this last episode poignantly suggests a degree of identification with Vathek by Beckford himself. While in earlier scenes the author seems to be standing back from the action, enjoying his creature's iconoclastic antics and making fun of the old and the reverent, in the end he no doubt projected some of his own sense of being rejected and isolated, young as he was when writing the novel, into Vathek's fate. Nouronihar, in her submission to Vathek and willingness to follow him into any crime, is another Louisa.

Vathek's message has been convincingly interpreted by Beckford's biographer Marc Chadourne, in the light of Jean-Paul Sartre's play *Huis clos* (*No Exit*), as a parable on the theme that "Hell is other people." (In *No Exit* one man and two women are condemned to live in a prison cell, and each is in love with the person who does not requite the passion. It reminds one of Mario Praz's comment on the spiral staircases in Piranesi's prisons, leading nowhere: "Anxiety with no possibility of escape is the main theme of the Gothic tales.") *Vathek*'s message, Chadourne says, is that hell is within ourselves as well: that passion is transformed into disgust, love into hate, and that one must say goodbye to all hope. However far one goes with Sartre or Beckford in that view, it is certainly the dark side of Beckford that especially appealed to such admirers as Lord Byron (who called *Vathek* his Bible) and Edgar Allan Poe.

The writings of Nathaniel Hawthorne, Charles Baudelaire, George Meredith, Algernon Swinburne, Stéphane Mallarmé, and Oscar Wilde can be found along the many trails that lead from *Vathek*. For the moment it is most relevant to note that in 1815 the poet Percy Shelley and Mary Godwin, his mistress, had been reading it.

MARY SHELLEY: FRANKENSTEIN

BECKFORD talks of Vathek's "insolent desire to penetrate the secrets of heaven"—in effect he sold his soul to the Devil, a decidedly Gothic motif that was taken up again later. *Frankenstein* (1818) is the story of a scientist who in creating a human being finds himself responsible for a monster and murderer; it displays strong affinities with *Vathek*, in that the impulse behind it is the desire to show how dangerous the attempt to discover the secrets of life can be. The tale became one of the principal progenitors of science fiction, and the scientist's tragedy is indirectly a criticism of the same "unnatural" curiosity that the author's husband, the poet Percy Shelley, showed in some of his work.

Mary Shelley (1797–1851) derived a marked independence of mind and spirit from her father, William Godwin, the political theorist and author of *Political Justice* (whose belief in the perfectibility of man through reason strongly influenced her husband), and from her mother, Mary Wollstonecraft, an ardent fighter for women's rights. Mary Godwin met Shelley when she was seventeen; he left his wife, Harriet, and the pair eloped to France and later moved to Switzerland, marrying in 1816, after Harriet committed suicide, and settling in Italy.

In the summer of 1816 the Shelleys were staying with Byron, his physician, Dr. John Polidori, and Matthew Lewis at a villa near Geneva. Byron read some German ghost stories and suggested they should each write one. Out of this came the first vampire story in English—Johann von Goethe had published a vampire work in 1797—Polidori's *The Vampyre*, developed from a sketch by Byron. Mary Shelley wrote *Frankenstein* after listening to conversations between her husband and Polidori about Erasmus Darwin's theories of evolution and being impelled by a dream concerning Darwin's experiments with the creation of artificial life.

On the surface level of a straightforward Gothic story, *Frankenstein* is creepier than most and is also moving. Pathos becomes tragedy, and the central conflict is of strong interest. It is an obsessive, dramatic, and symbolic hunt, like that of Samuel Taylor Coleridge's poem *The Ancient Mariner* (1798). The frenzy with which Frankenstein pursues the hidden knowledge; his disgust at the eight-foot-tall monster he has made; his destruction of a half-finished wife for the monster; his remorse when the monster kills his brother, friend, and wife; his chasing the monster in deepening despair—the reader is compulsively involved in this nightmarish experience.

One can also identify with the monster—one can recognize his misery at being repulsed in anger and hatred everywhere, and can see how his crimes derive from bitter resentment of his creator.

The dramatic effect of this struggle is achieved by plain language, on the whole, that unobtrusively keeps the story on the move. There is some awkwardness—Frankenstein is inclined to "gnash his teeth" too often, and where vivid detail is required, the narrative often lapses into abstractions. These abstractions are sometimes occasioned by the fact that Frankenstein keeps his dangerous discovery secret—which is somewhat irritating to the modern reader. For example, in Frankenstein's ghastly researches in graveyard, charnel house, and laboratory, where the author is expanding on a passage in Percy Shelley's poem *Alastor*, he has his eyes fixed on "every object the most insupportable to the delicacy of the human feelings" and dabbles in "the unhallowed damps of the grave," and so on.

Yet the description of the monster at the moment of coming alive is concrete enough:

His yellow skin scarcely covered the work of muscles and arteries beneath; his hair was of a lustrous black and flowing, his teeth of a pearly whiteness; but those luxuriances only formed a more horrid contrast with his watery eyes and straight black lips.

(ch. 5)

The description of typical romantic scenery in the Swiss mountains—somber pine forests, mists wreathed around the peaks—is straightforward: it suffices to set the scene or establish the atmosphere, but does not slow down the momentum of the story.

The characters, apart from the two protagonists, are weakly drawn; they are moved around in the background like cardboard figures in a toy theater, and all tend to speak in the same stilted way. There are some improbabilities. The account of the monster being built of dead limbs does not con-

vince, and many readers are incredulous at the way he lives undetected in a hovel from which he can see into a cottage, and is able to educate himself by eavesdropping when the family teaches English to an Arabian woman who visits them.

The structure of the narrative is confusing: the story begins and ends in letters from the sea captain, Walton, who is looking for the unknown in the polar regions of the north, with Frankenstein's story enclosed in his, and the monster's inside Frankenstein's. To compound this defect, some of the episodes are too long and drawn-out.

What overrides these flaws and gives the central conflict depth and resonance is something not fully appreciated until the last pages, when the monster bends over the dead Frankenstein in grief and remorse, saying he will now burn himself on a funeral pyre, and one realizes how much they have been part of one another. This theme has been hinted at several times—for instance, when Frankenstein says he considered the monster as his own spirit or as a vampire freed from the grave and impelled to kill those he loved. Their parallel lives, each hunting and being hunted by the other, suggest their interdependence as well as their hatred for one another.

The main message is thus dramatically and symbolically made clear: when reason is pushed to its limits, it breaks down; and the way in which the monster and his creator work toward each other's destruction implies that balance is the key to virtue, sanity, and wholeness. The psychological pattern of Frankenstein's progressive disintegration and the monster's growing evil are reflected in much later literature, notably in Robert Louis Stevenson's story of the respectable doctor who transforms himself, by a concoction he has discovered, into the evil obverse of his normal self, who leads a parallel but disreputable life: *The Strange Case of Dr. Jekyll and Mr. Hyde* (1886).

Frankenstein expresses moral and political lessons as well as psychological truths, most clearly in the monster's reproaches to Frankenstein when he asks for a wife. Frankenstein is convinced by the argument that his monster's vice derives from his misery, and that as his creator he is obliged to try to make him happy. This is developed as a political message in the description of the monster's experience of society as a whole, echoing William Godwin's socialistic theories. As the monster tries to adapt to society, he soon discovers that property is divided, that there is "immense wealth and squalid poverty," that man hates and repulses the poor and the wretched, and that poverty and isolation breed bitterness and crime.

Frankenstein, or the Modern Prometheus is the novel's full title, and the author's husband based his poetic drama *Prometheus Unbound* on the legend of the demigod who stole fire from heaven for the benefit of mankind and as punishment was chained by Zeus to a rock. The reproaches made by the monster to his creator also echo those made by John Milton's Satan in *Paradise Lost*. The creation of an artificial human being had earlier been treated in novels by Godwin and by Goethe.

Mary Shelley's book showed how the Gothic novel could widen its scope, and her kind of speculation on morality and man's scientific possibilities is a feature of the best of modern science fiction. However, the power and vitality of *Frankenstein* derive partly from the fact that Mary Shelley did not quite understand what she was doing. When she became more mature and had to understand what she wrote, her imagination lost its force. *Frankenstein*, the most enduring of the Gothic novels, is that very rare phenomenon: a classic that was originally a bestseller and has remained extremely popular. Several films in the 1930's based on the novel, together with translations in numerous foreign languages, have made the name Frankenstein synonymous with horror in many parts of the world.

THE GOTHIC GENRE

THREE other names are essential to the Gothic genre: Ann Radcliffe, Matthew Lewis, and Charles Maturin.

The novels of Mrs. Radcliffe have a sameness about them: they are not strong in characterization or in speculation. The story can build up toward a powerful climax, as it does throughout *The Italian* (1797), but in most of her books the author dissipates the interest by excessively complicated plots.

Nevertheless, she is very gifted. She added poetry to the novel. This poetry is found in her descriptions of landscape, and in the moods and feelings of her characters, who are for the most part "figures in a landscape"; they are in love with it, see divine order in it (as William Wordsworth did), are maneuvered by it (like some of Shakespeare's characters), and are dominated by it.

A Mediterranean landscape pervades her novels, and is used as the setting for her repeated theme: she presents a beautiful heroine who undergoes many dangers, and is made mysterious by apparently supernatural happenings, before being able to marry the man she loves. Because she did not actually see it, Mrs. Radcliffe took this landscape from the painters Claude Lorrain, Nicolas Poussin, Salvator Rosa, and others who satisfied eighteenth-century writers' fascination with what was called the "picturesque" (meaning at that time landscape that looked as if it had come out of a picture). She read the descriptions of travel journals and was influenced by the writing of Gray, James Thomson, and Jean Jacques Rousseau.

Thus to Otranto's castle she added abbey ruins, often wreathed in mist; majestic mountains, sometimes "frowning with forests of gloomy pine"; and sunlit or rainswept glades, reflecting every mood. She uses weather as Hollywood much later learned to use it.

The Mysteries of Udolpho (1794) and *The Italian* are her best works. Apart from the settings, the novels present many of Walpole's Gothic elements —old manuscripts revealing secrets, and so on—but she keeps the supernatural at a distance. Emily, the heroine of *Udolpho*, faints at a terrible sight: a corpse's face being consumed by worms. She later discovers it was a picture, an image of wax used by penitents in the past for contemplation. Strange shadows and weird music turn out to have equally rational explanations. Radcliffe referred to her work as "romance or phantasie," but her more concentrated later novel is less compromisingly Gothic.

Her wicked tyrants are her most interesting characters—Montoni in *Udolpho*, who marries Emily's aunt and tries to cheat her out of her inheritance, and the monk Schedoni in *The Italian* are lonely, strong-willed, handsome men with extraordinary passions, capable of great cruelty and also of great suffering. They show the strong influence of the bloodthirsty villains of the Elizabethan and Jacobean dramatists, while Walpole's Manfred (unconvincing though that character is) showed how some humanity could be added. On the other hand, it was mainly Mrs. Radcliffe's versions that inspired Maturin's, Byron's, and Scott's romantic villains. She also improved on Walpole's talkative servants, giving them more depth and humor.

Udolpho is mainly about sixteenth-century French people and *The Italian* about seventeenth-century Italians, but in Gothic fashion they have the mentality and concerns of Mrs. Radcliffe's contemporaries. In *The Italian* she makes use of what had become another fascinating milieu for the Gothic writer: the Roman Catholic church, with the secretive, ritualistic life of convent and monastery, and the terrors of the Inquisition, officers of which imprisoned those suspected of heresy and exacted confessions from them by torture.

Unlike other Gothic writers, Radcliffe is moderate in her exploitation of all this. Most of the information for the background had to be derived at second hand, from such German authors as Friedrich von Schiller—she had read his *Ghost-Seer, or Apparitionist* (1795)—and Marquis Grosse's *Genius*, which was translated as *Horrid Mysteries* in 1796. And she is typically vague, using the settings and rituals symbolically, rather than with any attempt at realism.

The author who first saw the huge potential in this subject matter was Matthew Lewis. In *The Monk* (1796) he used the scandalous accounts of goings-on in monasteries and in the prisons of the Inquisition to sensational and horrific effect. The exaggerations and implied condemnations were partly due to a desire to capitalize on a sudden resurgence of interest in such themes because of the revival of the Spanish Inquisition in 1768; the development of different kinds of secret societies, mostly liberal and revolutionary, before and after the French Revolution, also played a part.

In fact, the period contained many historical personages whose experiences were as amazing as most of those of its fiction. There was Giacomo Casanova, the most famous of lovers, and Anton Mesmer, whose magnetism developed into hypnosis, and many more. Most Gothic was the self-styled Count Alessandro di Cagliostro (1743–1795), "the last and greatest of the sorcerers." A physician, hypnotist, necromancer, alchemist, Rosicrucian, Grand Copt of the Egyptian rite of Freemasonry, he was idolized by the high society of London and Paris, where he lived in great splendor and organized spectacular demonstrations of his talents. He was also imprisoned several times. His origins are obscure, but apparently he was born in Palermo, Sicily, and named Giuseppe Balsamo. He was suspected of involvement in the notorious theft known as the Affair of the Diamond Necklace, but was acquitted. He was tried by the Inquisition in Rome in 1790, and sentenced to life imprisonment.

Cagliostro's name has reechoed in various litera-

tures, in plays by Goethe and Catherine II, in a novel by George Sand and several by Alexandre Dumas *père*, including the one translated as *The Memoirs of a Physician*, where he is portrayed as chief of the Illuminati, who aimed to overthrow the monarchs of Europe.

To return to Lewis' "horrific effect," that term needs a little explanation, for there is an important distinction within the Gothic genre between terror and horror. Mrs. Radcliffe's effects evoke terror, which implies "uncertainty and obscurity," as she herself, having avoided Walpole's mistake of too much clarity, expressed it. Terror awakens the faculties, whereas horror "contracts, freezes and nearly annihilates them." Horror includes repugnance as well as fear.

There had been horror in the last part of *Vathek* (1786) and there was to be horror in *Frankenstein* (1818), though not in a dominant mood, and the restraint of the latter owes much to Mrs. Radcliffe. But Mary Shelley's father, William Godwin, wrote some Gothic novels, notably *Caleb Williams* (1794) and *St. Leon* (1799), which have particular interest if seen as halfway houses between terror and horror: these books place the emphasis on psychology, clearly presented, and eschew mystery.

St. Leon has a Faustian theme, with a Schedoni-like character[2] ostracized by society conferring immortality on the hero. In *Caleb Williams* the eponymous hero discovers that two innocent people were hanged for a murder committed by a kind of superman figure called Falkland. Its use of crime in a novel format, with the story planned backward—the technique developed so skillfully by Arthur Conan Doyle—was the beginning of the detective story.

These stories took the Gothic novel a stage further in its evolution, but no one was ready for the shock of *The Monk*, which had the effect of releasing passions and breaking mental barriers with the force of an earthquake. While he lacked the poetry or the subtlety of Mrs. Radcliffe, whom he admired but found "spineless," Lewis possessed the energy and instinct to make a credible marriage of reality with the supernatural—something that Walpole had failed to do and that Mrs. Radcliffe did not dare to do.

Ambrosio, the abbot of a Capuchin monastery in Madrid about 1600, is a figure reminiscent of

---

[2]The villain of Mrs. Radcliffe's *The Italian*.

Macbeth. He is a devout man but also liable to strong passions; and once he yields to temptation, he suffers a rapid decline into evil and despair. Unknowingly he rapes his sister and kills his mother. In the prison of the Inquisition, his hands are smashed to a pulp and nails torn; to escape the auto-da-fe (death by fire) he sells his soul to a winged devil, who nevertheless drops him over a cliff onto a jagged rock.

In a subplot Agnes, the daughter of an aristocratic family living in a haunted castle, is compelled to become a nun; and when found to be pregnant, she is condemned by the prioress to spend the rest of her life in a dark dungeon below the convent, surrounded by rotting corpses, toads, and lizards, with "cold vapours hovering in the air, the walls green with damp." Agnes at one point is telling the story of her baby, which died a few hours after birth:

I vowed not to part with it while I had life: its presence was my only comfort, and no persuasion could induce me to give it up. It soon became a mass of putridity, and to every eye was a loathsome and disgusting object—to every eye but a mother's. In vain did human feelings bid me recoil from this emblem of mortality with repugnance. . . . I endeavoured to retrace its features through the livid corruption with which they were overspread. . . .

(ch. 11)

This is the most morbid passage in Lewis, perhaps, but he carries it off with headlong readability—not such a common attribute of best-sellers as may be imagined.

To the Gothic elements Lewis added unusual and "real" ghosts (notably a bleeding nun who had been murdered in life, and made a bloodstained appearance in the castle every five years), whose restlessness is often ended when their bones are buried; the Wandering Jew of European mythology, who insulted Christ and is compelled to wander the earth until Christ's Second Coming, and who in this version can stay no longer than fourteen days in the same place; wonderful demons; and sorcery.

Rich as Lewis' mixture is, the originality of his work, as with Walpole, resides in the recipe and the cooking rather than in the ingredients. His haunted castle comes from *Udolpho*; the evil monk Ambrosio derives from Montoni in the same work. (In turn, Ambrosio seems to have influenced Mrs. Radcliffe's Schedoni; and the latter's Inquisition scenes—though very much in the background of her

story—seem to derive from Lewis.) The gore and the eroticism of Lewis and the obsessive scenes of death in the vaults come from Elizabethan and Jacobean dramatists. Lewis was also well read in German literature, having studied part 1 of Goethe's *Faust* and Schiller. The bleeding nun story and Ambrosio's way of death were borrowed from German tales of terror.

Otranto influenced the Sturm und Drang (storm and stress) movement of the 1770's, and at the turn of the century numerous translations or adaptations of German novels were made in England, notably of Gottfried Bürger's *Lenore* (1796) and translations of Goethe and Schiller. There were three main kinds of German novel—chivalric novels, novels about robbers, and horror novels—and they added bandits, monks, poisonings, and tortures to the English Gothic elements.

The borrowings of course went back and forth. The German E. T. A. Hoffmann, for example, learned from Lewis and in turn influenced Maturin and Emily Brontë's *Wuthering Heights*. Lewis' work had numerous imitators, Percy Shelley's rather weak novels being among them, and later two very good writers on the supernatural: Edgar Allan Poe and Sheridan Le Fanu. French works enriched this traffic. The translation of Richardson into French generated numerous French heroines of sensibility, who were then imitated by British writers, together with Antoine Prévost's horror elements.

Maturin's *Melmoth the Wanderer* (1820) is as astonishing and, in its own way, as fruitful a work as *The Monk*. It is an amalgam of terror and horror; it displays an awkwardness and pretentiousness that at times make it exasperating reading; but it nevertheless contains in the eponymous hero/villain one of the most memorable of all Gothic diabolic characters. The necromantic Melmoth has bought with his soul 150 years of youth from the Devil, and in his wanderings through the seventeenth and eighteenth centuries attempts to find new victims: people undergoing extreme suffering are offered the chance of exchanging places with Melmoth if they give up their souls. They all refuse. This makes a unifying theme for a collection of different stories, although Maturin scarcely exploits its dramatic possibilities to the full. The subjects include the Englishman Stanton, who is losing his sanity in a London asylum, and Isadora, whom Melmoth marries in Madrid. They are married by the ghost of a dead hermit, and the witness is the ghost of a murdered domestic servant. Isadora suffers at the hands of the Inquisition. Her child by Melmoth dies in prison, and she herself dies of a broken heart after refusing Melmoth's offer.

More suggestive and less salacious than Lewis as he creates his worlds of torment, Maturin crammed into a very long novel most of the Gothic properties—there are a fair number of parricides and maniacs, monks whipping the flesh off a novice as he flees, Jews in cellars surrounded by the skeletons of their families—and learned from Lewis how to use the supernatural. But these elements are subsidiary to the terrors that go on inside people's minds. This is his original contribution to the Gothic novel: his analysis of the disintegration of the mind under extreme suffering and harassment.

An attempt to force the illegitimate son of the duke of Moncada into a vocation, made by his family and by monks, astonishingly incorporates many of the mind-bending techniques associated with the wars of the twentieth century. These episodes and the other Goyaesque prison, monastery, and asylum scenes stand out vividly in this rambling work. It suffers, though, from a surfeit of scholarly jokes and from the confusing Chinese-box structure of story within story that has been noted in *Frankenstein*, and was common in eighteenth- and early nineteenth-century novels.

Maturin was an inspiration not only for writers with Gothic associations, such as Poe, but also, directly or indirectly, for many different kinds of writers—for British writers of suspense stories such as Wilkie Collins and Stevenson, for psychological terror stories such as Henry James's *The Turn of the Screw*, for Oscar Wilde (especially *The Picture of Dorian Gray*), and for the modern detective novel. The great Italian classic of Alessandro Manzoni, *I promessi sposi* (*The Betrothed*, 1827), has a long section in which a young woman is forced to take the monastic vows. The most extensive influence of *Melmoth* was on French literature: on Victor Hugo, Alexandre Dumas *père*, and Honoré de Balzac (who wrote a sequel, *Melmoth Reconciled* in translation), among many others.

A disappointing ending—Melmoth, released from his wandering, suddenly ages and jumps off a cliff, leaving his handkerchief behind—does not detract from the powerful impression that the character leaves on the mind. His mysteriousness is enhanced by lack of detail about his appearance, except for references to his hypnotic eyes, lighted with "preternatural lustre," to his weird, desperate laugh, or to the furrows of agony that cross his face. The power he exerts over the imagination lies in the tremendous contradictions of his being: the force of his personality is such that he appalls and fascinates all who meet him—yet he fails to tempt any prospective victim. He scorns the weakness of some of the servants of the church, yet is impelled by satanic envy and destructiveness. He accepts his chosen fate, and yet is continually tormented by a glimmer of hope.

Melmoth, like Lewis' monk, as well as inspiring greater writers was of course vulgarized in many imitations. To add to the other "damned immortal" associations there is in him a strong suggestion of the mythical vampire, the "undead" who returns to life each night and sucks the blood of people, who then also become vampires. The most talented of the writers on vampires, such as Bram Stoker (1847–1912), whose best novel was *Dracula* (1897), put much of Melmoth into their protagonists, though there was also the example of Polidori's *The Vampyre*, published a year before *Melmoth*.

The work of E. T. A. Hoffmann (1776–1822), one of the finest writers of horror tales that Germany has produced, was among the German influences on Maturin, particularly in black magic. Hoffmann wrote one definitely Gothic novel, translated as *The Devil's Elixir* in 1824, about a monk succumbing to the Devil's temptations. He had the same interest as Maturin in powerful minds, whether strangely hypnotic or in league with the Devil; and this concern is much in evidence in the three *Tales of Hoffmann* that formed the basis of Jacques Offenbach's opera. In "The Sandman" a young student, under the spell of the evil magician Coppelius, falls in love with a doll, and finally jumps off a high building to his death. In the second tale a young man loses his reflection to his lover, and in the third a consumptive girl singer prefers singing herself to death to living safely and obediently.

Hoffmann can be overly morbid and lacks the psychological insights of Maturin; but for a hothouse originality that infected Dostoyevsky, among others, he deserves mention among the best practitioners of the Gothic genre.

GOTHIC AND POPULAR

The influence on English literature of the German terror-romance at the turn of the eighteenth century is illustrated by Jane Austen's satire upon the Gothic novel, *Northanger Abbey*, in which she shows how such literature could reduce its readers' capacity for enlightenment. Completed in 1803, it was held back by the publishers until 1818, who were apparently afraid that it would do harm to the Gothic market. In the city of Bath, Isabella Thorpe is recommended to read seven "horrid" novels (which have been analyzed in Michael Sadleir's *The Northanger Novels)*. Only one, *Clermont*, a rhapsodical romance dated between 1793 and 1798, is not German in provenance or inspiration. *The Castle of Wolfenbach, Orphan of the Rhine, The Mysterious Warnings,* and *Midnight Bell* are substantially Gothic and heavily German-influenced, the first strongly suggesting *Otranto*, the third, *Udolpho*. Then there are *Necromancer of the Black Forest*, with content directly borrowed from the German and pointing to *Melmoth*, and *Horrid Mysteries* (already mentioned), a translation from German.

The wholehearted Gothic novel lost favor and quality after 1820. It had fallen into the hands of unskilled, imitative writers: the result was either that the repetition of horrors in vulgar copies of Lewis blunted appetites, or that the dependence on Radcliffe-type explanations became tedious. The decline of the Gothic was assisted by different kinds of novels—notably Eaton Stannard Barrett's *The Heroine: Or The Adventures of Cherubina* (1813), Scott's *Waverley* (1814), and Jane Austen's *Northanger Abbey*. Both the first and the last of these satirized the genre, but it was a very slow process. (Jane Austen received £10 for *Northanger Abbey*, while more than twenty years earlier Mrs. Radcliffe had received £500 and £800 for *Udolpho* and *The Italian*, respectively.) From about 1830 a lurid kind of Gothic continued in series of magazine stories such as "Terrific Tales," or longer "shockers," with screaming covers.

As Gothic literature declined, popular literature of other kinds, much of it having Gothic attributes, boomed. For with the newly invented papermaking machines and rotary presses of the early nineteenth century, literature for the masses was being produced in quantity. Some of the appetite for the strange had been, and was being, deflected from Gothic to romantic—to Shelley, Byron, and Robert Southey, whose *Thalaba the Destroyer* (1801) used Oriental mythology and encouraged reprinting of *The Arabian Nights*. In spite of the Northanger list, the borrowings from German in popular literature as a whole were mainly romances, often without the

supernatural, such as Bürger's *Lenore*, translated as *The Chase* in 1796 by Scott, and folktales such as those collected by Jakob and Wilhelm Grimm. What is of interest at the moment is that some of the new kinds of popular literature exploited Gothic elements and qualities in various ways.

The supernatural, for instance, was often used as a divine agency to support the accepted morality that frequently provided the message. A typical plot, for example, shows the evil monk being thwarted in his designs on the maiden he has imprisoned when part of the monastery collapses on top of him, while the maiden makes her escape.

The influence of the German tales of terror spread beyond Gothic novels to many other kinds of popular literature. *The Monk* and *Melmoth* owe an obvious debt to the Faust legend: this was also combined very effectively, from the late 1830's, with the German werewolf theme—in G. W. M. Reynolds' *Wagner the Werewolf* (1847) a German peasant is given perpetual youth by Satan, provided he becomes a werewolf every seven years. Imitations of German stories often had German characters.

There were many satires of the Gothic novel, and the overly sensitive heroine of both the Gothic romance and the sentimental romance that preceded it was a frequent butt. Barrett's *The Heroine* (1813) provides at times a hilarious send-up of the excesses of Mrs. Radcliffe and Lewis, using phrases from the originals to make the parodies stick. Cherubina, a country girl who suffers various "Gothic" adventures while looking for her lost parents, says: "Oft times I sit and weep, I know not why; and then I weep to find myself weeping. Then, when I can weep, I weep at having nothing to weep at. . . ."

Jane Austen borrowed much of the situation of *Udolpho's* volume IV, chapter 4, for chapters 20–22 of *Northanger Abbey*. The heroine, Catherine Morland, is shown through the old abbey to her room, where someone had died twenty years before, by the old housekeeper, Dorothy. Catherine's head is full of Gothic novels, and she expects at least a secret passage, and perhaps an imprisoned wife somewhere and a few skeletons. But all she finds, in a japanned cabinet, is what appears to be an old manuscript that turns out, in the morning, to be a laundry list.

Jane Austen has a lot of fun with the Gothic conventions, and although the satire is gentle and subtle enough in the novel, her dislike of the unnaturalness of so much Gothic heroics is very clear. The message in this earliest completed major work—that the use of imagination without reason can dangerously damage one's judgment—was to be developed in her later novels. Like Catherine, the heroines of *Pride and Prejudice, Sense and Sensibility*, and the others would suffer in the real world, and lose their illusions.

Thomas Love Peacock, a friend of Shelley, satirized in *Nightmare Abbey* (1818) the way in which the poet and his followers derived their schemes for changing the world, not only from Shelley's father-in-law, Godwin, but also from Gothic romances and German tragedies and tales of terror—the way they made use, for example, of such secret societies as the Illuminati, founded by Adam Weishaupt in 1776, who considered that they possessed special enlightenment, believed in republicanism, and were organized like Freemasons. Shelley is represented by Scythrop Glowry in the book and Mary Shelley is Stella; but it is a problem for today's reader that many of the characters cannot be traced to the originals who suggested them, and since Peacock is very close to the events he was living through, the obscurities are many.

For the student of Gothic literature, nevertheless, the satirical wit of *Nightmare Abbey* provides plenty of compensation. There is a scene between Scythrop and Marionetta (based on Shelley's first wife, Harriet Westbrook), in which he suggests that they drink their mixed blood as a sacrament of love—(they would see "visions of transcendental illumination and soar on the wings of ideas into the space of pure intelligence")—that echoes a scene in *Horrid Mysteries* between Rosalia and Don Carlos. But Marionetta "had not so strong a stomach as Rosalia, and turned sick at the proposition." Peacock's aim in *Nightmare Abbey*, as he expressed it in a letter to Shelley, was to "bring to a sort of philosophical focus a few of the morbidities" of the literature of the time. It is lighthearted burlesque and is diffused over the wide target of both Gothic and romantic extravagances.

GOTHIC AND ROMANTIC

THE imaginations of the pre-romantic poets, notably Robert Blair, William Blake, Robert Burns, William Collins, and Edward Young, were strongly drawn to nocturnal themes, to graveyards haunted by ghosts and demons, and to the imagery of dreams and nightmares. They were stimulated by the treatment of such themes and imagery to be found here and there in Thomas Percy's *Reliques of Ancient English Poetry* (1765) and James Macpherson's *The Poems of Ossian* (1760–1763), in *The Arabian Nights*, and in cheaply printed collections of medieval legends such as those concerning Dr. Faustus and the Wandering Jew. And even earlier than this there is such a representative poem as Collins' "Ode to Fear" (1751):

> Thou to whom the World unknown
> With all its shadowy shapes is shown,
> Who see'st, appall'd, the unreal scene
> While Fancy lifts the veil between
> Ah, Fear! Ah, frantic Fear
> I see, I see thee near.

The romantic movement in poetry and the Gothic movement in the novel shared some of their origins—their interest in medievalism and in the supernatural, for instance. At times Gothic qualities appear to be one aspect of romanticism. Writers moved from one to the other. Mrs. Radcliffe, Lewis, and Maturin inserted verses into their novels; Lewis' ballads influenced the poetry of Scott, Shelley, Byron, and Coleridge; and the poets experimented with the Gothic novel and drama.

The Gothic principles expounded by Walpole in his preface to the second edition of *Otranto*—to create extraordinary, or supernatural, situations, but people them with believable characters behaving believably—have a strong affinity with Coleridge's recipe for romanticism, expressed thirty years later in the preface to the *Lyrical Ballads*. The interest in libertarian ideas, in spiritual worlds, and in the grotesque and the horrible in both Gothic and romantic has been sufficiently noted.

Where romanticism and Gothicism part company most conspicuously, perhaps, is in the insistence of the former that beauty is most closely associated with pain, desire, and sorrow. The Gothic novelists were well aware of the hypnotic appeal of their satanic villains, with their "virile beauty" (which Baudelaire attributed to the perfect type of Milton's Satan), which they flaunted as extravagantly as their suffering and cruelty; but whereas the novelists exploited the characters for dramatic and horrific effects, the romantic poets philosophized about the ways in which beauty associates with suffering.

"Our sweetest songs are those that tell of saddest

thought," Shelley says in "To a Skylark," and John Keats says in "Ode on Melancholy" that melancholy "dwells with Beauty—Beauty that must die." There are poems about the beauty of Medusa—one of the three Gorgons of Greek myth, with snakes for hair: a glance at her turned the beholder to stone. Shelley's poem "On the Medusa of Leonardo da Vinci in the Florentine Gallery" contains the line " 'Tis the tempestuous loveliness of terror." Baudelaire expressed his own and other spirits' attraction to the ugly and deformed as *"la soif de l'inconnu et le goût de l'horrible"* (the thirst for the unknown, the taste for the horrible).

The Gothic descriptions of corpses and skeletons, mingling fascination and loathing, are refined in the romantic poets to a longing for what is beyond death, in a spiritual or unknown world—for what cannot be described. Keats expressed this idealism most memorably in lines of "Ode on a Grecian Urn":

> Heard melodies are sweet, but those unheard
> Are sweeter. . . .

To the romantics death is a release from ugliness. On the death of Keats, Shelley rejoices that age would not spoil that beautiful spirit. The idea is extended by romantic extremists/outsiders such as Baudelaire, who searched for beauty where death and despair were near: in the hospitals for the poor and the brothels of Paris. Imagination was all; it was the feelings, rather than the mind, that were to be stimulated.

The erotic sensibility underlying the romantic attitude is the subject of Mario Praz's classic study *The Romantic Agony*, and there is space here only to mention the chief aim of the book, though it has suggested many of my comments in this essay. Praz pursues the relations between beauty and pain, sexual desire, and cruelty as one pattern in the carpet of romanticism. For his thesis he ransacked British, French, and Italian literatures, and naturally gave plenty of attention to the marquis de Sade (without overstating his few literary merits), the decadents, and various forms of algolagnia, including flagellation.

The term "romantic" has been obscured and devalued by its loose application to literature of all ages that emphasizes imagination and the subjective at the expense of the rational and the ordered, which follow rules. But even in the stricter, late eighteenth-century and early nineteenth-century sense, and confining the term to those writers who were consciously following a definite, romantic aim, the movement has a much less exact connotation of historical period than the Gothic. Romanticism is a current that can be traced right through to today, while Gothicism is a stream that goes underground, out of sight, for long periods, and then reappears in different forms. Part of the reason for the decline in Gothic as a genre was the absorption of many of its aspects by romanticism.

Byron, referring to Venice in *Childe Harold's Pilgrimage*, acknowledged that

> Otway, Radcliffe, Schiller, Shakespeare's art,
> Had stamped her image in me.
>
> (canto IV, 18)

The Byronic, or romantic, hero—the fatal man of the romantics—in the form of the Giaour, the Corsair, Childe Harold, Lara, and Manfred—all pale, beautiful, haunted by guilt, with amazing eyes, melancholy, superior, and proud, mostly also misanthropic, ruthless, mysterious, heroic, and villainous—clearly derives from the writers Byron singles out. Most directly they come from Mrs. Radcliffe's Montoni and Schedoni. The influence of Schiller's adventurous, suffering robbers came both directly and from Lewis' *The Monk* via Schedoni, and Milton's Satan is a shadow over all. Setting Mrs. Radcliffe's Schedoni—

His cowl, too, as it threw a shade over the livid paleness of his face, increased its severe character, and gave an effect to his large melancholy eye, which approached to horror . . . his physiognomy . . . bore the traces of many passions, which seemed to have fixed the features they no longer animated . . . his eyes were so piercing that they seemed to penetrate, at a single glance, into the hearts of men, and to read their most secret thoughts; few persons could support their scrutiny, or even endure to meet them twice. . . .

(*The Italian*, ch. 2)

beside Byron's Giaour—

> Dark and unearthly is the scowl
> That glares beneath his dusky cowl.
> The flash of that dilating eye
> Reveals too much of time gone by;
> Though varying, indistinct its hue,
> Oft will his glance the gazer rue,
> For in it lurks that nameless spell,
> Which speaks, itself unspeakable,

337

A spirit yet unquell'd and high
That claims and keeps ascendency. . . .
(*The Giaour*, 837–846)

the correspondences are clear.

As well as drawing together all these sources, Byron added much of himself, a man who lived, loved, and drank so hard that upon his death at thirty-six, his brain and heart showed the signs of very advanced age.

Byron's Manfred, talking of Astarte, provided the motto for the "fatal men" of romantic literature: "I loved her, and destroy'd her." Vampires are these fatal men in their most symbolic form. Byron mentions vampires in *The Giaour*, and gave Polidori the sketch that became the first vampire novel in English. Vampires were invariably men in the first half of the eighteenth century; thereafter they are mainly represented as women. Most vampire novels vulgarized Gothic themes.

The Wandering Jew, which became such a significant Gothic motif, has an unforgettable characterization in Coleridge's guilt-tortured *Ancient Mariner* (and later turns up in Keats's *Endymion* and Shelley's *Alastor*). Piranesi's etchings haunted Coleridge as well as Walpole and Beckford. In *Confessions of an English Opium-Eater* Thomas De Quincey tells how Coleridge described to him Piranesi's etching entitled *Dreams*: staircases, one after the other, with Piranesi standing at the top of each, before an abyss.

There is a close association between dreams—and their importance for the creative writer—and drugs. De Quincey in his *Confessions* held that dreams crystallized the particles of past experience into a symbolic pattern. In an opium-induced dream the writer could see how the crystallization took place. The influence of opium can be seen in Poe, Baudelaire, George Crabbe, Coleridge, Wilkie Collins, and Francis Thompson, who regularly took it; and De Quincey's thesis has much corroboration in the evidence from these writers that they learned from opium, by observing their imaginations at work.

In her study *Opium and the Romantic Imagination*, Alethea Hayter finds no clear pattern of influence on the works. Having acknowledged the benefits mentioned, she finds that the overall long-term effect is harmful because the drug "detaches the writer from sympathy with what is observed," and because it works against coherence and damages "the power to detect damage." She concludes her book brilliantly, imagining a writer's thoughts inside a typical Piranesi prison as a way of representing the effects of opium.

Both interior and exterior settings in the romantic poets often produce unmistakable echoes of the Gothic novels they read. Coleridge's ballad "Christabel" is a masterpiece of Gothic, with its haunted castle and moonlight gleaming through torn clouds. In his verse play *The Borderers*, Wordsworth, as well as borrowing a good deal of its content from Schiller's *The Robbers* and from various Gothic fictions, has learned from Mrs. Radcliffe how to put terror into the shapes and moods of natural scenery. Byron's drama *Manfred* has Gothic halls, a tower with a secret room, and demons; and his *Childe Harold* has picturesque passages that could have been written by Mrs. Radcliffe, as could many of those in Keats and Shelley. Keats in "The Eve of St. Agnes" plundered *Udolpho* for the castle, shadowy passages, moonlight, and feudal jollifications. When he attempts gorgeous descriptions, as in *Lamia*, it is Beckford that comes to mind. Shelley, apart from his two Gothic novels *Zastrozzi* (1810) and *St. Irvine* (1811), has bits of Gothic everywhere. The *Cenci*, in the words of D. P. Varma, has "the ferocity of algolagnic sensibility."

In early nineteenth-century prose fiction the Gothic spirit, unmistakable as it is, manifests itself in different ways. Scott, an admirer of Mrs. Radcliffe, took Gothic details to fill in his pictures and was rarely unfaithful to history. The Gothic manifestations of the Brontës are very interesting. Charlotte's Rochester in *Jane Eyre* and Emily's Heathcliff in *Wuthering Heights* have strong resemblances to Schedoni and Byron's Manfred; Rochester's locked-up mad wife is reminiscent of one in Mrs. Radcliffe's *A Sicilian Romance*; and *Wuthering Heights* has nightmares and ghosts. Both novels have Gothic weather; and when Emily falters, she has Heathcliff "crushing his nails into his palms, and grinding his teeth to subdue the maxillary convulsions." But the stories, with all their passions, are rooted in the reality of the simple, domestic life of the English countryside; their emotive power is enhanced by their credibility.

It is appropriate to end this section with a romantic-Gothic writer of great ability and seminal importance. With no author, perhaps, is the influences game easier to play than with the American Edgar Allan Poe (1809–1849). His heroes have affinities with the lonely outsiders of the American literary tradition in Herman Melville and Hawthorne, but more obviously and strikingly he learned a great deal from Coleridge, Byron, Keats, Shelley, and De Quincey. The main impulse for his tales of horror was the German Gothic literature.

Poe's reputation is much higher in France than in Britain or the United States; he is regarded as the leading spirit of symbolism, whom Baudelaire, Mallarmé, Paul Verlaine, and Arthur Rimbaud followed with reverence. Even more, if Jules Verne is the father of modern science fiction, Poe is its grandfather; and he also significantly developed the detective story, with lessons for Stevenson and Arthur Conan Doyle. "The Murders in the Rue Morgue" (1841) was based on an actual American case, transposed to Paris. Poe's powers of deduction were such that he could work out the ending of a Dickens novel by reading the first chapter.

"The Rue Morgue" is as much a story of horror as of detection. It is the horror tale that is Poe's forte—his only attempt at a novel was unfinished. At the beginning, under the influence of German tales, he had all the familiar Gothic machinery; but very speedily he developed his own, highly individual style. He then rejected the label of "Germanic," with its associations of extravagant gloom and "pseudo-horror," and wrote: "I maintain that terror is not of Germany but of the soul—that I have deduced this terror only from its legitimate sources, and only to its legitimate results."

Poe added psychology: his main interest, more so than Maturin's, was in what went on inside his protagonists' minds; and his descriptions of doom-laden settings and furniture are genuinely and symbolically relevant to the tale, not just spurious additions. The study is generally profound because most of the protagonists, like Usher in "The Fall of the House of Usher" ("there were but peculiar sounds, and these from stringed instruments, which did not inspire him with horror"), are endowed and cursed with an abnormally cultivated sensitivity. Estranged from reality, often inhabiting heavily curtained rooms, they lose their sanity and sometimes their lives. They are driven back into the prison of themselves. That is a horror symbolized in other tales by being drowned in whirlpools (as in "A Descent into the Maelstrom"), being buried alive (as in "The Cask of Amontillado"), and being subjected to the most ingenious tortures the Spanish Inquisition could devise (as in "The Pit and the Pendulum"). After Poe the Gothic spirit became diffused. The romantic movement had particularly exploited its super-natural aspects, and many different kinds of novel and tale would do the same.

MODERN GOTHIC

SINCE the 1830's there has been a flood of literature descended from the Gothic. Most directly there have been fiction about the supernatural, including stories of ghosts, vampires, werewolves, and other weird transformations; detective and thriller fiction; fantasy and science fiction. Some of this is mediocre, escapist stuff, but there are more great names to put beside those already mentioned, and many other writers of exceptional interest.

The better writers on the supernatural achieve their effects with the minimum of props; it is the interior, psychological effects that are significant. They learned from the great nineteenth-century novelists and from some of the master storytellers how to do it. Balzac's *Melmoth reconcilié* has been mentioned. In *The Wild Ass's Skin* (*Le Peau de chagrin*, 1831) he uses a magic device. The hero, Raphael, shares many of the characteristics of Faust as well as of the author himself. The plot pivots round a magic piece of leather, found in an antiques shop, that grants its owner's wishes but shrinks each time the spell is invoked, ironically shortening his life.

Another French writer, Alexandre Dumas *père*, apart from his long list of historical novels, dealt with the supernatural. *The Wolf Leader* (1857) uses that popular combination of Wandering Jew and werewolf themes, becoming a werewolf for periods being the Devil's condition for continuing life. Dumas also wrote a number of vampire tales. The American Nathaniel Hawthorne, in both tales and novels, makes considerable use of the supernatural or the weird to symbolize evil. *The House of the Seven Gables* (1851) involves a family curse—the ghosts of ancestors haunting a house because one of the family condemned an innocent man—a theme that Hawthorne handled in several works.

"The Queen of Spades" (1834), a short story by the greatest of Russian poets, Aleksander Pushkin, uses the supernatural in a simple but masterly way that combines irony and fantasy, and requires no aid from white sheets and clanking chains. It has reverberated in other literatures, was the basis of Peter Tchaikovsky's opera and the ballet *The Three-*

Card Trick. Hermann, an army officer, is an austere, self-absorbed, obsessed "hero" cast in a fatal, romantic mold; he won Dostoyevsky's acclaim and may have suggested the latter's Raskolnikov in *Crime and Punishment.* Hermann threatens an old countess with a pistol in order to learn a card trick that will win him a fortune gambling, and she dies of shock. The pistol was unloaded. Her ghost reveals the card trick to him, but he is foiled by her at the last round of the card game, when instead of the expected ace, the queen of spades turns up. The countess' features appear on the card; she winks, and he goes mad.

Nikolai Gogol in his short stories develops a Hoffmann-like fantasy. Such stories as "The Nose," in which that appendage, having been shaved off, takes on a life of its own and drives a carriage round St. Petersburg, is whimsical rather than witty, but there are few doubts about "The Portrait" (1835)—which continues living to express the evil of a wicked merchant—and "The Overcoat" (1842), one of the most famous of all ghost stories.

Charles Dickens wrote many supernatural tales within the novels and for the magazines he edited between 1850 and 1870, encouraging contemporaries, notably Wilkie Collins and Edward Bulwer-Lytton, to produce them. Henry James's *The Turn of the Screw* (1898) is about two children possessed by the evil spirits of dead servants. Franz Kafka, whose blend of allegory, fantasy, and horror, defying easy categorization, has been a strong influence on so much modern fiction, wrote three works that demand mention: *The Castle* (1930), *The Trial* (1937), and the long short story *Metamorphosis* (1937), in which a young man becomes a cockroach. Like Poe and Kafka, Guy de Maupassant put many of his own phobias and nightmares into his tales of supernatural terror before he died in 1893, at forty-two, syphilitic and insane.

The Irishman Sheridan Le Fanu (1814–1873) was, like Poe, a link between the Gothic and the psychological horror of modern times. In novels and numerous tales he dealt with all aspects of the supernatural, and his mastery of suspense and ability to sustain an atmosphere without slipping into bathos or unconscious humor (a tightrope for the best writers in the genre) have given him the status of a classic—though a neglected one. His tales, rather than his novels, show his strength. Among his masterpieces are the short stories "Carmilla," about a vampire countess, which achieves psychological insight into lesbianism without detracting from or vulgarizing the horrific effect, and "Green Tea," about a man haunted by a strange creature resembling a monkey.

Of the long list of British writers in this genre during the Victorian period, Lord Bulwer-Lytton (1831–1891), with the superb story *The Haunted and the Haunters* (1859) among historical and occult works; Lord Edward Dunsany (1878–1957), with his fantasies of other worlds, many containing a chilling evil presence at the heart of them; M. R. James (1862–1936), an ingenious but much less frightening successor of Sheridan Le Fanu, his inspirer; and the poet Walter de la Mare (1873–1956), who wrote collections of ghost stories and whose novels include *Memoirs of a Midget* (1921), about a woman two feet tall, are well worth reading.

Opinions vary on H. P. Lovecraft. His works, though readable, lack literary merit, and elements of racism and snobbery alienate many readers. But his fantasy worlds and weird tales are original, and enthusiasts of Gothic will admire his formidable knowledge of the literature of the supernatural. His critical work *Supernatural Horror in Literature* was published in 1927. Subsequent writers of supernatural stories have shown an interest in magic, witchcraft, and the occult in general.

A pattern for the development of the detective novel can be made out as follows: Godwin, Lewis, Poe (the key figure), Wilkie Collins, Le Fanu. Le Fanu's *The House by the Churchyard* (1863) is a fine example. Collins wrote two compelling detective novels: *The Woman in White* (1860) and *The Moonstone* (1868), well written, well worked out, and sustaining the "mysteries" (as much detective fiction used to be called) throughout. *The Woman in White* is one of the forerunners and best examples of what are called "thrillers." Added to the suspense/detection interest in this work are adventures and more recognizable (though controlled) Gothic elements, including a persecuted heroine and a devilish (though believable) criminal. *The Moonstone* is one of the best detective novels.

These labels are only rough guides, particularly since detective fiction is so voluminous. Both detective novels and thrillers use such Gothic techniques as ingenious murder methods, the theft of wills and other documents, wrongful suspicion, suspense, mysteries explained at the end. City streets replace castle corridors. The persecuted heroine is still there, if drier-eyed and more able to look after herself. The Gothic hero-villain may have become a mad scientist; a much nastier Frankenstein, as in Ian Fleming's thrillers; or he may be the detective, with an intellect far superior to that of anyone around him and the evil refined down to mere eccentricity. Perhaps the most famous detective in fiction is Arthur Conan Doyle's egotistic Sherlock Holmes, a pale thin man of astonishing deductive ability (like Poe's) who takes opium and plays the violin. He was the progenitor of a long line of detectives, including Dorothy L. Sayers' Lord Peter Wimsey, Agatha Christie's Hercule Poirot, and Georges Simenon's Maigret.

The three English writers were generally concerned with plot rather than sensation, but they did write books that contained horror. One of Doyle's best novels, in fact, is *The Hound of the Baskervilles* (1901), a Sherlock Holmes story in which the detective is confronted not by a werewolf but by a vicious hound with a villainous master. Sayers put together large anthologies entitled *Great Short Stories of Detection, Mystery and Horror* (1929–1934), and Agatha Christie also had a penchant for the weird, which surfaced in parts of many novels and in a fine volume of tales entitled *The Hound of Death* (1933).

Iris Murdoch, a philosopher as well as a novelist, uses Gothic elements in some of her novels, notably in *The Unicorn* and *The Time of the Angels*, the first set in a remote coastal region with a castle, a swamp, and cliffs above the sea. She gives the landscape a romantic power over the characters, and the castle is a prison for the chief character, Hannah Crean-Smith, cursed by her husband to remain inside for seven years. The Gothic setting and situation enable the author to fabricate a mythical environment in which she can explore various ideas about good and evil, guilt and innocence, and freedom. *The Time of the Angels* is set in a rectory.

The earlier mention of "mad scientists" suggests the link between the Gothic novel and science fiction. On the model of *Frankenstein* the best science fiction has some concern for the role of science in the future, and often has political and moral messages to deliver.

The works of Jules Verne, much of H. G. Wells, Aldous Huxley's *Brave New World*, and George Orwell's *1984* are among the most original kinds, but since the 1940's and 1950's, alongside an avalanche of science fiction pulp fiction, there has been a great variety of fascinating and vital literature in this sphere on both sides of the Atlantic, the "fantasy" and "pure science fiction" labels becoming increasingly difficult to keep distinct. The work of the American Ray Bradbury (born 1920), mainly in short story form, is better described as fantasy. Kurt Vonnegut, Jr., and Isaac Asimov, also American, are good as well as prolific.

Among the science fiction novels of Brian Aldiss is an ingenious commentary on Mary Shelley's novel called *Frankenstein Un-bound* (1973), in which Joe Bodenland, owing to a space-time rupture, is transported back from the United States of the twenty-first century to the Switzerland of 1816. Here he meets Mary Shelley; the poet Shelley, whose wife she is about to become; Byron; and the characters of the novel *Frankenstein* that is being worked on. J. G. Ballard has concerned himself with what he calls "inner space" (rather than outer). Many of his novels and stories deal with the effects on the mind of the environment and of natural disasters. Colin Wilson (born 1931) has written a combination of horror and science fiction in *Space Vampires* (1976). Michael Moorcock (born 1939) is an extremely prolific writer who exploits various techniques in fantasy, science fiction, and traditional genres, and is building a sizable reputation. Angela Carter's writings have been called, in some desperation, "Gothic science fiction." Mostly her works are an unusual blend of the two.

OTHER MEDIA

ANGELA Carter wrote a fantasia of the Dracula story for radio called *Vampirella*. "My daughter, the last of the line," Dracula says in this, "through whom I now project a modest, posthumous existence, believes . . . that she may be made whole by human feeling." There has been much work in the Gothic lineage done for radio, both adaptations and original work. What can misfire or become unconsciously absurd on the page or when represented on film or television may take compelling and frightening shape in the mind encouraged to imagine. As the child said, when asked why he preferred radio to television, "the pictures are better."

Where the effect has to be intimate, where the terror can be projected in subtle ways, where images can be unsensationally charged with symbolism, and where the atmosphere can be built up slowly and surely, then television can be a very effective medium. Ghost stories in a mainly domestic setting have tended to work best, but there have been satisfying television versions of such works as *Dracula* to confound these generalizations.

The attraction of Gothic horror for the cinema is obvious. One of the most influential films ever made is the classic German horror film, Robert Wiene's *The Cabinet of Dr. Caligari* (1919). The identity of Caligari, an eighteenth-century Italian showman who hypnotized a somnambulist and used him to commit murders, is taken over by the crazed director of a psychiatric institute. The script by Carl Mayer and Haas Janowitz has the flavor of Hoffmann. Mary Shelley's *Frankenstein* had been filmed in 1908, 1916, and 1920, but these versions no longer exist; Hollywood's *Frankenstein* of 1931 remains the classic, with Boris Karloff as the monster. This was followed by sequels adding to the story— *Bride of Frankenstein* (1935), the ambiguous title of which compounded people's inclination to make the name refer to the monster instead of the scientist, and *Son of Frankenstein* (1939); there have been many imitations since. "As a man I should destroy him, as a scientist I should bring him back to life," the scientist says in *Son of Frankenstein*. The effect of the films is to make fears and suspicions about the powers of the scientist explicit through the vivid imagery. The monster is galvanized into life in splendidly effective scenes—by harnessing electricity from lightning in the first film and through a generator (800° Fahrenheit, we are told) in the second—and Frankenstein is vulgarized from Shelley's idealistic and guilt-ridden scientist into an eccentric one getting crazier by the minute. The monster, in the first film of this series, was given a criminal's brain; and this is naively supposed to explain his evil nature from the start—Mary Shelley's socialistic message does not, of course, survive.

Bram Stoker's novel *Dracula* and later Gothic works were inspired by the much finer writer Sheridan Le Fanu, a point that needs emphasizing because the enormous success of Stoker's book has eclipsed the work of his fellow Irishman. Stoker receives more attention because it is his image of the vampire—the tall, pale count in the black cloak, repeated and imitated in many books and films—that has become standard and immediately comes to mind. Apart from that, he is extremely readable.

The striking, convincing patterns made by the logical system of beliefs deriving from the vampire legend and the vividness of the symbols make "suspension of disbelief" easy, and this explains the vast army of vampire buffs. The films have eminently cinematic attributes to play with: the vampire's need to operate between sunset and sunrise; the graves and coffins; his ability to travel as motes of dust or wisps of fog, and to change himself into a wolf, rat, bat, and some other animals (which often accompany him and which he can control); his superhuman strength and hypnotic power; his aversion to crucifixes, garlic, and wolfbane; his lack of reflection in a mirror; and the means of his destruction (a stake through the heart, after which decapitation and burning the corpse are extra precautions).

The first and greatly influential Dracula film was Friedrich Murnau's *Nosferatu*, made in Germany in 1922, in which the vampire was played by Max von Schrek. In 1931 the Hollywood version, *Dracula*, with Bela Lugosi as Dracula, launched the whole series of horror films, including the various sequels on the Dracula theme as well as on the Frankenstein one. One or two of the earliest are regarded as classics and have been repeated on television. In the 1960's Hammer Films of Great Britain returned to these and related themes—mummies, werewolves, zombies, and a number of "creepies" adapted from Poe. There have been half a dozen excellent film versions of *Dr. Jekyll and Mr. Hyde* and three of Doyle's *The Hound of the Baskervilles*, the most recent for television in 1974.

The best horror films, like the best Gothic literature, give shocking scenes a dramatic function and do not include them for mere sensation; most have been adapted from novels worth attention. Again, as in literature, suggestiveness—albeit visual rather than verbal—often has a more powerful effect than explicitness.

Psychopathic disorder has been a common motif in recent horror films. Usually it is associated with sexual repression and family tensions. *Psycho*, from the novel by Robert Bloch, published in 1959, is a good example, and the nearest to a Gothic horror film made by one of the masters of cinematic suspense, Alfred Hitchcock. This film achieved some of the most spine-chilling effects seen in the cinema with very little violent action. A famous scene is that of the stabbing to death of a woman taking a shower, behind a shower curtain, in which almost everything is left to the imagination while the blood is seen trickling away with the bathwater.

The central character of *Psycho* is a schizophrenic

who hates his mother, and the film inspired a number of "schizophrenic" films, including *Homicidal*, *Blood Sisters*, and *Schizo*. The threat to the family can, of course, be traced back to many different literary themes in the past; it is sufficient for the moment to trace it to *Frankenstein* and *Dracula* and their progeny. In some films the tensions are exteriorized and symbolized by violent upheavals in natural forces. In Hitchcock's *The Birds* (1963), from a story by Daphne du Maurier, when birds in thousands mass and terrorize a small town with sudden, ferocious invasions, the horror comes from realizing how vulnerable and artificial are the family's barriers against disintegration. The forces for destruction may be slumbering within the institution—they are easily awakened and turned against the institution itself. At the same time, the more widespread tensions of a civilized society may find outlet in the destruction of natural forces and, as in *The Birds*, these may take revenge.

Satanism, backed up by varying degrees of occult lore, has been the direction taken by horror novels and films in the past few years, and in the most striking examples the horror has been all the more suggestive and insidious by having the family background apparently happy, bourgeois, and well-ordered. In Roman Polanski's *Rosemary's Baby* (1968), from the novel by Ira Levin, the eponymous wife gives birth to an Antichrist with a cloven hoof, fathered by the Devil, and accepts the fact. In *The Exorcist*, from William Peter Blatty's novel (1971), the young, well-balanced daughter Regan is suddenly possessed, the furniture is hurled all over her bedroom, she emits obscenities and curses and vomits green bile (the film is in color). All is restored to normality after exorcism rites ending in a violent death.

The Omen (1976), film and novel by David Seltzer, is about an American ambassador to London and his wife, who have a demon-child, agent of the Devil's scheme to bring about the end of the world. The voice of reason is represented by a photographer who gets his head sawed off, and there is other violence and much occult business involving crucifixes. There are cheap effects in these films, but they have a flair and vitality to compensate.

The Gothic horror films, and the hybrid forms generated by combination with science fiction or with the occult, have a strong association with dreams, of the kind that inspired Walpole, Beckford,

and Mary Shelley. So we have not traveled too far from the original trinity after all.

CONCLUSION

Much of the content of Gothic literature was inspired by dreams or hallucinatory states that were self-induced or produced by drugs. The frequency of films based on Gothic literature is no accident—dreams are full of weird and vivid imagery that films can effectively present. Apart from that, both Gothic literature and Gothic horror films, aiming to be popular (even when also aiming to be art), are collective dreams, expressions of and safety valves for the unconscious of the age, expressions of generally experienced desires and fears that tend to be repressed by individuals. This is part of the reason why the Gothic spirit is so easily given different forms in different ages.

This essay has had two principal aims. The first has been to show that a literary genre too often dismissed as being of little merit, as being a freak that disappeared into a cul-de-sac, can be seen, when considered in a broader light, as very important, as being the product of a spirit that had antecedents in much great literature from ancient times, a spirit that was an essential part of romanticism—a spirit, moreover, that, far from dying out, divided itself and became the force behind other genres, notably supernatural fiction, detective fiction, thrillers, and science fiction.

The second aim has been to point out that although a vast amount of what I have called "Gothic literature"—all the literature that has a Gothic spirit and contains traces of direct influence from the Gothic novel of 1765–1820—is "popular" literature and was intended primarily as escapist entertainment, nevertheless there are some great writers and some very good ones who deserve attention, and do not get it, because a false distinction tends to be made nowadays between "good" and "popular." Shakespeare and Dickens were both, and so is Graham Greene. Perhaps Poe—in Britain, at least—and Sheridan Le Fanu are the greatest of the writers neglected because they were, and are, taken to be narrower than they are. Matthew Lewis, Bram Stoker, and H. P. Lovecraft are examples of writers who continue to be read, and deserve to be. Although they have faults, including awkward styles and a naiveté that produces unconscious humor, they nevertheless have more interest, more vitality and readableness, much less pretentiousness, and altogether more value than many a ponderous literary "classic" more honored in the histories of literature than by any significant number of readers.

An occupational hazard of the literary critic is to play the association game—to follow the trails suggested by the various aspects of a subject so as to give those aspects greater significance. The problem is that when a critic comes to the end of the game, he or she may find that he or she has arrived at a nebulous "universal significance" and has lost sight of the starting point.

I have tried to avoid that by staying close to the theme. But here it might be useful to give a little more emphasis to a few of the fascinating trails the student of the Gothic might be tempted to follow.

A compulsive interest in corpses and other manifestations of death, in demonstrating man's desire for immortality and fear of it, in developing understanding for the outcast, in analyzing erotic sensibility and the effects of sexual repression, in exploring sadomasochism—these are prominent among the concerns of the Gothic novel.

The interest in, and often obsession with, the paraphernalia of death is obvious enough, with its medieval associations and the various antecedents in medieval literature. Mention has already been made of how an attitude of antirationalism encouraged these interests. The rattle of skeletons and the hollow stare of skulls pursue the reader from Walpole's castle to Frankenstein's laboratory, and through hundreds of abbeys and cloisters. It is the mixed desire and fear of immortality behind this, expressed in Frankenstein's monster and in the various treatments of Faust, the various representations of the Wandering Jew and the vampire and combinations of these figures, that demand to be explored. Christopher Marlowe based his play *The Tragical History of Dr. Faustus*, first performed in the 1590's, on a popular tale published in 1587 by Johann Spiess, who brought in the idea of Faust's selling his soul to the Devil in exchange for immortality; the character was based on a real Dr. (Georg) Faust (1480–1540), an eccentric magician. The first part of Goethe's *Faust*, the most famous, appeared in 1808, and Thomas Mann's philosophical novel *Doktor Faustus* in 1947. In 1967 Marlowe's play was filmed as *Doctor Faustus* with Richard Burton and Elizabeth Taylor. There are many other versions to be explored and compared.

The original Wandering Jew was Cartophilus, Pontius Pilate's doorkeeper, who according to the legend struck Jesus Christ and told him to hurry. Christ replied, "I am going, but you must wait until I come again." Ever since, Cartophilus lives, every hundred years finding himself renewed as a thirty-year-old. Melmoth the Wanderer is the best-known of all developments of the legend and, like many other versions, combines it with the Faustian theme.

Longings for immortality, the shape that man's spiritual desires tend to take, accompany in the Christian world fantasies about the Devil; and the Devil or his agent, in the different forms he has assumed in Gothic literature—whether a Byronic fatal hero, an immortal wanderer, a Faustian figure, or a vampire—tends to be a romanticized image of freedom and power. In our dreams and in the Gothic novels this figure acts as we do not dare to act, lives as we do not dare to live, enjoys and suffers as we do not dare to: he represents our repressions.

Perhaps most conspicuously he represents our sexual repressions. Freud painted a picture of a Western civilization that had a dangerous quantity of sexual energy repressed by the institutions of the monogamous family. The Rochester of Charlotte Brontë's *Jane Eyre* and the Heathcliff of Emily Brontë's *Wuthering Heights* were fantasized outlets for this energy in the form of fiercely proud, antisocial, sexually dominating figures that towered over the other characters and were models for countless "romantic" heroes, mainly of women writers, to come. Of the Gothic litany the vampire in the form of Bram Stoker's Count Dracula is most obviously another manifestation of that outlet. The common love bite is, after all, aimed at the jugular vein, like the vampire's; and the eroticism of vampire novels is mainly disguised, implicit, symbolical, as it is in the Brontës.

Stakes penetrating the heart, the gushing of blood, and much other Gothic horror imagery in both films and novels were exploited for their erotic overtones when sexual explicitness was banned. Now that censorship is much laxer, the fact that there is little need for such disguise may be one reason why the traditional Gothic horror themes have tended in recent years to give way to the more suggestive psychological and occult themes. The demon-child that has appeared in several recent films is significant as a Freudian symbol, representing the repressed energies of the civilized family.

Mention has been made of Mario Praz's survey of the manifestations of erotic sensibility, including

344

algolagnia, in the romantic literature of three languages. The last two paragraphs above may suggest ways in which Praz's theme might be explored further.

Finally, Frankenstein's monster, Radcliffe's and Lewis' pale monks, Melmoth, the suffering outcasts of Poe, and all the other Gothic hero-villains or anti-heroes that compel attention and sympathy (even if also condemnation) have strong links with the "outsiders" in the novels of some of the greatest European writers of this century: Kafka, Albert Camus, Jean-Paul Sartre, Samuel Beckett, and others.

The perpetual attraction of the tale of terror, H. P. Lovecraft said, was "the scratching of unknown claws at the rind of the known world." That is certainly what one hears in the best of the Gothic novels, and when one hears it in the passages of the great writers who have forced their way into this essay, the sound, however intermittent, is unmistakable and unforgettable.

SELECTED BIBLIOGRAPHY

I. BIBLIOGRAPHY. T. J. Wise, *A Shelley Library* (London, 1924); M. Summers, *A Gothic Bibliography* (London, 1940); A. T. Hazen, *A Bibliography of Horace Walpole* (New Haven, 1948); R. J. Gemmett, "An Annotated Checklist of the Works of William Beckford," in *Papers of the Bibliographical Society of America*, 61 (1967), 143–158.

II. THE GOTHIC GENRE. H. Walpole, *The Castle of Otranto* (Chatto ed., London, 1907), with intro. by Sir W. Scott and preface by C. F. E. Spurgeon; M. Lewis, *The Monk* (Grove Press ed., New York, 1952), with intro. by J. Berryman; W. Godwin, *The Adventures of Caleb Williams, or, Things as They Are* (Rinehart ed., New York–Toronto, 1960), with intro. by G. Sherburn; W. T. Beckford, *Vathek*, R. Lonsdale, ed. (London, 1965), in the Oxford English Novels series; A. Radcliffe, *The Mysteries of Udolpho*, B. Dobrée, ed. (London, 1966), in the Oxford English Novels series; C. Reeve, *The Old English Baron. A Gothic Story*, J. Trainer, ed. (London, 1967), originally titled *The Champion of Virtue*; A. Radcliffe, *The Italian*, F. Garber, ed. (London, 1968), in the Oxford English Novels series; P. Fairclough, ed., *Three Gothic Novels: The Castle of Otranto, Vathek, and Frankenstein* (London, 1968), with intro. by M. Praz, in the Penguin English Library; M. Shelley, *Frankenstein, or, The Modern Prometheus*, M. K. Joseph, ed. (London, 1971), in the Oxford English Novels series; C. Maturin, *Melmoth the Wanderer* (Penguin ed., London, 1977), with intro. by A. Hayter.

III. GOTHIC-RELATED FICTION. E. Bulwer-Lytton, *The Haunted and the Haunters, or, The House and the Brain* (London–Glasgow, 1905), Gowan's International Library, no. 1; W. de la Mare, *Memoirs of a Midget* (London, 1921; repub. 1955); O. Wilde, *The Picture of Dorian Gray* (London–New York, 1925), illustrated by H. Keen; M. Summers, *The Supernatural Omnibus* (London, 1931); H. James, *The Turn of the Screw* (Penguin ed., London, 1946); S. Le Fanu, *In a Glass Darkly* (London, 1947), with intro. by V. S. Pritchett, contains the stories "Green Tea" and "Carmilla"; N. V. Gogol, *Tales of Good and Evil*, translated by D. Magarshack (London, 1949), contains "The Portrait"; H. P. Lovecraft, *The Haunter of the Dark, and Other Tales of Horror*, A. Derleth, ed. (London, 1951); A. C. Doyle, *The Hound of the Baskervilles* (London, 1957), illustrated by S. Hughes; F. Kafka, *The Castle*, translated by W. and E. Muir (Penguin ed., London, 1957); J. -P. Sartre, *No Exit*, translated by P. Bowles (New York, 1958), a one-act play originally titled *Les Autres* and retitled *Huis clos*; A. Pushkin, *The Queen of Spades*, R. Edmonds, ed. (London, 1962); E. T. Hoffmann, *The Devil's Elixir*, translated by R. Taylor (London, 1963), illustrated by H. Weissenborn; W. Collins, *The Moonstone* (London, 1963), in Everyman's Library; E. Brontë, *Wuthering Heights*, D. Daiches, ed. (London, 1965); N. Hawthorne, *The House of the Seven Gables* (Harper and Row ed., New York, 1965); A. Carter, *Shadow Dance* (London, 1966); W. Collins, *The Woman in White* (Penguin ed., London, 1966; 1974); E. T. Hoffmann, *Tales of Hoffmann*, translated by J. Kirkup (London–Glasgow, 1966).

B. Stoker, *Dracula* (Jarrolds ed., London, 1966); A. Carter, *The Magic Toyshop* (London, 1967); S. Le Fanu, *The House by the Churchyard* (London, 1968), in Doughty Library series; S. Le Fanu, *Uncle Silas* (Dover ed., London, 1968); F. Kafka, *Metamorphosis* (Penguin ed., London, 1970; 1974); W. P. Blatty, *The Exorcist* (New York–London, 1971); C. Brontë, *Jane Eyre* (Penguin ed., London, 1971); I. Murdoch, *The Unicorn* (London, 1971) and *The Time of the Angels* (London, 1971); J. Austen, *Northanger Abbey* (Penguin ed., London, 1972), with intro. by A. H. Ehrenpreis; A. Carter, *The Infernal Desire Machine of Dr. Hoffman* (London, 1972); N. V. Gogol, *The Diary of a Madman*, translated by R. Wilkes (Penguin ed., London, 1972), contains "The Nose" and "The Overcoat"; B. Aldiss, *Frankenstein Un-bound* (London, 1973); R. L. Stevenson, *The Strange Case of Dr. Jekyll and Mr. Hyde, and Other Macabre Stories* (by other authors) (Transworld–Corgi ed., London, 1974); T. L. Peacock, *Nightmare Abbey* (with *Crotchet Castle*) (Penguin ed., London, 1976), with intro. by R. Wright; E. A. Poe, *Selected Writings*, D. Galloway, ed. (Penguin ed., London, 1976); D. Seltzer, *The Omen* (London, 1976); H. de Balzac, *The Wild Ass's Skin*, translated by H. Hunt (Penguin ed., London, 1977); S. King, *The Shining* (New York–London, 1977); A. D. Foster, *Alien* (London, 1979); D. Seltzer, *Prophecy* (London–New York, 1979).

IV. CRITICISM. In addition to the works listed below, one may consult the *Oxford History of English Literature*, vols. IX and X. E. Birkhead, *The Tale of Terror. A Study of Gothic Romance* (London, 1921); E. Railo, *The Haunted Castle. A Study of the Elements of English Romanticism* (London, 1927); D. M. Stuart, *Horace Walpole* (London, 1927); K. Clark, *The Gothic Revival* (London, 1928; repr. 1974); M. Summers, *The Vampire: His Kith and Kin* (London, 1929), with bibliography; J. M. S. Tompkins, *The Popular Novel in England, 1770–1800* (London, 1932; repr. 1962); M. Praz, *The Romantic Agony* (London, 1933; 2nd ed., with new foreword by F. Kermode, London, 1970); M. Summers, *The Werewolf* (London, 1933), with plates and bibliography; M. Summers, *The Gothic Quest. A History of the Gothic Novel* (London, 1938); R. W. Ketton-Cremer, *Horace Walpole* (London, 1940; Ithaca, N. Y., 1966); B. Willey, *The 18th Century Background. Studies on the Idea of Nature in the Thought of the Period* (London, 1940; repr. 1962); H. P. Lovecraft, *Supernatural Horror in Literature* (New York, 1945); B. Willey, *Nineteenth Century Studies. Coleridge to Matthew Arnold* (London, 1949); M. Spark, *Child of Light: A Reassessment of Mary Wollstonecraft Shelley* (London, 1951).

H. Honour, *Horace Walpole* (London, 1957; rev. ed., 1970), in the Writers and Their Work series; D. P. Varma, *The Gothic Flame* (London, 1957), with foreword by H. Read and intro. by J. M. S. Tompkins; L. James, *Fiction for the Working Man, 1830–50* (London, 1963); W. H. Smith, ed., *Horace Walpole: Writer, Politician and Connoisseur* (New Haven–London, 1967); A. Hayter, *Opium and the Romantic Imagination* (London, 1968); T. De Quincey, *Confessions of an English Opium-Eater*, A. Hayter, ed. (Penguin ed., London, 1971), with an intro. by Hayter; M. Foucault, *Madness and Civilisation*, translated by R. Howard (London, 1971); G. Bataille, *Literature and Evil*, translated from the French by A. Hamilton (London, 1973); A. Camus, *The Rebel* (Penguin ed., London, 1974), contains the chapter "Byronic Outsiders"; M. Ashley, *Who's Who in Horror and Fantasy Fiction* (London, 1977); G. St. J. Barclay, *Anatomy of Horror* (London, 1978).

V. SHORTER ESSAYS AND ARTICLES. J. K. Folsom, "Beckford's 'Vathek' and the Tradition of Oriental Satire," in *Criticism*, 6 (1964), 53–69; M. Sadleir, *The Northanger Novels—a Footnote to Jane Austen* (Oxford, 1927; repr. as an English Association Pamphlet, London, 1968); R. D. Hume, "Gothic Versus Romantic: A Revaluation of the Gothic Novel," in *PMLA*, 84 (March 1969), 282–290; W. Crude, "Mary Shelley's Modern Prometheus: A Study in the Ethics of Scientific Creativity," in *Dalhousie Review*, 52 (1972), 812–825; K. W. Graham, "Beckford's Vathek: A Study in Ironic Dissonance," in *Criticism*, 14 (1972), 243–252; R. Wood, "Return of the Repressed," *Times Educational Supplement* (31 December 1976), on the implications of the horror film.